★ INSIDE THE ★ WHITE HOUSE

★ INSIDE THE ★

WHITE HOUSE

AMERICA'S MOST FAMOUS HOME
THE FIRST 200 YEARS

 BETTY BOYD CAROLI 

GUILDAMERICA
BOOKS

Doubleday Book & Music Clubs, Inc.
Garden City, New York

Front endsheet:
Eubie Blake playing ragtime on the South Lawn.

Back endsheet:
Olympics Winners at the White House.

Frontispiece:
North front of the White House

Book design, jacket, endsheets, and binding:
Richard Kopyscianski, Creative Director
Art Direction by Diana Klemin

Printed in the United States of America

ISBN 1-55859-438-8

For my mother, Edna Henry Boyd
and the memory of my father, Clyde Ford Boyd

CONTENTS

Foreword 9

Introduction

The White House: Two Hundred Years 11

Home to a Family 21

Office of the President 71

Museum of a Nation 123

House of the People 165

Presidents of the United States and Their Wives 211

Floor Plan of the White House 214

Photo Credits 216

Further Readings 217

Index 218

FOREWORD

Telling the White House story is not easy, nor can one book do it all. Dozens of volumes have already been written on topics as diverse as White House food and pets, architecture and music, gardens and furniture, glassware and automobiles. The occupants themselves and the building's staff have published countless memoirs about the time they spent in the White House, and historians and journalists have provided their own accounts (sometimes exposés) of what happened there.

Rather than duplicate any of these previous efforts, this book focuses on what the White House has come to mean at the time of its two hundredth birthday—the roles it plays and the uses it serves. Eleanor Roosevelt once titled an article "The White House Speaks" —she seemed to understand that the building took its own measure, confident of its own significance and permanence. More than simply surviving shifts in political thinking, the White House grows in prominence regardless of the criticism leveled at its occupants.

Organized thematically in four sections, the pages that follow go inside the White House in something other than a physical sense. Photographs, chosen from among countless available, have been selected to illustrate the four themes and show alterations over time. Readers will get a good idea of what the mansion looks like for its bicentennial celebration, but they will also understand the route it followed to achieve that look.

Readers who want more extensive coverage of any one topic will need to consult the list of additional readings on page 217. The volumes by William Seale, Elise Kirk, Jane Shadel Spillman, and Margaret Klapthor, as well as the White House guidebooks published and richly illustrated by the White House Historical Association, will be particularly useful. They prepared me for examining

In the era of bustles and parasols, before security considerations caused it to be closed off, the South Lawn provided a good vantage point for viewing White House residents who appeared on the South Portico.

documents at the White House, the Library of Congress, and the Houghton Library of Harvard University.

I have had generous assistance from many people. At the White House, Associate Curator Betty Monkman brought out files for me to look at and made other arrangements that facilitated the research. She and others in the White House Curator's Office, especially Assistant Curator William Allman and Angela Horton, answered countless questions and commented on portions of the manuscript. Staffs at the presidential libraries, Library of Congress, White House Historical Association, and White House Photo Offices cheerfully cooperated with me to find pictures. At Doubleday Book Clubs, an enthusiastic team, including Richard Kopyscianski, Diana Klemin, Barbara Greenman, Al Stiene, Joanne Willig, and Eleanor Tilvikas made my work a pleasure. Mary Sherwin Jatlow, Senior Editor, merits special thanks—for realizing that the White House bicentennial deserved a book and for her patience and good humor in seeing the project through.

INTRODUCTION

The White House: Two Hundred Years

After months of talk, the time had come to act, and the group that had gathered outside the Georgetown, Maryland tavern began walking southeast. In the lead were members of the local Masonic Lodge, whose fellow Mason, General George Washington, could not join them that Saturday—duties as President of the new United States of America detained him in Philadelphia. But Washington's wishes were very much on the men's minds—he had personally selected the spot where they were heading. There on a pleasant wooded knoll overlooking the Potomac River a home would be built for future Presidents of the nation: these men were going to lay the cornerstone for the White House.

It is doubtful that any of the Masons, stonecutters, or others who came together that October day in 1792 could have imagined the interest their actions would arouse two hundred years later. Only one newspaper account—from South Carolina—survives, and it does not record exactly where the cornerstone was placed. Most informed guesses put it somewhere on the southwest corner.

A drawing of the President's House after its burning in August 1814.

This photograph of the White House in the 1840s is the earliest known.

Ebullient over their accomplishment, the men returned to the Georgetown tavern and drank a toast to the future, but never in their wildest dreams could they have foreseen what the President's House would become. They could not have conceived that it would eventually add a bomb shelter to its basement and computer screens to every office; that one million visitors would walk through its rooms every year; and that live broadcasts would electronically transmit its picture around the world.

Had they been able to see into the future, the builders of the White House might have opted for a larger structure. George Washington would not have objected—he approved of the idea that Presidents should reside in style, and the city planner he selected in 1791, Frenchman Pierre L'Enfant, envisioned an American capital with majestic stone buildings and wide boulevards lined with fountains and monuments. The President's House in L'Enfant's plan would be enormous, about five times the size of the one eventually built.

Washington's approval, although very important, did not suffice to permit L'Enfant to proceed against the opposition of other Americans who wanted something more modest. Thomas Jefferson, who as Secretary of State had an important role in building the new Federal City, envisioned a setting that emphasized natural elements—rolling hills and small streams—like his beloved Monticello in Charlottesville. The three Commissioners selected to oversee the building project agreed with Jefferson—they had doubts about how Americans would react to a palace. Congress failed to appropriate any funds for L'Enfant, and then Jefferson fired him.

Now it was February 1792, and quick action was required. Thomas Jefferson suggested holding a contest to collect ideas for the President's House, and within months, nine entries came in. This was hardly an outpouring of enthusiasm in a nation numbering nearly four million people. Architects in Philadelphia and New York ignored the contest as though they considered it beneath their consideration, and Boston's renowned Charles Bulfinch declined to enter "on the grounds of modesty." But from among the nine proposals, one stood out and was quickly accepted by the Commissioners, perhaps because it had fewer of the features associated

Elaborate conservatories built in the 1850s provided presidential families with fresh flowers and a place to walk after dinner.

with a palace. The other entries, including some with large central courts and one with space for a draped throne, lost out to that of James Hoban who had been building homes for wealthy planters in South Carolina.

Historians would later agree that James Hoban's entry was not original, but then originality was not one of the requirements. He borrowed heavily from examples in his native Dublin: Leinster House (later House of Parliament) and the Lying-In Hospital both had Palladian façades and windows hooded in triangular shapes like those that would grace some of the windows in the President's House. When John Kennedy visited Ireland in 1963, he joked about how much the White House resembled "Dublin style" and concluded that James Hoban had wanted to make American Presidents of Irish descent feel at home. "It was a long wait," quipped Kennedy, "but I appreciate his efforts." Then the American President speculated on the rumor that Hoban had not been "fully paid."

Original or not, Hoban's design meshed nicely with the new nation's ideas about itself—simple in line yet big enough to qualify as the largest home in the nation. After George Washington prevailed on Hoban to add some stone embellishments to the exterior, take away the third floor, and increase the dimensions by one-fifth, building could begin. This would enable the cornerstone to be laid on October 13, 1792, just a bit behind schedule.

L'Enfant's plan for a stone structure survived, and Hoban took charge of construction. The surrounding area could not supply the workmen needed, and a call went out to other states (and even Europe) for help. Before it was finished many nationalities would help in the construction of the President's House, and although a complete roster of them does not exist, historians estimate that about one-half of those employed were foreign-born. The Irishman Hoban took up where the Frenchman L'Enfant left off, working alongside the Scottish stonemason Collen Williamson and other Scotsmen and many African-Americans hired by the day.

Eight years after the cornerstone was laid, John and Abigail Adams moved in. It should be noted that the exterior of the White House at that time had not yet achieved the look that we know today. Thomas Jefferson oversaw the addition of low wings to the east and west; James Monroe presided over the building of the rounded portico on the south; Andrew Jackson added a rectangular portico on the north. But over the years the four exterior walls—measuring 165 feet from east to west and 85 feet from north to

An office building—the West Wing of the White House—replaced the conservatories in 1902.

Over the years intricate stonework was covered up by dozens of layers of white paint so that in the 1980s a thorough cleaning was required to reveal its detail.

In 1927 extensive work on the White House provided more living space on the third floor that had previously been used for service and storage areas.

south—have retained their original dimensions and placement against every intrusion and change in occupants.

By the 1940s, the White House exterior had taken on icon status, as President Harry Truman learned when he suggested adding a second floor to the South Portico. Defending the change on both aesthetic and historic grounds, he insisted the porch offered an improvement over the current arrangement in which awnings, used to shut out the sun, became soiled and torn. Many Americans objected loudly to tampering with the White House façade but in the end, Truman got his way. Several of his successors, including Richard Nixon, spoke out in defense of the "Truman porch," but it caused some difficulty at the United States Mint: the engraving of the White House on twenty-dollar bills had to be redone.

The interior of the White House proved less impervious to alteration, and the basic structure incurred considerable weakening as one modern convenience after another was imposed on it: walls were cut up to accommodate gas pipes and electric wires; bathrooms and elevators took their toll.

In 1949, President Truman received warnings about the building's structural weaknesses that were even more alarming than those that had prompted a general renovation in 1902. Margaret Truman's piano had started to go through the floor, breaking the ceiling on a state room below, and the Commissioner of Public Buildings, W. E. Reynolds, was quoted as saying that the second floor "was staying up there purely from habit."

Thus began an enormous project taking more than three years in which the White House structure would be reinforced and its space expanded, while the basic four walls would not be budged even one inch. This remarkable feat was accomplished by gutting the interior and then installing a new steel frame inside. A renovation in 1927 had already added a third floor, recessed and concealed from public view by a balustrade. The 1949 modernization went in another direction to accomplish further expansion without visibly altering the exterior: excavating under the old basement. By 1952, when the Truman project was completed, the official total of rooms was set at 132, of which thirty-five are considered "principal."

The same stubbornness that protected the four walls from dem-

In 1949–52, the interior of the White House was completely gutted, and a steel frame was assembled inside the original stone walls.

olition and relocation also affected the naming of the building. Although it was originally known as the President's House (and that is how its flatware and linens were marked), references to the "white house" cropped up almost as soon as the gray sandstone was covered with its first coat of whitewash in 1798. After being rebuilt, following the burning by the British troops in the War of 1812, it was gradually renamed "Executive Mansion" (the word "mansion" commonly used in the nineteenth century to describe homes of wealthy citizens). But Americans persisted in calling it the "White House," and finally, in 1902, Theodore Roosevelt made that name the official one. He explained that every state had an Executive Mansion and the President of the United States deserved a residence of unique title.

Much about the White House went beyond an ordinary executive's home. Even before its site was selected, George Washington had decided that he would live and work at the same address. His successors followed his lead in spite of their own misgivings and the loud objections of their families. First Lady Edith Roosevelt likened the arrangement to a storekeeper "living above the store," and President Chester Arthur insisted no businessman would tolerate it: "You have no idea," he once told a reporter, "how depressing and fatiguing it is to live in the same house where you work."

As though the dual burden of serving as both home and office were not enough for one building, the White House gradually took on a third role—national museum. Special importance attached itself to the contents of the President's House: its glassware, china, and furniture attained exceptional value and aroused great interest. Americans who wanted the best examples of their nation's workmanship to grace the President's House donated prized furniture and art to it, and visitors lined up to see the exhibits. In 1988 the American Association of Museums accredited the White House as a museum.

The fourth role of the Executive Mansion, as the People's House, has been obvious and frequently acknowledged. From the beginning, Americans deemed it their property: they paid the bills and they meant to call the tune. Public tours throughout the year, enormous receptions for thousands of invited guests, concerts, and Christmas parties brought many people inside; crowds gathered on their own outside the gates to shout in victory when wars ended and protest in anger against policies they did not like.

What began as a relatively modest estate on the Potomac—a home for the President—has evolved in two hundred years into a national symbol of the first order. Unlike other important monuments such as the Statue of Liberty that speak to one part of the nation's past, the White House speaks to many. As home-office-museum-gathering place, it plays four roles in the nation's history, four parts on the world's stage. Any one of them would suffice to make the White House special; together they assure its unique importance and guarantee that millions of people will want to go inside.

In April 1989 George and Barbara Bush greeted visitors on the North Portico (with parts of the still unpainted north façade behind them).

HOME TO A FAMILY

Barbara Bush and new grandchild, son of Marvin and Margaret Bush.

★ Behind the pomp of diplomatic visits and state dinners, amidst the planning for public tours and cabinet meetings, the White House serves as home to the President and his family. Protocol and international crises are interwoven into the fabric of family life—marriages and anniversaries, births and deaths, illnesses and convalescences. Every President's family, except George Washington's, has lived at 1600 Pennsylvania Avenue (ranging from William Henry Harrison for only one month to Franklin Roosevelt for twelve years), and every occupant, no matter how short his residence there, has had to adjust to a multi-purpose White House.

To the uninitiated observer, a mansion of this size might seem to be able to accommodate easily the dual roles of home and

President Kennedy walks with his young son, John, Jr., outside the Oval Office.

In August 1974, before they moved in, Betty Ford joined her daughter Susan in a tour of the family quarters of the White House.

office—in fact, its management resembles that of a small hotel more than a private residence. By 1991 the White House boasted a budget of about seven million dollars and a staff of one hundred and three, including sixteen maids and housemen, seven butlers, nine cooks, and five ushers. To keep the building in tiptop shape, the mansion relies on ten engineers, four carpenters, six electricians, two plumbers, two storekeepers, two painters, and five florists. Additional employees come in on a part-time basis, and the National Park Service takes full responsibility for care of the grounds.

No wonder each incoming First Lady takes a tour of the premises before moving in. Traditionally, since 1909, the outgoing First Lady has introduced her successor to the mansion, and only rarely has she delegated the task to an assistant. Even personal inconvenience need not delay this visit. Just days after she had delivered a son by Caesarean section, Jacqueline Kennedy accompanied Mamie Eisenhower through dozens of White House rooms in order to make plans for moving in. Three years later Mrs. Kennedy went over housekeeping details with Lady Bird Johnson—one day after John Kennedy's funeral.

Even when the President and his family have campaigned in a bitterly contested election and lost, the tour takes place. Such events can be bittersweet, as when Lou Hoover, deeply disappointed that voters had rejected her husband's bid for reelection in 1932, walked with Eleanor Roosevelt through the family quarters on the second floor, or as when Rosalynn Carter, despondent after her husband's 1980 presidential defeat, escorted Nancy Reagan through the family section.

As each new President and his family move in, arrangements are made for the living quarters to suit their comfort. Betty Ford planned so that she and her husband had one room they could "crawl into and shut the door." She wanted their own favorite things there—the President's old blue leather chair, exercise bike, pipes and pipe rack. The valuable antiques in the White House collection were lovely but, like a lodger in the most finely appointed hotel, she insisted on a private space that she and her husband could call their own.

Most transitions from one administration to the next are sharp and precise. Clothing, personal furnishings, even pampered pets are all moved out, their substitutions in place in a matter of hours. All this is accomplished with very little fanfare. Back in 1909, Helen Taft noted that there is "never any ceremony about moving into the White House. You just drive up and walk in."

Within weeks of the change in administration, the domestic staff can feel an altered atmosphere—casual and friendly, or restrained and more formal—as bedrooms and sitting rooms on the second floor are rearranged to reflect their new occupants. Some families make few changes, bringing in only their most essential personal possessions—a favorite bed or special photographs—while other presidential families transform the upstairs quarters, installing new wallpaper and rugs. Color preferences are obvious: Mamie Eisenhower liked lots of pink, and Nancy Reagan's personal favorite was red.

What one family considers essential, the next one may discard. Lyndon Johnson insisted on shower heads that delivered a forceful spray but his successor, Richard Nixon, had them removed. The Hoovers added thirteen radios, many telephones, and matched furniture, while the Roosevelts just wanted "something comfortable."

Sometimes, having lived abroad or traveled extensively, the President and First Lady show their preference for a "foreign" flavor in furnishings. In 1911 *Good Housekeeping* described the Taft White House as "Oriental," with "cunningly carved teakwood chairs, tables, cabinets, and wonderful Eastern fabrics," all evidence of the Tafts' years in the Philippines. The Hoovers arrived with a sizable collection of Chinese vases, and Ellen Wilson, although she had never lived in Asia, redecorated the dark central hall in straw-colored Japanese paper. Nearly seventy years later Nancy Reagan brought her own special collection of tiny Chinese porcelain vases for display in the West Sitting Hall.

Besides an experienced staff to oversee the moving-in of the President and his family and the redecoration of the second-floor quarters, there are other enormous perquisites of White House living. After two years as First Lady, Barbara Bush told a reporter: "You'd have to be a little crazy not to like this." Former residents have recalled the thrill of traveling in limousines and private planes, arriving by helicopter on the South Lawn. The Fords' daughter Susan compared the whole experience to living "a fairy

Lyndon Johnson, who reportedly spent many hours on the telephone every day, speaks here from the West Sitting Hall on the second floor while daughter Lynda and grandson Patrick Lyndon Nugent look on.

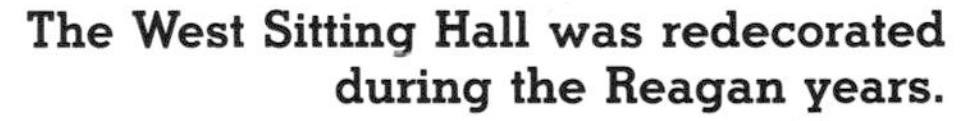

The West Sitting Hall was redecorated during the Reagan years.

Lady Bird Johnson wheels her grandson on the South Lawn, August 1967.

tale," and Lyndon Johnson's daughters talked of the excitement of meeting movie stars and world leaders every week. On one occasion in 1964 Lynda Bird, still a college student, helped host a lawn party where guests included Leonard Bernstein, Helen Hayes, George Balanchine, Willem de Kooning, Harper Lee, Walter Lippmann, Marya Mannes, Dr. J. Robert Oppenheimer, Ben Shahn, and many others equally famous. Luci Johnson, Lynda's younger sister, called White House living "a unique opportunity," one that anybody who had the chance should "savor" because "nothing like that will ever pass your way again."

Many White House families, however, feel overwhelmed by all the attention focused on them, and they complain about the lack of privacy. "Normal" routines now fall under the control of teams of staff members who schedule the family's mornings, afternoons, and evenings.

Most Presidents' families have never before lived in such a large residence and they must make their own rules about how to act around the domestic staff. The Nixons instructed employees to be as invisible and silent as possible, while Betty Ford wanted to be answered when she said "Good morning," and at "strictly family meals" President Ford liked to compare golf scores with the butler. The Hoovers, who were accustomed to having many servants in their homes in China and London, were often deemed cool and detached by White House staff members, while the Coolidges, who had always lived in modest rented quarters, treated the domestic staff almost as family.

Lack of privacy is perhaps the biggest complaint of Presidents' families. Sometimes the White House seems to have no walls, and as the ultimate "glass house," its every inch is considered open for viewing. In the early 1900s Edith Roosevelt noted that security agents watched her closely, even when she sat out on the porch. They must have thought, she observed wryly, that "I was about to hatch anarchists." Almost sixty years later Jacqueline Kennedy objected to losing her anonymity at the age of thirty-one when she became First Lady, and she tried hard to protect her two young children from reporters. Caroline, at age five, learned to hold up a warning hand and say, "No photographs." Lady Bird Johnson retreated to a small sitting room that had the virtue of "only one door," and she kept a little cushion to hang on the doorknob—tellingly imprinted, "I want to be alone."

This complaint about inadequate privacy was no twentieth-century development. In the 1840s the Polks, who had no children of their own, invited a niece, Joanna Rucker, for lengthy visits to the White House, and she wrote to a cousin in Tennessee that she was always being interrupted by some straggler who would pretend to lose his way to the President's office and stumble into the private family quarters. She laid the blame on the fact that the house belonged "to the Government and everyone feels at home."

Past residents of the Executive Mansion have also acknowledged the cost of putting one's life on hold as educations are shelved, friends distanced, hobbies and personal travel curtailed under the pressures of White House life. In 1964 Luci Johnson was only seventeen but she gave up her own social life to campaign for her father's reelection. Every weekend (except one) for about six months, she left the White House to go out and speak in his behalf. "From Friday noon until Sunday evening," there were, she recalled, "no dates and no parties." Once she escaped into a White House closet after hearing her mother and a presidential aide discuss sending her out to campaign on a weekend when she had already scheduled two dates.

Rosalynn Carter remembered that living in the White House changed the way people treated her. "Even my best friends looked at me differently," she admitted, and those who came to visit her in the White House were so in awe of the building that she found herself struggling to put them at ease. Susan Ford put it differently: the White House brings you "new friends," she said, and you have to be "cautious."

In that large house at 1600 Pennsylvania Avenue even the definition of the word "family" sometimes changes. The multiple facets of the President's job—social, political, executive—have encouraged the practice of inviting individuals outside the immediate family circle to serve in a supportive role. Widower Thomas Jefferson initiated the practice when he invited his married daughter, Martha Jefferson Randolph, to bring her family to stay in the Executive Mansion while her husband served in the U.S. Senate. The Presi-

Kennedy children, Caroline and John, Jr., join their father in the colonnade connecting the residence to the West Wing.

President Bush pauses to pose with granddaughters on his way to the West Wing.

dent also employed as secretaries two young men, Meriwether Lewis and William Clark, who worked and slept in a section of the East Room while Jefferson tutored them for their western expedition.

Martin Van Buren, whose wife had died nearly two decades before he assumed the presidency in 1837, took along his four sons when he moved into the Executive Mansion. Ranging from twenty to thirty years of age, they assisted their father in various ways, and the eldest, Abraham, served as his father's private secretary. In 1838 Abraham married Angelica Singleton, a relative of Dolley Madison, and he brought his bride to live at the White House where she presided as surrogate First Lady for the rest of President Van Buren's term.

Extended families residing in the White House—married sons and daughters, grandchildren and in-laws—came to be frowned on in the late twentieth century, as though voters objected to the cost or the privilege. Exceptions occurred, of course—Bess Truman's mother made lengthy visits to the White House and died there in 1952—but most presidential households in the twentieth century did not include the many relatives that were common earlier when voters approved, even applauded, this evidence that their leader was a solid family man. The only bachelor President, James Buchanan, was frequently written off as unfit for the job.

John Tyler eventually fathered fifteen children by two wives, more than any other President, and eight of them were born before he was called upon to lead the nation in 1841. The youngest son, then eleven years old, and three teen-aged daughters might have been expected to live with their parents, but President Tyler also arranged for his adult children and their spouses to live in the White House. The wife of Tyler's oldest son, Robert—an actress who appeared on the stage as Priscilla Cooper—often filled in as White House hostess.

Some Americans complained that Abraham Lincoln stretched the White House welcome mat a little too far. While Union forces were fighting a bloody war to put down the rebellion of Confederate states, Lincoln faced a delicate family situation. His wife's relatives were divided, and some of them, including her brothers, supported the South. When the husband of Mary Lincoln's youngest sister was killed in action, his widow, Emilie Helm, needed a place to stay and the President said, "Send her to me." Thus it happened that a Confederate widow slept in the White House while the Civil War continued, and rumors grew about traitors in high places.

Ulysses and Julia Dent Grant both had their fathers stay with them in the White House, and the elder Mr. Grant became famous for quarreling with the aged Mr. Dent. Their verbal assaults on each other, as reported with some glee in the national press, titillated the nation. One would accuse the other of being too deaf to hear anything, and the other would respond with coarser insults.

Sometimes the President's household reached outside the extended family to include employees or close friends in an attempt to make the pressured job of President a little less so. In December 1850, President Fillmore invited his law partner from Buffalo to come stay at the White House, explaining as he did so that it was "a temple of inconveniences" but had one room "neatly fitted up for guests." Franklin and Eleanor Roosevelt hosted several close aides and friends for months at a time. Harry Hopkins, a trusted adviser,

President Truman stopped for this photograph on the way to church on May 13, 1945, the day he set aside for prayerful thanksgiving for the end of the war in Europe. He is joined by his wife Bess, their daughter Margaret, Mrs. Truman's brother Fred Wallace, Mrs. Truman's mother, and the President's sister.

lived there with his daughter after his first wife died, and when he married again he stayed on for more than a year. Lorena Hickok, Eleanor's journalist friend, also had her own room at the White House for years.

★★★

All this activity could not have been predicted by architect James Hoban when he submitted the original plans for the President's House in 1792, but he did understand that this would be no ordinary residence. Like a wealthy planter's home, it featured spacious rooms of grand proportions on the first floor where parties and business meetings could accommodate dozens of guests. Above this "public" or "state" floor, the family's rooms were scaled to private uses—sleeping and family conversation.

Much like a latter-day hotel, the White House has always differentiated its three original floors according to function. Service areas—for food preparation, laundry and heating equipment—were relegated to the basement (actually the ground floor if viewed from the south). The first or "public floor" had large rooms with high ceilings and a grand entrance hall to serve for the most festive occasions, and upstairs on the second floor the family had its living quarters. Even that level had a public air about it, its spacious corridor running from east to west, providing parlor space for bedrooms on both sides.

From the beginning, circumstances encouraged considerable overlap between public and private uses of the mansion. Abigail Adams practically reversed Hoban's design—she invited visitors on business upstairs to the family floor because the first floor remained unfurnished and she requisitioned as a backyard the large East Room, which would later become the setting for the grandest White House social events. Her decision to hang laundry in the large "Audience Room" resulted partly from the season (it was December) but also from considerations of propriety (she recognized the indignity of putting out the President's underwear for all the neighbors to see).

The smaller parlors between the East Room and the Dining Room—later known as the Green Room, the Blue Room, and the Red Room, used for elegant public receptions—also were pressed into personal use by Presidents' families. Thomas Jefferson claimed the Green Room as a dining hall; William Howard Taft transformed

Frances Folsom Cleveland, the only White House bride of a President, sits in the West Hall on the second floor, near the Steinway piano that had been a wedding gift from William Steinway.

Esther Cleveland, the only child of a President ever born in the White House, is held by her mother, Frances Cleveland, while her older sister Ruth looks on.

the Blue Room into a music room, complete with Victrola and record collection; and Theodore Roosevelt's children used the Red Room as a play area and walked on stilts there.

Even with rooms serving dual purposes, the Executive Mansion was considered too small within decades of being built, and in 1857 one newspaper predicted that it would soon be used only for business and official entertaining. The Chief Executive could take his family to live in some more "salubrious" part of the capital city where he would not have to be "perplexed and annoyed at all hours by the crowd of licensed beggars and borers."

The First Family's housing problem worsened in the second half of the nineteenth century when the President's office staff took over the eastern end of the second floor. Large families had to subdivide the few rooms allotted to them in order to have a sufficient number of bedrooms. There were many complaints and several Presidents and their wives threatened to live elsewhere. Julia Grant thought she and her husband should keep their house on "I" Street—the President would commute to 1600 Pennsylvania Avenue for work and official entertaining. But the First Lady soon found that she was dealing with an inviolable tradition and the Grants put the "I" Street house up for sale.

Grover Cleveland was more successful than most Presidents in defying the tradition of residing year-round in the White House. Upon moving in he had found the building badly deteriorated, and although the living quarters were fairly well kept, the rest was shabby and dirty. One of his aides reported that the building had cockroaches; the attic contained "a terrible mess of junk"; and the basement was full of "rubble and overturned ash cans." Just before his marriage in 1886, President Cleveland announced that he needed a refuge so he could "go and be away from this cursed grind." He bought a house and thirty acres of land about three miles north of the mansion and lived there with his bride Frances for much of the year. From December to March when the social calendar peaked, the Clevelands slept at 1600 Pennsylvania Avenue, but in April the family's White House furniture was covered with large cloths, called "wraps," and the Clevelands moved out to their private retreat. The only President to serve two nonconsecutive terms (1885–89, 1893–97), Cleveland made a similar living arrangement

This postcard celebrated the fact that Grover Cleveland—reelected in 1892 after being out of the White House for four years—was the only President to serve two nonconsecutive terms.

Edith Kermit Roosevelt, Theodore Roosevelt's wife, assigned rooms on the west end of the second floor to herself and her husband, daughters Alice and Ethel, and sons Kermit, Quentin, and Archie.

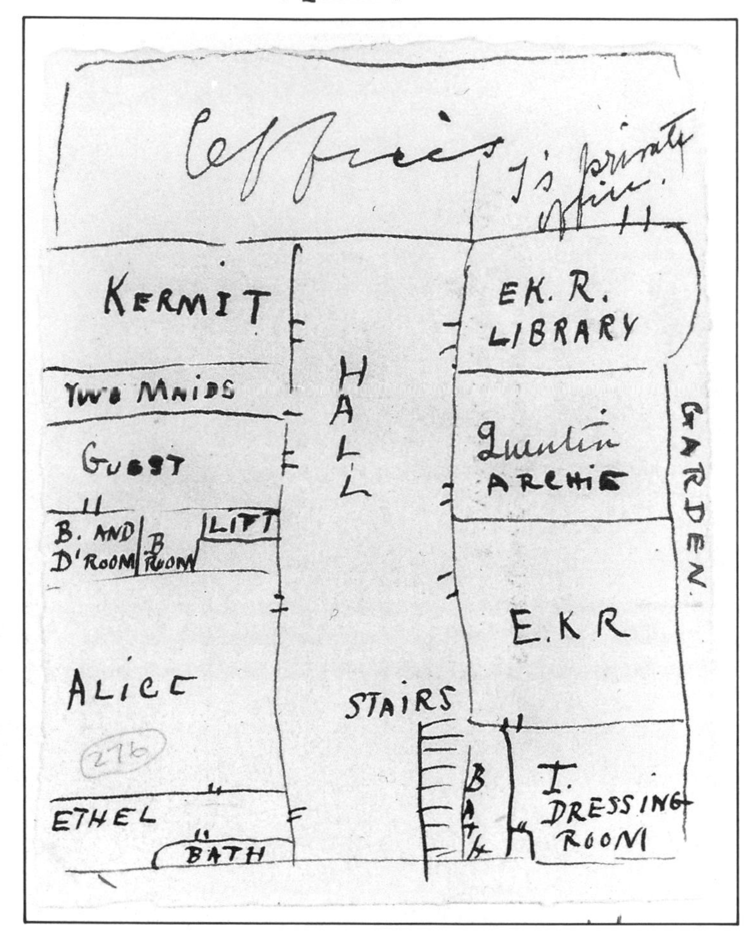

for his second term in office. By then he had young children and the privacy of his own home seemed even more important.

The White House, with its large staff, did have some advantages that the Clevelands could not ignore, however, and when First Lady Frances Cleveland was ready to give birth in September 1893, she remained there for the delivery. Her decision proved to be historic—the Clevelands' daughter, Esther, was the only President's child to be born in the mansion in two hundred years.

Benjamin and Caroline Harrison, who followed the Clevelands into the White House in 1889, agreed that they needed more room for their extended family. Because there were too few sitting rooms, at times the First Lady was required to invite female guests into her bedroom for conversation. Three possible solutions providing for more space were put forth. One called for building a separate residence for the President on Sixteenth Street and using the White House only for business and entertaining; the second plan outlined minor additions to the existing structure; and the third proposal, favored by the Harrisons, would have transformed the White House into a grandiose horseshoe with enormous conservatories. A fountain planned for the center courtyard would commemorate Christopher Columbus's arrival in America—thus noting the coincidence of the White House cornerstone being laid on October 13, 1792, the three hundredth anniversary of Columbus's first full day in the New World.

If the third proposal had been accepted, the President's House would look more like a palace than the White House we know today. But Congress balked at spending the money, and the Harrisons, like their predecessors, had to make do with minor renovations and a general cleanup.

Throughout the nineteenth century, Americans seemed content that the President and his family lived simply compared to royalty and heads of other nations. In 1884, a visitor to the White House wrote approvingly: "There is no sham or pretense . . . no effort to look like a temple or a cathedral or a castle. It tries to be a spacious and dignified dwelling and nothing more."

But by 1902, crowding at 1600 Pennsylvania Avenue had become serious. The family of Theodore Roosevelt included six children, ranging in age from seventeen-year-old Alice to four-year-old Quentin. Edith Roosevelt had struggled to divide the five bedrooms among them but even her best efforts resulted in some doubling up. Each of the Roosevelt daughters had her own space, but the two youngest boys shared a room, as did their brother Kermit whenever older brother Ted, Jr., came home from boarding school.

After the White House underwent a general renovation and refurbishing in 1902, the Roosevelts were able to reclaim the entire second floor as living space and guest quarters. The President retained an office in the residence but his staff moved to the separate, newly built West Wing. Business entertaining and official functions would be confined to the first and ground floors. Important guests might be invited to sleep on the second floor, and small confer-

Theodore Roosevelt's two young sons Archie and Quentin line up with White House police.

ences would occur there, but from this point on, the President's family considered "upstairs" to be their territory.

In 1927 renovations on the third floor provided several more rooms for the family and their personal guests. Formerly used only for utility functions, the top floor was recessed to make fourteen sleeping rooms, several bathrooms, and storage space. This upper floor, with its obvious advantage of being more distant from the public areas, became the choice of young residents. When Betty Ford toured the mansion prior to moving in, she suggested that her daughter use a room on the second floor, across from that of the President and First Lady. Susan, however, much preferred the privacy of a suite on the third floor—the same one that had been used by Julie and David Eisenhower during the Nixon years in the White House.

One area of the third floor became particularly popular. The sun porch or "sky parlor" built on the roof of the South Portico gave unobstructed views of many of the capital's monuments. Shielded from curious eyes, the President's family could enjoy a rare treat—privacy and sunshine at the same time. Margaret Truman played table tennis with her mother there and Bess Truman sometimes hit Ping-Pong balls into the skylight. Lyndon and Lady Bird Johnson's daughters, Luci and Lynda, entertained their young friends in that room, and when Luci married, the bridesmaids' party was held there. Eight years later, on the evening before Richard Nixon resigned the presidency, he and the First Lady

On the evening before Richard Nixon announced to the nation his decision to resign the office of President, his family joined him in the Solarium for this photograph.

Rosalynn Carter enjoyed the sunny views from the Solarium on the third floor of the White House.

assembled in the Solarium with their daughters and sons-in-law.

Even before the third floor was added in 1927, Presidents' families found a measure of privacy on the second floor. Several nineteenth century First Ladies spent so much time there that they became virtually invisible and Washingtonians would not have recognized them if they had walked down the street. Margaret Taylor, whose husband Zachary Taylor served little more than a year as President (1849–50), rarely ventured downstairs, and false rumors circulated to the effect that she smoked a pipe. Eliza Johnson, Mary Lincoln's successor as First Lady, saw almost no one outside her own immediate family. Jane Pierce, distraught over the death of her ten-year-old son just weeks before her husband's inauguration in

On Sunday evenings the Hayes family gathered in the second-floor Oval Room to sing hymns. *Frank Leslie's Illustrated Newspaper* pictured them in its April 3, 1880, issue.

1853, declined to go downstairs to attend public receptions. (Bennie, the last surviving son of the Pierces—two others had died earlier—had suffered mortal injuries in a train accident, from which both his parents emerged unhurt.)

While twentieth century White House residents abandoned attempts to isolate themselves on the second floor, they did persist in using the family rooms according to patterns set by their predecessors. The second-floor Oval Room remained a favorite, its central position and gracious proportions making it the preferred gathering spot for two centuries. Abigail Adams made it a priority to furnish this room, and her successor Dolley Madison settled on a color scheme that later became permanent: she chose yellow damask for the furniture and curtains.

In 1850 Abigail Fillmore put the family library in the upstairs Oval Room, and her daughter moved in a harp for evenings of music. Twenty-five years later the Hayeses sang hymns there; and in the 1930s and 1940s Franklin Roosevelt, whose mobility was limited, used it as a kind of salon, mixing business and social visits. In the same room, the Lyndon Johnsons celebrated their grandson Lyn's birthday and put up the family Christmas tree.

Most Presidents have chosen to sleep in the suite of rooms on the southwest corner of the second floor. From there they have a long, expansive view out over the South Lawn. The morning sun cannot reach them at dawn, and they are protected a bit from the street noise of Pennsylvania Avenue on the north. During the 1991 war against Iraq, President George Bush complained that the war protesters' drums kept him awake, but he would have been disturbed more if his bedroom had faced north. (Only a few Presidents, suspected to be particularly late sleepers, have chosen a bedroom facing north.)

Over the years some changes in White House facilities have been necessary in order to meet the special requirements or requests of the Presidents and their families. President Taft, who weighed over three hundred pounds, needed a super-sized bathtub installed for his private use. President Garfield's mother (the first to witness her own son's inauguration) required assistance in walking, and the first elevator in the White House was purchased

The Johnson family celebrated Christmas 1968 (their last in the White House) with a tree in the second-floor Oval Room.

for her. President Franklin Roosevelt, paralyzed from the waist down, later relied on the same elevator to move him from floor to floor and, fearful of fires, had the building inspected frequently. Fires in fireplaces were extinguished whenever he remained alone in a room—a marked contrast to President Nixon, who kept the fireplaces going even in summer because he liked the look of an open fire. Fortunately he could control the temperature by running an air conditioning system at the same time. By 1969, when Nixon became President, the White House's cooling system worked efficiently and well, a far cry from the primitive air conditioning hoses that had first been strung through the building in the hot summer of 1881 as President Garfield lay dying.

Because of its importance as the presidential residence, the White House is specially equipped to deal with any minor illness that occurs. In fact, its medical facilities come closer to that of a hospital than a home, and since the 1850s a doctor has usually been close at hand. President Buchanan was the first to invite a physician friend to live in the family quarters, and four decades later William McKinley was the first President to appoint an official White House physician, Surgeon General Presley Marion Rixey. Subsequent Presidents' families came to rely on a staff of military nurses and doctors to attend to minor illnesses, give vaccinations for foreign travel, and advise members of the household.

In the nineteenth century taking a month or more off for recuperation was acceptable, but twentieth-century Presidents (as well as their wives) have been expected to get back to work quickly, even under difficult circumstances. President Reagan struggled to keep a partial schedule as soon as possible after the assassination attempt in March 1981, and after subsequent surgeries. Nancy Reagan and Betty Ford, who underwent mastectomies during their White House years, cited demands of their official duties as reasons for keeping their convalescences short.

The period following a death in the President's immediate family has always been a particularly difficult, trying time in the White House. The first occurrence was in 1800—thirty-year-old Charles Adams, son of John and Abigail Adams, died within days of his parents' move into the Executive Mansion. Abigail Adams had recently visited him in New York and she understood that he was an alcoholic and ill. But word of his death, although not entirely unexpected, rendered her and the President disconsolate for weeks. In 1862 President Lincoln's ten-year-old son Willie died of typhoid fever, and after his body was embalmed in the Green Room, Mary Lincoln vowed that she would never set foot in that room again. Sixty-two years later, Calvin Coolidge's younger son Calvin, Jr., contracted blood poisoning from a blister he got while playing tennis on the White House court, and within weeks the sixteen-year-old died.

Despite such enormous emotional strains, along with the pressure of presidential responsibilities, those who have lived in the White House find that something about the place pushes them on. Many of the Presidents and First Ladies have expressed a kind of awe at "living with history" and a desire to measure up to the legacy of their predecessors. Theodore Roosevelt was not easily impressed, but even he spoke of the effect those corridors had on him: he could almost see Lincoln (whose presence was strongest for T.R.) moving in and out of different rooms.

Others who have stayed at the White House, even for short visits, have encountered the mysterious "ghost" of the martyred President in the Lincoln Bedroom. Britain's Winston Churchill and Holland's Queen Juliana reported that they had glimpsed something strange. In 1987 Maureen Reagan, the President's daughter, who had slept in the Lincoln Bedroom with her husband Dennis Revell (six feet seven inches tall, he found the Lincoln bed the only one to his liking), admitted that they both had seen the "ghost." It was "an aura," she said, "sometimes red, sometimes orange" that appeared during the night. Even the Reagans' dog, Rex, seemed to sense something strange in that area and he would bark when he passed the Lincoln Bedroom but would refuse to enter.

Special tributes to famous predecessors can be daunting. Lyndon and Lady Bird Johnson, moving into the presidential bedroom, found two inscriptions on the mantel. One noted: "In this room Abraham Lincoln slept during his occupancy of the White House as President of the United States." The other, in small letters, read: "In this room lived John Fitzgerald Kennedy with his wife Jacqueline during the two years, ten months and two days he was President of the United States." Lady Bird Johnson concluded that this is one house where "history thunders down the corridor at you."

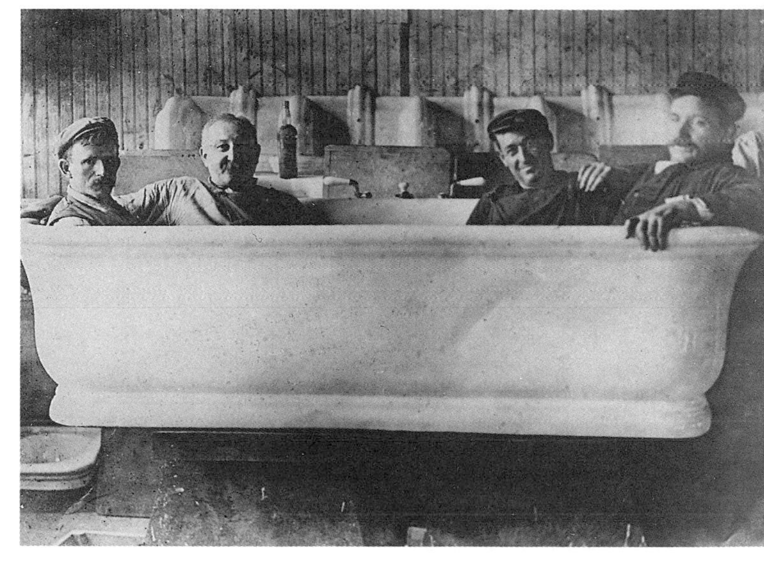

Four men could sit in the super-sized bathtub installed in the White House by President Taft (opposite page).

The Nixon family eats in the second-floor family dining room. Counterclockwise: President Richard Nixon, daughter Tricia, First Lady Pat Nixon, son-in-law David Eisenhower, daughter Julie Eisenhower.

Regardless of their prominence in the nation's annals, all White House families have had to give some attention to paying the bills—a matter complicated by the fact that family and business have shared the same roof. George Washington set the precedent in rented quarters in New York City when he hired a chef and proceeded to pay out of his own pocket for the food consumed. More than two hundred years later that practice continues, although somewhat altered. The President's family pays for whatever it eats and uses—groceries, flowers, and laundry—but since the 1920s the government has picked up the bill for "official" guests.

More than one family has complained about the strain on its purse. Abigail Adams worried that she could not pay the food bills and remain solvent. William Henry Harrison, who was President for only one month, tried to control expenses by going out with a market basket and doing his own shopping. Calvin Coolidge went over the meat bills himself, and Mamie Eisenhower clipped coupons to get discounts. Some First Ladies attempted to cut costs by hiring professional caterers; others relied on their own employees to find ways to save.

In the original plan for the President's House, architect James Hoban located the kitchen in the middle of the ground floor on the north side of the building. Surrounding the kitchen were pantries and storage compartments for stocking provisions and storing pans, silver, china, and glasses. During two centuries the main kitchen has moved only once, to the northwest corner of the ground floor, and it has adapted well to the need to feed dozens of guests at some meals, hundreds of people at receptions, and the President's family every day.

A smaller kitchen alongside the main kitchen sufficed for occasions when the President's family dined alone, and several Presidents have installed their own experienced cooks to preside over that area. Sometimes different tastes within a family have necessitated two cooks. Franklin Roosevelt's preferences tended toward more sophisticated fare than his wife's housekeeper provided, and anyone looking over her menus will understand why—Henrietta Nesbitt's repertoire did not go beyond basic meat-and-potato dishes.

Eleanor Roosevelt had hired Mrs. Nesbitt, a Dutchess County, New York, neighbor, because she preferred "someone I know" in

A steward works in the pantry to prepare for a state dinner given by the Fords.

the job rather than a professional housekeeper. The First Lady, who took scant interest in food and probably would not have complained if served rice, potato, and cream sauce at the same meal, also approved of her housekeeper's dedication to economy. Mrs. Nesbitt once boasted that she served a meal to White House guests (who happened to be war veterans) for just over thirty cents per person.

The original White House kitchen, organized like that of a hotel or very large estate, featured two mammoth stone fireplaces and barred windows to let in natural light from the north. An annual coat of whitewash camouflaged greasy walls. Over decades, the kitchen changed to incorporate new technology. Electricity, installed in the White House in 1891, was the first step toward a fully electric kitchen by 1933. Further modernization added deep freezers, huge ranges, and all the trappings of the most demanding professional chef.

Being in the public eye, White House families must suffer the indignity of having even their food preferences scrutinized by the nation. Not all Presidents boasted the sophistication of Thomas Jef-

The White House family kitchen on the ground floor as it appeared in the 1890s.

ferson, whose wine cellar would have pleased a prince, or the polish of Chester Arthur, who brought his own French chef to the White House. Lyndon Johnson was known to make midnight refrigerator raids on the tapioca pudding and to object to beef-wrapped pâté as "spoiled meat"; Richard Nixon, although revealing himself to be a connoisseur of wine after leaving office, was known to pour catsup on his luncheon cottage cheese while he was President; and George Bush's veto on broccoli was broadcast beyond the White House kitchen to vegetable haters across the land.

Until 1961, the President's family had no dining room of its own on the second floor. Everyone had to come downstairs to eat in the private dining room on the state floor level or, as they would have in a hotel, request room service on a tray to be delivered upstairs. Housekeeper Henrietta Nesbitt's careful records during the 1930s show how frequently this latter option was exercised. Alongside every menu—carefully typed so that historians would know exactly what the Roosevelt family ate on any given day—Mrs. Nesbitt noted the number of people served. Sometimes, while two or three people might venture downstairs to the dining room, six others would ask for trays upstairs.

Jacqueline Kennedy objected to downstairs family meals and arranged for a smaller dining room on the second floor. The space she designated had already gone through several transformations. Once the bedroom of Theodore Roosevelt's daughter Alice, it had doubled as hospital when she had to have an appendectomy.

Alice Roosevelt Longworth's detailed accounts of the years she resided in the White House (including the story of her appendectomy and her confession that she used to go to the roof to smoke cigarettes) fascinated Americans. Eager to capture favorable public attention, many Presidents and their wives also provided interesting or amusing anecdotes for publication. The Grants, with their four attractive children and penchant for the public spotlight, permitted the press to quote their youngest son, Jesse, talking about his difficulties with dogs and with relatives. After daughter Nellie married in an extravagant celebration, and son Fred wed a Chicago socialite and then brought her to live at the White House, an entire nation seemed to want to read all the details—where everyone was sleeping and how the Grants' new granddaughter (weighing in at a

First Lady Nancy Reagan made a point of pretasting all dishes to be served to her guests.

The Carter family dines in the second-floor family dining room, its wallpaper restored after the previous family in residence, the Fords, substituted yellow painted walls. Clockwise from top: First Lady Rosalynn Carter; a family friend; daughter Amy; Lillian Carter, mother of the President; daughter-in-law Judy Langford Carter; son Chip; and granddaughter Sarah Rosemary Carter.

whopping twelve pounds at birth) was doing. First Lady Julia Grant obliged by doling out information as though she were a public relations agent.

Few White House families have included small children, and their rarity has increased the public's curiosity about them. Only Frances and Grover Cleveland, Edith and Theodore Roosevelt, and Jacqueline and John Kennedy had children less than five years old when they moved into the White House, although many others had young grandchildren. Caroline and John Kennedy, Jr., were the first young children of a President to live in the White House in more than fifty years, and photographers eagerly sought pictures of them whenever their mother permitted them to appear. Tourists inquired of White House guards where the baby slept and where Caroline's pony, Macaroni, was kept.

Growing up in the White House spotlight is not easy; public criticism can be loud and frequent. Franklin Roosevelt's granddaughter, Eleanor Dall Seagraves (Sistie), recalled as an adult that she had heard herself referred to as "that brat in the White House." Amy Carter was widely scolded for reading at the dinner table (as were her parents for permitting it).

Like typical grandparents, Presidents and First Ladies have been pleased whenever their young grandchildren have visited, and they have set aside parts of the lawn for them to play on. Despite criticism, Eleanor Roosevelt had an outdoor swing put up for grandchildren Sistie and Buzzie Dall after they came with their mother to live at the White House. Lyndon and Lady Bird Johnson, who had two grandchildren by the time they left office, created a tiny, secret garden for all young residents to enjoy.

Visits from grandchildren are singled out by staff as particularly pleasant times at the White House. During the difficult years following the Civil War, Andrew Johnson's wife, Eliza, made one of her very rare public appearances to attend a party honoring her grandchildren and their four hundred guests. One longtime White House employee, William Crook, observed that "there had never been a children's party so wonderful."

Ava Long, Head Housekeeper during the Hoover years, said that the only time she saw Lou Hoover in an exuberant mood was when her grandchildren came to stay with her. Their father began

The wallpaper in the second floor family dining room was removed during the Ford administration and the walls were painted yellow.

Eleanor Roosevelt encountered criticism when she decided to install a swing for her grandchildren Sistie and Buzzie Dall on the White House lawn.

In the early 1890s, President Benjamin Harrison's grandchildren became the most photographed children in the nation.

treatment for tuberculosis in December 1930, and while their mother attended to him, the three children, their nurse, and a governess moved into 1600 Pennsylvania Avenue. Ranging in age from Peggy (four and a half years) to Joan (eight months), the Hoover grandchildren remained half a year at the White House, and they could occasionally be seen with their grandparents greeting well-wishers from the South Portico steps.

White House residents worry about the safety of small children, and before each member of the household had security protection, every family took its own precautions. Frances Cleveland thought she could safely send her children and their nurse for a walk on the lawn until she observed the frightening result—strangers picking up her young daughter in admiration. Subsequently the First Lady insisted that the gates to the grounds be closed, and even when vicious rumors circulated about the children's physical and mental deficiencies, she refused to relent.

Julia Grant had objected earlier to the public's easy access to

The number of Roosevelt grandchildren had grown by the time the President began a fourth term in 1945.

the White House. "I closed those gates," she later wrote in her autobiography, and although there "was a public outcry against our exclusiveness, my children and I had a wonderful time."

Cameras had become popular by the 1890s and tourists stalked White House families, intent on getting their own personal snapshots. Benjamin Harrison's grandchildren could be seen on the lawn, pulled by their ponies or walked by their nurses, thus bringing a human touch to an otherwise distant President. Harrison's young grandson had his picture taken so many times that he became, according to some reports, the most photographed child in America. The child's fame grew until one southern congressman composed a verse about him, ending with the words: "Baby rules the White House / and damn it there you are."

Woodrow Wilson's first grandchild was born in the Executive Mansion in January 1915, but the baby failed to arouse the curiosity that had surrounded the Harrison grandchildren. A number of youngsters had moved through the White House in the intervening years, including the notoriously energetic and ingenious six children of Theodore Roosevelt. Journalist Jacob Riis, a good friend of T.R.'s, recalled seeing them slide down the banister to the state floor and parade their pet reptiles across the dining-room table. He was not present, however, for their most famous caper. When Archie Roosevelt became ill, his younger brother Quentin decided to comfort him by taking his favorite pony to the sickroom. The feat required coaxing the pony into the small White House elevator, but the visit cheered Archie and attracted considerable public attention. When a modern elevator was installed, the old one went on display at the Smithsonian Institution, mannequins of Quentin and the pony appropriately posed inside.

The Roosevelt boys sometimes intruded on their father's guests in very direct ways. John McIlhenny, a Rough Rider friend of the President's, was staying overnight at the White House and using a room separated from the Roosevelt boys' bathroom by a makeshift partition. Suddenly he got a wet sponge on top of his head.

Even the generally sedate daughters of President Wilson were tempted to mischief in the White House. They would join tourists walking through the mansion and then, without revealing their identity, make comments about the Wilson family—to the amuse-

President Woodrow Wilson, whose first grandson was born in the White House in January 1915, holds his first granddaughter, born later that same year.

President Theodore Roosevelt's son Quentin sits on the pony that later achieved fame for riding on the White House elevator.

Rosalynn and Amy Carter admire the White House garden.

This photograph of Abraham Lincoln and his son Tad in the White House appeared in *Harper's Weekly,* May 1865, just weeks after Lincoln's assassination.

ment of a few others who were in on the ruse and the shocked disbelief of those who were not.

If a President's children are of school age, several choices are available. Instruction can take place at one of the capital city's public schools (Amy Carter attended Thaddeus Stevens School) or one of the private academies (Luci Johnson enrolled at National Cathedral School). Presidential offspring can go away to boarding school or college, as the Coolidge sons did, or bring teachers in to start their own White House school class, as when the Kennedys arranged for a group of about twenty children to join daughter Caroline.

Abraham Lincoln's sons invited a few friends to share a tutor, and Julia Bayne, whose brothers went to the Lincoln White House school, implied that they all learned less than they could have and that Mary Lincoln, a particularly indulgent mother, went too far in her edict to "let the children have fun." The Garfield sons had their own tutor—Dr. Hawkes, who complained to the President that his charges talked too much and worked too little. The President reacted by saying he would check their assignments himself; the quality of their work immediately improved.

Choosing a school for one's children is usually no simple matter; the fishbowl nature of the White House ensures that it will be complicated. The security of the student must be considered and conditions assured for at least some scholarly progress. At the same time, most Presidents' families, aware that their White House years are limited, want to include children in as many of the special events and celebrations as possible. Almost as soon as Lyndon Johnson was inaugurated, Lady Bird began thinking of ways to persuade college-aged daughter Lynda to leave the University of Texas "and come back and live in Washington with us." The First Lady admitted to herself that this would be "no easy job."

A kind of camaraderie, reaching across generations and political party lines, develops among those with White House ties, and reunions occasionally occur. One such meeting in 1966 brought together members of seven Presidents' families to reminisce. Several of those present had actually lived in the White House—Mamie Eisenhower and her granddaughters, Franklin Roosevelt's son and granddaughter, and elderly Marthena Harrison Williams, who had caused a stir seventy-four years earlier when the White House was

put under quarantine while she recuperated from scarlet fever.

At another of these reunions, Margaret Truman joked that she was happy to meet her "fellow inmates," and President Taft's son Charles recounted how he had enlisted the help of young Quentin Roosevelt to plaster spitballs on all the White House paintings. The caper evidently inspired David Eisenhower, who admitted that on the last night he spent in the White House during his grandfather's second term he had put notes behind all the pictures, promising "I shall return"—and sure enough he did, as the son-in-law of President Nixon eight years later.

★★★

During their years in the White House, the President's family can turn to a variety of activities to fill any free time. If they choose to

Members of several Presidents' families posed at the White House for this photograph on November 28, 1966. Seated: (left to right) Julia Grant Cantacuzene, granddaughter of Ulysses Grant; Marthena Harrison Williams, granddaughter of Benjamin Harrison. Standing: (left to right) Eleanor Seagraves, granddaughter of Franklin Roosevelt; Mamie Eisenhower; Lady Bird Johnson; Lawrence Hoes, descendant of James Monroe; Mary and Barbara Ann Eisenhower, granddaughters of Dwight Eisenhower; Elliott Roosevelt, son of Franklin Roosevelt; Susan Eisenhower, granddaughter of Dwight Eisenhower; Barbara Eisenhower, daughter-in-law of Dwight Eisenhower; Mary Virginia Devine, great-granddaughter of Benjamin Harrison; John Roosevelt, son of Franklin Roosevelt; John Roosevelt's wife; and Helen Taft Manning, daughter of William Howard Taft.

read, there are plenty of books, at least since 1850 when Abigail Fillmore moved in and found that there were none. A former schoolteacher who had always liked having her own library, the First Lady persuaded Congress to appropriate two thousand dollars to buy volumes for the upstairs Oval Room. This collection was supplemented by additional purchases, and in the 1930s when the American Booksellers Association volunteered to donate reading matter, the library was relocated on the ground floor.

Presidential families need not leave the premises to view their favorite film or to take a class. In 1942 Franklin Roosevelt installed a movie theater in the East Colonnade, and it has provided relaxation for many Presidents. Jimmy Carter reportedly held the record for the most films watched there until he lost that distinction to Ronald Reagan (who sometimes preferred seeing films on a video in the upstairs family quarters). Bess Truman started a Spanish class for Washington wives and although Mamie Eisenhower, who enrolled, insisted that they learned little, the classes met regularly. Lady Bird Johnson called the White House "one big seminar," and Rosalynn Carter relied on experts to tutor her on many important national and international issues.

When Presidents and their families want recreation, the facilities are usually provided on the premises—at least they have been

For Christmas 1960 (their last in the White House), Dwight and Mamie Eisenhower invited relatives and friends to join them for a holiday meal.

The day after his inauguration, President George Bush chatted with his mother, Dorothy Walker Bush, in the Oval Office.

President Jimmy Carter enjoyed frequent tennis games on his own White House court.

during the twentieth century. John Quincy Adams had to take his morning swims in the Potomac (reportedly in the nude), but a hundred years later Franklin Roosevelt had the luxury of a pool. Limited by his paralysis, he had turned to swimming for exercise, and his doctors spoke publicly of how much he benefited from it. Schoolchildren from across the nation sent in their dimes and quarters to finance the construction of a White House pool, which was located in the colonnade connecting the West Wing to the residence. Roosevelt's four immediate successors enjoyed the pool, but Richard Nixon covered it up and converted the space to a pressroom. During Gerald Ford's presidency, funds were obtained from private sources to build another pool on the South Lawn.

Harry Truman turned to other types of recreation—poker or bowling—and had an alley installed in the West Wing. More than twenty years later Pat Nixon would go to relax in another bowling alley on the ground floor of the White House, near the area where Edith Wilson had once learned to ride a bicycle.

Among the top White House "perks" is a private tennis court, complete with courtside table and soft drinks. When President Bush, who interspersed jogging with horseshoes in his recreation program, put son Marvin in charge of allocating playing time, someone joked that he had captured "one of the most powerful jobs in the new administration."

The new outdoor swimming pool, built with private donations, served President Ford as the setting for a press conference.

President Hoover (second from left) joined aides and reporters for thirty minutes of medicine ball each morning at seven before beginning work.

For other leisure moments there are pets, and the White House has sheltered an incredible variety of animal life in two hundred years, rivaling a zoological park in its array of rabbits, snakes, turtles, and tropical fish. In 1969 Margaret Truman published an entire book on the subject, *White House Pets.*

The tradition of keeping animals at the White House began when Thomas Jefferson had cages built on the White House lawn for bears brought back from the Western journey of Lewis and Clark. Forty years later, the first American expedition to Japan returned with many souvenirs, including some tiny "sleeve dogs" for the President and his friends. The minute dogs resembled birds, and one observer noted that "a coffee saucer made ample scampering ground."

Personal pets often have to be cared for by the White House staff who, when the job becomes too burdensome, find ways of cutting back. The Grants' young son Jesse acquired several dogs, but one after another they died. Finally the President announced that the entire staff would be fired if another dog died, and the next one survived the remainder of Grant's presidency.

First Lady Grace Coolidge, famous for her fondness for animals, is shown with her raccoon Rebecca.

President and Mrs. Ford and their daughter Susan pose with Liberty and her first litter of puppies.

President Bush relaxes with the family dog, Millie.

The names of many of the dogs belonging to the Presidents and their families have become household words. Millions of Americans came to recognize Warren Harding's airedale, Laddie Boy, and Lyndon Johnson's beagles, Him and Her. Franklin Roosevelt's Scotty Fala and the Fords' golden retriever Liberty became familiar White House figures, and television viewers often saw First Lady Nancy Reagan trailing at the leash of her dog Rex after she stepped out of the presidential helicopter onto the South Lawn. Barbara Bush endeared herself to millions of animal lovers when, almost as soon as she had moved into the White House, she provided a birthing room for the family dog, Millie (the same area that had once been used by Nancy Reagan as a hair salon). In 1990 *Millie's Book* appeared in print, the first autobiography of a presidential pet.

★★★

President Roosevelt's dog Fala became a favorite of the nation and was frequently photographed alongside the President.

President Johnson's grandson Patrick Lyndon Nugent (center) celebrates his first birthday with a White House party in June 1968.

Every family marks some milestones of its own—wedding anniversaries, birthdays, marriages of sons and daughters—and the First Family is no exception. Some have struggled to keep these observances private, drawing a firm line between themselves and the world, while others have willingly transformed these dates into public celebrations. Nineteenth century Presidents, in particular, scheduled large parties to observe personal milestones, but that practice gradually became less popular. The Hoovers were noted for having many dinner guests throughout the year, but on their wedding anniversary they dined alone. The Franklin Roosevelts paid little attention to special days—at least for adults—and housekeeper Henrietta Nesbitt's records show only a cryptic notation: "birthday cake" on the menu.

Children's birthday parties in the White House illustrate once again how its public and private roles merge. Franklin Roosevelt's grandchildren had their celebrations arranged by the First Lady's secretary, who carefully preserved the records which can now be found in the Library of Congress. Edith Helm, who worked for several Presidents' wives, noted the names of young friends of Sistie Dall who agreed to attend her party on March 24, 1934, and those who declined—almost as though this were a state dinner or important political event. The invitation to Sistie's party came in two sections—one a typical juvenile card and the other featuring the presidential seal. Like so many other things in the Roosevelt White House during the years of the Great Depression, the invitations show a touch of frugality. They were evidently ordered in bulk, and the same one (with the day and hour changed) sufficed for several different occasions.

While in residence at the White House, Presidents' families find it hard to ignore the public's curiosity; gifts exchanged among themselves become part of the national record. The Reagans dutifully listed for the press the practical items they presented each other—often riding gear or ranch equipment for their California retreat.

Gifts from outside the family are another matter. Congress sets a limit on the value of items that a Chief Executive may accept, and the limit applies to his spouse and children as well as to himself. Items worth more than a designated amount become public property, to be turned over to a museum or left for the nation's use.

But such restrictions are recent, as a look through presidential papers shows. Lou Hoover hesitated to take a new Cadillac but then accepted in a note appropriate to this woman who loved horseback riding: "We decline most of the commercial gifts offered us," she wrote the donor, but "this Cadillac seems so much like a new colt just come in from the pasture that we cannot resist adding her to our Cadillac stable."

When gifts were offered to celebrate a personal event such as a wedding anniversary, lines between personal friends and business associates merged in uncomfortable ways. Helen and William Howard Taft celebrated their twenty-fifth anniversary with a huge party on the South Lawn of the White House in June 1911. Thousands of invitations went out (the First Lady insisted that she kept no record of the exact number) and hundreds of costly gifts came in.

Young friends of Sistie Dall received this invitation to her White House birthday party.

Miss ISOBEL HARRIS, Composer-Pianiste

Miss EMILY WOOLLEY, Soprano

Saturday, March 24, 1934
The White House

Helen Taft, the first President's wife to ride with her husband from the inauguration to the White House, caused even more comment when she held a large party at the Executive Mansion to celebrate her silver wedding anniversary.

One aide admitted, "I never knew there was so much silver in the world." One judge whom "the President hardly knows" sent a tureen two hundred years old costing eight thousand dollars. Embarrassed by the generosity and the appearance of impropriety, the President decreed that nothing should go on exhibit, but the First Lady stored all the gifts away with a later use in mind. She could erase the monograms on many pieces and pass them on as gifts to other people.

★★★

White House weddings, especially those that involve a member of a President's immediate family, are almost never entirely private affairs, as several brides have learned. The very first White House wedding almost escaped public attention—perhaps because its principals were President James Madison's widowed sister-in-law, Lucy Payne Washington, and Supreme Court Justice Thomas Todd. Even a bride could not upstage First Lady Dolley Madison, who reportedly "stole the show."

Within a decade, her successor Elizabeth Monroe upset Washingtonians by refusing to make her daughter's wedding a part of the capital's social season. Elizabeth Monroe insisted that the marriage of daughter Maria to her cousin, Samuel Gouverneur (who had served as the President's private secretary), be a strictly family affair. When the diplomatic community objected to the exclusion, the First Lady dispatched the Secretary of State to set them straight. Maria Monroe, the first daughter of a President to marry in the

White House, had her private "family" wedding in the first-floor Oval Room on Thursday evening March 9, 1820, and then five days later a reception was held for the newlyweds in the East Room.

While such small, relatively private ceremonies would continue to dot White House history (President Tyler's daughter married in a quiet ceremony in January 1842), larger, more public celebrations became common in the late nineteenth century. In 1874 President Grant's only daughter Ellen (Nellie) wed Algernon Sartoris, whom she had met during a trip to Europe. At first the President objected—that Nellie, at eighteen years of age, was too young to wed—but then he relented and invited several hundred guests to what was later described as the "greatest social event" of Grant's presidency and "the most brilliant wedding in the history of the White House."

The East Room, newly redecorated in an ornate style characterized as "steamboat palace," was embellished further by numerous large flower arrangements. Orange blossoms were brought in

The East Room, in its rococo-revival style of the late 1800s, provided a festive party room.

from Florida, and one of those attending described the room as a "perfect bower of bloom." The Marine Band played as Nellie, attended by eight bridesmaids, made her way to a small, flower-covered platform to recite her vows.

For a while it seemed that Nellie Grant's marriage was the most interesting news story in the nation. Special newspaper supplements, printed with pictures and details of the ceremony, sold out as quickly as they could be printed. When the marriage failed a few years later, a national magazine, *Public Opinion,* noted that the entire nation was saddened because it "had assumed a half-way responsibility for the match."

If the wedding ceremony featured the Chief Executive as bridegroom, Americans showed even more interest. When Grover Cleveland married Frances Folsom on June 2, 1886, the guest list was considerably smaller than for the Grant wedding, but public interest for the first (and only) marriage of a President in the White House, was even greater.

Although she did not provide the press with photos of her wedding dress, Frances Folsom posed for this picture for her family.

The young bride (one month short of her twenty-second birthday) had just returned from Europe and so most of the arrangements were left to the President. A wedding in a bridegroom's home was hardly typical, but so many of the circumstances of this match went beyond the ordinary. The bride's grandfather, whose home might have served for the ceremony, had just died, and no one else in her family could provide a place that guaranteed the necessary privacy. The President, who belonged to no church, disliked the idea of being married in one. A hotel did not offer the desired setting nor could adequate security and privacy be guaranteed there. Almost by default, the White House was chosen, and the President himself penned the invitations to cabinet members and a few close friends, about twenty-eight in all.

Guests gathered in the Blue Room, and the Marine Band played Mendelssohn's "Wedding March." The bride and groom walked in together, took their vows, and then led their guests to the State Dining Room where everyone feasted on a twenty-pound salmon (one of the largest ever recorded as coming from the Connecticut River) and tasted the four-tiered wedding cake that had been baked in New York. The man responsible for transporting the cake to Washington had taken the overnight train and had gone

When the Clevelands barred the press from covering the wedding ceremony, *Harper's Weekly* published its own version.

without sleep in order to make sure the cake arrived in perfect condition.

Many years later a Washington woman recalled how she had been only ten years old at the time of President Cleveland's marriage and that she and her young friends had stood with noses pressed against the White House fence to see as much as they could. Although she never had a glimpse of the bride and groom, she had heard the Marine Band and had seen "the huge banks of flowers and ferns in the windows."

Journalists went wild. Many camped on the White House lawn and others tried to hide among the catering staff and musicians. Barred from the mansion for the ceremony, reporters simply made up their own versions of what happened. The President had insisted that he wanted none of the sentimental trappings typically

After her marriage to Nicholas Longworth, Alice Roosevelt posed with him and her father, President Theodore Roosevelt (right).

associated with weddings, such as horseshoes and flower arrangements in the shape of wedding bells, but one national magazine printed a picture of him and his bride standing under both a horseshoe and a wedding bell. When the couple left for a honeymoon in nearby Maryland, reporters dogged their steps, hid in the shrubbery surrounding the honeymoon cottage, and took photographs whenever the Clevelands emerged for some fresh air.

Edith Roosevelt hoped to avoid some of this circus setting when her stepdaughter, Alice, married Nicholas Longworth, a prominent Republican congressman, on February 17, 1906. Arrangements were not simple, since a thousand guests were invited, and three separate entrances were designated for their use. The East Room had just been redecorated in 1902, and Nellie Grant Sartoris (who was a guest at the Roosevelt wedding) must have been struck by the contrast between this wedding and her own. Only a few tasteful flower arrangements adorned the room, and the bride, without any attendants, walked with her father to an improvised altar. The bride's stepmother had benefited from the Clevelands' experience with the press, and the First Lady permitted photographs of the bride's dress to be distributed. But in spite of all her cooperation, errors in journalism did creep in. Reports that the wedding party paraded down the big White House staircase were unfounded. Edith Roosevelt said, "We descended in the elevator."

Details of Alice Roosevelt's wedding became part of the White House social record and a model for others that followed. When two of Woodrow and Ellen Wilson's daughters decided on White House weddings, the staff looked to the Roosevelt nuptials for hints on arrangements. The first to wed, Jessie, chose Tuesday November 25, 1913, a day that turned out to be mild for late autumn. Invited guests (including military officers, foreign diplomats, cabinet members, relatives, and family friends) were told to present their admission tickets at the White House gates.

The bridegroom, Francis (Frank) Sayre, had an uncomfortable moment when he arrived for the ceremony and realized that he had neither a ticket nor any identification documents. He had been out walking on the Virginia shore with a friend that day and had come directly to the White House, where he found unusually tight security arrangements. When a guard asked who he was, Sayre recalled, "I told him I was the bridegroom but he replied that anyone could

President Wilson's youngest daughter married in a small White House ceremony in May 1914.

claim to be the groom. I suggested he call the Captain, because if I did not get inside there would be no wedding."

As in the two previous East Room weddings, Frank Sayre and Jessie Wilson took their vows in front of a low dais set up near the long outside wall, and the Marine Band played. Guests filed through the Blue Room, had refreshments in the State Dining Room, and then returned to the East Room, where the carpets were rolled back for dancing.

The bridegroom recalled that he and Jessie had a "tricky time getting away." Rumor had it that newsmen were vying for the best story about the couple's wedding trip plans, and a one-thousand-dollar reward awaited the winner. Frank and Jessie enlisted the help of a friend who let them use his car rather than a more recognizable White House vehicle, and a Secret Service man on a motorcycle cooperated by tying up traffic while they escaped. Then, after crossing over into Virginia, the newlyweds exchanged the first car for another one (equally inconspicuous) and, on their way to Baltimore, drove back past an unsuspecting crowd gathered outside the White House.

When President Wilson's youngest daughter, Eleanor (Nellie), married William Gibbs McAdoo six months later, circumstances made a smaller ceremony appropriate. The bridegroom was widowed and the bride's mother was ill with Bright's disease, which would prove fatal three months later, so only eighty guests were invited for the 6 P.M. ceremony in the Blue Room. This time the ruse to outwit reporters went a little differently. The bridegroom arranged for several White House cars and his own personal automobile to be parked conspicuously in different places. Then, after the ceremony, McAdoo enlisted the help of several guests; pretending to be the bridal party, they ran to the various cars and sped away, thus confusing reporters and dividing their attention while the real newlyweds escaped in another automobile that had been hidden behind some bushes.

A hiatus occurred in White House weddings—at least for Presidents' daughters—until the 1960s, when there were three. Luci Johnson, dubbed the "first White House bride" in fifty-two years, did not actually marry in the Executive Mansion. She had converted to Catholicism and her wedding mass was celebrated on August 6, 1966, at the Shrine of Immaculate Conception. But just about every

At the White House reception following Luci Johnson's marriage to Patrick Nugent, guests feasted on an enormous seven-tiered cake.

other element of the festivities took place at 1600 Pennsylvania Avenue: intricate planning, photography, and reception.

Since curiosity was at such a peak, newspapers wanted to publish a picture of the bridal gown before the wedding, but Luci was superstitious (or romantic) enough to want the bridegroom, Patrick Nugent, to see it for the first time when she wore it to the altar. Great effort went into helping her keep the secret. J. B. West, Chief Usher, noted that the white gown was locked in the Lincoln Bedroom, and no one was permitted to enter. When Luci decided she wanted to be photographed in the dress in the East Room, the entire White House had to be declared off-limits until she accomplished her mission. For an hour and a half no one, not even the housecleaners, walked through the White House corridors. Chief

Lynda Bird Johnson descends the main staircase on the arm of her father for her marriage in the East Room, December 9, 1967.

Usher West recalled that there was "tighter security than there had been during the Cuban missile crisis."

On the day of the wedding, the Executive Mansion was transformed. The upstairs hall was screened off into a beauty shop so bridesmaids could get their hair and makeup done by experts. Downstairs the state rooms were beautifully decorated and all set for the reception. After the ceremony, on a day Lady Bird described as the hottest of the summer, guests returned to the air-conditioned White House where a receiving line formed to greet them in the Blue Room. Then everyone filed into the East Room to watch the President's daughter cut the seven-tiered wedding cake.

On this one occasion, the White House staff proved overly efficient. When the bride prepared to change into her going-away outfit, she found that it had already been packed and taken away. Her mother admitted to having some nervous moments until the outfit was found and brought back.

Luci's older sister, Lynda, married on a crisp day in December 1967, and she chose a White House ceremony for her wedding to Charles Robb (whom she had met when he served as a military aide at the White House). Lynda's wedding followed the model set by Alice Roosevelt—with the ceremony in the East Room—but, unlike Alice and her father, Lynda and her father really did descend the famous stairway.

Julie Nixon, whose marriage to David Eisenhower, grandson of the former President, was scheduled to occur one month before her parents moved into the White House, chose another site—a New York church—but two years later her sister Tricia decided on a White House wedding when she married New York law student Edward F. Cox. Actually, the site was the Rose Garden, thus achieving a "first" for a President's daughter. Outdoor ceremonies are always risky in June, and no tent had been set up—in case of rain, the ceremony would have to be moved inside.

Julie Eisenhower recalled that the day of the wedding was gray with intermittent drizzle all through the morning. By about three o'clock, when guests began arriving for the 4 P.M. ceremony, no decision had yet been made to move inside. Julie and Tricia were "almost comically taking turns pacing in front of the beautiful arching window of the West Hall overlooking the Rose Garden." They could see the altar already set up under an iron gazebo covered with hundreds of white flowers. Military aides were trying to keep

President and Mrs. Nixon leave the Rose Garden after the marriage of their daughter Tricia in the first outdoor wedding of a President's daughter at the White House.

the guests' chairs dry, wiping them off and then preparing to carry them inside, only to change their minds and put them back in their previous places.

The President had retreated to a hideaway office across the street, and Pat Nixon left the final decision to the bride, who, in telephone conference with her father (who had conferred with the Air Force weather station), decided to rush the ceremony into a fifteen-minute storm clearing predicted for 4:30. The President escorted his daughter down the South Portico steps and along a path to the Rose Garden. The weather forecast proved accurate, and the ceremony was completed without rain. Then guests moved inside for dancing in the East Room. It was, Julie Eisenhower recalled, one of the first times her parents had danced in the White House.

Enormous publicity surrounded the Nixon Cox wedding. Sixteen hundred reporters requested credentials and a separate tent was set up for them over the tennis court. As though to justify their presence, they published detailed, very personal information about the bride and groom, including her weight (ninety-eight pounds), her school record, and the fact that she collected Dresden and Meissen china. Exact wording of the vows went out on news wires. Besides biographical information on the bride and groom, press releases described the bandleader and told where he went to school, the ages of his three children, and his wife's first name. The bridegroom's souvenirs of the event—along with a piece of the wedding cake—went into the files at the Library of Congress, helping to document another White House family's records.

Few homes in America can match the White House as an elegant setting for a daughter's marriage or any other celebration. Nor can other private residences compete with it as a medical facility, travel agency, and communications network. Every family who lives there remarks on the advantages and the responsibilities of this once-in-a-lifetime opportunity. First-time visitors and long-time employees understand that the White House is, first and foremost, a residence for the President—a place for private moments, intimate family gatherings, and leisure activities with friends. In its first two centuries, the venerable mansion shared its fame with thirty-nine different families, and none of them would ever forget it.

After their daughter Tricia's Rose Garden wedding on June 12, 1971, President and Mrs. Nixon joined the bride and groom in a waltz in the East Room.

OFFICE OF THE PRESIDENT

In 1968 Lyndon Johnson announced from the Oval Office that he would not run for re-election.

★ When newspapers run headlines such as "The White House says . . ." or television reporters sign off "from the White House," they mean the office, not the residence. That small complex of offices, nestled in an extension on the west side of the mansion, looks more like the headquarters of a moderately successful corporation than the workplace for a world leader. From a modest, oval-shaped office, the Chief Executive presides over a staff that is spread out into the East Wing and fills two entire buildings nearby.

In some ways the President's office functions like a sizable city—apex of political power, center of a communications labyrinth, network of expert advisers and trusted staff. Even when a President leaves the

President George Bush, seated at a partners' desk in the Oval Office, speaks on one telephone while General Colin Powell uses another, during Operation Desert Storm, February 1991.

premises, the machinery and personnel continue to operate twenty-four hours a day, sifting reports, maintaining communications, and staying prepared to change course and implement new policy on a minute's notice. A score of telephone operators stand ready to put staff in contact with dozens of specialists familiar with the most obscure, distant parts of the world. The official phone directory of the Executive Office of the President lists more than four hundred people (although not all of them work in the White House complex), and that does not begin to cover the men and women, machines and operations that are considered part of the network.

When George Washington decided to combine residence and office under one roof he could hardly have anticipated the complex problems that twentieth century Presidents would confront—threats of terrorists and hostage takers, international trade arrangements, and the demands of a nation of 240 million people. George Washington's staff was small—hardly larger than that needed by any gentleman who oversaw a sizable plantation, and most of his contemporaries employed relatives or friends, thus reinforcing the link between family and office.

The temptation to hire relatives was strengthened by the tradition that each President paid his secretaries from his own pocket. Not until 1857 did Congress approve an annual salary of $2,500 for an employee to handle secretarial duties. Even then, the custom of the President's office as a kind of multigeneration family club was so strong that James Buchanan, a bachelor with no sons of his own, employed his nephew James Buchanan Henry. Working for a relative, even one highly placed, had its drawbacks, and the young man, citing unreasonable demands by the President, quit after two years on the job.

Presidents forced to reach beyond relatives to find secretaries often brought them into the family circle and treated them like sons. Abraham Lincoln employed John Nicolay, a German-American from Illinois who had edited a small newspaper and worked for the fledgling Republican party in the 1860 election. Nicolay enlisted another young man from Illinois, John Hay, as his assistant, and the two were soon ensconced down the hall from where the Lincoln family slept.

For the President, "living above the shop" had its special problems as work and family matters overlapped and schedules merged into a seamless day that mixed children and business appointments, politics and pleasure. As long as the nation was small and the decisions few, the President worked at a leisurely pace and easily confined his office to part of the first floor. In the first administrations the few letters received each day at the White House could be piled on a single silver tray, opened at a small writing desk, and answered by a lone scribe or even by the recipient himself.

The first person to serve a full four-year term in the White

President Kennedy met with top advisers amidst scattered children's shoes.

George and Barbara Bush pose with Queen Elizabeth II and Prince Philip in May 1991.

House, Thomas Jefferson, had eight years in which to organize his work space inside the mansion and get the office functioning efficiently. Unfortunately, he showed little administrative talent. Although he was a brilliant writer of memorable prose, Jefferson spoke poorly, without authority or clarity, and put little importance on office efficiency. Jumbled, irregular schedules often satisfy geniuses, and Jefferson's creative mind, which moved as easily from architecture to agronomy as it did from viticulture to vivisection, could thrive in a disorganized setting. Famous for announcing that he had no use for protocol at social events, Jefferson was just as casual about business, and the disorder that characterized seatings at his dinner table applied equally to his office.

The sunny, spacious room on the southwest corner of the White House that would later become the State Dining Room was Jefferson's choice for working, and one of his contemporaries described this "cabinet room" as holding a motley combination of furniture. In the center was a "long table, with drawers on each side" where the President kept his important papers alongside carpenter's tools and garden equipment. Maps lined the walls, and books, charts, and globes were interspersed with flowers and plants on the shelves. A mockingbird, Jefferson's "constant companion in his solitary and studious hours," remained in its cage while visitors were present, but when the President was left alone he would take the bird from the cage and permit it to fly around the room.

However informal Jefferson's office may have appeared, it did function as reception hall for the nation's leader, and it was here that representatives of other peoples came to call. The United States still commanded little attention from major European countries, but the North American Indians (as Native Americans were referred to at the time) already realized a need to make friendly gestures toward the President of the United States.

In 1804 a delegation of Osage Indians arrived at the President's House—the result of an invitation Jefferson had issued through Meriwether Lewis to come "at public expense." Their appearance and apparel intrigued Washingtonians, and one French artist profited from the curiosity by producing and selling crayon drawings of them.

Minor dignitaries from abroad also visited the President, often as much out of curiosity about this new American republic as out of a need to discuss matters of mutual interest. In 1805, when the

Osage delegation returned to Washington, their visit coincided with that of a Tunisian minister by the name of Meley Meley, who was traveling with his own large entourage. Accounts vary as to which of the two delegations appeared more exotic.

Meley's "numerous suite" came dressed in "Turkish costume, rich as silk, velvet, cashmere, gold and pearls could make it," while the "strangely contrasted" Osages wore deerskin moccasins and leggings, their faces and bodies painted. They must have made a colorful group as they sat down together at the President's table, where Jefferson surprised them by serving ice cream made from a recipe he had acquired during his stay in France. In the middle of a hot, humid Washington summer, the cold dessert caused no end of marveling and the President's guests carried away memories of an unforgettable dinner.

Of all the exotic foreigners who would visit the President's House during the next two centuries, none would arouse more curiosity than Marquis de Lafayette, whose assistance during the Revolution was still remembered by grateful Americans when he returned for a celebratory visit in 1824. The capital city still resembled a rough farming village in comparison to elegant European capitals, and one of Lafayette's aides expressed disbelief that the President of the United States would consent to reside in such unimposing surroundings. No important person in his own country would have received visitors in such a modest building.

American reporter Ann Royall also expressed her disappointment, describing the President's House as "unsavory," rendered more so by "a pack of the most insolent miscreants, in the character of his domestics, who guard the avenues to his presence."

None of this criticism could dampen Lafayette's welcome, and he found crowds everywhere eager to honor him, even putting his name on the top of ginger cakes. During that visit, he received the ultimate accolade: the park on the north side of the President's House was renamed to honor him.

As the United States grew and enhanced its importance in the world, a long line of distinguished foreign visitors made their way to the President's door. Skilled translators were not always available or present, especially in the nineteenth century, and there were many opportunities for misunderstanding. When a Chinese diplomatic

President Ford and Queen Elizabeth dance during the state dinner in honor of the Queen and Prince Philip at the White House, July 7, 1976.

On June 25, 1954, a meeting on the South Lawn included Secretary of State John Foster Dulles, British Prime Minister Winston Churchill, President Dwight D. Eisenhower, and British Foreign Secretary Anthony Eden.

President Rutherford B. Hayes greeted a delegation from China in the Blue Room, 1878.

delegation visited in 1878, dinner guests reported that they had to resort to childish mime. Royal guests could not be suitably accommodated overnight at the President's House, and in 1860 when the Prince of Wales visited, only he and two aides could sleep in the White House; the rest of his entourage stayed at the British Embassy.

The twentieth century saw an increase in foreign dignitaries and envoys, and by the 1940s Washington had become a virtual magnet for royalty and foreign heads of state. Eleanor Roosevelt wrote her daughter in some exasperation: "We've had the Dutch royal family for a night, all the Quezon family from the Philippines . . . and await the King of Greece . . . I forgot the President of Peru."

A visit by Winston Churchill during the Christmas season of 1941 turned out to be chaotic, and Eleanor Roosevelt remembered his stay as one of her most difficult times in the White House. The President's residence already carried an aura of being under siege —blackout curtains had gone up soon after the attack on Pearl Harbor—and the British Prime Minister arrived in some secrecy. An aide, a secretary, two Scotland Yard men, and a valet accompanied Churchill, and he expected all of them to be housed with him on the second floor of the White House.

Very quickly it became apparent that the British entourage expected to have considerable service and the run of the floor. They turned the Monroe Room (which the Roosevelts had used as a sitting room) into a map room and office, then proceeded to impose their own erratic schedules on an overworked domestic staff. Afternoon naps kept the Britons fresh, while the Roosevelts, who did not permit themselves the luxury of resting after lunch, tried to keep up the hectic pace. Even the energetic First Lady admitted that it always took several days to catch up on sleep after Churchill left.

At the conclusion of Mideast peace talks at Camp David in September 1978, President Jimmy Carter invited Egyptian President Anwar Sadat (seated on the left) and Israeli Prime Minister Menachem Begin back to the White House to sign the historic peace treaty.

Job seekers crowded the stairs on their way to the President's second floor office.

Almost from the day it was first occupied, the President's House hosted a steady stream of congressional representatives and office seekers (whose numbers grew along with the nation). After 1800, new states entered the Union in rapid succession, each one sending representatives and their families to the capital. Agencies and departments multiplied, and individuals came seeking jobs and favors for themselves, their relatives, and their friends.

Responding to the added responsibilities of the office, President Andrew Jackson began using part of the second floor for work, and John Tyler, upon taking office in 1841, ordered new desks equipped with cubbyholes and dividers. Andrew Jackson had used three rooms on the south side of the second floor, but the staffs of his successors claimed the entire east end.

Demands for the President's time were enormous. Each Chief Executive took responsibility for making hundreds of appointments, and job seekers descended on Washington after each presidential election to see the winner. Heading directly to the Executive Mansion, they congregated on the main floor and tried to take their case to the President or, failing that, to his closest assistant.

The stairway between the public first floor and the family-office second floor became famous and congested with traffic in both directions. Abraham Lincoln admitted to fleeing the residence just to avoid the crowds, and when he came down with a mild case of smallpox after delivering the Gettysburg Address he mused, "Now let the office seekers come for at last I have something I can give all of them."

After the Civil War ended in 1865, wealthy Southerners who had supported the rebellion against the Union flocked to Washington to ask for pardons. Their requests carried a certain urgency, since they were barred from political activity—including voting and holding office—until their mission was accomplished. President Andrew Johnson, a Tennesseean not unsympathetic to the Southern argument, thrived on the visible power his position gave him as men and women trooped up the White House steps to ask his forgiveness for themselves and members of their families.

Although Lincoln's wartime presidency left him little time for reorganizing the office, his successor—the tailor-turned-politician from Tennessee, Andrew Johnson—began to put some order into operations on the second floor. He permitted the installation of a telegraph in the mansion in 1866, thus beginning changes that would eventually turn that part of the White House into a maze of wires and cables necessary for communications. To accommodate a larger staff, Johnson put up partitions to make cubicles, and he installed file cabinets and additional desks. A receptionist sat in a room at the top of the stairs to sift out unnecessary intrusions.

Nineteenth-century Presidents maintained a private office of their own on the second floor, usually one of those rooms overlooking the large South Lawn. Ulysses S. Grant worked next door to the oval room where his children and wife would gather to talk and read. With a few steps he could move from a difficult political decision to relaxation with his family.

New inventions gradually made their way to the second floor of the White House, further complicating the split between its roles as home and office. The first telephone, installed in 1879 with the symbolic number "1," remained a single phone for three decades and it serves as a humble forebear of the hundreds of lines as-

Before a separate West Wing was built in 1902, the President's business callers went up a stairway located close to the north entrance, checked in with a receptionist, and then were ushered into one of the main offices.

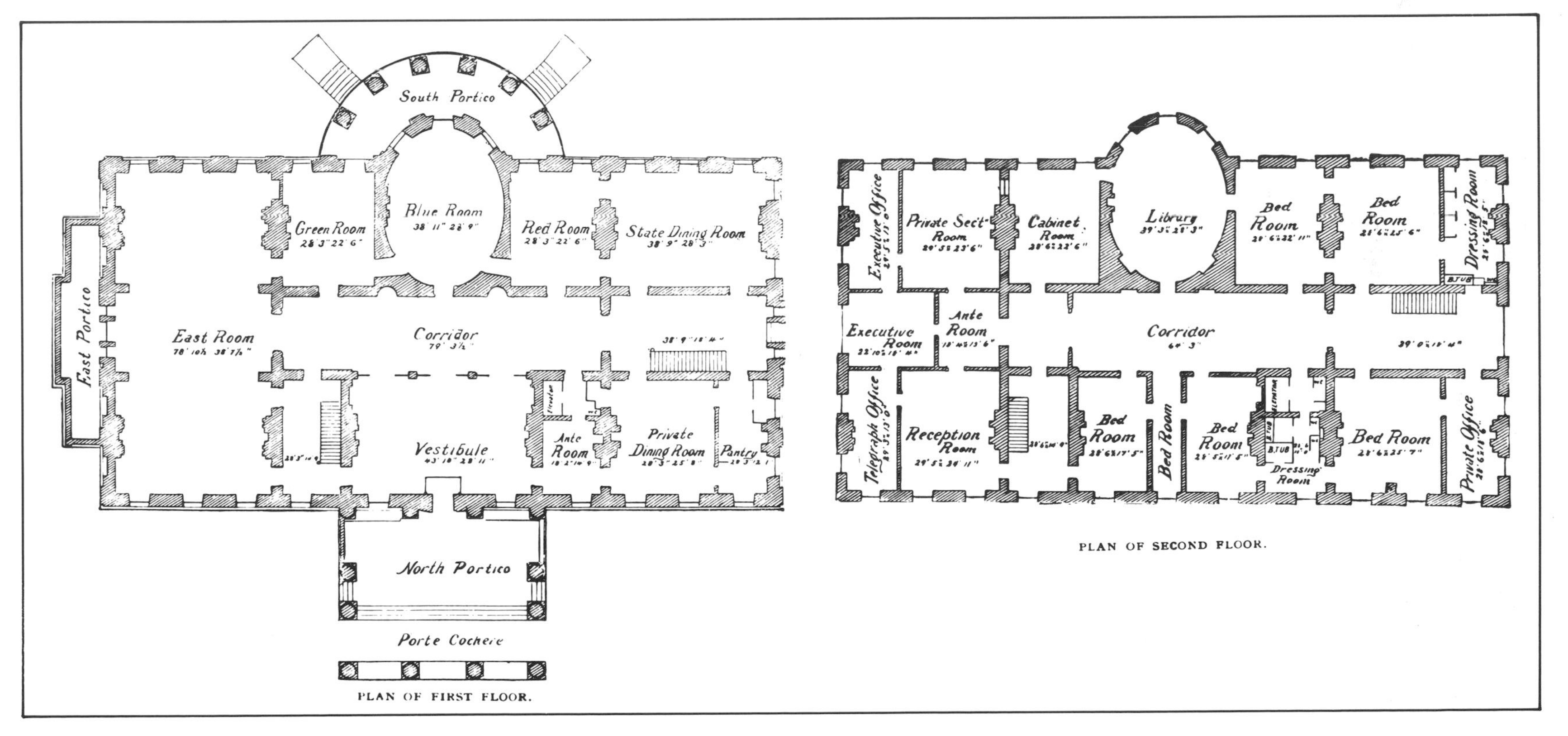

signed to the Executive Office a century later, when one month's telephone bill approached forty thousand dollars.

The typewriter was introduced into White House offices in 1880, bringing new noise levels with it and also, eventually, women workers who were needed to handle the ever increasing amounts of correspondence. Like most office staffs of the time, the President's remained entirely male until 1889 when Benjamin Harrison hired Alice B. Sanger as a stenographer. A veteran of Harrison's Indiana law office, she became the first woman to be employed in the White House in a job other than domestic service.

The increasing importance of the United States in the world—especially at the time of the Spanish-American War in 1898—helped keep the White House office growing. In 1900 Congress recognized the heavy workload and agreed to pay for two assistants and a "Secretary to the President." These staff members and their equipment cluttered much of the second floor, leaving President William McKinley and his wife Ida to confine their residence to cramped quarters in the west end.

In 1901 Theodore Roosevelt, McKinley's successor, felt compelled to make changes. Advisers, warning him that it was no longer safe to entertain crowds in the White House, suggested that whenever he anticipated large gatherings, he should arrange to have the floors reinforced with thick timbers. Earlier Presidents had

The President's staff, entirely male until 1889, worked in makeshift offices that also served as communications center, map room, and conference space.

A maze of wires cluttered the offices of the presidential staff after the first telephone was installed in 1879.

Before 1935, Presidents typically fled Washington for most of the summer, and this cartoon implies that Theodore Roosevelt took the White House with him to his Long Island estate.

used this safeguard at receptions for hundreds of guests, but now it would be routine for much smaller groups.

Theodore Roosevelt also faced the problem of finding enough seats for dinner guests. The President planned extensive entertaining, but the State Dining Room could accommodate no more than forty, and when he wished to host more, additional tables had to be set up in the large central hall or in the East Room—an unacceptable makeshift arrangement for a world leader.

Almost everyone agreed that the President's staff had outgrown the space they occupied on the second floor of the mansion, but no one wanted to ask the Roosevelt family to double up more than they had already done. Of course the President could have moved his family elsewhere, leaving the entire mansion for office space and official entertainment. But such an arrangement struck most Americans as wrong, and Theodore Roosevelt concurred in that view. When he was misquoted on the subject, he immediately set the record straight, saying: "Mrs. Roosevelt and I are firmly of the opinion that the President should live nowhere else than in the historic White House."

If the family stayed, then the question was where to build an office. Anything too close to the main house would impinge on its lines and mar its beauty; any sizable structure on the surrounding lawn would clutter and detract from the residence. The solution, described as "temporary" so as to disarm any critics, provided for an inconspicuous rectangular structure to the southwest of the White House, so close that the President could walk through a connecting colonnade and reach it in a few seconds.

The West Wing, as the office building became known, is traditionally off-limits to all but the President, his staff, and specially invited guests. Its heart is the Oval Office, the one room that more than any other has become synonymous with the presidency. An elliptical shape had not been part of the 1902 West Wing, but when the office building was enlarged in 1909 during William Howard Taft's administration, an Oval Office was designed. Rumors circulated that the shape derived from the President's rotund form—humorists joked that he had just lain down on the lawn while architects drew the outline of the room around him.

The real story behind the oval shape reaches back into Ameri-

One of the earliest photographs of the Blue Room in about 1867 shows use of the oval shape in floor coverings and ceiling decoration.

can history before there was a White House. President Washington followed the custom of his day by entertaining at levées—gatherings of men for conversation and refreshment in the late afternoon. Because his New York house could not accommodate sufficient seats, the President stood, and his guests typically formed a circle for conversation so that all participants appeared equal, with no one taking either the "head" or the "foot" of the room.

Eighteenth-century architectural styles promoted the idea of elliptical rooms. Bow windows were much in vogue in English Regency architecture around 1800, and President Washington

President Jimmy Carter's West Wing Oval Office.

showed a pronounced fondness for them. When the capital moved to Philadelphia and he rented the "largest house in town," the President included bow windows in his suggestions for remodeling. Washington may have communicated his preference to White House architect James Hoban, who designed an oval room on the south side of each floor.

With the oval shape so firmly entrenched in the history of the President's House, it is not surprising that architects echoed it in the West Wing. In delivering his design plans, Taft's architect, Nathan Wyeth, implied that its shape was no accident. "I have endeavored to show a dignified treatment," he wrote, "in keeping with the high purpose it is to serve." Although Franklin Roosevelt would later redesign the West Wing and put the Oval Office in the southeast corner, Taft's Oval Office was at the center, thus underlining the fact that it stood at the hub of operations.

Like all busy executives, Presidents retain space for several private studies and hideaways, one of the most convenient being a small suite just off the Oval Office. President Carter reportedly went there to work early in the morning, and occasionally he scheduled lunches there. In that same area President Bush put his personal computer and installed a private dining room.

After much of the office work was removed from the residence, an invitation to the second floor of the White House took on special cachet. In his first year as President, George Bush frequently invited congressmen and their spouses to visit the family quarters. He showed them the view from the "Truman balcony," snapped their photos in the Lincoln Bedroom, and walked them through bathrooms where they could observe the damp towels still on the floor. Such socializing might not change many votes but anyone who has wondered what the House looks like at the top of the stairs will understand that such visits cannot hurt.

★★★

Most twentieth century Presidents have divided their working time between the West Wing and the residence. Lyndon Johnson improvised conferences in many different rooms, and his Secretary of Defense, Clark Clifford, later wrote that he had learned of Johnson's decision not to seek reelection in 1968 when the President, still getting dressed for his televised speech to the nation, invited him into his bedroom to read the manuscript. Theodore Roosevelt used a room on the family floor for conferences, and his wife Edith jokingly said that the windows had to be opened frequently to "let out the politicians." Woodrow Wilson, who liked to type out his own letters and speeches, at least in a first draft, had his trusty portable typewriter transported many times from the Oval Office to his private study on the second floor. When the time came for signing the Underwood Tariff Act into law in 1913, Woodrow Wilson invited fifty of the law's backers to the Oval Office to witness his signature.

Such signature sessions had formerly been confined to the residence; the most famous one occurred on January 1, 1863, when Abraham Lincoln signed the Emancipation Proclamation. Turning to Secretary of State William Henry Seward, he explained that it was not uncertainty that caused him to dip his pen more than once before placing it on the paper: "I have been receiving calls and shaking hands since nine o'clock this morning till my arm is stiff and numb. Now this signature is one that will be closely examined. If they find my hand trembled, they will say 'He had some complications.' " Then Abraham Lincoln carefully signed his name.

So long as the office staff remained as small as that of Lincoln or of Wilson (the latter employed no more than forty), the West Wing's space sufficed, and even ceremonial events could be held there. As an example, in January 1915 Woodrow Wilson invited friends to witness the first transcontinental telephone call ever made from the Oval Office. What he did not know was that several staff members, eager to witness this unprecedented presidential communication, had arranged to eavesdrop on the call. They had placed an extension in the ushers' office just inside the north entrance to the residence and listened in awe as their President spoke with someone in San Francisco. Isabella Hagner, social secretary to First Lady Ellen Wilson, admitted that she had been one of those who had witnessed "this marvelous achievement."

After the death of his first wife in August 1914 and his remarriage in December 1915, Woodrow Wilson went less willingly to the Oval Office, preferring the privacy of the residence. Telephone and telegraph messages multiplied, especially after the entry of the United States into World War I in April 1917, and the increased number of clerks and employees required to keep the office functioning around the clock augmented the confusion. Wilson re-

In 1979 Jimmy and Rosalynn Carter welcomed
Pope John Paul II to the White House,
the first Pope to visit there.

treated to a study near the upstairs library where he kept his books. It was the only place, he wrote to a friend in May 1917, where "I can get things done."

Calvin Coolidge conducted most of his business in the West Wing, but by 1929 President Hoover found the space too small. Having come to the job from the business world, he was intent on efficiency and orderliness. The Republican nomination in 1928 was his first call to elective office, and he had little use for the kind of office management that most of his predecessors, schooled in the disarray of lesser political posts, took for granted.

President Gerald Ford talked with Japanese Emperor Hirohito in the Blue Room during a state dinner held in honor of the Emperor and the Empress Nagako, October 2, 1975.

President Hoover began by employing three private secretaries and about forty staff members, but that number quickly grew far too large to work in five small rooms on one floor of the West Wing. The building provided little opportunity for expansion. Low ceilings on the second floor reduced possibilities for its use as more than an attic, and the basement required further excavation before it could accommodate anything other than storage.

Staff members argued for expansion or even the more drastic alternative of transferring the President's office to a different location. But once again tradition proved inviolable, and the decision was made to hollow out additional rooms at the basement level.

The Director of Public Buildings, Ulysses S. Grant III (whose grandfather had once resided in the White House), took charge of the project. Excavation made space for a telegraph room, stenographers' and clerks' offices, locker rooms, and lounges on the lower level. Offices on the main floor were also redesigned so that the President's and his staff's offices were set off from the lobby and waiting rooms on the north.

By the summer of 1929 the West Wing was finished and functioning, but by year's end it required rebuilding again. Hoover's work space, so carefully renovated and enlarged, had caught fire and burned on Christmas Eve. The Hoovers were inside the residence that evening, enjoying a holiday dinner with family and friends, when an employee came to inform them of the flames coming out of the office building.

Guests in dinner jackets pitched in to help rescue files, and the President, who stayed on the west terrace to direct the action, reminded them that a small dog had been locked in the building that night so as to be given as a surprise to a child on Christmas morning. In an ironic twist, the President who would soon earn his countrymen's wrath for appearing insensitive to their economic plight remembered to order the dog's rescue.

In spite of the help offered from volunteers and the city's fire fighters, the building burned, except for some skeletal walls and partitions. Coming so soon after the debacle on Wall Street in October 1929, this did not seem a propitious time for talk about new construction; and accounts of the rebuilding disguised it as "general repairs." This was a ruse that had worked after the 1814 burn-

As part of their official duties President and Mrs. Kennedy prepare to meet guests at a State Dinner in honor of the Grand Duchess of Luxembourg.

President Herbert Hoover addressed a crowd gathered on the lawn outside his Office.

ing of the White House by the British and it would be used again when the residence was gutted and restored in the 1940s.

As soon as the work was finished, Hoover's large staff quickly made use of all the increased space, setting new records for the number of communications sent and received. In 1930, the first full year of the Hoover presidency, 77,055 telephone calls originated in the West Wing and nearly five times that number were received. The staff had to commandeer space in rooms that connected the main building to the West Wing, and in the process they pushed domestic services, such as laundry, into other areas.

The Great Depression crippled Hoover's presidency and limited him to one term, paving the way for Franklin Roosevelt to take office in the bleakest days of the economic downturn. Roosevelt's physical disability, resulting from poliomyelitis (infantile paralysis) twelve years earlier, made the trip to the Oval Office difficult (although he later used the elevator and an armless wheelchair with great ease) and for his first few days as President he worked in the residence.

Just hours after his own inauguration, Roosevelt summoned his cabinet members for a meeting. The Hoovers had just vacated the White House, leaving the upstairs Oval Room furnished with only a few chairs, a sofa, and a bare desk. Frances Perkins, assuming her title of Secretary of Labor—the first woman to hold cabinet rank—noted that "it never looked so tidy again as it did that night."

Roosevelt would continue to use the Oval Room for ceremonial parts of his job and for entertaining. He signed the Emergency Banking Act of 1933 and held some of his press conferences in that room, but he also liked to intersperse socializing with business, mixing drinks for colleagues or inviting them to join him for a meal served on a tray there.

Roosevelt's first trip to the West Wing had its bad moments. His valet wheeled him over, assisted him onto a desk chair, and then left him alone—more alone than he would have liked, he later explained. The drawers had been emptied, all writing matter removed, and he could not even find a buzzer with which to summon help. Finally, the man just elected to pull the nation out of the worst depression in its history leaned back in his chair and shouted.

The next year, 1934, Roosevelt enlarged the West Wing and

President Franklin Roosevelt became famous for delivering radio speeches from various rooms in the White House.

President Kennedy made this style rocking chair famous, although his wife objected to its effect on her plan to restore the White House. "A rocking chair is a rocking chair," she said, "and there is not much you can do to cover it up."

reorganized his staff. A larger space was allocated to the Oval Office, now situated in the southeast corner where it looked out over the Rose Garden and occupied the same area that Ellen Wilson had once designated for drying laundry. When television viewers watch their Chief Executive deliver a speech from the Oval Office, it is this room, 36 feet long and 30 feet wide, that they are seeing.

Space is tight in the West Wing, which measures only about 60 by 90 feet. During Jimmy Carter's presidency, one employee estimated that each staff member assigned there got an average of about 70 square feet, although few would have relinquished that tiny space for larger quarters elsewhere. One Nixon aide explained the advantage of a basement cubicle within a few steps of the Oval Office. "Never underestimate the importance of proximity."

Even these modest dimensions had been achieved with some trepidation, and President Roosevelt carefully prepared public opinion to accept his expansion of the West Wing. In one of his Fireside Chats in June 1934, the President explained that he had no intention of impinging on the plans of the original designers, but his office required modernization. During the summer, while he went on an extended trip to the West Indies and Hawaii, work began to install "modern electric wiring and modern plumbing and modern means of keeping the offices cool in the hot Washington summers." The underground rooms would be expanded and a third floor of offices added. But the President assured his listeners that the "magnificent pattern" they all recognized would not be changed: "The artistic lines of the White House were the creation of master builders when our Republic was young. The simplicity and the strength of the structure remain in the face of every modern test."

Franklin Roosevelt was back working in the enlarged office building by December 4, bringing with him an executive staff that now numbered 120. But the stresses of the Great Depression, the multiplication of federal agencies, and World War II would soon render that number hopelessly inadequate. Bulletproof windows were installed in the Oval Office during World War II, and other changes were made to increase security, but the building's dimensions remained untouched.

Attempts to enlarge the West Wing during the Truman administration foundered, partly because of outrage at what seemed to be the desecration of a national monument. One cabinet member voiced his own objections in a letter to the President. He was concerned, he wrote, for the "thousands of people who came every day to see [the White House] as they would visit a shrine, not only because it houses the Chief Executive of the Nation but for what it represents in the hearts of the people."

Over the years each new administration has decorated the Oval Office to fit its own tastes. Colors change and paintings shift to reflect new heroes and hobbies. Americans who visit a presidential library such as that of Lyndon Johnson in Austin, Texas, or Jimmy Carter in Atlanta, Georgia, will understand how varied the same room can look. Each has a model of its namesake's Oval Office,

Caroline Kennedy (left) joins a friend under her father's Oval Office desk in June 1963.

John F. Kennedy used the "Resolute" desk, given to President Rutherford B. Hayes by the British in 1880.

and in comparison they seem like entirely different places.

Sometimes the changes are unplanned. In an ironic twist, Lyndon Johnson moved into a freshly decorated Oval Office immediately after the Kennedy assassination. Jacqueline Kennedy had chosen the red carpet weeks earlier, but the installation had been delayed because of an air-conditioning problem. Just as the carpet was finally being installed, word came from Dallas that President Kennedy had been shot. Work continued—but for a different occupant.

Lyndon Johnson replaced Kennedy's famous rocking chair with one of his own and substituted family photos for the naval paintings and watercolors that had pleased his predecessor. A larger, simpler desk replaced the famous "Resolute" desk, a favorite of many Presidents and the one that doubled as play space for the Kennedy children when they visited their father in his office.

The "Resolute" desk first came into the White House in 1880 when the British government sent it to President Rutherford B. Hayes as a symbol of amicable relations between their two nations. Timber used to make the desk had come from the oak of a British ship, the HMS *Resolute,* abandoned in the Arctic in 1854 and then rescued for the Britons by American whalers.

Whether a President chooses to use this desk or another one, to have the presidential seal woven in the middle of the rug or not, to make the walls blue or yellow, is up to him, but virtually no President leaves the room unchanged. Each occupant tries to underplay the cost of redecoration. President Ford had his wife's press secretary issue a tiny announcement in November 1974 that he would be furnishing the Oval Office to reflect his own taste and provide a "warmer feeling" than that in President Nixon's office. The carefully phrased announcement left the impression that the cost would be negligible since most of the furniture would come from storerooms and other parts of the White House collection.

Even successive Presidents of the same political party customize the Oval Office furnishings to their own liking. Ronald Reagan installed a wooden floor of Kentucky oak and walnut (in place of the "wood-appearing" vinyl that had been there since 1969) and covered it with a salmon colored rug featuring the presidential seal. President Bush chose a moderate-size partners' desk (so-called be-

President Reagan looks over papers in the Oval Office, decorated during his tenure with Western art, including the sculptures in the background.

cause drawers on both sides permit two people to work there simultaneously) and a large blue rug featuring the presidential seal prominently in the center.

Although the Oval Office has remained central (symbolically, if not physically) to the West Wing since 1909, assignment of the space around it has shifted. As in any business operation, the size of one's office helps signal status. Even the waiting room (how big it is and whether every caller is treated the same) conveys a message about how the President does business, and the press and political insiders scrutinize the assignments made by each new administration. In 1985, as President Reagan began a second term by

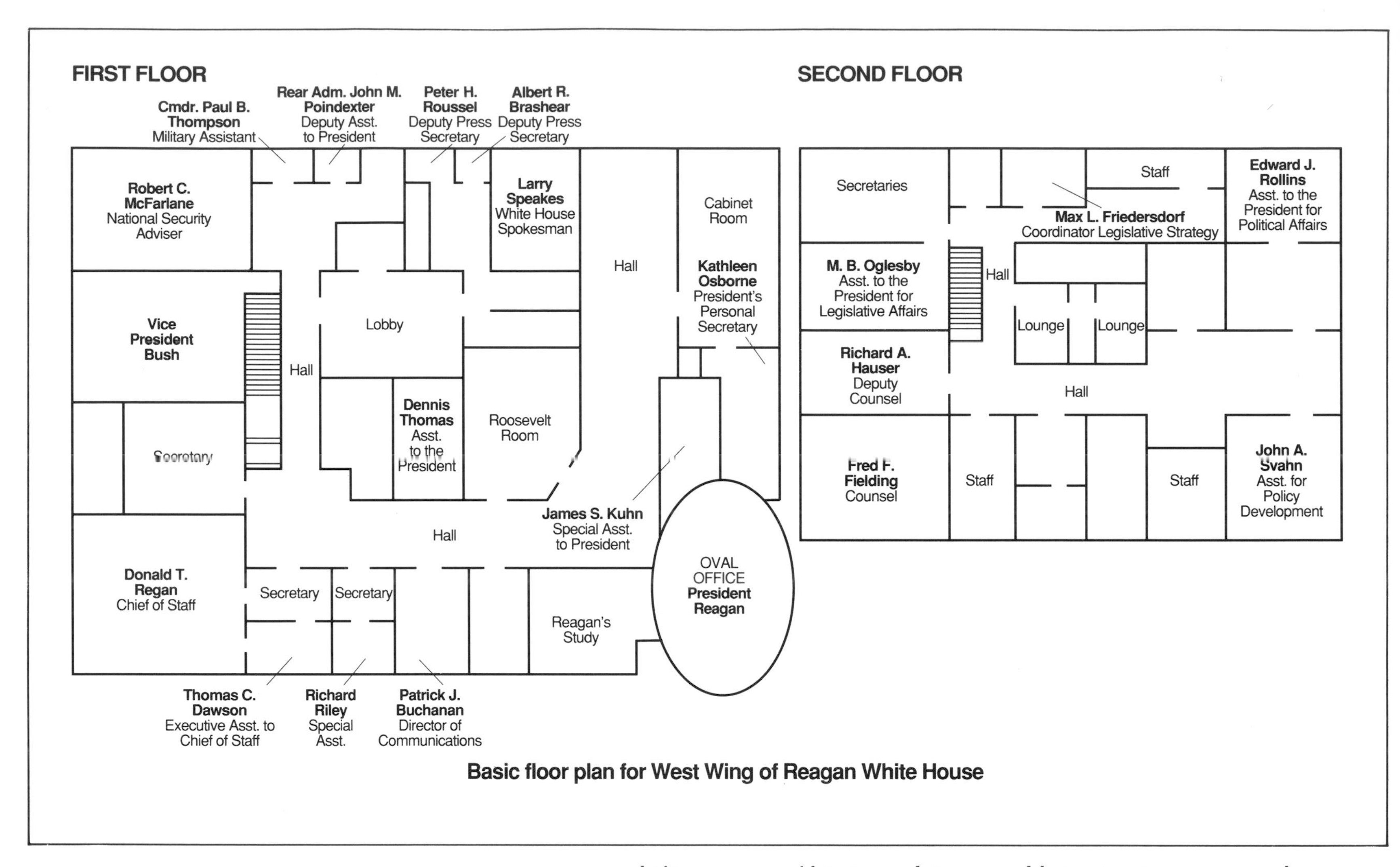

Basic floor plan for West Wing of Reagan White House

shifting some of his top advisers and bringing in new people, a major newspaper provided a diagram of the West Wing. It showed the President's Chief of Staff, who oversees the entire operation of the Office of the President, ensconced in a large corner room that is closer to the Oval Office than is the Vice President's office. The National Security Adviser, Robert C. McFarlane, was using a first-floor office—he had previously been assigned basement quarters.

★★★

To an uninformed visitor, the West Wing's basement looks more like the underpinnings of a moderately successful corporation than the setting for decisions of world importance. Much of the space is set aside for services—a plaque on one door identifies it as a barbershop, a tiny 10-by-10-foot cubicle where Milton Pitts trimmed hair for President Nixon and then remained through three subsequent administrations. From across the corridor wafts the aroma of food from the staff's dining rooms. The paneled walls and blue fittings project a nautical feeling, hardly an accident since the Navy runs the dining hall and boat-loving Franklin Roosevelt oversaw its construction.

Staff dining (or "mess") privileges are among the most coveted perks of White House employment. The three small dining rooms can serve ninety people at one sitting, but even two shifts cannot accommodate all who claim the privilege. Family and friends of staff members beg to be included, and in 1979 one announcement of promotions implied that the biggest effect would be in the dining room—the new titles carried with them eligibility for eating in the White House mess.

Diligent control keeps many prospective diners out. A reporter for *The New Republic* learned that no journalists were allowed, and in January 1989, just as the Bush administration was settling in, Brent Scowcroft, the President's National Security Adviser, opened a meeting of the National Security Council staff by announcing that all matters were up for discussion except the "White House mess and parking privileges."

Within a few steps of the dining room is an inconspicuous area of special importance called the Situation Room, which is always staffed around the clock. Its origins date back to the failed Bay of Pigs invasion in 1961 when President Kennedy decided to convert this room, formerly used for storage and utilitarian plumbing, to a communications room for monitoring information affecting national security. Wherever he goes, the Chief Executive is always linked to this small room by complicated electronic equipment (commonly called the "football" and carried by a military aide). Information is relayed to the President within minutes of its being received. Next door to the Situation Room is a conference area, encased in a lead shield that can stymie the most sophisticated eavesdropping equipment.

In 1972 President Nixon had the Situation Room remodeled, and computer terminals, two safes, and wall-to-wall carpeting were installed so that it resembled thousands of offices across the country. One visitor described it as visually disappointing—with a dozen or so technicians going quietly about the work of monitoring video terminals, filing papers, and waiting for the moment when they would be expected to act quickly. Workers have been known to complain of boredom, but each knows that major change is always imminent. An almost infinite number of events at any spot in the world might require the President, through his National Security Adviser, to look to the people in this room for fast, accurate information on which to base a decision.

Especially in times of crisis, Presidents make frequent visits to the Situation Room. Lyndon Johnson went there often to monitor developments in Vietnam, and he was there in January 1968 when word came that the North Koreans had taken command of the American intelligence ship *Pueblo*. Information was crucial—the North Koreans charged that the Americans had violated the twelve-mile limit at sea, while the Americans insisted they had remained within international waters.

In contrast, Presidents rarely venture to the West Wing's second floor where low ceilings—a necessity if the building was to remain an inconspicuous adjunct to the large main structure—make the small offices appear cramped. Its leaky roof has become famous and resistant to change. As one spokesperson explained, no administration wants to undergo the disruption caused by a thorough repair, and each President leaves the leaks for a successor to plug up. On occasion, buckets have had to be strategically placed on the first floor to catch water that has leaked from the second floor.

Power radiates from the main floor of the West Wing where, in addition to the individual offices and the waiting room, two meeting rooms provide conference space. The first, which is centrally located, was dubbed the Fish Room by Franklin Roosevelt and decorated with memorabilia from his fishing trips. But in 1969 President Nixon renamed it the Roosevelt Room for his fellow Republican Theodore Roosevelt, who had presided over the original construction of the West Wing. Reporters noted a bipartisan nod, made possible by the room's exhibition of quotations from both Theodore and Franklin Roosevelt. But most of the room celebrates T.R.—his Nobel Prize, and his love of horses and the West.

The Roosevelt Room in the West Wing, used for small conferences and meetings, was called the Fish Room by President Franklin Roosevelt.

Until the Nixon administration, Presidents had no permanent studio for press conferences, and John Kennedy (here seated in his special rocking chair) sometimes used the Oval Office for interviews.

The other conference room, just a few steps away and facing out onto the Rose Garden, is known as the Cabinet Room, which should be familiar to every viewer of television news. The brown leather chairs surrounding the table are only temporary, and most of them are purchased by their respective occupants upon leaving the job. Each is marked with a small plaque identifying who sits there, and two of the chairs—belonging to the President and Vice-President—are distinguished from the others by their slightly higher backs. When he was President, Lyndon Johnson further enforced the notion of "having his own turf" by installing several buttons at

Flanked by Secretary of State Dean Rusk and Secretary of Defense Robert McNamara in the Cabinet Room, President Lyndon Johnson holds Courtney Valenti, daughter of White House staffer Jack Valenti.

his place under the table—one of them a command for his favorite diet soft drink.

A few steps across the hall from the Cabinet Room, a Press Office underscores how much the Chief Executive's job has changed in two centuries. The first Presidents would not have understood the title or felt the need for a Press Secretary—someone to hand out news about what the President was doing and why. Twentieth-century Americans, however, came to know the names of several Press Secretaries better than those of the Vice Presidents: Pierre Salinger for Kennedy, Ron Ziegler for Nixon, Jody Powell for Carter, and Larry Speakes for Reagan.

The move toward having a separate spokesperson for the President began slowly. In the West Wing of 1902, Theodore Roosevelt allotted space for reporters next to his secretary's office. Journalists accustomed to hanging around the White House entrance, scrutinizing exits and entrances in hopes of scooping an important story, found themselves invited inside and thus acknowledged as a legitimate part of the governmental process. Reporters even merited their own telephones so they could phone their stories to the office rather than rely on a corps of young messengers to run back with the news.

Nothing so formal or organized as a press conference existed yet, although Theodore Roosevelt seemed to relish chats with individual reporters. Often these talks would occur while the President went about some other task such as reading and answering his mail. Oscar King Davis ("O.K." to his friends), a *New York Times* reporter, described how he would see the President two or three times a week, generally in the evening when Roosevelt came back to the office to clear up his desk before going to dress for dinner. Roosevelt "would glance over a letter, make an addition or alteration with his pen, and sign his name at the same time he was keeping up a steady fire of talk about whatever subject happened to be under discussion." This kind of exchange did not appeal to Woodrow Wilson, who, while still a political science professor, had recognized that he did better lecturing to large groups than talking with individual students in his office. Wilson invited reporters to come *en masse* to the Oval Office so he could set them straight on matters of public interest. More than one hundred showed up in March 1913, but the exchange did not go well. Edward Lowry, one of the reporters present that day, described how a few questions were asked, tentatively, and answered "crisply, politely, and in the fewest possible words. A pleasant time was not had by all."

Reluctant to abandon the idea of talking with reporters, Wilson scheduled another press conference a week later. When nearly two hundred correspondents appeared, the small Oval Office could not accommodate them and so the meeting adjourned to the East Room in the residence, thus setting a pattern that continues to this day for very important or celebratory press conferences.

Presidents following Wilson dealt with reporters in their own individual ways. Warren Harding, a newspaperman before going into politics, agreed to meet with them twice a week, and then he followed up this friendly overture by inviting them to play poker and referring to them genially as "our newspaper family." Even the taciturn Calvin Coolidge invited newspaper writers into his office, and Franklin Roosevelt thrived on the exchanges. As many as two hundred reporters would try to crowd around his desk which was, according to one observer, "covered with dolls, totems, and knickknacks. It was like a meeting of a club."

Most Presidents preferred a little more distance between themselves and their interrogators, so they relied on a staff member whose job eventually got its own title, Press Secretary. The assignment had its special stresses—as an extreme example, two Press

Pierre Salinger, Press Secretary to President Kennedy, briefed reporters on White House decisions.

Secretaries serving Truman died on the job. Nevertheless, gradually Americans came to expect to hear much of the news about their President not from the man who held the office but from his Press Secretary.

In its attempt to distribute favorable reports about the President, the Press Office showers news organizations, fraternal associations, sports groups, and ethnic alliances with hundreds of press releases. So much activity requires a large staff, and in the 1980s one estimate placed the total number employed in presidential press activities at one hundred fifty—all of them under the direction of the Press Secretary, although not all working in the West Wing. Some had to be assigned space across the street in the Old Executive Office Building or in some more remote quarters.

This mushrooming growth in the President's Press Office had more than one explanation—the number of correspondents assigned to cover the President had also multiplied. In the early 1950s, television typically designated only fifteen minutes each day for national news, but by the 1980s several hours of programming went into people's homes every day. Correspondents assigned to cover the President had to fill up much of that time, and the White House "beat" became a popular one. Morning viewers came to expect their own favorite reporter on the screen at 7 A.M. talking directly "from the White House."

Since the West Wing predated the development of either radio or television, studio space for the Chief Executive was not provided, and Presidents struggled to make their own media arrangements. Calvin Coolidge gave the first radio speech by a Chief Executive in the White House, and First Lady Lou Hoover set up a tiny workplace on the second floor where she could practice with microphones before giving her talks on national radio.

Franklin Roosevelt, a natural master of radio communications, used the medium extensively, broadcasting from various rooms in the White House, including the Diplomatic Reception Room on the ground floor. He was bothered by the fact that his "Fireside Chats" were first staged in a room where there were no fireplaces. The one that had been there was covered up, and in 1941 the President had the fireplace restored, complete with mantel.

Roosevelt's successors continued to use the radio to address the nation, and Ronald Reagan scheduled weekly broadcasts on

Saturday mornings, but gradually Americans came to rely on television for news from their President. By 1969, ninety-five percent of American homes boasted at least one television set, and many had more. Lyndon Johnson understood the popularity of the medium—he had chafed at the limitation of seeing only one channel at a time and installed a giant console of three screens in the Oval Office so that he could watch three networks simultaneously.

Television cameras and the accompanying paraphernalia of teleprompters invaded every part of the White House. As the cameras became more maneuverable and required less light, almost any corner of the mansion was suitable. Nancy Reagan appeared in front of television cameras in the Map Room, and Barbara Bush scheduled interviews in the ground floor Library.

Presidents have sought a more permanent arrangement. John Kennedy experimented with answering reporters' questions in auditoriums outside the White House compound, but Lyndon Johnson wanted something more convenient. James Hagerty, who had served as Eisenhower's Press Secretary, came forward with a plan to turn the Fish Room, just steps from the Oval Office, into a full-time broadcast studio. If various branches of the media split the bill (estimated at a million dollars), the President could appear in front of cameras and be shown in homes across America several times a day. That project failed, but eventually Lyndon Johnson arranged for a makeshift studio to be set up in the White House theater so that he could rehearse his remarks before delivering them to the press.

Johnson also courted the press by improving their workplace. The Fourth Estate's status in the West Wing had not improved much since the days when Theodore Roosevelt permitted the press to wait in the lobby rather than outside. The lobby provided few amenities, and it resembled the waiting room of a train station more than part of the Executive Office. Coats and discarded paper cups piled up on the center table as reporters lounged around, waiting for a story worth writing. Johnson had the lobby refurbished and provided more seating. The table was removed and a portrait of George Washington hung over the receptionist's desk as a reminder of the dignity of the office.

When Richard Nixon visited reporters one Sunday in 1969, he found their quarters cramped and unattractive, and he inquired with some disdain of one reporter present, "Is this where you

President Lyndon Johnson's Oval Office included a triple-screen television console.

work?" The result was a completely new facility, in the space where Franklin Roosevelt's swimming pool had once been—in the colonnade connecting the office wing to the residence.

Finally, reporters had their own turf—a lounge equipped with telephones and individual radio booths, seats for listening to the President or one of his spokespeople, a raised platform for cameras, and a podium with its own blue curtain and White House logo. At the rear of this low-ceilinged room is a hodgepodge of Formica-topped tables, making the space seem more like part of a thriving newspaper than part of the President's office. Seats can accommodate sixty to seventy reporters, but the room expands for an unknown number of standees when a big story breaks. On a typical day when the President is at work, twenty or so reporters might wait at any one time for a story, but on a Saturday or a quiet summer day, when the President is out of town, the area is deserted, with only a cleaning crew and perhaps one late-filing reporter on the premises.

Some journalists caviled that the Press Room gave them a less advantageous point from which to see who was entering the President's office—their former quarters had provided more proximity—but they remained downstairs. Additional remodeling in 1981 pushed amenities back, as lounging chairs and coffee machines gave way to more work areas. The Reagan administration assigned permanent seats in the Press Room for each network or major newspaper so that the President could more easily recognize individuals and call them by name.

Television correspondents like to deliver their remarks from outside the Oval Office so that the West Wing forms a graceful, low backdrop. Tourists and other visitors learn to recognize the reporters, each of them outfitted with a microphone and trailed by cameras and wires necessary to transmit their observations across the continent and around the world.

In spite of the efficient organization of the West Wing offices, the White House residence continues to offer some very obvious advantages for Presidents to work. The mansion's size and multiple entries conceal entrances and exits. An adviser or covert messenger can make an appearance without alerting the press, and the President can be awakened during the night or interrupted at lunch for a decision or a briefing.

Jody Powell, Press Secretary to President Carter, spoke with journalists in the Press Briefing Room.

During World War II, President Roosevelt set up a Map Room on the ground floor of the residence and limited access to a very few people. It served as a communications center for vital information related to the war, including the movement and progress of Army and Navy units. President William McKinley had followed naval maneuvers during the Spanish-American War in a map room that he improvised on the second floor of the residence, but Roosevelt was probably more impressed by the example of Winston Churchill who designated one room in his underground London bunker as a map room.

In the White House version, large wall maps with different-colored pins marking positions and progress of troops appealed to President Roosevelt. He did request one personal favor, though, quite outside normal operations: One pin marked the ship on which his son was serving in the Pacific. It was the first pin the President looked for whenever he entered the room.

Roosevelt's Map Room served more than cartography purposes. Secret communications came in for decoding, and the President's messages went out. A dozen men, equally divided between Army and Navy, filed materials and maneuvered the map pins to reflect the latest intelligence. Because it was considered a military facility, the Map Room was off-limits to all but the President and a half dozen of his most trusted advisers. Even his cabinet members, his Secret Service guards, and his family were barred. Doors to the room were either sealed off (as to the adjoining Diplomatic Reception Room) or guarded around the clock by a White House policeman.

Only the energetic First Lady, Eleanor Roosevelt, seems to have breached the security precautions, rushing past an amazed guard one day in order to learn the whereabouts of one of her sons in combat. She even took Madame Chiang Kai-shek, wife of the Chinese Nationalist leader, on a tour of the room, but this time the staff had some warning, and they scrambled the map pins and rearranged the room before the women arrived.

Although security precautions require very limited access to parts of the White House, the President seeks to appear open to constituents' comments and criticisms, even maintaining a listed phone number. In addition to the regular switchboard, there is another manned by the military, and this is the one that takes care of the President's communications when he is traveling. Exceptions are sometimes made, though, as when Lyndon Johnson objected to the male voice of a Signal Corps officer asking "Number, please" and ordered a female White House operator to go along to handle calls.

For White House telephoning, President Johnson relied on a crew of twenty operators—actually he relied on them a lot because he broke all records in using the telephone to confer with advisers and to cajole congressmen into taking a particular position or casting a needed vote. The operators, justly fabled as able to find anyone, anywhere, work in shifts around the clock. Because they typically stay from one administration to the next, they develop enormous expertise and compile large files of unlisted, hard-to-find numbers that they closely guard and rarely share. Even Jimmy

The Map Room, used as a situation room during World War II, now serves as a meeting room.

Nancy Reagan met with media advisers in the Map Room on the ground floor of the residence.

Carter, after leaving the White House, was refused when he requested numbers from the operators' files, but he did get an offer of personal help whenever he wanted to place a call.

One of the most famous stories about the White House switchboard concerns the Kennedy years. The President decided to test the skill of the operator on duty by requesting the whereabouts of a man who was at that very moment standing beside him in the Oval Office. The solution came in minutes.

Sometimes even an experienced operator cannot produce the desired result, however. When President Eisenhower asked the switchboard to reach his assistant, Sherman Adams, who was driving to New Hampshire, the operators calculated where Adams would be, then contacted a farmer at about that place to ask him to flag down a blue Oldsmobile tagged New Hampshire 22. The farmer spotted the car and hailed it, but Adams refused to stop.

President Ford stopped by the White House switchboard in the Old Executive Office Building to thank the operators.

President Kennedy's young daughter Caroline had more luck. When she wanted to speak to Santa Claus, she called the switchboard, and when a repairman working down the hall was pressed into an acting role, she gave him her Christmas list—including a helicopter for her brother who saw their father use one "all the time."

By 1991, the switchboard registered almost 40,000 calls every week. Two or three times that number come in at particularly eventful times such as during the U.S. bombing of Libya in April 1986, or during Operation Desert Storm in early 1991. Sometimes the switchboard is inundated for reasons unrelated to national events. When a television evangelist encouraged viewers to call the President, thousands of them did, swamping the switchboard for hours.

Since the Nixon years, volunteers have assisted the switchboard staff in answering calls directed to the President. Typically political supporters of the incumbent Chief Executive, they answer routine queries, direct callers to a particular source, and keep a tally of opinions expressed. These same unpaid workers address the President's greeting cards, which are sent out each year to wish people happy birthday and happy anniversary. In 1990 the Bushes mailed more than 750,000 of these cards.

If the President and his staff had only telephone messages to answer, their load would be considerably lighter, but many Americans choose to write letters to the President with their opinions, concerns, and requests. As the population of the nation has grown, letters to the White House have multiplied. President Reagan received more than four million written communications in 1986, a far cry from the few that appeared on George Washington's desk when the Republic was young.

Actually the number of letters has grown remarkably even when the population has remained almost static. In 1954–60, President Eisenhower received about 700,000 letters annually; in the 1960s that figure doubled, and by the 1970s the Carter White House reported about 3.5 million each year. By the time George Bush took office, the number had risen to six million.

The letters come in foreign languages (these are forwarded to the State Department for translation), in Braille (answered in Braille), in the awkward block printing of young children (these writers receive a booklet telling them how the White House operates), and in the cramped, careful script of people needing help (these are referred to appropriate agencies).

Perhaps the President's high visibility (and that of his family) make the White House an easy focus for the people's wrath. Certainly its address is easy—probably the only location in the United States for which postal authorities need only two words—White House. The city and street location are superfluous, and even a zip code is deemed unnecessary on White House stationery. In at least one case, just a sketch sufficed. Theodore Roosevelt, whose toothy grin was as famous in his time as Jimmy Carter's became later, received an envelope addressed only with a simple drawing of teeth.

If architect James Hoban could stroll through the White House offices two hundred years after the cornerstone of the mansion was laid, he would see flickering computer terminals on many desks. After the White House Information Systems was set up in the early 1960s to improve communication, the first functions to be computerized were those of national security and military operations. The office staff continued to rely on typewriters and telephones.

The Carter years brought change. Just as personal computers moved into many American homes, they also entered the President's House. Terminals appeared on desks to help schedule cabinet meetings, analyze federal budget data, and create a digital version of the President's signature on letters. The visitors' office and the Curator relied on computers, and by 1982 the clerical staff had learned to use them as well. Finally upper echelon management were assigned terminals on which they could hook up to wire services, peruse personnel and financial data, and contact one another.

Last of all, the President got his own personal computer. In April 1991 George Bush became the first Chief Executive to have a fully automated office—although he gave little indication that he meant to master the new technology. Weeks after the terminal's arrival, his Press Office announced that he had had little time to familiarize himself with it and that his first lesson had involved nothing more than learning how to turn it on. First Lady Barbara Bush was already ahead of her husband in this respect, having become adept at using her compact laptop computer.

Although he was inaugurated at the Capitol, Richard Nixon gave his resignation speech in the White House and then walked to a helicopter on the South Lawn.

While the President's office is in the White House, the presidential oath of office is rarely taken there. That ceremony is reserved for the Capitol, and only under very special circumstances has a presidential inauguration occurred at 1600 Pennsylvania Avenue. Vice presidents who succeed to the office following the death of the incumbent are sworn in wherever they are, and Harry Truman took his oath in the Cabinet Room of the West Wing after Franklin Roosevelt's death in April 1945. Duly elected Chief Executives rarely had that option.

Rutherford B. Hayes's inauguration, in March 1877, is one of the exceptions. He had won the presidency in a very close election —a special commission had ruled him victorious over the Democrat Samuel Tilden, who actually got more popular votes—and some people expected trouble when Hayes took office. The date of the inauguration that year fell on a Sunday and so two oathtakings were planned. The first—unannounced even to people who were dining in the White House that Saturday night—took place in the Green Room, and then a public ceremony followed at the Capitol on Monday.

White House inaugurations remained rarities until the 1940s

President Harry Truman talked with former First Lady Eleanor Roosevelt at his desk in the West Wing Oval Office.

and '50s, when there were two. In both cases incumbents were involved, so there was no question of the nation being without a Chief Executive, even for a very short time. Franklin Roosevelt's fourth term began in January 1945, while World War II continued and the President, seriously ill, prepared to travel to the Soviet Union to meet with Churchill and Stalin at Yalta for peace talks. An extravagant or time-consuming inauguration seemed inappropriate and so a simple, practical ceremony was held at the White House. Crowds watched from a snow-covered South Lawn as Franklin Roosevelt appeared briefly on the portico and took the oath for an unprecedented fourth time.

In 1957 Dwight Eisenhower's second inauguration, which also fell on a Sunday, took place first in the East Room but was reenacted later in a public ceremony on Capitol Hill. The White House ceremony was a very private affair, and Pat Nixon, wife of the Vice President-elect, was called upon to hold the family Bible for her husband's swearing-in. She inadvertently set an example that her successors followed; and after Lady Bird Johnson held the Bible for her husband in 1965, the tradition became established that spouses would participate in the inaugural ceremony.

Neither this nor any other aspect of the First Lady's job had been spelled out in the Constitution. Her role gradually evolved from a purely social one to one with considerable clout, and Americans came to take for granted that the spouse of the Chief Executive would become involved in the administration in very visible and potentially valuable ways. Eleanor Roosevelt called herself "the eyes and ears" who could observe for her husband and report back to him. Lady Bird Johnson, with the assistance of a large and competent staff, made her "Beautification" program an important part of Lyndon Johnson's legislation package.

The stage for the emergence of strong First Ladies had been set in the early days of the Republic when George Washington decided to combine office and residence. Wives of men who work at home would understand why many presidential spouses complained that they could not avoid being drawn into political discussions. Talk concerning problems that the nation faced surrounded them each day. Virtually no visitor paid a purely social call; each came with a business motive.

Every invitation issued from the President's House carried polit-

One of the most activist First Ladies, Eleanor Roosevelt is shown here with the President outside the Oval Office.

ical consequences, and each First Lady who participated in the scheduling of social events entered a partisan thicket. How she manipulated her way through the maze of party alignments and personal enmities could affect her husband's record. Dolley Madison went out of her way to treat opponents as kindly as supporters, and historians credited her as being an important part in James Madison's reelection to the presidency in 1812. Mary Lincoln, less shrewd in such matters, caused her husband some trouble as when, for example, she demanded that guests enter the White House through designated doors, according to their official titles. Judges, senators, and foreign ministers were to be separated from congressional representatives and common folk.

More than social planning was involved if a First Lady wanted to be an asset to her husband. Americans learned to approach the President by making their requests to his wife. As soon as the First Lady became a familiar figure, through coverage in national magazines and newspapers, letters addressed directly to her came in asking for advice and help on everything from temperance to polygamy.

Not until the 1950s did Congress recognize the office of First Lady and supply it with a staff. Presidents' wives before that time were left to fend for themselves: providing their own secretarial help, asking friends to volunteer time, or borrowing workers from other government offices. In the 1870s, when men still monopolized secretarial positions at the White House, Julia Grant employed a man as secretary. Explaining to a reporter why she preferred working with him rather than with a woman, she noted that a woman "might in the beginning prove a perfectly seaworthy vessel but after all, without any warning, spring a leak."

Edith Roosevelt deserves credit for being the first to acquire a secretary at government expense to assist with the First Lady's responsibilities. In 1901 Isabella Hagner, who had previously worked for a relative of Edith Roosevelt, came "on loan" from the clerical section of the War Department. Conditions were so crowded that she had to set up a desk in the First Lady's bedroom and then move "bag and baggage" to the hall when Mrs. Roosevelt needed the room. It was Isabella Hagner who handed out information to reporters on social events—the food and beverages served, the attire of the guests, and the flower arrangements.

Edith Roosevelt's example evidently inspired successive First Ladies to communicate directly with the press rather than to rely entirely on their husbands' staffs. Florence Harding once even invited women reporters up to her second-floor bedroom where she received them in a rose negligée.

Eleanor Roosevelt took women reporters on a tour of thc mansion the day after her husband's inauguration and set the following Monday morning at eleven for her first news conference in the Red Room. For the next twelve years she met with reporters regularly whenever she was in Washington. As many as seventy-five women showed up, and the conferences moved from one room in the White House to another—sometimes the Green Room on the main floor or the Monroe Room on the second floor. The First Lady would enter last, often still in riding clothes, and pass around a box of candy or serve some lemonade.

The First Lady's staff remained small until the 1960s but its

As part of her job as First Lady, Jacqueline Kennedy inspected plans for Lafayette Square, on the north side of the White House.

First Lady Rosalynn Carter maintained her own office in the East Wing.

growth is easily documented. In 1953 the *Congressional Directory* showed official recognition of the distaff side of the White House when it listed as part of the Executive Office one "Acting Secretary to the President's wife." Jacqueline Kennedy hired her own press secretary (another first), and Lady Bird Johnson assembled the largest and most accomplished First Lady's staff in history. The exact number of people working for Mrs. Johnson and her projects remains in doubt. Some came "on loan" from federal agencies and remained for years without ever going on the First Lady's payroll. Others appeared for temporary stints and then left when the job was done.

Located in the East Wing, near the Correspondence Office where invitations are addressed, the office of the First Lady has become an important component of the President's office. Rosalynn Carter, who sometimes went there in a business suit and frequently mentioned the "working lunches" that she shared with the President, helped define the job as a separate and important one. Both Barbara Bush and Nancy Reagan kept an office in the family quarters, and each First Lady maintained a busy schedule involving projects she had chosen to support, speaking engagements, and meetings. By 1990 much of the information about how the White House operated and all photographs of the President's family came not from the West Wing but from the First Lady's Press Office.

Large as it has become, the office of the First Lady is only a tiny part of the President's Office, which extends outside the White House compound into surrounding office buildings and across the city, encompassing a complex network of advisers and messages, equipment and responsibilities. Only a fraction of the work accredited to the Chief Executive actually occurs at 1600 Pennsylvania Avenue. After two hundred years, the White House has come to mean not just a place or a job, but a large and powerful operation.

MUSEUM OF A NATION

Glassware ordered by President and Mrs. Benjamin Harrison.

★ A beautiful classically designed building, the White House makes an impressive showcase for the nation's treasures, its prized collection of period furniture and artwork. Portrait gallery of Presidents and exhibition hall of fine antiques, it contains furnishings of historic as well as artistic interest. Visitors walking through the public rooms immediately sense that they are in a museum—high ceilings and roped-off walkways make this house seem too grand for everyday living and too gracious for an office. The aura of history is strong, and even First Lady Jacqueline Kennedy expressed awe at walking near objects that had belonged to legendary past residents—their influence remained so strong, she said, that for her first two years in the White House she rarely spoke above a whisper.

The Lincoln Bedroom exhibits furniture, artwork, and documents of the period 1850–70.

In November 1988 the American Association of Museums accredited the White House as a museum, thus giving a nod of approval granted to only about one tenth of all institutions in the country that call themselves museums. That decision was not automatic; it followed a two-year review of White House operations and the care of its collections. The Association concluded that the President's House had moved beyond being simply a home and office for the Chief Executive and had become, in the words of one scholar, "the nation's oldest important showcase for the arts." From now on it would have to answer to more than its occupants whenever a change of furnishings or decoration was considered.

No complete catalogue of White House holdings exists, but if one could be designed from the computerized inventory it would be immense, including thousands of items in several categories: furniture (1,942), ceramics (15,661); glassware (3,145); metalware (13,092); lighting fixtures (1,121); paintings (338); prints and drawings (451); and sculpture (69). The list requires regular updating as new donations and acquisitions arrive.

For nearly a century, occupants of the President's House gave little attention to preserving its historical record. In 1801 John Adams carefully listed the furnishings right before his presidential term was up, but he was probably motivated more by the need to protect himself against charges of theft than by the wisdom of starting an archive. His successors were no more systematic than he, and few of them left anything beyond sketchy descriptions of the various rooms. Historians trying to reconstruct the mansion's appearance at a particular time must turn to letters, government vouchers, and cryptically written notes that survive from that period.

As it neared its one-hundredth birthday in 1892—and perhaps because of this milestone—the White House began to take on historic importance of its own, and occupants, especially First Ladies, tried to compile a record of the building's past. Lucretia Garfield set out to research the topic in the Library of Congress in 1881 because, her husband wrote in his diary, "so little is known." But she soon became ill with malaria, and before she had recovered, her husband was assassinated, thus ending any scholarship on the mansion she may have envisioned.

The first archival projects of Presidents' wives centered on prized collectors' pieces used by previous administrations, and books about the White House focused on the people who lived and worked there. Nineteenth-century historians and Executive Mansion employees penned dozens of volumes, detailing their research, experiences, and opinions, but no one catalogued the physical objects. Even in 1908, when Gilson Willets published *Inside History of the White House,* he devoted more pages to "Relatives as First Ladies" and "Holidays at the White House" than to "Public and Private Rooms" or "White House Portraits."

Not until the 1920s was any concerted effort made to document the mansion's holdings and to attract donations that would enhance its archival significance. Grace Coolidge, stymied by her husband in so many of her personal projects during her years as First Lady, set an important precedent when she appointed the first advisory committee ever named to oversee the selection of furnishings and artwork for the White House. The First Lady wisely chose experts with broad experience as collectors, donors, and advisers

Lady Bird Johnson, in a small ceremony in the East Room in June 1964, accepted a donation to the White House Collection.

at other historic sites and at the newly opened American Wing of New York's Metropolitan Museum of Art.

Grace Coolidge's project focused on the family quarters, but since furniture and artworks were moved from one floor to another at residents' requests, she had to consider furnishings for the entire mansion. Money was a major consideration, and in 1925 an obliging legislature increased appropriations from the twenty thousand dollars routinely granted each new administration to fifty thousand dollars, the same amount that is allocated today to each incoming family for redecorating their own quarters. Even in the 1920s that sum was insufficient to purchase valuable furnishings to upgrade the interior, and so Congress passed additional legislation permitting the First Lady and her committee to seek donations directly from private sources, as a typical museum staff does.

Because of a combination of personalities and events, Grace Coolidge never attained the reputation of Jacqueline Kennedy as restorer of the White House. Mrs. Coolidge's Advisory Committee members disagreed over what kind of furniture was preferable, and a national debate erupted over whether "colonial" styles were more appropriate to the mansion than "Victorian" pieces or those identified with beaux arts or "foreign" designs. Americans who had never before given much thought to the subject joined in the argument, and one magazine invited its readers to send in their opinions. Finally President Coolidge abruptly halted the project by announcing that nothing at all would be done. Other than a dozen or so pieces of furniture that were donated and a coverlet that Mrs. Coolidge crocheted for the Lincoln bed, there is little trace left of her project to refurbish the White House.

Learning from the Coolidge experience, successive administrations were slow to embark on new restoration projects. The years of the Great Depression hardly offered the right setting for talk of upgrading the White House, although Lou Hoover did instruct one of her assistants to begin a history of the mansion (never published), and she arranged to have reproductions made of some of President James Monroe's furniture. Mrs. Hoover had admired the pieces that Monroe's descendants had donated to a museum dedicated to their famous ancestor in Fredericksburg, Virginia, and, realizing that the original furniture was unattainable, she had several pieces copied for a parlor that she had set aside for her family on

Delegates from the National Society of Interior Designers presented President and Mrs. Eisenhower with furniture for the Diplomatic Reception Room on the ground floor, the first room to be furnished entirely with authentic antiques.

the second floor. Coincidentally, the Monroes had designated that room for the same use, and the Hoovers initiated the practice of calling it the Monroe Room.

The two subsequent Presidents did not continue the Hoover restoration project. Franklin Roosevelt proposed including a separate museum in the new East Wing (built in 1942 and eventually the location of the office of the First Lady), and Harry Truman endorsed the idea, but neither Eleanor Roosevelt nor Bess Truman indicated much interest.

By the late 1950s, attitudes appeared to be changing. Just as Dwight and Mamie Eisenhower prepared to retire to their Gettysburg farm, the National Society of Interior Designers [NSID] donated furniture for the Diplomatic Reception Room (so named because diplomats traditionally gathered there in the oval room on the ground floor). The NSID had worked two years to collect the necessary funds (about $100,000) and to locate enough appropriate pieces to furnish this room entirely in "early American antiques." It was the only room in the White House, the designers noted proudly, with that distinction.

With the publicity surrounding the arrival of the furniture in June 1960, an idea may have been planted in the mind of Jacqueline Kennedy, whose husband was about to capture the Democratic party's nomination for President. Almost immediately after John Kennedy's election in November, his wife announced her project as First Lady—to make the White House a "showcase of American art and history." Only three years (to the day) intervened between that announcement and President Kennedy's assassination, but it was

Jacqueline Kennedy conducted camera crews on a preview tour of the White House prior to filming a televised tour in early 1962.

time enough for her to build a reputation as the most successful of the several First Ladies who attempted to restore the White House.

Jacqueline Kennedy set the stage for an entirely new way of viewing the White House. In January 1961 she named a twelve-member committee to help locate appropriate furniture and works of art and to raise the money for further purchases. A few months later Lorraine Pearce, a twenty-six-year-old curator on loan from the Smithsonian Institution, went to work full-time cataloguing everything in the building. Congress put its own important stamp of approval on the project by passing a law to make removal of objects difficult: "furniture, fixtures and decorative objects of the White House, when declared by the President to be of historic or artistic interest," would be permanent—future occupants could not discard them at whim.

Public enthusiasm was enormous, and hundreds of donations came in. Some were large, others very small. One fourth grader in Kansas sent a dollar and encouraged his friends to contribute too, so that more antiques and paintings could be purchased.

President Kennedy, sensitive to the political consequences associated with projects termed "elitist," hesitated to endorse the restoration program, and Mrs. Kennedy wrote that she was "warned, begged, and practically threatened" not to undertake it. She persisted, she explained publicly, because she wanted the house to be one that all Americans could take pride in, and she wanted schoolchildren especially to understand its significance. Jacqueline Kennedy had first visited the White House when she was eleven years old, and she remembered being impressed by its uniqueness. Returning in 1960 for a private tour with Mamie Eisenhower, Mrs. Kennedy had an entirely different reaction; she confided to a friend that she had been disappointed with the undistinguished furnishings, some of them in rather worn condition.

In order for the restoration project to support itself, a guidebook to the White House was published and put on sale in the summer of 1962. Since the sales actually occurred on White House premises, complaints about "commercialization" came in, but success at the cash register mitigated the sting of disapproval. At one dollar per copy, the guidebooks sold well and nearly two million of them were printed in the next two years.

The organization that actually oversaw the project was the

White House Historical Association, formed in November 1961 under the First Lady's aegis for the purpose of increasing "the understanding, appreciation, and enjoyment of the Executive Mansion." The Association also collected private funds to be used for purchasing items that would enhance the collection—whether a painting, a piece of furniture, or an important document.

In 1961 the White House began a systematic listing of every new acquisition, and three years later it published a catalogue or inventory, setting a precedent that later administrations would follow. Each item in the catalogue had a number, indicating the date it was "accessioned," and a description, including size, period, materials, and the source that provided it for the President's House. For example, a mahogany writing table, made in America "circa 1850" and measuring thirty-six inches wide and twenty-six inches deep was described as "Victorian, with rectangular top covered in black leather. Single drawer opening in front with Victorian gilt pulls. Four cabriole legs carved at knees and feet." Julia Grant had used the desk as First Lady, and it was donated in 1961 by a couple who lived in South Wellfleet, Massachusetts.

The catalogue divided its new holdings into four categories (Furniture, Furnishings, Fine Arts, Documents) and then subdivided each of these into twenty-two smaller groups. Among the forty-seven chairs donated to the White House in 1961 was one armchair from the original set that President Monroe had ordered from France in 1817. Six chairs were purchased with "general funds" and although none of them could be directly connected to a White House family, all were excellent examples of American craftsmanship around 1800.

Jacqueline Kennedy went in "working clothes" to look through White House storage rooms and sort out those pieces worthy of display. Some valuable items, formerly kept under lock and key except for the most important visitors, went on permanent exhibit for every tourist to see. The enormous gilt plateau centerpiece, comprising seven sections capable of extension to thirteen feet, which had impressed dinner guests at the President's House since 1817 and had been described as "the chief historic treasure of the White House," was now set out on the table for all visitors to admire.

Jacqueline Kennedy's personal popularity drew people to the

White House where they viewed the dazzling vermeil collection which the Eisenhowers had quietly put on display in 1957. Margaret Thompson Biddle, an American heiress who spent years in Paris accumulating artwork and silver had died the previous year, and although some of her estate was auctioned off in Europe, much of the vermeil collection had been willed to the American President's House. Vermeil, a process in which silver pieces are dipped in gold, had been popular in 1817 when President Monroe bought furnishings for the Executive Mansion, and he included vermeil flatware in his order. The Biddle gift, valued at $100,000, would complement what remained of Monroe's original order, and its urns and trays would become the focus of one entire room's exhibit on the ground floor.

The Vermeil Room on the ground floor highlights the White House collection of vermeil (gold-dipped silver).

During the Kennedy administration the White House was transformed into a fledgling museum with its own curator, advisory committee of experts, and fund-raising outfit, but it took the endorsement of successive administrations to ensure the development of the collection. Lyndon Johnson cooperated by signing an important executive order: one part created a Committee for the Preservation of the White House to advise on the "museum character" of the public rooms so that the House could become "a living testament to the history of our country"; the second section provided for a full-time curator to be appointed by the President.

Now that the White House holdings were protected by the 1961 law, Americans more willingly donated treasured objects. CBS turned over the microphone used by Franklin Roosevelt for his Fireside Chats. A Salt Lake City attorney sent in a dinner plate that he said had been a gift to his uncle from Theodore Roosevelt more than fifty years earlier. The plate's purple border surrounding an American eagle established it as part of the dinner service purchased for the White House by Mary Lincoln. According to the donor's letter, his uncle, a Boston newspaper editor, had been accompanying President Roosevelt through the White House one day and had noticed the plates. When he announced that his wife would be "thrilled" to own one, T.R. obligingly opened the cupboard and handed one over.

While donations of historic White House items were welcomed, such pieces were not sufficient to raise the collection to the showcase status that its backers envisioned. The Committee for the Preservation of the White House actively sought additions, making specific requests for portraits of Presidents and their wives, as well as paintings by such distinguished American artists as Mary Cassatt, Thomas Eakins, and George Caleb Bingham.

In January 1967, Joseph Hirshhorn, a New York philanthropist who owned a large collection of Eakins paintings, obligingly donated a 1903 portrait of a young girl. The subject of the painting, which was of enormous value at the time, was Ruth Harding, the niece of one of Eakins's closest friends. Lady Bird Johnson was delighted with the gift and saw that it immediately went on display in one of the public rooms, but she was somewhat nonplussed a short time later when, escorting a group of visitors, she remarked how sad the painting's young subject looked. One elderly man in the group spoke up in Ruth Harding's defense—she really was not a sad woman at all, he said, and he should know because he married her.

During the Nixon administration, efforts to restore the White House continued—in fact, they accelerated. A new curator, Clement E. Conger, was appointed in early 1970, and he brought a remarkable enthusiasm and singleness of purpose to the job. Complaining of Congress's stinginess with "the most important house in the world," he described himself as "passionately dedicated" to transforming the mansion into the world's finest repository of American art and antiques.

Besides the lack of money, Conger encountered other problems as White House Curator. He found that each new First Family had quite different ideas about what furnishings they wanted on the second floor of the residence. Jacqueline Kennedy put wallpaper featuring scenes from the American Revolution in the family dining room, but Betty Ford had the paper removed and painted the room yellow. The scenes were inaccurate anyway, a history buff pointed out—the nineteenth-century French artist had placed battles at sites where none had occurred.

Almost immediately on assuming the curatorship, Conger created a stir by telling the *New York Times* that Jacqueline Kennedy's contribution to White House restoration had been exaggerated by the press who had "created an optical illusion that the White House contained a great collection of American antiques." Conger was particularly critical of Stephane Boudin, the Frenchman who had advised Mrs. Kennedy on wall coverings and draperies for the public rooms on the state floor. Boudin's previous experience had been at Malmaison, and Conger judged him untrained in restoring American period houses. The result was more French than American, critics charged, and Conger initiated what became known to insiders as the "de-Kennedyization" of the White House. He began with the Green and Red rooms, and during the next five years all the principal rooms on the main and ground floors were redecorated to reflect the views of Conger and the Committee for the Preservation of the White House.

The Green Room may have gained its designated color before any of the other rooms, since Thomas Jefferson (who dined there)

First Lady Pat Nixon conferred with Curator Clement Conger on paintings added to the White House Collection.

The Green Room, furnished in the Federal style, boasts many fine pieces that date from 1800–15.

and the Monroes (who made it their Card Room) all used green floor coverings, upholstery, and draperies. Under Clement Conger's direction, the room was refurbished in 1971 and furnished with outstanding pieces from the first two decades of the White House's use. Duncan Phyfe, the nineteenth-century Scottish cabinetmaker who made a reputation for himself in New York, is represented by several pieces, including the desk-bookcase on the south wall; and Lawrence Ackerman, who upholstered for Duncan Phyfe, signed one of the chairs. The two mahogany worktables near the fireplace conceal multiple tiny drawers and compartments which, when opened out, form a labyrinth of intricate workmanship. The early Presidents are well represented: the Sheffield silver coffee urn on the long table in front of the sofa once belonged to John and Abigail Adams; and the marble mantel, moved here from the State Dining Room, is one of James Monroe's purchases.

Another of the marble mantels ordered by Monroe is in the Red Room, a favorite parlor of Dolley Madison (interestingly, the room was decorated in yellow when she was First Lady). Furnished in the American Empire style of 1810–30, the Red Room is the setting for one of the most important and best documented pieces of furniture the White House owns from those years: a small round table, labeled by its maker Charles-Honoré Lannuier, is made of mahogany and other woods, its marble top of magnificent geometric inlay and its legs exquisitely curved. This room frequently served for musical performances in the nineteenth century, and coincidentally the Empire style featured the stringed lyre as a decorative motif in chair backs and table legs.

Refurbishing these state rooms required public and private support, and Clement Conger, in appealing to Americans to donate rare antiques, gave multiple reasons for doing so: tax deductions, national pride, and family pride. Sometimes it takes all three, he admitted. His plea for donations became all the more important when he found himself shut out of competitive bidding for fine furniture and artwork that came up for sale. He simply could not match the prices offered by well-heeled collectors buying for themselves.

During Jimmy Carter's presidency important American paintings were added to the White House collection, and when he left as

President in 1981 the time seemed right for major refurbishing of the second floor. To help cover expenses, a fund drive was organized, and after the original goal of $850,000 was quickly reached, a total of $1.2 million in private contributions came in. This money, augmented by sums raised by the White House Historical Association and funds appropriated by Congress, provided for painting the exterior, conservation treatment of 150 objects inside, and purchase of additional artworks.

The refurbishing of the private quarters alone cost $730,000 and provided new wall coverings in ten rooms, seven closets, and eight bathrooms. The master bedroom was decorated with hand-painted wallpaper in eighteenth century style. Thirty-three mahogany doors were refinished, as were the floors in twenty-four rooms. Eighteen carpets were replaced, along with many draperies and lamp shades.

Congress agreed to pay for restoring the White House exterior and work began in 1980 with plans for completion by 1992. This complicated stone cleaning, which started on the east wall and concluded on the west façade, required that the mansion wear unattractive scaffolding for more than a decade. Visitors making their first trip to Washington would have to choose their photo backgrounds carefully, since much of the mansion was covered up. In fact, tourists' comments might have echoed those of a woman who, during the 1920s renovation, mistook the scaffolding for a fire escape and concluded that the White House must be a real firetrap.

Cleaning revealed many details in the stone façade and enhanced the building's appearance. Multiple coats of paint (as many as thirty-two in some places) had been put on top of the first layer that had been used to seal the porous Virginia sandstone in 1798. Intricate carvings at the tops of the windows and on the pilasters and columns had been completely obscured, and twisted ropes and delicate roses, the result of months of skillful chiseling, had disappeared under multiple coats of white paint.

After experts settled on a complicated process combining a chemical stripper with a water spray, hunks of paint came off, revealing delicate molding and "tooth tooling" that formed tiny ridges. Remnants of paint remained, but workmen proceeded cautiously, using special plastic scrapers so as to avoid causing further damage. After the stonework had been repaired, the entire surface was ready to be painted with two coats of a specially tailored formula, but restorers decided to leave uncovered one small section under a north window, where ominous scorch marks from the burning by the British in the War of 1812 were still visible.

These markings remind Americans that the White House is a unique record of their past, and whenever anyone suggests altering its basic structure, objections are heard loud and clear. More than once (and with most publicity in the 1890s, 1920s, and 1940s), elaborate plans were drawn up to change the exterior significantly, adding new wings to accommodate an expanded office on the west side and an extensive museum on the east side. Each time the plan was scrapped so that the basic dimensions of the White House remained as they were drawn in the 1790s.

The Library on the ground floor houses a large selection of books by American writers on American topics.

The Blue Room contains several pieces of furniture ordered for it by President James Monroe in 1817.

The first residents of the President's House, Abigail and John Adams, lived there with very sparse furnishings. Abigail complained that although she had two hundred bushels of coal, the only mirrors in the place were "fit for dwarfs." The large, full-length painting of George Washington that Congress had just purchased was of little use when she really needed tables and chairs.

Widower Thomas Jefferson showed scant interest in furniture but he did install some ingenious inventions. One of the most novel featured a revolving door with shelves so that new dishes could be served and old ones taken away at meals without the drafts and noise caused by servants' opening and closing doors.

Appearance conscious Dolley Madison showed no inclination to entertain in spartan surroundings and she quickly enlisted the help of Benjamin Latrobe, whom President Jefferson had appointed as Surveyor of Public Buildings, to help her select curtains and furniture. Within weeks she had several of the main rooms ready for visitors' inspection, but only a tiny fraction of the nation ever got to see them before British soldiers set them on fire during the War of 1812.

In 1817, the task of furnishing the rebuilt mansion fell to President James Monroe, a patrician Virginian, and his stylish New York-born wife, Elizabeth. The Monroes brought considerable European experience and strong personal tastes to the job, having lived in Paris for several years. When Congress appropriated $20,000, the Monroes quickly spent that amount and more, the bulk of their budget designated for a large order placed in France. The President explained to the legislature that the cost had been high because he wanted the furniture to be worthy of its surroundings, or, as he put it, "not less deserving attention than the building for which it is intended."

Monroe compiled a long list for his French agent, including clocks, silver, wallpaper, console tables, and carpet with the United States coat of arms featuring the bald eagle. For the prized oval room on the first floor he ordered two sofas, thirty-eight chairs (two of them were armchairs with closed and upholstered sides, called bergères), six footstools, and two screens. Eagle symbols were plentiful in France since Napoleon (who had claimed it as his own insignia) had been banished to Elba, and Monroe's purchases fea-

The "Minerva" clock, one of several clocks ordered from France by President James Monroe in 1817, met his requirement that all figures be fully clothed.

tured countless eagles woven into upholstery fabric, rugs, and curtains. His ban on furnishings with representations of nude figures was not so easily respected. A bronze clock showing a clothed Roman goddess (currently in the Entrance Hall) came with the purchasing agent's apologies—he had found the selection small.

Even today, evidence of Monroe's taste in furnishings is visible throughout the White House, especially in the Blue Room. Remnants of the shipment he received (including many treasures that have been returned to the White House since 1961) include a mahogany marble-top table and a pier table, the only two pieces of furniture to remain in the White House continuously since 1817. Not for another twenty years after Monroe placed his order did the Blue Room take on its famous hue, but the French Empire-style furniture, clocks, and vases, embellished with olive leaves, stars, and classical figures, are all his choices.

Monroe's order had specified that everything be in dark wood, but the French purchasing agents had substituted gilded beechwood for mahogany in most of the pieces, explaining that "mahogany is not generally admitted" into even "private gentlemen's houses" and thus could not be condoned in a President's palace. Historians suspect that the real reason had to do with cost. With mahogany in short supply because of a ban on its importation, local woods offered a cheaper alternative. On color, there would be no economizing—the furniture would feature red fabric although it was acknowledged to be twice as "dear."

The Monroes bestowed a kind of elegance on the President's House that twentieth-century occupants would try to imitate. One guest, describing a Monroe dinner table as the "most stylish" imaginable, singled out the silver "waiter" or plateau centerpiece as particularly beautiful, although she thought the forks contained so much silver "you would call them clumsy."

Despite all Monroe's expenditures, an inventory compiled when he left office showed several rooms empty. A guest at one of his dinners recalled eating in a "vast, cold hall," and in 1829 a congressman offered his own description of a bizarre East Room—"an unfinished barn" adorned by "four immense French" mirrors.

Successive Presidents made their own changes in the mansion's appearance in accordance with their whims, the size of their purse, and their inclination to keep the domestic staff diligent.

Opinions were mixed on the results. One visitor noted that the straw carpet on the second-floor Oval Room was filthy from tobacco juice that had missed the spittoons, but another described the East Room as "fit for a king." Economy, more than aesthetics, shaped judgments about what hung on the walls and filled the rooms, and Presidents had no qualms about discarding things they did not like or sending wagonloads off for auction.

By 1860 Empire furnishings had gone out of style, and President Buchanan sold most of the Monroe furniture. Not until the 1960s—when the White House made an effort to bring back furniture originally purchased by the Presidents rather than accept reproductions or period pieces—did much of the Monroe furniture reappear. One settee and seven chairs in the Blue Room are the same ones that Monroe bought—and plaques on the backs of four chairs identify them as the work of French cabinetmaker Pierre-Antoine Bellangé.

Buchanan and other late-nineteenth-century Presidents preferred the massive, ornately carved pieces that marked the most stylish interiors of their time. Woodworking machines had been perfected to turn out elaborate carvings of curlicues and flowers, and the most fashionable furniture revealed—even flaunted—this new technology. President Buchanan and his niece Harriet Lane ordered several pieces in this Victorian rococo-revival style and they transformed the Blue Room with plush, heavily upholstered chairs and sofas. Not everyone approved of Buchanan's choices even then, and a New York reporter described the fringes, flowers, and tufts as "a perfect *cholera morbus* of drapery and furniture."

The Lincoln suite on the second floor of the White House exhibits outstanding examples of the Victorian style and serves as a memorial to the martyred President. The centerpiece is a dark rosewood bed with an ornate headboard so high that it seems more fitting for a throne. Although the Lincolns bought the bed, they probably never used it, in spite of the fact that its size—eight feet long and six feet wide—suggests that it may have been purchased with the tall President in mind. Other furniture in these two rooms, which once served him as offices, touched Lincoln's life in some way: a chair resembling the one he sat in at Ford's Theatre the night he was shot; chairs used by his cabinet members at meetings; the desk he wrote at while staying at the summer White House a few

This portrait of Angelica Van Buren, painted in 1842 after she left the White House, hangs in the Red Room, furnished in the Empire style, 1810–30.

miles away. The desk displays Lincoln's most famous words—the Gettysburg Address, the only copy in existence that he titled, signed, and dated.

Mary Lincoln bought extravagantly for the White House (exceeding by $6,700 the normal $20,000 allotment made by Congress), and her husband protested. It "would stink in the nostrils of the American people," he explained, if he approved an overrun for the purchase of plush hassocks or "flub dubs" while Union soldiers went without blankets. The First Lady may have slowed her spending, but finding many merchants willing to extend credit, she continued to buy draperies and linens for the White House and clothing and jewelry for herself.

Subsequent administrations (Johnson, Grant, and Hayes) alternated between frugality and extravagance. One spent heavily on the mansion and the next ignored it, or at least permitted deterioration. The family of Andrew Johnson behaved as though they had been taking the money from their own pockets, whereas the Grants introduced a free hand entirely in keeping with their "Gilded Age," and later Rutherford and Lucy Hayes boasted of rummaging in attics and basement storerooms to furnish the various rooms.

Calling the White House poorly outfitted, Chester Arthur refused to stay there until improvements were made. He auctioned off wagonloads of furniture and engaged his fellow New Yorker Louis Comfort Tiffany to design a huge screen of colored glass for the front hall.

Tiffany's ornate style survived until the state floor was completely redecorated during Theodore Roosevelt's presidency. In place of the dark, heavy furnishings and wall coverings, the Roosevelts chose simple shapes and light colors. The East Room was left largely unfurnished; its gleaming parquet floors and elegant Steinway grand piano seemed adequate adornment. Ellen Slayden, wife of a Southern congressman, remarked that the White House had been transformed from "a gilded barn" into a comfortable residence.

★★★

From the very beginning, portraits had been considered vital to the White House collection, and they account for much of the feeling of being in a museum that visitors have as they walk through the mansion. The famous full-length portrait of George Washington that hangs in the East Room is only one of many that Gilbert Stuart produced of the nation's first President. Another, more familiar portrait—since it approximates the one on the dollar bill—hangs in a different room. The East Room painting is actually a copy that Stuart produced of an earlier portrait done while Washington was alive, and it has some unusual features. The mouth is clenched, and at least one friend of Washington stated that it was not a good likeness.

The portrait of George Washington in the East Room is best known as the sole artwork that survives from the Executive Mansion prior to August 24, 1814, the date when Dolley Madison provided

Visitors gathered in the East Room for music, dances, and receptions.

Louis Comfort Tiffany designed this large screen for the White House main entrance hall in 1882.

for its rescue. President James Madison had been out inspecting his troops that day—every indication pointed to a British assault on the capital—but the First Lady refused to leave the White House and even flouted the prospect of danger by ordering that the dinner table be set for forty guests. Friends solicitous of her safety urged her to flee, and Dolley admitted in a letter to her sister that one of them is "in a very bad humor with me because I insist on waiting until the large picture of Gen. Washington is secured." Finally, after making one last tour of the state rooms where she salvaged small silver items that she could take with her, Dolley Madison left, confident that the portrait was safe.

Always one of the most prized possessions of the White House, the painting of George Washington inspired later Presidents to have their likenesses done. James Monroe, who as Secretary of State had responsibility for such matters, commissioned John Vanderlyn, who had studied with Gilbert Stuart, to do President Madison's portrait. For his own portrait as Chief Executive, Monroe turned to Samuel F. B. Morse, the man better known to later generations as the inventor of the telegraph.

Additions were made sporadically to the White House portrait gallery until 1857 when Congress commissioned George P. A. Healy, one of the country's foremost portraitists, to do several of the unrepresented Presidents. Healy completed portraits of John Quincy Adams, Martin Van Buren, James Polk, Millard Fillmore, Franklin Pierce, and John Tyler, but after the War between the States started, money was not available to have the pictures framed. After the war ended, Andrew Johnson's daughter, who found the canvases rolled up in the attic, arranged for their framing and display in the large transverse hall on the state floor. This came about, ironically, because the President, who was a poorly educated man and the only Chief Executive to be impeached (but not convicted), took great pleasure in showing visitors through the Presidents' portrait gallery.

Very quickly the collection of paintings outgrew the main hall. Only a few of the nation's Chief Executives, often the most recent, enjoy the honor of being represented in the heavily traveled first-floor corridor. Other portraits, the works of a distinguished roster of American painters, appear throughout various rooms of the residence, and favorites of the incumbent hang in the Cabinet Room of

George Washington's portrait by Gilbert Stuart has been hanging in the White House since 1800 — the only item to have been there so long. (detail)

the West Wing. Healy's famous portrait of Abraham Lincoln commands a special place above the mantel in the State Dining Room, and another picture, a miniature of President Lincoln and his son Tad, hangs in the Lincoln Bedroom. The latter was probably done in the 1870s and is the work of Francis Carpenter, who had stayed at the Lincoln White House for several months to paint a picture of the President and his cabinet as they appeared at the time of the signing of the Emancipation Proclamation. On meeting Carpenter for the first time Lincoln had asked skeptically, "Do you think you can make a handsome picture of me?"

Posing for an official portrait becomes part of every President's job, although most delay it until leaving office. Jimmy Carter sat for painter Herbert E. Abrams in 1982, more than a year after leaving Washington, D.C., and although he appears seated in a chair from the Red Room, Carter actually posed in Plains, Georgia. Gerald Ford's portrait was painted in 1977 by Everett Kinstler while the ex-President was at his home in Vail, Colorado.

The main stairway near the North Entrance serves also as portrait galley for ex-Presidents.

More than one Chief Executive has had second thoughts about his official portrait after it was finished. Lyndon Johnson made headlines by rejecting the one done of him by Peter Hurd. Commissioned by the White House Historical Association (at a reported fee of six thousand dollars, which was half of Hurd's usual price for a color portrait), the painting took several months to complete. When Hurd delivered it to the Johnson ranch in Texas he received a very cool reception. The President greeted him with "icy politeness," Hurd reported, and Lady Bird Johnson described the meeting between the two men as the grimmest she ever expected to witness if she "lived to be one thousand." Johnson called the painting "the ugliest thing I ever saw" and showed the artist a likeness he much preferred—one done by the popular illustrator Norman Rockwell. The President's opinion no doubt explains its banishment from the White House, although the First Lady's office gave other reasons: it was "inappropriate" (with the Capitol in the background), not consistent in style with other Presidents' portraits, and (at 40 inches by 48 inches) "too big."

Lyndon Johnson was not the only person to worry about how he would appear in the permanent White House gallery. Richard Nixon switched portraits after leaving office, preferring one by J.

Edith Roosevelt posed for only a portion of this portrait painted by Théobald Chartran while she was First Lady.

Anthony Wills, who had also done Eisenhower's portrait. In 1991 Ronald Reagan sent a portrait of himself done by Everett Kinstler to replace one done earlier by Aaron Shikler. Calvin Coolidge took more time to change his mind. At the conclusion of his presidency he left a portrait in which he appeared dressed in a cutaway coat; three years later he returned to retrieve it and replace it with one that showed him in a business suit.

Coolidge, known for his thrift, did not cut corners when it came to portraits. He had expected to sit for the painter Howard Chandler Christy, but finding a full schedule that day, he arranged for his wife to be the subject. That portrait, showing the vivacious First Lady in a red dress standing beside her collie Rob Roy, is very much a product of the 1920s; the dog's name—also the name of a cocktail—is a spoof on the prohibition decade.

Since 1902 the entry corridor on the ground floor has exhibited portraits of the First Ladies.

At least the First Lady posed for it herself. In 1902, Edith Roosevelt arranged to have her portrait painted by Théobald Chartran, but finding that her large family and busy White House schedule left her too little time, she prevailed on a friend of roughly the same body proportions to substitute for her. The First Lady posed only while her face was being sketched, and that may account for the fact that neither she nor her husband liked the finished product. Such substitutions were fairly common. In 1878 when President Hayes asked his Ohio artist friend Eliphalet F. Andrews to do a portrait of Martha Washington to hang as a companion to the full-length portrait of George Washington, a niece of Hayes, Emily Platt, served as the model.

By the time the Executive Mansion had been officially renamed the White House in 1902, Presidents' wives had become prominent national figures, and Edith Roosevelt thought it appropriate to organize a portrait gallery featuring them all ("myself included," she specified) on the ground floor. The wide corridor seemed a perfect place for exhibiting portraits, and although not all White House wives left their likenesses—some of those from the nineteenth century provided no painting or photograph or drawing even for their own children—all since 1869 (except Ellen Wilson) are represented in the White House collection.

Jacqueline Kennedy's portrait, one of those eagerly sought by tourists, often meets puzzled responses. The First Lady most closely associated with White House restoration posed for painter Aaron Shikler in her New York apartment, and there is nothing in the painting to connect her with the Executive Mansion or with the energy and vigor that characterized the Kennedy administration. A much-imitated fashion plate when she lived in the White House, Jacqueline Kennedy is shown not in the pillbox hat or simple sleeveless dress that she helped popularize in the early 1960s, but in a full-length, long-sleeved robe that defies identification with any particular period. Actually, she had remarried—becoming the wife of Aristotle Onassis, the Greek shipping tycoon—before this portrait was done in 1970.

Before 1960, White House art was limited almost entirely to portraits of the Presidents and their wives, but during the next three decades the collection widened so that it showed many different regions of the nation. Paintings that now hang in the White House

First Lady Jacqueline Kennedy posed for her official White House portrait in 1970. (detail)

A decanter given to President James Madison in 1816.

include cityscapes of Philadelphia and New York; a Connecticut "Farmyard in Winter"; "Florida Sunrise" (the first Southern scene to be acquired for the White House); "Niagara Falls," and "Cliffs of Green River, Wyoming."

Western themes were favored by President Reagan, and several artworks selected for exhibit in the West Wing during his two terms reflected that interest. The Oval Office boasted a Remington sculpture, "Bronco Buster," and in the lobby were several paintings with Western motifs, including "Crossing the River Platte" and "Point Lobos, Monterey, California." Additional valuable paintings featuring Western subjects came into the White House collection as gifts during the Reagan years—Albert Bierstadt's landscape "View of the Rocky Mountains," and Charles Russell's "Fording the Horse Herd."

Although the White House had a policy of acquiring works of artists no longer living, in 1970 the Nixons drew attention to the White House's collection by holding an exhibit of a contemporary painter. The first one-man show in the building's history featured Andrew Wyeth, a favorite of the President and First Lady. Some of the twenty-one Wyeth paintings that hung in the East Room had never been previously exhibited.

Not all of the painters featured in the White House are American. One of the most poignant reminders of John Kennedy's brief presidency is a painting by a French impressionist that was donated by Kennedy's family in his memory. The work of Claude Monet, "Morning on the Seine," with its misty early morning blue, catches a scene as transitory as the presidency of the man whose memory it honors.

Also of great historic and artistic interest are the china, glassware, and metalware acquired by the White House over two centuries. Remnants of large purchases made by many different Presidents are exhibited in various parts of the public floors—in display cases in the east foyer and on the large table in the State Dining Room.

Among the most fragile White House holdings are the 3,145 pieces of glassware, including 870 surviving from the nineteenth century. This represents only a fraction of what was bought, since many dozens of glasses were broken at receptions and din-

This painting by Claude Monet was a gift to the White House from John F. Kennedy's family, donated in memory of the late President.

ners. Other pieces were given out as mementos of special occasions.

In the earliest days of the nation's capital, European diplomats sold off their household furnishings and silver when departing from their posts, and the President's House could pick up quality silver at bargain prices. No one seemed to mind that it was secondhand. Soon, however, the idea developed that the Executive Mansion deserved its own custom-made or at least specially selected furnishings. In 1826 a federal law mandated that purchases be American-made, unless nothing suitable was available.

A glass compote purchased for the Jackson administration.

Glass-making was among the first skills sufficiently developed in the United States to satisfy White House buyers. In 1817 an Englishman wrote that he was "astonished" to "witness such perfection on this side of the Atlantic" and especially in western Pennsylvania, "that part of America which a New Yorker supposes to be at the farther end of the world."

President Monroe evidently agreed with that assessment because that same year he placed an order for glassware with Benjamin Bakewell, whose factory he had visited the year before. Pittsburgh and the surrounding area had several glass factories, and local residents took pride in their reputation for producing quality products. The *Pittsburgh Gazette* boasted that an order from the President for a full set of "decanters, wine glasses and tumblers of various sizes and different models, exhibiting a brilliant specimen of double flint, engraved and cut by Jardelle," would put the region on the map; the firm of Bakewell & Page was to be congratulated for making Pittsburgh manufactures "known to the world." Not a single glass from that shipment survives—only the bill showing a hefty price of fifteen dollars per dozen for one hundred forty-four "cut Tumblers" with the "U.S. arms engraved on each."

The oldest surviving glassware at the White House was ordered by President Andrew Jackson from the same Pittsburgh firm in 1829. Later Presidents added to the supply with purchases of their own in the flat panel cut glass patterns with engraved vines, grapes, and the American eagle.

Monroe's order and those that followed show how closely the Seal of the United States became associated with the presidency. Most Americans see it often, since it appears on every dollar bill, but few realize that it predates the Constitution. In 1782, when the Revolution was not yet formally concluded, the seal began to appear, showing an eagle (symbolizing authority) holding in one talon a sheaf of arrows (signifying preparedness) and in the other talon an olive branch (symbolizing peace). Thus Americans seemed to be announcing, very early in their struggle toward nationhood, that they were prepared for both war and peace.

Over time the seal would vary in small details, depending on who designed it. The Jackson glassware shows a curious deviation. Although Jackson was known for his belligerent military initiatives, the glassware purchased for his administration featured an eagle devoid of arrows, clutching in one talon a palm frond and in the other a laurel branch.

New Yorker Martin Van Buren had little use for the "plain" table settings of his predecessor in the Executive Mansion, and as soon as he took office in 1837 he began planning elegant dinner parties. The President enjoyed fine wine and evidently had his own ideas about what kind of glasses he wanted to offer his guests. Instead of relying on the Pittsburgh firm for all the necessary glass replacements, Van Buren ordered from importers, thus stirring up many objections. One critical congressman from Pennsylvania, Charles Ogle, complained that the President was "spending the People's cash on *foreign Fanny Kemble green finger cups* in which to wash his pretty tapering, soft, white lily fingers, after dining on *fricandeau de veau* and *omelette soufflé*."

Van Buren did buy some of his countrymen's products, including the first pressed glassware for the mansion. This technique, in which glass is pressed for its shape and design rather than blown, was still a novelty in the 1830s, and American craftsmen were particularly skilled at it. Colored finger bowls were much in vogue in the 1830s, at least among the fashionable, and Van Buren braved Congressman Ogle's disapproval to provide his guests with tiny bowls filled with water and a slice of lemon or an orange leaf.

Other Presidents would add to the glass service, disposing in various ways of the odd pieces left over from their predecessors. Mary Lincoln included in her many purchases an entirely new set of glassware which she specified should be "rich-cut & engraved with the U.S. Coat of Arms." In this case the eagle on the seal reverted to the original pose, wielding both arrows and an olive branch. This pattern endured, with subsequent administrations adding to it over the next four decades, and it held the record as the longest in use.

Many items disappeared in one way or another. Some were broken at crowded receptions or during the process of being washed and stored. Others were probably removed by souvenir hunters who could not resist the chance to walk off with evidence of their visit to the White House. Sometimes odd pieces were sold to help raise money for a new set, and at least one glass in the White House collection is a gift from the descendants of people who happened to find it at an 1850 auction.

By the 1890s styles in glassware had shifted, and thicker, heavier glass forms (called "blanks") were being cut into intricate patterns featuring diamond shapes and stars. One of these "rich-cut" designs, the popular "Russian" pattern, was selected by First Lady Caroline Harrison when she purchased additional glassware in 1891. Although she tried to economize and ordered only sixty of each item, the number of different pieces required by each diner (water goblet, champagne glass, claret, sauterne, sherry, Apollinaris tumbler, finger bowl, and ice cream plate), shows how very complicated a table setting had become. Dinner guests who became bored with the table conversation might have noticed that the eagle in the Harrison glass pattern faced left toward the arrows rather than right, as had been the case with the Lincoln glassware.

In the major refurbishing of the White House in 1902, First Lady Edith Roosevelt changed the way breakables were discarded. She considered it inappropriate that the President's china and

Jacqueline Kennedy's choice of glassware for the White House (left) contrasts sharply with the ornate styles preferred by her predecessors. Mary Lincoln's selection (right), reordered by other Presidents until 1891, featured the presidential seal.

China purchased during the Monroe administration.

glassware could be parceled out to friends or auctioned off to the highest bidder, and so she arranged for a more dignified demise. Any rejects from the pantry, no longer usable because of chips or insufficient numbers, were to be broken in pieces and thrown into the Potomac. One White House aide, an ardent admirer of the First Lady, concurred in her decision although it troubled him to implement it. In a letter to his family, he wrote wistfully: "When I think how I should value even one piece of it, it hurts to smash it, but I am sure it is the only right thing to do."

Subsequent Presidents bought supplements or new glassware in the intricate patterns offered by American firms, until 1961 when Jacqueline Kennedy ordered plain unmarked glassware from Morgantown, West Virginia, not far from where President Monroe had placed an order in 1817. She explained that she wished to help an economically depressed area, and when the manufacturer began publicizing the "President's House Crystal" at ten dollars a dozen, the First Lady said that she did not mind at all.

The Kennedy glassware, made by Lenox since the Morgantown firm went out of business, still appears at state dinners. It features no design or insignia (although glassware with the Seal of the United States is still used in American embassies around the world), and every White House guest who raises a toast—no matter how impressive the occasion—is drinking from an inexpensive glass indistinguishable from that used in thousands of American homes.

The democratization of the White House glassware is not echoed in its china, nor is the reliance on American workmanship. No administration before the twentieth century purchased American-made china. Francophile James Monroe bought from a French company and later Presidents followed his lead, adding to the service he had started. Julia Grant considered purchasing her countrymen's products but rejected each sample as inferior. Finally she selected a pattern made at Haviland's French factory. It featured a gold band, with the traditional presidential seal at the top and a delicate floral arrangement in the center.

The Grants' dinners broke tradition in several ways. Now that the nation had developed into a major industrial, economic, and political power, its leader could afford to vie in elegance and style with the royal houses of Europe. President and Mrs. Grant em-

The China Room on the ground floor of the White House exhibits dishes used by Presidents for nearly two centuries.

First Lady Lucy Hayes liked to show guests through the White House conservatory after dinner. Here she is photographed with three of her children.

ployed an Italian chef who had practiced his skills in America's most fashionable hotels, and he came well equipped to plan and execute elaborate menus. Dinners of many courses—sometimes twenty-nine—became the rule, and guests had the opportunity to try intricate concoctions never before encountered on this side of the Atlantic. One reporter described a dinner beginning with a French vegetable soup better than ever before tasted, and then "croquet of meat" and partridges. Six wineglasses and a bouquet of fresh flowers marked each place and a well-trained staff, in white starched uniforms and kid gloves, served each guest. Clearly this was a dinner meant to compete with the palaces of Europe rather than reflect the simplicity of a frontier people.

As so often happens in American history, the trend toward "royal" china was interrupted by a backlash from provincial America. Lucy Hayes, an Ohioan who lived in the White House for only four years, stamped her Midwestern print on the china collection in a remarkable way. By the 1870s it had become accepted that each administration would select a new state china, its quality and appearance being taken as a mark of the First Lady's style, and Lucy Hayes decided to order a set of plates featuring painted ferns. Theodore Davis, a young artist employed by *Harper's Weekly*, met her by chance and became friendly with her entire family, especially her son Webb. Davis suggested that Mrs. Hayes expand the fern motif to show the full variety of flora and fauna in North America. The First Lady liked the idea, and Davis labored for months over the designs. The result was a set of state china showing a good selection of the plants and animals of North America—from buckwheat to cactus to raccoons and shad—a virtual cornucopia of the continent. One White House aide later judged it "about as ugly as it is possible for china to be," but the wife of a Maine senator disagreed and argued: "It is worth a trip from New York to Washington to see the table at a state dinner at the White House." In 1975 historian Margaret Klapthor called the Hayes china a peak in the "Nationalist period" (1845–93), when the emphasis was on "American themes."

In 1889, when First Lady Caroline Harrison found that she had too few plates of any one pattern to serve a state dinner unless she used the Hayes china, she opted for something new. An accom-

A serving platter from the Hayes china.

plished artist, the First Lady continued the nationalist theme but in a more restrained way, working with a designer to produce a pattern that combined goldenrod and corn with the presidential seal. She had hoped to use an American company in order to underline her commitment to American workmanship, but none of the samples submitted measured up to her requirements and in the end she ordered the china from France.

Edith Roosevelt, recognizing how much interest Americans showed in the presidential china, bought special display cabinets, and Edith Wilson later designated one entire room on the ground floor for its exhibition. Eventually, the collection of White House china became one of the most popular displays at 1600 Pennsylvania Avenue. Subsequent First Ladies selected their patterns with exhibition in mind, and since 1966 an extra place setting is routinely ordered for the Smithsonian Institution.

Selecting a Lenox pattern, Edith Wilson was the first to purchase American-made china for the White House. She took her time in the matter and examined several samples made especially for her before finding one that suited her taste for color and pattern. The winning design, later reordered by the Harding, Coolidge, and Hoover administrations, makes a table about as regal as any democratic nation can condone. The plates are bordered in gold and feature the presidential seal, with the eagle clutching a laurel branch with thirteen leaves on one side and a sheaf of thirteen arrows on the other. Never known for skimping, Edith Wilson placed an order for $11,251 worth of dishes including ten dozen plates for each of the following: dinner, soup, fish, entrée, dessert, and salad. The order also included after-dinner cups as well as lesser numbers of platters and serving pieces. Marked in gold on the back of each is:

THE WHITE HOUSE
1918

Fifteen years later the nation struggled through a deep depression but newly installed First Lady Eleanor Roosevelt faced the same dilemma as several of her predecessors. Additional china had been ordered during the 1920s but not enough to compensate for breakage. When newspapers announced that Mrs. Roosevelt had requested 1,000 pieces (at a total cost of about $9,000), criticism mounted and she felt obliged to explain in one of her news conferences that it was more economical to buy an entire new service than to purchase piecemeal replacements. Her actual order was nearly twice that originally announced (1,722 pieces) and was filled, as the Wilson order had been, by Lenox.

The Roosevelt porcelain, ready for use at a dinner for ninety-nine guests honoring the heads of foreign missions on January 24, 1935, won praise from the press. More blue than gold, it acknowledged its national role by featuring the presidential seal and a band of forty-eight stars (the number of states then in the Union). But the design chosen made a personal statement as well—the narrow gold scroll inside the blue border comprised roses and three feathers, details taken from the Roosevelt family coat of arms. The back of the plate is stamped "The White House 1934."

By 1951 Bess Truman faced a perennial problem—insufficient matching dishes to serve a state dinner. When she ordered a new set, her husband, who was a history buff, saw that an old error was corrected. The presidential seal, variously drawn over the years, was now standardized. According to an executive order of October 25, 1945, the eagle would forever face the peaceful olive branch, and the words *E Pluribus Unum* would issue from its beak. To coordinate colors with the new "Williamsburg green" walls of the State Dining Room, the Truman china had a large green band. Its cost, almost three times that for which Eleanor Roosevelt had been criticized earlier, reflected the inflated prices of post-World War II America. The china was ready for use on April 3, 1952, the first time the Trumans were able to entertain in the White House after a lengthy period of renovation; their guests that day were Dutch Queen Juliana and her consort Prince Bernhard.

The Truman china, combined with pieces from sets purchased by previous administrations, served the White House for more than a decade. Then, in 1966, Lady Bird Johnson ordered a pattern designed by Tiffany featuring delicate wildflowers and the presidential seal that had by then become *de rigueur.* It was paid for by an anonymous donor and the First Lady chose not to reveal its cost.

By 1981, when the Reagans moved into the White House, the lack of suitable china again became a matter of concern. The John-

China purchased during the Lyndon Johnson administration.

Nancy Reagan ordered a china pattern that featured the presidential seal.

son pattern seemed too casual for a state dinner, and at a dinner for King Hussein of Jordan in 1980, the Carters mixed plates from different sets in order to produce a formal look. An article in *Newsweek* complained about the indignity of combining patterns but noted that a sufficiently large new service would cost $300,000.

Nancy Reagan turned to Lenox to make a new state service, and the result featured a gold band around a red border. She applied many tests before making her final selection, including close observation under candlelight. The bill, totaling $209,508 for 4,372 pieces, reflected the general rise in prices and included no profit for Lenox, who did the job at cost. Paid for by the Knapp Foundation through the White House Historical Association, the Reagan china was ready for use on February 3, 1982, when Egyptian President Hosni Mubarak and his wife came to dine.

Although the china cost considerably less than *Newsweek* had predicted, many Americans thought the sum exorbitant, especially since it coincided with a White House announcement of cuts in public programs such as child care and school lunches. The Reagan china was retained, however, and joined its predecessors in the White House china exhibit, rounding out nearly two centuries of presidential plates.

★★★

More than a million people walk by the White House china exhibit every year, then up the wide staircase to the state floor. Proceeding like visitors to any of the nation's museums, they move along a designated path with brief stops to admire the superb portraits of the Presidents and First Ladies, the exquisitely crafted furniture and antique accessories, and the elegant serving pieces that have been used by presidential families dating back to the Madisons. Encompassing a remarkable collection of American furnishings, art, and design, the White House is not only a national landmark—it is a living museum.

In 1936, Eleanor Roosevelt greeted a large crowd on the South Lawn.

HOUSE OF THE PEOPLE

★ The White House has always served as the People's House—a place to celebrate important holidays and unite at times of national mourning, a place to receive distinguished visitors and showcase the nation's talent. When tensions run high, such as at a war's beginning or conclusion, the crowds around the White House swell, but even at other times throughout the year a steady stream of Americans of all ages and backgrounds converge at 1600 Pennsylvania Avenue. Parents stand in line for hours so that their children can tour the public rooms, and people from across the country and even from abroad come to demonstrate and to make their opinions heard. Legislators on Capitol Hill might like to think that they work more closely with the people,

In June 1978 Eubie Blake, at age 95, played ragtime on the South Lawn.

but it is the President's House that draws the largest crowds, making the White House a magnet in every season.

In the first decades of the Republic, Presidents underlined the public's ownership by referring to "the People's House" and opening the residence to visitors. In the 1860s when fears for the President's safety caused the welcome mat to be retracted, the number of invitations climbed as a kind of compensation, and crowds continued to congregate outside the gates as if the White House were a town square or public hall. In the twentieth century, when the population grew too large and the distances too great for most Americans to make their way to 1600 Pennsylvania Avenue, television took the building to them, and they were invited to watch their President speak from the Oval Office and listen to celebrities "In Performance at the White House."

Unlike the homes of other world leaders, the President's House is open year-round for public viewing. Many visitors share the sentiment of the youngster who, when reprimanded for jumping on a sofa at Andrew Jackson's inauguration party, replied defiantly, "It is one-millionth part mine."

White House residents have publicly acknowledged the American people's proprietary interest. When Eleanor Roosevelt moved into the White House during the Great Depression, she explained she did so with a heavy heart; no woman could do otherwise, she noted, if "she accepts the fact that it belongs to the people and therefore must be representative of whatever conditions people are facing." Lady Bird Johnson echoed those feelings when she called the White House a "rich storehouse of recollections" not just to Presidents but to the "whole nation."

More than any other dwelling in the United States, the White House arouses curiosity—people want to know about the foods served, the exercise taken, the pets kept, and the music played. When the purchases appear excessive, Americans complain of "royal" trappings—but then they object at least as loudly if the President and First Lady settle for out-of-style clothing or less than elegant dining. Although it is strictly forbidden, visitors during a tour have been known to run their fingers over a windowsill to check its cleanliness. Others comment on the height at which the grass is cut—as though this were their own backyard.

During the Carter presidency, large picnics were scheduled for the South Lawn.

★★★

Even before its plaster had dried, back on January 1, 1801, the President's House opened its doors to the public. The tradition had already been established by George Washington that the nation's Chief Executive would receive callers on the first day of the year. Aware of the value of appearing close to his constituents, Washington had immediately announced upon taking office in 1789 that he would entertain at two weekly parties at his home throughout the year: Men would visit him on Tuesday afternoons at a levée (or reception) and all were welcome with their wives at Martha Washington's party on Friday evening.

That very first year of his presidency, the levée happened to fall on January 1, and George Washington decided, in an act of generosity or an attempt to win public approval, to open his home to everyone. Each guest would be greeted by the President of the United States and his wife, drink a cup of punch, and mix with the others present. In eighteenth-century America an open house of this sort was common on New Year's Day—some employers invited their workers to come by for a toast to the future, and apprentices were permitted to enter homes closed to them the other 364 days of the year. But for heads of state, such parties were rare.

Not everyone in New York City, the nation's temporary capital, was inclined to call on the Washingtons. Ideas about deference and propriety kept many of the poor away from their leader's house. Even in the aftermath of the Revolution, Americans could not shed some old traditions, nor could they break accepted rules about who called on whom. A liveryman or an apprentice shoemaker who did not work for the President would not have ventured into his house. If asked why, he would have been surprised by the question. He had never voted, nor did he expect to, and he felt little inclination to approach the President. His wife might have been curious about the interior of the President's House but would have been too uncomfortable with the idea of entering it to venture through the front door.

Fashionable New Yorkers who put themselves on a social par with the President were not so reticent and welcomed the opportunity to see how the Washingtons entertained. When one of the women guests judged the cream in the dessert trifle a bit rancid, word spread that Lady Washington had a few things to learn.

Philadelphians proved just as curious, and when the federal government moved to the City of Brotherly Love in 1791, they lined up for the New Year's Day reception. Eleven of these receptions occurred prior to November 1800, when John and Abigail Adams moved to Washington, and the Adamses felt they could do no less than open the doors of the President's House to the public on January 1.

Washington City, as it was called then, had fewer than five hundred households, so the turnout was only a fraction of what it would later become. The oval room on the second floor was made as presentable as possible and, to add a festive note, the President and First Lady invited the Marine Band to play, making it the first

As part of her First Lady duties, Jacqueline Kennedy welcomed many visitors to the White House.

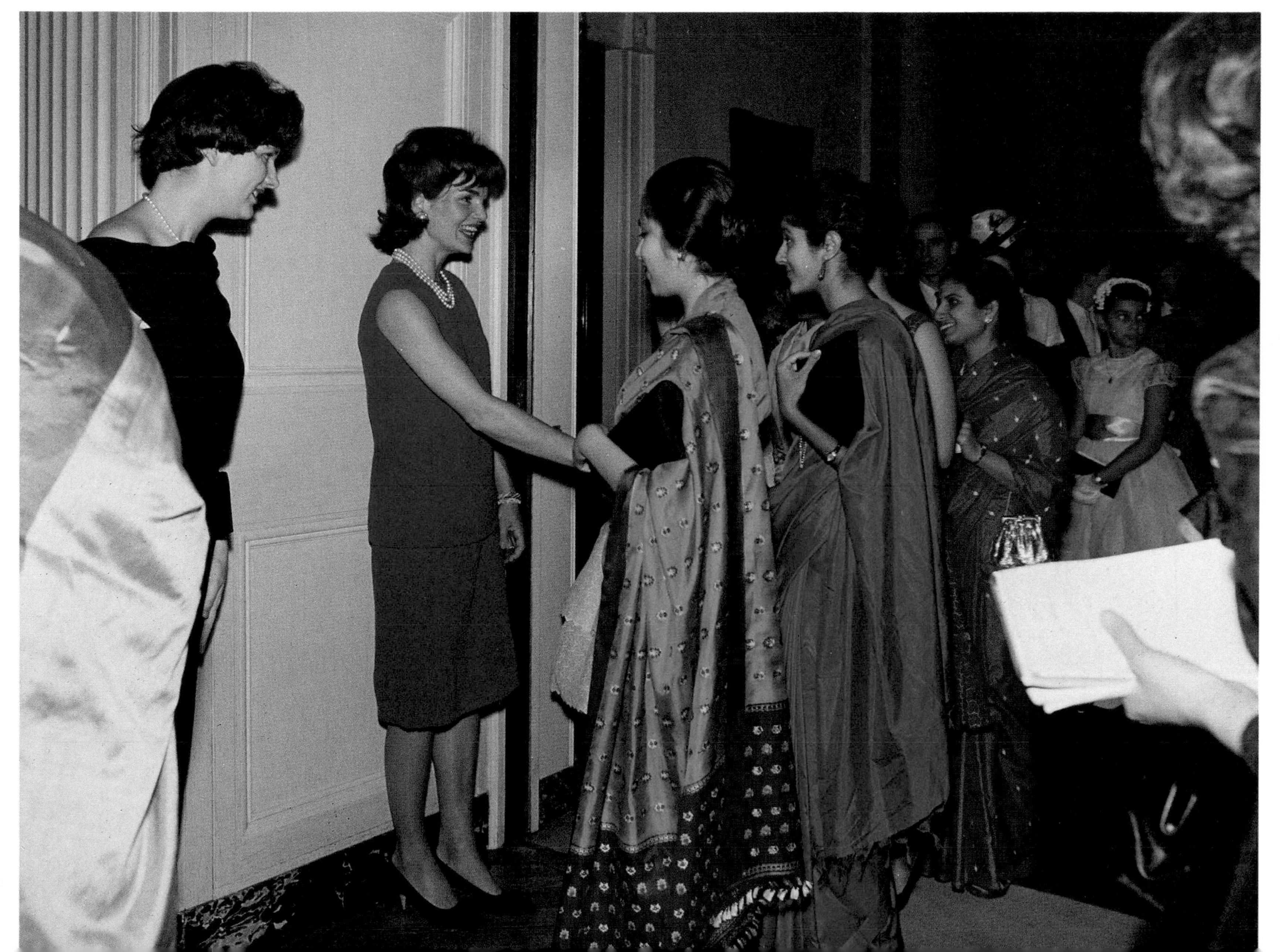

musical group to perform in the White House. Forming a tiny ensemble of two French horns, two clarinets, and a bassoon, the bandsmen, in red jackets and blue pantaloons, provided the brightest color in the room. They could not know, nor could the guests as they filed upstairs to greet John and Abigail Adams, that they were initiating a tradition that would last, with some interruptions, for 132 years—without invitation, anyone could visit the President's House on New Year's Day.

The following year (1802), Thomas Jefferson continued the tradition of inviting in the public to celebrate on January 1. Although the refreshment served was a bit unorthodox, it appropriately carried strong partisan overtones at a time when political parties were still taking shape. Jefferson's Republican admirers in West Chester, Pennsylvania, had sent him a wagon drawn by six horses and carrying a 1,235-pound cheese that they claimed was made from the milk of "Republican" cows. New Year's guests, more heavily Republican that year than previously, ate with particular

Rosalynn Carter poses with a group of Girl Scouts in the State Dining Room.

gusto, pleased that they controlled the presidency—the ultimate "big cheese."

In the summer of 1801, during his first year as President, Thomas Jefferson decided to open the lawn around the President's House in celebration of the day independence was declared. He arranged for a large party on July 4, and the event quickly became the best attended of the year. Whether the Chief Executive was in residence or not, people flocked to his house for the festivities. The tradition would continue into the twentieth century, and when the grounds were eventually closed off, people expected fireworks on the Mall or concerts at the Capitol building to supplement their celebration.

In addition to the January 1 and July 4 holidays, the White House opened for smaller groups of visitors at other times. Thomas Jefferson permitted public tours, and Dolley Madison, a First Lady who combined an unusually large measure of political savvy with the sure hand of a seasoned hostess, followed his lead. She recognized the political value of being popular, and every Wednesday evening between six and nine anyone could visit the Madisons at home. Technically, only those who had been introduced to the President and his wife (or knew someone who had been) were invited, but that was a latitude easily stretched, and on the designated day "Open House" prevailed.

A wide range of people accepted. When author Washington Irving visited the capital in 1811, he "swore by all my gods" that he would attend one of Dolley Madison's parties. So did hundreds of clerks and congressmen's relatives. The First Lady moved among them all, greeting strangers warmly and conversing with her husband's enemies as much as with his friends. President Madison, brilliant with a pen but a failure at party talk, stayed on the sidelines, willing to respond to those who sought him out but never comfortable as a host.

Massachusetts congressman Elijah Mills, a political opponent of Madison's, complained that the drawing rooms were "full of intrigue, political and moral" and the guests were not those he would have chosen: "all classes of people are there from men from Russia to underclerks of the Post Office and the printer of a paper—greasy boots and silk stockings"—and many of the women showed "very much the manners and appearances of 'high life below the stairs.' "

To speed the flow of traffic, this bridge was built so that guests could exit directly from the East Room to the lawn. ***Frank Leslie's Illustrated Newspaper,*** **March 16, 1889.**

Crowding was common, and one woman who attended an 1814 reception at the Executive Mansion described how people had to "compress themselves as small as they could" in order for everyone to get inside. Unfortunately, in their zeal they caused some damage, and "in the excessive heat of the apartments, the rouge, which had been applied with 'an unsparing hand' began to run together with powder, dust and perspiration, making their wearers 'altogether unlovely to soul and eye.' "

As the nation grew and the capital city expanded, the crowds multiplied. Lines of three or four abreast formed outside the Executive Mansion, curling down the hill as people waited to shake hands with the President. Eventually a temporary bridge was added from the East Room to the lawn so guests could exit directly rather than wind around through the house again, clogging the traffic flow.

New Year's Day 1818 was an especially important celebration, since that day had been selected for reopening the President's House after its 1814 burning. Workmen rushed to meet the deadline, and curious Americans lined up to see the results. One congressman estimated that a thousand people appeared that day, but President James Monroe and his wife Elizabeth stood through the ordeal of greeting each one, "nodding, bowing, smiling and talking. . . . The fatigue must have been very great."

For the diplomatic corps and the congressmen (who, beginning in 1818, were admitted ahead of the general public), an appearance at the President's House on January 1 became practically obligatory. A newspaper editor's wife thought attendance was "generally deemed a test of loyalty" no matter what the weather. Torrents of rain came down on New Year's Day 1823, but a New England congressman reported that virtually everyone he knew went to "the palace." Louisa Adams, wife of John Quincy Adams, then Secretary of State, noted in her diary that she had attended the President's reception although she was "miserably sick."

Americans looked for other chances during the year to visit the White House, and they were often obliged by Presidents who realized the advantages of remaining accessible. Andrew Jackson chose Washington's birthday to give the last public reception of his presidency (in February 1837) and he offered as refreshment a "mammoth cheese" (weighing 1400 pounds) that had come as a gift from admiring farmers in Oswego County, New York. According to some who were present that day, the smell of cheese filled the entire house and went beyond, reaching the Capitol building where congressmen, after filling their pockets with cheese, had gone to work.

Andrew Jackson became famous for attracting huge crowds wherever he went. For his first inauguration in 1829 so many people descended on the capital that room-and-board prices soared, and one report had a dozen eggs selling for eighty cents, more than most working people earned in a day. After Jackson's inaugural ceremony the crowd at the President's House surpassed all previous gatherings, a fact that was noted with some displeasure in newspaper accounts of the day. Supreme Court Justice Joseph Story fled the scene, saying that he wanted to avoid a mixture of

Supporters of Andrew Jackson sent him a mammoth cheese which he served at a White House reception.

people ranging "from the highest and most polished down to the most vulgar in the nation."

A Pennsylvania congressman who was present that day described a White House so crowded that waiters could not serve the barrels of orange punch they had prepared. People rushed the doors, "glasses were broken, pails of liquor upset and the most painful confusion prevailed." The congressman claimed to have seen men and boys, "boots heavy with mud," standing on satin damask-covered chairs. Not until waiters carried the punch out onto the White House lawn did the crowd inside begin to thin out.

Presidents dared not offend voters by closing the White House gates too abruptly. When President Martin Van Buren, who had a reputation for fancy manners and high living, tried to dispense with the Fourth of July party in 1839, he was loudly criticized. Presidents soon learned that if they wished to flee hot, humid Washington in July, they should arrange for the celebration to proceed without them. Even President Polk, reputedly a workaholic, took time to visit with callers, and twice a month he and his wife Sarah gave a reception following the Marine Band concerts. As many as two hundred people showed up.

Carriages lined up outside the North Portico, the principal public entrance during the nineteenth century.

Union soldiers camped in the East Room during the Civil War.

By the 1860s, this kind of open house seemed inappropriate and Mary Lincoln tried to put a stop to it. The city had grown, bringing many more people into visiting proximity. The mood in Washington was bitter, with the nation divided in a Civil War. President Lincoln wanted to hold the receptions even in wartime, and he continued to schedule them, but he feared for his own safety and that of his family. Anxiety ran so high, President Lincoln's private secretary William Osborn Stoddard wrote, that Mary Lincoln asked him to open every letter and parcel addressed to her.

The large number of invitation cards that she issued—as many as five hundred for a single event—suggests that Mary Lincoln went beyond inviting just the capital elite. Those honored with a card were expected to show it at the door, go up to the second floor to deposit coats and hats, and then return to one of the state rooms on the main floor (often the Blue Room) to be greeted by the President and First Lady. All evening the Marine Band supplied "sweet music" in the background, and about 11 P.M. a procession led by the Lincolns moved down the grand hallway to the dining room, where

Regardless of cold weather and snow, people lined up for blocks to greet the President and his wife on New Year's Day.

a table provided "one of the finest displays of the confectioner's art ever seen in this country."

Some criticism greeted this kind of restricted, invitation-only affair and critics used it as ammunition in their crusade against Mary Lincoln, but in the end it was accepted as necessitated by circumstances. Anyone with even a little clout or minimal acquaintance could arrange for a place on one of the guest lists, but the right to attend on whim—except on January 1—was taken away.

Popular First Lady Frances Cleveland greeted an exceptionally long line of visitors on New Year's Day 1887. Just months earlier, she had become the first to marry a President in the White House. Only twenty-two years old at the time, she created a sensation and her picture appeared in magazines across the country. A nineteenth-century version of Jacqueline Kennedy, "Frankie" Cleveland was imitated in dress and hairstyle by thousands of women. People willingly stood in line for hours on New Year's Day just to shake her hand, and some reportedly claimed the privilege more than once. The First Lady obligingly greeted each one, but to ease the strain she had to resort to brief massages of her hands and arms.

First Lady Edith Roosevelt clutched a bouquet of orchids to avoid shaking hands. That ruse was insufficient, however, to keep people in line moving quickly, and the Marine Band conductor developed another strategy to influence the flow of traffic. After starting with slow, soft pieces, orchestrated without drums or cymbals, he introduced a little light opera music as diplomats and congressmen filed past; then as the general public was admitted and the crowds grew, the band played loud marches. The President and his wife reported that they saw a change—people seemed to flow with the music, moving faster when it was faster, thus permitting more of them to be greeted in less time and leaving the hosts less fatigued at the end of the day.

Unfortunately there were pranksters, and some of them were dangerous. Fear escalated after President McKinley was shot while greeting the public in 1901. The assassination took place in Buffalo while the President attended the Pan-American Exposition, but the effect back in Washington was direct and immediate. McKinley's successor, Theodore Roosevelt, announced a new rule: no one—not even a close friend—could go through the receiving line and

Although Americans allow their Presidents some latitude in decorating the White House, one cartoonist implied that Theodore Roosevelt had gone too far with his wild game theme.

approach the President while carrying a muff or bundle of any kind.

The Roosevelt rule had little effect on two men intent on playing a practical joke at a New Year's Day reception. From the front they appeared appropriately dressed, but from the back they were walking billboards: the placards attached to their jackets promoted a well-known mineral water. The President was not amused and amended his rules so that only those who were "clean and free of bodily advertising" were to be admitted.

During Theodore Roosevelt's second term, between 5,000 and 9,000 people filed through the White House every New Year's, and an extra aide was assigned to stand opposite the President to watch for dangerous people. Security men were rotated so as to encourage vigilance.

Occasionally the receptions had to be canceled because of a national emergency, illness, or extenuating circumstance, but the decision was not made lightly. Of course none could be held immediately after the 1814 burning of the President's House, and Benjamin Harrison had to call off the party in 1893 after his granddaughter, Marthena Harrison, was quarantined with scarlet fever. The child was confined to two rooms on the northwest corner of the second floor, but prudence dictated keeping crowds away from the entire mansion. Harrison's presidency must have seemed jinxed by then; his wife had died the previous October, and he had lost his November bid for reelection.

The cancellation of the New Year's White House reception by the Harrisons was noted by Woodrow Wilson in 1915 when he, too, considered calling it off. His wife had died only five months previously and the Great War had already started in Europe. Celebration was hardly the feeling of the day. Even then Wilson hesitated, not willing to risk being called "elitist." Finally he was persuaded, one of his secretaries reported, by the Harrison precedent. Word went out that the President would not be greeting visitors that day.

Not everyone in Washington looked forward to the January 1 reception. Diplomats and congressional representatives had other opportunities to see the interior of the White House, and many of the capital's elite attended various dinners and receptions during the year. Janet Richards, a lecturer and suffrage leader, received invitations to White House parties over five decades, beginning with the McKinley administration in 1897, and she explained to her friends that she had more interesting things to do on January 1 than mix with the masses and shake hands with the President.

In 1932 when bad weather deterred many people from standing in line to greet the Hoovers, Richards noted in her diary that it had been an altogether miserable day—a "pouring down rainy day! Such a disappointment to the thousands who had planned to storm the White House . . . for their one annual 'look in' on the . . . great."

The poor turnout in 1932, added to the disenchantment of Washington officials and the President's own disappointment with the continuing economic depression, combined to put a stop to the New Year's receptions. By January 1933, Herbert Hoover had presided over a depression-torn country for nearly four years, and when he had run for reelection the previous November he had lost. Hardly in the mood for a party, Hoover had no reason to think other people were, and considering his unpopularity, the number of callers might have been embarrassingly small. During the last four-month interval between the presidential election and inauguration (beginning in 1937, Presidents would take the oath on January 20 rather than on March 4), the Hoovers decided to take off for a much-needed rest in the South rather than stay around Washington to shake hands.

The President's New Year's reception was not revived again, and the long line of Americans shaking hands with their President on January 1 became a thing of the past. Invitations would now become the rule for all White House events, although tourists would still be permitted to walk through the state rooms during designated hours.

The number of names on guest lists soared in order to compensate for the decreased accessibility. Each year thousands of average citizens received cards admitting them to garden parties, receptions, luncheons, and teas—their names carefully typed and indexed in the White House social records prepared by the staff. Edith Helm, secretary to Eleanor Roosevelt, noted that during the 1935–36 season more than 27,000 people accepted an invitation to the White House: 906 for lunch, 1099 for dinner, 5672 for state

New Year's Day receptions drew large crowds for more than a century.

receptions, and 19,713 for tea. The presidential family shared quarters with 378 overnight guests, and sightseers walked through the state rooms at the rate of more than 70,000 per month.

Music was often a central feature of White House parties, and after its very first appearance in 1801 the Marine Band became a regular attraction at all but the smallest, most casual events. Bands of other military branches would eventually rotate in the White House performance schedule but the Marine Band was most closely associated with the Chief Executive and became known as the "President's own."

In the 1840s the Marine Band began regular concerts on the White House lawn, and these free events attracted a loyal following. Frederika Bremer, a Swedish visitor to the capital in early July 1850, reported what she had observed when she attended. People sat on the grass, munched picnic lunches, and strolled about, greeting their friends and stopping, if they chose, to chat with the President. Zachary Taylor, the military hero who had reluctantly assumed the presidency, evidently enjoyed this part of the job, and one visitor noted that he was always ready to "shake hands with anyone who chooses to present himself."

Eventually the band concerts were shifted temporarily to Wednesdays because First Lady Jane Pierce insisted on tranquillity as she prepared for religious services on Sundays, but she dared not stop the music. People expected the lawn to be open to them, and they took it as their right to use it without any special invitation.

The intrepid Mary Lincoln asked that the concerts be stopped after her son Willie died in 1862, but she was loudly criticized. The music and laughter grated on her nerves, she said, at a time when her life was so full of grief. Abraham Lincoln liked listening to the music but objected to the attention he attracted whenever he appeared. The President had stepped out on the South Portico one Saturday afternoon to hear the band better, but as soon as the audience caught sight of his tall, gaunt figure, they requested a speech. He immediately retreated, remarking to a friend, "I wish they would let me sit out there quietly and enjoy the music."

The band's membership remained largely foreign—mostly Germans and Italians—throughout the nineteenth century because the United States had not yet developed many of its own music

Band concerts, first held on the South Lawn in the 1840s, continued to draw large audiences like this one, photographed about 1920.

Maestro Dino Anagnost (second from left) paused for this photo on the South Lawn after conducting the New York Metropolitan Singers/Greek Choral Society in a concert in the East Room. The concert and reception honored his Eminence Archbishop Iakovos, Primate of the Greek Orthodox Church in the Americas (on the left).

schools. Nor did it have a sufficiently large number of musicians to apprentice younger ones. Until 1880 foreigners conducted the Marine Band, when American-born John Philip Sousa took over. With an emphasis on patriotic themes in his music, Sousa composed more than one hundred marches including such classics as "Semper Fidelis," "Stars and Stripes Forever," and the "Washington Post March."

Musical entertainment had been popular inside the President's House from the very beginning. Thomas Jefferson, an accomplished violinist himself, arranged for music at his receptions, and he personally owned several keyboard instruments. Louisa Adams kept her harp and sheet music handy, and the newly wed John and Julia Tyler teamed up for duets.

These musical programs remained private until the middle of the nineteenth century when the mansion began receiving world-famous artists. Adelina Patti, one of the most sought-after sopranos of the late 1800s, came to visit the President but she did not sing. Perhaps she had qualms about performing without being paid, since she was used to receiving five thousand dollars for such appearances. The tradition of performing for free, however, still continues into the White House's third century. An artist invited to entertain at the White House receives a plaque or a signed photo—perhaps even a dinner and a chance to stay overnight—but not a check from the President.

Rutherford Hayes deserves credit for introducing "musicales" at the White House, and during his four years as President he scheduled fifty such events, combining a private concert with a chance to socialize. One featured Maria Selika, the first African-American to sing at the White House. Chester Arthur arranged for the first concert in the East Room, and during Theodore Roosevelt's administration the White House blossomed with music. Hundreds of people came to hear world figures such as pianist Ignace Paderewski, who first performed in the East Room in 1902. He returned to play nine times for seven different Presidents, eventually bringing his own piano with him so he could practice in the Queens' Bedroom (where he also slept).

Regardless of personal preferences, each presidential family tries to invite performers and present compositions popular with the

American people. In 1905 the Marine Band learned Scott Joplin's "Maple Leaf Rag" in response to pressure from Theodore Roosevelt's family; Mamie Eisenhower scheduled the bands of Lawrence Welk and Fred Waring in the 1950s; in the early 1960s the Kennedys presented the legendary cellist Pablo Casals (who had first performed at the White House in 1904); and ten years later the Nixons invited country-western singer Johnny Cash.

Struggling artists profit from the boost of a White House appearance and marginal figures move into the mainstream. First Lady Helen Taft, an accomplished pianist herself, favored keyboard music in making up her concert list, and nine of the eleven pianists that she invited to the White House were women. In 1935 Eleanor Roosevelt's invitation to Antonia Brico, to conduct the New York Women's Symphony in a concert of Mozart selections came at a time when women musicians were rare and women conductors even more so. Brico's career was just beginning and the White House appearance paved the way for her to conduct later at major concert halls in the United States and Europe. In 1962 Grace Bumbry was still an unknown opera singer when she appeared in the East Room, but her career soared after just one performance at the Kennedy White House.

Before the Kennedy Center for the Performing Arts opened in 1971, the White House frequently functioned as a theater, presenting such shows as *Hello Dolly,* whose cast gathered to celebrate its fourth anniversary on January 17, 1967.

In December 1990, Barbara Bush showed visitors the Christmas tree in the Blue Room.

By the end of its second century, the White House had been the setting for just about every variety of musical performance—ranging from the Beach Boys to Isaac Stern (who played the violin for seven Presidents). The jazz group that had shocked Lou Hoover's guests at a Christmas party for her son would now no longer create a stir, and when the Carters arranged for televising the programs, the audience for "In Performance at the White House" became potentially almost as large as the nation itself. Rosalynn Carter explained that the idea of televising musical performances resulted from the realization that "so many people who had never been to the White House would be thrilled to come."

Although musicians have most often been the featured performers at White House programs, other entertainers have also appeared, including dancers, monologists, and theatrical groups. Before Kennedy Center opened in 1971, the White House functioned as a leading theater for professional readings of Shakespeare, ballet performances, and Broadway shows.

★★★

Just as Americans have gathered at the President's House for various performances, they have also come to it for holiday celebrations. First Lady Nancy Reagan recalled that as a child she had rolled Easter eggs on the South Lawn, a tradition that Lucy Hayes is credited with beginning. Children of employees or friends of the Chief Executive eagerly anticipated the annual lawn party, and the numbers attending were particularly large if the President had young children.

In 1885, an oversight resulted in no preparations being made for the party, but when bachelor President Cleveland heard of the mistake, he immediately ordered the grounds opened for all to enjoy. Thousands arrived, carrying colored eggs they meant to roll and exchange before settling down to picnic lunches. Thirsty crowds converged on the mansion, and President Cleveland sent word that he would greet them in the East Room. He had not foreseen how many would take advantage of the offer and finally he was advised to retreat—otherwise he would have been shaking youngsters' hands until dark.

The Easter egg roll continued to draw ever increasing numbers. In April 1961, an estimated ten thousand people converged

One of President Bush's granddaughters joins him with a basket of Easter eggs in the Oval Office.

Military bands and choruses, with a long tradition of performances at the White House, join in most festivities, including this 1990 Christmas party.

on the White House lawn even though the Kennedys had gone to Florida. In the absence of the presidential family, the Air Force Band played and the city's recreation department organized games. Even this gigantic turnout did not break the record set in 1941 when an estimated 53,248 people showed up.

That same year marked an unusual Christmas tree lighting. Since the 1890s, White House families had put a Christmas tree inside the mansion and, since 1923, another tree outside. Placement of the exterior tree varied—sometimes it was on the Ellipse (south of the White House) or in Lafayette Park (to the north). But whatever the location, the tree drew large crowds and its brilliant colored lights added to the city's Christmas festivities.

In 1941 the Secret Service protested. Civil Defense precautions blacked out the city at night, and protection of the President (and Winston Churchill, who happened to be a guest) required that the White House not be targeted by anything so prominent as a lit Christmas tree. President Roosevelt objected that he would not be denied his tree, and by means of compromise the community tree was moved to the South Lawn—within the fenced White House grounds so the President could be more closely protected.

Christmas Eve 1941 turned out to be a particularly mild winter

In November 1918, when word spread through the capital that World War I was finally over, crowds gathered at the White House.

night, and thousands of men and women gathered to sing carols and hear short speeches by Franklin Roosevelt and Winston Churchill, the first meeting of a President and British Prime Minister on Christmas Eve. The men spoke from the South Portico while other distinguished guests, including the Crown Prince and Princess of Norway, stood behind them. Then the President pushed a button and the giant tree was lit, thus beginning the tradition of a "national" Christmas tree near the President's House.

Crowds have gathered many times on that same lawn to celebrate military victory. The President may actually sign the peace document inside the White House—as William McKinley did in 1898 when he went to a second floor room (now known as the Treaty Room) and put his name on the document that ended the Spanish-American War—but the real signature belongs to the people shouting outside. In November 1918, throngs of Americans gathered near the White House gates. Actually they gathered too soon, having heard a false report that the Great War was already over four days before it actually was. They had to be sent away, Edith Wilson explained, but then on Monday November 11, they returned, and this time their shouts were justified. Jubilant crowds also gathered to celebrate V-E day and V-J day in 1945 at the end of World War II.

Not all Americans come to the White House in celebration—some come in anger, frustration or concern, as they would to a community meeting house. Then Lafayette Park becomes a mass of signs announcing opinions and demanding action. South of the White House, the Ellipse can become packed, a sea of angry voices reaching up to the President's office and to his bedroom.

No one can be sure what single protester deserves credit for first taking his case directly to the President in a public way, but John Tyler came up against more than one of them. Tyler's presidency began inauspiciously in April 1841, when he became the first Vice President to take over after the death of an incumbent, William Henry Harrison. Tyler alienated the Whig party leaders by insisting on being granted full discretionary powers as President and by vetoing a fiscal bill drawn up by the Whigs. After a few drinks at local saloons, an ugly mob moved toward the Executive Mansion. Finding the gates closed, they began screaming, throw-

On a wet, snow-covered lawn, Americans gathered in January 1945 to witness an unprecedented fourth inauguration for Franklin D. Roosevelt as President.

ing rocks, and firing guns. A particularly irate group took up space right across the street and burned the President in effigy—surely a frightening sight for the Tyler family inside a relatively unguarded house.

Unanimity is rare in a democratic society where the Constitution ensures the right to freedom of speech, and the White House continues to serve as a focal point for differing ideas. In the 1960s Lafayette Park became a permanent protest ground, providing the space for thousands of demonstrators to make their opinions known directly to the President. The family of Lyndon Johnson endured twenty-four-hour-a-day chanting, and his daughters, whose husbands were serving in Vietnam, could not help but be distressed by shouts of anti-war demonstrators: "LBJ/ LBJ/ How many boys/ did you kill today?" The Nixons learned to eat lunch inside the White

Suffragists converged on the White House in 1917 to gain President Woodrow Wilson's support for women's voting rights.

House, the unmistakable smell of tear gas wafting up to them.

Betty Ford, after publicly supporting the Equal Rights Amendment to bar discrimination on the basis of sex, suffered the indignity of seeing her views disparaged in the park in front of the White House. Then, on the televised evening news, she saw a replay—black-clad figures parading through the park carrying placards denouncing her for pressing "second-rate manhood on American women."

All important national questions get debated on White House space, or as close to it as proponents of different views are permitted to come. Sometimes that seems very close. In the fall of 1990, when the United States and its allies considered how to move Iraqi soldiers out of Kuwait, Lafayette Park filled with people and signs opposing military action. Their numbers grew, and in January 1991, when President Bush went on television to announce that air attacks were beginning on Iraqi forces, he spoke above the shouts of protesters outside.

Like London's Hyde Park, the area outside the White House fence offers a remarkable platform. It charges no rent and guarantees immediate press coverage—reasons enough to make it a favorite site of protest. Young men and women often make a White House demonstration the reason for their first trip to Washington, and the President's House remains their strongest memory.

Sometimes the demonstrations appear to get quick results. In early 1917 advocates of the vote for women, convinced that Woodrow Wilson's failure to support a national amendment had stymied their progress, converged on the White House. Some of the suffragists chained themselves to the gates and others were dragged away. But their signs made their point, and the President shifted his position and came out for a suffrage amendment in early 1918.

President Wilson considered the suffragist demonstrators of little danger to him personally; he even invited them in for tea—and could not understand why they declined. Each day as he went out for his afternoon ride, he tipped his hat to them in a courtly gesture that infuriated them.

Presidents have not always viewed the demonstrators so benignly. Previous Chief Executives, going as far back as Madison, put security guards on the grounds in order to protect their own

When Abraham Lincoln's body lay in state in the East Room, poor lighting precluded photographs, but an artist made this sketch so that Americans across the nation could participate vicariously in rites for their martyred President.

safety and that of their family. Gradually, and almost imperceptibly, the President's House would change into the barricaded, highly guarded and less accessible White House that Americans would come to know in the 1990s. Protection for the leader from the people stood as the very antithesis of what democracy was supposed to be about. A representative of the people should have no reason to fear, popular reasoning went, as long as he remained responsive to constituents' needs and wishes. Only in the face of attempted assassinations and increased fear did the cement barriers and a sophisticated security force come into use.

In the initial discussions of security in the early nineteenth century, the word "guard" rarely appears, and the first hired were called "watch" men as though they were merely keeping a ship on course or attending to fires that might go out. Even when John Tyler persuaded a reluctant Congress to pay for a permanent security force in the 1840s, only four men were hired and they were called "doormen." To the uninformed, they appeared to be more social fixtures than security measures as they stood around nonchalantly and mingled with guests at receptions.

In 1853 Franklin Pierce, a Democrat from New Hampshire, became the first President to have a full-time bodyguard. He had made the South Lawn into a park and hired two men to guard it at night, but he wanted reinforcements closer at hand. Having witnessed violence more than once, he was not inclined to put himself at risk. He had seen the assassination attempt on President Jackson in 1835 and had lost a close friend in a duel waged over politics. Pierce may have felt particularly vulnerable, having lost all three of his sons before any reached maturity.

Whatever his reasons, Pierce asked Thomas O'Neil, who had been his orderly in the Mexican-American War, to attend to his safety. O'Neil escorted the President down the capital's streets and went riding with him. When Pierce worked inside the White House, O'Neil ensconced himself in the entrance hall where he observed everyone who came through and, if necessary, could respond to calls for help.

A combination of events contributed to increased security measures. Abraham Lincoln's assassination in 1865 (the first of a

After President Garfield's death in 1881, the White House was draped in mourning.

After President Garfield was shot in 1881, well-wishers converged on the White House. *Frank Leslie's Illustrated Newspaper,* July 30, 1881, showed a young African-American girl presenting a bouquet of flowers.

Florence Harding greeted tourists and posed with delegations, including this group of Masons.

President) and James Garfield's in 1881 both occurred outside the Executive Mansion, but they resulted in many discussions about how to protect the President. Whenever the United States went to war, the need for extra vigilance was obvious. By the 1980s terrorist attacks around the world resulted in closing off the entire avenue east of the White House. A new visitors' entrance was built to screen everyone who passed through. At first glance, the visitors' entryway blends so well with the Palladian lines of the original mansion that it might seem part of it—but in function it is nearly two centuries removed. Its metal detectors, like those in most airports, check thousands of people every day, and guards personally inspect handbags and identification cards.

Breaches sometimes occur. White House security forces were shaken in January 1985 when a Denver man, vacationing in the capital, infiltrated the Marine Band and got up to the State Floor of the White House where he poked around for about ten minutes before the guards noticed him. Jailed for five days, he was ordered to undergo a psychiatric examination—but not before the entire building was checked for hidden explosives.

Such precautions would have shocked early nineteenth-century Americans who claimed the right to walk into the White House at any hour of the day—at least as far as the East Room. During the presidencies of Jefferson and Madison, visitors could wander in at will, and although the elusive Monroes liked their privacy and tried to keep people out, their successors opened the doors again. President Andrew Johnson announced that the East Room would be open for visitors every day except Sunday between 9 A.M. and 3 P.M. Guests could enter the north door, walk through the wide hall, and stand in the East Room for as long as they liked. Some even brought along a minister and exchanged vows so they could boast that they had been "married at the White House."

Subsequent administrations restricted access but Florence Harding brought back some of the nineteenth-century openness when she reintroduced public tours. Although self-centered in many respects, she seemed intent on making every visitor feel welcome, and staff recalled that she would frequently go downstairs from the living quarters to shake hands with tourists and have her photograph taken with whatever delegation wanted to pose.

Even after security precautions transformed the White House

into a barricaded fortress, White House residents sought ways to stay physically close to the public. Lyndon Johnson could be seen reaching through the iron fence to shake hands with tourists; Rosalynn Carter made frequent trips to the ground floor to be photographed with one delegation or another, referring to each of these picture sessions as a "bottom-of-the-elevator"; and George Bush often detoured to surprise visitors with a personal greeting.

★★★

Although it would seem that royal figures might find no welcome mat in the "People's House," in fact they have been popular guests. In 1860 the visit of the Prince of Wales (later to become King

A women's sorority posed with Florence Harding (fifth from right) on the White House portico.

Edward VII) resulted in what White House historian William Seale called a "public spectacle."

Monarchs' visits continued to dot American history in the following decades, but none aroused quite the interest accorded King George VI and Queen Elizabeth in 1939. Never before had a reigning British monarch favored the United States with a stopover, and the White House went through months of cleaning and refurbishing in preparation. In her weekly news conferences, Eleanor Roosevelt was besieged with questions on how she would accommodate her royal guests, feed them, and dress for them—and whether they merited a curtsy. Reporters felt obligated to assure readers that the nation's most visible guest house was being properly run.

For most royal visitors of the late twentieth century, the White House is simply too small to accommodate them and their entourage overnight, so they are housed across the street at the official guest quarters in Blair House. But one second-floor bedroom of the White House did earn the name of "Queens' Bedroom" in honor of the five who had stayed there. Decorated in rosy pink, this was the room Mamie Eisenhower chose as her own when she returned to visit the Nixons.

The same room also appealed to the entertainer Sammy Davis, Jr, when he was an overnight guest of the Nixons. He had been shown first to the coveted Lincoln Bedroom but had demurred,

When Britain's reigning monarchs made their historic visit to Washington in June 1939, Eleanor Roosevelt accompanied Queen Elizabeth on the ride from the train station to the White House.

The Queens' Bedroom takes its name from the fact
that many royal guests have slept there.

The domestic staff in 1877 included one cook, two waiters, a house maid, a messenger, a watchman, two laundresses, and a nurse.

joking later, "I thought to myself, now I don't want [Lincoln] coming in here talking about 'I freed them, but I sure didn't mean for them to sleep in my bed.' "

Davis touched on a delicate subject. Eighty percent of the domestic staff was black at the time of his visit and large numbers of African-Americans had worked in the residence since it was first occupied, their records inevitably tied to the house's history. Thomas Jefferson installed several of his Monticello slaves there, and one of them gave birth to a baby—who died less than two years later, resulting in what historians think is the first funeral held in the White House. Other Southern Presidents, notably Madison, Jackson, Polk, and Taylor, used their own personal slaves as part of the domestic staff, in an attempt to cut expenses paid out of their own pockets.

Guest status came more slowly. A small number of African-Americans joined the July 4 celebration on the White House lawn in 1864, and even more attended a reception in the Blue Room the following New Year's at which President Lincoln shook hands with all his guests. A few years later, when Julia Grant was asked if all races were welcome at her receptions she avoided the issue, saying that she expected only whites would care to attend.

Very few prominent African-Americans were entertained at the White House in the late nineteenth century, and their appearance, if publicized, did not always meet with public approval. The onetime abolitionist who later became Minister to Haiti, Frederick Douglass, accepted—without incident—a blanket invitation extended to all Washington, D.C., officials to attend a reception after Grover Cleveland's second inauguration in 1893. A few years later, in 1901, Theodore Roosevelt invited educator Booker T. Washington to dinner at the White House but found himself chastised in newspapers throughout the South. No one seemed to care that the President's sister, Corinne Robinson, invited the same guest to lunch at her New York apartment a few weeks later; she did not live in the People's House.

Public opinion had not changed much by 1929 when Lou Hoover invited Jessie DePriest, spouse of the first African-American to be elected to Congress in twenty-nine years, to a tea that the First Lady regularly gave for congressmen's wives. Some white Southerners were outraged, and several newspapers published editorials

Pat Nixon welcomes children to the East Room.

insisting that the First Lady had "defiled" the Executive Mansion.

Finally in the 1930s, groups that had formerly been barred began slowly to achieve guest status without incident, and in the following decades their numbers grew. When the Nixons paid tribute to jazz musician and composer Duke Ellington, one journalist noted that more African-Americans were present than at any previous time in the nation's history.

Gradually the White House welcome mat has extended to people of diverse ethnic backgrounds. Italian-Americans, whose countrymen had provided musical entertainment for decades, began receiving invitations to come as guests in the 1930s. Jerre Mangione, a young Sicilian-American who worked with the Federal Writers' Project, found himself dining at the White House and around the table were Jewish and Chinese individuals—all listening to the First Lady discuss race relations. Mangione, the son of a Rochester paperhanger, would return to the White House for a weekend with the Roosevelts, and Joseph Lash, son of a Jewish storekeeper, became a frequent guest.

Visits from average Americans increased while Pat Nixon was First Lady. She wanted as many people as possible to have the special thrill of receiving a personal invitation to the White House. During the first year of the Nixon presidency, a record-breaking 60,000 people got their names on guest lists at 1600 Pennsylvania Avenue. A dinner party on the South Lawn honoring returning prisoners of war drew thirteen hundred people, making it the largest such event ever held there. On Thanksgiving day, 225 elderly Washingtonians were bused in from all around the city to eat at the White House.

Pat Nixon also reached out to people in other ways. She refused to use a facsimile of her signature and paid the price for that decision by signing autographs for several hours each day. Tourists found her a warm hostess who sometimes hugged those who seemed a little frightened by the place. When one little boy objected that it could not be the President's House because there was no washing machine, the First Lady led him by the hand upstairs to see one.

No matter how determined the President and his family are to open the White House to everyone, the size of the nation dictates that only a tiny fraction can ever set foot inside. Television brings the mansion into the homes of most of the others. Harry Truman introduced the idea of a televised White House tour after gutting and rebuilding of the interior was completed in 1952, and Jacqueline Kennedy led television cameras through the public rooms a decade later. Tricia Nixon, the President's daughter, also consented to act as hostess for a televised tour of the mansion, and in 1990 George and Barbara Bush issued a public invitation to "the first live tour of the White House in over twenty-five years" on the television show *Prime Time Live*.

President Jimmy Carter helped stir a barbecue on the South Lawn.

★★★

Americans' vicarious "invasion" of the President's House began on the printed page over a century ago. As national magazines increased their circulation in the late nineteenth century and tried to appeal to more women readers, they hired women reporters. The subject of politicians' family life became a popular one. Emily Briggs, writing as "Olivia" for the *Philadelphia Press,* got her scoops from a White House steward, and other reporters relied on guests and employees to tell how things were done inside.

In 1873 a fictional "Aunt Mehitable" (pseudonym for Harriet Hazelton) began contributing a monthly column to *Godey's Lady's Book,* one of the biggest women's magazines. Taking the part of an uneducated country woman, "Aunt Mehitable" described in detail a visit to the Grant White House with its gold wallpaper and fancy

Harry Atwood landed an airplane on the White House lawn in 1911 after President Taft declined his invitation to go for a ride.

chandeliers. When she wrote how the First Lady was so "ugly" that she resorted to shuttered windows and gas lights in the middle of the afternoon to avoid scrutiny, readers could participate vicariously in both the glamour and the glee.

That same curiosity about White House families continued, even accelerated, in the twentieth century when electronic and print media competed among themselves to furnish the most information. Newspapers published details about every state dinner—the guest list, the menu, and what the President, First Lady, and honored guests wore. Even recipes for main dishes were sometimes included, along with a mention of the hour that the President went to bed.

Demands to share in the White House often appear boundless, extending even to using it for personal celebrations. A White House wedding might be considered the exclusive domain of those who reside or work there, but as late as 1944 one Navy Department stenographer with no particular connection to the presidential family wrote to Eleanor Roosevelt requesting to be married in the White House "on the 11th or 12th of this month." The First Lady's secretary was left the duty of declining. Refusals must be carefully phrased, like those of a renter objecting to a landlord's request, and Presidents make a point of acknowledging frequently their debt to the American people.

★★★

A loyal staff reinforces the White House's role as the People's House. Employees tend to think of themselves as servants of the nation, much as they would if they worked at any other public monument or government office. They often remain for decades, regardless of the turnover in Chief Executives and political parties, and in so doing they develop considerable expertise in how to run the White House.

In the 1960s when Lady Bird Johnson noted that the staff went on with its work no matter who the occupants were, she reiterated a point made by a reporter who wrote in 1909 that the President's House, with its thirty employees, "pretty much ran itself." In the 1920s, strong-willed Florence Harding, acknowledging that she felt somewhat superfluous, explained in a letter: "In this big house I do not have quite the same feeling of running the wheels myself as I

Barbara Bush conducts invited visitors through the Lincoln Bedroom.

President and Mrs. Kennedy talk with Pearl Buck and Robert Frost in the East Room after a dinner in honor of Nobel Prize winners.

did in a smaller establishment but I do keep my hand on the helm and give it a turn now and then."

Betty Ford, who assumed First Lady duties after the Nixon resignation in August 1974, learned that a state dinner had been planned for the next week. The Fords had not yet moved into the White House and had known nothing of the dinner plans. At first Mrs. Ford felt overwhelmed but then realized that "the White House is filled with people who can do anything—cook, bake, serve, design and hand-letter place cards, arrange flowers and choose music. All you have to do is know what you want and ask for it."

Presidential families seeking to impose their own tastes on White House management find that the establishment runs largely on rules of its own under the direction of a Chief Usher. That job gained in power because it has typically been held for many years by the same man. Irwin ("Ike") Hoover first came to the White House as an electrician in the spring of 1891 and he remained employed there a total of forty-two years, twenty of them as Chief Usher. Coincidentally, one President he served had the same family name (although the men were not relatives) and Lou Hoover insisted that he be addressed as "Mr. Usher" in order to avoid any confusion that might result from having two Mr. Hoovers in the same household. "Mr. Usher" Hoover was succeeded in 1933 by Howell G. Crimm, who served a remarkable twenty-four years.

The usher position started out as a kind of steward—someone who intercepted visitors and relayed their calling cards to the President's secretary. As early as the 1840s, the British term "usher" sometimes attached itself to this intermediary, who also took on the responsibility of approving food orders, accepting deliveries, and performing other household management tasks.

Lady Bird Johnson chose the Lincoln Bedroom for her meeting in April 1964 with poet Carl Sandburg (center) and photographer Edward Steichen (left).

President and Mrs. Reagan invite guests to join them in dancing at the White House.

By 1897 when the title "Chief Usher" became official, the job, as well as that of his assistants, was highly coveted. Ushers stood well above domestic servants—they dressed in frock coats during the day, worked closely with the First Lady, played with the President's children, and enjoyed the perquisites that naturally come to anyone with frequent access to a powerful person. From an office just inside the north entrance, they monitored all entrances and exits.

Ushers became enormously valuable to Presidents and their families, and when J. B. West published his account of his years as Chief Usher, he subtitled it *Upstairs at the White House: My Life with the First Ladies.* Presidents' wives repaid him with many compliments, and when he died, Jacqueline Kennedy Onassis made one of her rare intercessions with the Reagans to get special permission so that West could be buried in Arlington National Cemetery.

By the end of the White House's second century, the job of Chief Usher had become a demanding management position. The incumbent, Gary Walters, heads a staff of more than one hundred, and additional employees come in for special occasions such as state dinners or whenever unusual skills are required. The office of the Chief Usher, still situated inside the north entrance as it has been since the 1840s, boasts state-of-the-art technology; a computer screen flashes the location of any member of the President's family who is on White House grounds as well as the whereabouts of the President, in order to help coordinate activities occurring simultaneously in the mansion. All workers and visitors to the residence are cleared through the Chief Usher. If the White House were a city, he would be town manager.

Even lesser staff jobs have shown remarkable longevity, thus underlining the fact that the staff serves a nation rather than a particular President. Elizabeth Jaffray, hired as head housekeeper by Helen Taft in 1909, remained seventeen years and worked for four different families before leaving to write her book, *Secrets of the White House.* Isabella Hagner, the young War Department clerk employed at the White House in 1901 to help with the First Lady's correspondence, remained there eight years, resumed her job at the War Department during the Taft administration, and was re-

Dinner in the State Dining Room with President Lincoln's portrait over the fireplace.

Chief Usher Gary Walters oversees the mansion's operation from an office inside the north entrance. Here he is shown in the ground-floor library.

called to the White House by Woodrow Wilson's wife in 1913. Her return was remarkable—the 1912 election had been a bitter three-way contest in which Wilson had defeated both the Republican nominee William Howard Taft and the insurgent Bull Moose candidate Theodore Roosevelt, but even the acrimony of that contest did not negate Hagner's value as secretary to the new First Lady.

The expertise of social secretaries and Chief Ushers might be offered as reason for keeping them on after their original employers have left, but strictly domestic workers have also remained through changes in administrations. One of Helen Taft's hirees, Maggie Rogers, came to work as a maid in 1909 and was still there when her daughter took a similar position twenty years later. Robert Taylor Smith from Wooster, Ohio, took a job as White House messenger in 1897 when he was a young man of twenty-two and stayed for fifty-two years; and Edmund Starling, who began working at the White House in 1914, boasted that he had known every President from Woodrow Wilson to Franklin Roosevelt.

Staff members learn to keep a low profile and respect privacy. Distinguished visitors, elaborate security arrangements, complex scheduling, and high pressure are all part of every day's work. On hand for the funeral of one President, they can assist more usefully at the next; present for one war, they can help to prepare the house for the next one.

After Pearl Harbor, those who had worked in the White House during the World War I years would recall how the American people looked to the presidential residence and its First Family as models of how to keep up morale. In 1917 Edith Wilson served "meatless" and "wheatless" meals and arranged for twenty Shropshire black-faced sheep to graze on the White House lawn. Then when the time came to shear them, she contributed to the war effort the $52,828 from the wool, which states competed among themselves to auction at the highest price. Rolling bandages for the Red Cross and chauffeuring soldiers around the capital, the First Lady might have been the wife of any CEO intent on helping her country. President Wilson's three daughters all joined in the effort. Margaret, the eldest, who was just starting a singing career, donated all her earnings to the war, and Jessie and Nellie rolled bandages and helped at servicemen's canteens.

White House Social Secretary Linda Faulkner briefs social aides, officers of the Armed Forces, on how to greet guests at the East Entrance and escort them to the state floor for lunch in the Family Dining Room.

Twenty-five years later, during World War II, First Lady Eleanor Roosevelt also spent a great deal of time and attention on the war effort and took much of her work on the road. Canceling the White House social season, she went off to inspect troops in England and the Pacific. Americans who looked to the White House for leadership during those years knew that the Roosevelt sons were all in uniform, and saw the President's house as just one more American residence that had sent its sons to fight.

★★★

In wartime or peace, the shrewdest Presidents remember that they occupy public property and hold a limited "lease" at 1600 Pennsylvania Avenue. Ever since the White House was built, Americans have demanded that it reflect their tastes, answer to their criticism, and serve as a model for the best that they themselves could become. A loyal staff maintains the mansion in the best possible condition—for the President and his family; for the national and world leaders who arrive to meet with the President; for the millions of average people who tour the public rooms or are invited as special guests; and, as a legacy, for the many generations still to come.

During its first two hundred years the stone walls of the White House have grown remarkably elastic, expanding to accommodate ever larger numbers of visitors, staff, and offices, as well as multiple roles and functions. Individual Presidents may call it home, but through two centuries it has remained the People's House—and its importance as a symbol of the American people has never diminished.

In May 1956, President Eisenhower and First Lady Mamie Eisenhower greeted veterans at a garden party on the South Lawn.

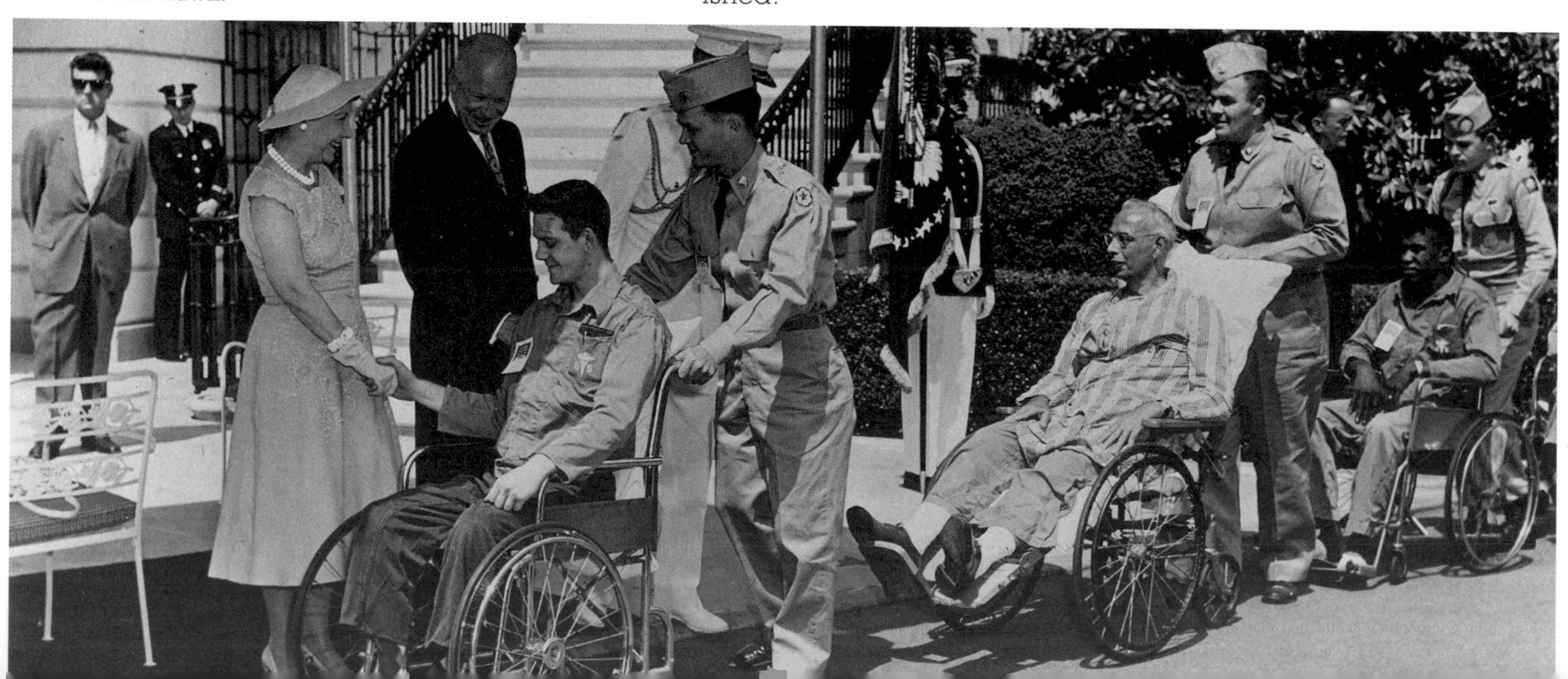

In October 1988, special Olympics winners gathered at the White House to celebrate their victories.

While Americans seek a closer look inside the White House, Presidents and their families have a special vantage point from which to see others. The Kennedy family is shown looking out from the South Balcony, November 13, 1963.

PRESIDENTS OF THE UNITED STATES AND THEIR WIVES

	Years in Office
WASHINGTON, George (1732–1799) Martha Dandridge Custis Washington (1731–1802)	**1789–1797**
ADAMS, John (1735–1826) Abigail Smith Adams (1744–1818)	**1797–1801**
JEFFERSON, Thomas (1743–1826) Martha Wayles Skelton Jefferson (1748–1782)	**1801–1809**
MADISON, James (1751–1836) Dolley Payne Todd Madison (1768–1849)	**1809–1817**
MONROE, James (1758–1831) Elizabeth Kortright Monroe (ca. 1763–1830)	**1817–1825**
ADAMS, John Quincy (1767–1848) Louisa Johnson Adams (1775–1852)	**1825–1829**
JACKSON, Andrew (1767–1845) Rachel Donelson Robards Jackson (1767–1828)	**1829–1837**
VAN BUREN, Martin (1782–1862) Hannah Hoes Van Buren (1783–1819)	**1837–1841**

	Years in Office
HARRISON, William Henry (1773–1841) Anna Symmes Harrison (1775–1864)	**1841**
TYLER, John (1790–1862) Letitia Christian Tyler (1790–1842) Julia Gardiner Tyler (1820–1889)	**1841–1845**
POLK, James (1795–1849) Sarah Childress Polk (1803–1891)	**1845–1849**
TAYLOR, Zachary (1784–1850) Margaret Smith Taylor (1788–1852)	**1849–1850**
FILLMORE, Millard (1800–1874) Abigail Powers Fillmore (1798–1853)	**1850–1853**
PIERCE, Franklin (1804–1869) Jane Appleton Pierce (1806–1863)	**1853–1857**
BUCHANAN, James (1791–1868) [never married]	**1857–1861**
LINCOLN, Abraham (1809–1865) Mary Todd Lincoln (1818–1882)	**1861–1865**
JOHNSON, Andrew (1808–1875) Eliza McCardle Johnson (1810–1876)	**1865–1869**
GRANT, Ulysses (1822–1885) Julia Dent Grant (1826–1902)	**1869–1877**

	Years in Office
HAYES, Rutherford (1822–1893) Lucy Webb Hayes (1831–1889)	**1877–1881**
GARFIELD, James (1831–1881) Lucretia Rudolph Garfield (1832–1918)	**1881**
ARTHUR, Chester (1829–1886) Ellen Herndon Arthur (1837–1880)	**1881–1885**
CLEVELAND, Grover (1837–1908) Frances Folsom Cleveland (1864–1947)	**1885–1889** **1893–1897**
HARRISON, Benjamin (1833–1901) Caroline Scott Harrison (1832–1892) Mary Lord Dimmick Harrison (1858–1948)	**1889–1893**
McKINLEY, William (1843–1901) Ida Saxton McKinley (1847–1907)	**1897–1901**
ROOSEVELT, Theodore (1858–1919) Alice Lee Roosevelt (1861–1884) Edith Carow Roosevelt (1861–1948)	**1901–1909**
TAFT, William Howard (1857–1930) Helen Herron Taft (1861–1943)	**1909–1913**
WILSON, Woodrow (1856–1924) Ellen Axson Wilson (1860–1914) Edith Bolling Galt Wilson (1872–1961)	**1913–1921**
HARDING, Warren (1865–1923) Florence Kling De Wolfe Harding (1860–1924)	**1921–1923**

	Years in Office
COOLIDGE, Calvin (1872–1933) Grace Goodhue Coolidge (1879–1957)	**1923–1929**
HOOVER, Herbert (1874–1964) Lou Henry Hoover (1874–1944)	**1929–1933**
ROOSEVELT, Franklin (1882–1945) Eleanor Roosevelt Roosevelt (1884–1962)	**1933–1945**
TRUMAN, Harry (1884–1972) Bess Wallace Truman (1885–1982)	**1945–1953**
EISENHOWER, Dwight (1890–1969) Mamie Doud Eisenhower (1896–1979)	**1953–1961**
KENNEDY, John (1917–1963) Jacqueline Bouvier Kennedy (1929–)	**1961–1963**

	Years in Office
JOHNSON, Lyndon (1908–1973) Claudia (Lady Bird) Taylor Johnson (1912–)	**1963–1969**
NIXON, Richard (1913–) Patricia Ryan Nixon (1912–)	**1969–1974**
FORD, Gerald (1913–) Elizabeth (Betty) Bloomer Warren Ford (1918–)	**1974–1977**
CARTER, Jimmy (1924–) Rosalynn Smith Carter (1927–)	**1977–1981**
REAGAN, Ronald (1911–) Jane Wyman Reagan (1914–) Nancy Davis Reagan (1921–)	**1981–1989**
BUSH, George (1924–) Barbara Pierce Bush (1925–)	**1989–**

President and Mrs. Hoover, accompanied by two of their grandchildren, greet a crowd gathered outside the South Portico.

FLOOR PLAN OF THE WHITE HOUSE

Ground Floor

G1 Library
*G2 Ground Floor Corridor
G3 Vermeil Room
G4 China Room
G5 Diplomatic Reception Room
G6 Map Room

First Floor

*F1 East Room
*F2 Green Room
*F3 Blue Room
F4 South Portico
*F5 Red Room
*F6 State Dining Room
F7 Family Dining Room
*F8 Cross Hall
*F9 Entrance Hall

**An asterisk marks rooms open to the public*

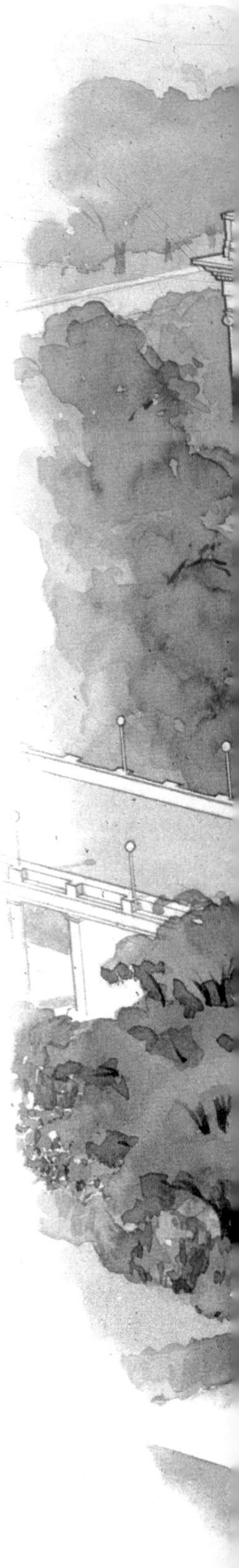

*F6
F7
*F9
*F8
*F5
*F3
*F2
F4
*F1
G1
G6
*G2
G4
G5
G3
ROBERT W. NICHOLSON

PHOTO CREDITS

Grateful acknowledgment is made to the sources whose photographs and illustrations appear on the following pages:

AP/Wide World Photos: 17, 30, 35, 49, 128, 224
Susan Biddle, The White House: 19, 25 (bottom), 74
Jimmy Carter Library: 44, 48 (top), 52 (top), 79, 86, 109, 120, 167, 170, 199
Corning Museum of Glass: 123, 150, 152, 155
Culver Pictures, Inc.: 38, 39, 62, 63
Dwight D. Eisenhower Library: 50, 77, 127, 208. Also courtesy of National Park Service: 77, 127, 208.
Gerald R. Ford Library: 22, 41, 45 (top), 52 (bottom), 54 (top), 76, 90, 112
Rutherford B. Hayes Presidential Center: 78, 158, 191, 196
Herbert Hoover Presidential Library-Museum: 53 (top), 92, 213
Houghton Library, Harvard University: 32, 84, 177
Lyndon B. Johnson Library: 4, 23 (top), 24, 37, 56, 65, 71, 102, 107, 125, 183, 203
John F. Kennedy Library: 20, 25 (top), 73, 91, 94, 95, 96, 101, 104, 119, 169, 202, 210
John Kordel, Metropolitan Singers/Greek Choral Society: 182
Library of Congress: 9, 11, 12, 13, 14, 15, 27, 29, 31, 33, 36, 46 (top), 47, 48 (bottom), 53 (bottom), 57, 58, 59, 60, 61, 67, 80, 81, 82, 83, 85, 116, 143, 144, 172, 173, 174, 175, 176, 179, 181, 188, 190, 192, 193, 200, 218, 220
National Archives: 34, 69, 186, 187
National Park Service: 16
The New York Times. Copyright © 1985 by The New York Times. Reprinted by permission: 98
Richard Nixon Library, National Archives: 115, 133, 198
Y.R. Okamoto, Lyndon B. Johnson Library: 66, 217
Carol T. Powers, The White House: 21, 184 (top), 201, 223
Ronald Reagan Library, National Archives: 97, 111, 204, 209, back endsheet
Franklin D. Roosevelt Library: 45 (bottom), 46 (bottom), 55, 93, 118, 165, 194. Also courtesy of UPI/Bettmann: 45 (bottom), 165.
David Valdez, The White House: 51, 54 (bottom), 70, 184 (bottom), 185
White House Historical Association: front endsheet, 2, 7, 23 (bottom), 40, 42, 43, 89, 100, 110, 122, 131, 134, 137, 138, 139, 141, 145, 146, 147, 148, 149, 151, 156, 157, 159, 161, 162, 164, 195, 205, 206, 207, 214–15. Also courtesy of National Geographic: front endsheet, 7, 43, 89, 164, 207. Also courtesy of Leet-Melbrook, Inc.: 42.

FURTHER READINGS

Kirk, Elise K. *Music at the White House.* Chicago: University of Illinois Press, 1986.

Klapthor, Margaret. *Official White House China: 1789 to the Present.* Washington, D.C.: Smithsonian Institution Press, 1975.

Ryan, William, and Desmond Guinness. *The White House: An Architectural History.* New York: McGraw-Hill Book Company, 1980.

Seale, William. *The President's House.* 2 vols., Washington D.C.: White House Historical Association, 1986.

Spillman, Jane Shadel. *White House Glassware.* Washington, D.C.: White House Historical Association, 1989.

White House Historical Association. *The White House: An Historic Guide.* 17th ed. Washington, D.C.: White House Historical Association, 1991.

White House Historical Association. *The Living White House.* 8th ed. Washington, D.C.: White House Historical Association, 1987.

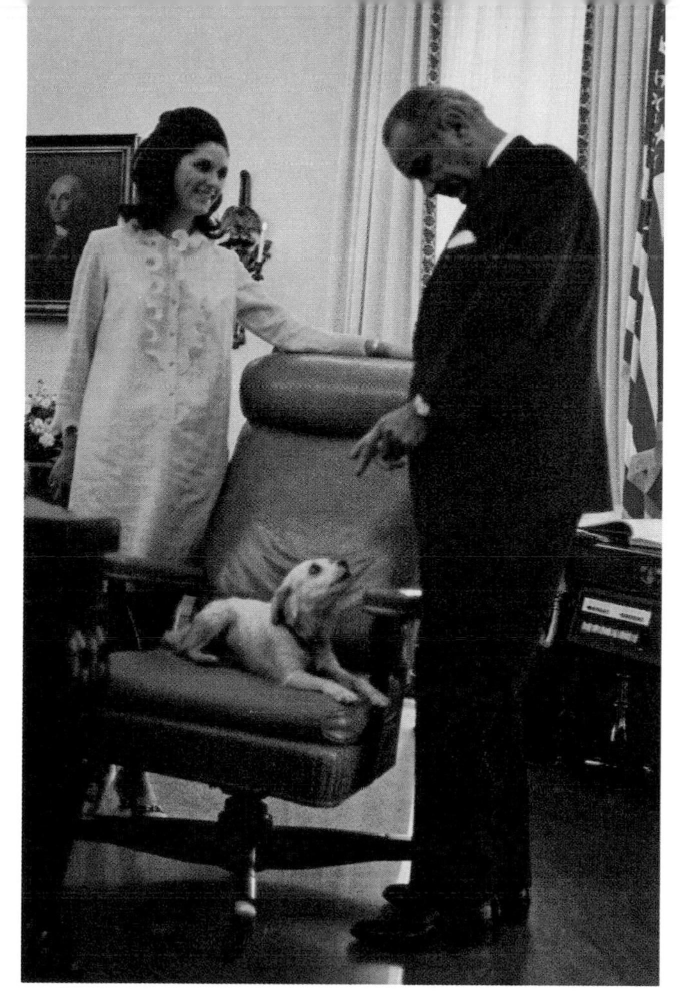

President Lyndon Johnson let one of his dogs try out his desk chair in July 1968, after he had announced that he would not run for another term.

First Lady Grace Coolidge, famous for her fondness for animals, is shown with her dog Rob Roy.

INDEX

(page numbers in **boldface** refer to illustrations)

Abrams, Herbert E., 146
Ackerman, Lawrence, 135
Adams, Abigail, 14, 28, 36, 38–39, 41; and furnishings, 135, 139; and receptions, 169–70
Adams, Charles, 38–39
Adams, John, 14, 38–39, 124, 169–70; and listing of furnishings, 124, 135, 139; and receptions, 169–70
Adams, John Quincy, 52; portrait of, 145; and receptions, 172
Adams, Louisa, 172, 182; and musical entertainment, 182; and receptions, 172, 182
Adams, Sherman, 112
African-Americans, 197–98
Allman, William, 10
American Association of Museums, 18, 124
American Booksellers Association, 50
American Revolution era, 76, 133, 168–69. *See also* specific developments, individuals
Anagnost, Dino, **182**
Andrews, Eliphalet F., 149
Animals. *See* Pets
Anniversaries, 57–58; gifts and, 57–58; greeting cards and, 113. *See also* specific anniversaries
Archives (historical records). *See* Catalogues
Arthur, Chester, 18, 43; and concerts, 182; and furniture, 142
Artists, musical, appearance of, 182–84. *See also* Painters
Atwood, Harry, **200**
"Audience Room," 28
"Aunt Mehitable" (*pseud.* for Harriet Hazelton), 200–1

Bakewell, Benjamin, 153
Balanchine, George, 24
Band concerts, 180–83, **181**, **185**
Bayne, Julia, 48
Beach Boys, 184
Begin, Menachem, **79**
Bellangé, Pierre-Antoine, 141
Bernhard, Prince, 161
Bernstein, Leonard, 24
Biddle, Margaret Thompson, 131
Bierstadt, Albert, "View of the Rocky Mountains" painting by, 150
Bingham, George Caleb, 132
Birthday parties, 56–57; greeting cards and, 113
Blue Room, 28, 31, **85**, **138**, 140, 141, 175, 197
Boudin, Stephane, 133
Bremer, Frederika, 180
Brico, Antonia, 183
Briggs, Emily ("Olivia"), 200
Buchanan, James, 26, 38, 72; and furnishings, 141; as the only bachelor President, 26
Buck, Pearl, **202**
Bulfinch, Charles, 12

Bumbry, Grace, 183
Bush, Barbara, **19**, **21**, 23, **74**, 106, 114, **184**, **201**; and grandchildren, 21; and her pet dog, Millie, 54; role of, 121; and televised tours, 199
Bush, Dorothy Walker, **51**
Bush, George W., **19**, **25**, **51**, 52, **54**, **70**, **71**, **74**, 99; and computer use, 114; and food preferences, 43; and Gulf War protesters, 189; letters to, 113; and office space, 87, 114; and televised tours, 199; and visitors, 87, 193, 199
Bush, Marvin, 52

Cabinet Room, 101, 103
Cantacuzene, Julia Grant, **49**
Carpenter, Francis, 146
Carter, Amy, **44**, 45, **48**
Carter, Chip, **44**
Carter, Jimmy, **44**, 45, **79**, **86**, **89**, 95–96, 112, 114; and films, 50; letters to, 113; and music, 184; and office space and staff, **86**, 87, 94, 95–96, 103, 121; portrait of, 146; and telephone switchboard use, 110–12; and tennis, **52**
Carter, Judy Langford, **44**
Carter, Rosalynn, 22, 24, **35**, **40**, 45, **48**, **89**, **120**; and music, 184; role of, 121; and schooling and tutors, 50; and tourists and photos, **170**, 193
Carter, Sarah Rosemary, **44**
Casals, Pablo, 183
Cash, Johnny, 183
Cassatt, Mary, 132
Catalogues (archives, historical records, inventories), 124–26, 130, 140
Ceramics, 124. *See also* China collection
Chartran, Théobald, 147, 149
Chiang Kai-Shek, Madame, 110
China collection, 150, 156–63
China Room, **157**
Christmas celebrations and parties, 18, **184**, 185–86
Christy, Howard Chandler, 148
Churchill, Winston, 39, **77**, 78–79, 109, 117, 185–86
Civil War era, 26–27, 45, 80–81, **175**, 190–92, 197. *See also* specific developments, individuals
Clark, William, 26, 53
Cleveland, Esther, 30, 31, 32
Cleveland, Frances Folsom, **29**, **30**, 31–32, 45, **60**, **61**; and her children's security, 46; and receptions, 176; her wedding in the White House, 60–63
Cleveland, Grover, 31–32, 45, **61**, 197; and Easter egg roll celebration on White House lawn, 184; wedding in the White House of, 60–63
Cleveland, Ruth, **30**
Clifford, Clark, 87
Columbus, Christopher, fountain planned for, 32
Committee for the Preservation of the White House, 132, 133
Computers, use in the White House of, 114
Conger, Clement E., 133–35, **133**
Congress, and the White House as a national museum, 126, 129, 136, 139, 345
Coolidge, Calvin, 24, 39, 41, 48; and the first White House radio speech, 105; portraits of, 148; and reporters, 104; and work space, 90
Coolidge, Calvin, Jr., death of, 39
Coolidge, Grace, **53**, 125; and archives, 125–26; and pets, **53**; portrait of, 148–49
Cooper, Priscilla (Mrs. Robert Tyler), 26
Cornerstone, placement and laying of, 11, 32
Cox, Edward F., **34**, 67–68, **69**
Cox, Tricia Nixon, 34, **40**, 67–68, **69**; her marriage to Edward F. Cox, 67–**69**; and televised tours, 199
Crimm, Howell G., as Chief Usher, 203
Crook, William, 45
Curators, 132, 133–35

Dall, Buzzie, 45, **45**
Dall, Eleanor (Sistie), **45**, **49**, 57
Davis, Oscar King ("O.K."), 103
Davis, Sammy, 194–97
Davis, Theodore, 159
De Kooning, Willem, 24
Demonstrations. *See* Protest demonstrations
DePriest, Jessie, 197–98
Devine, Mary Virginia, **49**
Dining (dining rooms, dinners, kitchens and cooking facilities, services), 28, 41–43, **42**, 60–61, 99, 132, 135, 156, 202, **205**, **207**; glassware and china collection, 150, 156–63; and "mess privileges," 99. *See also* Receptions
Dining Room (Green Room), 28
Diplomatic Reception Room, 127–28
Douglass, Frederick, 197
Dulles, John Foster, **77**

Eagle symbol, use on furnishings of, 139–40, 153–54, 161
Eakins, Thomas, 132–33
Easter egg roll celebrations, 184–85
East Room, 28, **59**, 140, 141, 142, **143**–45, 172, 182, 183, 184, 192
East Wing, 127
Eden, Anthony, **77**
Eisenhower, Barbara, **49**
Eisenhower, Barbara Ann, **49**
Eisenhower, David, **34**, **40**, 49, 67; wedding of, 67–68
Eisenhower, Dwight D., 49, **50**, **77**, 106, 112, 127, **127**, 131, **208**; letters to, 113; portrait of, 148; second inauguration of, 117
Eisenhower, Julie Nixon, **34**, **40**, 67–68; marriage to David Eisenhower, 67–68
Eisenhower, Mamie, 22, 23, 41, 48, **49**, **50**, 127, **127**, 129, 131, 183, 194, **208**; and band music selections, 183
Eisenhower, Mary, **49**
Eisenhower, Susan, **49**
Electricity, installation in the White House of (1891), 42
Elizabeth, Queen, 194, **194**
Elizabeth II, Queen, **74**, **76**
Ellington, Duke, 198
Executive Mansion, use of term, 17. *See also* President's House; White House
Extended families, use of White House by, 25–28

Fala, 54

President Harding's dog inside the White House shortly after his owner died in August 1923.

Faulkner, Linda, **207**
Fillmore, Abigail, 36–37, 50
Fillmore, Millard, 27; portrait of, 145
Films (theater), 50, 183
Fires, 17, 91–92; burning of the White House by the British in the War of 1812, **11**, **17**, 137, 139, 178
First Ladies, 22–49; and archives, 124; portraits of, 148–49 (*see also* individual First Ladies); and the press, 118–19; and restorations and furnishings, 123–63 *passim;* role of, 117–21; and staff and offices, 118–21; and visitors and receptions, 165–208 *passim* (*see also* Receptions; Visitors); *See also* individual First Ladies
Fish Room (later the Roosevelt Room), **100**, 106
Food (cooking, dining, kitchens, services). *See* Dining
Ford, Betty, **22**, 24, 25, 34, 38, **54**, 133; and protesters, 189; and the White House staff, 202
Ford, Gerald, 22, 24, **52**, **54**, **76**; and office space, **90**, 96–97; portrait of, 146
Ford, Susan, **22**, 23–24, 34, 54
Fourth of July celebrations, 171, 174, 197
Frost, Robert, **202**
Furnishings (furniture), 124–63 *passim*. *See also* specific individuals, kinds, locations, uses

Garfield, James, 37, 38, 48, 124; assassination of, **191**, **192**; mother of, 37–38
Garfield, Lucretia, 124
George VI, King, 194
"Ghosts," 39; Lincoln's, 39, 197
Gifts, 57–58
Glassware, 124, 150–63, **155**
Godey's Lady's Book, 200–1
Good Housekeeping (1911), 23
Gouverneur, Maria Monroe, 58–59
Gouverneur, Samuel, 58–59
Grandchildren, 44–49, 57. *See also* specific individuals
Grant, Ellen (Nellie), 43, 63; White House wedding of, 43, 59–60, 63
Grant, Fred, 43
Grant, Jesse, 43, 53
Grant, Julia Dent, 27, 31, 43–45, 118, 197, 200–1; and dinners, 156–59; and furnishings and restorations, 130, 156; and her children's security, 46–47
Grant, Ulysses S., 27, 31, 43–45, 53, 59, 81, 91, 142, 200–1; and daughter's White House wedding, 59–60; and dinners, 156–59; and family anecdotes, 43–45
Grant, Ulysses S., III, 91
Great Depression era, 92, 94, 166, 179; and restorations, 126, 160–61. *See also* specific developments, individuals
Great War. *See* World War I era
Green Room, 28, 39, **133**–35
Greeting cards, 113
Guidebooks, 129–30
Gulf War. *See* Iraq

Hagerty, James, 106
Hagner, Isabella, 88, 118–19, 204–6
Harding, Florence, 119, **193**; and public tours, 192; and staff, 201–2
Harding, Ruth, portrait of, 132–33
Harding, Warren, 54, 133, **192**; and reporters, 104
Harrison, Benjamin, 32, 47, 82; and grandchildren, 32; and receptions, 178; and wife's death, 178
Harrison, Caroline, 32; and glassware and china collection, 155, 159–60
Harrison, Marthena, **46**, **48**–49, 178
Harrison, William Henry, 21, 41, 46, 186
Hawkes, Dr., 48
Hay, John, 72
Hayes, Helen, 24
Hayes, Lucy, **36**, 37, 38, 142, **158**, 182; and china collection, 159, **159**; and Easter egg roll celebration, 184
Hayes, Rutherford B., **36**, **38**, **78**, 96, 142, 149; inauguration of, 115; and "musicales," 182
Hayes, Webb, **36**, **158**, 159
Hazelton, Harriet, 200–1
Healy, George P.A., 145, 146
Hello Dolly cast, **183**
Helm, Edith, 57, 179
Helm, Emilie, 26–27
Henry, James Buchanan, 72
Hickok, Lorena, 28
Him and Her (LBJ's pet beagles), 5
Hirohito, Emperor, **90**
Hirshhorn, Joseph, 132–33
History of the White House (Willets), 125
Hoban, James, 13–14, 28, 41, 87, 114
Hoes, Lawrence, **49**
Holiday celebrations, 184–86. *See also* specific holidays
Hoover, Herbert, 23, 24, 46, **53**, 90–**92**; and work space and staff, 90–92; and visitors and receptions, 179
Hoover, Irwin ("Ike"), as Chief Usher, 202–3
Hoover, Joan, 46
Hoover, Lou, 22, 23, 24, 105, 126–27, 203; and African-Americans, 197–98; and gifts, 57; and her grandchildren, 45–46; and musical entertainment, 184; and restorations, 126–27; and visitors and receptions, 179, 184, 197–98
Hoover, Peggy, 46
Hopkins, Harry, 27–28
Horton, Angela, 10
Housekeepers, 41–42, 43, 45. *See also* specific individuals
Hurd, Peter, 146
Hussein, King (Jordan), 163

Iakovos, Archbishop, **182**
Inaugurations, 115–17. *See also* individual Presidents
"In Performance at the White House," 166, 182–84
Invitations, 57, 121
Iraq, Gulf War and, 37, 80, 189; protest demonstrations and, 37, 189
Irving, Washington, 171
Italian-Americans, 198

Jackson, Andrew, 14; and cheese gift, **173**; and glassware, 153–54; inauguration of, 173–74; and receptions, 172–74; and slaves,

197; and work space, 80
Jaffray, Elizabeth, 204
Jefferson, Thomas, 12, 14, 25–26, 28, 42–43; and caged bears kept on the White House lawn, 53; described, 75; and Green Room, 133–35; and inventions, 139; and music, 182; and slaves, 197; and visitors and receptions, 170–71, 182, 192; and wine cellar, 43; and work space, 73–76
Jewish-Americans, 198
John Paul II, Pope, **89**
Johnson, Andrew, 45, 80–81, 142, 145; and portraits, 145; and visitors, 192; and work space, 80–81
Johnson, Eliza, 35, 45; and her grandchildren, 45
Johnson, Lady Bird, 22, 24–25, 34, 37, 39–40, 48, 49, **56**, **65**, **66**, 117, **125**, 132–33, 166, **203**; and "Beautification" program, 117; and china collection, 161–62; and daughter Luci's wedding, 67; and furnishings, 132–33, 161–62; and her grandchildren, **24**, 45; and staff, 121, 201
Johnson, Luci, 24, 25, 34, **37**, 48, **56**, **65**; marriage to Patrick Nugent, 64–67
Johnson, Lynda Bird (Mrs. Charles Robb), 23, 24, 34, **37**, 48; wedding of, 67
Johnson, Lyndon B., **23**, 24, 25, 34, **37**, 39–40, **56**, **65**, **66**, 67, **71**, 95–96, **102**, **107**, 110, 117, 132; and food preferences, 43; and his grandchildren, 45; and his pet beagles, 54; portrait of, 146; and protesters, 188; and telephones, 110; and Situation Room, 100; and television and the press, 106; and tourists, 193; and work space and staff, 87, 95–96, 101–3, 117
Joplin, Scott, "Maple Leaf Rag" by, 183
Juliana, Queen, 39, 161
July 4 celebrations, 171, 174, 197

Kennedy, Caroline, 24, **25**, 45, 48, **95**; and her pony, Macaroni, 45; and phone switchboard, 113
Kennedy, Jacqueline, 24, 39, 43, 45, 48, **91**, 96, **119**, 123, 128–32, **169**, 176, 185, **202**, **210**; and Chief Usher West, 204; and glassware, **155**, 156; and music concerts, 183; and Onassis, 149, 204; and own press secretary, 121; portrait of, **149**; and restorations, 123, 126, 128–32, 133; and televised tours, 127, 199
Kennedy, John F., **20**, **25**, 39, 45, 48, **73**, **91**, **94**, 96, **101**, 103, 149, 150, 151, 185, **202**, **210**; and music, 183; and phone switchboard, 112, 113; and the press, 101, 106; and restorations, 128–32; and Situation Room, 99
Kennedy, John, Jr., **20**, **25**, 45
Kennedy Center, 184
Kinstler, Everett, 146, 148
Kirk, Elise, 9
Klapthor, Margaret, 9, 159

Laddie Boy (Warren Harding's pet airedale), 54
Lafayette, Marquis de, 76; park named for, 76 (*see also* Lafayette Park)
Lafayette Park, 76, 185; protesters and, 186–89
Lane, Harriet, 141
Lannuier, Charles-Honoré, table by, 135
Lash, Joseph, 198
Latrobe, Benjamin, 139
Lee, Harper, 24
L'Enfant, Pierre, 12, 14
Lenox glassware and china, 156, 160, 161, 163
Letters (mail), 113–14, 118
Levées, George Washington's, 168
Lewis, Meriwether, 26, 75
Liberty (Fords' pet golden retriever), **54**
Library, 50, **137**
Library of Congress, 124
Lincoln, Abraham, 26–27, 39, **48**, 72–73, 80, 118, 141–42, 175–76, 197; assassination of, 48, **190**–91; Bedroom, 87, 126, 141–42, 146, **189**, 194–97, **201**, **203**; and Gettysburg Address, 80, 142; and "ghosts," 39, 197; and office seekers, 80; portrait of, 146, 205; and signing of the Emancipation Proclamation, 88, 146; and visitors and receptions, 175–76, 197; and work space and staff, 72–73, 80
Lincoln, Mary Todd, 26–27, 35, 39, 48, 118, 132, 180; and furnishings, 132, 142, 154, 155; and glassware, 154, **155**; and music concerts, 180; and receptions, 175–76
Lincoln, Tad, **48**, 146
Lincoln, Willie, death of, 39, 180
Lippmann, Walter, 24
Long, Ava, 45–46
Longworth, Alice Roosevelt, 32–33, 42, **62**, 67; her appendectomy, 43; wedding of, **62**, 63, 67
Longworth, Nicholas, **62**, 63
Lowry, Edward, 103–4

McAdoo, Eleanor (Nellie) Wilson, wedding of, 64
McAdoo, William Gibbs, 64
McFarlane, Robert C., 98
McIlhenny, John, 47
McKinley, Ida Saxton, 82
McKinley, William, 38, 82, 109, 186; assassination of, 176; and parties, 179
McNamara, Robert, 102
Madison, Dolley, 26, 36, 58, 118; and furnishings, 135, 139; and Red Room, 135; and visitors, 171; and Washington's portrait, 143–45
Madison, James, 58, 118, 145, 189; portrait of, 145; and slaves, 197; and visitors, 171, 192
Mail (letters), 113–14, 118
Management (staff). *See* Staff
Mangione, Jerre, 198
Mannes, Marya, 24
Manning, Helen Taft, **49**
Map Room, 109–**10**, **111**
Marine Band, and music concerts, 169–70, 174, 175–76, 180–82, **181**, 183, 192
Medical facilities, 38–39, 61
Meley, Meley, 76
Metalware, 124, 150
Military victory celebrations, 186. *See also* specific events
Millie (Barbara Bush's pet dog), 54
Millie's Book, 54
Mills, Elijah, 171

"Minerva" clock, **139**
Monet (Claude) paintings, 150, **151**
Monkman, Betty, 10
Monroe, Elizabeth, 58–59; and furnishings, 139–41; and visitors and receptions, 171, 192
Monroe, James, 14, 58; described, 139; and furniture and furnishings, 126–27, 130, 131, 135, 139–41, 153, 156; and glassware and china, 153, 156; and Green Room, 135; portrait of, 145; and visitors and receptions, 172, 192
Monroe, Maria (Mrs. Samuel Gouverneur), 58–59
Monroe Room, 79, 127
"Morning on the Seine" (Monet painting), 150
Morse, Samuel F. B., 145
Mubarak, Hosni, 163
Musical entertainment, 169–70, 174, 175–76, 180–84. *See also* specific individuals, kinds

Nagako, Empress, **90**
National Park Service, 22
National Society of Interior Designers (NSID), 127–28
Nesbitt, Henrietta, 41–42, 43
Newspapers (the press), 103–8, 200–1; First Ladies and, 118–19
New Year's Day open house and celebrations, 168–71, 172, **176**, 178–**79**
New York Women's Symphony, 183
Nicolay, John, 72
Nixon, Julie, **34**, **40**, 67–68; marriage to David Eisenhower, 67–68
Nixon, Pat, 24, **34**–35, **40**, 52, 67, 68, **69**, 117, **133**, 150, **198**; and visitors, 198
Nixon, Richard M., 16, 23, 24, **34**–35, 38, **40**, 49, 52, **67**, **69**, 99, 103, 117, 194, 202; and African-Americans, 198; and daughter's wedding, 68, 69; and food habits, 43; and paintings, 150; and phone switchboard, 113; portraits of, 146–48; and the press, 106–8; and protesters, 188–89; resignation of, **34**, **115**; and restorations, 133; and Situation Room, 99, and work space and staff, 94, 96, 100
Nixon, Tricia, **34**, **40**, 67–68, **69**; marriage to Edward F. Cox, 67–**69**; and televised tours, 199
North American Indians (Native Americans), 75, 76
Nugent, Luci Johnson, 24, 25, 34, **37**, 48, **56**, **65**; marriage to Patrick Nugent, 64–67
Nugent, Patrick, 64–67
Nugent, Patrick Lyndon, **23**, **24**, **56**

Oath of office, Presidential, 115
Offices (work space), President's, 71–121 *passim*. *See also* specific Presidents
Office seekers, **80**
Ogle, Charles, 154
Olive (laurel) branches as peace motifs, 153, 154, 161
Olympic winners (1988), **209**
Onassis, Aristotle, 149
Onassis, Mrs. Aristotle, 149, 204. *See also* Kennedy, Jacqueline
O'Neil, Thomas, 190
Oppenheimer, J. Robert, 24
Osage Indians, 75, 76
Oval Office, 85–88, **86**, 92–95, 101, 103–4, 107, 108, 158, 166; origin of shape, 85–86
Oval Room, 36–37, 50, 139, 141, 169

Paderewski, Ignace, 182
Painters (paintings), 95, 124, 132–33, 135–36, 139, 149–50. *See also* Portraits; specific painters, paintings
Patti, Adelina, 182
Pearce, Lorraine, 129
People's House, Executive Mansion as the, 18, 165–208
Perkins, Frances, 92
Pets, **53–54**, 55, 166. *See also* specific animals, individuals
Philip, Prince, **74**
Photography (cameras, photos), visitors and, 47, 121
Phyfe, Duncan, 135
Pierce, Bennie, 36
Pierce, Franklin, 35–36; portrait of, 145; and security concerns, 190
Pierce, Jane, 35–36, 180
Pitts, Milton, 99
Platt, Emily, 149
Polk, James, 25, 145, 174; portrait of, 145; and slaves, 197; and visitors and receptions, 174
Polk, Sarah, 25; and visitors and receptions, 174
Portraits (portrait gallery), 132–33, 139, 142–49. *See also* specific individuals
Powell, Colin, **70**
Powell, Jody, 103, **109**
Presidential seal motif, 160, 161
President's House, planning and construction of (1792), 11–18, 28, 41; 1902 renovation, 16, 33; 1927 renovation, 16, 34; 1949 modernization, 16; 1952 renovation, 165; rebuilt after War of 1812, 17
Press, the, 103–8, 200–1; First Ladies and, 118–19; women reporters, 200–1
Press conferences, 103–8. *See also* specific individuals
Press Office, 103–8, 114, 121
Press Room, 108
Press Secretary, 103, 104–5, 120, 121
Prints and drawings, 124. *See also* Painters
Privacy, lack in the White House of and provision for, 24–25, 35, 46–47
Protesters (protest demonstrations), 18, 37, 186–90, **188**
Public Opinion, 60
Pueblo incident, 100

"Queen's Bedroom," 194, **195**

Race relations, 197–98
Radio broadcasts, **93**, 94, 105–6, 132
Randolph, Martha Jefferson, 25
Reagan, Maureen (Mrs. Dennis Revell), 39
Reagan, Nancy, 22, 23, 38, **43**, 54, 106, **111**, **204**; and china collection, 161–62; and dog, Rex, 54; and Easter celebrations, 184; and gifts, 57; role of, 121
Reagan, Ronald, 38, 39, 57, 96, **97**–98, 103, **204**; and china collection, 161–62; and films, 50; and letters (mail), 113; and

paintings, 150; portraits of, 148; and the press, 108; and radio talks, 105–6; and work space and staff, 96, **97**–98, 103
Receptions, visitors and, 75–79, 80, 82–85, 87, 95, 117–18, 168–97 *passim*. *See also* Visitors; specific individuals
Recreation facilities, 49–**52**
Red Room, 28, 31, 133–35
Remington, Frederic, "Bronco Buster" sculpture by, 150
"Resolute" desk, **96**
Restorations (modernizations). *See under* President's House; specific individuals, kinds
Reunions, 48–49
Revell, Dennis, 39
Revell, Mrs. Dennis. *See* Reagan, Maureen
Revolutionary War era, 76, 133, 168–69. *See also* specific developments, individuals
Rex (Reagans' pet dog), 39
Reynolds, W. E., 16
Richards, Janet, 178–79
Riis, Jacob, 47
Rixey, Presley Marion, 38
Robb, Charles, 67
Robb, Lynda Bird Johnson, 23, 24, 34, **37**, 38; wedding of, 67
Robinson, Corrine, 197
Rob Roy (Coolidge collie), 148
Rockwell, Norman, 146
Rogers, Maggie, 206
Roosevelt, Alice. *See* Longworth, Alice Roosevelt
Roosevelt, Archie, 32, **33**, 47
Roosevelt, Edith Kermit, 18, 24, 32, 33–34, 45, 88, 118–19; and china collection and glassware, 155–56, 160; and portrait and portrait gallery, **147**, 149; and stepdaughter Alice's wedding, 63
Roosevelt, Eleanor, 9, 22, 23, 27–28, **45**, **46**, 110, **116**, **118**, 127, **165**, 166, **194**; and china collection, 160–61; and food preparation, 41–42, 43; and grandchildren, 45, **46**, 56–57; and music concerts, 183; and receptions and royal visitors, 78–79, 176, 179–80, 183, **194**, 201; role of, 117, 119; and war effort, 208; "White House Speaks" by, 9
Roosevelt, Elliott, **49**
Roosevelt, Ethel, 32
Roosevelt, Franklin D., 21, 22, 23, 27–28, 37, 38, 45, **46**, 48, **55**, 79, **93**, 99, 115, 117, **118**, 119, 206; and Christmas celebrations, 185–86; and Fala, 54; and films, 50; and Fireside Chats, **93**, 94, 105, 132; and food preferences, 41, 43; and fourth-term inauguration, 117; and Map Room, 109–10; and physical disability, 92; and the press, **52**, 104, 119; and restorations, 127; and swimming pool, **52**, 108; and work space and staff, 87, 92–94, 100
Roosevelt, Mr. and Mrs. John, **49**
Roosevelt, Kermit, 32, 33
Roosevelt, Quentin, 32, **33**, **47**, 49
Roosevelt, Theodore, 17, 31, 32–34, 39, 43, **47**, **62**, 67, **84**, 100, 114, 132, 142, 149, 176–78, 206; and African-Americans, 197; and furnishings, 142; and grandchildren, 45, 47; and music concerts, 182, 183; and the press, 103, 106; and Roosevelt Room, **100**, 106; and receptions and visitors, 82–85, 176–78; and security, 176–78; and work space and staff, 87–88, 103
Roosevelt, Theodore, Jr. (Ted), 33
Roosevelt Room (formerly the Fish Room), **100**, 106
Royall, Ann, 76
Royal visitors, **74**, 78–79, **90**, 193–**94**, 195. *See also* specific individuals
Rucker, Joanna, 25
Rusk, Dean, **102**
Russell, Charles, "Fording of the Horse Herd" by, 150

Sadat, Anwar, 79
Salinger, Pierre, 103, **104**
Sandburg, Carl, **203**
Sanger, Alice B., 82
Sartoris, Algernon, 59
Sartoris, Nellie Grant, 59–60, 63
Sayre, Francis (Frank), 63–64
Sayre, Jessie Wilson, 206; wedding of, **63**–64
Schools (education, tutors), Presidents' children and, 48, 50
Scowcroft, Brent, 99
Sculpture, 124, 150
Seagraves, Eleanor Dall (Sistie), **45**, **49**, 57
Seale, William, 194
Seal of the United States motif, 153, 154
Secretaries (office staff), 72, 80, 82–85, 88, 91, 99, 114, 118, 121; social, 206
Secrets of the White House (Jaffray), 204
Security, 94, 99, 110, 175, 176–78, 185, 189–93; children's, 46–47, 48; protest demonstrations and, 189–90; weddings and, 63–64, 67
Selika, Maria, 182
Seward, William Henry, 88
Shahn, Ben, 24
Sheffield silverware, 135
Shikler, Aaron, 148, 149
Signature signing sessions, 88, 186
Situation Room, 99–100, **110**
Slayden, Ellen, 142
Smith, Robert Taylor, 206
Solarium (sun porch; "sky parlor"), **34–35**
Sousa, John Philip, 182
Spanish-American War era, 82–85, 109, 186
Speakes, Larry, 103
Spillman, Jane Shadel, 9
Staff (employees, management), 22, 23, 24, 32, 41–42, 201–8; Chief Ushers, 202–4, 206; head housekeepers, 204–6; social secretaries, 206 (*see also* Secretaries). *See also* specific functions, individuals, kinds
Stalin, Joseph, 117
Starling, Edmund, 206
State Dining Room, 75, 85, 135, 150, 161, **205**
Steichen, Edward, **203**
Stern, Isaac, 184
Stoddard, William Osborn, 175
Story, Joseph, 173–74
Stuart, Gilbert, George Washington portraits by, 143–**45**
Suffragists, 188, **189**
Swimming pool, **52**, 108
Switchboard, telephone, **83**, 111–13. *See also* Telephone

President George Bush and new grandchild, Charles Walker Bush.

President Harry Truman tried out the new White House bowling alley—but did not change his shoes.

Taft, Charles, 49
Taft, Helen, 23, 57–**58**; and anniversaries, 57–**58**; and music concerts, 183; and staff, 204–6
Taft, William Howard, 23, **38**, 57–**58**, 85, 87, 200, 204–6; and anniversaries, 57–**58**; and Oval Office, 85, 87; special bathtub for, 37, **39**
Taylor, Margaret, 35
Taylor, Zachary, 35, 180; and slaves, 197
Telegraph, first use in the White House of, 81, 88
Telephone, first (1879), 81–82, **83**; and first transcontinental call (1915), Wilson and, 88
Television, 106, 108, 166; correspondents and the news and, 106, 108; and music performances, 184; and public tours, **127**, 199
Tennis courts, **52**
Theater (films), 50, 183
Tiffany (Louis Comfort) designs, 142, **144**, 161; glassware and china, 142, 161; screen, **144**
Tilden, Samuel, 115
Todd, Lucy Payne Washington, 58
Todd, Thomas, 58
Tourists (tours), 46–47, 165–208 *passim*. *See also* Visitors
Truman, Bess, 26, **27**, 34, 50, 127; and china collection, 161; and her mother, 26, 34
Truman, Harry, S., 16, **27**, 52, **116**, 127, 161; "balcony," 87; and oath of office, 115; and press secretaries, 105; and televised tours, 199; and work space and staff, 95
Truman, Margaret, 16, **27**, 49; *White House Pets* by, 53
Tyler, John, 26, 80, 145; and music concerts, 182; portrait of, 145; and protesters and security, 186–88; and White House wedding of his daughter, 59
Tyler, Julia, and music concerts, 182
Tyler, Robert, 26
Tyler, Mrs. Robert (Priscilla Cooper), 26
Typewriters, first White House use of (1880), 82
Underwood Tariff Act, Wilson's signing of, 88
Upstairs at the White House: My Life with the First Ladies (West), 204

Valenti, Courtney, **102**
Van Buren, Abraham, 26
Van Buren, Angelica Singleton, 26; portrait of, **141**
Van Buren, Martin, 26; and glassware, 154; portrait of, 145; and visitors, 174
Vanderlyn, John, 145
Vermeil Room collection, 131, **131**
Vietnam War protesters, 188–89
Visitors, 46–47, 75–79; reception of, 75–79, 80, 82–85, 87, 95, 117–18 (*see also* Receptions); royal, **74**, 78–79, **90**, 193–**94**, 195 (*see also* specific individuals); the White House as a national museum and, 123–63 *passim*; the White House as the People's House and, 165–208 *passim*. *See also* Tourists

Wales, Prince of (later King Edward VIII), 78, 193–94
Wallace, Fred, **27**
Walters, Gary, Chief Usher, 204, **206**
Waring, Fred, 183
War of 1812, burning of the White House and, **11**, **17**, 137, 139, 172, 178
Washington, Booker T., 197
Washington, George, 41, 106, 113, 117, 172; and levées, 168; and planning and construction of the President's House, 11, 12, 14, 17–18; portraits of, 139, 143–**45**, 149; and work space, 72, 86–87
Washington, Lucy Payne (Mrs. Thomas Todd), 58
Washington, Martha, 168; portrait of, 149
Weddings (marriages), 43–45, 56–68; Cleveland as the only President married in the White House, 60–63; first in the White House, 58–59. *See also* specific individuals
Welk, Lawrence, 183
West, J. B., 65–67, 204
West Wing, **14**, 33, 85, 87, 90, 91, 92–95, 97–105, **98**, 106, 108, 115; basement, **98**–100; Cabinet Room, 115, 145
White House, **12**; as a national museum, 122–63; as the home of the President and his family, 17, 21–68; as the People's House, 18, 165–208; as the President's office, 71–121; made official name, use of term, 17; placement and laying of the cornerstone, 11, 32; roles of, 17–18
White House Historical Association, 9–10, 130, 136, 146
White House Pets (Margaret Truman), 53
Willets, Gilson, 125
Williams, Marthena Harrison, 46, 48–**49**, 178
Williamson, Collen, 14
Wills, J. Anthony, 148
Wilson, Edith, 52, 160, 161, 206
Wilson, Eleanor (Nellie), 206; wedding of, 64
Wilson, Ellen, 23, 63–64, 88, 94, 149; death of, 178
Wilson, Jessie, 206; wedding of, **63**–64
Wilson, Margaret, 206
Wilson, Woodrow, **47**–48, 63–64; children and grandchildren of, **47**–48, 63–64; death of his first wife, 178; and the press, 103–4; and receptions, 178; and suffragists, 188, **189**; and work space and staff, 88–90
Women: first employment in the Executive Office of, 82; musicians, 182, 183; reporters, 200–1; suffragists, 188, **189**. *See also* First Ladies; specific individuals
World War I era (the Great War), 88–90, 178, 186, 189, 206
World War II era, 78–79, 94, 109–10, 117, 161, 185–86, 206, 208
Wyeth, Andrew, 150
Wyeth, Nathan, 87

Ziegler, Ron, 103

W9-CBH-773

FROM LUCY TO LANGUAGE

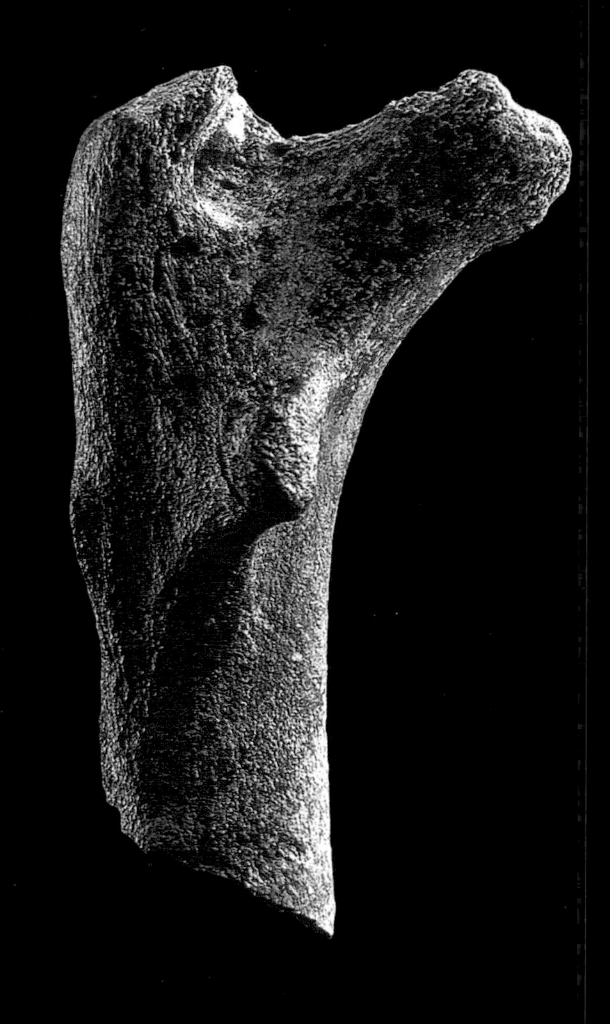

Femur of *Australopithecus afarensis* from Maka, Ethiopia. The anatomy of the bone's head and neck indicates that it came from a hominid that walked on two legs nearly 4 million years ago. Actual size. *Photograph by David Brill; courtesy of National Museum of Ethiopia.*

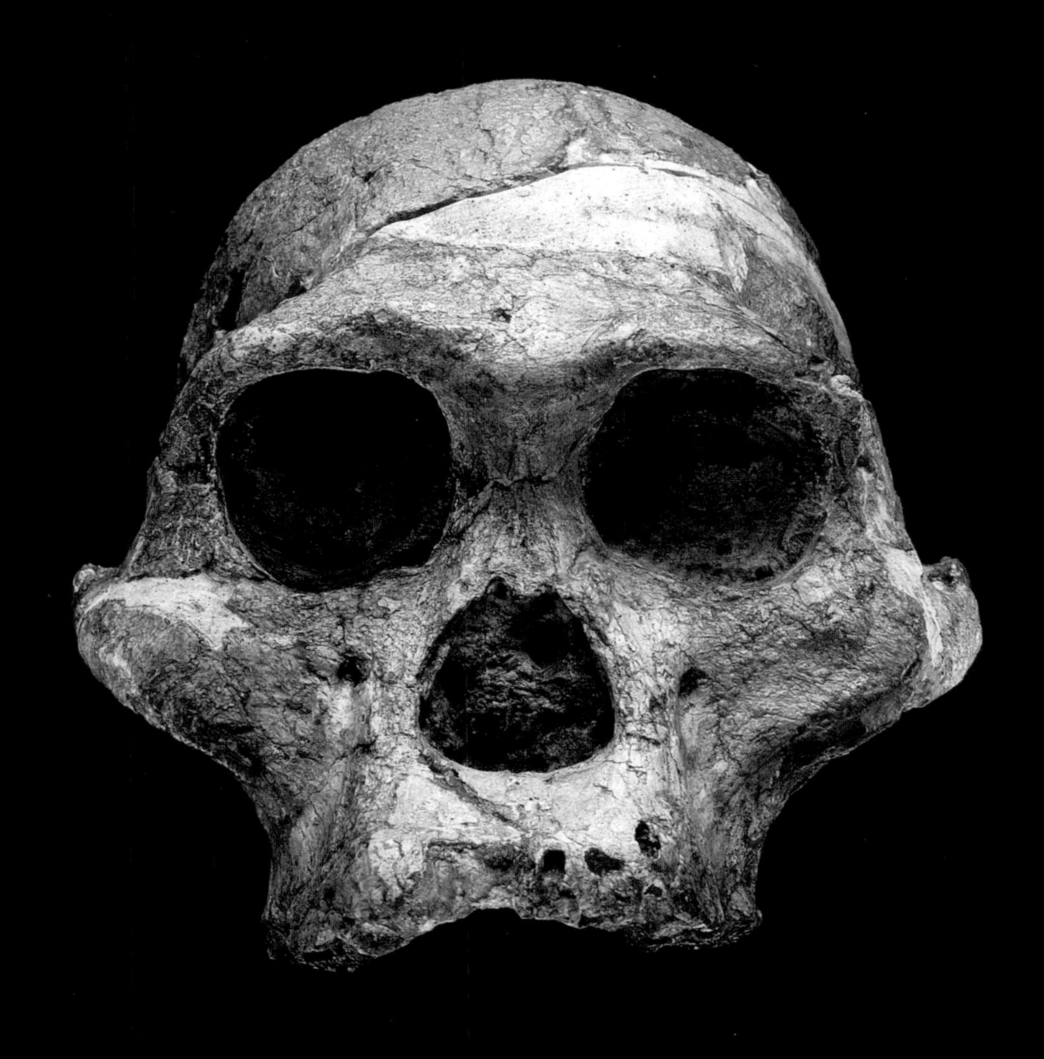

***Australopithecus africanus*, Sts 5.** An examination of the anatomical details of this 2.5 million-year-old cranium demonstrates that "these small-brained, man-like beings were very nearly human." Actual size. *Photograph by David Brill; courtesy of Transvaal Museum.*

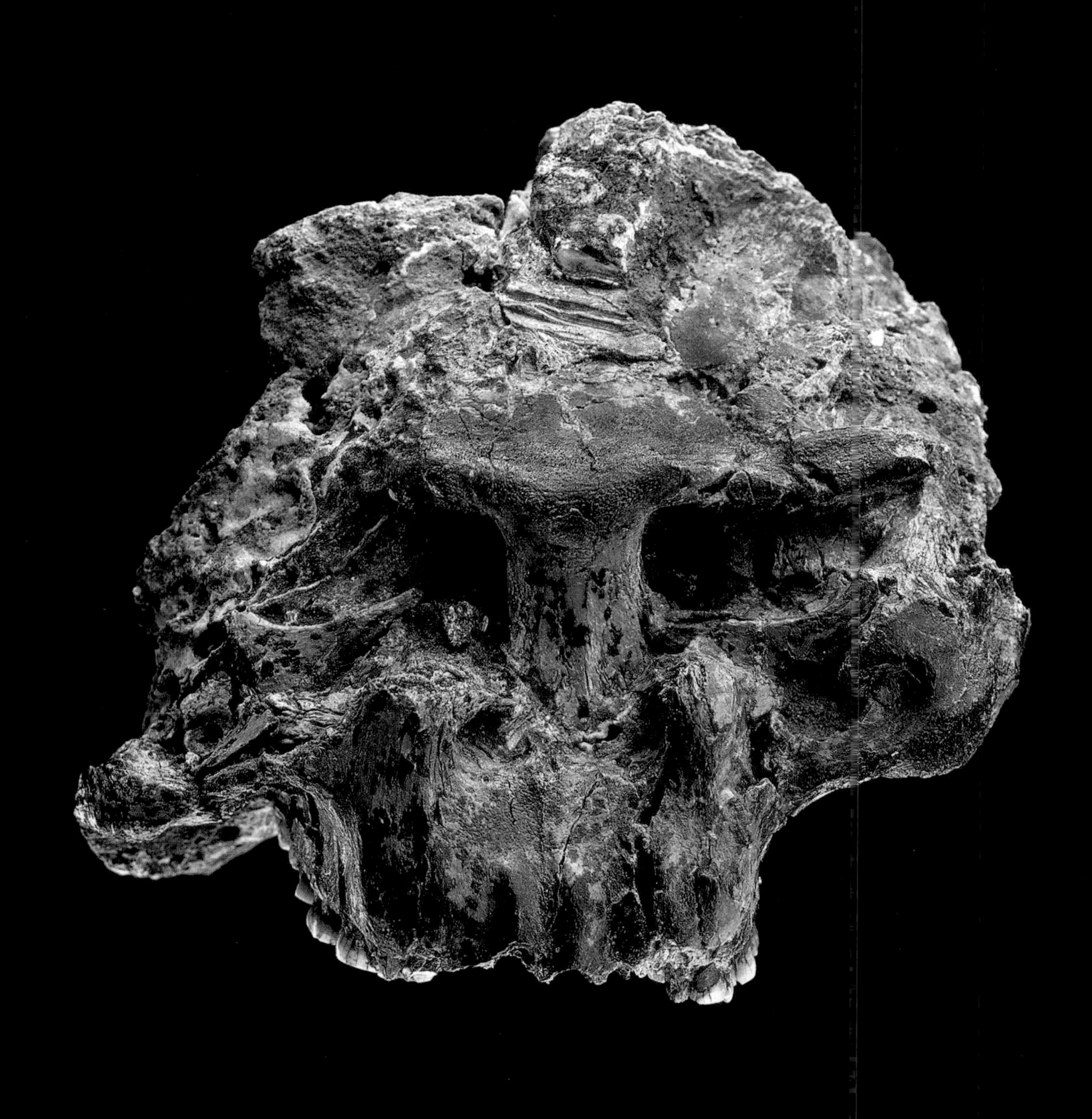

***Australopithecus robustus*, SK 79.** The tremendous pressure put on bones during the slow process of burial and fossilization is evident in this 1.5 to 2.5 million-year-old cranium from Swartkrans, South Africa. Actual size. *Photograph by David Brill; courtesy of Transvaal Museum.*

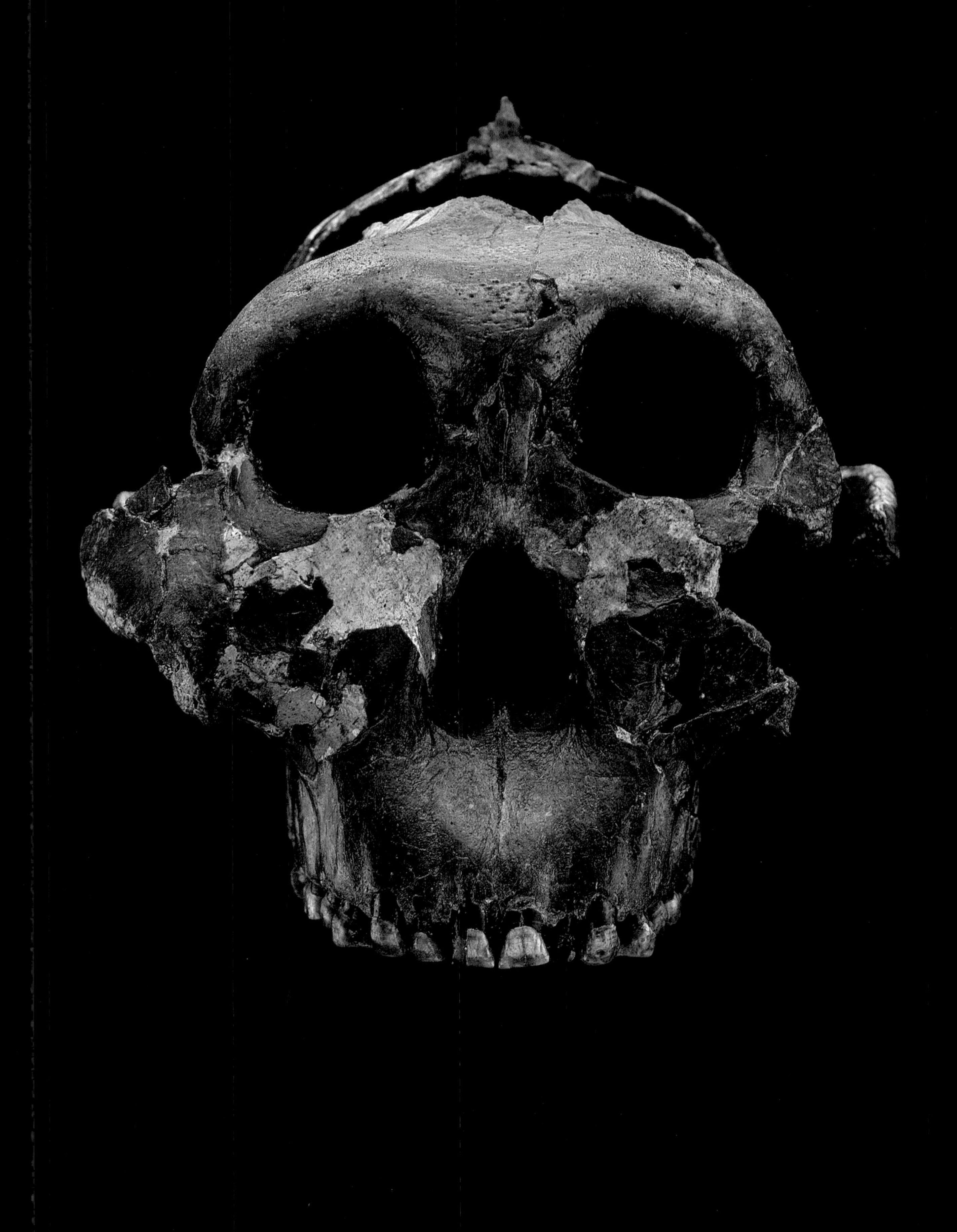

***Australopithecus boisei*, OH 5.** *A. boisei* was a truly impressive creature, dominated by a massive skull with a broad, concave face—a face like no other in human evolution. Actual size. *Photograph by David Brill; courtesy of National Museum of Tanzania.*

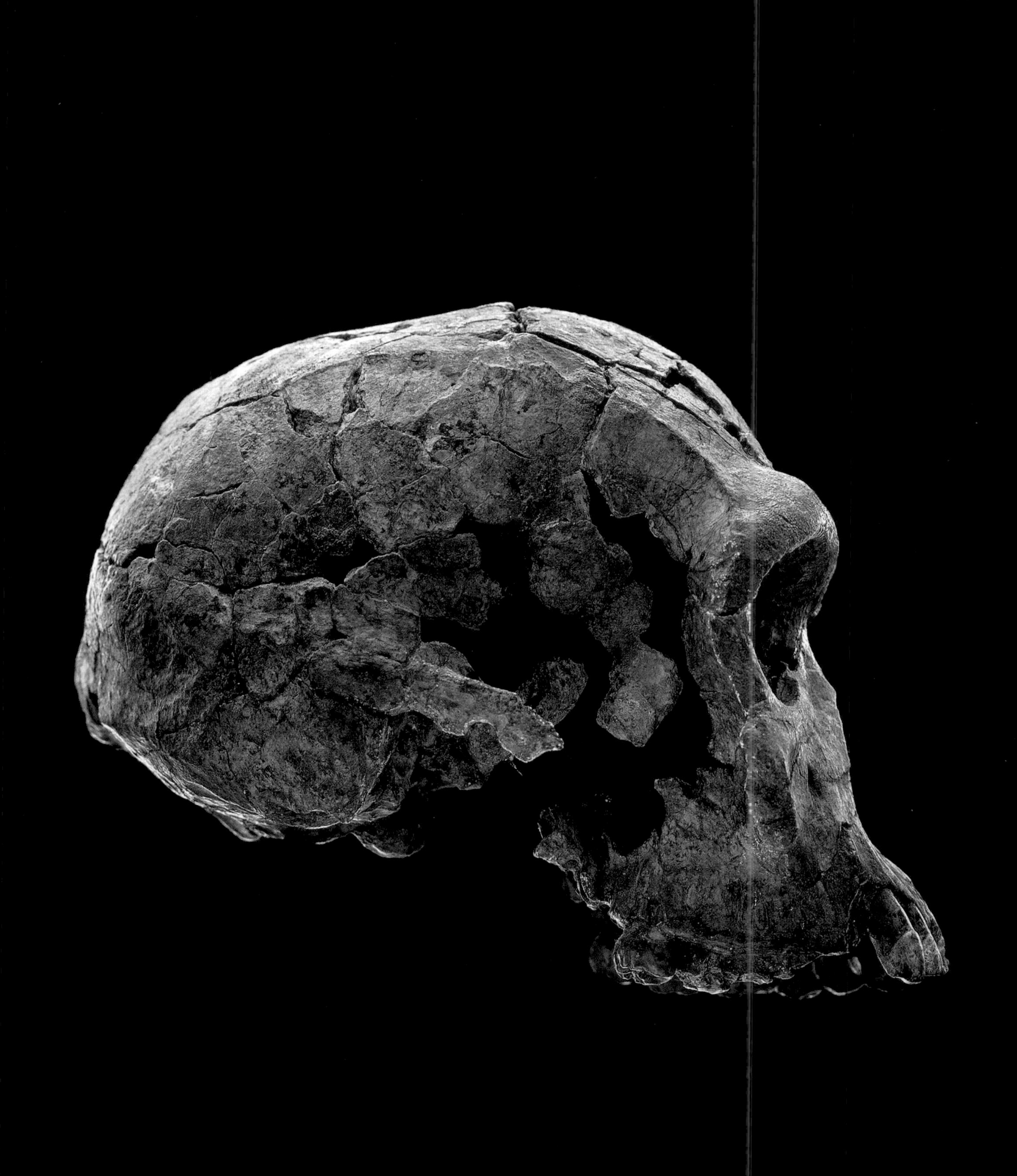

***Homo habilis*, KNM-ER 1813.** Anatomy and stratigraphy support the idea that 1813 belongs in *habilis* and that this species is a good candidate for ancestor to all later species of *Homo*, including modern humans. Actual size. *Photograph by David Brill; courtesy of National Museums of Kenya.*

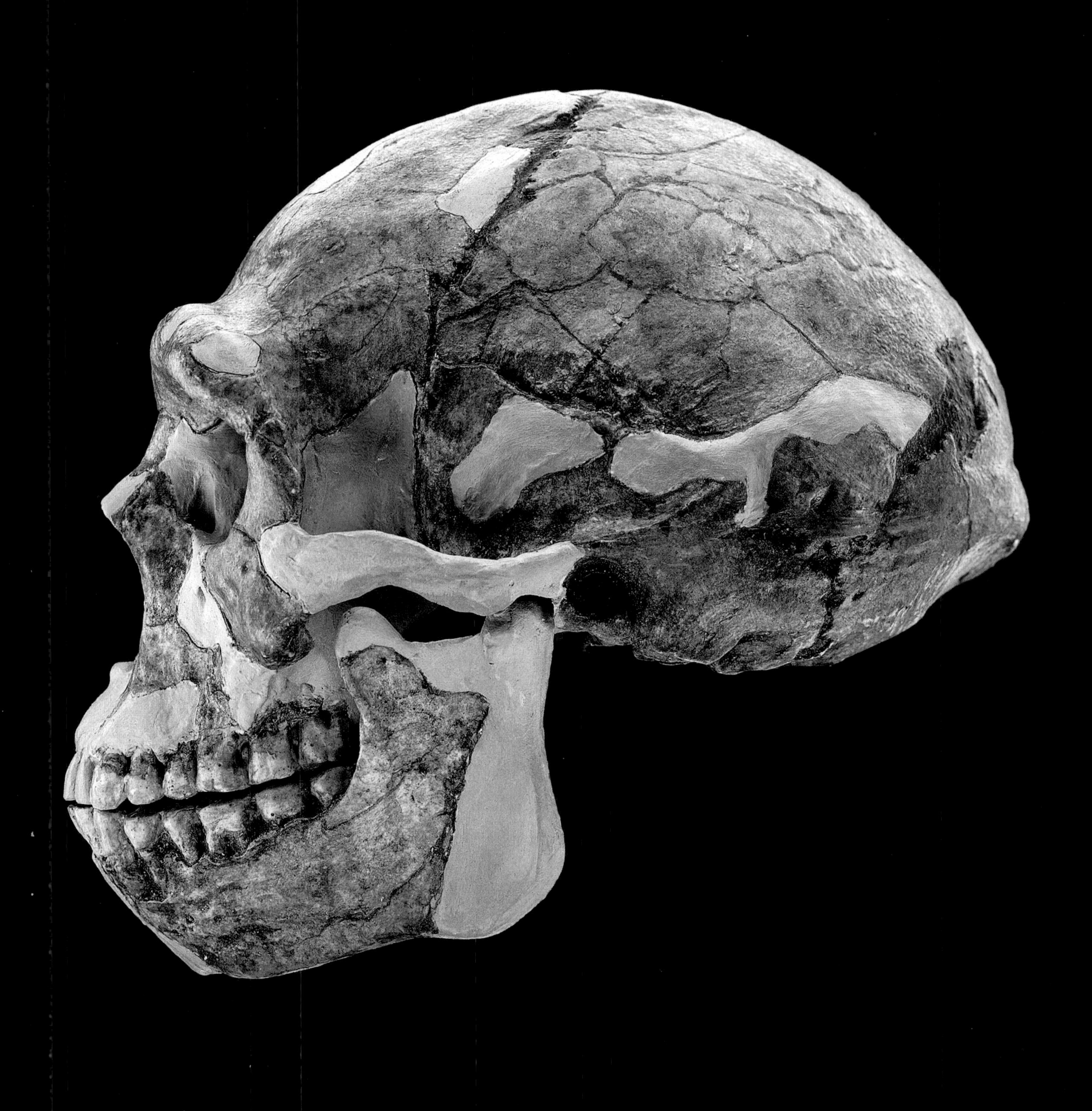

***Homo erectus,* reconstructed skull of Peking Man.** The cave of Zhoukoudian, or Dragon Bone Hill, about 40 kilometers south of Beijing, China, in which the original 400,000 to 500,000 year old fossils that were used to make this reconstruction were found, has also yielded the earliest evidence of fire outside of Africa. Actual size. *Photograph by David Brill; courtesy of American Museum of Natural History.*

Homo heidelbergensis, **Petralona 1.** With some Neandertal-like features and others that are much more primitive, this 300,000 to 400,000 year-old cranium underscores the difficulty of trying to pin a species designation to a poorly dated, singular fossil. Actual size. *Photograph by David Brill; courtesy of Paleontolgical Museum, University of Thesaloniki.*

***Homo neanderthalensis*, La Ferrassie 1.** This 50,000 year-old cranium exhibits the "classic" Neandertal anatomy that evolved in glacier-covered western Europe midway between this species appearance and extinction. Actual size. *Photograph by David Brill; courtesy of Musée l'Homme.*

***Homo sapiens*, Skhul V.** Skhul V belongs to a population whose anatomy is overwhelmingly similar to that of modern humans but whose Mousterian technology is similar to the Neandertals with whom they periodically shared the Middle Eastern landscape for 40,000 years. Actual size. *Photograph by David Brill; courtesy of Peabody Museum of Archaeology and Ethnology, Harvard University.*

FROM LUCY TO LANGUAGE

DONALD JOHANSON

& BLAKE EDGAR

Principal Photography David Brill

A Peter N. Nevraumont Book

Horse head figurine from Isturitz, France. Bone carvings became a more common form of art in Europe during the Magdalenian period from 18,000 to 12,000 years ago, when some of the most spectacular decorated caves were also painted. Actual size. *Photograph by David Brill; courtesy of Musée des Antiquités Nationale.*

Other Books by Donald Johanson

Ancestors: In Search of Human Origins
(co-authors Lenora Johanson and Blake Edgar)

Journey from the Dawn: Life with the World's First Family
(co-author Kevin O'Farrell)

Lucy's Child: The Discovery of a Human Ancestor
(co-author James Shreeve)

Lucy: The Beginnings of Humankind
(co-author Maitland Edey)

Blueprints: Solving the Mystery of Evolution
(co-author Maitland Edey)

SIMON & SCHUSTER EDITIONS
Rockefeller Center
1230 Avenue of the Americas
New York, New York 10020

A Peter N. Nevraumont Book

10 9 8 7 6 5 4 3 2 1

Library of Congress Cataloging in Publication Data

Johanson, Donald C.
From Lucy to language / Donald Johanson & Blake Edgar:
principle photography by David Brill.
p. cm.
"A Peter Nevraumont book."
Includes bibliographical references and index.
ISBN 0-684-81023-9 (alk. paper)
1. Human evolution. 2. Fossil man. 3. Australopithecines.
I. Edgar, Blake. II. Title.
GN281.J57 1996
573.2—dc20 96-31576
CIP

ISBN 0-684-81023-9

Printed and bound by Editoriale Bortolazzi-Stei, Verona, Italy

Designed by José Conde, Studio Pepin, Tokyo, Japan

Created and Produced by
Nevraumont Publishing Company
New York, New York

Ann J. Perrini, *President*

To my wife Lenora and our son Tesfaye for support and understanding.

– D.C. Johanson

To Aidan, who couldn't wait. – B.E.

contents

PART 1

Central Issues of Paleoanthropology

WHAT IS A HUMAN?
1 · The Human Creature *page 18*
2 · The Quest for Origins *page 18*
3 · Is Human Evolution Different? *page 21*

EVIDENCE
4 · The Science of Paleoanthropology *page 21*
5 · The Early Human Fossil Record *page 22*
6 · Discovering Early Human Fossil Sites *page 23*
7 · Recovering the Remains of Early Humans *page 25*
8 · Dating Fossils and Artifacts *page 26*
9 · Climate and Human Evolution *page 27*
10 · Teeth *page 28*
11 · Proteins, DNA, and Human Evolution *page 30*
12 · Why is Paleoanthropology So Contentious? *page 31*

ANCESTORS
13 · Our Closest Living Relatives *page 32*
14 · The Last Common Ancestor of Apes and Humans *page 32*
15 · Drawing the Human Family Tree *page 37*

LINEAGES
16 · African Genesis *page 38*
17 · Early vs. Modern Humans *page 40*
18 · Eve, and Adam *page 41*
19 · The Earliest Fossil Evidence of Anatomically Modern Humans *page 43*

MIGRATION
20 · Out of Africa *page 46*
21 · The First Americans *page 47*
22 · Peopling the Globe *page 49*

DIVERSITY
23 · Defining Human Species *page 52*
24 · Co-Existing Human Species *page 53*
25 · Human Diversity Today *page 56*
26 · What Is Race? *page 56*

ANATOMY
27 · The Size of Early Humans *page 57*
28 · Sexual Dimorphism *page 73*
29 · Gestation *page 76*
30 · Maturation *page 78*
31 · Evolution of the Human Brain *page 80*
32 · Reconstructing the Appearance of Early Humans *page 83*

SOCIETY
32 · Primate Societies and Early Human Social Behavior *page 83*

BIPEDALISM
34 · Evidence for Bipedalism *page 86*
35 · The Origins of Bipedalism *page 88*

TOOLS
36 · The Oldest Stone Tools *page 89*

CUSTOMS
37 · Hunters, Gatherers, or Scavengers? *page 90*
38 · Diet *page 91*
39 · Cannibalism *page 93*
40 · Fire *page 96*
41 · Shelter *page 97*
42 · Clothing *page 99*

CULTURE
43 · Burial *page 100*
44 · Art *page 102*
45 · The Origins of Language *page 106*

IMPONDERABLES
46 · The Problem of Consciousness *page 107*
47 · Will Humans Become Extinct? *page 107*
48 · Place of Humans in Nature *page 111*

PART 2

Encountering the Evidence

Ardipithecus ramidus, ARA-VP-6/129, Juvenile Partial mandible *page 116*

AUSTRALOPITHECINES *page 117*

Australopithecus anamensis, KNM-KP 29281, Adult mandible *page 122*

Australopithecus afarensis

Australopithecus afarensis, A.L. 288-1, Lucy, Partial adult skeleton *page 124*
Australopithecus afarensis, A.L. 333, Fragments of thirteen individuals *page 126*
Australopithecus afarensis, A.L. 444-2, Adult cranium *page 128*
Australopithecus afarensis, A.L. 129-1a+1b, Adult female knee joint *page 130*
Australopithecus afarensis, L.H. 4, Adult mandible / Fossil hominid footprints *page 131*

Australopithecus africanus

Australopithecus africanus, Sts 5, Mrs. Ples, Adult cranium *page 134*
Australopithecus africanus, Sts 14, Partial adult skeleton *page 136*
Australopithecus africanus, Sts 71 and Sts 36, Adult cranium and mandible *page 138*
Australopithecus africanus, Taung Child, Juvenile skull *page 142*
Australopithecus africanus, TM 1517, Adult partial cranium and mandible *page 144*
Australopithecus sp., Stw 252, Adult cranium *page 146*

Australopithecus robustus

Australopithecus robustus, SK 6, Adolescent mandible / SK 48, Adult cranium / SK 79, Adult cranium *page 148*

Australopithecus aethiopicus

Australopithecus aethiopicus, KNM-WT 17000, Black Skull, Adult cranium *page 152*

Australopithecus boisei

Australopithecus boisei, OH 5, Zinj, Adult cranium *page 156*
Australopithecus boisei, KNM-ER 406, Adult male cranium / KNM-ER 732, Adult female cranium *page 158*

HOMO *page 162*

Homo sp., A.L. 666-1, Adult maxilla *page 168*

Homo habilis

Homo habilis, OH 7, Juvenile male partial skeleton *page 170*
Homo habilis, OH 24, Adult female cranium *page 172*
Homo habilis, KNM-ER 1813, Adult cranium *page 174*
Homo habilis, OH 62, Partial adult skeleton *page 176*

Homo rudolfensis

Homo rudolfensis, KNM-ER 1470, Adult cranium *page 177*

Homo ergaster

Homo ergaster, KNM-ER 3733, Adult cranium *page 180*
Homo ergaster, KNM-WT 15000, Juvenile male skeleton *page 182*
Homo ergaster, SK 847, Partial adult cranium *page 184*

Homo erectus

Homo erectus, Trinil 2, Java Man, Adult partial cranium *page 187*
Homo erectus, Peking Man, Adult skull reconstruction *page 188*
Homo erectus, Sangiran 17, Adult male cranium *page 191*

Homo heidelbergensis

Homo heidelbergensis, Bodo cranium, Adult cranium *page 194*
Homo heidelbergensis, Mauer 1, Adult mandible *page 196*
Homo heidelbergensis, Arago XXI, Adult cranium *page 198*
Homo heidelbergensis, Petralona 1, Adult cranium *page 200*
Homo heidelbergensis, Steinheim, Adult female cranium *page 202*
Homo heidelbergensis, Atapuerca 5, Adult skull *page 204*
Homo heidelbergensis, Broken Hill 1, Adult cranium *page 208*

Homo neanderthalensis

Homo neanderthalensis, Krapina C, Adult female partial cranium *page 211*
Homo neanderthalensis, Saccopastore I, Adult female cranium *page 212*
Homo neanderthalensis, Teshik-Tash, Juvenile partial skeleton *page 215*
Homo neanderthalensis, Kebara 2, Adult male skeleton *page 218*
Homo neanderthalensis, Amud 1, Adult male skeleton *page 220*
Homo neanderthalensis, Amud 7, Partial infant skeleton *page 222*
Homo neanderthalensis, La Chapelle-aux-Saints, Adult male skeleton *page 224*
Homo neanderthalensis, La Ferrassie 1, Adult male skeleton *page 226*
Homo neanderthalensis, Neandertal 1, Adult calotte *page 228*
Homo neanderthalensis, Gibraltar 1, Adult female cranium *page 230*
Homo neanderthalensis, Saint-Césaire, Partial adult skeleton *page 232*

Homo sapiens

Homo sapiens, Dali, Adult male cranium *page 234*
Homo sapiens, Omo I and Omo II, Partial adult skeleton and cranium *page 236*
Homo sapiens, Qafzeh IX, Adult female skeleton *page 239*
Homo sapiens, Skhul V, Adult male skeleton *page 242*
Homo sapiens, Cro-Magnon I, Adult male skeleton *page 244*
Homo sapiens, Kow Swamp 1, Adult male skeleton *page 247*

PALEOLITHIC TECHNOLOGY *page 250*

Oldowan tools *page 250*
Acheulean tools *page 254*
Mousterian tools *page 256*
Upper Paleolithic tools *page 258*

APPENDIX 1: TYPE SPECIMENS FOR HOMINID SPECIES *page 262*
APPENDIX 2: HOMINID FOSSIL AND ARCHEOLOGICAL *page 263*
ACKNOWLEDGMENTS *page 264*
SELECTED REFERENCES *page 265*
INDEX *page 269*

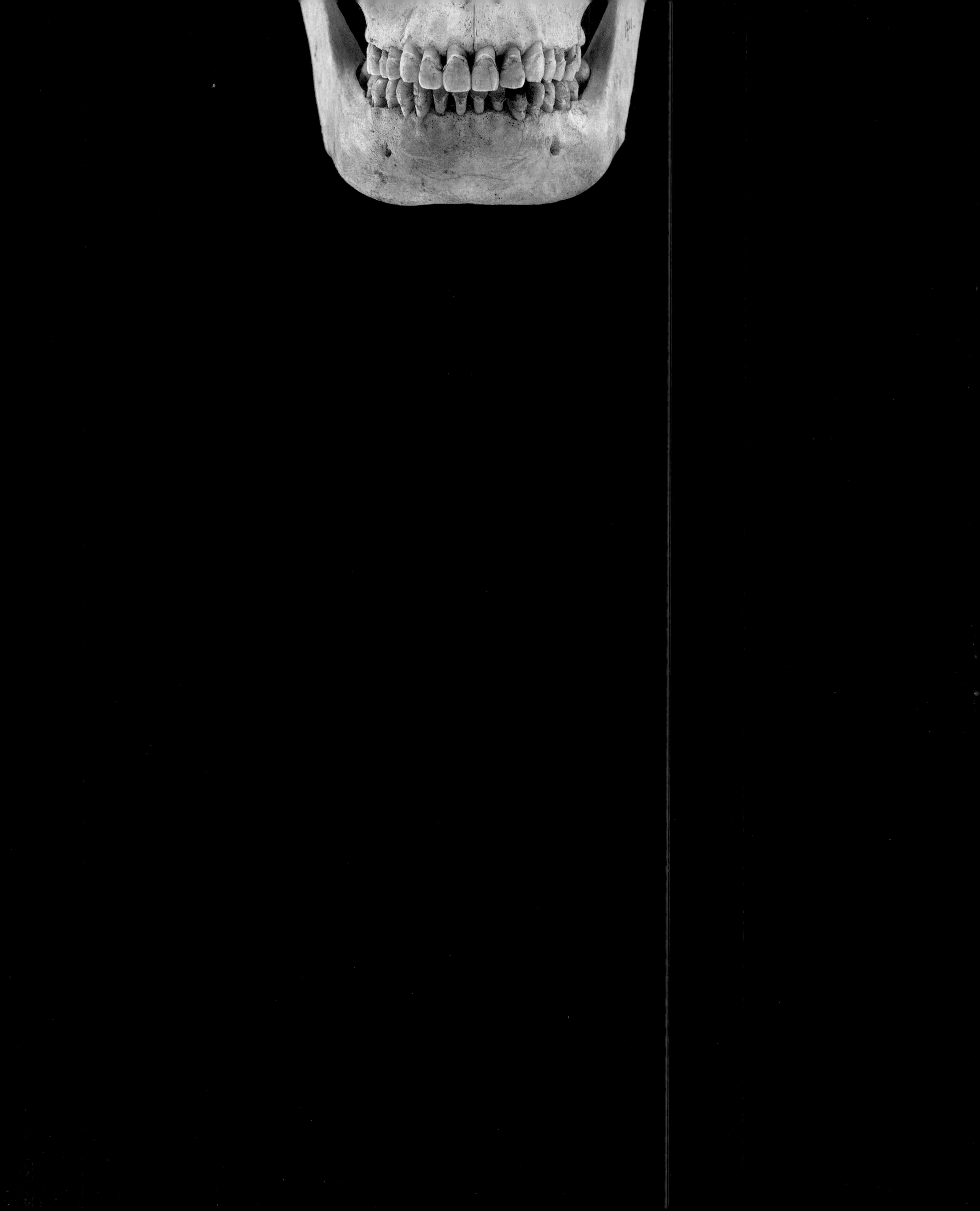

Part 1

CENTRAL ISSUES OF PALEOANTHROPOLOGY

1 · The Human Creature

A HUMAN is any member of the species *Homo sapiens* ("wise man"), the only living representative of the family Hominidae. The Hominidae, or hominids, are a group of upright-walking primates with relatively large brains (see page 33). So, all humans are hominids, although not all hominids could be called human. ❡ Next, all humans are primates. The mammalian order of Primates includes about 180 species of prosimians (such as lemurs, tarsiers, and lorises), monkeys, apes, and ourselves. Primates are unusual mammals, for they have evolved such distinctive traits as highly developed binocular vision (and a corresponding enclosed eye socket in the skull), mobile fingers and toes with flat nails instead of claws, and with sensitive pads at the tips, a shortened snout with a reduced sense of smell, and large brains relative to body size. ❡ If primates are unusual for mammals, humans are even more unusual for primates. We are essentially elaborated African apes. We share almost 99 percent of our genetic material – the information that codes for our proteins, bones, brains, and bodies – with chimpanzees. Yet, despite such similarities, there are significant genetic and pronounced physical differences between humans and apes. ❡ Clearly, that distinctive portion of our DNA must involve some regulatory genes that code for our unusual features. Humans also possess 46 chromosomes to an ape's 48, and our version of the extra ape genes has been lumped together on chromosome 2; perhaps in that process some crucial mutations arose, but we would have to sequence and study all human and ape DNA to solve this paradox. Our close genetic affinity to apes has prompted some authorities, notably Jared Diamond in his book *The Third Chimpanzee*, to argue that it is fallacious to separate humans and apes into two separate families (African apes constitute the family Pongidae). ❡ We walk upright on two limbs, and to accommodate such a strange posture we have developed a specialized pelvis, hip and leg muscles, and an S-shaped vertebral column. We have tiny canine teeth and flat faces with a protruding nose. Males have a pendulous penis, while in females the physical signs of ovulation are concealed, something that happens in no other primate. ❡ Humans are highly social animals, a trait we inherited from our primate past, but we have taken it to new extremes through the development of complex written and spoken language which enables us to communicate nuances of feeling as well as information, and a material culture that includes symbolic art. We are also called a moral animal. Besides that strange habit of walking upright, perhaps it is our inventiveness and our introspective nature that truly distinguish humans among the primates. ❡ Our species, *Homo sapiens*, was first described in 1758 by the Swedish botanist Carl von Linné, whom we know better as Carolus Linnaeus. Most early descriptions concentrated on a very few traits, the most obvious being brain size. If we were to create a richer, more complete biological characterization of our species, many other traits would need to be included. Humans have a relatively long life span that begins with immaturity at birth and a prolonged infancy. Physical maturation is delayed during childhood, then occurs quickly during the adolescent growth spurt. We are polytypic in morphology and skin and hair color but genetically very homogeneous. Our behavior is marked by habitual tool use, communication through spoken and written language, and the symbolic representation of objects. We are culturally adapted to survive in a broad range of physical environments, climates, and temperatures. We are omnivorous and share food extensively with others, another mark of our social being. Our body is relatively hairless except for the head and face, axilla (arm pits), and pubic region. Skeletal features include a hand with an opposable thumb that endows us with a power grip and precise, fine hand movements; relatively straight and slender limb bones; a pelvis, lower limbs, and associated muscles specifically modified for bipedal locomotion; an enlarged hallux, or big toe, in line with the rest of our toes rather than opposed to them; and a foot with a weight-bearing arch to absorb the stresses of two-legged locomotion. ❡ This list and the aforementioned traits provide a hint of who we are biologically. Many other features of anatomy, behavior, and diversity in *Homo sapiens*, as well as in other hominids, provide the basis of content for this book. As we query the remains of our extinct relatives for clues to who we are and how we got that way, we will discover that we are much nearer to them than we think, even if separated by millions of years.

2 · The Quest for Origins

SINCE at least the Upper Paleolithic, some 40,000 years ago, every human society has devised a creation myth to explain how humans came to be. The need to explain our origins is one of the universals of being human. Creation myths are based on cultural beliefs that have, in one manner or another, been adopted as legitimate explanation by a particular society. To a large extent, creation myths glorify the specialness of humans. In the broadest view, such myths undertake to explain our differences from all other creatures-our humanness. ❡ In contrast to cultural myths about human origins, the science of paleoanthropology, which also tries to construct a narrative about how humans came to be, is rooted in the scientific method. This method, based on objective observation and evaluation, is governed by a set of rules that permit the testing of hypotheses, and the results of such tests may lead to the rejection or modification of the original construct. The success of paleoanthropology rests on integrating two different fields: Darwinian evolutionary theory and the study of Earth's geological history (see page 21). ❡ Much like a detective story, the quest for clues to our origins is exhilarating and filled with surprises. The goal, however, is not to figure out "who done it" but to understand why and how: why we differ from our closest relatives, the African apes, and how we became a bipedal, large-brained, culturally dependent animal. We are the last species in the zoological family Hominidae (hominids, in the vernacular), and to understand something of our place in nature (see page 111) we need to explore the lessons held by the past. ❡ As we learn more about our origins, it becomes apparent that although an ape ancestor became bipedal several million years ago, there was nothing in that development that ensured the eventual evolution of *Homo sapiens*. Bipedalism, a basic feature of hominids, did not make modern humans inevitable. Paleoanthropological discoveries make it clear that the human family tree is not a single lineage in which one species succeeded another, leading relentlessly to the appearance of modern humans. Instead, the hominid fossil record suggests that our ancestry is better thought of as a bush, with the branches representing a number of bipedal species that evolved along different evolutionary lines. All of those species were successful, sometimes for long periods, and all went extinct. At the probable time of a common ancestor for humans and African apes, 6 to 8 million years ago, there was no guarantee that humans would evolve. Yet we did evolve, and because we turned out to be inquisitive creatures with the ability to reflect on

Donald Johanson, Hadar, Ethiopia.
Johanson holds an Oldowan stone artifact more than 2 million years in age.
Photograph by Enrico Ferorelli.

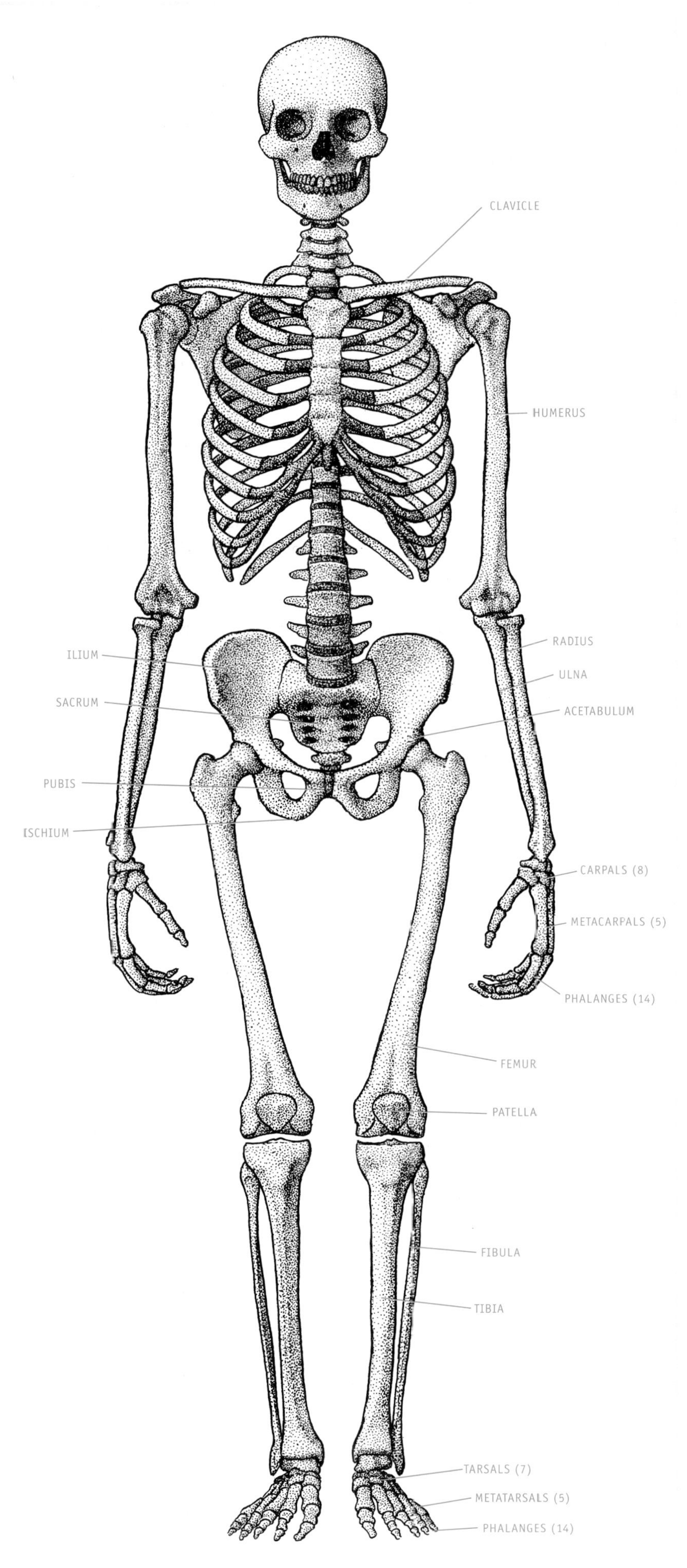

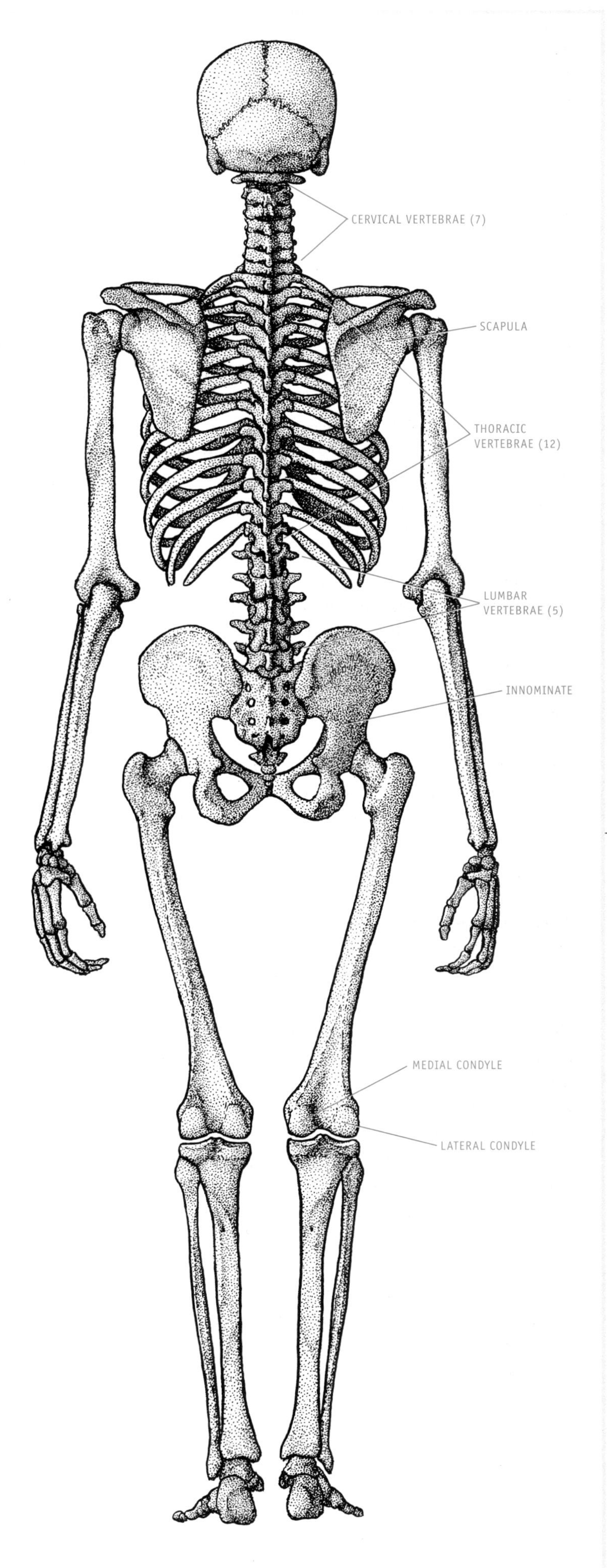

Frontal and Posterior Views of the Human Skeleton.
The human skeleton generally contains a total of 206 bones, which are a type of living tissue that grows and changes throughout life. *Illustrations by Diana Salles.*

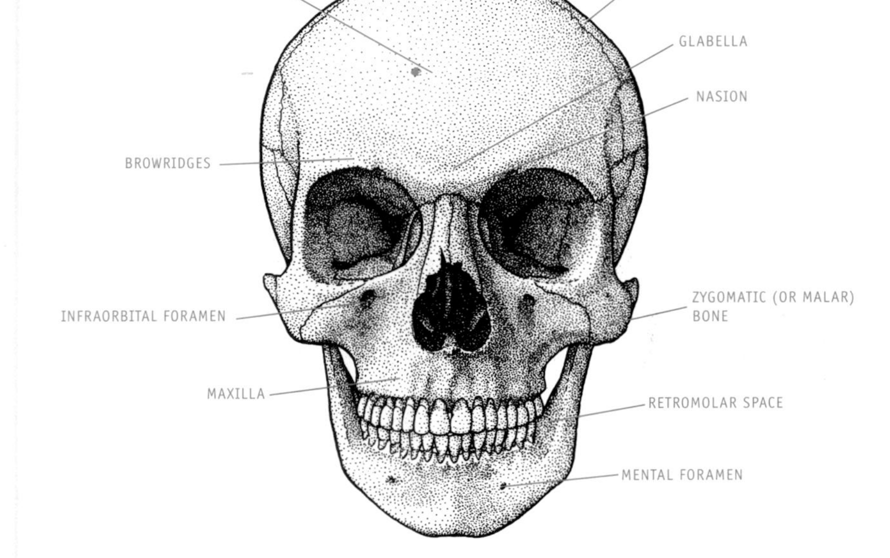

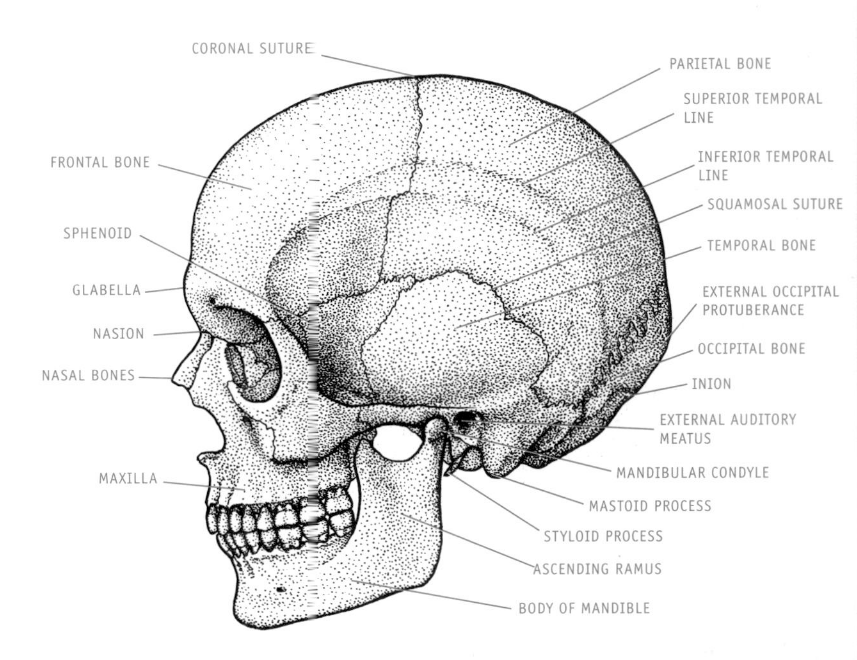

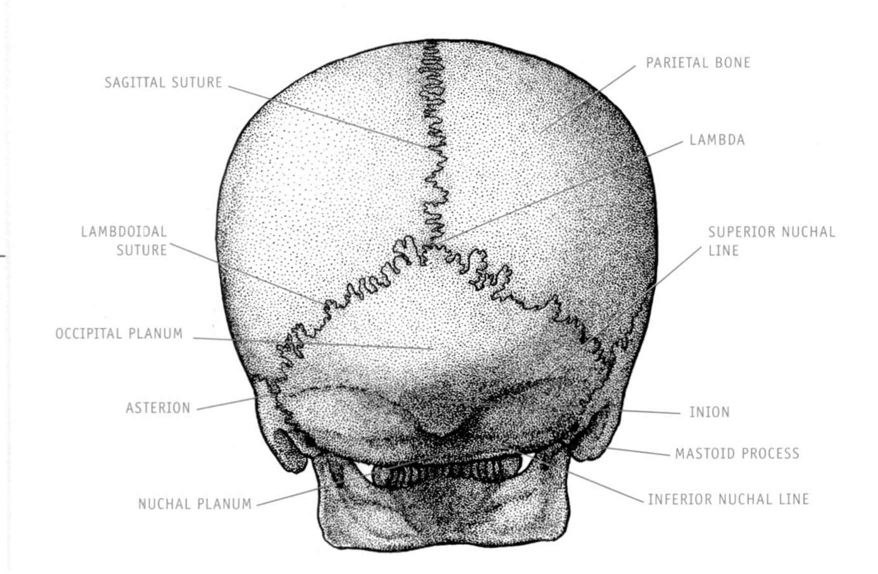

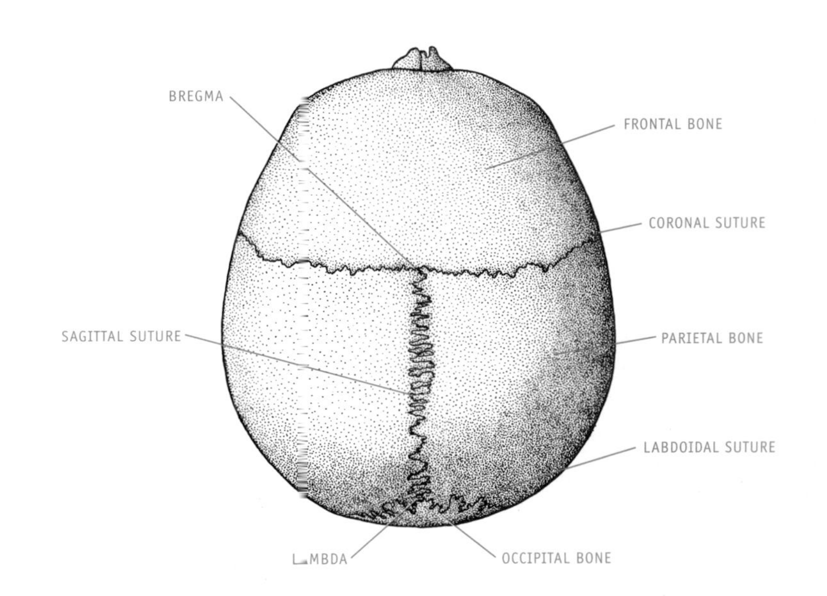

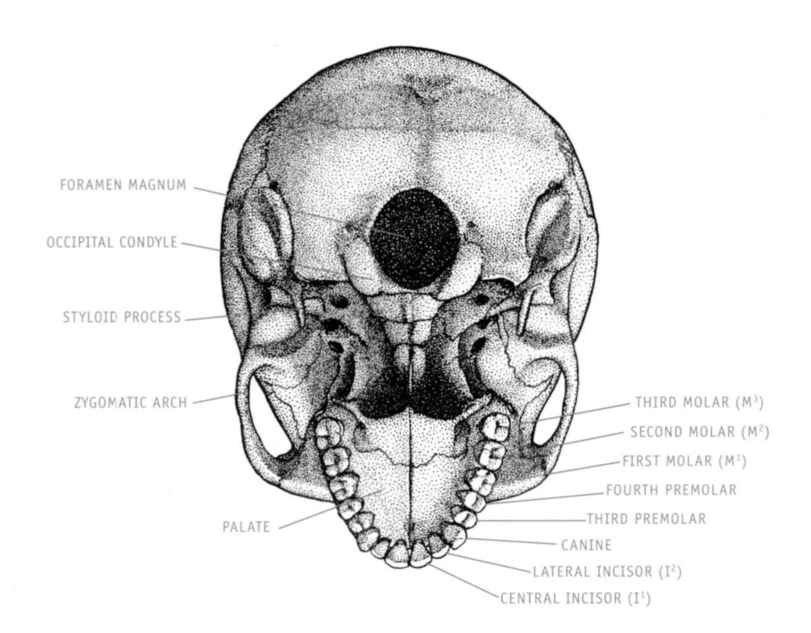

Five Views of the Human Skull: Frontal, Lateral (left), Posterior, Superior, and Basal. An adult human skull consists of a cranium and a mandible, or lower jaw. The cranium contains 27 bones, including six unpaired bones, eight paired bones, and a total of six inner ear bones. *Illustrations by Diana Salles.*

our past, we have done so avidly. ¶ Paleoanthropology in part plays to that inquisitive, exploratory part of our makeup. Expeditions to remote terrains feature prominently in paleoanthropology, and whereas living for months in a tent, usually under desert conditions, is not to everyone's liking, the pursuit of our origins can be enjoyed in other ways. Each new find, it seems, receives front-page coverage in newspapers, and magazines featuring reconstructions of our ancestors on their cover become the best-selling issues of the year. Hominid fossils touch a responsive chord in people everywhere, who seem to have an inherent drive to know their beginnings. We want to know what the fossils have to say to us. ¶ There seems to be a magic in the fossilized bones that transcends time. Specimens like Lucy, a 3.2 million-year-old partial skeleton from Hadar, Ethiopia, have become touchstones for discussing human origins. Although older human ancestors have now been discovered, Lucy, with her affectionate name, has become a benchmark by which people judge new hominid discoveries. Even though distant relatives like Lucy lived very different lifestyles from us modern humans, the message they bring, after millions of years of suspended animation, is important to us all. ¶ Ultimately our fascination with the study of human origins nourishes our need for exploration and for understanding both our uniqueness and our close link to the natural world. Today more than ever, people are thinking about the future of the universe and the survival of humankind. For many, the lessons we can learn from our past give us a better perspective on ourselves, our place in nature, and how we view our future.

3 · Is Human Evolution Different?

FOR MOST of human evolution, cultural evolution played a fairly minor role and did not pick up speed until the Upper Paleolithic, 40,000 years ago. If we look back to the time of the australopithecines, some 4 million to 1 million years ago, it is obvious that culture had little or no influence on the lives of these creatures, who were constrained and directed by the same evolutionary pressures as the other organisms with which they shared their ecosystems. So, for most of the time during which hominids have existed, human evolution was no different from that of other organisms. ¶ Once our ancestors began to develop a dependence on culture for survival, however, a new layer was added to human evolution. According to Sherwood Washburn, professor emeritus at the University of California, Berkeley, there is a definite relationship between biology and culture that he terms "biocultural feedback." Washburn suggests that the unique interplay of culture change and biological change could account for why humans have become so different. His basic premise is that as culture became more advantageous for the survival of our ancestors, natural selection favored the genes responsible for such behavior. Those genes that improved our capacity for culture would have had an adaptive advantage. The ultimate result of the interplay between genes and culture was a significant acceleration of human evolution, as manifested in, among other features, the growth of our brain and its mental capacity over the past 2 million years. ¶ Cultural and biological evolution contrast in a number of ways and are very different processes. Biological change, or evolution, is facilitated by the transmission of genetic information from one generation to a succeeding one by the configuration of DNA in genes. Cultural evolution is the passing on of information by behavioral means and involves the processes of teaching and learning. By these definitions, a bird might make a tool or a nest, but it does not learn how to do this; it is born with the genetic endowment which, at the appropriate time, "turns on," and a nest is constructed. Although humans are genetically equipped with basic biological imperatives, our sophisticated cultural behavior must be learned by teaching, and, most important, this learning is associated with a symbolic mode of communication, usually language. ¶ Information transmitted by DNA involves passing that information from one individual to another, which can only be done at a single point (conception) in the life span of that individual. Cultural evolution, on the other hand, is not passive but active and incorporates lifelong teaching and learning. Further, any one individual can teach one or many and a single individual can learn from one or many. In cultural evolution, in contradistinction to biological evolution, where the information is stored as a DNA sequence, information can be memorized, written, videotaped, audiotaped, and transmitted using sound, pictures, and words. ¶ Culturally transmitted information is behaviorally very flexible and not restricted. A bird can sing a mating song beautifully, but a tenor can sing many romantic arias in several different languages with noticeably distinct levels of passionate commitment. The plasticity of learned cultural information is a true hallmark of being human, as is evidenced by the myriad societies around the world. ¶ Cultural behavior is passed on by communication and therefore can spread to many more individuals than a genetic novelty that is transmitted only in the DNA. Biologically based behavior requires an enormous number of generations to spread, whereas cultural innovations, especially with the information revolution, spread exceedingly quickly. ¶ Human evolution is an intriguing interplay of biological evolution and cultural evolution. And in the view of sociobiologists Charles Lumsden of the University of Toronto and the noted E. O. Wilson of Harvard University, who have dubbed this interaction "gene-culture coevolution," humans have been shaped through the synergetic interaction of genes and culture. In the final analysis, human evolution is different from the evolution of all other life on this planet. We are distinguished by our capacity for culture, which ultimately has biological roots.

4 · The Science of Paleoanthropology

PALEOANTHROPOLOGY calls on a broadly conceived and strategically implemented multidisciplinary approach to discover and interpret the evidence for human evolution. It is the responsibility of the paleoanthropologist to coordinate activities in the field and in the laboratory, carefully integrating knowledge contributed by specialists in geology, biology, and the social sciences. The goal is to understand, as thoroughly as possible, the process by which we became human. ¶ The major coordination of a field project seeking to recover important clues to our ancestry is customarily under the leadership of an individual with a background in anthropology (the study of mankind). The paleoanthropologist (one who studies ancient humans) works closely with scientific colleagues to raise funding to support field projects, with a primary expectation being the recovery of the fossilized remains of our ancestors. The paleoanthropologist has the ultimate responsibility for overseeing the research from the planning stages, to actual fieldwork, to the recovery and in-depth laboratory study of particularly the hominid fossils, and finally to the publication of research results in the scientific literature. ¶ Once sites have been located (see page 25), an interdisciplinary team enters the field for weeks to months to undertake exploration and excavation focused on finding hominid remains. In the case of cave sites, the process of excavation is slow and tedious. In open-air sites such as those found in the Great Rift Valley in East Africa, exploration takes the form of foot survey, with teams of expedition members scouring the landscape in search of hominid fossils that have eroded from ancient geological strata. ¶ Hominids are not all that a survey team might fruitfully uncover, however. In the past, hominids were a rather small and insignificant component of paleocommunities. Vertebrates such as elephants, antelopes,

Afar fossil hunters at Hadar, Ethiopia. Finding bones of hominids and other vertebrates requires much legwork and a little luck. *Photograph by Enrico Ferorelli.*

monkeys, pigs, hippos, and many others ranging in size down to small rodents were much more dominant elements on the landscape. The study of nonhominid fossil vertebrates is the purview of a cadre of paleontologists (scientists who study ancient animals), each concentrating on a particular group of animals. Some paleontologists work only in the laboratory, identifying and studying fossil specimens collected in the field by others; some make forays into the field to make their own collections. ◖ Paleontologists not only contribute to a more complete understanding of the evolutionary history and diversity of particular faunal groups but, by studying the composition of the fossil assemblages, help reconstruct the ancient ecology of the site. Further appreciation of the paleoenvironment is contributed by paleobotanists, who study fossil wood and fruits, and by palynologists, who identify past vegetation from fossilized pollen grains. ◖ Some animal groups, such as pigs and elephants, underwent fairly rapid evolution, and certain species in these groups are important indicators of a specific time period. The use of animals for dating a site is known as biostratigraphy, and at some sites where precise geochronological dating is impossible, this is the only way to estimate the age of the site. ◖ In the field, the paleoanthropologist, while monitoring all aspects of the field campaign, often works with a team of highly experienced surveyors who have been trained to search for hominid fossils. The training, largely the result of extensive field experience, also benefits from instruction in osteology (the study of bones). Comprehensive and strategic foot survey in search of hominids demands keen eyesight and special dedication, for it is often conducted under very harsh and remote conditions. ◖ If artifacts, usually made of stone, are found, the field archeologist undertakes painstaking and exacting excavation, carefully mapping and labeling each artifact or fossil uncovered. Such archeological information aids in understanding how our ancestors may have used tools in hunting, scavenging, and food-processing activities. ◖ The paleoanthropologist, most often trained as a physical anthropologist with a specialized interest in some aspect of human anatomy such as the dentition, the postcranial bones, or skull morphology, works in the laboratory with other scientists who have their own area of anatomical expertise. During the anatomical study, following preparation and cleaning of the field specimen, each one is identified, measured, photographed, described, compared with other fossil specimens and ultimately published. Experts in the area of biomechanics assist greatly in understanding the function of fossil hominid bones, often providing insights into the nature of the locomotor and masticatory systems and the possible use of hands for manipulation.

◖ Discoveries of hominid and nonhominid fossils and artifacts are of little use unless we know something about the context in which they were found and their geological age. Of overriding importance in the study of paleoanthropology are the geological sciences. One of the major undertakings of the geologist is to map the geological layers in which discoveries have been made. These stratigraphic geologists provide the depositional framework in which to place the discoveries, and often provide detailed descriptions of the sediments that assist in understanding the environment of deposition, such as a delta, river, lake, or back swamp. ◖ Geochronologists employ various methodologies for determining the exact age of the geological sequence. After field collecting appropriate samples for analysis, they spend long hours in the laboratory applying radiometric techniques to dating (see page 26). The strata of interest are usually, but not always, sediments of volcanic origin. The precise dating of fossil hominid-bearing sequences is crucial when trying to place a find within the broader framework of human evolution. ◖ Mapping specialists assist in drafting accurate maps on which to record discoveries and employ aerial photographs and satellite imagery to assist in the search for potential new sites (see page 25). Highly mobile global positioning technology now permits the precise location of important sites and finds to within a few meters on Earth's surface. ◖ Field research at any hominid site is an ongoing process, whether it be in an open-air site in East Africa, a cave in the Middle East, a quarry in Asia, or a rock overhang in Europe. The paleoanthropologist must constantly refine the research strategy, thoughtfully integrate a diversity of disciplines, carefully phrase questions, apply new methodologies, and implement targeted survey and excavation to significantly augment our knowledge of human evolution.

5 · The Early Human Fossil Record

HOW MUCH fossil evidence of our hominid ancestors has been recovered? To answer this question, one can consider either the number of individuals represented at different sites or the absolute number of fossil specimens (that is, individual bones or fragments) from those sites. An individual hominid can be represented by anything from a single tooth to a complete skeleton, but thinking in terms of the number of individuals gives a sense of the rarity of hominid fossils and the odds against their preservation. Hominids were certainly relatively rare animals on the landscape anyway, which only increases the challenge of finding their fossilized remains. ◖ The contents of any fossil sample will be biased by the specific conditions for preservation at a site. A host of variables, including the environment where an individual died, the potential for trampling by animals or transport of bones by water, carnivores, or other agents, the durability of the bones themselves, and damage or loss of the bones after exposure by erosion will influence what individuals will be successfully preserved as fossils, what fossils will be found, and their state of preservation. ◖ Compared to the extensive fossil record of some mammals—pigs, rodents, horses, and antelopes, for example—the fossil evidence of human evolution is relatively spotty. About half of the time span in the last three million years remains undocumented by any human fossils. From those periods that are documented, however, we have obtained a reasonably impressive sample that tells us much about the biology, ecology, and diversity of our ancestors. This would not have been possible without the dedicated and diligent efforts of many professional and amateur fossil hunters during the past 150 years, and many of the fruits of those labors are displayed and described in this book. Fossil hunters continue to add significant new finds—lately even new species—every year, ensuring that our fossil record will only grow richer. For now, consider the following as a brief, provisional inventory of species and specimens. ◖ From the earliest period of hominid evolution, more than 4 million years ago, only a handful of largely undiagnostic fossils had been found, including the mandible fragments from the Kenyan sites of Lothagam and Tabarin (see page 39). The situation improved in this decade with the recent discovery and naming of *Ardipithecus ramidus*, which lived about 4.4 million years ago. This species is known from forty-three specimens of several individuals (see page 116), including a partial skeleton that has yet to be described. All the specimens come from the site of Aramis in the Middle Awash region of Ethiopia. There are twenty-four specimens, about half of them dental remains, of *Australopithecus anamensis* (see page 122), a species from Kanapoi and Allia Bay in northern Kenya that lived just before 4 million years ago. ◖ The best represented early hominid is *Australopithecus afarensis*, which lived between 4 and 3 million years ago in East Africa. Its remains number 324 specimens of at least 111 individuals from Hadar, Ethiopia, and thirty-one specimens from Laetoli, Tanzania. The best known specimens are the partial skeleton A. L. 288-1, or Lucy (see page 124), and 214 bones from thirteen individuals from the single locality A. L. 333 (see page 126). Other fossils that most likely belong to this species include a 3.9 million-year-old partial frontal bone from Belohdelie, Ethiopia and some fragmentary remains from Omo Shungura and Fejej, Ethiopia, and Koobi Fora, Kenya. ◖ In South Africa, the species *Australopithecus africanus* is represented by at least 120 individuals from Sterkfontein (see page 148) alone, plus the single individual from Taung (see page 142), and a few from Makapansgat. The most abundant South African hominid site is the cave of Swartkrans, where painstaking excavation of breccia has yielded about 200 *Australopithecus robustus* (see page 148) and six *Homo* fossils, which can attributed to a minimum of eighty-five individuals and six individuals, respectively. ◖ The earliest form of robust australopithecine in East Africa is *Australopithecus aethiopicus* ("southern ape of Ethiopia"). It appeared about 2.5 million years ago and is known from three specimens belonging to three individuals: the toothless partial mandible Omo 18, from Ethiopia, and from west Lake Turkana, Kenya, the partial mandible KNM-WT 16005 and the cranium KNM-WT 17000, better known as the Black Skull (see page 152). A fourth specimen that might be attributed to this species, or alternatively to early *Homo*, is the mandible KNM-ER 1482 from Koobi Fora. ◖ From between 2.4 and 1.2 million years ago, the period in which genus *Homo* evolved in Africa and began populating other continents, the hominid fossil record of East Africa consists of about 300 specimens of crania, mandibles, and teeth. A third of these belong to *Australopithecus boisei*, such as the crania OH 5 (see page 156) and KNM-ER 406 (see page 158), eighty-five belong to *Homo*, and the rest cannot be identified to a particular hominid. An additional fifty postcranial bones round out the hominid sample from this time period. ◖ African *Homo* fossils from this period can be assigned to the species *habilis*, *rudolfensis*, and *ergaster*. The sample of *H. habilis* fossils includes thirty-three specimens from Olduvai Gorge, including seven partial crania (see pages 170 and 172), four mandibles, assorted limb bones and teeth, and a fragmentary partial skeleton (see page 176). About half a dozen specimens from Koobi Fora can be included in this species, the most complete being the cranium KNM-ER 1813 (see page 174). Several teeth, two mandibles, and a very fragmentary cranium from Omo may also belong to *H. habilis*. *Homo rudolfensis* is represented by several specimens from Koobi Fora, most notably the cranium KNM-ER 1470 (see page 177), which was the type specimen used to name this species in 1986, and the mandible of a separate individual, KNM-ER 1802. Another probable *H. rudolfensis* specimen is the 2.4 million-year-old mandible UR 501 from Malawi. *Homo ergaster* is better represented by several specimens from Koobi Fora and West Turkana, Kenya, including the type specimen mandible KNM-ER 992, the crania of KNM-ER 3773 (see page 180) and 3883, and the skeleton of KNM-WT 15000 (see page 182), as well as the partial cranium SK 847 (see page 184) from South Africa. ◖ Outside of Africa, the oldest hominid remains belong to *Homo erectus*. Specimens from at least forty-eight *H. erectus* individuals—a third of the total worldwide sample of this species—have been found in Java, mainly at Trinil (see page 187), Sangiran (see page 191), Ngandong, and Modjokerto. These fossils include crania, skullcaps, and skull fragments from thirty individuals, jaws or jaw fragments from nine individuals, plus some limb bones and numerous teeth. Another third of the world's *erectus* fossils come from China, mainly from the single site of Zhoukoudian, where forty-five hominid specimens from fifteen individuals were recovered (see page 188). ◖ From the Middle Pleistocene, *Homo heidelbergensis* is represented by hundreds of bones from at least thirty individuals from Atapuerca (see page 204) and four individuals at the nearby site of Gran Dolina (see page 46), plus twenty others, usually partial or complete crania, from elsewhere in Europe and Africa. Much more abundant are the Neandertals, the probable direct descendants of *H. heidelbergensis*. Remains of about 500 *H. neanderthalensis* individuals have been discovered (see pages 211-233), largely in western Europe, central Europe, and the Near East. ◖ From this brief inventory, it is clear that paleoanthropologists have accumulated a large sampling of fossil evidence from at least some hominid species, although disagreement as to how to classify and interpret this evidence persists. Only by gradually filling in the gaps in the fossil record can we hope to arrive at the correct interpretation of our past.

Olduvai Gorge, Tanzania. Located in the Great Rift Valley, where eruptions, uplift, and erosion create ideal conditions for preserving fossils, this was one of the first sites in Africa to be explored for evidence of our ancestors. *Photograph by Emory Kristof: copyright National Geographic Society.*

6 · Discovering Early Human Fossil Sites

CONTEMPORARY paleoanthropologists are greatly assisted in their search for fossil hominid sites by the use of sophisticated remote sensing data, such as satellite images, and computerized geographical information systems. In the past, the majority of sites were located by chance. Olduvai Gorge in Tanzania, for example, was found by a German entomologist exploring what was then German East Africa. While chasing a butterfly, so the story goes, Wilhelm Kattwinkel almost fell off a cliff into the gorge. During the course of Kattwinkel's natural history expedition he collected fossils at Olduvai and sent them back to Berlin, where they aroused the interest of paleontologists. ◖ Many sites

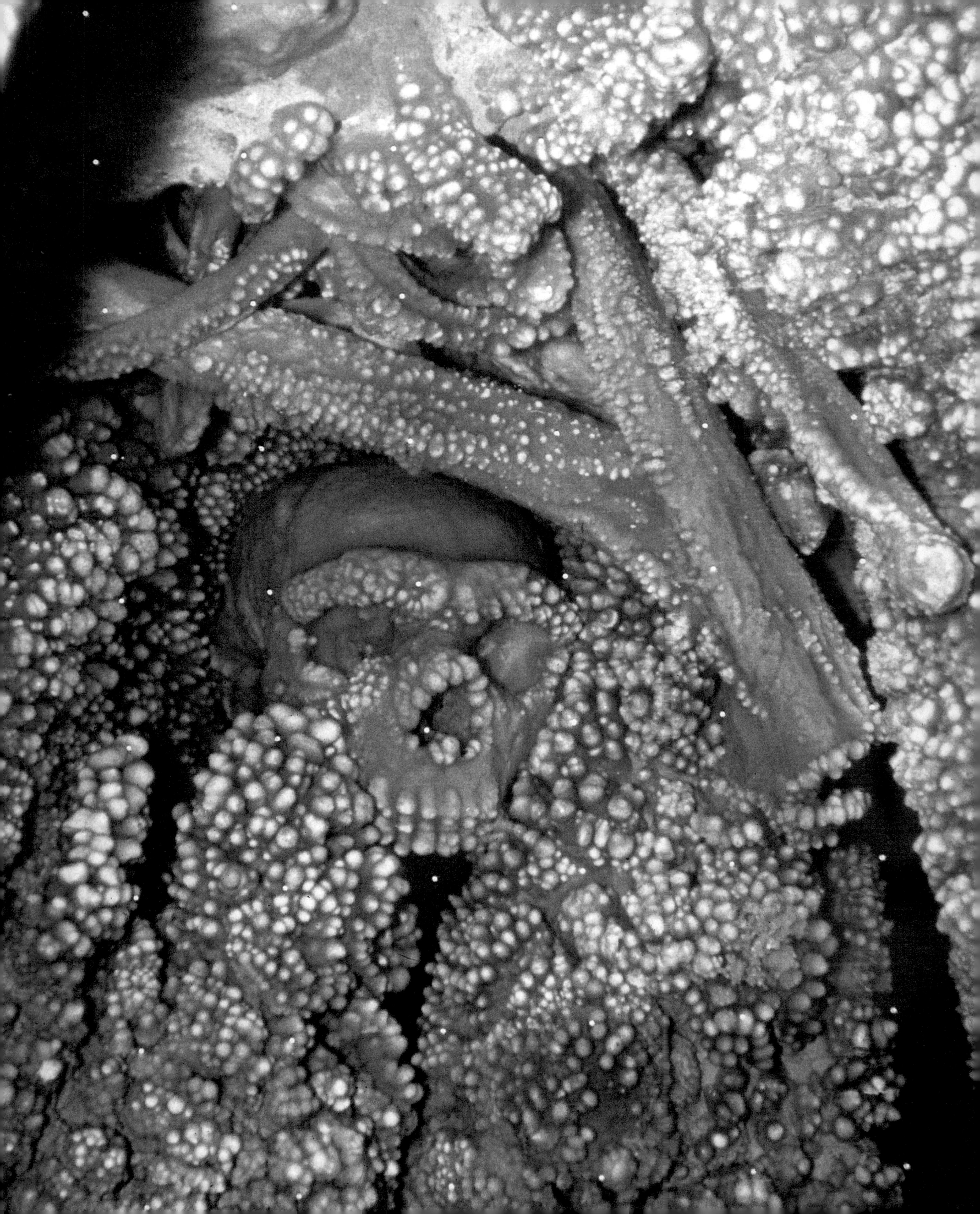

in East Africa were found as an adjunct to geological exploration of the Great Rift Valley, where the vagaries of volcanism, uplift, and erosion have created an ideal setting for the preservation, and later the exposure, of vertebrate fossils. An example is the site of Hadar, Ethiopia, where the partial skeleton of Lucy was found in 1974. In the late 1960s the French geologist Maurice Taieb, while mapping the geology of the little-known Afar depression, recognized abundant vertebrate fossils and stone tools eroding from ancient strata. He brought these to the attention of paleoanthropologists, and there began an important series of ongoing expeditions to the region. ◖ Sites in Europe have often been discovered by amateur archeologists, who systematically search caves, rock overhangs, and fields where plowing brings up artifacts or fossils. In the absence of surface occurrences of artifacts or fossils, it is virtually impossible to predict where excavation might prove fruitful. ◖ Mining operations resulted in the recovery of the first Neandertal in Germany, in 1856, the first *Australopithecus* at Taung, South Africa, in 1924, and the Mauer mandible in gravel pits near Heidelberg, Germany, in 1907. The famous Cro-Magnon fossils in southwestern France were found during construction of a railroad. Speleologists discovered the remarkably productive cave of Atapuerca in Spain, as well as important caves with Paleolithic art such as those at Chauvet and Cosquer. One of the most spectacular finds by cavers is the 1993 discovery of a still unexcavated, virtually complete Neandertal skeleton at Altamura, Italy. ◖ Today, paleoanthropologists are aided in their search for new sites by space-based imagery. It was fortunate for the Paleoanthropological Inventory of Ethiopia that portions of the Ethiopian rift had been flown over in October 1984 by NASA's space shuttle, the *Challenger*. On board, a large-format camera recorded images on negatives roughly 23 by 46 centimeters that produced high-resolution stereoscopic photographs. The photographs were of great assistance in locating geological structures such as faults, as well as in differentiating certain rock types. They subsequently proved indispensable for research expeditions on the ground, navigating over terra incognita. ◖ Satellite-produced Landsat thematic mapper images further enhance the space-based imagery. Whereas photographs can register only visible and near infrared wavelengths, the satellite images are recorded in digital form and transmitted back to Earth, where computer enhancement can reveal hidden structures in the data. Multispectral scanners record a wide spectrum from blue to short-wavelength infrared. The brightness of one spot, or pixel, on Earth is recorded by a string of numbers. Pixel size has a spatial resolution of some 30 meters, but new images from the European remote sensing satellite *SPOT* has a pixel size of about 10 meters. ◖ Because different rock types have varying reflectance, Landsat images can be used to distinguish between volcanic rocks and sedimentary deposits. Shuttle photographs and Landsat images permitted the Paleoanthropological Inventory of Ethiopia team to predict the possibility of fossiliferous beds in a previously unexplored region of Ethiopian rift. The next step was to survey, on foot, those areas initially outlined using remote sensing. On the ground, rich fossil deposits older than 2 million years were encountered, and Acheulean tools were found in apparent association with vertebrate fossils. Satellite data have also proved useful in pinpointing fossil-bearing sediments at Fejej in southern Ethiopia, where in 1990 4 million-year-old *A. afarensis* specimens were collected. ◖ Now that remote sensing techniques have proved their usefulness in locating important paleoanthropological sites, they will probably be more widely employed. However, the finding of hominid specimens will always rely on the untiring efforts of a dedicated ground survey team.

Skeleton of *Homo neanderthalensis* from Altamura, Italy. In 1993, spelunkers discovered this apparently complete skeleton with the skull partly obscured by a stalagtite. *Courtesy of Bari State University.*

7 · Recovering the Remains of Early Humans

THE PROCESS of recovering fossil hominid remains is inherently destructive. As soon as a fossil is picked up from the ground or excavated from an ancient stratum, the specimen is no longer in its original context, and some information is lost. With awareness of this problem, modern recovery and excavation techniques are far more rigorous than the "treasure hunting" approach of earlier eras. The search for and excavation of hominid remains today incorporates a carefully articulated research design intended to preserve as much information as possible. ◖ Once a fossil-bearing set of deposits has been located, a strategic plan must be implemented to search for fossil hominid remains. Fossils at open-air sites are rare and widely scattered. Accordingly, an intense and thorough foot survey with, at times, crawling on the outcrops is obligatory. The searchers must have good visual acuity and a thorough knowledge of vertebrate anatomy to sort out the hominid fragments from the background scatter of nonhominid fossil bones. A missed hominid fragment may wash away with the next rainstorm or disintegrate with additional weathering. ◖ Once a hominid fragment is recognized, a specific protocol is followed. Photographic and even video recording of the fossil may precede recovery of the specimen. A locality number is assigned and a general description of the locality is recorded in a field notebook. The exact location of the find is also identified by a pinprick on an aerial photograph of the site. ◖ If close examination of the specimen reveals that any breaks in it are fresh, other portions might be nearby. A larger area surrounding the initial find is delimited by a perimeter of string, and team members, on hands and knees, carefully search for additional fragments. If other bits are found, a string grid is established over the area most likely to yield more bone. Each square meter of the grid is intimately examined and all fossil fragments are collected, identified, numbered, and plotted on graph paper using a coordinate system. After this initial collection, the loose sediment is scraped up with a trowel or small shovel, placed in a bucket, carried away from the hominid locality, and sifted through a fine mesh screen. ◖ Stone matrix adhering to a fossil will often reveal the precise geological horizon from which the fossil came, because layers of sand, clay, or silt each have their own characteristic composition. Sometimes a decision will be made to excavate into a hillside in the hope of finding additional bones that have not yet weathered out of their matrix. First the sterile overburden is removed, using everything from a portable jackhammer and picks to loosen the compacted sediments, to small rock hammers and trowels as the fossil horizon is approached. Dental tools, sharpened nails, and other pointed digging tools allow slow, controlled excavation. When bones are encountered, dental picks and soft brushes are used to expose the limits of the fragment. ◖ After the specimen is exposed, it is not immediately removed. A small drawing is made of the specimen and its precise position is measured using metal tapes and plotted on graph paper. The compass orientation is noted and even the dip, or angulation, of the bone, which can be used to help establish the direction of water flow, for example. Because the horizons from which specimens are excavated are uneven, the depth of a specimen is recorded using a plumb bob or a surveyor's transit and stadia rod. For a datum point, a metal stake is driven into the ground. This serves as a reference point for horizontal and vertical measurements and may allow reconstruction of the spatial relationships of the find in a three-dimensional computer program. ◖ While the specimen is still in the ground, it may be treated with a preservative like Butvar, an acetone-soluble polyvinyl acetate, to prevent any further fragmentation. After the preservative is dry the specimen is lifted, labeled, put into a plastic bag, and carefully transported back to the field laboratory. ◖ Every care is taken in the field to chronicle in notebooks as much information as possible. All stages of

The cave of Swartkrans, South Africa. Most South African hominid fossils, encased in concrete-like breccia, have been blasted or dug from limestone caves. Swartkrans yielded the largest known collection of *Australopithecus robustus* fossils. *Photograph by David Brill.*

excavation must be written up immediately and in detail, including measurements, stratigraphic information, the names of the excavators, the date and time of the discovery, and so on. Because excavation is destructive, the field notebooks become the new record for the original locality. The information contained in the notebooks is invaluable for writing up scientific articles and becomes a reference for future investigators. ❡ Some countries, anticipating future innovations in paleontological excavation and recording techniques, limit the extent of work at any given site. For example, in Israel only one third of any site may be excavated, with the remainder reserved for other expeditions. Preservation of portions of a site also plays a crucial role when the rethinking of a scientific problem can only be solved by renewed excavation at a specific site and a reformulation of the research strategy.

8 · Dating Fossils and Artifacts

WITHOUT a way to estimate the antiquity of paleontological and archeological discoveries, it is impossible to construct a chronology for the events in human evolution. Fortunately, several techniques are available, and usually at least one of them can be used at a particular site by geologists or geochronologists. ❡ Two broad categories of techniques exist: relative and absolute dating. Relative methods indicate whether a given fossil, artifact, or site is younger or older than another one but cannot pinpoint an age in years. For instance, by the nineteenth-century geological principle of superposition, rock or sediment layers closer to the top of a vertical sequence should be younger than the underlying layers if the layers have not been disturbed. A common technique of relative dating, used to compare the ages of distant fossil sites, is biostratigraphy, which relies on the fossil remains of widespread animals that change distinctly during their evolutionary history. Rodents, elephants, antelopes, and pigs have proved particularly useful as biological markers of time in Africa or the Near East. Biostratigraphy has helped establish a chronology for the fossil-rich limestone caves in South Africa, such as Swartkrans and Sterkfontein, which lack volcanic or radiogenic rock material suitable for absolute dating methods. Biostratigraphy also provides a system of checks-and-balances for evaluating age as determined by the more technical absolute methods. For instance, it was analysis of pig teeth that revealed an error in the potassium-argon age estimate for the KBS Tuff at Koobi Fora in Kenya and forced a revision by more than a half million years of the age for such hominid fossils as KNM-ER 1470 (see page 177). ❡ Absolute dating methods are a more powerful and precise tool for pinpointing evolutionary events. Many of the methods are radiometric: they rely on the constant rate of decay of certain radioactive isotopes—varieties of a chemical element—in rocks to act as a clock that reveals a specific age in years. These methods tend to be quite new, and even the earliest absolute techniques have had important refinements in the last decade or so. ❡ Perhaps the most famous absolute dating technique is the radiocarbon method, which was developed in the 1940s and first applied to date a piece of acacia wood collected from the oldest Egyptian pyramid, the step pyramid of Saqqara. Radiocarbon dating can be applied directly to bone or other organic matter. An age can be determined by measuring the amount of carbon-12 (the stable, predominant form of natural carbon) in an object and deducing how much carbon-14 (the rare, radioactive isotope) had been present when the object was living. Because carbon-14 decays into nitrogen at a known rate after death, it is possible to determine, after measuring the current amount of this isotope, an age for the object. The wood from Saqqara indicated that this first Egyptian pyramid was built 4,600 years ago. ❡ The radiocarbon method only works for relatively young organic objects because the half-life of carbon-14 is 5,730 years (meaning that half of the carbon atoms in a sample will have disintegrated after the passage of this amount of time). Because a given sample of carbon-14 is reduced in size by half every 5,730 years, radiocarbon effectively runs out of time after 40,000 years. A newer approach, called accelerator mass spectrometry (AMS) radiocarbon dating, has the promise of extending the technique's viability further into the past, perhaps as far as 75,000 years ago. Because the AMS method can be applied to much smaller samples—a speck rather than a gram—than conventional radiocarbon decay methods, the new technique has been able to date directly for the first time such important archeological discoveries as European Upper Paleolithic paintings in some of the decorated caves. ❡ For more ancient sites, geochronologists have turned to elements with much longer half-lives. Potassium is an abundant element in Earth's crust, and about 0.01 percent of all potassium is the radioactive isotope potassium-40, which has a half-life of 1.3 billion years. Potassium-40 decays naturally into argon-40. The more argon-40 a rock contains, the longer the rock clock has been ticking: the more argon that is present, the older the rock. By measuring the amount of potassium present and the amount that has already decayed into argon, an age for the rock can be determined. ❡ Developed in the 1950s, the potassium-argon method was soon put to work dating the volcanic ash and tuffs that bracketed fossils or artifacts in Olduvai Gorge's layers of rock. Its application at Olduvai Gorge and later at many East African hominid sites revolutionized our concept of the span of human evolution. Since the 1980s the technique has itself been revolutionized through the use of lasers to melt individual rock crystals for dating, rather than relying on a larger sample that might be contaminated by older or younger crystals that would give a false date. Also, a single sample can be used to measure both the argon and potassium content, whereas the conventional potassium-argon technique required two separate samples. The new method, called single-crystal laser-fusion argon-argon dating, measures the ratio of argon-40 to argon-39, an artificial isotope created in a nuclear reactor from stable potassium-39 and which serves as a proxy to indicate the amount of potassium. This technique can also be carefully controlled to get a series of ages from the outside to the core of the rock sample. Recently, the argon-argon method was used to fine-tune the age of Lucy and the First Family fossils from Hadar to 3.2 million years. ¶ Several dating methods have been developed to cover the broad span of time that is either too old for the radiocarbon method or too young for potassium-argon to handle – that is, the period between about 300,000 and 40,000 years ago. Three of these methods – electron spin resonance (ESR), thermoluminescence (TL), and optically stimulated luminescence (OSL) – work by counting electrons trapped by flaws in the microscopic structure of crystals. ¶ Electrons accumulate over time as radiation released by radioactive elements in the rock and in surrounding sediment continues to punch holes into the crystal lattice. The electrons can be freed as light, in the case of TL and OSL, and the amount of escaping light can be carefully measured to estimate the time elapsed since a stone tool, for instance, was last heated by a campfire or exposed to the sun before burial. Rather than expel electrons from a rock, ESR excites them with a cascade of microwaves in a magnetic field. In response, the electrons flip their direction, or spin, through a process called resonance. The energy of resonance gives off a spectral signal – related to the number of trapped electrons – the magnitude of which can be measured and used to calculate an estimate of the sample's age. A sample can be tested repeatedly by ESR but only once with TL or OSL. ¶ Neither TL nor OSL can be used to date bone directly, but they work well on burned flint tools, ceramics, or sediments. ESR works on a range of natural material including tooth enamel, coral, and mollusk shells. Both TL and ESR have shed much light on the origins of modern humans, especially at cave sites in the Levant, where Neandertals and early modern humans overlapped in time for 50,000 years. OSL has been used at archeological sites in Australia, where the results indicate that modern humans may have first arrived on that island continent as long as 60,000 years ago (see page 52). ¶ Still other dating methods have helped shed light on questions in human evolution. These methods include paleomagnetism, fission-track, uranium series, and amino acid racemization. So, paleoanthropologists have many tools at their disposal to estimate the age of their finds. No dating method comes without constraints or potential pitfalls, however, and great care must be taken in selecting appropriate samples in the field and preparing them in the laboratory. Ideally, as many methods as possible should be tried independently to provide a confident date for a fossil, artifact, or site.

Dating volcanic ash from Hadar, Ethiopia. Geologist Bob Walter collects a sample of from the BKT-1 tuff at Hadar for dating in a Berkeley laboratory. The single crystal laser-fusion argon-argon dating method relies on a laser to melt individual rock crystals containing a radioactive isotope that decays at a known rate and calibrates the rock's age. *Photographs by Enrico Ferorelli.*

9 · Climate and Human Evolution

LOCAL and even regional environmental and climatic changes apply pressures or open opportunities for flora and fauna alike. Species unable to adapt to the new conditions will perish. Much attention has focused in recent years on the role of global-scale climatic events in shaping evolutionary history. Attempts have been made to link specific environmental changes to several biological and cultural milestones in our evolutionary history. How close a fit do we find between climate change through time and the various speciations and extinctions traced by our fossil record? ¶ First, let's examine the evidence for climate change in Africa during the span of hominid evolution. The evidence comes from both land and sea: carbon isotopes in tooth enamel that document prevailing plant cover and soil, and dust from deep-sea drilling cores. Most plants, including trees, shrubs, and certain grasses, convert carbon into compounds with three-carbon chains in their chemical structure (and so are called C3 plants). Plants in dryer, more seasonal environments, especially temperate and tropical grasses (called C4 plants), build four-carbon chain compounds by an alternative process. Because C3 and C4 plants contain different proportions of stable carbon isotopes, the ratio of these isotopes can be studied to determine whether C3 or C4 plants – that is, whether woodland or grassland – predominated at times in the past. The same carbon isotope ratios show up in the tooth enamel of animals that have ingested and digested this vegetation. ¶ The enamel evidence suggests that between 6 and 8 million years ago in Africa, ocean surface temperatures dropped and a shift occurred from previously dominant C3 plants to dry-adapted C4 plants, the sort found in the savannas that cover nearly two thirds of Africa's land today. Although C4 plants began appearing in East Africa as long as 15 million years ago and occurred in patchy distribution mixed with woodland trees and shrubs, savanna grasses dominate the East African landscape as of 7 million years ago – about the time that the first hominid split off from its last common ancestor with African apes.

◖ Wind-blown dust from the African continent settles on the sea floor, where it gradually collects as an uninterrupted record of climate for the past several million years. Thicker dust layers form, for example, during particularly dry periods with strong winds. Seafloor dust accumulations indicate that after 2.8 million years ago, the ice sheets in the northern latitudes expanded vastly, causing a severe drying and cooling in Africa that favored arid-adapted plants and animals. The sediments from this time contain greater amounts of phytoliths, or bits of silica from grass. Similar cool, dry periods recurred 1.7 and 1 million years ago. ◖ According to the turnover pulse hypothesis proposed by paleontologist Elisabeth Vrba, the climate changes triggered new directions in evolution. Fossils of both large and small mammals—bovid antelopes and rodents—show that these habitat-specific animals had a turnover of extinctions and speciations 2.5 million years ago in which the arid-adapted kinds survived in both southern and eastern Africa. Hominids, Vrba believes, responded in the same way to the swings in vegetation and, presumably, in rainfall and temperature. ◖ Sometime between 3 and 2.5 million years ago the hominid lineage split into two branches: one with the first member of genus *Homo* and a second with the first robust australopithecines. What is possibly the earliest fossil of *Homo*, a maxilla from Hadar, Ethiopia, was recently dated to 2.5 million years ago, about the time of the global cooling and drying. And the most ancient stone tools occur at this same time (see page 168). The coincidence is certainly provocative, but *Homo* may well have evolved closer to 3.0 million years ago, before the drop in temperature. ◖ A potential problem also arises with linking the emergence of robust australopithecines to this climate change. Antelopes switched from being woodland browsers to being grassland grazers at 2.5 million years ago, but the Black Skull, KNM-WT 17000 (see page 152), indicates that a primitive robust australopithecine had already evolved by 2.6 million years ago. ◖ Another cautionary tale comes from Konso-Gardula, Ethiopia, where the oldest known Acheulean artifacts, dated to 1.4 million years, have been found, along with a hominid mandible. This earliest evidence for a profound change in human technology falls in between the global cooling of 2.5 million years ago and the subsequent cooling that began a million years ago. By the time of the more recent cooling, which has been credited with spurring the migration of *Homo erectus* out of Africa, *H. erectus* had already been in Asia for almost 800,000 years. If the recently reported dates from Java (see page 46) are correct, *H. erectus* made huge leaps in its geographic range long before the alleged climatic catalyst. ◖ Establishing links between past climate change and evolutionary change depends on being able to pinpoint the first and last appearances of species in the fossil record, because these data theoretically should indicate, respectively, speciation and extinction events. But to determine these events reliably requires a thorough sampling of the fossil record across time, across different habitats, and across the range of a species. Then there is the challenge of accounting for the natural rarity of some species (and hominids were likely to have been relatively rare animals) as well as the problem of recognizing different species from fossil evidence. ◖ Even if these obstacles of sampling and interpreting fossils can be surmounted, it still is not easy to make the connection to climate change. Paleoclimatic studies of sediments in the Tugen Hills near Lake Baringo, Kenya, point out some of the difficulty in linking climatic and evolutionary events over a broad span of time and from global to local scales of space. This region spans the time from about 13 to 2 million years ago, and a few hominid fossils have been found there. By spanning such a broad time period, the Tugen sequence should reveal the local impact of major climatic events. Carbon isotope analysis of the soils showed that the mix of forest and grasses has changed little during the past 15 million years. It has always been a mosaic of habitats: savannas did not abruptly replace rain forests, and the cooling event 2.5 million years ago left no abrupt change in vegetation. In the Tugen Hills, at least, major climatic events apparently had little influence on plant cover or, presumbably, on changes in animal populations. ◖ Alhough a broad-scale correlation exists between climate changes and changes in hominid species, there is no way to show that one triggered or drove the other. We are gaining a fine-grained understanding of the early climate, but the picture provided by scarce and fragmented human fossils remains too coarse-grained to allow definite connections to be drawn between the two lines of evidence. We should also remember that hominids seem to have been good ecological generalists, able to tolerate a wide range of environments, and as such they may have been less sensitive to climate change than habitat specialists.

10 · Teeth

BECAUSE teeth are capped by enamel, the most durable biological substance known, and because they possess a core made of a very hard mineralized tissue called dentine, they constitute the majority of fossil hominid specimens. Teeth are extremely informative about the age, sex, diet, health, and taxonomic identity of extinct hominids, and we are fortunate to find them so plentiful in the fossil record. The informative power of teeth is the reason why paleoanthropologists are often well versed in dental anatomy and spend considerable time describing and analyzing remains of fossil dentitions. ◖ Hominids, like all Old World monkeys and apes, possess thirty-two adult teeth: sixteen upper and sixteen lower teeth. In each jaw there are two central and two lateral incisors, two canines, four premolars, and six molars. Each tooth type has its own function: incisors are for slicing, canines for grasping or piercing, and the cheek teeth, premolars, and molars for crushing and grinding. Our baby teeth, sometimes called the milk or deciduous dentition, number ten and consist of two central and two lateral incisors, two canines, and four molars in both the upper and lower jaws. Each hominid tooth has its own distinctive crown anatomy, permitting identification of its exact position in the dental arcade. It is relatively easy to tell right from left and upper from lower. Upper molars, for instance, have four cusps, while lower molars generally have five cusps. Detailed knowledge of dental anatomy also permits specific identification of the tooth's position—for example, first or second premolar. Each bump (cusp), groove, or crest has its own specific name, which permits detailed description of each tooth and facilitates easy comparisons between samples. The root number and structure also help identify teeth: upper molars have three roots and lower molars only two. ◖ Among mammals, teeth are so diagnostic of each species that often the taxonomic identity can be determined from a single tooth, usually a molar. For example, in 1935 the German paleontologist Ralph von Koenigswald purchased fossil mammalian teeth in a Chinese apothecary shop, where they were being sold as "dragon teeth" to be used for medicinal purposes. One tooth, an enormous lower third molar, caught his eye. It had a diagnostic groove pattern, common to all hominids and apes, called the *Dryopithecus* pattern. On the basis of this single specimen von Koenigswald erected a new genus, *Gigantopithecus* (giant ape), which remains the largest known primate ever to have lived. ◖ In virtually every diagnosis of a new species of fossil hominid, teeth play a vital role. This is not solely because teeth constitute the bulk of the fossil samples but because in each species there is a diagnostic set of anatomical features in the dentition. For example, each species of *Australopithecus* (see page 117-121) is distinguished by a unique constellation of dental traits. ◖ Insight into the diet of early

Teeth and jaws of *Australopithecus afarensis* from Hadar, Ethiopia. Dense and durable, teeth and jaws constitute the majority of the human fossil record and provide a range of vital information about an organism's identity and life history. Actual size. *Photograph by John Reader, Science Source/Photo Researchers.*

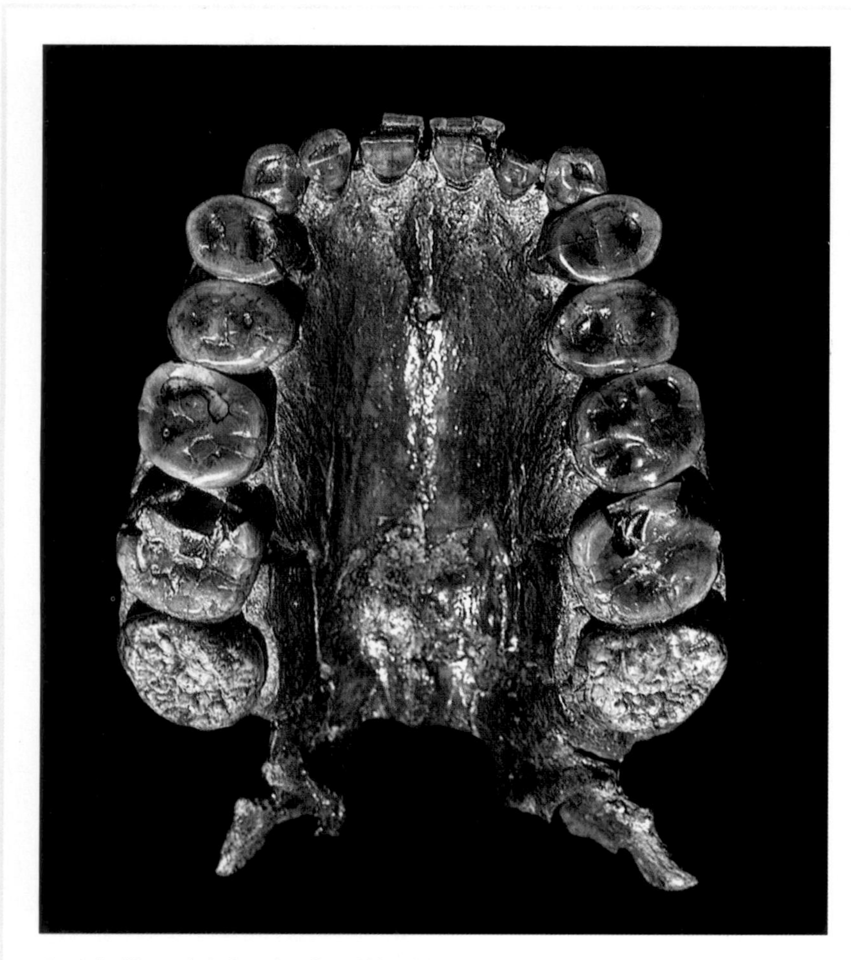

***Australopithecus boisei* cranium from Olduvai Gorge, Tanzania.** The massive molars that characterize this species can be seen in this occlusal view of OH 5. Actual size. *Courtesy of Donald Johanson, Institute of Human Origins.*

hominids can be gleaned from studies of the shape of the cusps, the relative sizes of the teeth, the enamel thickness, and dental wear, including microwear. Thick dental enamel, such as that found in hominids, serves to extend the life of a tooth. This probably reflects an adaptation to a heavily masticated diet before the cooking of food became common. Robust australopithecines, which are thought to have subsisted on a diet of tough, low-quality food, had the thickest enamel of any primate. ◖ Within any species of hominid there is considerable overlap in the size of male and female teeth, but sometimes differences in canine size make it possible to assign a particular specimen to one sex or the other (see page 73). The approximate age at death of a hominid specimen can be determined by the state of dental eruption as well as by the degree of wear on the teeth. In Lucy's mandible, for example, the third molar, the wisdom tooth, is erupted and just beginning to show wear, leading to the conclusion that Lucy was fully adult when she died. ◖ Sometimes the health of an individual can be judged from the condition of the teeth. For instance, disease or poor nutrition can promote an interruption in dental development that is manifested as pits or grooves on the enamel surface, a condition know as hypoplasia. Where teeth have been broken, exposing the root canal, an abscess can develop, which is seen in resorption of the bone around the roots of the tooth. Because of the lack of refined sugar in the prehistoric diet, dental caries are rare but not unknown in early hominids (see page 242). ◖ Microscopic study of the dental enamel adds substantially to what we can learn from the gross anatomy of the crowns. Dental enamel is composed of prisms of apatite crystals that are formed in an incremental manner. By looking at two different types of incremental markings, usually with a scanning electron microscope, it is possible to estimate the period of crown formation for individual teeth. Recent studies of hominid dental development suggest that australopithecines probably matured more quickly than modern humans, retaining a more apelike pattern of maturation (see page 80). ◖ Teeth were obviously important to the survival of our ancestors, being, to a large degree, the sole source of food preparation. For paleoanthropologists teeth are also crucially important, and odontology—the study of teeth—is sure to provide further insights into various aspects of the biology and behavior of our ancestors.

11 · Proteins, DNA, and Human Evolution

FOR MOST of the history of paleoanthropology, fossils and artifacts provided the only clues to the course of human evolution. Although these remain the most tangible and evocative sources of evidence, since the early 1960s significant contributions to the field have come from the analysis of proteins and genes in humans and other living primates. During the past three decades, data from the growing science of molecular evolution have in fact revolutionized our understanding of hominid evolution. ◖ Because all life shares an underlying biochemical foundation of DNA, studies of genetic molecules and the proteins they design permit comparison between very distantly related organisms in a quantifiable way. Before the molecular techniques were developed, estimates for the date when African apes and humans split from a common ancestor ranged from 4 to 30 million years ago, with most fossil experts choosing a date somewhere in the middle. But the biochemists came to a very different conclusion, namely, that African apes and humans had diverged much more recently, perhaps only 5 million years ago. ◖ That meant that *Ramapithecus*, the purported hominid whose taxonomic status had to be revised in the wake of molecular evidence, was far too old to qualify as a hominid, but paleontologists were loathe to exclude this and other ancient fossils from the hominid family tree. Over time, and after much contentious debate, paleoanthropology has accepted this more condensed molecular time scale for human evolution. The cumulative evidence could not be ignored. Two techniques were primarily responsible for enhancing our understanding of the molecular relationships among primates: immunological reaction to blood proteins and DNA-DNA hybridization. (See page 41 for a discussion of how studies of mitochondrial DNA have contributed more recently to human origins research.) ◖ Proteins evolve over time and thus have ancestral forms, much as fossils reveal an ancestral or primitive anatomy. Because they are manufactured directly from a genetic blueprint, proteins have a structure that closely reflects the genetic makeup of an organism, so they can provide a good measure of genetic relatedness between different species. These two characteristics—that proteins evolve and have a structure that is genetically determined—form the basis of the immunological technique developed by biologist Morris Goodman in the late 1950s and early 1960s. ◖ The technique measures the magnitude of immunological cross-reaction as an indirect means of determining the degree of similarity between the proteins of two species. For example, a human blood protein, such as albumin, is injected into a rabbit, which will produce antibodies against any parts of the molecule that differ from its own albumin. The rabbit's anti-human albumin serum, rich with antibodies, can then be extracted and placed in test tubes. Albumins from a range of primates are added to the serum samples in the test tubes to measure the extent of immune reaction, visible as a precipitate that forms in the solution. The stronger the reaction, the more closely related are the human and the other species being tested. ◖ In 1962, Goodman announced that according to immunological data, humans, chimpanzees, and gorillas were equally related to one another. This countered the previously accepted belief that chimps and gorillas were each other's closest relative and that they had a common ancestor long after the first hominid split off from an ape evolutionary lineage. Few listened to Goodman at the time. ◖ But in that same year, biochemists Linus Pauling and Emile Zuckerkandl proposed that proteins evolved at a steady, determinable rate and thus had the constancy of a clock. The amount of genetic divergence must then be proportional to time, and so, knowing the amount of difference between molecules in two species and the rate of evolution in the molecule, one should be able to determine when the two species shared a common ancestor. Differences between the amino acid sequences in the same protein of two different creatures constitute the ticks in the molecular clock. The most accurate physical clock, however, is radioactive decay, so molecular divergence dates need to be calibrated based on radiometrically dated fossil or geological evidence. A common calibration point used in molecular studies of human evolution is the split between Old World monkeys and hominoids (humans, apes, and their ancestors), which, based on fossil evidence, is generally accepted as having occurred around 30 million years ago. ◖ In 1967, Goodman's technique was carried further by biochemists Vincent Sarich and Allan Wilson using the blood serum protein albumin. Their work confirmed Goodman's conclusion that humans, chimps, and gorillas were each other's closest living relatives. They found a stronger reaction between both human and chimp albumins and between human and gorilla albumins than between human and orangutan albumins. So the African apes were closer relatives to humans than the red Asian ape. Even more distantly related were the Asian lesser apes, the gibbon and siamang. ◖ Then Sarich and Wilson added the dimension of time. Because they had previously demonstrated that albumin evolution in primates occurs at a steady rate, Sarich and Wilson suggested that the human and ape lineages had evolved at equal rates since their divergence and that albumin molecules could serve as a clock that had continued ticking along each lineage since that divergence. By establishing a relationship between immunological distance and time, they reached the conclusion that the human and African ape lineages diverged only 5 million years ago. ◖ The immunological technique has since been used with a host of proteins, including transferrin, hemoglobin, and cytochrome c. One drawback to this technique is that only a small amount of genetically coded information gets analyzed. Another molecular technique developed in the early 1960s, DNA-DNA hybridization, offered the promise of establishing evolutionary relationships using most of the genetic information contained within chromosomes. Like the immunological technique, this is an indirect method of ascertaining two species' similarity. ◖ In the DNA-DNA hybridization technique, DNA molecules, which consist of double strands wound into a helical shape, from two different species are boiled until the strands separate. Then the solution containing the separate strands is cooled, allowing the strands to anneal, often forming a hybrid of one strand from each species. A certain number of complementary bases from each strand will recognize each other and bond together. The more closely related the two species are, the more bases on their respective DNA strands will bond after the strands collide, and the more cohesive the resulting hybrid helix will be. The melting point-the temperature at which hybrid DNA separates again upon being reheated-is the quantitative measure of similarity: the lower the melting point, the less related are the two species under study. ◖ This technique was pioneered by Charles Sibley and Jon Ahlquist, who established the evolutionary relationships among birds before turning their attention to primates. Once they did, they found that DNA seems to be evolving at the same rate in all hominoids, so the average rate of evolution can be assumed to be steady along any two diverging lineages. Sibley and Ahlquist found a closer link between chimps and humans than either has with gorillas. This conclusion has been borne out more recently by other molecular studies (see page 32). As for specific dates, Sibley and Ahlquist put the chimp-human split at between 6.3 and 7.7 million years ago, while the common ancestor with gorillas lived 8 to 10 million years ago. ◖ Alhough these and other molecular techniques, and their revisionist conclusions, have become broadly accepted by anthropologists, elements of them remain controversial. The idea of a molecular clock, for instance, may hold for certain molecules, but there is no single, universal molecular clock, as evidence suggests that proteins and molecules evolve at varying rates. If such obstacles can be overcome, the study of molecular evolution should continue to provide a vital counterpoint to the hard evidence obtained from fossils.

12 · Why is Paleoanthropology So Contentious?

PALEOANTHROPOLOGY faces contentions from within and without. Often these arguments provide an opportunity to reexamine the evidence, shore up an argument, or educate the public in the issues that drive the field. Some debates originate in discoverers' egos, and their ramifications may be of interest only to the professional anthropologist. But the larger questions taken up in this book – where we come from, our relationship to the apes, how we should conduct ourselves in the future – touch hot nerves in American public life. The discussion of these issues has sent shock waves through our religious and educational institutions, and sometimes has to be resolved with the aid of our judicial system. ◖ The realization that humans, along with all other organisms on Earth, arrived here through a haphazard process that was guided by the natural selection of random variations ran counter to the belief that supernatural intervention guided human affairs. Darwin's exploration of biological rather than divine mechanisms as shaping human life, in exactly the same way those mechanisms shaped the lives of other creatures, struck a dissonant chord in many. Evolutionary theory was regarded as distasteful at best, sacrilege at worst. Most unsettling was the prospect that human existence was not inherently progressive and deliberate but the result of random forces – which would continue to operate through us, and on our progeny. ◖ Even today, with a vast storehouse of fossil evidence for human evolution, there are still dedicated scientists and lay people who continue to embrace a creationist view of our origins. But evolution is a fact. Evolutionary theory seeks to understand and describe the biological and environmental mechanisms that drive evolution. Evolutionary theory passes the test of scientific hypothesis; creationism does not and is not a science. It is a cultural orientation. As anthropologist Ashley Montagu once wrote, tongue in cheek, "Science has evidence without certainty, creationism has certainty with evidence." ◖ Controversy within the science of paleoanthropology is rampant and has always been, ever since the first remains of fossilized humans came to light in the mid-nineteenth century. There are some concrete explanations for why human evolutionary studies have been plagued by debate and controversy. The reasons for argument over a fragment of a jaw, a partial skull, a handful of teeth, or an uncertain geological date are not that difficult to understand. Often a scrappy fossil generates diverse interpretations of how it fits into the bigger picture of human evolution. Sometimes it is impossible to be certain about the actual significance of a fossil find, and it is better to postpone judgment until more complete specimens are recovered. ◖ Other reasons relate to the personalities in the discipline. The search for hominid fossils has attracted many strong-willed investigators who devote their lives to discovery and interpretation. It takes tremendous dedication to obtain funding and permits for exploration and to do fieldwork in remote areas without amenities. Even years of exploration do not guarantee discovery of significant fossils. The stakes are high. Hominid fossils are glamorous and bring scientific and popular success to those who find them, more so, say, than rodent fossils. The fossils themselves become revered and coveted. In some instances, unfortunately, access to fossils has been hindered because of a sense of proprietorship or differences of opinion between scientists. ¶ No scientist in any endeavor can say that he or she is entirely free of certain beliefs and preconceptions. We all carry with us opinions that play an important role in how we formulate our interpretations of the fossil evidence. The appearance of discordant evidence is sometimes met with a sturdy reiteration of our original views. The discovery of a new fossil has the potential to alter our picture of human evolution, but it takes time for us to give up pet theories and assimilate the new information. In the meantime, scientific credibility and funding for more fieldwork hang in the balance. ¶ The science of paleoanthropology is still young. However, a number of investigators are attempting to move the field onto a new plane by developing robust strategies for understanding what the fossils can tell us about our origins. The next step is to encourage cooperation, discussion, and the sharing of fossil discoveries with all colleagues. Paleoanthropologists who work together, freely engaging in discussion and debate, will reap the biggest rewards. ¶ Fossils are deeply fascinating. They speak from a remote past, and there is magic in them. The time has come to work collegially toward teasing out of each find information that will enhance our knowledge of our beginnings. Only in this way can we fully appreciate what messages were left behind by our ancestors eons ago. That is the real magic.

13 · Our Closest Living Relatives

THOMAS HENRY HUXLEY first attempted to explain the relationship between humans and African apes from an evolutionary perspective in his 1871 book, *Man's Place in Nature*. Everything we have learned since then has only affirmed and elaborated on Huxley's intuition. Huxley conjectured that we did not descend from living apes, but rather that both humans and apes descended from some distant common ancestor. Unfortunately, when he made his arguments, Huxley had only a pair of Neandertal skulls to turn to for fossil evidence. We continue to dig deeper into the human fossil record, but the African ape fossil record remains almost nonexistent, probably because of the poor prospects for fossilization in the sorts of forest environment that apes have always favored. ¶ Nonetheless, African apes, we now know, are our closest living relatives, with whom we most likely shared a common ancestor within the last 6 to 8 million years. Without all the fossils to firmly establish this kinship, scientists have turned to behavioral observation (see page 83), comparative anatomy, and genetic studies. Despite the odd juxtaposition of significant anatomical differences and insignificant genetic differences between African apes and humans, both anatomy and genetics point toward the same result for our closest living nonhuman kin. ¶ Humans clearly depart from apes in several significant areas of anatomy. Many of our anatomical differences stem from our adaptation to bipedal locomotion. Because we walk on two legs, our vertebral column is more curved than an ape's, with the skull more centered at the top of the column. At the opposite end, our pelvis has become squatter and broader, with the ilia (the large bones that form the bowl shape of our pelvis) curving forward to support the upper body. The hip and knee joints, the bony heel, and the foot, in which our big toe no longer splays sideways but follows in line with the other toes, further reveal our anatomical departure from the apes. ¶ More differences come to light when we compare ape and human limb lengths and proportions. As might be expected for a biped, we humans carry much of our body weight in the lower limbs, which are longer than our upper limbs. The arms make up some 7 to 9 percent of our body weight, but the legs comprise 32 to 38 percent. In African apes the upper and lower limbs (or forelimbs and hind limbs) are much more similar to each other in this regard. In bonobos, for instance, the upper limbs account for 14 to 17 percent of the total body weight and the lower limbs account for 20 to 28 percent. In gorillas, the upper limbs account for 14 to 16 percent of body weight and the lower limbs for about 18 percent. The evenly balanced proportions of a gorilla's upper and lower limbs reflect this ape's adaptation to knuckle-walking on all fours, while chimps and bonobos will more readily take to two legs for short distances. If we look only at relative body size and limb proportions, it appears that chimpanzees resemble humans more closely than gorillas do. ¶ An astonishingly close genetic similarity exists between African apes and humans. Chimpanzees and bonobos share 99.3 percent of their total nuclear DNA, so these are obviously extremely close relatives. But chimps and humans still share 98.4 percent of their nuclear DNA. Despite our substantial anatomical and cultural differences from them, we depart from chimpanzees in only 1.6 percent of our genetic makeup. Such a short genetic distance is typically found among sibling species of the same genus, yet chimps and humans have been arbitrarily separated into distinct biological families. Gorilla DNA differs from human DNA by only 2.3 percent. Given such close numerical kinship, it is likely that mutations in regulatory mechanisms that control how genes get expressed underlie our biological divide with the apes. ¶ These genetic differences also reflect the varying amounts of time since each species split off from a common ancestor. Chimpanzees (*Pan troglodytes*) in West and East Africa have existed in separate populations for about 1.5 million years, and bonobos (*Pan paniscus*) split off from other chimps around 2.5 million years ago. Gorillas split off from this ape line much earlier, at least 8 million years ago. Sometime after the gorilla lineage diverged, the common ancestor of all hominids split off from this line to begin the evolutionary journey traced in this book. ¶ Was this common ancestor more like a gorilla or a chimp? Fossil evidence from *Australopithecus afarensis*, *A. anamensis*, and what we know of the even earlier species *Ardipithecus ramidus* suggests that a chimp is the closest modern comparison to this earliest common ancestor. We can speculate that in appearance and behavior, this animal was a black-haired, quadrupedal, large-brained, thin-tooth-enameled, forest-dwelling frugivore. ¶ The bulk of evidence from numerous nuclear and mitochondrial DNA studies now also supports a closer genetic kinship between *Homo* and *Pan* than between either *Pan* and *Gorilla* or *Homo* and *Gorilla*. The rates of genetic change appear quite similar among humans, chimps, and gorillas, and for some time it was thought that these species split off from a common ancestor over such a brief period that genetic studies might fail to resolve a closest related pair. But a recent and comprehensive review of the relevant sets of DNA sequence data concluded that eleven supported *Homo* and *Pan* as the closest related pair, while only two favored the *Pan-Gorilla* pair and one favored the *Homo-Gorilla* pair as closest relatives. In other words, among the apes, our closest kin are chimpanzees.

14 · The Last Common Ancestor of Apes and Humans

THE TERM "missing link" is widely used but greatly misunderstood. In 1871, Charles Darwin in his book *The Descent of Man* suggested that humans and the African apes were descended from a common ancestor. Many have interpreted Darwin's idea of a common ancestor for humans and modern African apes as a species that stood halfway between human and ape, blending the characteristics of each. What Darwin meant was that modern humans and apes could be traced back in time, through a series of separate species that converge at a common ancestor. So, in a sense, the discovery of nearly every fossil hominid is the discovery of another link in the long evolutionary chain from the common ancestor to modern humans today. They were all, each and every one of them, missing links. ◖ Following Darwin, "we must not fall into the error of supposing that the early progenitor of the whole Simian Stock, including man, was identical with, or even closely resembled, any existing ape or monkey. " We must never lose site of the fact that every one of our ancestral species was successful in its own right. It was not some imperfect version of modern humans or apes but a thriving organism with its own specific adaptations. ◖ It is often asked why, if we evolved from apes, are apes still here? This question misses two important points. First, humans did not evolve from any living ape but from one in the past that was more generalized in its anatomy. Second, and following on the first point, contemporary African apes, like humans, have evolved a set of adaptations, such as knuckle-walking, that were not present in the common ancestor. Because the common ancestor was a generalized ape, more ancient hominids will be more apelike in their appearance. ◖ During the 1970s and 1980s it was widely held among paleoanthropologists that the common ancestor for hominids and apes must have lived deep in the Miocene, some 15 to 20 million years ago. This made us very comfortably distant from the African apes which pleased those committed to the view that human distinctiveness has deep geological roots. ◖ This view was the result of a 1932 discovery of a fragmentary jaw with teeth, in the Siwalik Hills of northern India. The discovery was made by G. Edward Lewis, a paleontology graduate student at Yale University, who named the specimen *Ramapithecus*, after the Hindi deity Rama. At the time, Lewis assigned the 7 to 8 million-year-old maxilla to the Hominidae. Most scientists ignored this suggestion, but in the 1960s the idea that *Ramapithecus* was a hominid gained popularity when similarities between it and later hominids were pointed out. In addition to the thick dental anatomy, presumed short face, hominid dental eruption pattern, and small canine, it was the reconstructed parabolic shape of the tooth rows (apes have U-shaped tooth rows) that seemed to clinch its affinities with the hominids. ◖ Even older corroborating evidence came from Fort Ternan in western Kenya, where Louis Leakey found jaw fragments dated to 14 million years ago that appeared virtually identical to the Siwalik maxilla. Some paleoanthropologists were so enthusiastic about these putative early hominids that they speculated *Ramapithecus* was a bipedal tool-making creature that prepared food and whose offspring had an extended juvenile period necessary for prolonged social learning. ◖ Debate raged in the anthropological community until the early 1970s, when the hominid status of *Ramapithecus* came under heavy criticism. The most damaging blow was the realization that, because of a basic error in interpreting anatomy, the upper jaw of *Ramapithecus* had been reconstructed incorrectly. In order to reconstruct the correct shape of the dental arcade it was necessary to have a midline. The Siwalik maxilla lacked a midline, and as other fossils with a midline were recovered from Kenya, their dental arcade appeared more U-shaped – more apelike. ◖ Corroborating evidence for a more U-shaped dental arcade in *Ramapithecus* came when paleontologist Peter Andrews, at The Natural History Museum, in London, and Alan Walker, anthropologist at Penn State University, published a reconstruction of the Kenyan *Ramapithecus* mandible. Other than the thick dental enamel, there was little to link *Ramapithecus* with later hominids. But a particular difficulty arose with using thick enamel as the sole feature suggestive of hominid status: in Pakistan, wherever *Ramapithecus* remains were found, a thick-enameled ape known as *Sivapithecus* ("Siva's ape") also turned up at the same site. Ultimately enough *Sivapithecus* remains were found to validate the notion that what had been called *Ramapithecus* was only a smaller version of *Sivapithecus*, an ape. ◖ The *coup de grâce* came in 1981, when Harvard University anthropologist David Pilbeam described an 8 million-year-old partial cranium and mandible of *Sivapithecus* that had been found in Pakistan. The resemblance of this specimen to a modern orangutan was so striking that some thought it should be placed in the genus of the orangutan, *Pongo*. Ironically, David Pilbeam, along with his mentor, Duke University paleontologist Elwyn Simons, were the two scientists who had proposed and staunchly defended the hominid status of the Siwalik *Ramapithecus* in the 1960s and 1970s. ◖ Further criticism of the alleged hominid status of *Ramapithecus* came from an entirely different quarter – the developing discipline of molecular anthropology. Very simply, it was thought that the more closely related creatures were, the more similarities they would share in their blood proteins. With the aid of such techniques as electrophoresis, which can separate individual protein molecules for identification, it was found that humans and African apes were astonishingly similar, and the Asian apes, just as the fossil evidence suggested, were significantly more dissimilar. In fact, a bold suggestion was made to place humans and the African apes in the same zoological family, the Hominidae. ◖ To some researchers, such closeness in blood proteins implied that the common ancestor for modern humans and the African apes must be much more recent than the date assigned by the *Ramapithecus* evidence. In the late 1960s and early 1970s it was determined that the degree of difference in certain blood proteins between different primates was directly related to the length of time elapsed since they last shared a common ancestor. ◖ Calibrating the molecular clock – a method of determining the timing of evolutionary divergence based on relative rates of mutations (see page 78) – on the basis of the last common ancestor for Old World monkeys and apes, roughly 30 million years ago, led to the astonishing conclusion that humans and African apes shared a common ancestor no earlier than 8 million years ago! So emphatic were the researchers who arrived at these conclusions that one, Vincent Sarich, anthropologist at the University of California, Berkeley, wrote, "one no longer has the option of considering a fossil older than about 8 million years as a hominid ***no matter what it looks like.***" ◖ Recent DNA studies indicate that we share more than 98 percent of our genes with African apes. Although the molecular clock does have some potential shortcomings, such as the assumption of a constant rate of genetic mutation, it appears that the DNA and molecular studies are in agreement that a common ancestor for African apes and humans is much more recent than the *Ramapithecus* episode led scientists to believe. Only the fossil record, however, will be able to tell us what the anatomy of that last common ancestor was, the kind of world it lived in, and what sorts of behavior characterized the species. With bipedalism being the defining characteristic of early hominid evolution, one of the most important controversies this fossil evidence can address is the locomotor mode of the common ancestor of humans and African apes. ◖ All three modern African apes are quadrupedal knuckle-walkers. They share a distinctive mode of locomotion whereby they support their weight on the back side of their middle finger bones or phalanges. Other terrestrial primates, such as monkeys, use the palm surface of their hands for support. Hominids, of course, are bipedal. ◖ There are three competing theories as to the locomotor mode of our common ancestor. The first suggests that the common ancestor was a knuckle-walker and that the African apes retained the feature of knuckle-walking while humans lost it. The second theory postulates that the common ancestor was a generalized arboreal climber. According to this theory, bipedalism evolved in our direct ancestors, while knuckle-walking evolved independently at least twice in gorilla and chimpanzee ancestors. The third theory, which seems most likely, suggests that the common ancestor was an arboreal climber and that subsequent to the split between hominids and the African apes, we became bipeds. In this scenario, however, the apes evolved knuckle-walking as a specialized adaptation to terrestriality before diverging into the three extant species. ◖ The absence of anatomical features commensurate with

Skull of male chimpanzee, *Pan troglodytes*. Anatomical evidence and, more recently, much molecular evidence reveals that the common chimpanzee, is the living species most closely related to ourselves. Actual size. *Photographs by David Brill; courtesy of National Museum of Natural History.*

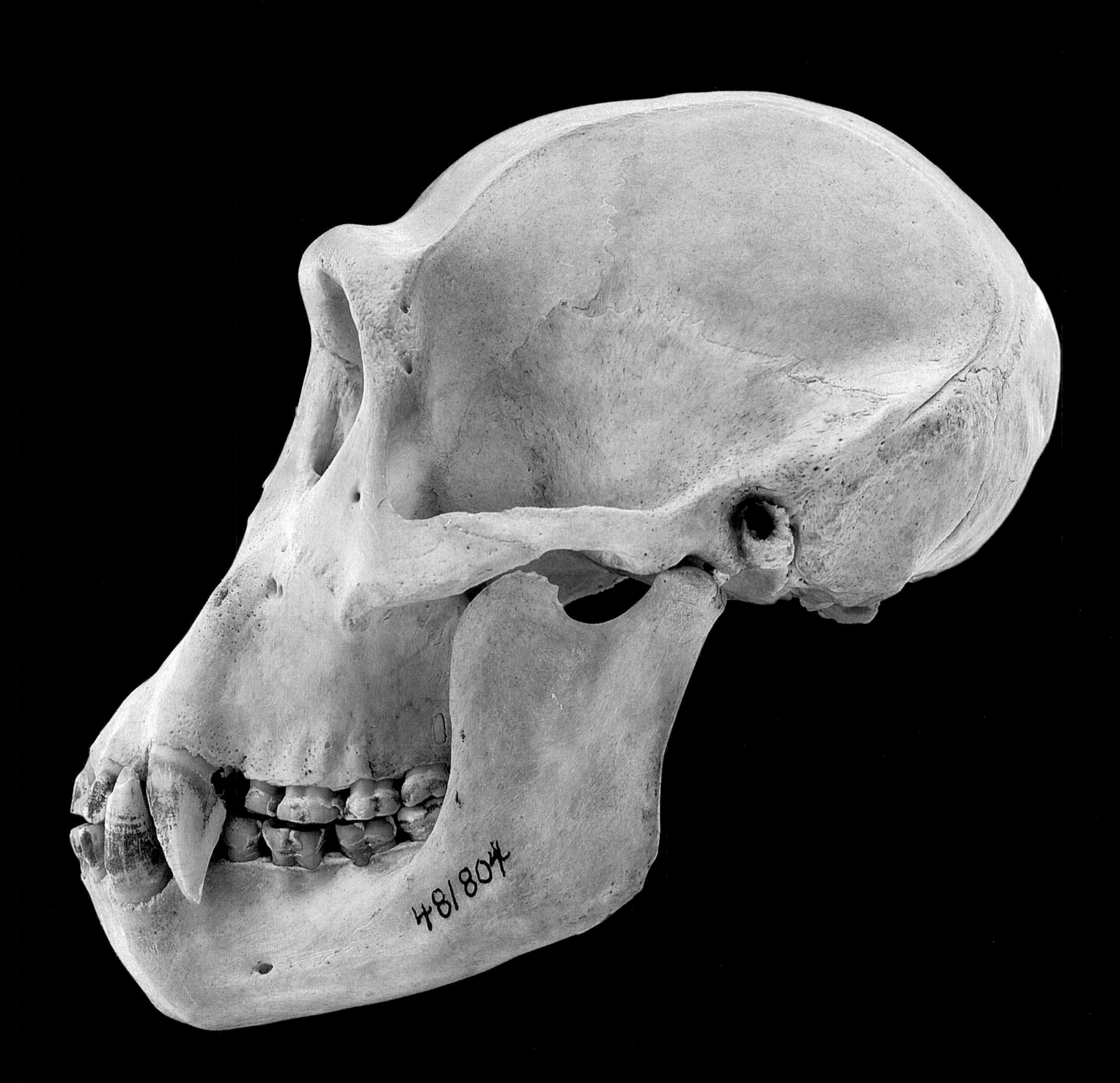
481804

Skull of *Sivapithecus* from Potwar, Pakistan. Once considered to be in direct ancestry to humans, fossils of *Ramapithecus* are now considered the same as those of *Sivapithecus*, a likely ancestor of the orangutan. Actual size. *Photograph by David Brill; courtesy of Peabody Museum of Archaeology and Ethnology, Harvard University.*

knuckle-walking in the best-known early hominid, *Australopithecus afarensis*, appears to rule against the view that this adaptation was in our ancestry. It also seems to make more evolutionary sense to see knuckle-walking as so specialized an adaptation that had our direct ancestors employed such a mode of locomotion, bipedalism might not have arisen. Therefore, alternative number one is rejected. The third alternative is preferred over the second, since knuckle-walking appears to be such a specialized and unique locomotor mode that it is unlikely to have arisen more than once-but we could be wrong. ◖ The fall from grace of *Ramapithecus* as an early hominid serves as an excellent example of a hypothesis which was tested and ultimately discarded after further investigation and the discovery of more complete specimens. Unfortunately, we know so little about hominid and ape evolution during the late Miocene, roughly 5 to 10 million years ago, that it is impossible at this time to identify the last common ancestor.

15 · Drawing the Human Family Tree

THE VARIETY of human family trees now cluttering the literature makes it virtually impossible to identify the correct tree because of the forest. A family tree is supposed to reflect genealogy; that is, trees are constructed by tracing lines of descent back into the past through distinct ancestral species. Some scientists claim there is no infallible method for discriminating a bona fide ancestor from one that was only an extinct relative. Put the other way around, whereas we can be certain that we had ancestors, it is much more difficult to be certain that a particular fossil species actually left descendants, and, if it did, whether we are among them. ◖ We know that some fossil groups, like the robust australopithecines, which disappeared from the fossil record about 1 million years ago, were not on a direct line of descent to modern humans but were a separate group of dietarily specialized hominids. It is when we try to identify our direct ancestors that things become clouded. Although Lucy is widely embraced as one of our most ancient ancestors, we can never be positive that she herself left descendants. Her skeleton has no diagnostic anatomy to indicate that she even bore children. Nevertheless, since her species, *A. afarensis*, is the sole hominid group thus far known to have existed between 3 and 4 million years ago, *some* members of her species must have left descendants. ◖ Identification of the genuine ancestor becomes more complex when more than one possible candidate exists. Recent hominid finds, the earliest so far known in the fossil record, dated to between 3.9 and 4.4 million years ago, suggest the temporal overlap of at least two hominid taxa, making correct conclusions of ancestor-descendant relationships far from straightforward. This may also be the case for early *Homo*, which may contain at least three species: *H. habilis*, *H. ergaster*, and *H. rudolfensis*. In this instance a consensus as to the identity of the species ancestral to later hominids has proved problematic. A similar predicament exists for a much later time period, when Neandertals and anatomically modern humans overlapped in time. Depending on one's theoretical framework, Neandertals did or did not leave genes in modern human populations. ◖ The spate of hominid finds in the past fifty years, and with them evidence bearing out the Darwinian concepts of branching and diversification in evolutionary pathways, has made erecting our own family tree more difficult. The concept of a direct evolutionary relationship between fossil ancestors and modern humans was easy to defend when few fossils had been discovered. The unilinealists, for example, around the turn of the century saw a simple progression: apes to Java Man to Neandertals to modern humans. It was all very simple: We began with an apelike ancestor and, because of some general evolutionary trend, a particular inertia, light-skinned European hominids emerged. Such linearity, however, flew directly in the face of the Darwinian evolutionary processes. Why should human evolution be different from the evolution of any other organism? The notion that modern humans represent not only the ultimate goal of hominid evolution but the goal of evolution itself died hard. ◖ If the process of evolution is one of splitting and divergence, this has strong implications for the number of human species that have existed (see pages 23 and 40). If, as some believe, there were many more species of human ancestors than we are able to recognize, then ancestor-descendant relationships become bewildering, making the building of evolutionary trees even more complex. Family trees become more similar to broad bushes with multiple branches of various lengths. ◖ In 1866 the German biologist Ernst Haeckel, a contemporary of Darwin, published the first evolutionary trees. With a fondness for coining scientific terms, such as ecology and ontology (the study of embryological development), he invented the word *phylogeny* for the study of ancestor-descendant relationships among organisms. So enthusiastic was Haeckel about the construction of family trees that he devised one for humans. On this tree he placed a missing link, calling it *Pithecanthropus alalus* ("speechless ape-man"). This was an inspiration to Eugène Dubois, who named his Java find *Pithecanthropus erectus* ("erect ape-man"). ◖ Following Haeckel, early attempts at classifying organisms and constructing family trees tended to consider only overall similarities and differences among various organisms. This method was suspect because it contained a great degree of subjectivity. More recently, in an attempt to bring more scientific rigor and objectivity to the process, a system known as cladistics was introduced. In cladistics, evolutionary relationships are examined by tabulating primitive versus derived character states for specific anatomical traits. Organisms are grouped into clades (branches) on the basis of shared derived characters inherited from a recent common ancestor, but not shared with more ancient ancestors. ◖ Anatomical characters are determined to be derived or primitive, and the cladogram that most economically explains the patterns of relationships of these features is considered the best. For example, among hominids, bipedalism is a primitive trait, meaning that it is a trait shared by all hominids and therefore of little value in differentiating one hominid species from another. This is why primitive traits are not of great value in assessing relationships between species, because all species possess these. In contrast, a character state such as significant brain expansion is a derived feature that can be used to separate *Homo* from *Australopithecus*. It is generally true, therefore, that the greater the number of derived characters shared by two species, the closer is their evolutionary relationship. ◖ The evolutionary relationships determined by cladistics are translated into a phylogenetic tree, which requires the addition of time and the supposed ancestor-descendant relationships of the different taxa. A tree, therefore, is a visual representation of the pattern of hominid evolution through time. ◖ How a hominid family tree is drawn depends on the current state of knowledge of taxonomic diversity in the past. Although some species and time periods are moderately well represented by actual fossil finds, others are not. Because of the incomplete fossil sample as well as time gaps in our knowledge, we have not constructed a hard-and-fast phylogeny but include dotted lines in an attempt to express alternative views. In one case, the evolutionary connection between *Ardipithecus ramidus* and later hominids is indicated by a question mark. So little is known about *A. ramidus* that it is difficult to definitively place it on the tree. ◖ A comparison of the dental and jaw anatomy in *A. anamensis* and *A. afarensis* establishes a fairly plausible evolutionary connection. Although characters such as tooth shape and the buttressing of the anterior part of the jaw are different in these two species, the more primitive character state in *anamensis* makes it a good precursor to *afarensis*. If it turns out that *A. afarensis* overlaps in time with *A. anamensis*, the tree will get bushier in the 4 million-year time slice, indicating

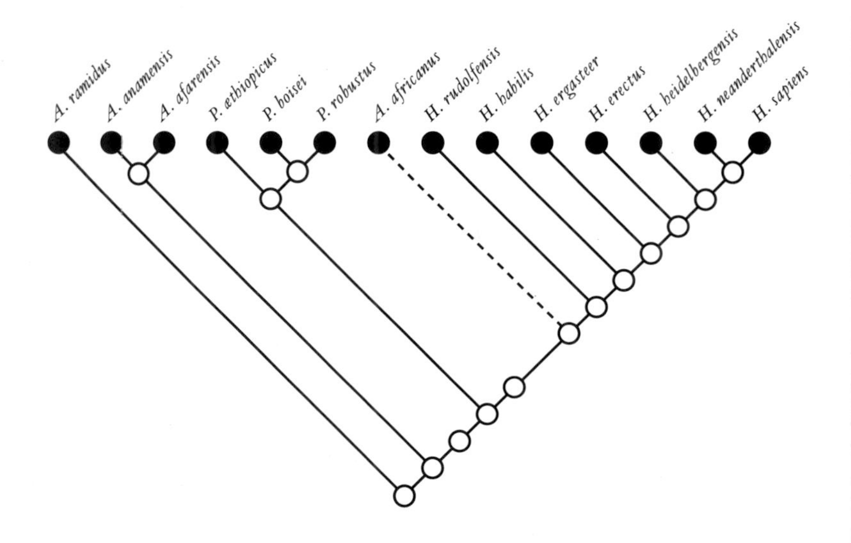

Cladogram (above) and Phylogenetic Tree (below) of Human Evolution. Shared anatomical features indicative of common ancestry can be used to sort organisms into related groups on a branching diagram called a cladogram, which illustrates how these features have been distributed in the organisms' evolutionary history. An alternative diagram, the phylogenetic tree, adds an axis of time and arranges species into a more explicit pattern of ancestors and descendants. *Cladogram after Tattersall, 1995, phyologenetic tree after Wood, 1994.*

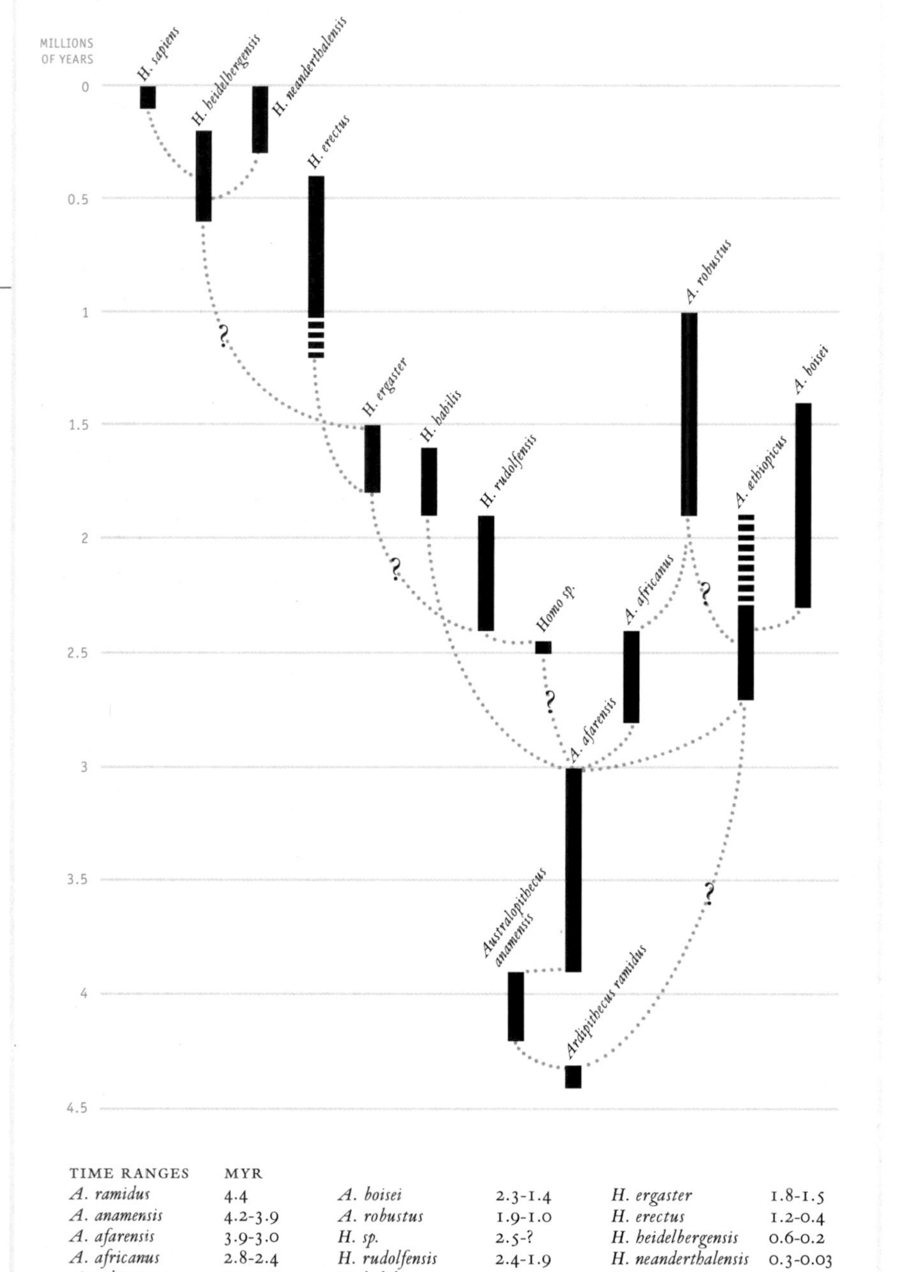

TIME RANGES	MYR				
A. ramidus	4.4	*A. boisei*	2.3-1.4	*H. ergaster*	1.8-1.5
A. anamensis	4.2-3.9	*A. robustus*	1.9-1.0	*H. erectus*	1.2-0.4
A. afarensis	3.9-3.0	*H. sp.*	2.5-?	*H. heidelbergensis*	0.6-0.2
A. africanus	2.8-2.4	*H. rudolfensis*	2.4-1.9	*H. neanderthalensis*	0.3-0.03
A. æthiopicus	2.7-1.9	*H. habilis*	1.9-1.6	*H. sapiens*	0.1-0.0

that perhaps the latter species diverged from the former and overlapped with it for a brief period of time. ◖ *A. africanus* is judged to be a sole ancestor to *A. robustus* and, because it displays a host of features derived in the robust direction, it is not viewed as an ancestor to *Homo*. Confirmation that *A. aethiopicus* shares a number of primitive features with *A. afarensis* suggests that a separate lineage leading to *A. boisei* evolved in East Africa, parallel to that seen in South Africa. A minority view holds that *africanus* went extinct without leaving descendants and that both *robustus* and *boisei* evolved from *aethiopicus*. ◖ The genus *Homo* presents several problems. First, there is a long gap in the fossil record between 2 and 3 million years ago where convincing intermediates between *A. afarensis* (the presumed ancestor to *Homo*) and earliest *Homo* are essentially absent. Second, some investigators have postulated as a second species at Sterkfontein a *Homo*-like contemporary of *A. africanus*, referred to *Homo* species novum. Third, *H. habilis*, as recognized by some, has made it increasingly difficult to nail down precise evolutionary relationships between taxa. *H. habilis* from Olduvai could be a dead end, leaving *H. rudolfensis* as an ancestor to *H. ergaster*. Some interpretations see *ergaster* as a common ancestor to *H. erectus* and *H. heidelbergensis*, while others see *ergaster* as ancestral to *erectus*, which in turn would be ancestral to *heidelbergensis*. There is increasing support for recognizing *H. neanderthalensis* as a separate species from *H. sapiens* and one that ultimately went extinct. *H. sapiens* would therefore have evolved from *H. heidelbergensis*, a common ancestor to Neandertals and to anatomically modern humans. ◖ This evolutionary tree stops with us, *Homo sapiens*. An intriguing question is, where will the tree lead? Will there be more speciation? Will we evolve into a different species, *Homo computerensis*? The answer is that the conditions that bring about speciation are currently absent in the modern world. Humans are no longer reproductively isolated, a necessary condition for sufficient differences to develop in populations to bring about speciation. Instead, we have become a highly mobile species aided in our movements by modern modes of transportation, and as a result of this mobility we have become homogenized as a species. Reestablishing the conditions for speciation would require isolating some part of the human population—through space colonization, say. If that island of humans in space remained out of contact with Earth long enough, then we might see the appearance of a new species of *Homo*.

16 · African Genesis

THE GREAT RIFT VALLEY in East Africa has yielded the most ancient fossilized remains of our ancestors and relatives. Although there is no reason to believe that early hominids were confined to eastern Africa, as a recent find of *Australopithecus* in the Central African country of Chad has shown (see page 200), it is the unique geological history of the Rift Valley that is responsible for the concentration of finds. From what is known, however, it does appear that the earliest hominids were confined to Africa, since no remains of australopithecines have been found elsewhere in the world. ◖ Molecular studies confirm that African apes are more closely related to modern humans than either group is to the Asian orangutan. The African ape-human clade shared a relatively long common evolutionary history, subsequent to the time when orangutans followed their own evolutionary trajectory. There is a growing consensus, partly as a result of molecular studies, that the last common ancestor to the African ape-human clade will eventually be found somewhere between 6 and 8 million years ago, undoubtedly in Africa. ◖ Until recently, hominids older than 4 million years were limited to less than a half-dozen specimens. These specimens include a right mandible fragment with a first molar found at the site of Lothagam, in northern Kenya, and dated to approximately 5 to 6 million years ago. Although its

Right mandible from Lothagam, Kenya. This fragmentary fossil exceeds 5 million years in age but is not complete enough to identify to species or even to classify as a hominid or an extinct ape. Actual size. *Photographs by Robert I.M. Campbell; courtesy of National Museums of Kenya.*

Mandible from Tabarin, Kenya, KNM-TI 13150. An age of between 4 and 5 million years makes this fossil broadly contemporaneous with Ethiopian fossils of *Ardipithecus ramidus.* This mandible has been identified as *Australopithecus praegens.* Actual size. *Photograph by Robert I.M. Campbell; courtesy of National Museums of Kenya.*

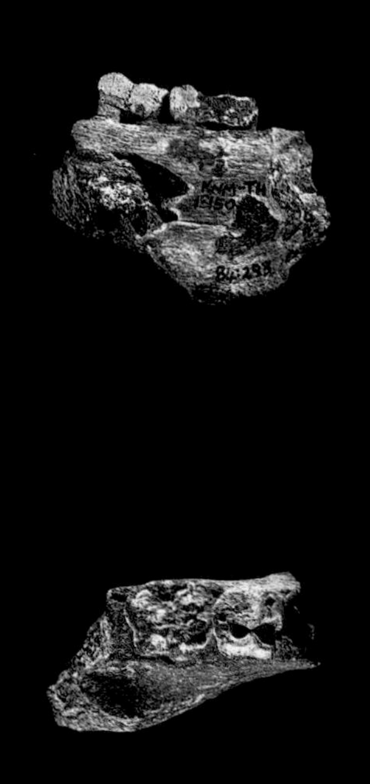

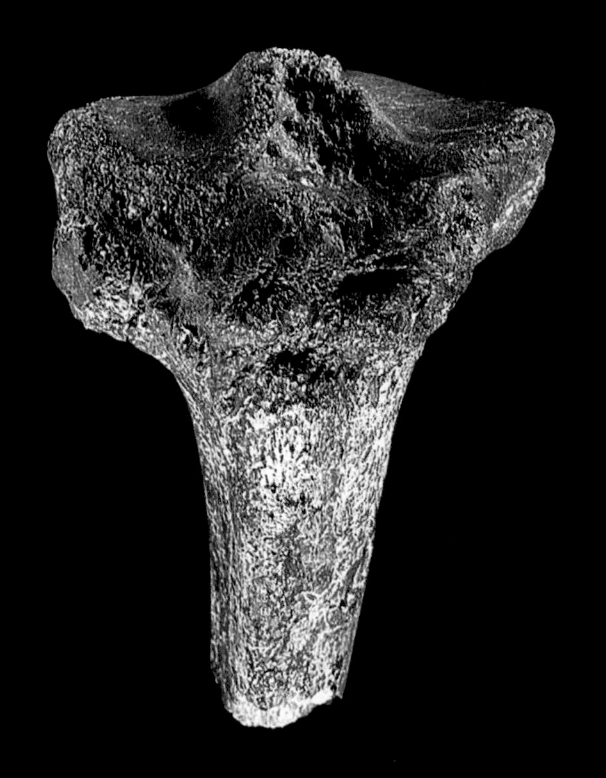

Tibia of *Australopithecus anamensis* from Kanapoi, Kenya. The earliest known evidence for bipedalism is this specimen, KNM-KP 29285. Both upper and lower ends were recovered, and the articular surface for the knee joint is clearly expanded from front to back as in a biped. Actual size. *Photograph by Robert I.M. Campbell; courtesy of National Museums of Kenya.*

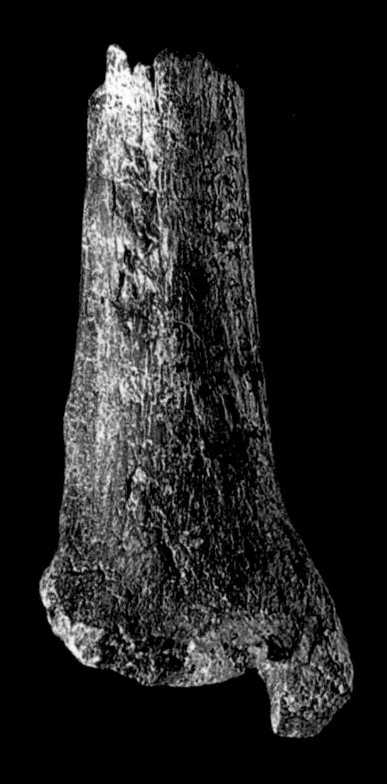

anatomy is consistent with placement in the family Hominidae, the fragmentary nature of the Lothagam specimen makes assignment to genus or species impossible. A proximal humerus from Lake Baringo, Kenya, dated to approximately 4.2 million years ago, shares morphological similarities with *Australopithecus afarensis*. ◖ A mandible fragment from Tabarin, northern Kenya, with worn right first and second molars dates from between 4.15 and 5.15 million years ago. It has been designated a new species, *Australopithecus praegens*. The site of Fejej, in southern Ethiopia, dated to 4.2 million years yielded a handful of fossil hominid teeth that are placed in *A. afarensis*. ◖ With such a small collection of hominid fossils from deposits more than 4 million years old, the recent discoveries from Aramis, Ethiopia, and Kanapoi, Kenya, dated respectively to 4. 4 and 4.2 million years, are a welcome addition to the very earliest part of our fossil ancestry. ◖ In 1994 a team led by paleoanthropologist Tim White of the University of California announced the discovery of fossil hominid specimens from Aramis, a site situated in the Middle Awash river valley in Ethiopia. Consisting of teeth, jaws, bits of skull, and postcranial bones, the Aramis material, radiometrically dated to 4.4 million years, possesses a unique constellation of anatomical features (see page 116), which stimulated the naming of a new species, *Australopithecus ramidus* ("ramid" is from the Afar people's word for root). After further consideration and the discovery of a nearly complete skeleton at Aramis, the entire collection was allocated to a new genus, *Ardipithecus* ("ardi" means ground or floor in the Afar language; thus "basal root ape"). ◖ In August 1995 Meave Leakey, a zoologist at the National Museums of Kenya and her colleagues reported the discovery of hominids from the Lake Turkana region in northern Kenya. These finds, predominantly from the site of Kanapoi, range in age from 3.9 to 4.2 million years and consist mostly of teeth and jaws. They show strong similarities with *A. afarensis*, but the Kanapoi hominids are characterized by a series of anatomical features (see page 112) that distinguish them as a new species, *Australopithecus anamensis* ("anam" is from the Turkana word for lake; thus, "southern ape of the lake"). A distal humerus found at Kanapoi in 1965 has now been attributed to this new species. Now that the 4 million-year barrier has been breached, it is possible that more sites such as Kanapoi and Aramis will be found with early hominids. ◖ The fossil finds from Kanapoi and Aramis offer a tantalizing look at an early part of the hominid fossil record that was previously unavailable. These finds will no doubt generate debate, as happens with the announcement of any new hominid species, but finally we are able to delve deeper into the phylogenetic roots of our unique zoological family, the Hominidae.

17 · Early vs. Modern Humans

THE HUMAN family includes both living and extinct species of bipedal primates that have been evolutionarily distinct since their separation from a common ancestor with the African apes. The formal zoological category for this group of bipedal primates at the family level is the Hominidae, which in its more popular or vernacular form is abbreviated as hominid. ◖ The traditional classification, which places humans in the family Hominidae and the great apes (chimps, gorillas, orangutans) in the family Pongidae, has recently been challenged on the basis of biochemical and molecular studies. These studies have established the closeness of humans and African apes, to the exclusion of the orangutans. To more accurately reflect the evolutionary relationships between these apes and humans, some scientists include them all in the Hominidae. To stress the close evolutionary connection between humans and African apes, they are put into the subfamily Homininae, while orangutans and their ancestors are placed into the subfamily Ponginae. Although these newer groupings more closely reflect the evolutionary history of apes and humans, the more traditional classification cited above is followed here, because it is widely used in the paleoanthropological literature. ◖ The family Hominidae is divided into early hominids and later hominids. In this book all early hominids, with the exception of *Ardipithecus ramidus*, are placed in the genus *Australopithecus* ("southern ape") and collectively called australopithecines. Later hominids are all placed in the genus *Homo*. The Hominidae constitute a diverse zoological family, united by the ability to walk bipedally. Some of the greatest anatomical differences in hominid species become clear if we look at the differences between early and later hominids, that is, between australopithecines and *Homo*. ◖ Early hominids are placed by most paleoanthropologists in a single genus, *Australopithecus*, which contains seven species: *anamensis*, *afarensis*, *bahrelghazali*, *africanus*, *aethiopicus*, *robustus*, and *boisei*. The recently named genus *Ardipithecus*, considered an early hominid, contains a single species, *ramidus* (see page 116), which some paleoanthropologists consider an eighth species of *Australopithecus*, *A. praegens*. In this book the term australopithecines is employed as a collective term for all species of *Australopithecus*. Some researchers object to this usage because it implies a subfamilial rank, Australopithecinae, and prefer the term australopith. ◖ Australopithecines, sometimes called early hominids (or even early humans), have thus far been found exclusively in African deposits ranging in age from more than 4 million years old to roughly 1 million years old. Although their postcranial bones—those occurring "after the cranium," or below the skull—attest to committed terrestrial bipedalism, some species show features such as relatively long arms and curved finger and toe bones that are reminiscent of an arboreal ancestry. Australopithecines were vegetarian, and some species, the robust australopithecines (*A. robustus*, *aethiopicus* and *boisei*), developed extreme masticatory adaptations such as very large postcanine teeth with thick, fast-growing enamel, thick mandibles, and massive chewing muscles such as the temporalis, sometimes associated with bony crests that anchor these muscles on the cranium. Faces range from being very prognathic (projecting) in earlier forms to flat and even dish-shaped in the later, robust forms Australopithecines have postcanine megadontia, meaning that the molars and premolars are relatively large compared to the anterior teeth. ◖ The australopithecine skull has a small braincase, ranging from less than 400 cc to approximately 530 cc, and is dominated by a relatively large face. The cranial vault is relatively thin-walled and, when viewed from above, shows marked postorbital constriction. An anteriorly situated sagittal crest along the midline of the cranial vault, for attachment of the temporalis muscles, is sometimes present, particularly in robust males. Pronounced nuchal crests that anchor neck muscles occur in the occipital region, and foreheads range from flat and low to slightly more vertical. The mastoids are heavily pneumatized (full of air cells). ◖ Associated postcranial remains are not common, but australopithecines ranged in stature from 1 to 1.5 meters and in body weight from 27 to 45 kilograms (about the weight of a 10-year-old modern American child). Where sufficiently well known, species exhibit marked sexual dimorphism, with males substantially larger than females. ◖ *Homo*, the genus in which modern humans are placed, was named in 1758 by Linnaeus. It contains seven species: *rudolfensis*, *habilis*, *ergaster*, *erectus*, *heidelbergensis*, *neanderthalensis*, and *sapiens*. The genus probably originated in Africa roughly 2.5 million years ago, but today it is global in distribution. *Homo* is distinguished from the australopithecines by a larger cranial capacity, ranging from roughly 530 cc in earlier species to upward of 2,000 cc in modern humans. There tends to be an increase in stature (especially lengthening of the lower limbs) and body weight, and a reduction in sexual dimorphism. The entire facial skeleton with its associated masticatory apparatus, including the dentition, is reduced relative to that of the australopithecines. True browridges, absent in australopithecines, become strongly developed in some species. In general, muscle markings on the skull and on the postcranial bones are reduced. The bones of the cranial vault are noticeably thicker than in australopithecines. ◖ Modern *Homo sapiens* is also distinguished by a number of anatomical features. Modern humans have fairly gracile skeletons with very reduced browridges and cranial buttressing. Our teeth and jaws are strongly reduced and our faces are vertical and flat, with a prominent nose. Our thinly built mandibles have a mental eminence (a chin). Our short skulls are distinguished by a high, vertical forehead and dominated by a very large brain. ◖ Perhaps the most distinguishing feature of our species is our dependence on culture for survival. Culture and symbolic language are central themes in distinguishing modern humans (beginning some 40,000 years ago). We communicate symbolically through language and have become dependent on culture for survival. Although some anatomical variation exists in *Homo sapiens*, making our species polytypic, these differences are insignificant.

18 · Eve, and Adam

IN 1987, a Berkeley biochemistry lab sent shock waves through the scientific community with the announcement that modern human genetic heritage had been traced back through time to our species' very origin. That origin occurred in Africa around 200,000 years ago. The study relied on a portion of our genetic reserves, called mitochondrial DNA (mtDNA), that is inherited only from one's mother, so the proposed founding mother of humanity naturally got dubbed "mitochondrial Eve" and this origins story became the Eve hypothesis. ◖ The scenario written in the mtDNA data had some staggering implications. Humans resulted from a relatively recent speciation event and rapidly spread out from Africa around the world. Moreover, all the more archaic populations of *Homo erectus* and *Homo heidelbergensis* already living outside Africa made no contribution to the modern human genome. Because the mtDNA failed to show any deep Asian roots for our species, for instance, Peking Man and Java Man were dead ends. ◖ The now-classic mtDNA study by the late Allan Wilson, Rebecca Cann, and Mark Stoneking examined gene diversity among 147 people from the United States, New Guinea, Australia, Asia, and Europe. The scientists homed in on DNA in the mitochondrion, an organelle outside the nucleus that generates energy for a cell. Mitochondrial DNA evolves much more rapidly than nuclear DNA, so it can be used to explore questions about recent evolutionary divergences by studying the differences between populations due to accumulated genetic mutations since some past divergence. In this case, the results showed that Africans had greater mtDNA diversity (reflecting a longer period of evolution) than other populations, and a human genealogical tree could be rooted in Africa with a founding mother between 140,000 and 290,000 years ago. ◖ Paleoanthropologists arguing for an ancient human lineage stemming directly from *erectus* populations on several continents couldn't abide by Eve. After the shock waves passed, the Eve hypothesis met with some stiff criticism: for using a less exact analytical method called restriction analysis instead of more detailed comparisons between complete genetic sequences; for using African Americans as a substitute for African populations; and for not including some sort of nonhuman genetic outgroup (a more distantly related species, such as a chimpanzee), to help root the human genetic family tree. In response, the study was refined and repeated, adding mtDNA from 189 people, including 121 Africans from six sub-Saharan regions. Chimpanzee mtDNA was examined to calibrate the molecular clock by comparing the differences between chimp and human mtDNAs accumulated since the two species diverged from each other. These results, published in 1991, also suggested that humans arose in Africa between 166,000 and 249,000 years ago. As before, the new Eve tree had two main branches, one leading to six African mtDNA types and the other to everyone else. Eve's support was shored. ◖ But not for long. The computer program used in both Eve studies, called PAUP, for Phylogenetic Analysis Using Parsimony, ranks different trees by the principle of parsimony: the tree requiring the fewest genetic mutations, or steps, to explain its pattern becomes the most plausible. It turns out, though, that the computer's results may depend on how data gets entered, how many runs are made, and how many trees it analyzes. A study by geneticist Alan Templeton found 100 trees more parsimonious than the 1991 Eve tree, while another scientific team obtained 10,000 trees that were more parsimonious than the 1987 Eve tree and had a mix of geographic roots. In addition, the range of potential error in pinpointing a date for human origins meant that Eve could have lived anytime between 100,000 and a million years ago. Suddenly, the African origin for modern human mtDNA no longer appeared so clear cut. ◖ Although the Eve hypothesis remains controversial, the accumulated genetic evidence still suggests a recent origin, and probably an African one. A different segment of mtDNA, the cytochrome oxidase subunit II (CO II) gene being studied by Maryellen Ruvolo and others, indicates that, assuming chimps and humans shared a common ancestor 6 million years, modern humans apparently originated 222,000 years ago. And one study of the complete mitochondrial genome, albeit from only two humans, came up with an origin date of 176,000 years ago. Africans also have the greatest mtDNA and nuclear gene diversity of any population, which suggests that their genes have greater antiquity. ◖ If Eve has proved elusive, Adam has been even more so. A few teams of geneticists have undertaken the task of identifying appropriate portions of the Y chromosome, the male sex chromosome, for clues to when and where humanity's founding father(s) lived. Much of this chromosome never recombines with the X chromosome (the sex chromosome found in both males and females) and persists unchanged except for the occasional mutation, so like mtDNA the Y chromosome offers another potential way to trace human prehistory to its starting point. ◖ One Y chromosome study in the early 1990s concluded that Adam was a pygmy living 200,000 years ago in the forest of what is now the Central African Republic. Three studies published in 1995 made further attempts to locate Adam. The first study using a small sequence of the ZFY gene, which may determine the development of sperm and testes, found an optimal date for Adam of 270,000 years ago, in close correspondence with the mtDNA dates for Eve. A pair of subsequent research papers offered slightly different stories. One pinned to the ancestral human Y chromosome a date of 188,000 years ago and suggested a pattern of male migration from Africa to Europe and Asia; the other concluded that the modern human origin was much more recent, only 37,000 to 49,000 years ago. ◖ Nuclear DNA has also been employed to determine the timing of modern human origins. Some analyses suggest an African origin around the same time as indicated by the mtDNA, but increasingly the evidence points to an even more recent emergence. The analysis by Luigi Luca Cavalli-Sforza and colleagues of microsatellites in nuclear DNA from an ethnic sampling of 150 people concluded that Eve lived no longer ago than 133,000 years. A newer, more comprehensive nuclear DNA study by a large team of geneticists in six countries used two parts of the CD4 gene of chromosome 12 from a global sample of 1,600 individuals in forty-two populations. Again, the most diversity occurred among sub-Saharan African populations, while a startling uniformity characterized all groups outside of Africa. After spreading throughout Africa, apparently, groups of these early modern humans embarked from the northeast corner of the continent into the Middle East about 102,000 years ago. From there they entered Europe and continued spreading eastward into Asia and beyond. ◖ It is important to realize that mention of Adam or Eve does not mean that we are all descended from just one pair of individuals, as in the Bibli-

Fossils of *Homo sapiens* from Klasies River Mouth, South Africa. Four mandibles and several cranial fragments from these coastal caves date to between 80,000 and 100,000 years ago, supporting the idea that modern humans evolved recently in Africa. Actual sizes. *Courtesy of South Africa Museum.*

cal story of Eden. Mitochondrial Eve represents not the ancestral mother from whom all humans descend, but rather the specific carrier of an ancestral mtDNA molecule that gave rise to all modern human mtDNA. Many other men and women were Eve's contemporaries, and considering that mtDNA constitutes only 1/400,000th of our total genome, these contemporaries almost certainly contributed to other parts of our present genetic makeup. In order to have maintained our current level of genetic diversity, it is likely that populations of the first modern humans would have totaled at least 10,000. So our species did not derive from a single ancestral couple, an Adam and Eve, but did originate relatively rapidly from a founding population that lived in Africa sometime in the vicinity of 200,000 years ago.

19 · The Earliest Fossil Evidence of Anatomically Modern Humans

IN the early part of the twentieth century, scientists like the English anatomist Sir Arthur Keith, who served as Louis Leakey's intellectual mentor, and the French paleontologist Marcellin Boule postulated that modern humans were of great antiquity. The pre-sapiens theory, articulated in large part by Boule and Keith, held that Neandertals could not be among the ancestors of modern humans not only because they were too brutish, but because modern humans had already existed long before the Neandertals evolved. Boule strongly influenced his onetime student, French anthropologist Henri Vallois, who, after Boule's death in 1942, continued to champion the pre-sapiens theory well into the 1950s. ◖ The pre-sapiens theory influenced Boule's description of the Neandertal remains found at La Chapelle-aux-Saints. He stressed the skeleton's primitive anatomy, saying it was so apelike that no self-respecting European would want it in his ancestry. Keith's work on the Piltdown specimen, a skull of presumed great antiquity, reflected a similar theoretical framework. He gave the skull a larger cranial capacity than others had done, reflecting his view that brain expansion led the way in hominid evolution. He also turned a blind eye to any primitive features of the skull. It was from these two directions that Neandertals were squeezed onto a side branch.
◖ Strangely enough, Boule, Vallois, Keith, and others were correct in thinking that very ancient modern humans did exist, and most likely Neandertals were not our direct ancestors (see pages 56 and 232). However, they were correct for the wrong reasons, because the specimens on which they based their conjectures were not as old as they thought. Piltdown Man was exposed as a hoax, a modern human cranium combined with an orang jaw and buried with ancient fossils. Also, skulls with modern anatomy, like the specimen from Galley Hill, England, were found to be burials of modern humans in older strata. Eventually, candidates such as the skeletons from Grimaldi, once thought by Boule to be ancient "Negroids," turned out to be geologically more recent than Neandertals. ◖ The real challenge to establishing the antiquity of anatomically modern humans was and remains dependable dating. The important events in the origin of modern humans occur in the time range between 200,000 and 40,000 years ago. During that period of time both Neandertals and anatomically modern humans made their appearance, but it is precisely that period that is not adequately addressed by traditional radiocarbon and potassium-argon dating methods, which are more suitable for fossils older or younger than the age range in question. The newer techniques of thermoluminescence, electron spin resonance, and uranium-thorium series dating (see page 26) do address the period of 200,000 to 40,000 years ago, and with their use paleoanthropologists have been able to fill in some of the blanks in our early history. ◖ The most persuasive case for early anatomically modern humans comes from Jebel Qafzeh, a cave located near Nazareth, Israel. Parts of more than twenty well-preserved skeletons with skulls, some fairly complete, are known from this site. (see page 239) With the application of both thermoluminescence and electron spin resonance dating techniques, the Qafzeh hominids have been dated to between 90,000 and 100,000 years ago. Although the Qafzeh hominids possess some primitive features, overall the skulls are astonishingly modern looking. They have high, short braincases with fairly vertical foreheads, only slight browridges, and an average cranial capacity of roughly 1,550 cc, comfortably within the range of modern humans'. The mandibles have well-marked chins, further attesting to the modernity of the Qafzeh hominids. Additional evidence of *Homo sapiens* comes from the rockshelter at Skhul at Mount Carmel in Israel, a site roughly the same age as Qafzeh. Remains of at least ten individuals were recovered from Skhul, including several probable burials. ◖ In East Africa, in an area known as Omo-Kibish in southern Ethiopia, just north of Lake Turkana, remains of a partial skeleton, Omo I (see pages 45 and 236), were recovered in 1967. This skull associated with postcranial bones is very modern looking in having a rounded vault and an expanded parietal region. The associated mandible has a prominent chin. The braincase of a second individual, Omo II, was found some distance away and appears more *Homo erectus*-like. Although the dating of the Omo-Kibish fossils is uncertain, uranium-thorium dating of shells found with the fossils suggests the specimens may be as much as 130,000 years old. ◖ At the southern tip of Africa, the fossil specimens from Klasies River Mouth are associated with a Middle Stone Age archeological assemblage. Age estimates based on uranium-thorium and electron spin resonance dating suggest that the hominids lived there between 120,000 and 75,000 years ago. Some specimens are more robustly built, but a partial mandible has a strongly developed chin and is relatively lightly built. A small portion of the lightly built frontal bone lacks a supraorbital torus and thus has a modern human morphology. ◖ An adult skull from Border Cave in South Africa is often cited as an example of a very early anatomically modern human cranium. (see page 44) The specimen is indeed modern looking, but since it lacks the sort of damage seen on other fossils from a Middle Stone Age horizon, this may be a case of a more recent burial into older sediments.
◖ Outside of Africa, the evidence for anatomically modern humans is unconvincing until roughly 40,000 years ago. For example, in Europe the earliest appearance of modern humans, usually referred to as Cro-Magnon Man, is always associated with artifacts typical of the Upper Paleolithic (see page 258). In the Near East, remains of modern *Homo sapiens* are few and far between, but the earliest, from Ksar Akil, in Lebanon, is roughly 37,000 years old. Evidence for modern humans in eastern Asia is not very convincing owing to the scarceness of sites and fossils and the uncertainties of dating these finds. ◖ Based on what is currently known, *Homo sapiens* first appeared in Africa (biogeographically, the sites in present-day Israel are here considered part of Africa). One remarkable aspect of the earliest *sapiens* is that although they are anatomically modern, their associated stone tool technology, variously called the Mousterian or Middle Stone Age technology, suggests that they were not behaviorally modern. ◖ The implication from these finds is that *Homo sapiens* did not arise as a direct result of some major behavioral change, at least not one that can be detected in the fossil record. The postcranial bones of early *sapiens* were robustly built, suggesting that they were still dependent to a large degree on brawn and not on tools for many activities. ◖ This generates the obvious question of why a modern anatomy preceded a modern behavior. This is one of the key unanswered questions in paleoanthropology today. Is it possible that the brains of early *Homo sapiens* were simply not yet wired for sophisticated culture? The modern capacity for culture seems to have emerged around 50,000 years ago, and with it, behaviorally modern humans who were capable of populating the globe.

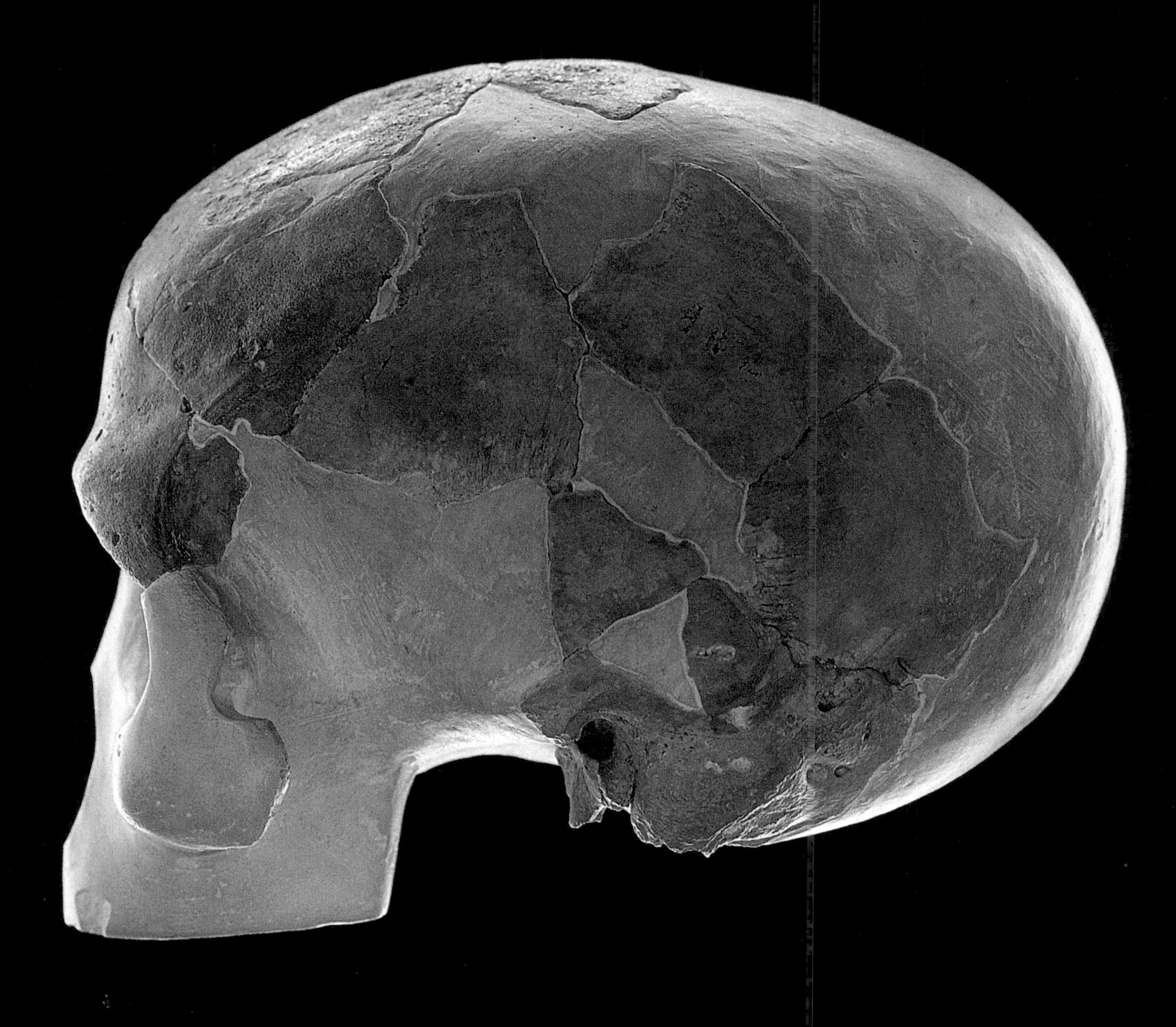

Cranium of *Homo sapiens* from Border Cave, South Africa. This specimen, Border Cave 1, was unearthed during mining for guano in the cave. It may date to between 70,000 and 80,000 years ago. Actual size. *Photograph by Gerald Newlands.*

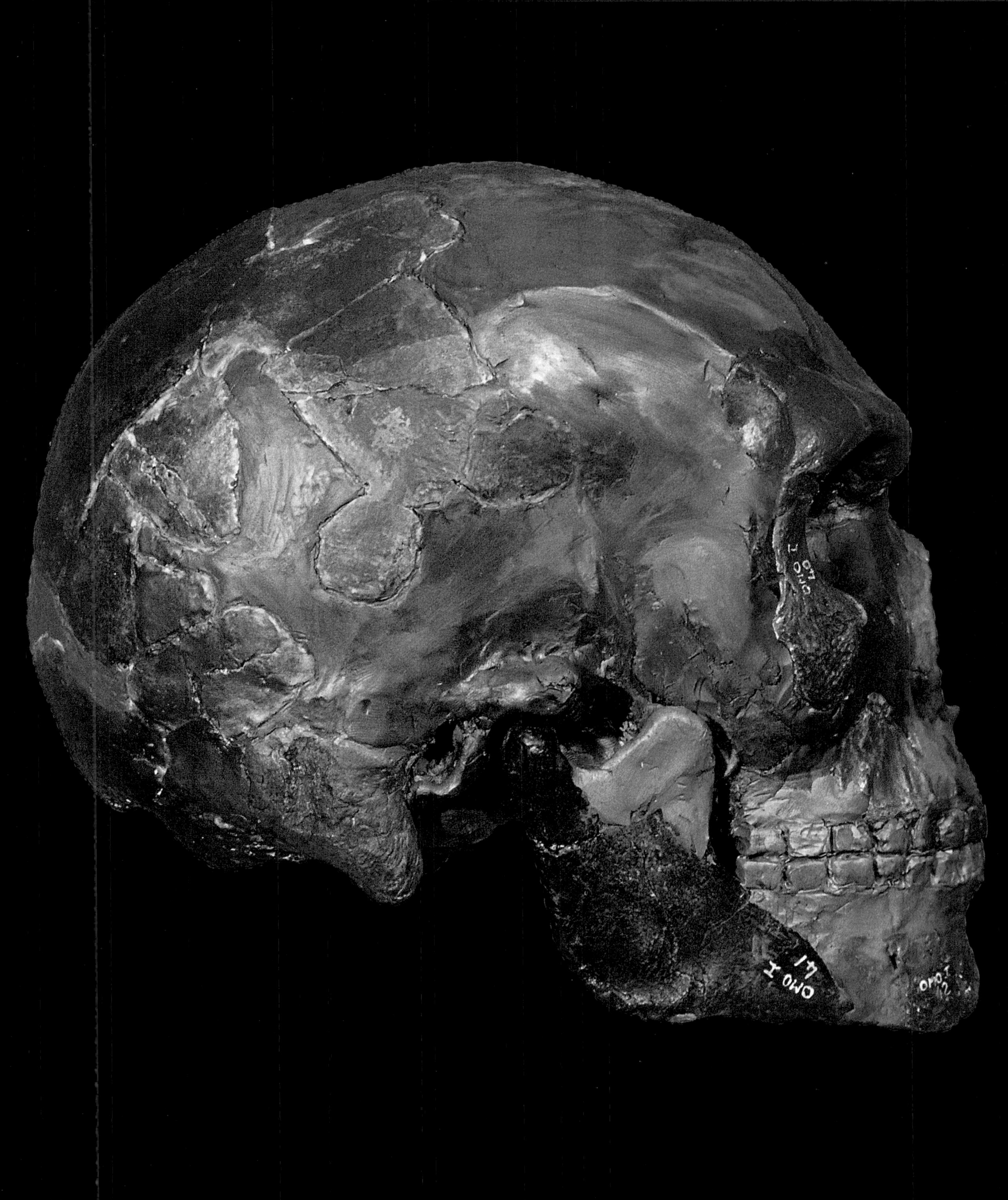

Skull of *Homo sapiens* from Omo-Kibish, Ethiopia. A lateral view shows this specimen's long, curved parietal bones, high forehead, and developed chin—all traits found in modern human fossils less than half this old. Actual size. *Courtesy of Michael Day.*

20 · Out of Africa

SEVERAL important discoveries in the 1990s have reopened the question of when our ancestors first journeyed from Africa to other parts of the globe. Traditionally, *Homo erectus* is credited as being the prehistoric pioneer, a species that left Africa about 1 million years ago and began to disperse throughout Eurasia. But recent evidence indicates that emigrant *erectus*, or perhaps its ancestor *Homo ergaster*, made a much earlier departure from our continental cradle. ◖ In 1994, reports of new dates for some old bones shocked anthropologists and made the cover of *Time* magazine. The bones in question come from Modjokerto and Sangiran, two sites on Java, the island where the first remains of *H. erectus* anywhere were found in 1891 (see page 187). The partial skull lacking a face or teeth from Modjokerto, discovered in 1936, belonged to a five- or six-year-old child *erectus*. Its geological age had been estimated at about a million years. With recent redating, however, it is thought that the child lived at least 1.8 million years ago. Other *erectus* fossils from Sangiran, including the face and back of two different skulls and a lower jaw, revealed an age of over 1.6 million years. ◖ The relatively new high-precision argon-argon dating method, which uses a laser to determine the amount of argon gas inside single rock crystals, provided the age estimates for sediments at the two sites. Some have questioned whether the dated sediments come from the same spots as the fossils, with the suggestion that the fossils may be much younger. Nonetheless, the fact that sediment from two sites 240 kilometers apart had similar ages lends support to the earlier dates. These dates remain striking due to the absence of any other firm evidence for early humans in East Asia prior to a million years ago, and the individuals from Modjokerto and Sangiran would have certainly traveled through this part of Asia to reach Java. The earliest *erectus* specimens in east Asia include the cranium from Gongwangling (Lantian), China, which may be a million years old or closer to 800,000 years old, and some isolated teeth from Yuanmou and other Chinese sites that probably date to around 700,000 years ago. ◖ If *erectus/ergaster* left Africa nearly a million years earlier than anyone had suspected, then what enabled this hominid to move onward? It had been argued that a new tool technology, the Acheulean industry, attributed to *erectus* and typified by hefty hand axes and cleavers, gave this species an ecological edge in expanding its range. But the situation cannot be that simple, especially if *erectus* arrived in Asia before the first Acheulean tools appeared in Africa around 1.7 million years ago (which explains the long-noted absence of Acheulean tools in eastern Asia). ◖ New fossil evidence also points to an earlier than anticipated arrival for *H. erectus* in Eurasia. In 1991, archeologists excavating a grain-storage pit in the medieval east Georgian town of Dmanisi uncovered the mandible, or lower jaw, of an adult *erectus* along, with other ancient animal bones and stone tools. The jaw has since been dated by three independent techniques, including potassium-argon and paleomagnetism dating, to 1.8 million years ago, making this the first early human in Eurasia and a rival with Modjokerto for being the first outside of Africa. The Dmanisi specimen more closely resembles contemporaneous African jaws than later Asian ones, so it may belong to *H. ergaster* or some other hominid species. ◖ Early African emigrants may have skirted the eastern edge of the Mediterranean Sea before heading east. In Israel's Jordan Valley, the site of 'Ubeidiya has yielded stone tools from both an early chopper-core industry and crude Acheulean-like hand axes dated to between 1.2 and 1.4 million years ago by three different methods. The 'Ubeidiya tools resemble those of comparable age excavated from middle and upper Bed II at Olduvai Gorge, Tanzania. At the same site were found part of a hominid skull and some teeth. Acheulean hand axes and cleavers dating to 600,000 years ago have also been found at Gesher Benot Ya'aqov, another site in Israel's Jordan Rift Valley, a northern extension of the Great Rift Valley that may have had similar lake and woodland ecology to hominid habitats in East Africa. ◖ One lingering mystery is did *Homo erectus* only head east into Asia, altogether bypassing Europe? No unequivocal fossils of *erectus* have emerged in Europe. Although some specimens, including the crania from Petralona, Greece and Arago, France (see pages 200 and 198, respectively) have been proposed as *erectus*, they belong to the more recent species *Homo heidelbergensis*. ◖ Many paleoanthropologists believed that no early humans entered Europe until 500,000 years ago, citing evidence such as a lower jaw from Mauer, Germany, the Heidelberg Man, the type specimen of *H. heidelbergensis*, which was discovered in 1907 (see page 196). In 1994, the announcement of a tibia, or shin bone, from Boxgrove, England, confirmed that by 500,000 years ago, early humans had reached Great Britain, when the island was a peninsula of Europe. ◖ The discovery of new fossils from Spain, published in 1995, secured a more ancient arrival of early humans in Europe. Three dozen bone fragments and a hundred stone tools were collected in the cave of Gran Dolina in the Atapuerca Mountains from sediments dated by the paleo-

Fossils of *Homo heidelbergensis* from Gran Dolina, Spain. The earliest Europeans may be represented by these 780,000-year-old remains of at least four individuals, including an adolescent and child. Actual sizes. *Photograph by Javier Trueba, Madrid Scientific Films; courtesy of Juan-Luis Arsuaga.*

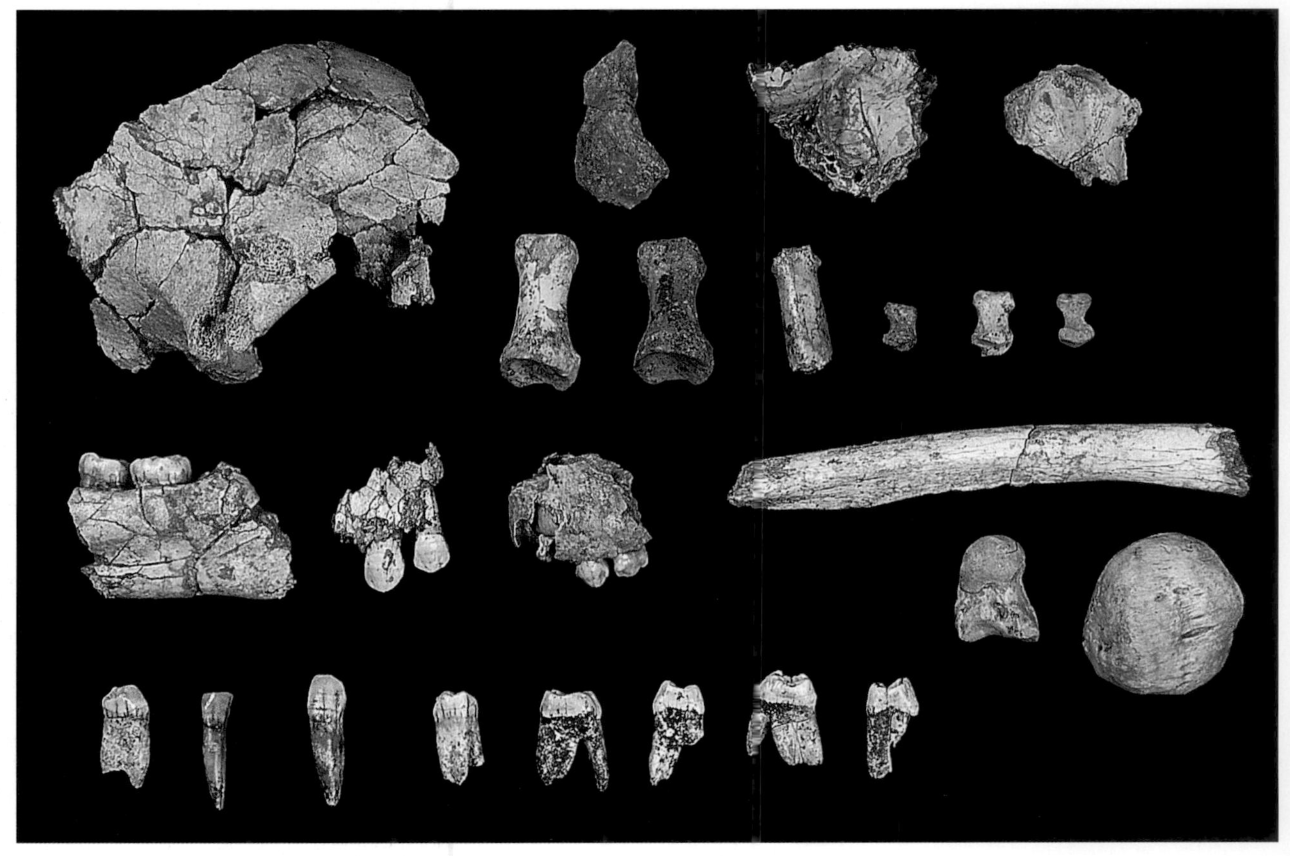

magnetism method to 780,000 years ago. The fossils – several teeth, jaw and skull fragments, and hand and foot bones – come from four individuals, including a child and an adolescent. Unlike either *erectus* or the later Neandertals in form, the Gran Dolina bones probably belong to a primitive form of *H. heidelbergensis* or to an earlier, as yet unrecognized species. Whether some cave harbors an even earlier European remains to be seen.

21 · The First Americans

IN 1932 near Clovis, New Mexico, while exploring the shore of a driedup lake, archeologists found some unusual stone tools between the ribs of extinct mammoths. Nothing like the elegant, finely flaked spear points had been found before. The base of the point was fluted: a large rectangular flake had been knocked off each side, permitting the stone to be hafted onto a wooden shaft that could then be hurled at an animal. The tool came to be called a Clovis point. The Clovis people were biggame hunters who may have been lured to North America by the migrations of huge herds of herbivores, such now extinct animals as mammoths, mastodons, musk oxen, camels, horses, and ground sloths. Excavation at the site uncovered the remains of four mammoths associated with more Clovis points, all beneath layers containing smaller Folsom points, which until the Clovis discovery had been the oldest known technology in the Americas. ◖ Other sites with Clovis points made from chert and chalcedony turned up subsequently in each of the lower forty-eight states, southern Canada, and as far south as Tierra del Fuego. Radiocarbon dates have consistently placed these artifacts within the time period of 11,000 to 11,500 years ago. No widely accepted archeological sites of greater antiquity have been found, which suggests that modern human PaleoIndians first entered the Americas at this time, crossing the Bering Sea land bridge from Asia around the end of the last Ice Age. ◖ This date, often called the Clovis barrier, has been rammed many times by evidence purporting to be a little or a lot older, but it has yet to crumble. There have been many pre-Clovis contenders in North and South America, but most have withered under critical scrutiny. Either the evidence for the antiquity of human bones and artifacts or the evidence that tools were made by human hands tends to evaporate. Perhaps nothing in American archeology receives more critical scrutiny than the latest pre-Clovis claim, but a few sites have weathered the criticism better than the rest. ◖ One such site is Meadowcroft Rockshelter, in the Ohio River basin of Pennsylvania. Sediments excavated at Meadowcroft contained numerous artifacts, animal bones, and plant remains interlaced with charcoal from fire pits that provided organic material for a series of more than fifty radiocarbon dates. The most ancient deposits at the site date to between 31,000 and 21,000 years and contain no artifacts. But evidence of humans appears soon afterward. The oldest artifact, apparently a small piece of a bark basket or mat, has been dated to 19,600 years ago, plus or minus 2,400 years. A cut and charred chunk of deer antler was dated to around 16,175 years ago. ◖ Finished stone tools and flakes come from the same occupation level in the site, including retouched knives, blades, and other slicing implements. A single short, leafshaped projectile point may date to around 13,000 years ago. None of the tools closely resemble Clovis technology, but the unusual blades have broad similarities with blade tools from the European Upper Paleolithic. ◖ Another enduring pre-Clovis contender comes from the Chilean site of Monte Verde in South America. Unlike Meadowcroft, Monte Verde is an openair, creekside marsh site, where a peat bog preserved stones and bones as well as wooden tools, logs and branches arranged to form foundations of huts, and even a piece of mastodon flesh. These peat deposits have been dated to around 13,000 years ago. The remains of a separate structure had a foundation of sand and gravel mixed with animal fat where the occupants apparently stored

Stone artifacts from Monte Verde, Chile. Two basalt projectile points and a possible drill made of black slate were excavated from an archeological layer dated by the radiocarbon method to 12,500 years ago. Actual sizes. *Courtesy of Tom D. Dillehay, University of Kentucky.*

Rock painting from Monte Alegre, Brazil. Among the oldest known paintings in the Americas, this image was made some 11,000 years ago by a hunter-gatherer culture contemporaneous with Clovis people, the earliest generally accepted culture in North America. *Photograph by Anna C. Roosevelt; courtesy of Field Museum of Natural History.*

(*left*) **Projectile point from Meadowcroft Rockshelter, Pennsylvania.** The leaf-shaped Miller lanceolate comes from the top of the earliest artifact-bearing level, indicating human hunters lived at this site at least 13,000 years ago. Actual size. *Photograph by J.M. Adovasio; courtesy of Mercyhurst Archaeological Institute.*
(*right*) **Quartz crystal spear point from Monte Alegre, Brazil.** Excavated artifacts and charred remains of tropical fruits and small animals from this rockshelter demonstrate human occupation of Amazonia between 10,000 and 11,000 years ago. Actual size. *Photograph by Romulo Fialdini; courtesy of Museo Goeldi and Banco Safra.*

food and used tools of stone, bone, and wood to prepare meat and hides. A few dozen people may have lived at Monte Verde at one time, surviving on a broad diet of gathered plants and hunted animals. ◖ Although archeologists may be willing to accept an age of 13,000 years for Monte Verde, deeper deposits at the site have sparked greater controversy. These deposits contain more ambiguous artifacts associated with charred wood that was dated by the radiocarbon method to 33,000 years ago. Even the excavators remain somewhat skeptical of this earlier occupation date, which would precede the burials of Cro-Magnon in France. ◖ Pre-Clovis critics claim that the charcoal in some of the Meadowcroft Rockshelter sediments has been contaminated, skewing the radiocarbon results toward an earlier age. Monte Verde's critics question not the accuracy of the dates but the authenticity of the artifacts and their association with the ancient sediments (suggesting that younger tools may have filtered down into an older sediment layer). ◖ Other sites with possible evidence of an even earlier human arrival in the Americas have received much attention recently. Pendejo Cave in New Mexico contains two dozen living floors that may date as far back as 39,000 years ago. The evidence includes purported pebble and flake tools made of stone transported to the cave from a distant source, charcoal, a human hair, and apparent fingerprints impressed into clay some 30,000 years ago. The site does contain an amazing array of mammals that lived in the area between 30,000 and 40,000 years ago, but most archeologists are withholding judgment about whether humans were among them. ◖ Further south, excavators of the Pedra Furada Rockshelter in Brazil contend that humans occupied the site beginning nearly 50,000 years ago-when Neandertals still prevailed in Europe-until 14,000 years ago, and again between 10,000 and 6,000 years ago. The youngest layers show clear signs of human use: finely made stone knives, stone hearths, and abundant rock art. Paintings on the walls of Pedra Furada-one of about 200 decorated rockshelters at the base of the same sandstone cliff-are thousands of years old. ◖ Beyond 14,000 years ago, however, the organic remains become scarce, hearths become ambiguous, and art disappears. Several hundred crude quartzite cobble "tools" constitute the main evidence of human presence. A trio of American archeologists-including the lead excavators of Meadowcroft and Monte Verde-recently examined the earlier evidence at Pedra Furada firsthand and concluded that the cobbles had broken naturally after falling from the cliff above the site. ◖ For now, Meadowcroft and Monte Verde remain the best bets for a pre-Clovis peopling of the Americas. If the antiquity of either holds up, then PaleoIndians must have entered North America long before 12,000 years ago in order to reach these remote locations. ◖ Further clues to a somewhat earlier arrival in the Americas come from the Caverna da Pedra Pintada, a cave site in the Brazilian Amazon. A battery of radiocarbon dates from burnt wood and seeds plus thermoluminescence and optically stimulated luminescence dates of burnt quartz tools and quartz grains, respectively, place human occupation at this site between 11,200 and 10,000 years ago. And these people had a culture quite distinct from that of the Clovis hunters. The early Amazonians painted cave walls, crafted triangular stemmed spear points, and subsisted on a broad diet of tropical fruits, fish, small mammals, and other game. ◖ Although these cave dwellers were approximate Clovis contemporaries, perhaps the first Americans had a similarly broad foraging strategy that only later shifted to the big-game hunting associated with Clovis culture. The scarce and scattered nature of solid preClovis contenders should still give pause, however. If humans were abundant in the Americas before the almost ubiquitous makers of Clovis culture, why did they leave so little trace of their existence?

22 · Peopling the Globe

AFRICA was the sole setting of human evolution for the first 3 or 4 million years of hominid existence. It is only within the past 2 million years that any hominid exodus from Africa occurred (see page 46). The first species to begin a spread into new continents was *Homo erectus*, which is found throughout eastern Asia and possibly in Europe. But the travels of *Homo erectus* pale by comparison to the global colonization achieved by our species, which now occupies almost every terrestrial habitat on the planet in numbers approaching 6 billion. Indeed, the ability to colonize new habitats, prompted by such cultural developments as clothing, shelter, and boats, is a key human trait. We got to everywhere, eventually, because we could get there, and the trek took as few as 5,000 generations. ◖ Genetic differences in the nuclear DNA of human populations on various continents can be used to estimate when one population split off from others, or essentially when each continent first became populated. The scattered migration of individuals tends not to leave any genetic traces and in fact will reduce total genetic diversity by blending traits that would otherwise distinguish more isolated populations. Mass migrations of people, however, do tend to increase diversity by stimulating genetic drift—in which novel mutations will more likely arise and be inherited by subsequent generations—and adaptation to new environments. It is the genetic traces of these mass migrations that inform us when we came to occupy the globe. According to this gene geography, Africans became separated from other groups around 100,000 years ago. Groups in southeast Asia and Australia split off around 60,000 years ago. Asia and Europe became occupied by 40,000 years ago, and northeast Asia and the Americas harbored humans only within the last 30,000 years. In the vast Pacific, those parts closest to Australia and Sahul were colonized first, while Polynesia has probably been populated only for about 3,500 years. ◖ A separate nuclear gene study of two segments from chromosome 12 suggests a recent modern human migration out of northeast Africa about 100,000 years ago. The gene patterns then followed a distinctive eastward cline, as though these first human emigrants then entered the Middle East and Europe and continued east through Asia, across the Pacific, and into the Americas. ◖ From the Eurocentric perspective of paleoanthropology, Australia was long seen as a final frontier that was inhabited fairly recently. New dating evidence from the Malakunanja II rockshelter in Arnhem Land, near the northern tip of Australia, suggests that humans first arrived there 60,000

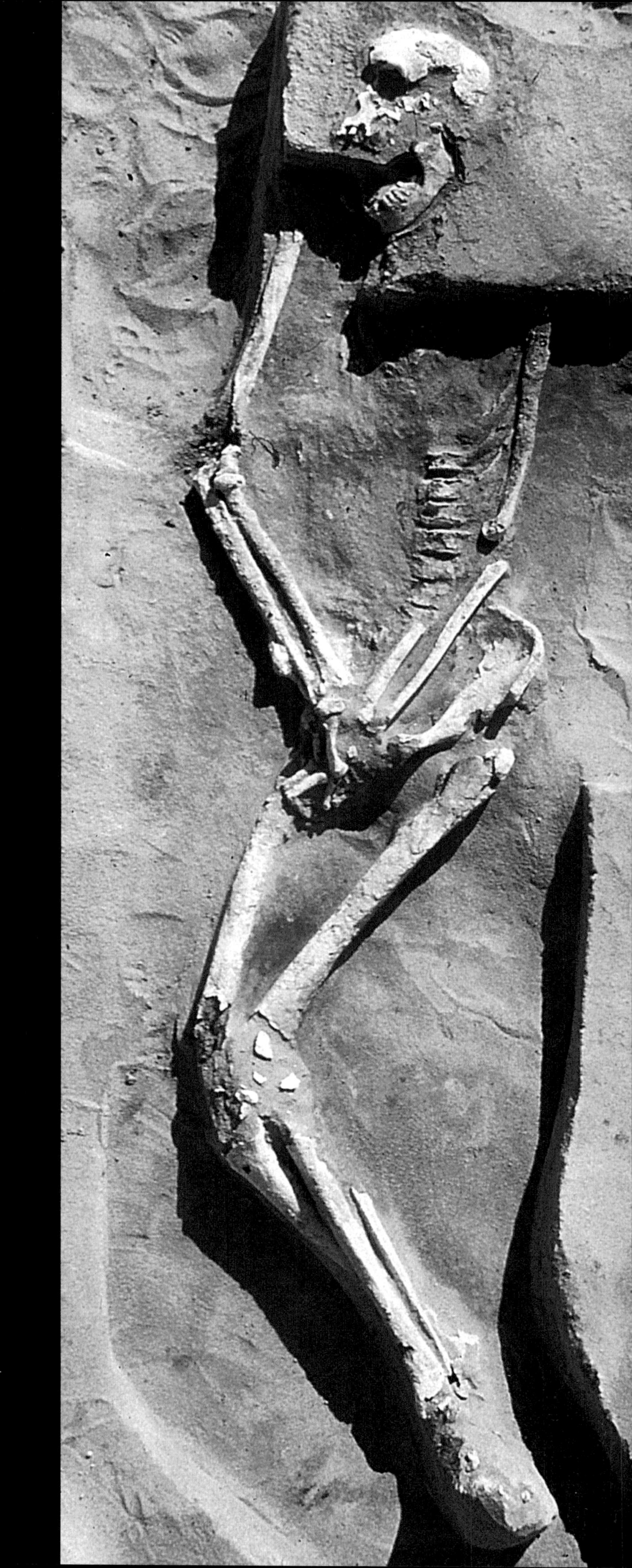

Rock painting from Kakadu National Park, Australia. The earliest Aboriginal art dates to at least 40,000 years ago and was part of a tradition of rock painting that continued until nearly the present day, including such recent works as these from northern Australia. *Courtesy of Donald Johanson, Institute of Human Origins.*

***Homo sapiens* burial at Lake Mungo, Australia.** The Mungo III male skeleton dates to nearly 30,000 years ago, but other evidence from northern Australia indicates that people first arrived on the continent 20,000 years earlier. The body was sprinkled with red ochre, a practice known from burials of similar age in Europe. *Courtesy of Alan Thorne, Australian National University.*

years ago. The site of Nauwalabila I in the Northern Territory's Deaf Adder Gorge contains hematite used for pigment at a level dated to 53,000 years. Archeological sites on the southern side of the island continent show that humans had spread across Australia as long as 40,000 years ago. ◖ Australia reveals in microcosm what became a global phenomenon after 50,000 years ago: a burst of colonization that put people all over the Old World, initially, and then across Australasia and the Western Hemisphere. Humans suddenly learned how to cross expanses of water and ice and how to find food in high mountains and parched deserts, even frozen tundra. What sparked this intrepidness? Intriguingly, this increase in colonization coincides roughly with the first archeological signs of behaviorally modern humans; anatomically modern humans had existed for at least the previous 50,000 years, but 50,000 years ago there appear the first signs of art, of diversified tools for specific functions, and other clues to enhanced culture. Increasingly intricate and far-flung networks of trade and cooperative social alliances between groups probably facilitated human range expansion. ◖ With the advent of agriculture and animal domestication just 10,000 years ago, people could export not only themselves but the skills for cultivating staple crops. Human societies became more sedentary and structured, and a far greater population size could be maintained than under any hunter-gatherer lifestyle. Human population densities today exceed those at the end of the Paleolithic by as much as 10,000 times. But it is only recently that our numbers have reached such staggering sums. The planet gained its billionth human around 1800. It took only 130 years more for the population to double to 2 billion and little more than three decades to add a third billion. In the last 30 years alone, the population has nearly doubled again. ◖ Today we worry, with good cause, about our cumulative effect on the global environment. Many threats today stem from our sheer numbers and our demand for space and resources, but our impact on wildlife seems to have begun with the colonization of new continents. In the past 40,000 years, 85 genera of large mammals have gone extinct, including such charismatic creatures as woolly mammoths and rhinos, club-tailed glyptodonts, giant ground sloths, and saber-toothed cats. Some strong correlations exist between the time these animals disappeared and when humans entered their habitats. North America may have experienced a Pleistocene overkill of large mammals not long after Clovis-point-wielding PaleoIndian hunters arrived from Asia. Birds also experienced severe extinctions, especially on islands, where many flightless species lived. The Pacific islands, for instance, may have lost 2,000 bird species within the short span of human occupation. Whenever we reached new places, extinctions of previously secure animals apparently followed. Knowing this history, can we afford to find out just how many humans can occupy Earth?

23 · Defining Human Species

SINCE the time of Linnaeus, in the mid-eighteenth century, species, the lowest category in the Linnaean hierarchy of organisms, have been known as the basic unit of biological classification. The prevailing view during Linnaeus's time was that species were fixed, unchanging types that had been created through divine intervention. Darwinian thinking of the following century, by contrast, emphasized "descent with modification." Species were not static but dynamic—they changed, and they came and went. ◖ In the late twentieth century further definitions of species have appeared. The biological species concept, a product of the Modern Evolutionary Synthesis in the 1940s, states that a species is a group of organisms that is reproductively isolated from other such groups. The recognition species concept, which enlarges on this statement, holds that species are the most inclusive group that shares a fertilization system. This definition implies that members of a species have a specific mate-recognition system so that species breed with their own kind—lions do not mistake cheetahs, for example, as potential mates. These views of species have added strength to the idea that species are real, distinct, and readily identifiable entities in nature. ◖ Certain mating behaviors can be observed in living species, and genetic analysis can further strengthen the case for a particular species, but we do not have these advantages in studying fossils. How can we ever know if *A. boisei* and *A. robustus* were reproductively isolated from one another, or whether their different mate-recognition systems would have prevented them from mating? It seems that the biological species concept and the recognition species concept simply are not very useful for recognizing paleospecies. Even in the case of living organisms it is not always easy to ascertain what characteristics in the mate-recognition system keep individuals of the same species together. Moreover, with few exceptions, the morphological features that reinforce reproductive isolation are not found in the hard parts, which are all that we have available in the fossil record. ◖ Another aid to recognizing a living species is that its representatives live at the same time (*synchronic*) and in the same geographic location (*sympatric*). Hominid fossils are patchily distributed over 4.5 million years of time and spread across the globe. Very seldom do we have instances such as at Olduvai Gorge, where two distinct hominids, *Australopithecus boisei* and *Homo habilis*, not only overlapped in time but apparently occupied the same landscape. ◖ How, then, do we recognize paleospecies? How do we take a group of newly discovered fossils, such as those recently found at Kanapoi, and determine whether they belong to an already recognized species, such as *A. afarensis*, or to a new species? As a general guide, we look at modern species of primates that we know belong to a reproductively isolated group. For example, a series of features in the skeletons of bonobos and common chimpanzees, which do not interbreed (they are reproductively isolated from each other), are taken as a measure of species differences in the genus *Pan*. If we find, as was true for the Kanapoi hominids, that the fossil assemblage differs from other species of early hominids by a series of morphological features equal to or greater than the differences seen between the two species of *Pan*, we can conclude that it is a distinct species—in this case, *A. anamensis*. ◖ This procedure is not always clear cut, which is why paleoanthropologists continue to disagree over the number of hominid species that have ever existed. Evaluating the significance of morphological differences is not always easy. Only first-hand experience with the skeletal anatomy of numerous mammalian groups, especially primates, provides the necessary perspective from which to distinguish between variation within a species, or *intraspecific variation*, and variation between species, or *interspecific variation*. For instance, understanding the pattern of variation in a primate species that results from sexual dimorphism will prevent us from placing the males of a fossil assemblage into one species and the females into another species. ◖ Early workers in paleoanthropology tended to place every new fossil specimen found into a new species. This approach, known as "splitting," led to such a bewildering array of names that it was impossible to understand and discuss hominid evolution in a meaningful manner. In part, the splitter mentality was due to discoverer ego, but it also reflected the view that differences seen between fossils mirrored actual species distinctions. With the development of the Modern Evolutionary Synthesis and an increasing appreciation of population variability, the pendulum began to swing in the other direction. At that time, rather than emphasizing the individual variation seen in fossils, the idea that morphology could vary within a species began to influence the way in which fossil samples were partitioned. Perhaps as an overreaction to the previous splitting of fossil specimens into several species, the number of taxa was severely reduced, by those now known as lumpers. ◖ In the view of some researchers, the lumpers may have overreacted and, in so doing, underestimated the number of hominid species that existed and thereby oversimplified the complexity of hominid evolution. In fact, we will probably always underestimate the number of species in the hominid fossil record. One reason is that fossil samples tend to be fragmentary, and it may not be possible to garner sufficient evidence to justify establishing a new species. But, and even more important, there seems to be little correlation between species and morphological differences. Some groups of primates – for example, lemurs – consist of numerous species that are distinct on the basis of behavior and skin and hair coloration. These aspects do not fossilize, and if all we had were the skeletons, we would severely underestimate the number of lemur species. Two fossil femurs that look identical might not, in fact, belong to the same species – a sobering thought for those dealing with paleospecies. ◖ The problem of recognizing paleospecies is linked to a more fundamental problem in taxonomy – determining how species should be segregated. If an evolving lineage is continuous, as it must be, at least until it terminates in a final extinction, then dividing one species from another would appear to be arbitrary. If species A evolves into species B, and so on, how is this evolving lineage subdivided into species? Such thinking has given rise to the extreme view that *Homo sapiens* should be projected into the past to include *Homo* fossils dated to 2 million years ago. Rather than giving different species names when morphological changes are seen, it was suggested that different stage designations be given. Such a rendition contributes little to our understanding of change and diversity in human evolution. ◖ When the nature of speciation became better understood through an increasingly complete fossil record for a number of animal species, it became clearer that species appear very suddenly in the geological record. Throughout their life span as a species, they seem to be in a state of stasis, exhibiting little or no change, and then they disappear rather abruptly. It was easy to ascribe the suddenness of species' appearances and departures to the incompleteness of the paleontological record. ◖ The key to resolving this quandary is that an evolutionary lineage should not be likened to a continuous ladder of evolution but to a bush that reflects divergence and branching. The manner in which speciation, the process whereby new species are born, operates is that some splinter group of a species, a population, becomes geographically isolated and develops into a new species. The geographically isolated population, unable to exchange genes with the parent population, begins to diverge as a result of genetic drift and mutations. Presumably it is in these smaller outlying populations, with smaller gene pools, that speciation occurs. ◖ The Darwinian view of phyletic gradualism, which points to slow, minute change over extremely long periods of time, has been severely challenged by the more recent concept of punctuated equilibrium. The basic tenet of punctuated equilibrium is that new species arise by splitting off from ancestral species. This splitting is presumed to occur rapidly and sporadically. Therefore, the absence of fossils showing intermediate, smooth transitions between species is explained by this model as a result of sudden splitting, and incompleteness of the fossil record need not be invoked to account for missing intermediate forms. A corollary to the punctuated equilibrium model is that descendant species closely resemble the ancestral species only for a short period of time. ◖ One final point requires consideration. Punctuated equilibrium does not ignore natural selection or adaptation. In this model, natural selection and adaptation are not panspecific forces but operate differentially on various local populations. Insofar as environmental and climatic fluctuations occur over relatively short periods, there are probably many opportunities for speciation – another reason to expect a greater number of species than is currently recognized for the Hominidae. ◖ Turning to the hominid fossil record, it is interesting to note that from its first appearance, roughly 4 million years ago, to its disappearance 1 million years later, *A. afarensis* (in its skeletal remains) appears relatively unchanged. Although we can make this statement about the hard parts, which fossilize, nothing can be said about possible changes in behavior or the soft tissue. It is likely that when other taxa are as well known as *afarensis*, this pattern of long periods of stasis will prove to be typical of hominid evolution. ◖ Hominid evolution is similar to that of other organisms. Splitting and divergence would seem to be the rule, and in this case, as more hominids are found, the tree will undoubtedly become bushier. From a theoretical point of view, because morphological change and speciation do not necessarily go hand in hand, it is more than likely that some species will go undetected. ◖ Paleoanthropologists often wonder how many hominid species have ever existed. The answer is that we do not know, and it is highly likely that we will never know.

24 · Co-Existing Human Species

THERE is a theoretical concept in ecology called the competitive exclusion principle. According to this principle, only one species of a particular kind of animal can inhabit a specific ecological niche (which can be thought of as that animal's place and profession) at any particular time, because the existence of any contemporaneous species filling an identical niche in the environment would cause intense competition for food and other resources. Eventually all but one of the competing species would be forced out. This principle, once it was applied to human evolution, generated what became known as the single species hypothesis. ◖ As intelligent, large-bodied bipedal primates with presumably similar ecology and a dependence on tools and culture, it was thought, hominids could only have existed one species at a time. Only one hominid species lives today, of course, but was this always the case? ◖ Although fossil discoveries from Olduvai Gorge, Tanzania in 1959 and the early 1960s suggested that two distinct kinds of hominids might have occupied the environment at the same time, confirmation of this conjecture had to wait another decade, when in 1975, a nearly complete cranium of *Homo ergaster*, KNM-ER 3733 (see page 180), was found in sediments at Koobi Fora, in northern Kenya. Six years earlier, another complete cranium known as KNM-ER 406 (see page 158), a classic example of *Australopithecus boisei*, had been unearthed from the same sediment layer. That meant the two specimens, representing two distinct species, had lived, broadly speaking, at the same time. The simple story of only one hominid species living at any one time throughout human evolution was clearly wrong. ◖ If two distinct kinds of hominids shared the same landscape in East Africa nearly 2 million years ago (and apparently did so in South Africa as well), scientists needed to consider how those species would have divided the resources in the environment to permit their coexistence. In the case of these two species, *H. ergaster* may have been a wide-ranging omnivore with a large carnivorous component to its diet. The heavy-duty tools of *ergaster* suggest that this hominid was a butcher *par excellence* of hunted or scavenged game meat. Because its jaws and teeth were specially designed for crushing and chewing, *A. boisei* is often characterized as a herbivore, focusing on a diet of hard foods, perhaps including nuts and seeds. ◖ But have more than one hominid species always coexisted? For the earliest period of human evolution, the existing evidence indicates that perhaps only a single species lived at any one time. More than 4 million years ago, we have evidence of *Ardipithecus ramidus* and *Australopithecus anamensis*, the former preceding the latter in time. Between 4 million and 3 million years ago in East Africa, the only known hominid was *Australopithecus afarensis*. ◖ By about 2 million years ago, however, at least one split in the family tree had occurred, as both the robust australopithecines and the first members of genus *Homo* had evolved. There were at least three species of

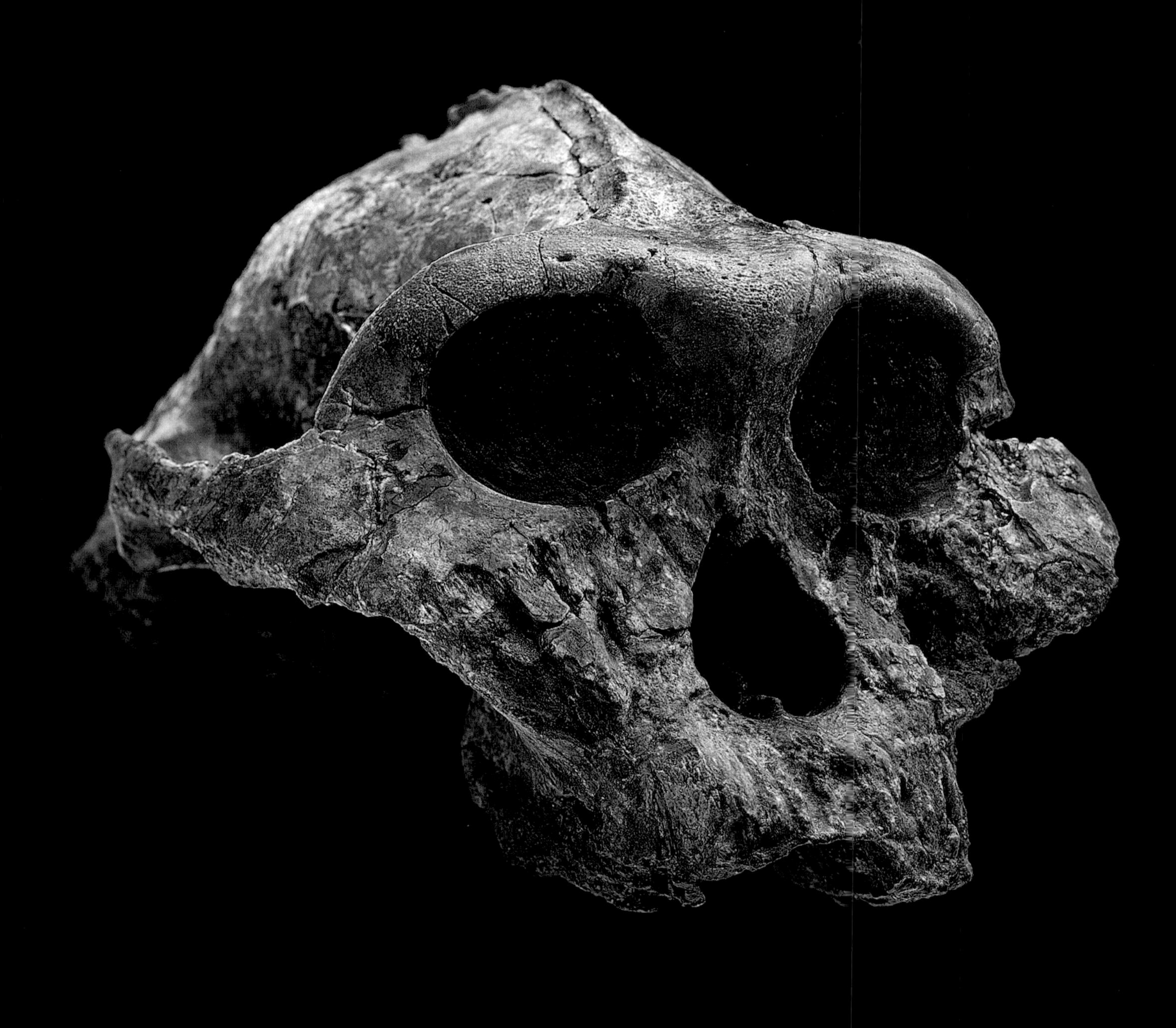

Crania of *Australopithecus boisei* and *Homo ergaster* from Koobi Fora, Kenya. Discovery of these very different specimens, KNM-ER 406 (*left*) and KNM-ER 3733 (*right*), in sediments of the same age invalidated the hypothesis that only a single hominid species could survive in a habitat at any one time. Actual sizes. *Photographs by David Brill; courtesy of National Museums of Kenya.*

robusts, including the East African one represented by the 406 cranium and several other crania, jaws, and teeth. Many paleoanthropologists believe that at least three species of early *Homo* also lived in East Africa at this time. These would be the species *H. habilis*, *rudolfensis*, and *ergaster*, which included 3733 (see page 162). ◖ The most compelling case of hominid coexistence, however, involves ourselves as one of the characters. We now have ample evidence from the Near East, particularly from several caves on Mount Carmel in Israel, that Neandertals, or *Homo neanderthalensis*, and modern *Homo sapiens* overlapped in time and space for about 50,000 years. Did these similar species live together and interact, or did they lead essentially separate lives? Scenarios range from the evolution of Neandertals directly into modern humans, to coexistence and hybridization between these distinct populations, to the replacement of Neandertals by their more modern counterparts through violent confrontation or more subtle ecological competition. The first idea seems untenable given the length of time that moderns and Neandertals overlapped in the Near East. Hybridization is unlikely, although possible, if the two groups were biologically distinct, as suggested by their disparate anatomies. And although modern humans ultimately outlasted Neandertals, there is no hard evidence of violent or rapid replacement anywhere (although modern humans do appear rather suddenly in the archeological record of western Europe). ◖ The single species idea resurfaced recently in a modified form when two South African researchers, Maciej Henneberg and Francis Thackeray, argued that the anatomical differences used to distinguish hominid species disappear in a particular statistical analysis to the degree that only one species can be identified at any single period during human evolution. Each hominid species, they concluded, was no more variable in body size or cranial capacity than humans are today. Yet, despite our underlying genetic homogeneity, modern humans have dramatically variable anatomy, more so than many of our ancestors. Comparing fossil populations to the more variable modern ones, however, obscures the distinctive features that mark separate species. We need only to look at 3733 and 406: it is hard to imagine how such different creatures could ever constitute a single species.

25 · Human Diversity Today

AROUND the world, humans appear very different from each other. To some extent, we are. There are differences in skin color, body size, limb proportions, hair texture, and other physical features. Certainly, there are differences in dress and countless cultural customs. But despite our visible variety of sizes, shapes, and features, humans are remarkably similar beneath the surface of our skins—tediously uniform, in the words of one geneticist. In fact, two random people may differ by only one to three letters per thousand in the alphabetic code of their DNA. Put another way, the genetic sequences of two unrelated individuals may be as much as 99.9 percent identical. (see pages 58–71) ◖ Human populations do differ in the presence or frequency of certain genetic alleles and their associated, tangible traits. Of the human genetic variation that exists, however, some 85 percent occurs between individuals of the same nationality. Most of our genetic variation occurs within the same population group rather than between two given groups. If all but one population were wiped out, much of our species's genetic diversity would still survive. ◖ Because our species is so homogeneous, it is not possible to delineate any solid genetic boundaries that correspond with our culturally constructed categories of race. Minor genetic differences underlie about three quarters of the color variation seen in our skin, hair, and eyes, with the rest of the variation due to such factors as sunlight exposure and nutrition. ◖ But why are we so depauperate in genetic variation compared with our closest living relatives, the African apes? We split off from the apes around 6 to 8 million years ago, yet they seem to have accumulated much more genetic variation than us since that time. One possible answer is that our present limited genetic diversity stems from a relatively recent origin for modern humans. Perhaps we went through a genetic bottleneck early in our evolutionary history—a drastic reduction in total population that winnowed much of our previously accumulated diversity. Given the rapid rate at which humans migrated around the globe and our current population size, although, such a scenario seems hard to fathom. We continue to probe the genetic legacy contained in present populations to find the answers to our evolutionary history.

26 · What Is Race?

THE CONCEPT of race has engendered more anger, animosity, and bloodshed than any other idea in human history. Setting aside the contentious social connotations of race, what does the word mean in human biology? Among animal species, the term race applies to geographic varieties that can be distinguished at the level of a subspecies. But among humans, what are considered races are groups that are not distinct enough—and never have been—to be subspecies. Individuals from any two human populations have always been able to intermingle and interbreed. ◖ Nevertheless, because we tend to choose mates from people living in similar social groups in the same area, certain traits have been preserved in certain human populations. So, populations do possess different physical features that result from a combination of geographic location and genetic inheritance. These features have been used as the basis for establishing racial differences. Many of them, however, are superficial traits that help people adapt to a certain environment or climate. ◖ Consider, for example, skin color, the most commonly cited signature of racial differences. Fewer than ten genes control the range of variation in human skin color, from the darkest to the lightest tones. These genes occur in every human to produce melanin, skin pigments that can be black, brown, yellow, or red. All humans have the genetic capacity to become black or white—or any shade in between. It is the action or inaction of the enzyme tyrosinase that actually determines how light or dark our skin will be, and that depends on the environment where we live. Aboriginal Australians, with a history on the island continent that goes back perhaps 60,000 years, have evolved very dark skin, but the recent European immigrants to Australia have not had enough time to adapt to its harsh sun and thus suffer from epidemic rates of skin cancer. ◖ Skin color turns out to correspond largely to latitude, and a continuum of change can be seen along a north-south line. This holds true for other physical traits as well. The wider apart two populations live, the more differences can be counted between them, but if we consider the range between any extremes, a pattern emerges of a geographic gradient of variation for any trait. ◖ It becomes difficult, then, to impose artificial boundaries on such variety, and doing so simply obscures the real patterns of human diversity. Who qualifies, for instance, as "black": all African Americans, African Brazilians, Caribbean peoples, and Africans? The group "Africans" alone combines an incredible geographic, linguistic, and physical (not to mention cultural) diversity of people, and also obscures the fact that North African populations more closely resemble those of southern Europe than they do sub-Saharan African populations. ◖ Populations themselves are the real units of human diversity. A more realistic approach that does not involve lumping vast groups of humans into dubious categories such as Caucasian, Mongoloid, Negroid, Capoid, and Australoid—the five divisions named by anthropologist Carleton Coon in the early 1960s, but which lack biological bearing—would be to identify people by cultural or specific geographic groupings. Humans, by nature, like to categorize nature, but races represent empty categories. They will no doubt continue to crop up in social and political contexts, but they have increasingly lost meaning for anthropologists. ◖ As a result, the American Association of Physical Anthropologists recently prepared a revised version of the official Statement on Race for UNESCO, which was first developed in 1951 and updated subsequently. Among the points raised in the most recent Statement on Race are that human populations have been isolated at times, but never for long enough to create genetic barriers to mating; we thus cannot be divided into specific genetic or geographic categories that have any biological value. Genetic diversity occurs in all human populations and reflects the influence of both natural and cultural environments. There is no evidence that truly homogeneous or "pure" populations have ever existed. Those human traits that appear to have biological value do not show up more frequently in any particular population. The global process of urbanization may result in reducing the differences between human populations. Finally, there is no necessary concordance between biological characteristics and cultural groups, and none of the latter can be said to constitute a race.

27 · The Size of Early Humans

WE cannot directly measure the weight of our ancestors, but estimates of body weight can be obtained by comparing the fossilized remains of early humans with modern apes and living humans of similar dimensions. To begin these comparisons, we must first decide what parts of a fossil hominid would be diagnostic for our purposes. Until recently such attempts were hampered by the availability of only fragmentary skeletal material but a plenitude of teeth. Initially it was thought that there must be a close relationship between tooth size and body size. For example, reconstruction of body weight, based on its massive molars, for an australopithecine found in South Africa yielded an estimate of 72 kilograms. When researchers switched to the ankle bone as the reference point, however, a more realistic estimate of 34 kilograms was obtained. Thus, although fossil teeth constitute the vast majority of early hominid remains, using them to reconstruct body weight can produce unsatisfactory results. ◖ Common sense suggests why estimates of body weight based on measurements of teeth would be incorrect. Body weight is not reflected in the size or mass of teeth. Furthermore, we have learned that australopithecines in particular were large-toothed relative to body size, a condition known as megadontia. Disproportionately large teeth in small bodies lead to estimates of body weight that are too high. ◖ Rather than measuring teeth, it is more appropriate to examine the weight-bearing postcranial skeleton (everything below the skull) for clues to body weight. Our body mass is transmitted to the ground through the pelvis, lower limbs, and feet—the skeletal segments that must be able to support our weight. Here researchers encountered another problem: not only have postcranial remains been quite fragmentary until recently, but the postcranial anatomy is very similar in different species of australopithecines and even in early *Homo*, making it difficult to distinguish species. Both shortcomings have been overcome in part by the recovery of a number of more complete skeletons such as Lucy. ◖ With postcranial skeletons at hand, and with the postcranial skeleton selected as the element to be compared in an estimate of body size, we can now turn to modern taxa. For comparison we have modern humans and the living apes. The living apes must now be put to one side, because they evolved a significantly different method of locomotion that led to different limb ratios than in humans. Because modern apes are quadrupedal and transfer some weight through their forelimbs, their hind limbs account for proportionately less of their body weight than in humans. So, estimates of the body weight of our ancestors are best based on comparisons with contemporary humans, for both are bipeds. ◖ Next, the postcranial bones of extant humans of known weight are measured. Statistical methods establish a close correlation between measurements of postcranial bones and body weight. For example, the diameters of the femoral head and top and bottom ends of a tibia closely correlate with body weight. The greater the body weight, the larger are these diameters in modern humans. ◖ The associated skeletal elements of the Lucy specimen offered an unprecedented opportunity for evaluating the accuracy of predicting body size using a variety of skeletal measurements. (see page 124) When measurements taken on a human sample, including some small individuals such as pygmies, were used for comparison, Lucy's weight was reconstructed as 27.3 kilograms. Confidence in this estimate is high, since measurements of seven of Lucy's individual bones from shoulder to ankle and comparisons with the human sample gave estimates ranging from 24.2 to 30.2 kilograms. As might be expected for a biped, the best predictors of body weight were the lower limb joints. ◖ A cursory glance at the postcranial bones assigned to *Australopithecus afarensis* reveals that there is considerable range in size. In fact, there appear to be two size groups: one large and one, like Lucy, small. Assuming the smaller individuals are female and the larger ones male, reconstruction of body weight in this species pointed to an intriguing aspect of the biology of *A. afarensis*: a large size discrepancy between males and females. Males, at about 45 kilograms, are roughly 40 percent heavier than females, which average 29 kilograms. The relatively small size of females and the rather pronounced sexual dimorphism have important implications for behavior (see page 73). Stature estimates for *A. afarensis*, based on comparisons with modern humans, also confirm sexual dimorphism, with males averaging about 1.5 meters tall and females about 1 meter tall. ◖ A number of postcranial specimens are now known from both eastern and southern Africa for the time range between 4 and 1 million years ago. However, because species of *Australopithecus* and *Homo* were contemporaries for nearly 1.5 million years and because their postcranial anatomy is nearly identical, it is not an easy task to assign isolated finds to a particular species. Therefore, postcranial elements can be positively identified only when diagnostic craniodental material is associated with the find. Such associations are rare, and in the case of *A. boisei* estimates of weight are based on only one specimen of each sex. Estimates for *A. robustus* and *A. africanus* are derived from several individuals, thanks to the larger samples from southern Africa. Estimates of body weight and stature are given in the chart below.

	BODY WT. (kg)		STATURE (m)	
	male	*female*	*male*	*female*
A. afarensis	45	29	1.5	1.1
A. africanus	41	30	1.4	1.1
A. robustus	40	32	1.3	1.1
A. boisei	49	34	1.4	1.2

There is certainly room for improvement in the estimates of body weight and stature for early humans, and perhaps greater accuracy will be forthcoming with the recovery of additional individuals. However, a number of observations can be made based on what is already known. Male australopithecines are generally larger than females, an observation that supports sexual dimorphism in all australopithecine species. Although *A. robustus* and *A. boisei* are often referred to as "robust" australopithecines, the adjective applies to their large teeth, not their body size, because they are not much bigger than the other two species, *afarensis* and *africanus*. ◖ It is apparent that during the australopithecine phase of human evolution there was stasis in body size, with males weighing between 40 and 50 kilograms and females weighing between 28 and 34 kilograms. This does

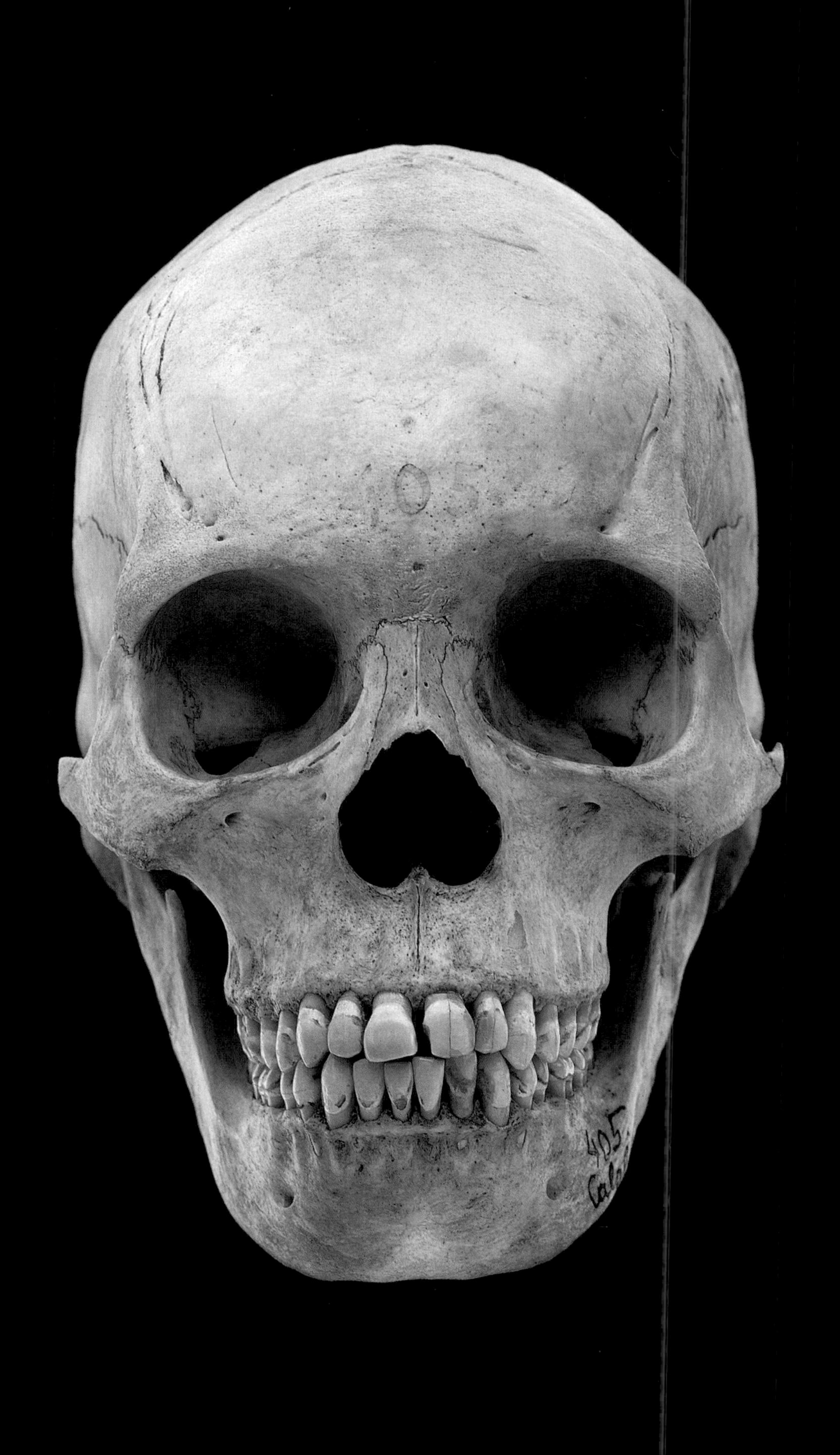

Skull of modern *Homo sapiens* from Zaire. Actual size. This African male is between the ages of 35 and 45. Actual size. *Photographs by David Brill; courtesy of American Museum of Natural History.*

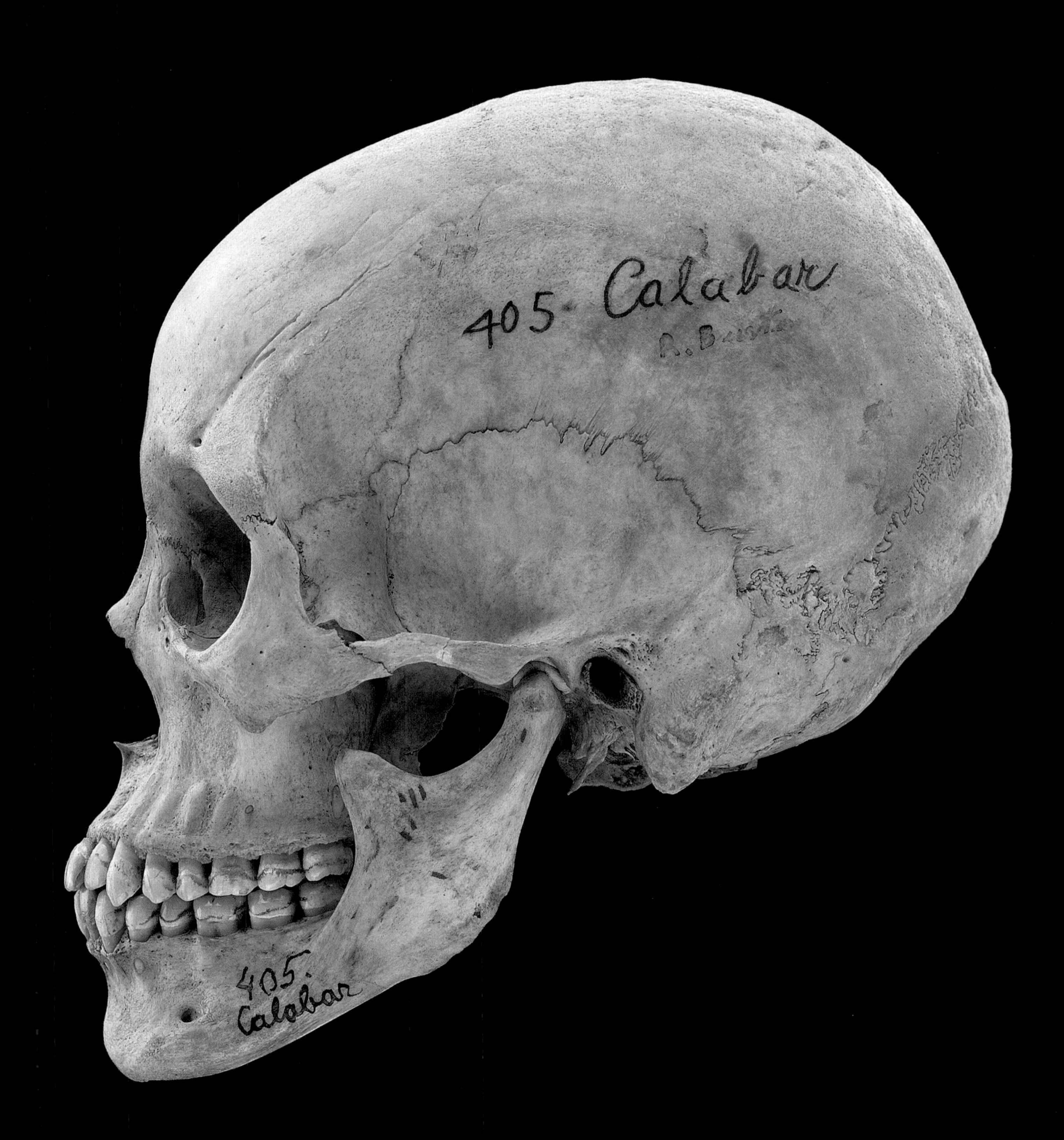
405. Calabar
405.
Calabar

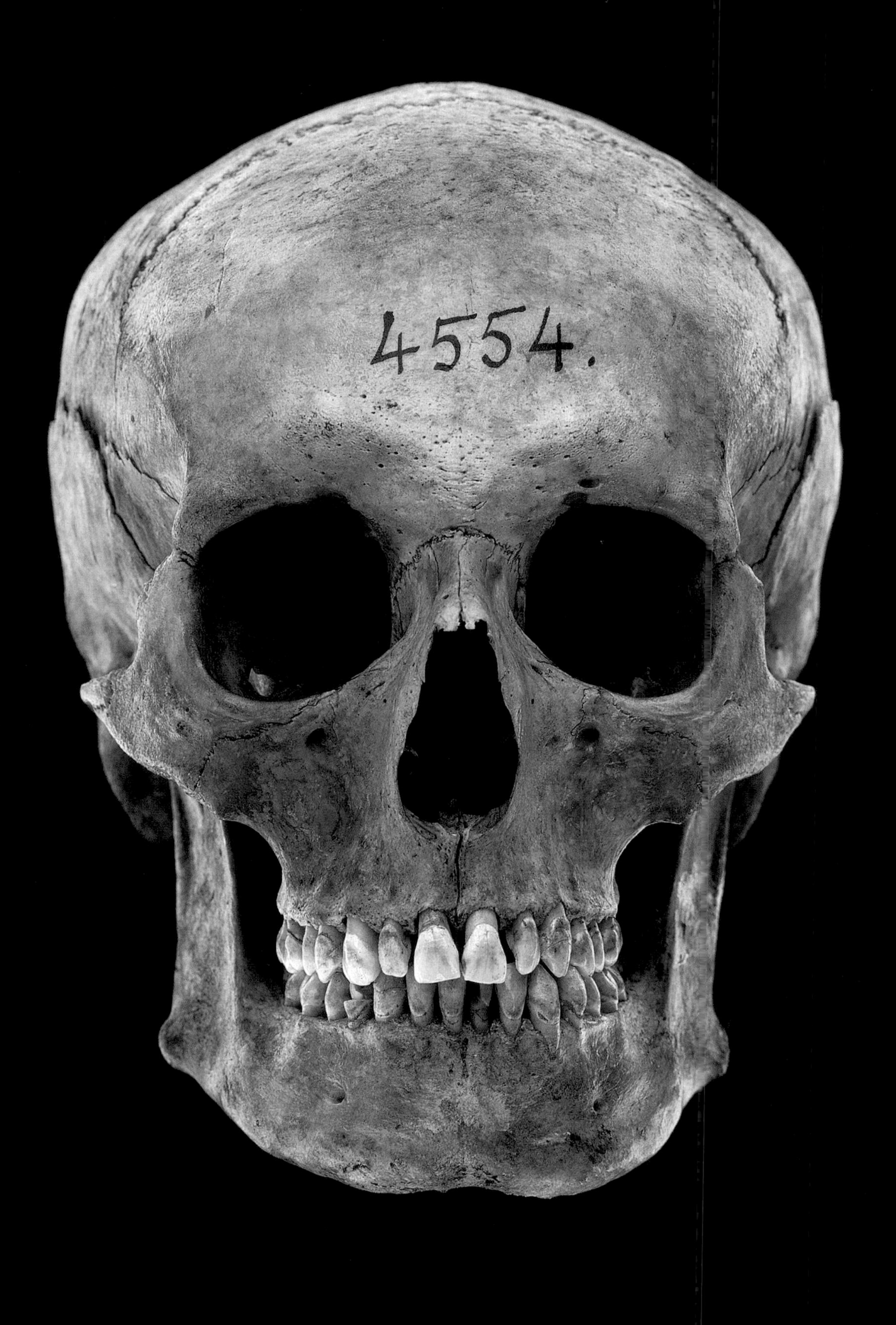

Skull of modern *Homo sapiens* from Germany, Europe. This skull comes from a young male between the ages of 25 and 30. Actual size. *Photographs by David Brill; courtesy of American Museum of Natural History.*

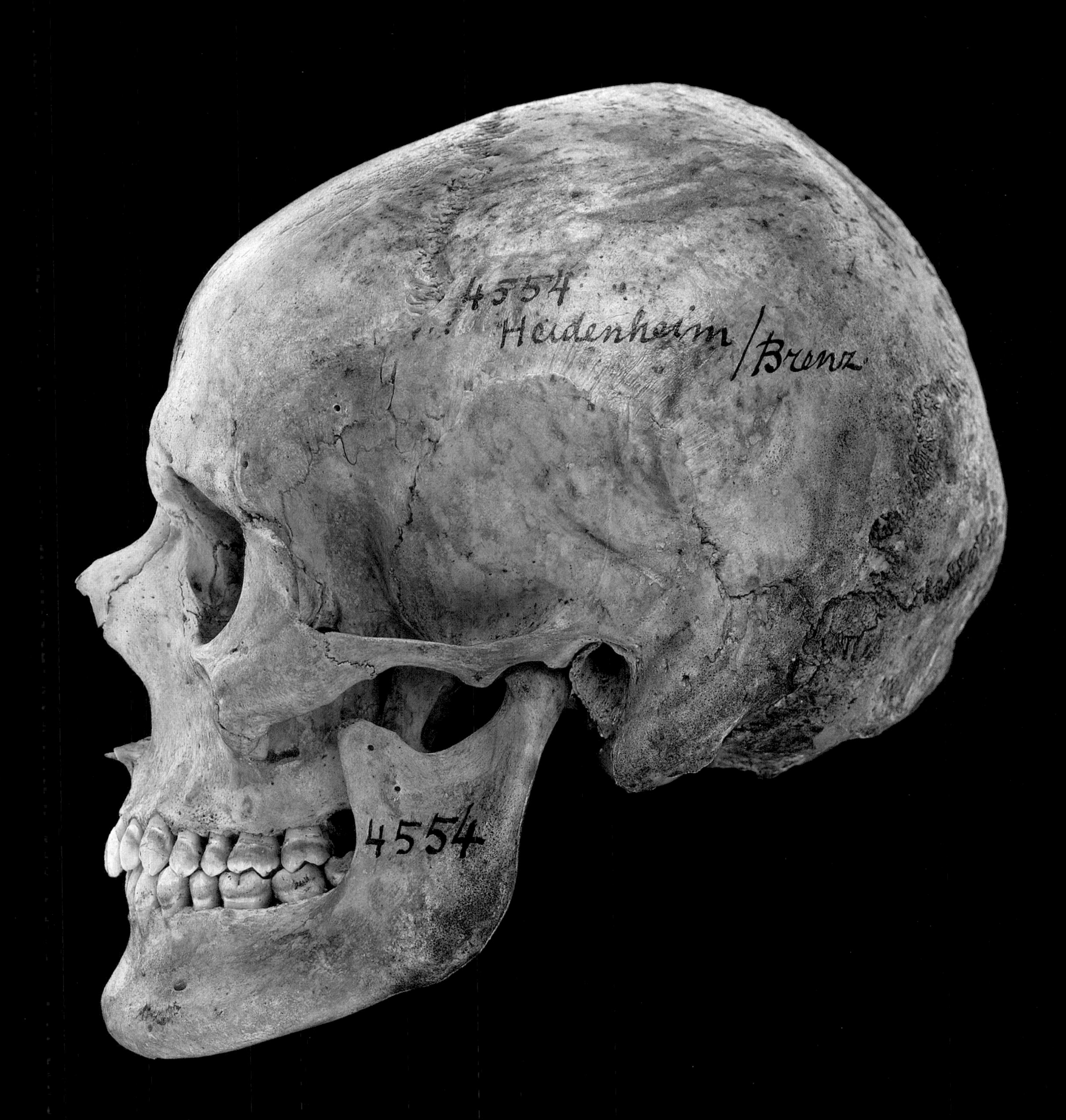
4554
Heidenheim /Brenz
4554

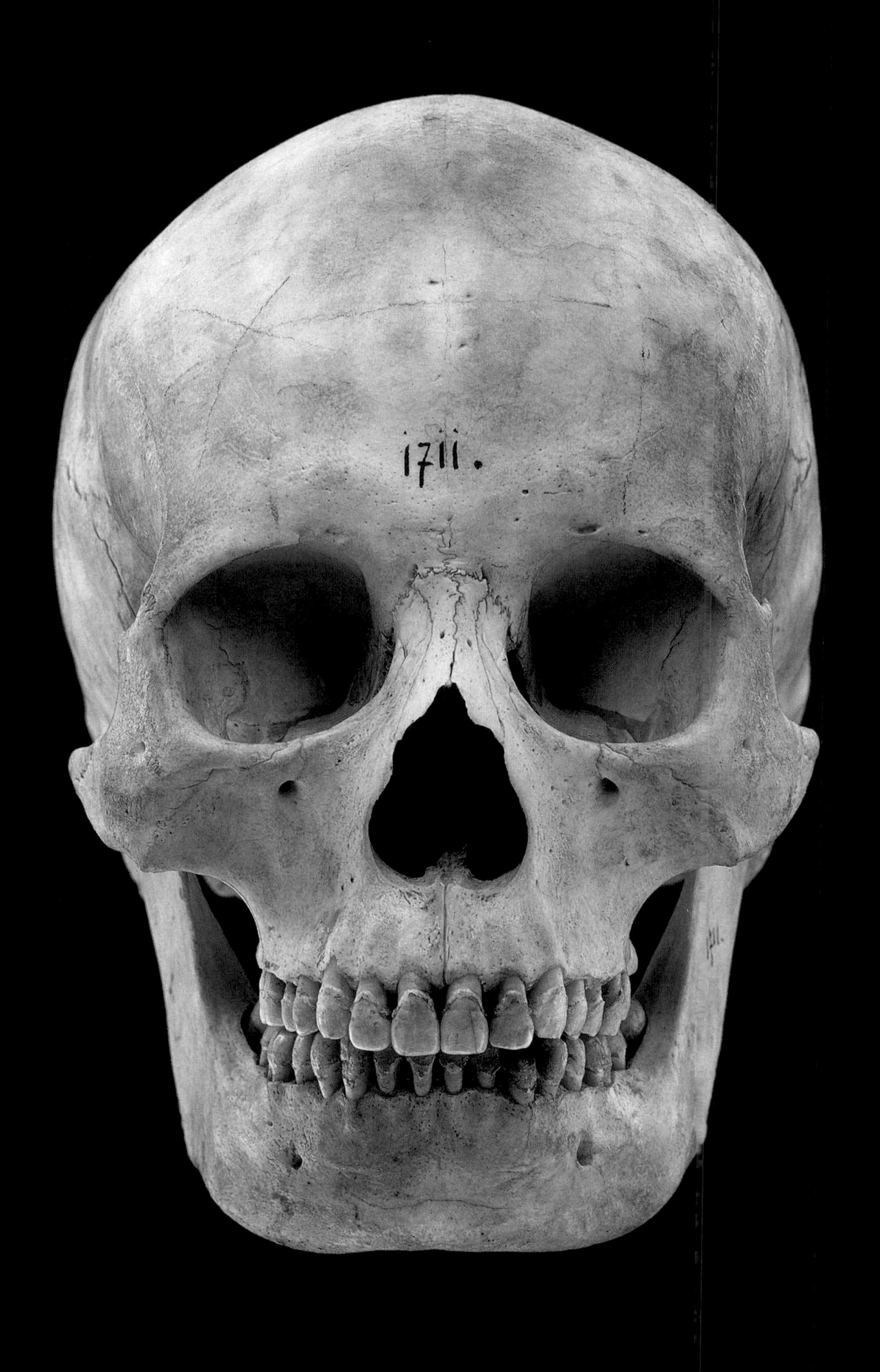

Skull of modern *Homo sapiens* from Borneo, Asia. Though collected in Indonesia, this skull comes from a Chinese woman between the ages of 25 and 30. Actual size. *Photographs by David Brill; courtesy of American Museum of Natural History.*

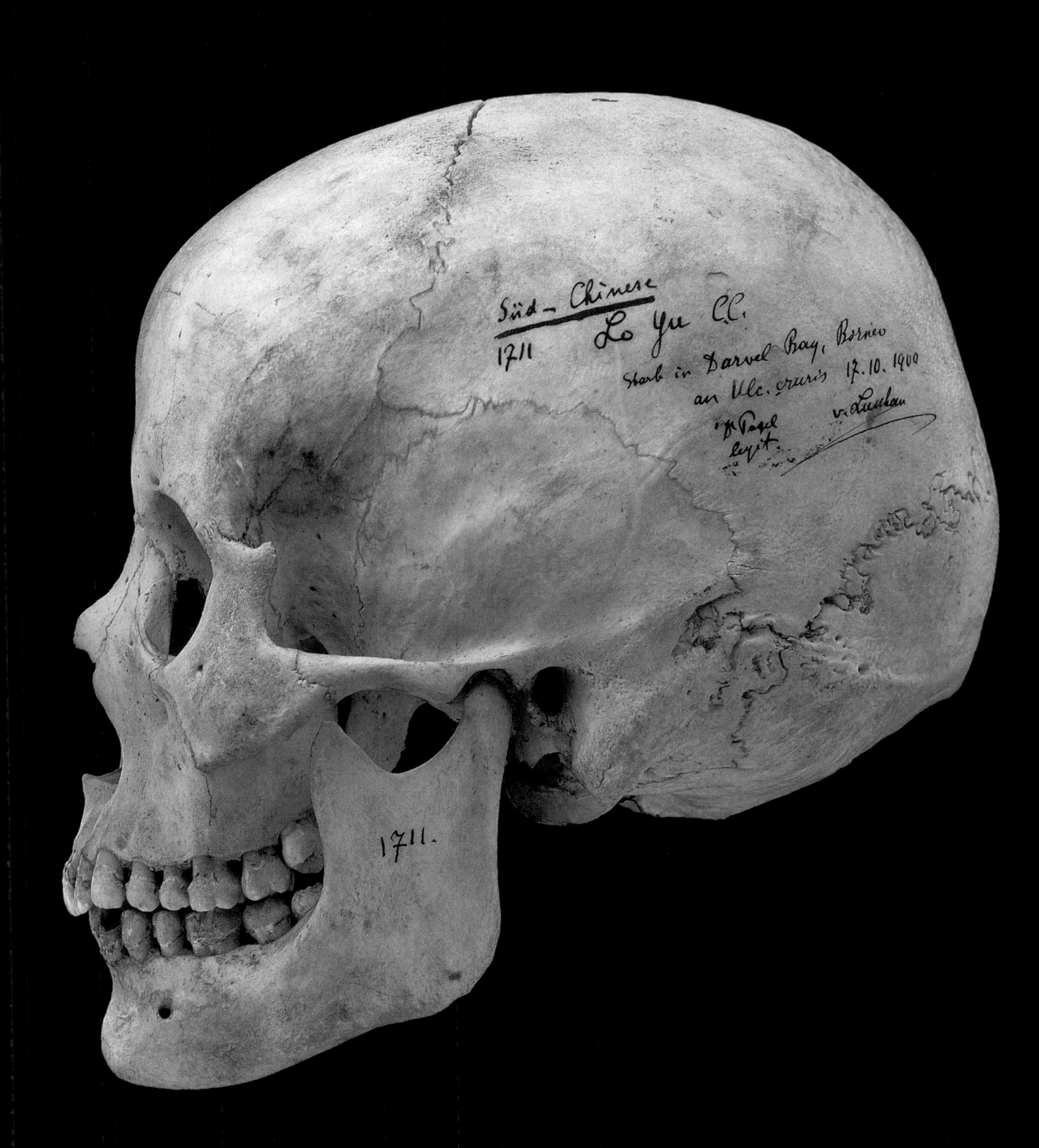
Süd-Chinese
1711 Lo Yu C.C.
Starb in Darvel Bay, Borneo
an Ulc. cruris 17.10.1900
legit v. Luschan
1711.

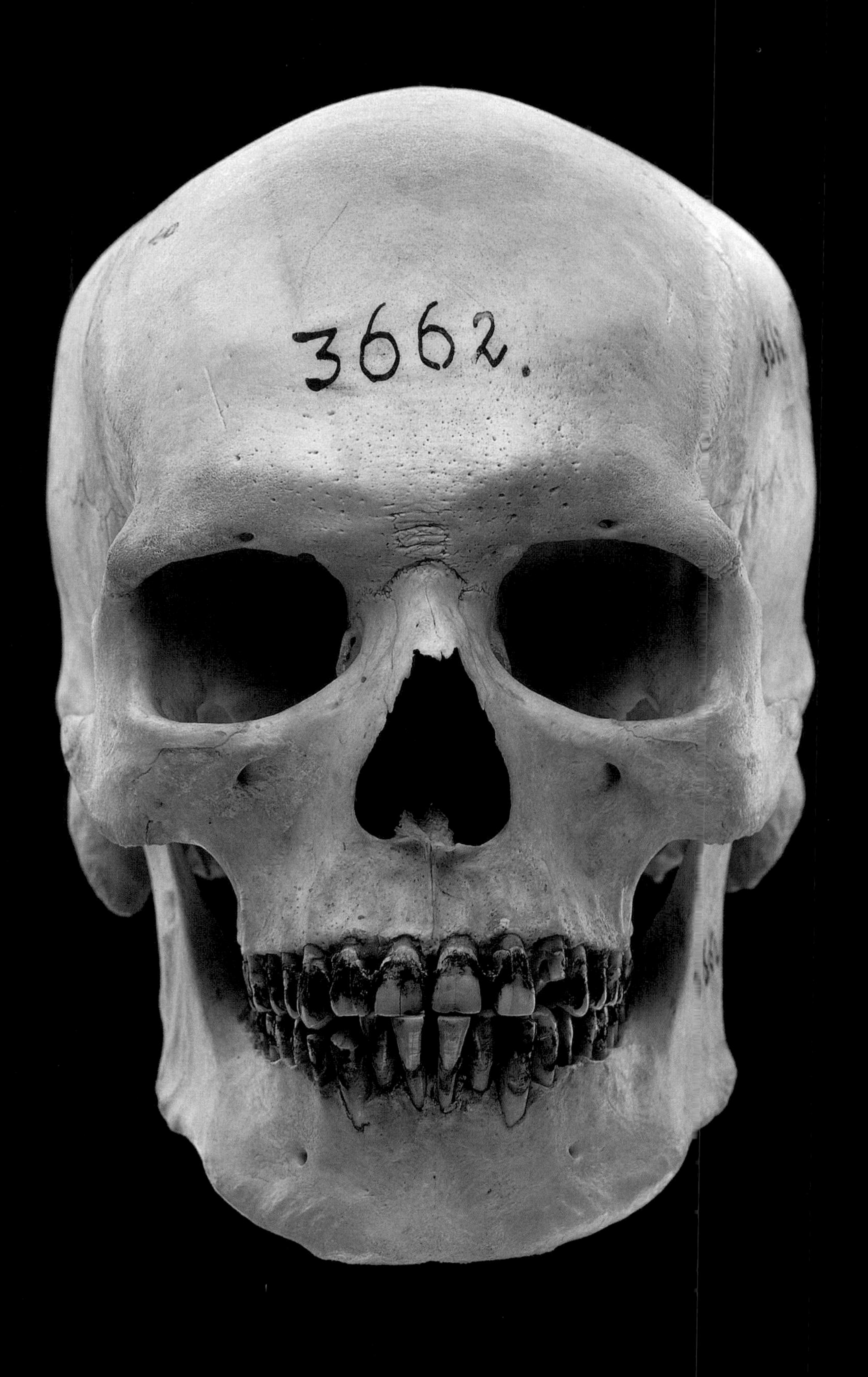

Skull of modern *Homo sapiens* from India, Asia. The teeth of this young Bengali male are stained from eating betel nut. Actual size. *Photographs by David Brill; courtesy of American Museum of Natural History.*

Skull of modern *Homo sapiens* from Solomon Islands, Australasia. This male specimen was collected in 1893 at Guadalcanal. Actual size. *Photographs by David Brill; courtesy of National Museum of Natural History.*

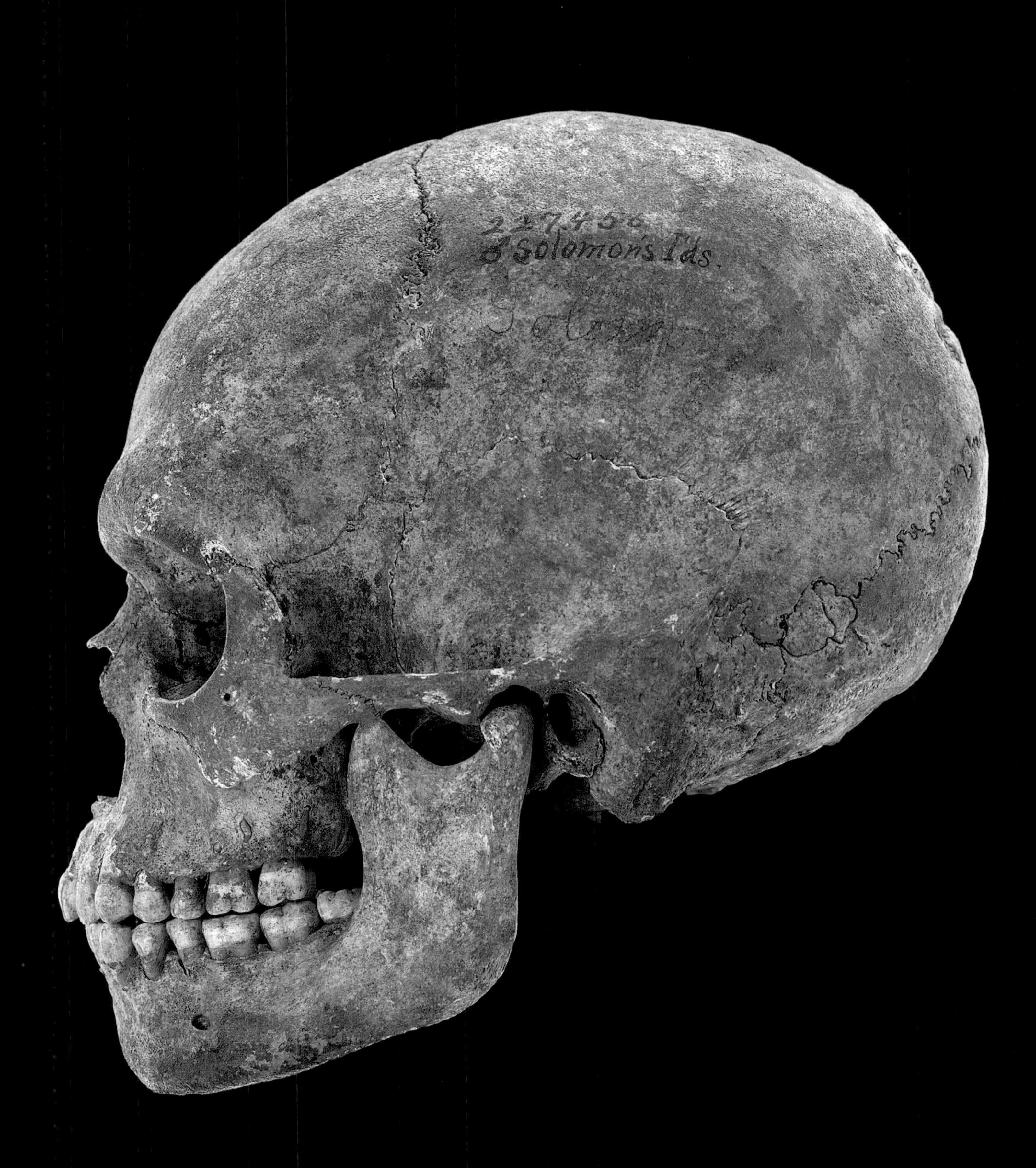
Solomon's I'ds.

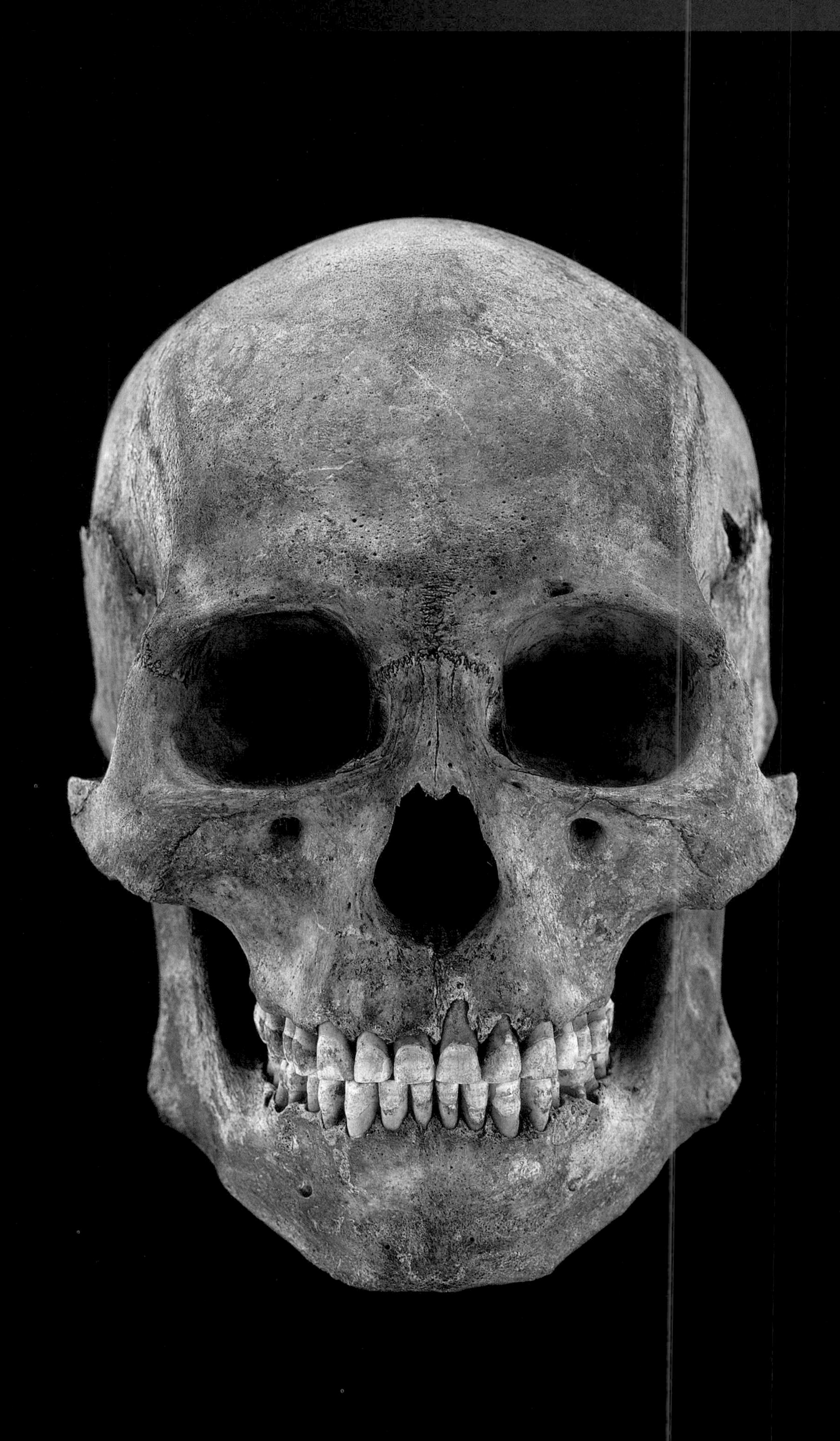

Skull of modern *Homo sapiens* from North America. This male Alaskan eskimo is between the ages of 35 and 40. Actual size. *Photographs by David Brill; courtesy of American Museum of Natural History.*

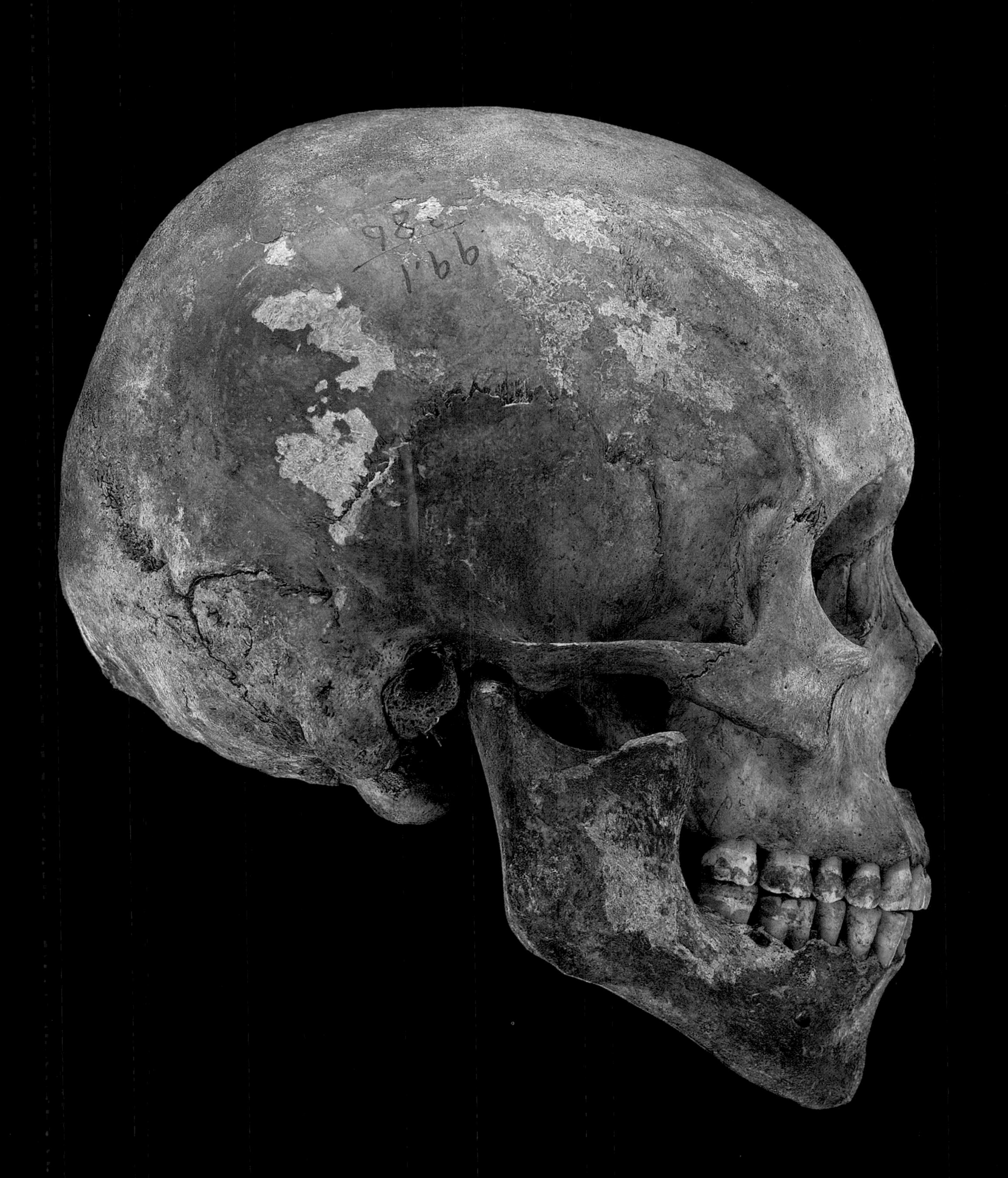

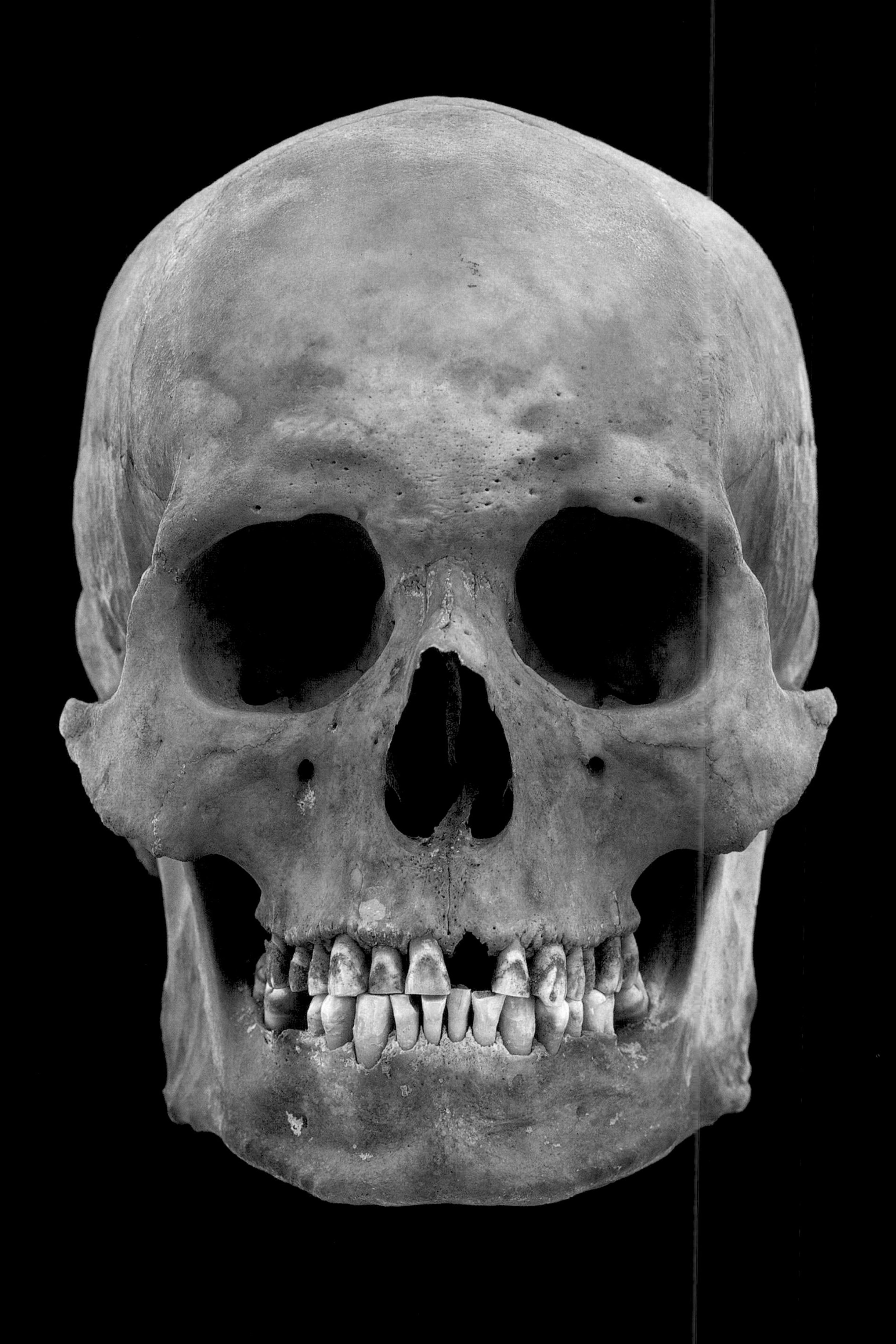

Skull of modern *Homo sapiens* from Peru, South America. This male from Chilca, Peru dates to about the fifteenth century. Actual size. *Photographs by David Brill; courtesy of National Museum of Natural History.*

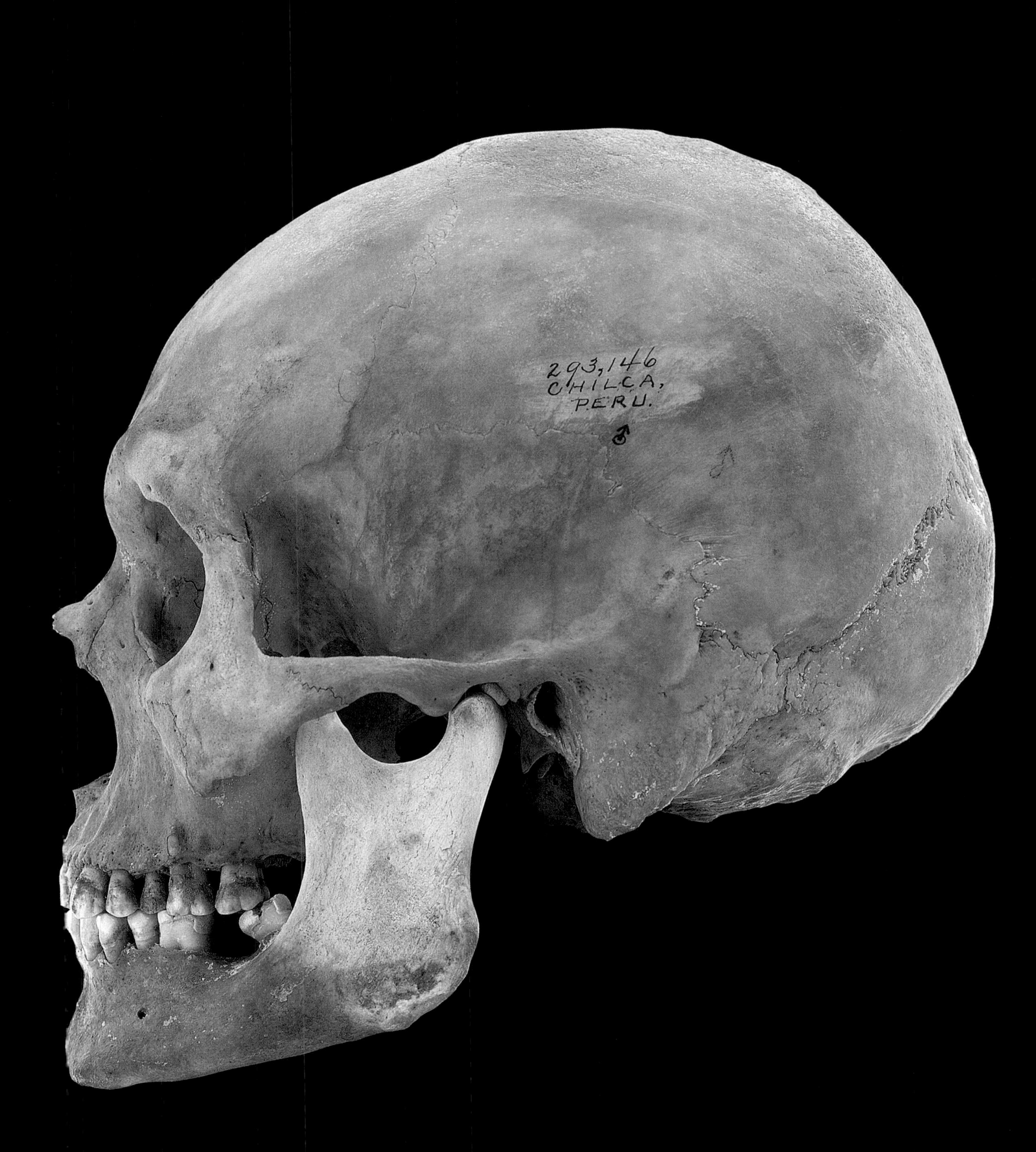
293,146
CHILCA,
PERU.

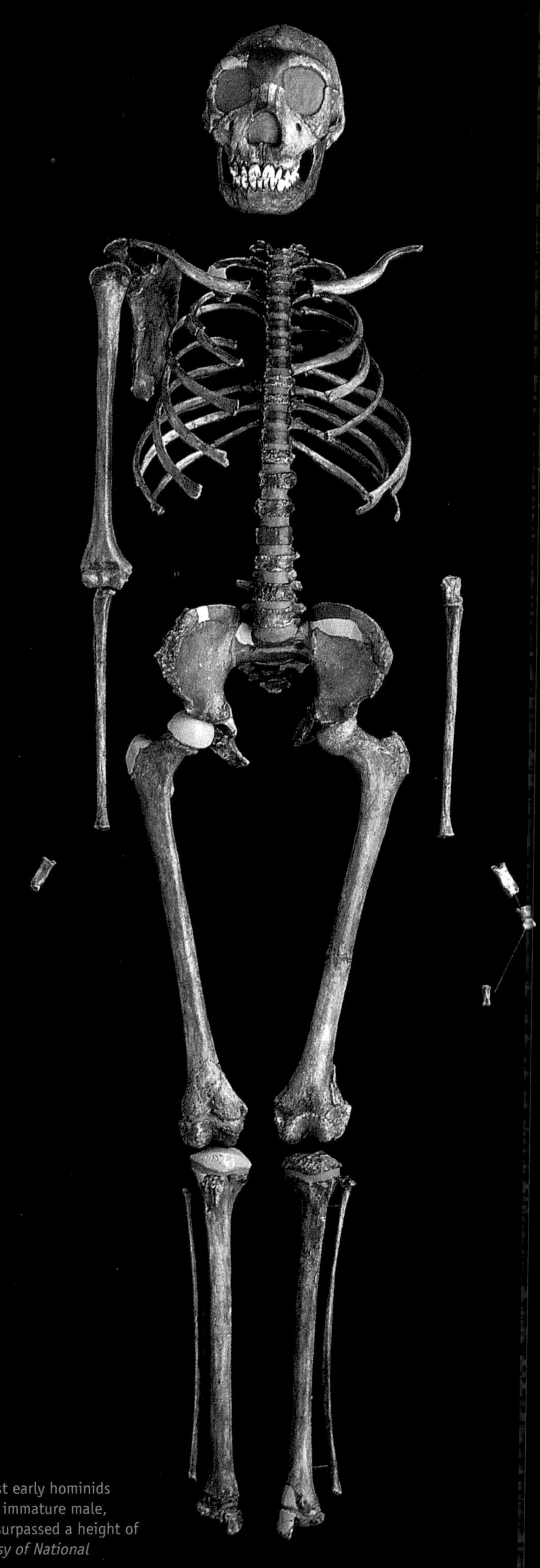

Skeleton of *Homo ergaster* from Nariokotome, Kenya. Most early hominids were not much larger than modern chimpanzees, but this immature male, WT 15000, evolved a tall, thin physique and had already surpassed a height of five feet when he died. *Photograph by David Brill; courtesy of National Museums of Kenya.*

not fit with a trend of increasing body size in hominids through time. Indeed, a specimen from Olduvai Gorge, OH 62 (see page 176), that has been assigned to *Homo habilis* and dated to 1.8 million years ago, has the surprisingly small body size of a mere 24 kilograms. In fact, a significant increase in body size does not seem to have occurred until the appearance of *Homo ergaster*, as represented by the Turkana Boy, KNM-WT 15000, (see page 182). This remarkably complete skeleton is estimated to have weighed close to 67 kilograms and to have stood about 1.6 meters tall — a stunning increase in size at 1.6 million years ago.

28 · Sexual Dimorphism

HUMANS, like virtually all mammals, are characterized by distinct features in size, shape, and behavior that differentiate between males and females — a condition known as sexual dimorphism. For example, human males tend to be larger and stronger than females. Human males and females differ in growth rate, the distribution of subcutaneous fat, and many other features. But the most obvious contrasts are seen in the secondary sexual characteristics such as the genitals, patterns of hair distribution, and breasts. ◖ Following Darwin, it is widely thought that reproductive competition among males leads to selection for physical and behavioral traits that enhance their success in siring more offspring. This increased competition to mate with females may lead to larger male body size and to the development of weapons such as large canine teeth or antlers. The selection for larger body size in males increases the level of sexual dimorphism in a particular species. Darwin first drew attention to this sequence and called it sexual selection, the evolutionary process that favors adaptations that increase mating success. This form of sexual selection often takes the form of male-male mating competition in which the larger, more aggressive males breed more offspring, thus passing on to them those genes responsible for the characteristics that were advantageous for mating. ◖ The degree of sexual dimorphism, therefore, would seem to have some connection with mating systems. As a rough generalization, primates that exhibit little or very reduced dimorphism tend to be monogamous. On the other hand, where sexual dimorphism is extreme and males are twice or more the size of females, the males tend to be polygynous and to live either in groups having a single mature breeding male (such as gorillas) or in multi-male, multi-female groups (such as baboons). However, closer study of body size in relation to sexual dimorphism shows a more mixed picture. Some monogamous species are quite dimorphic, and some species with reduced dimorphism are polygynous. ◖ Another generalization is that the overall body size of a species is directly correlated with the degree of sexual dimorphism. Usually cited is the gorilla, which is the largest in size and among the most dimorphic of all primates (see pages 84-85). Again, there are exceptions to this generalization. ◖ The need for males to protect females that are foraging or looking after infants is another factor determining the degree of sexual dimorphism. In an open savanna setting, where potential predator pressure is high, large males possessing formidable canines would have a distinct advantage in defending the troop and driving off predators. ◖ Sexual dimorphism can also be examined from the point of view of its advantages for females, and here we note that in most dimorphic species, the females are smaller than the males. If being large is good, allowing males to challenge competitors and predators, why aren't females also large? Field studies of baboon troops have shown that pregnancy and lactation place severe energy demands on females. Subsisting on a fairly low-quality vegetarian diet, female baboons are hard-pressed to eat enough to nourish their fetuses or continue to produce sufficient milk to provision their offspring. Therefore, smaller females have an advantage over larger females because they are able to eat enough to keep themselves alive and meet other energy demands of child-rearing. ◖ There also seems to be a division of labor by sex that is partly related to body size. In baboons and chimpanzees, where occasional hunting has been observed, it is the males that habitually hunt. Although females have been observed hunting in close proximity to the troop, they tend to concentrate on gathering plant foods. Perhaps this exploitation of different resources functions to reduce feeding competition between the sexes. For example, in the extinct huia birds of New Zealand the males had short, stout beaks which they used to peck away at branches in search of insects. Females used their long, curved beaks to probe into crevices. In this way, the sexes were not competing for the same food. ◖ The larger samples of fossil hominids from Africa exhibit marked sexual dimorphism, as manifested in the size of teeth, jaws, and other skeletal elements. Estimates of body size (weight) based on lower limb joint size for the best-known early australopithecine, *Australopithecus afarensis*, suggest that males were considerably heavier than females. The average size for six *A. afarensis* males is 45 kilograms, and for three females it is 29 kilograms. The ratio of male to female body weights gives an estimate of the degree of sexual dimorphism. In *A. afarensis* this ratio is 1.52, a value exceeding that of 1.35 for *A. africanus*. For comparison, ratios in modern humans and apes are as follow: humans, 1.22; chimpanzees, 1.37; orangutans, 2.03; and gorillas, 2.09. Clearly, the ratio for *A. afarensis* far exceeds that seen in modern humans and chimps, but it falls short of the large values for gorillas and orangs. ◖ Precisely why *A. afarensis* is so dimorphic is not totally understood, but in part the answer has to do with its terrestriality. In all species of primates that are predominantly terrestrial, we see substantial size dimorphism. However, what is most surprising about *A. afarensis* is the reduced size of the canines in males and the low level of canine dimorphism. In most but not all primates there is a correlation between body size dimorphism and canine dimorphism. That is, in primates of low body size dimorphism there is low canine dimorphism and in species with large body size dimorphism there is large canine dimorphism. Furthermore, large canine dimorphism seems to be related to high levels of aggression or male-male competition. ◖ The smaller canines in *A. afarensis* males may therefore suggest that, for whatever reason, there was reduced male-male aggression. Another important consideration is that male primates are largely responsible for warding off predators. In the case of baboons, for example, males are large and have dagger-like canines, both useful features for impeding predator attacks. ◖ In *A. afarensis*, whose males lacked large canines, large body size may have been selected for as part of a strategy for protecting against predators. A presumed reduction in male-male aggression, because of the lack of large canines, might also have led to more cooperation between males to drive off the large predators that occupied the same territory as these early hominids. Chimpanzees, in which males within a group are genetically closely related, have been observed to collectively drive off leopards. ◖ Large predators roamed the landscape at Hadar and Laetoli, and *A. afarensis* would have been subject to predation. In addition, Hadar was more heavily wooded, like the environment in which baboons live today, where incidents of predation are highest. It is in such a habitat, with impaired visibility, that these early hominids would have benefited from larger male body size and male cooperation. Such model building must be viewed cautiously, but it is an interesting example of the importance of features such as sexual dimorphism, body size, and canine size in trying to understand the behavior of our earliest ancestors.

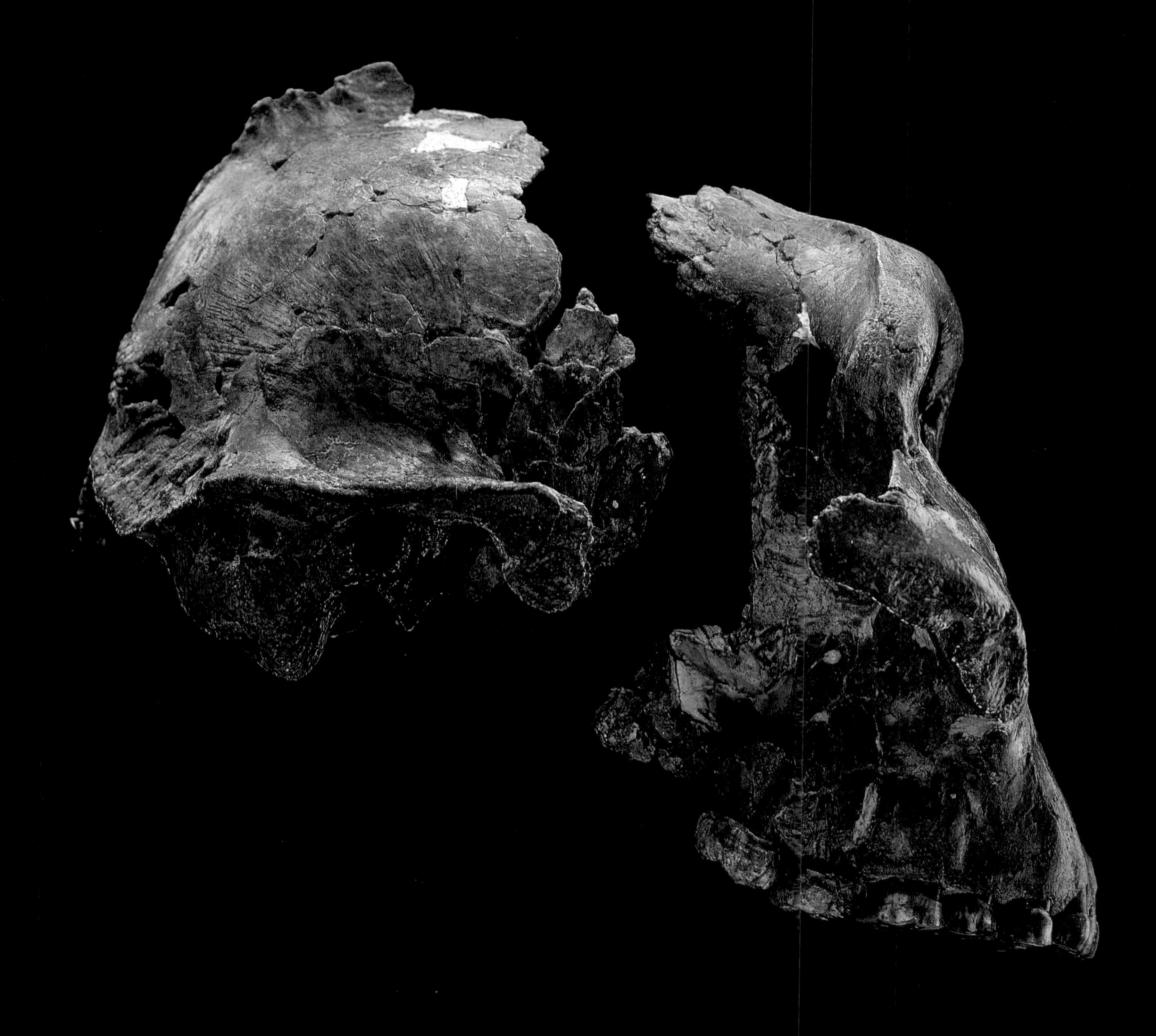

Crania of male and female *Australopithecus boisei*. Early hominid males and females exhibit considerable body size differences, dramatically shown by the male OH 5 (*left*) and the female KNM-ER 732 (*right*) specimens. Actual sizes. *Photographs by David Brill; courtesy of National Museums of Kenya.*

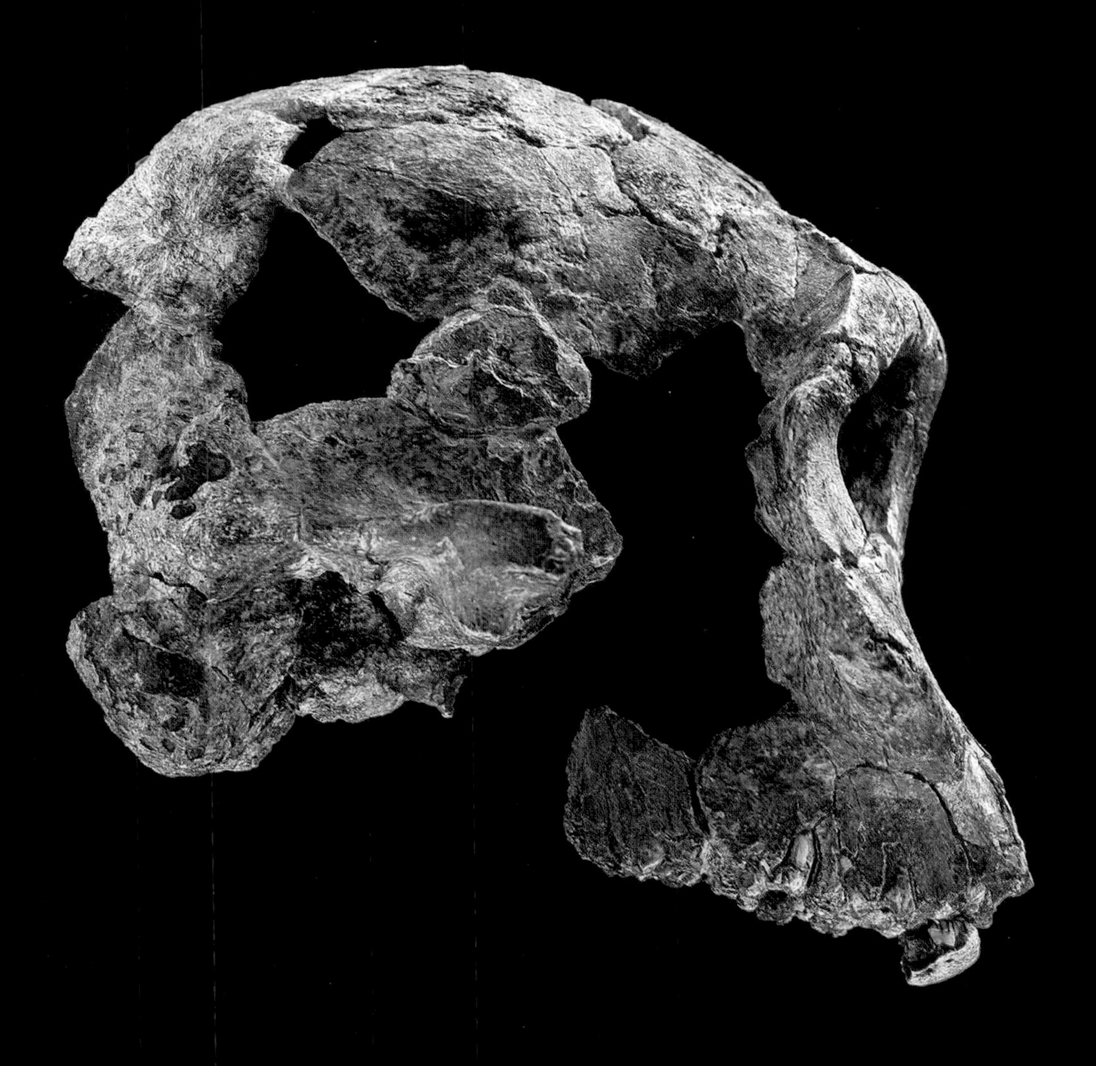

FOR our relatively modest mammalian body size, humans have a long period of gestation in the womb, lasting anywhere from thirty-eight to forty-two weeks. But we live long lives, and life span does correlate with length of gestation. The longest gestation of any mammal – twenty-two months – occurs in the female elephant, which lives an average of fifty-five years.

29 · Gestation

Brain size also correlates with gestation length. Mammals with larger brains at birth have a longer gestation, and based on our brain size relative to brain size in other mammals, humans should have an even longer gestation than we already do. ◖ Our gestation fits the general primate pattern of slow fetal body growth rate but rapid fetal brain growth, relative to growth rates in other mammals that give birth to well-developed offspring, such as a zebra foal that soon springs to its feet after a birth on the savanna. Even though human gestation is relatively long and the infant emerges large for its mother's body size, the human brain is born immature. A newborn chimpanzee's brain, for comparison, has already reached half its adult weight, but a newborn human's brain has only a quarter of an adult brain's weight. To compensate, the fetal pattern of rapid brain growth continues after birth for the first year of life, during which the brain more than doubles in size from its newborn dimensions. And as any parent knows, newborn human babies, compared to almost any other animal, are extremely dependent in this first year of life. As far as our brains our concerned, human gestation lasts twenty-one months (almost as long as an elephant's). This growth pattern, termed *secondary altriciality*, is unique to humans, and it evolved because we have struck a compromise between having big brains and being bipedal. ◖ A newborn human may be the twice the weight of a newborn ape, but the human mother probably weighs only half as much as the mother ape. That is why the process of human birth is among the most difficult for any animal. For a chimpanzee, birth comes easily; the infant's head passes through the birth canal without much constriction. The human pelvis, however, has been extensively reconfigured for two-legged locomotion, and in order to accommodate a large-brained baby, it has expanded from front to back and contracted slightly from the sides, creating a rounder birth canal. Because the birth canal starts out widest from side to side, the human infant's head must enter it turned sideways and then flex chestward and rotate 90 degrees in order to squeeze through the narrow middle of the birth canal, which is widest from front to back. The baby exits facing a different direction than when it entered. ◖ Australopithecines apparently came much closer to apes than humans in gestation length and difficulty of birth. From the shape of two fossil pelvis specimens of *Australopithecus africanus* (Sts 14) and *Australopithecus afarensis* (A. L. 288-1, or Lucy)(see pages 87 and 137), it is possible to infer that these hominids gave birth to infants with heads close in size to those of newborn chimpanzees. Birth was probably pretty quick and easy, although Lucy's pelvis is constricted from front to back and the infant's head most likely entered the birth canal sideways. Some recent radiographs of monkey and baboon births show that these primates also rotate in the birth canal, so it may be that, like humans, early hominid infants went through a similar rotation, perhaps to let their shoulders pass through the narrowest section of the canal. ◖ But if australopithecines generally had an apelike gestation and birth, when did the human gestation pattern appear? One recent hypothesis holds that Neandertals had a longer gestation period than ours. This argument relies on evidence from a particular part of the pelvis. Although most of the pelvic bones – the ilium, ischium, and sacrum – are similar in shape and size in Neandertals and modern humans, the two groups differ in the anatomy of the pubis, the bone that forms the front of the pelvis. Neandertals possess an extremely long, slender and flat superior pubic ramus, a bar along the top of the bone, whereas the pubis of early modern humans and their descendants has a short, thick ramus. (In this detail of

Pelvis of *Homo neanderthalensis* from Kebara, Israel. The elongated superior pubic ramus at the top of a Neandertal pelvis was cited as evidence that this species had a longer gestation and birthed larger, better developed babies than modern humans. Recovery of this pelvis from the Kebara 2 skeleton showed that the birth canal was not significantly larger than a human's, however, so Neandertal gestation was probably not any longer. Actual size. *Photograph by David Brill; courtesy of Sackler School of Medicine, Tel Aviv University.*

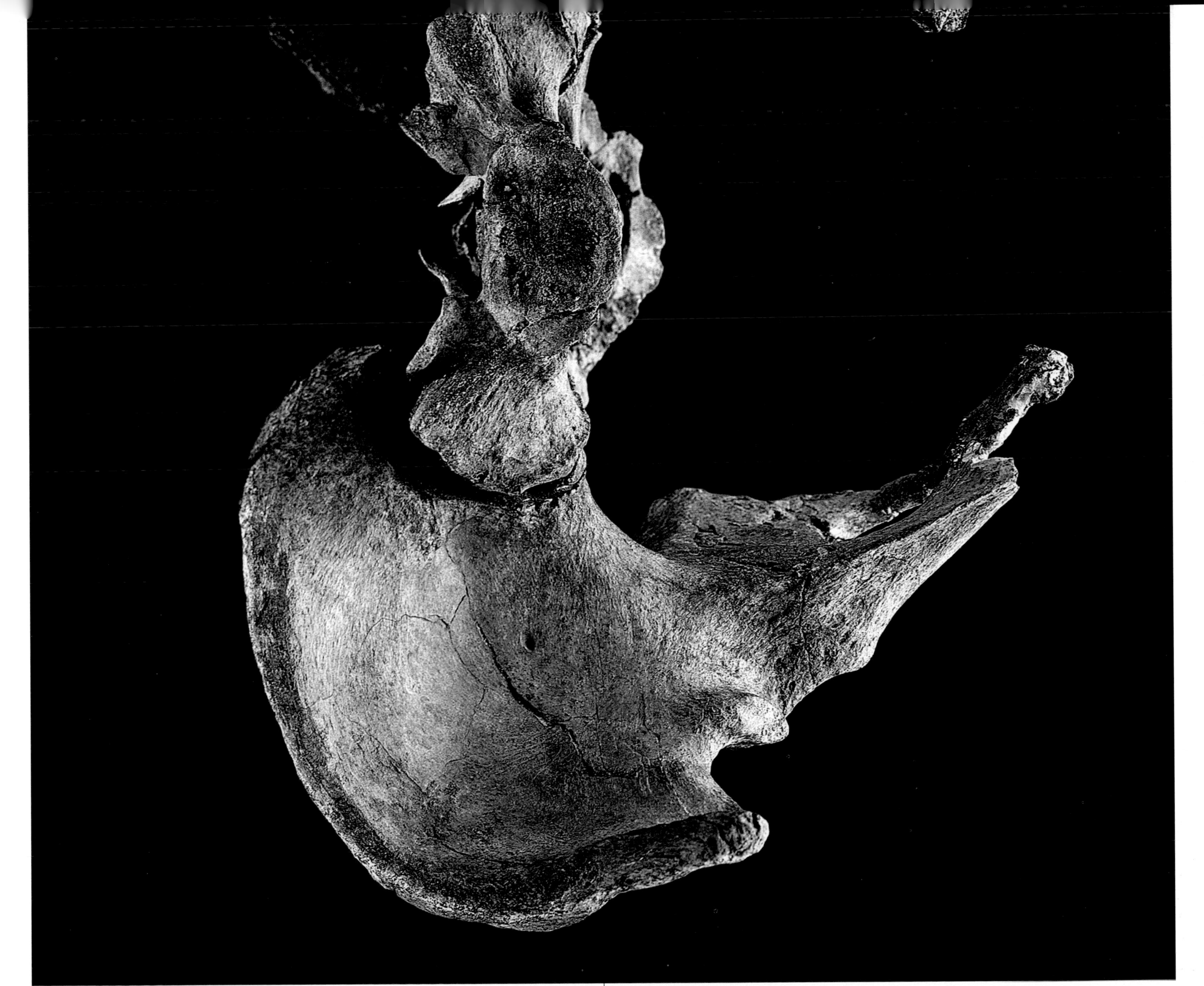

anatomy, at least, modern humans appear to be more strongly built than the burly, barrel-chested Neandertals.) ◖ After studying the seven Neandertal pubic bones then available, paleoanthropologist Erik Trinkaus proposed that the long, thin ramus would have broadened the pelvis and thus enlarged the birth canal of Neandertal mothers by up to 25 percent, allowing mothers to give birth to bigger, more developed, less dependent babies. Neandertals might therefore have had a longer gestation than modern humans, perhaps as long as twelve months. ◖ This idea generated lots of speculation about whether Neandertal babies were born more mature and whether the shorter gestations of modern humans required the evolution of greater social support to care for and protect the underdeveloped infants. A shorter gestation would have led to reduced time between births and might have given modern humans a reproductive edge that eventually allowed them to outproduce and outcompete Neandertals. Further evidence soon forced a revision of this whole story. ◖ The 1983 discovery of the Neandertal skeleton from Kebara Cave in Israel singlehandedly refuted the idea of longer gestation periods in Neandertals. This specimen, Kebara 2, included the most complete Neandertal pelvis ever found. The specimen's superior pubic ramus measures about 90 millimeters long, longer than that any other Neandertal and nearly a third longer than the ramus of modern human males. Yet the pelvic inlet width is only 13 percent wider in the Neandertal. So the pelvis was wider from side to side but not deeper from front to back, and the volume of the birth canal did not change. Although Kebara 2 is a male, we can assume that a female Neandertal's pelvis would have similar proportions, and that the greater length of the pubic ramus still did not contribute to a larger birth canal. ◖ Evidence from another complete skeleton, the 1.6 million-year-old *Homo ergaster* specimen KNM-WT 15000 (see page 182), suggests that the human pattern of postnatal brain gestation may have arisen in this species. This skeleton belongs to an adolescent boy, but its pelvic width is so narrow that it is hard to imagine an adult female of the species being able to birth a baby with the presumed brain weight—perhaps 20 grams—of this hominid. Unless, that is, this hominid had a pattern of brain growth more like that of modern humans, with brain weight at birth relatively small but continued rapid growth outside the womb to build an absolutely bigger brain. The implication is that *Homo ergaster* also gave birth to infants that required long-term constant care after birth, and perhaps in this strange twist on primate gestation lies the seeds of the elaborate socialization and prolonged learning that came to characterize our species.

30 · Maturation

ALONG with bipedalism, relatively large brains, and symbolic language, one of the unusual aspects of human life history is our delayed development and growth. Humans take twice as long as living apes to reach maturity. For instance, chimpanzees mature after eight or nine years, but human females become sexually mature at around age thirteen and continue to grow for five more years. Humans, unlike any other primate, also have inserted a spurt of rapid growth, between puberty and maturity, known as adolescence, when a significant amount of total growth occurs throughout the skeleton. Our extended childhood and adolescence has often been considered a means of enhancing our capacity for learning and thus may be a critical trait of our species. We clearly differ from apes in this respect, but what was the case for our hominid ancestors? ◖ Although hard data about the rates of hominid development are somewhat elusive, intriguing techniques have been developed to answer this question. It is possible to estimate the age of death for a skeleton by careful scrutiny of the bones. Joints offer one set of clues. The growth plates, or epiphyses, at the ends of limb bones fuse to the bone shafts at different rates. In humans, the joints tend to fuse completely in this order, beginning at an average age of 18 years: elbow, hip, ankle, knee, wrist, and shoulder. ◖ Teeth provide an excellent record of growth and development as revealed by their sequence of eruption. In humans, the three molars on one side of each jaw erupt about six years apart, beginning with the first molar at age six. The second molar's appearance corresponds with the onset of puberty and adolescence, while the third molar erupts as an adult height is reached. Other teeth can be used to pinpoint similar periods of early development. ◖ A more innovative aging technique considers the incremental growth lines that form like tree rings within the tooth enamel. Such lines inside the enamel are called the striae of Retzius, but as the tooth grows these lines become visible on the outer surface of the enamel and are called perikymata. Although the actual cause of the lines remains uncertain, it is thought that a new line appears each week as the tooth forms and grows, so the lines provide a ruler of the individual's age. Under a microscope, perikymata can be seen on human and hominid incisors. Because they are among the first teeth to form, incisors become particularly useful for making age estimations of very young individuals. Similar studies have been made of incremental growth in molar crowns of late juvenile or adult specimens. ◖ In order to make accurate estimates of the age at death of hominid specimens, it is necessary to know whether their growth rates were more like apes or closer to our own. Initial studies by paleoanthropologist Alan Mann in the 1970s suggested that early hominids had maturation rates similar to that of modern humans. Mann based this conclusion on a collection of juvenile australopithecine teeth from South African cave sites such as Swartkrans. Mann's estimated ages for isolated teeth in the sample led him to conclude that australopithecines had a pattern of tooth eruption widely spaced over time, and hence a long period of immaturity. ◖ More recently, the detailed analysis of perikymata and a broader understanding of ape dental development have caused paleoanthropologists such as Holly Smith and Christopher Dean to rethink this idea and conclude instead that early hominids had shorter growth periods and matured at rates more like those of modern apes. This rethinking forces a revision in the age estimates for juvenile fossils. By shifting from a human to an ape growth model for australopithecines, the estimated age at death for a specimen like the *Australopithecus africanus* skull from Taung, for example, gets halved from seven years to slightly more than three. ◖ Judging from the rate and sequence of enamel deposition on their molars and the formation of incisors, robust australopithecines apparently had a unique growth pattern, different from that of apes, modern humans, and other australopithecines. In robust australopithecine molars, enamel was applied quickly and mostly to the tops of molar crowns, creating a pattern similar to that of human baby teeth. It is as though the robusts retained this juvenile

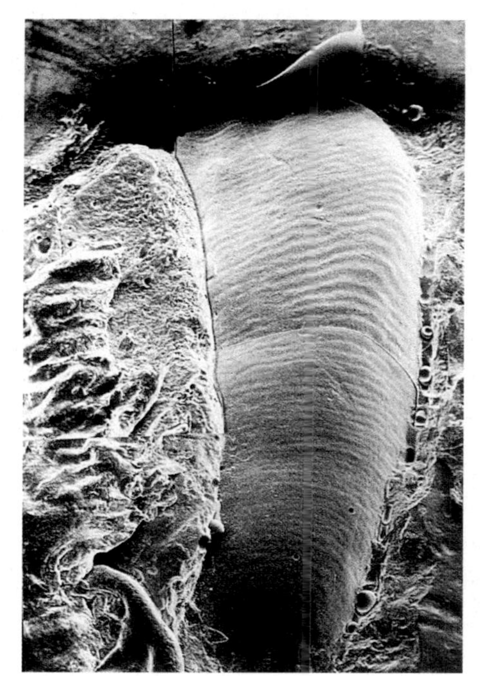

Growth lines on tooth of juvenile *Australopithecus robustus*. Growth lines, or perikymata, on teeth can help determine the age at death of an individual. This tongue-side view of the SK 62 incisor from Swartkrans, South Africa shows several parallel perikymata. *Courtesy of Christopher Dean, University College London.*

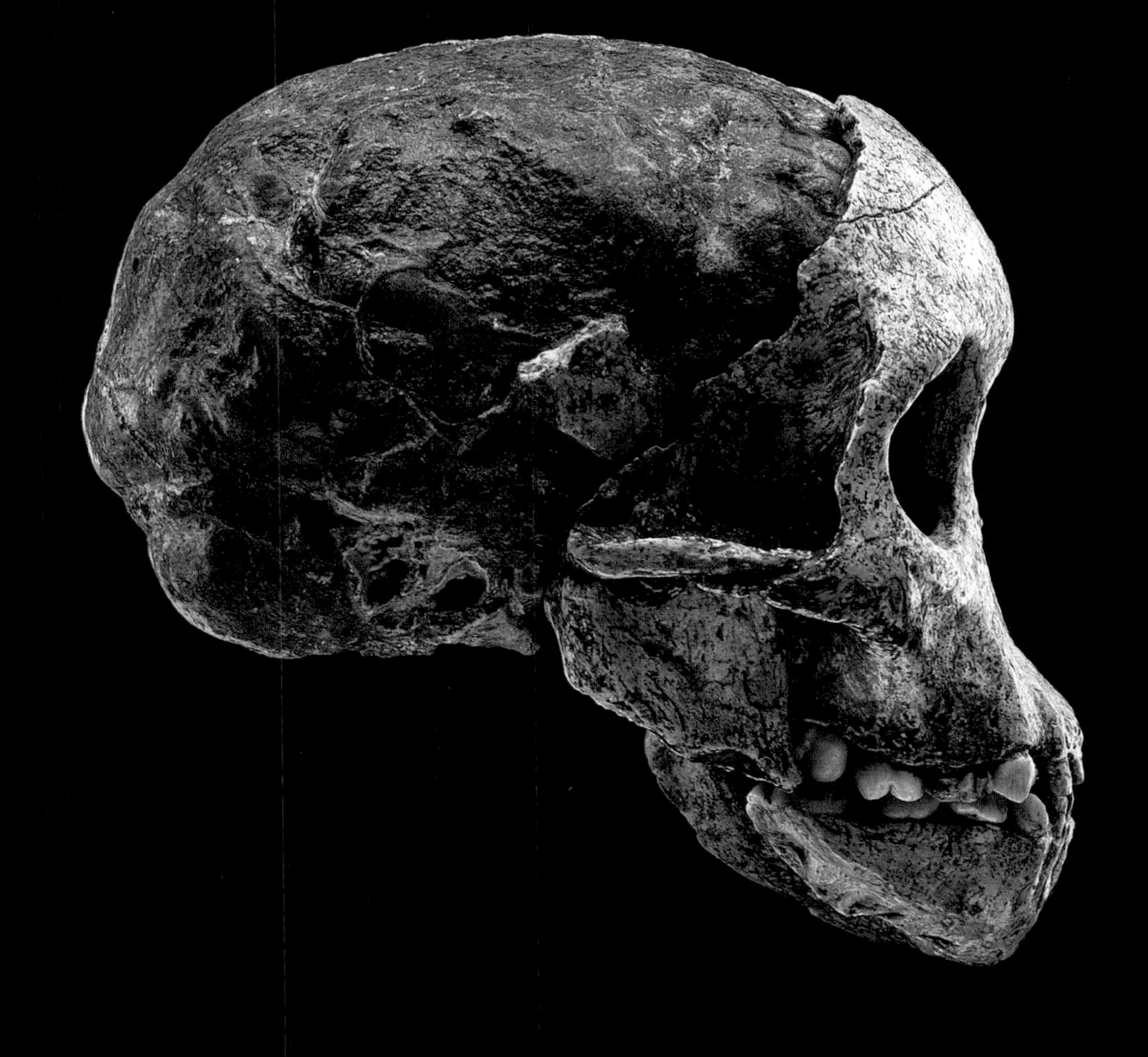

Skull of *Australopithecus africanus* from Taung, South Africa (see also page 143). If the famous Taung child matured at a rate similar to modern apes, then its estimated age at death was three years. This individual was probably preyed upon by an eagle. Actual size.
Photograph by David Brill; courtesy of University of the Witwatersrand.

trait in response to some evolutionary pressure — perhaps their probable diet of hard nuts and seeds — to produce teeth quickly and erupt them early. ◖ It may be that even early members of genus *Homo*, including *Homo habilis*, had apelike rates of growth. Data for two juvenile dental specimens from Koobi Fora, KNM-ER 820 and KNM-ER 1590, suggest that early *Homo* kept the primitive pattern of growth and had not yet evolved delayed maturation. If an apelike pattern of growth characterized human evolution for the first few millions of years, when did this pattern change? ◖ The discovery of the 1.6 million-year-old KNM-WT 15000 skeleton (see page 182) at Nariokotome, Kenya, in 1984 provided a unique opportunity to study a nearly complete juvenile skeleton with its associated skull and teeth. Estimating WT 15000's age at death depends on just what skeletal evidence is used and whether the specimen is compared to an ape or a human growth model. Judging from tooth eruption, the Nariokotome boy had not reached adulthood. His permanent first and second molars had come in, but the third molars (wisdom teeth) had not, and there are still milk canines in the upper jaw. Fewer than half of his permanent teeth had completely formed, suggesting that he died while in the first half of adolescence, perhaps around age eleven years. ◖ Evidence from other parts of the skeleton, including the degree of fusion in the upper arm bone epiphyses and the presence of cartilage between the pelvic bones, puts the specimen at younger than fifteen years and probably close to thirteen years. But based on overall stature — he stood 1.6 meters tall — the skeleton matches a modern human of at least fifteen years. By any human standards, this was a big boy. ◖ Based on a human scale of growth, WT 15000 was somewhere between eleven and fifteen years old when he died. If an ape scale is used instead, the age estimates drop to between seven and nine years. The ape growth model seems to fit WT 15000's molar development, but the anterior teeth have already reached a more advanced stage of growth when compared to apes. The correct answer to the skeleton's age may lie somewhere in the middle of the estimates derived from ape and human standards, say nine or ten years, and it is reasonable to conclude that maturation in this species occurred at some intermediate rate. ◖ As for our relatively recent contemporaries the Neandertals, there is some evidence that they may have matured more quickly than modern humans. The perikymata of an unerupted incisor from a Neandertal child skull found at Devil's Tower on Gibraltar suggested that this child had died at three or four years of age. Yet the skull already had well-developed molars for its age and a brain size of 1,400 cc, approaching the average for modern humans. So Neandertals, in contrast to us, may have grown up quickly, and perhaps this accelerated growth contributed to their bigger heads and brains. ◖ Since Alan Mann's pioneering work two decades ago, we have assembled techniques to help us arrive at an understanding of how other hominids developed and grew. While the answers should become clearer with the addition of new juvenile fossils and more sophisticated analyses, we have already learned that the rate of maturation was as important an adaptation in the lives of our ancestors as it is for ourselves.

31 · Evolution of the Human Brain

THE SPONGY, 1.3-kilogram organ inside our skulls consists mostly of water, but it contains the key to the past 2 million years of our evolutionary story. With its estimated 100 billion neurons — as many communicating nerve cells as there are stars in the Milky Way — and a trillion glial cells to support those neurons, the brain regulates our behavior, our motions and emotions, our instincts and ideas — all that distinguishes the human experience. ◖ In absolute size, the human brain breaks no records. Elephant brains exceed ours by a factor of four, and some whale brains are even bigger. Apparently, bigger bodies require larger brains in order to operate. Brain weight increases about two thirds as fast as body weight over a range of small to large mammals, so that the biggest mammals have absolutely larger but relatively smaller brains. ◖ Regardless of body size, however, primates tend to have relatively large brains. Primates are visually oriented animals, and color stereoscopic vision must require some complicated neural connections. Monkeys, apes, and humans possess the biggest brains relative to body weight of any terrestrial mammals. So, part of the answer is that the human brain is just a highly elaborated ape brain. ◖ Yet there is still something different, something unique, about the size of the human brain. Our brain is three times larger than the predicted size for a hypothetical non-human primate of average human body size. Almost all of this added size has evolved within the past 2 million years. But size isn't everything. ◖ Our brain also differs significantly from those of apes in the proportion of various parts. It did not just uniformly grow bigger and thus endow us with intelligence. Some parts of the human brain changed little, while others became barely recognizable. The pons and medulla, primitive parts of the hindbrain, have not been especially enlarged in humans. We show some enlargement of the midbrain, but the real difference lies elsewhere, in the cortex or gray matter of the forebrain. ◖ Human brains display an amazing inflation of the cerebellum and neocortex (which covers much of the cerebrum), areas that play crucial roles in many aspects of learning. The cerebral cortex constitutes 80 percent of our brain mass The primitive forebrain functioned primarily in the sense of smell. Although our forebrain remains connected to the olfactory lobes, these have become reduced, and our forebrain now serves a new function. ◖ That function is reflected in the role of the prefrontal cortex of the left hemisphere. An average primate with a brain blown up to the size of ours would still have a prefrontal cortex that is more than 200 percent smaller than that of the human brain! The prefrontal cortex includes those regions of the brain, such as Broca's and Wernicke's areas, that are strongly associated with the production and understanding of language. Compared to apes, we have greatly enhanced the size and neural connections in that part of the brain. In contrast, the part of our brain devoted to controlling motor skills takes up only about a third of the space it does in a monkey's brain. (We won't be leaping agilely through forest canopies anytime soon.) As a result, we sacrificed some capability for seeing and smelling but gained new capacity for symbolic and computational thought. ◖ In addition, the human brain is a sponge that soaks up sensations and observations, and it is a masterful organ for storing, retrieving, and processing a wide range of detailed and complicated information. To borrow a metaphor from biologist Christopher Wills, "We differ from other animals not in the ability to juggle but in the number of balls that we can keep in the air simultaneously. " Our brains have permitted us to evolve culture and enhance it to an unprecedented degree in the history of life on Earth (see page 21). ◖ So, size alone does not explain our unusual mental abilities. What counts is what's inside the package and how it is all arranged. Cognitive neuroscience is an exciting and rapidly expanding field of inquiry, but we are still just scratching the surface of figuring out how the human brain works. We should not expect to find a simple relationship between brain size, complexity, and intelligence. ◖ We cannot answer exactly why we evolved our large brains, but fossil evidence tells us when we evolved them. During the Lower and early Middle Pleistocene (between 2 million and around 700,000 years ago), hominid brain size doubled, from about 440 cc to more than 900 cc. This change affected mainly the side-to-side and back-to-front dimensions of

Brain endocasts and cranium of *Australopithecus* from South Africa. A trend toward larger brains occurred in the course of human evolution. Australopithecines like these had brains less in 500 cc in volume, while brain volume in genus *Homo* ranges from 600 cc to about 2,000 cc. Actual sizes. *Photograph by John Reader, Science Source/Photo Researchers.*

the cranium, especially the frontal and occipital bones and the cranial base. In part, this doubling occurred because of a general increase in body size, but its rate and extent suggest that natural selection was also focused specifically on adding cranial capacity. ◖ The biggest burst in brain size, however, occurred during the Middle to Upper Pleistocene (around 500,000 to 100,000 years ago), the span of time from late *Homo erectus* to early *Homo sapiens.* This change in both size and shape represents one of the most remarkable morphological shifts that has been observed in the evolutionary history of any mammal, for it entailed both an enhanced cranial capacity and a radical reorganization of brain proportions. It affected the vertical dimensions of the frontal and occipital bones, allowing for growth of the neurocranium. ◖ Subsequent changes in our cranial capacity, as seen in the shape of the skull, were minor by comparison and included more upward expansion of the frontal bone, a higher and broader biparietal arch, and a rounding of the occipital bone. Thereafter, from the Upper Paleolithic through the present, our skulls and brains have undergone no significant change. Modern human brains weigh an average of 1.3 kilograms and have an average volume of at least 1,350 cc. ◖ People often wonder why Neandertal brains were bigger than ours. Were they smarter, and if so, why are they extinct? The reason for their bigger brains has to do with the relationship between body size and ambient temperature. The "classic" Neandertals of western Europe were adapted to a late Pleistocene cold climate, and part of that adaptation was a relatively larger brain corresponding to their stout stature. Male classic Neandertals had a mean cranial capacity of 1,582 cc. A similar pattern of reduced limb length, stouter body proportions, and larger cranial capacity occurs in modern populations living at high latitudes, including the Lapps or Sääme people and the Greenland Inuit.

32 · Reconstructing the Appearance of Early Humans

IF THERE is a single topic in paleoanthropology that excites more general interest than who our ancestors were, it is what early humans looked like. Piecing together dozens or hundreds of delicate fragments into skulls and limb bones requires both scientific knowledge and puzzle-solving skills, but taking the next steps of adding muscle and flesh to these bones constitutes a marriage of science and art. The challenge, essentially, is to perform a dissection in reverse, and few people are up to the task. Two who have made this task their calling are American paleoartists and anatomists Jay Matternes and John Gurche. ◖ Matternes has spent more than thirty years mastering his techniques and is best known for carefully reasoned depictions of early hominid life in his paintings. In addition to representing a group of some hominid species in exacting anatomical detail, these works include a meticulous reconstruction of the habitat. His painting of *Australopithecus afarensis* for the November 1985 *National Geographic Magazine* shows a troop of eleven individuals, from infant to adult, foraging for figs on the ground of a dense montane forest. His interpretation of Neandertal life has two women and a boy skinning an ibex with stone tools beside the entrance to a rockshelter, while a man uses a piece of antler to strike sharp flakes from a flint core. Matternes's murals of various extinct primates and hominid ancestors in their environmental context can be seen in the Hall of Human Biology and Evolution at the American Museum of Natural History, in New York. ◖ To make a graphic reconstruction of a specific specimen, Matternes may photograph the fossil – taking care to avoid any parallax distortion – and project its image on a wall for tracing. He orients the skull projection and subsequent drawings to be in Frankfurt Horizontal, a standard anatomical position defined by taking a straight line between the porion, the craniometric point just above the ear canal opening, and the orbitale, the lower rim of the eye socket. This position replicates the natural angle of a human head. (Nearly all of David Brill's fossil portraits in this book were made in Frankfurt Horizontal.) Matternes uses a series of tissue overlays to draw in muscles and ultimately skin and hair over the bones. ◖ For his reconstruction of a male *A. afarensis* that was reproduced in *Lucy: The Beginnings of Humankind*, Matternes opted for a hairy, dark-skinned body, although he decided against adding much facial hair or a beard, surmising that beards had yet to evolve as secondary sex characteristics, as well as to show better the actual facial features. ◖ John Gurche, a painter and sculptor, has recreated the heads of several hominids for the National Museum of Natural History, in Washington D. C. He has also created a reconstruction of a male *A. afarensis*, but in three dimensions. Unlike Matternes, who in 1981 relied on a composite skull comprised of bones from several *afarensis* individuals, Gurche had the advantage of basing his head on the A.L. 444-2 cranium (see page 128) discovered in 1992. The result of Gurche's 700 hours of work appeared in the March 1996 *National Geographic.* ◖ In any reconstruction, Gurche, like Matternes, refers often to notes, casts, and photographs made during dissections of heads from ape cadavers. He first molds and casts the face, and then takes subsequent casts of each layer as he dissects down through skin and muscle to the skull. He studies the original skull or a faithful cast, to which he adds muscles of modeling clay and plasticene by following the bone's natural contours – the bumps, ridges, crests, and tubercles that mark the origin and insertion of muscles and allow an estimation of their size during life. Pockets of fat tissue, also plasticene, help fill out the face. Epoxy is used to construct nasal cartilage, which is deduced from the size and shape of the nasal septum in the facial skeleton. Finally, a layer of skin, individually placed hairs, and colored acrylic eyes complete the face. ◖ Although these artists collaborate closely with paleoanthropologists in the course of a commission, such work relies on informed speculation and assumption as well as on science. We cannot be certain of the color of a certain hominid's eyes or skin, the exact shape of the nose, or how much hair covered the head or body. But by using their artistic and interpretive talents to flesh out hominid fossil finds, Matternes and Gurche have brought our ancestors much closer to us. When we look at these creations, we see both how far we have come and how near we remain.

Reconstruction of male *Australopithecus afarensis*. Artist John Gurche created this face using the A.L. 444-2 cranium discovered at Hadar, Ethiopia in 1992. (see page 128) *Photograph by John Stum; copyright © 1995 John Gurche.*

32 · Primate Societies and Early Human Social Behavior

LONG-TERM field studies in recent decades have shed an immense amount of light on the behavior of our closest living relatives, the African apes. As more primatologists observe more populations in more places, it has emerged, for instance, that chimpanzees in different forests possess separate traditions and learned behaviors. These differences are expressed in many aspects of life, such as the making and using of stone, leaf, or twig tools, types of grooming, diet and attitudes toward prey animals, and the extent of cooperation in hunting. In other words, chimps have distinctive cultures. They may be the most behaviorally variable animal of all, after humans. But the apparent diversity and complexity of chimp behavior make it more difficult to tease out just which behaviors might have been shared by the earliest hominids or the last common ancestor of humans and apes. One approach to this problem taken by primatologist Richard Wrangham was to compare and contrast salient behaviors among chimpanzees, bonobos, gorillas,

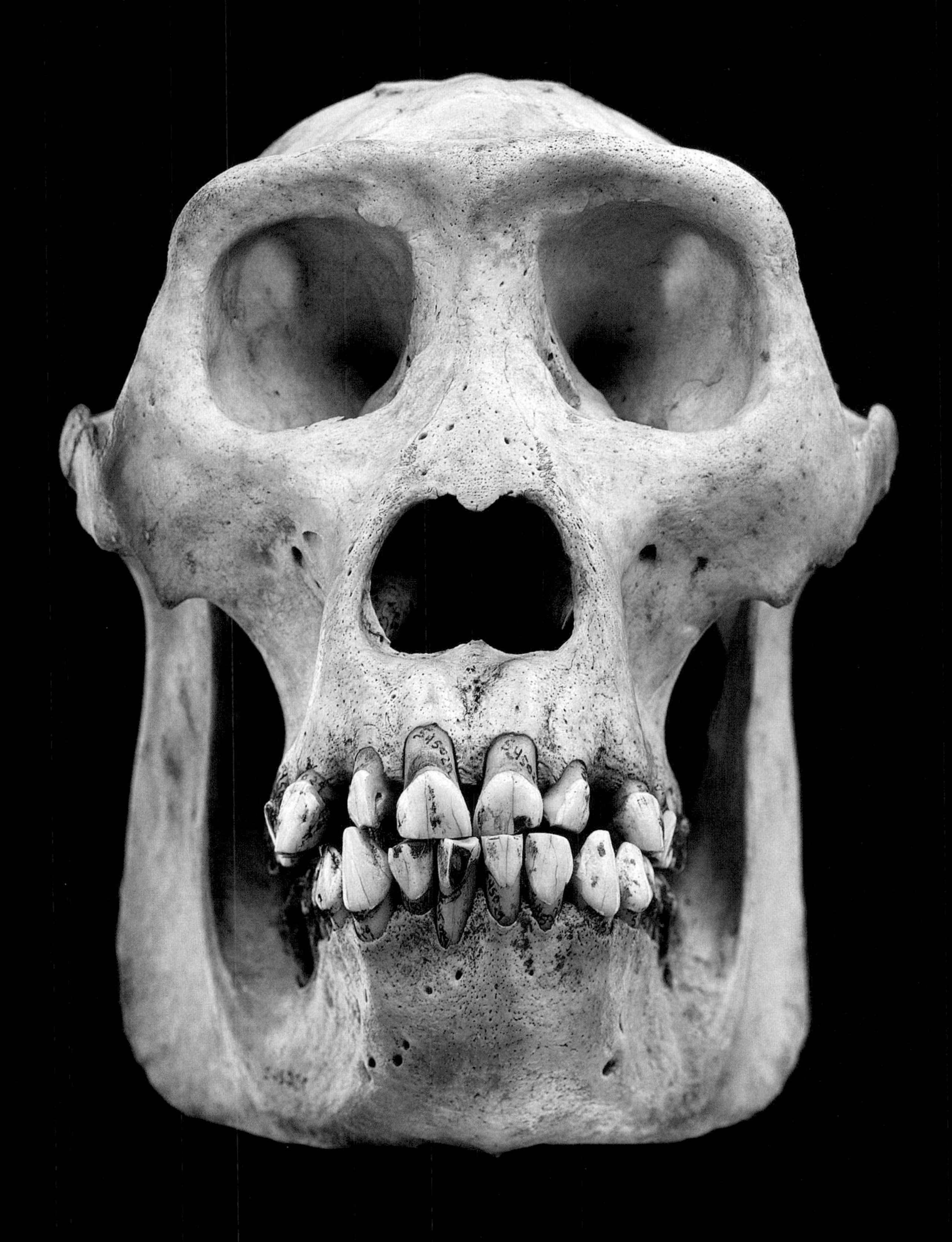

Skulls of male (*left*) and female (*right*) mountain gorilla, *Gorilla gorilla beringei*. These specimens come from the Virunga Mountains of Rwanda, site of Dian Fossey's long-term study of this most endangered ape. Gorillas form social groups in which only a single dominant male mates with females. Actual sizes. *Photographs by David Brill; courtesy of National Museum of Natural History.*

and humans to determine what behaviors are shared by all, because those behaviors are more likely to have evolved in a common ancestor. If each living species differs in a given behavior, then nothing can be confidently concluded about the likely behavior of the common ancestor.

◖ Wrangham selected several important elements of social organization, including adult group patterns, relationships among males and females, sexual relationships, and relationships between unrelated groups. He then examined how each takes shape in various human cultures and the African apes to find a pattern of shared conservative features. For example, many human societies and all African apes have a tendency toward female exogamy, or the forced migration of female members from the group in which they were born, which means that mothers generally associate with adult females who are not close relatives. The unity of this feature among living species suggests it was present also in the common ancestor.

◖ However, when Wrangham looked at sexual behavior, no clear pattern emerged. Gorillas are polygynous, meaning that one male mates exclusively with several females. Both chimpanzees and bonobos are promiscuous, so neither sex mates exclusively. As for humans, our sexual tastes and traditions vary within and between social groups. So, little can be said about the sexual behavior of a common ancestor. Even so, the fact that male African apes normally mate with more than one female and the prevalence of polygyny in many human societies suggest that similar behavior occurred in our mutual ancestor. ◖ This hypothetical common ancestor thus took form as a primate whose females migrated out of their birth group and formed tolerant, possibly friendly relationships with other females, though did not forge coalitions to gain a social advantage; whose males spent some amount of time living and traveling alone and did not form tight social bonds with other males; whose males mated with more than one female, whether in short-term or long-term relationships; who lived in a closed social network or community; and who had hostile relationships with other groups of its kind that gave rise to attacks and fighting among males. ◖ Aspects of the common ancestor's behavior that remained elusive in Wrangham's study because of variation among apes and humans included the stability of groups gathered to feed or travel; the degree of territoriality; the duration of sexual relationships and whether they were polygynous or just promiscuous; whether males ever mated with close relatives; and whether males formed alliances with each other. ◖ Another researcher, Michael Ghiglieri, followed Wrangham's lead and refined a behavioral model for the most recent common ancestor. He argued, based on genetic evidence, that humans, chimpanzees, and bonobos could be considered apart from gorillas as a more closely linked group (see page 32), and so certain behaviors shared by these three primates, but not found in gorillas, would have presumably characterized the common ancestor. ◖ So, the social structure of Ghiglieri's hypothetical common ancestor included closed, stable groups with many males and females; strict retention of male offspring in their birth group (male endogamy) and female exogamy; the establishment of a male kin-group community system with cooperative behavior among related males to form alliances against rivals, who might have been stalked and attacked; weaker bonds between females; polygynous mating; males active in defending group territory; fusion-fission sociality (individuals stay in large groups even during environmentally stressful periods but also temporarily travel alone); and moderate sexual dimorphism (body size differences due to sex). Male endogamy led to the creation of male kin groups that provided communal defense of females and territory. Ghiglieri further surmises that males of the hominid ancestor formed stable and exclusive mating bonds with one or more females and made a greater investment in the care of offspring, which increased the odds of successful reproduction. ◖ Of course, such models that seek to characterize a common ancestor should be seen simply as guidelines to exploring questions about early hominid behavior.

Our ancestors were each unique biologically, ecologically, and behaviorally, with specific adaptations that shaped behavior. Bipedalism, for instance, a form of locomotion not practiced habitually by any ape, would certainly have influenced the behavior of early hominids considerably in terms of how food was obtained and processed, what size territory was occupied or explored, and perhaps even provided the foundation for much of hominid mating and social strategy (see page 89).

34 · Evidence for Bipedalism

QUADRUPEDALISM has served untold numbers of primate species for tens of millions of years. However, natural selection, the process that molds living organisms, focused on upright, two-footed walking in our ancestry as the primal behavioral adaptation that launched our evolutionary journey. The major anatomical features associated with bipedalism are seen in the extensive reorganization of the trunk, pelvis, lower limb, and foot. The ability to walk upright reflects an interdependent set of alterations in the soft (muscle) anatomy and, most significantly for paleoanthropologists, in the bony anatomy. ◖ The pelvis of a bipedal hominid differs from all other primate pelves in having broad, vertically short blades that are rotated inward to form a pelvic basin, which supports the viscera in an upright creature. Such an arrangement repositions our large hip muscles to the side, making them useful in balancing our trunk over our lower limbs when walking. Enhanced balance also stems from repositioning the center of gravity within the basin-like pelvis, due in part to the S-curvature of our spine. ◖ The thighbone, or femur, is critical since it supports our entire body weight during locomotion. The relatively long, stout femur fits into the hip socket via a large head. The knee end, due to the oblique orientation of the femoral shaft, is positioned directly beneath the body, adding to the fluidness of our walk by diminishing side-to-side tilting. Features in the knee are designed to facilitate maximal weight transfer and to prevent kneecap dislocation. ◖ It is our foot that ultimately contacts the ground and has become especially well adapted to terrestrial bipedalism. Unlike all other primates, which have a grasping great toe, we have a great toe that is aligned with the other toes, is not opposable, and forms the focal point for forward propulsion-toe-off. Two arches formed on the sole of the foot by strong ligaments act as shock absorbers during locomotion. ◖ Considerable debate has focused on the capacity of the earliest species in our family tree, the australopithecines, for bipedality. Fortunately for the paleoanthropologist, the fossilized remains of our ancestors exhibit an extensive suite of skeletal landmarks that bespeak bipedalism. The skulls, teeth, and isolated skeletal fragments that until recently constituted most of the hominid finds were not able to show the anatomical arrangements of pelvis and lower limb that would resolve the issue of early bipedality, but one skull feature was almost as good. In hominids the foramen magnum, the hole at the base of the skull through which the spinal cord emerges, faces downward, allowing the skull to sit at the top of the vertebral column and spinal cord. In quadrupedal primates, by contrast, the foramen magnum is positioned toward the back of the skull. The position of the foramen magnum eventually proved diagnostic for bipedalism, and when Raymond Dart in 1925 described the skull of the Taung Child, from South Africa, and used it to erect a new taxon, *Australopithecus africanus*, he confidently asserted that it belonged to a bipedal hominid ancestor on the basis of the position of the foramen magnum. ◖ Although portions of the pelvis and lower limb are known for the South African australopithecines, the most comprehensive case for bipedalism is made by the extensive postcranial elements of East African *A. afarensis*. The pelvis and lower limb bones found at Hadar, Ethiopia, and dating to between 3.2 and 3.4 million years ago, provide more than

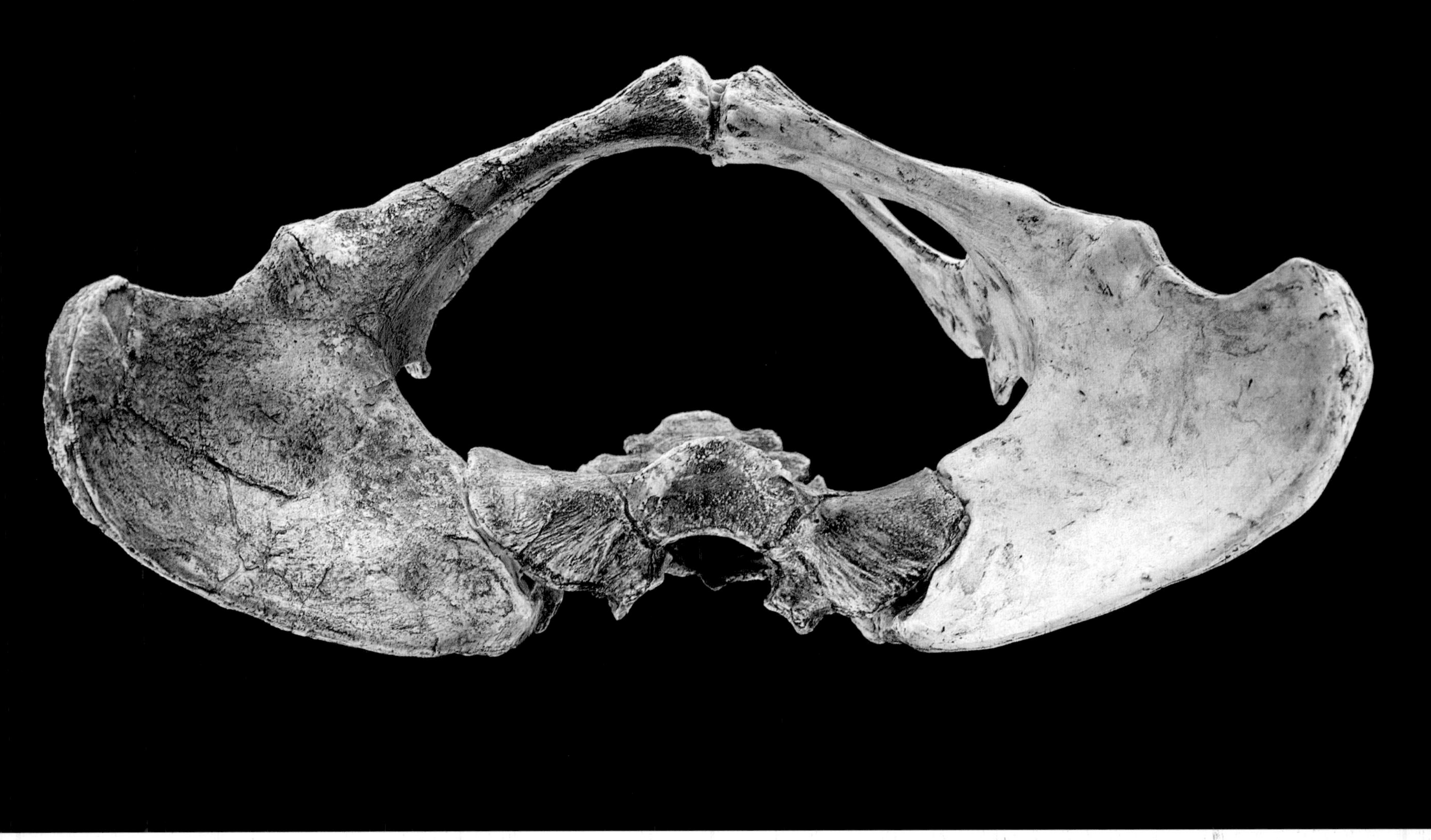

Pelvis of *Australopithecus afarensis* from Hadar, Ethiopia. The partial skeleton of A.L. 288-1, or Lucy, included the left half of her pelvis and a complete sacrum, the five fused vertebrate that make up the rear of the pelvis. The right side was carefully reconstructed to reveal a remarkably humanlike form to the pelvis, indicating that Lucy had been bipedal. Actual size. *Photography by David Brill; courtesy Owen Lovejoy, Kent State University.*

ample evidence that *A. afarensis* was an accomplished biped. The bones of Lucy play a vital role here, but other lower limb bones from Hadar further attest to bipedal behavior in this early hominid. ◖ Restoration of Lucy's complete pelvis from an intact sacrum (tail bone) and left innominate (hip bone) revealed all of the major landmarks of a modern human bipedal pelvis. Her pelvis is short, with the blades rotated inward. Slight differences from a modern pelvis are to be expected, such as the flare of the blades, which may have added increased stability to the pelvis during locomotion. Adjacent to a relatively large femoral head, the femoral neck has thickened bone on its lower margin, to prevent breakage from the bending forces generated during walking. ◖ The shaft of Lucy's femur is oblique to the horizontal, an arrangement that causes weight to be transferred primarily through the lateral condyle, the outside knob at the bottom end of this bone. This condyle is also flattened, enhancing contact with the tibia (shin bone) for maximum weight transfer. The broad notch on the front of the femur has a raised ridge that prevents lateral displacement of the kneecap. (see pages 2 and 130) ◖ Anatomical details of the ankle, especially the articulation of the tibia and the talus (ankle bone), support the bipedal nature of *A. afarensis*. A careful look at the articulation of the large toe with the main portion of the foot shows that this important joint was incapable of the rotation and divergence seen in an apelike grasping foot. ◖ The locomotor skeleton of *A. afarensis* is not identical with our own, an outcome we should expect because of the skeleton's antiquity. In fact, a number of primitive features, such as a short femur, slightly curved finger and foot bones, narrow rather than broad fingertips, a highly mobile wrist, powerful arms, and so on, are unlike those found in modern humans. The intriguing mixture of specialized bipedal features and primitive features in *A. afarensis* is not in dispute. It is the interpretation of what this amalgam of primitive and advanced traits means for locomotor behavior that is open to debate. ◖ Some scientists stress the bipedal features of *A. afarensis* and conclude that this hominid did not participate in any arboreal activities but was a committed terrestrial biped. The primitive features are interpreted as evolutionary baggage left over from an arboreal ancestor. Other, equally powerful voices have spoken out for the probability that *A. afarensis* spent a considerable amount of time in the trees. Those scientists believe that the primitive features are consistent with the idea that *afarensis* was foraging for food, escaping from predators, or even sleeping at night in the trees. However, the critical anatomical adaptations seen in the hip, knee, and foot for bipedalism suggest that climbing behavior was not adaptively important and that bipedalism had been under strong selection for some time. ◖ Substantial insights into the locomotor capabilities of *A. afarensis* come from the remarkable discovery of a 27-meter-long trail of 3.6 million-year-old hominid footprint impressions in a volcanic ash at Laetoli, Tanzania (see page 133). The discovery of this hominid trackway in 1978 permitted an unprecedented evaluation of the soft anatomy of a very ancient human ancestor. The hominid footprints found at Laetoli must have been made by members of *A. afarensis*, because the only fossil hominids recovered from Laetoli belong to this species. ◖ Painstaking excavations by Mary Leakey and her team revealed footprints astonishingly like those made by *Homo sapiens* in wet beach sand. The Laetoli prints show a strong heel strike, followed by transfer of weight to the outside of the foot, then across to the ball of the foot, and finally concentrated on the great toe. The great toe is not divergent; there is only a slight gap between it and the lateral toes, similar to that seen among people today who do not wear foot coverings. The impression left in the ancient volcanic ash also reveals an energy-absorbing arch to the foot. ◖ Although other hominid prints from cave sites in Europe date to the Upper Paleolithic, they are from our own species, *Homo sapiens*. The Laetoli prints provide conclusive evidence that hominid bipedality reaches back 3.6 million years in time and undoubtedly stretches even deeper into the past.

35 · The Origins of Bipedalism

EARLY in the twentieth century, substantial debate centered on the sequence of events in human evolution. One school was committed to the view that our brains grew big first and then we became bipedal, while another school saw bipedalism as a precursor to the big brain. To many, bipedalism was a locomotor response in our ancestors to a terrestrial habitat after they left the familiar arboreal one behind. Those who favored the brain first scenario speculated that human intelligence was a necessary precursor for making the decision to walk upright and move out of the forests onto the grasslands. In more elaborate forms, flight from the forest was consistent with the notion of expulsion from the Garden of Eden. Those who saw bipedalism as the initial adaptation claimed that it was the first step toward freeing our forelimbs to manufacture and use tools. This set up a classic feedback mechanism: bigger brains, better tools; better tools, bigger brains. ◖ Resolution of the sequence of events derives from the recovery of a significant storehouse of ancient fossil hominids in Africa. These fossils have provided definitive evidence for bipedalism extending back to roughly 4 million years ago, and a growing consensus postulates that the acquisition of bipedalism may have occurred somewhere between 5 and 8 million years ago. Substantial brain expansion is not seen until roughly 2 million years ago, thus firmly establishing the sequence of development for these two diagnostic features of human evolution. ◖ It is also necessary to abandon the view that our ancestors became bipedal to make and use tools, for the bipedal australopithecines apparently did not manufacture stone tools. Lithic artifacts first appear in the geological record about 2.5 million years ago, at least 1.5 million years after our ancestors became bipedal. Hence the connection between big brains, tool use, and bipedalism has been effectively uncoupled. ◖ Any explanation for why we became bipedal must also take into consideration that, compared with quadrupedalism, bipedal locomotion is slow, clumsy, and fraught with opportunities for injury. And contrary to much that has been written, walking on two legs is not energetically more advantageous than getting around on four legs. ◖ Some explanations point out that upright posture permits hominids to reach up and pick fruit from a tree or use their hands in special social displays. But nothing prevents a quadruped from doing these things as well, just as chimpanzees and gorillas do. ◖ An often quoted but overly simplistic explanation for bipedalism contends that it enabled our ancestors to stand up and see over the tall savanna grass when they left the forest. From a practical point of view, it is difficult to think of a more vulnerable time to try out a major behavioral change than when moving into an unfamiliar habitat, especially one containing successful predators. Imagine how easily large cats could have taken a slow, lumbering hominid that announced its presence by standing up. Chimps and baboons do look over tall grass to assess the surrounding area, but in case of danger they can resort to four legs and quickly escape. From this perspective, it makes more sense to develop a scenario in which we became bipedal while still in the familiar surroundings of the forest. ◖ Another line of thinking about early upright bipedalism has focused on bodily thermal regulation, the heat load sustained on the open savannas, and how evolution might have helped humans cope with it. The English physiologist Peter Wheeler has postulated that the upright stance of bipedalism would have reduced the amount of body surface area exposed to the sun's

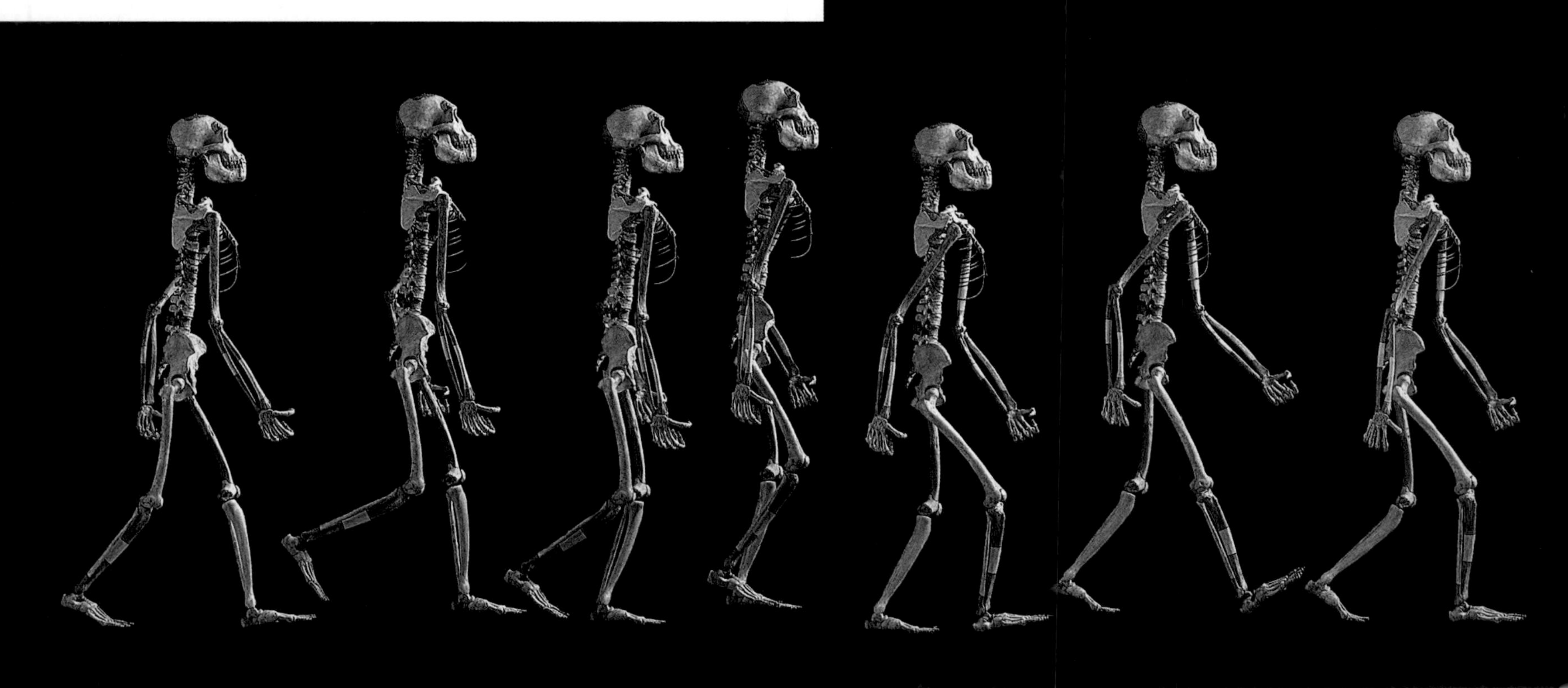

Articulated reconstruction of *Australopithecus afarensis*. The plaster skeleton created by anthropologist C. Owen Lovejoy and his students depicts this hominid as fully adapted to habitual bipedal locomotion. *Photograph by David Brill; courtesy C. Owen Lovejoy, Kent State University.*

rays. An added benefit, he suggests, would have come from our bodies being elevated above the hot ground and exposed to cooling breezes. The underlying idea is that faster dissipation of the heat load would extend the daily foraging times for hominids. Other studies, however, have pointed out that the added foraging time would have been minimal and that hominids, like other animals on the savanna, would have derived greater benefit by resting during the hottest part of the day. Upright bipedalism does reduce the amount of incoming heat due to direct sun exposure, but reduction in the heat load was not the driving force for bipedalism. ◖ Bipedalism is a major evolutionary innovation, and separate from the issue of its numerous advantages for hominids, its source must be sought in behavioral change that enhanced the reproductive success of early hominids. One of the most comprehensive scenarios explaining bipedalism has been offered by Kent State University paleoanthropologist C. Owen Lovejoy. Lovejoy has placed his model within the framework of natural selection. Upright walking was selected for in response to some behavioral advantage. Lovejoy has focused on what he calls the "fundamental selective triad," the three areas in which an organism consumes most energy — reproduction, feeding, and safety. The goal of any species is to stay alive, to eat, and to reproduce. Lovejoy points out that beyond a certain point, there is no advantage in expending more energy for feeding and safety, but additional energy spent on reproduction would have a significant evolutionary impact. If a female could dedicate more time to reproduction by reducing birth intervals and caring for more than one dependent offspring at a time, there would be an evolutionary payoff in terms of a greater likelihood that each generation would survive long enough to produce the next. But a faster reproduction rate would require that the female not have to expend energy foraging for food or worrying about the safety of herself and her offspring. ◖ One manner in which this could happen would be if males provided high-quality food to females, allowing the females to invest more energy in infant care. Nourishment provided by males would reduce females' foraging time and reduce their exposure to accidents and predation. Thus, the development of longer-term relationships between males and females, the beginnings of pair-bonding, could have had evolutionary significance for hominids. ◖ On the one hand is the notion that males, now bipedal, used their upper limbs for carrying food, to provision females who did not mate with other males, thus securing known paternity. On the other hand, females who selected mates based on their dependability in providing food would gain higher odds of increased survivorship of their young. Following upon these we can look at two possible consequences. ◖ Lovejoy notes that since human females lack external signs of ovulation (estrus) such as sexual swelling and olfactory clues, frequent copulation is necessary for conception to occur. Lovejoy suggests that males were attracted to females who did not display outward symptoms of ovulation, and as a result the males could have avoided competition with other males for those females in obvious estrus. ◖ Lovejoy points out that male and female humans are distinguished from one another by features that serve to attract the opposite sex. For example, males and females have distinctive scalp hair, distinctive voices, and specialized scent glands in their armpits and pubic region. Furthermore, males are some 20 percent larger than females, exhibit facial hair, and have a large penis, the largest among all primates. Human females have permanently enlarged breasts (chimps have enlarged breasts only during lactation) and a particular distribution of body fat. Perhaps penis and breast size were important sexual signaling devices that served to attract potential mates. ◖ An important feature of the unique mating structure seen in hominids is that each sex has something to offer the other. The male provides a reliable source of food as well as added protection for the female and the young. The female guarantees that the male's genes will be passed on to the next generation; and it is precisely the increased survivorship of the offspring in Lovejoy's model that is the key. Because both ape and human infants have extended periods of childhood learning and take a long time to mature, their reproductive rate is low. So, the opportunity to conceive and raise multiple overlapping offspring would have a significant impact on the reproductive rate of a particular species. ◖ In late Miocene times, 5 to 10 million years ago, cooler climates brought about a diminution of the tropical forests, long the stronghold of the apes. The apes were forced to hang on in more widely dispersed clumps of forest. In contrast, the fast-breeding monkeys proliferated and even began to adapt to the savannas. Thus began the steady decline, which continues today, in the diversity and number of apes. The only ape that flourished was the hominid one, which developed a unique and successful breeding package, an important element of which was bipedalism.

36 · The Oldest Stone Tools

A BONOBO named Kanzi, living at the Language Research Center in Atlanta, Georgia, was given an incentive to make stone tools. Fruit was placed in boxes that were tied shut with cord. After Kanzi was shown how the sharp edge of a stone flake could be used to cut the cord, he was offered a choice of several flakes for cutting open a box. He chose well, easily cutting the boxes open, and even began occasionally to strike one rock against another to produce his own flakes. ◖ This experiment was conducted to see what kinds of stone tools might be made by a chimpanzee, our closest living relative, and to compare those with the oldest known stone tools in the archeological record. At first glance, there was an overall similarity between Kanzi's tools and the earliest stone tools, usually referred to as the Oldowan industrial complex because they were first recognized at Olduvai Gorge, in Tanzania. (see page 250) However, closer inspection by an archeologist who specialized in stone tool technology indicated that Kanzi's work, even after several months, did not show the level of cognitive complexity that is seen in the Oldowan material. Kanzi's tools looked much like the broken stones that occur naturally in riverbeds, glacial deposits, and other geological situations where rocks might be haphazardly knocked about. These geofacts lack a distinct pattern of manufacture. Their random pattern of breakage and flaking is easily discerned by experienced archeologists. ◖ What diagnostic features would allow us to recognize the earliest stone artifacts? Chimps are not alone in the experimental manufacture of stone tools; some archeologists have become accomplished stone knappers and as a result have come to know a great deal about stone tool technology. Direct percussion — the striking of one rock, called a hammerstone, against another, called a core — produces a flake. The manufacture of high-quality flakes incorporates knowledge of where and at what angle to strike a rock. Even more fundamental is the selection of the raw material for tool manufacture. Fine-grained rocks like chert and obsidian produce finer tools than coarser-grained rocks like basalts. ◖ Flakes made through the purposeful behavior of a hominid show a number of features referred to as conchoidal fracture. This kind of fracture is normally absent from naturally cracked stones, which usually break along natural fractures. Artifact flakes bear a striking platform where the hammerstone knocked off a flake. The inner side of the flake exhibits a bulb of percussion immediately below the striking platform and a convex, rippled surface resulting from the shock waves moving through the stone from a hammerstone blow. The core from which the flake was struck bears a flake scar, the negative impression of the bulb of percussion on the flake. ◖ When Louis Leakey first visited Olduvai Gorge, in 1931, he observed an abundance of stone flakes and cores scattered throughout the gorge that showed signs of purposeful and repeated patterns of manufacture. This archeological assemblage consisted of rock types such as lavas and quartzite that must

Oldowan artifacts from Gona, Ethiopia. Candidates for being the world's earliest known stone tools these Oldowan flakes and cores are believed to be about 2.5 million years old. *Photograph by Enrico Ferorelli.*

have been transported in from several kilometers away. Moreover, in certain areas concentrations of these stone artifacts were associated with broken or butchered animal bones. ◖ The earliest stone tools from Olduvai come from the lowest strata at the site, which are close to 2 million years old. Other East African Rift Valley sites stretch further back into time, permitting exploration of the possibility of even earlier traces of stone tool technology. The Omo region of southern Ethiopia, immediately north of Kenya's Lake Turkana, has been investigated since the 1930s because of the fossil-rich strata known as the Shungura Formation. Many claims have been made for the "oldest" stone tools, but the best documented and most firmly dated ones, thanks to a series of volcanic ashes, come from 2.3 to 2.4 million-year-old geological horizons in the Shungura Formation. The artifacts consist of quartz pebbles associated with abundant flakes and quartz chips. ◖ Oldowan stone tools are known from localities around Lake Turkana and are especially numerous at Koobi Fora, east of the lake, in deposits roughly 1.9 million years old. Preliminary work west of Lake Turkana has identified stone artifacts that may be roughly the same age as those from the Shungura Formation. ◖ Excavations in the western portion of Hadar, Ethiopia, in the Gona drainage, have recovered numerous cores made from lava cobbles and associated flakes. At the moment these artifacts are undated, but they conform to the character of an Oldowan industry. Age estimates as old as 2.5 million years have been suggested for the Gona artifacts, but it is equally possible that they are not much older than those from Koobi Fora and Olduvai. Another site at Hadar, A. L. 666, has recently yielded twenty stone flakes and cores associated with a hominid maxilla that is dated to 2.3 million years ago (see page 168), making this the oldest known association between a hominid fossil and stone artifacts. ◖ The overall evidence from East Africa suggests that by roughly 2.3 to 2.5 million years ago, the Oldowan industry tool tradition was well established. Perhaps even older stone tools will be found, but unless their makers returned to a specific spot on the landscape where concentrations of artifacts would be obvious, these sites may be difficult to find. The use of naturally occurring rocks to break open nuts, a behavior that has been observed in chimpanzees in West Africa, probably extends far back into our past, but recognition of such behavior from the archeological record may be impossible. ◖ Although there is no question that the stone tools of the Oldowan industrial complex were fashioned by a hominid hand, there is equally no consensus as to who made the tools. Australopithecines existed throughout the range of time during which Oldowan tools have been found, roughly between 2.4 and 1.5 million years ago. It is virtually impossible to be absolutely certain of the identity of the toolmaker, but most paleoanthropologists credit the larger-brained *Homo habilis* or *Homo rudolfensis*. ◖ A stronger case for *Homo* as the toolmaker is the simple observation that stone tools do not become part of the geological record until *Homo* appears on the scene. Even more convincing is the fact that tools of the Acheulean industrial tradition, mostly hand axes, very quickly replaced the Oldowan tools about 1.5 million years ago, just after the appearance of *H. ergaster*. If robust australopithecines had been making Oldowan tools, one would have expected the tradition to have continued until the extinction of australopithecines, around 1 million years ago, but this was not the case.

Oldowan flake tool from Hadar, Ethiopia. The A.L. 666 site has yielded a fossil upper jaw of *Homo* as well as several stone cores and flakes. With an age of 2.3 million years, these are the oldest known stone tools in direct association with a hominid fossil. Actual size. *Courtesy of Donald Johanson, Institute of Human Origins.*

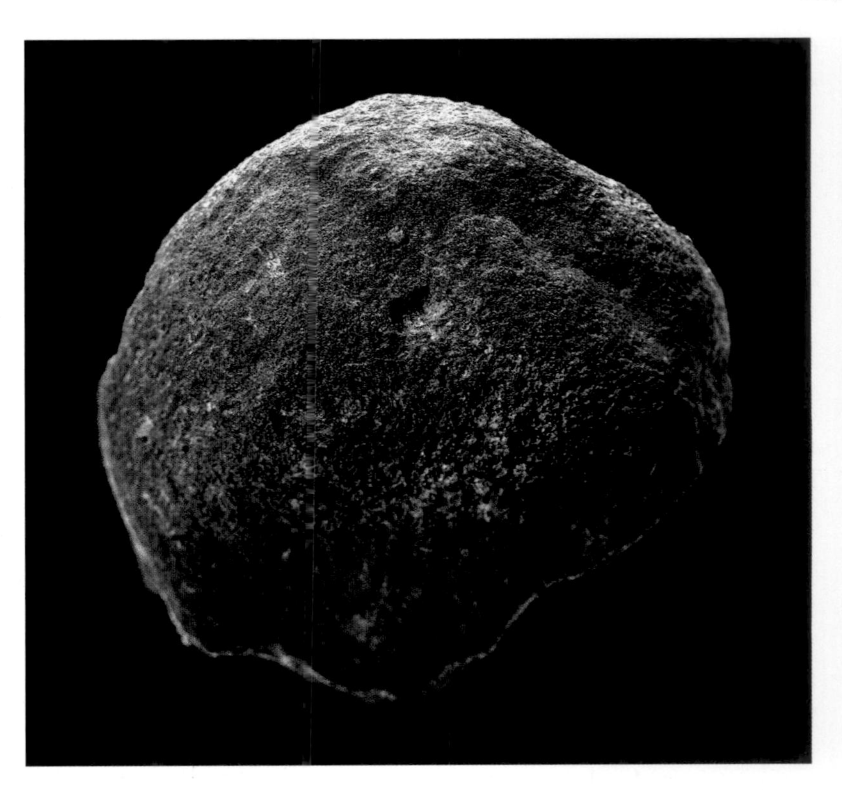

Hammerstone from Olduvai Gorge, Tanzania. This 1.8 million year-old artifact may closely resemble the earliest type of stone technology. A rounded, unmodified cobble can be used to strike sharp flakes from another rock, creating an effective cutting tool. Actual size. *Photograph by David Brill; courtesy of National Museum of Tanzania.*

37 · Hunters, Gatherers, or Scavengers?

OUR earliest ancestors' subsistence behavior is the focus of tremendous attention, but because behavior does not fossilize, teasing details out of the archeological record has proved arduous. Some attempts to understand early hominid lifeways have involved nothing more than projecting into the past an impoverished version of modern hunter-gatherers' lifeways. Although hunter-gatherers provide a comparative base, we must not lose sight of the fact that early hominids undoubtedly had their own unique and highly successful set of lifeways that were probably behaviorally distinct from any living model. The most pervasive single explanation for the survival strategy of our ancestors has been the "hunting hypothesis." Hunting, as understood by predominantly male anthropologists, seemed to be *the* key activity, one that explained nearly every aspect of humanity. Hunting took cognitive skills, prompting brain expansion; it took cooperation, possible only in more complex societies, and perhaps it even took language to plan and conduct the hunt. ◖ The late archeologist Glynn Isaac erected a larger framework of

behavior that still embraced hunting as a core activity. The more elaborate scenario became known as the "home base hypothesis" and could, Isaac believed, explain the emergence of humanness. Hunting depended on cooperation and planning, which demanded enhanced intelligence and communication skills. Food was brought to a specific place, a home base, where it was shared. This served to establish strong social bonds and stimulated reciprocal behavior, a sort of economic interdependence between males and females based on a division of labor. Males hunted for food and protected the group, females collected plant foods and cared for the children. ◖ Support for this hypothesis was sought in the excavations at Olduvai Gorge, Tanzania, where numerous stone tools were found associated with broken-up animal bones, some of which even showed stone tool cut marks. At this locality, known as FLK I, dated to roughly 1.8 million years, remains of *Homo habilis* were also recovered. The association of tools, bones, and hominids was taken as proof of the home base hypothesis, and FLK I was designated a home base where our ancestors left remains of their meals. ◖ Lewis Binford, an archeologist at Southern Methodist University, has objected strenuously to interpreting the assemblage at FLK I as evidence for hunting by early hominids. If we look into the past with a preconceived notion, such as hunting, the remains at Olduvai will appear to offer proof of that notion. Binford stressed that analogy with modern hunter-gatherer societies grossly biases interpretation of the actual archeological evidence by inference. All that can be inferred from FLK I, according to Binford, is that early hominids collected stones and used them to break open bones. He proposed that, at best, our ancestors at FLK I were processing bones they had scavenged from carnivore kills. In other words, our early ancestors were scavengers, not hunters. ◖ To test Binford's theory, a critical study was undertaken in the 1980s by Rob Blumenschine, an archeologist at Rutgers University, who studied the composition of modern bone accumulations on the Serengeti. He observed numerous feedings by lions, hyenas, cheetahs, and jackals and noted that after these predators had dined on the flesh and crunched up the ribs, the leftovers consisted mostly of limb bones and the skull. He further noticed that roughly 15 percent of those bones showed carnivore tooth marks. ◖ Blumenschine collected the bones left behind by the carnivores and, using an unmodified stone cobble, broke open the bone to extract the marrow, carefully noting the pattern of bone breakage. He then compared his observations on the modern sample to the evidence from FLK I and concluded that the Olduvai bone collection, like the ones on the Serengeti, was probably the result of scavenging behavior. The Olduvai assemblage consisted mostly of limb bones, many of which showed carnivore tooth marks and stone tool damage. The implication was that our ancestors scavenged carnivore kills made by lions, leopards, saber-toothed cats, and even hyenas, collecting predominantly long limb bones and breaking them open to benefit from the bone marrow, a fatty, high-energy food source. Most carnivores, including hyenas, would have been unable to crack the thick-walled bones, but a hominid with a simple stone tool would have had no problem doing so. The emerging view of "man the scavenger" did not have quite the heroic proportions of "man the hunter." ◖ *Homo habilis* may have benefited from bone marrow, but was doubtless also fairly flexible in its subsistence behaviors, relying on different food resources for which it developed special foraging strategies. This was especially true for seasonally available vegetable food sources. We can also assume that because hominids must drink every day, our ancestors remained close to permanent sources of water.
◖ Blumenschine's work further suggests that scavenging would have put an evolutionary premium on intelligence. To be successful at scavenging, early hominids would have had to detect and locate carcasses. They needed to know quite a bit about the behavior of predators — where they hunt, and when. Most important, they needed to know when not to interfere with predators that might have turned on them for a meal. Perhaps some of the skills acquired during scavenging were a prelude to including more meat in the hominid diet. ◖ The time when hunting *did* become a major aspect of hominid subsistence behavior continues to be the center of much debate in paleoanthropology. Many archeologists contend that hunting is an ancient human subsistence strategy going back hundreds of thousands of years, perhaps even a million years, to the time of *Homo erectus*. Often cited are the associated remains of large mammals like elephants with hand axes and cleavers. Lewis Binford, however, continues to be cautious and hesitates to accept the association of stone tools and butchered bones as evidence for hunting rather than scavenging. Rather, he takes a contrarian view and suggests that hunting large animals on a regular basis did not become an important element in human subsistence behavior until the Upper Paleolithic, beginning some 40,000 years ago, when spears and arrows were regularly used.

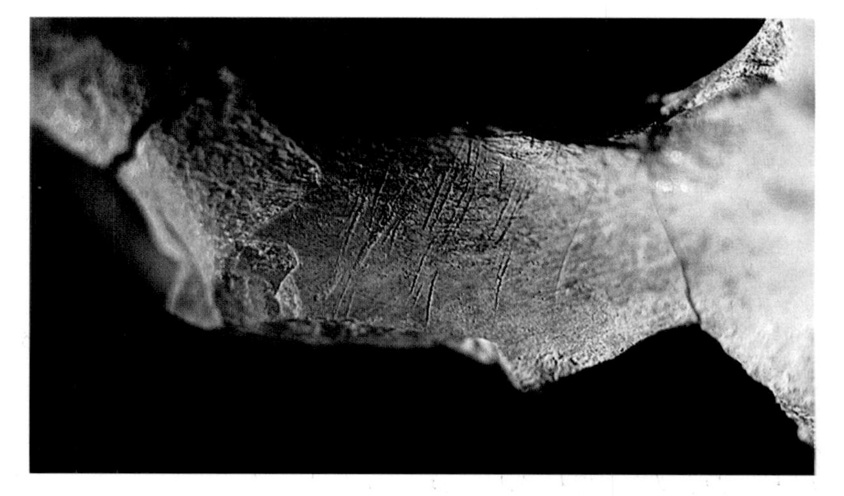

Cut marks on a bone from Olduvai Gorge, Tanzania. These parallel incisions were made by a sharp-edged stone flake in the hand of a hominid. *Photograph by David Brill; courtesy of National Museum of Tanzania.*

38 · Diet

FOOD is an endless source of conversation in Western nations, and the struggle against obesity supports a billion-dollar dieting industry. The same was not true for our ancestors, who struggled to get enough of the right kinds of food to survive. To reproduce — the Darwinian goal of the individual and the species — an animal must stay alive, which means it must eat. Our ancestors were successful in getting enough to eat, for we are here today. What remains conjectural is the type of diet they had and how the foodstuffs were processed. ◖ The first discoveries of australopithecines in South Africa immediately elicited some imaginative speculation about their dietary preferences. For example, *Australopithecus africanus* was quickly pictured as a carnivorous, bloodthirsty ape. The distinctive cranial and dental anatomy of *A. robustus* was thought to be a response to an herbivorous diet that demanded extensive mastication of low-quality vegetable foods. These early inferences about the diet of australopithecines rested on a combination of preconceived ideas about the importance of meat eating to early humans and observations of gross dental wear and anatomy. More recently a number of strategies have been employed to more precisely assess the diets of early hominids. Most of these strategies have been applied to teeth, which are shaped differently to accommodate different diets and also bear the signatures of the types of food consumed.
◖ Comparisons of dental anatomy between groups of animals that subsist on varying types of foods provide some insight into specific dietary adaptations. For example, carnivores, which are specialized meat eaters, have a set of scissors-like back teeth that are used to cut through flesh. Grass

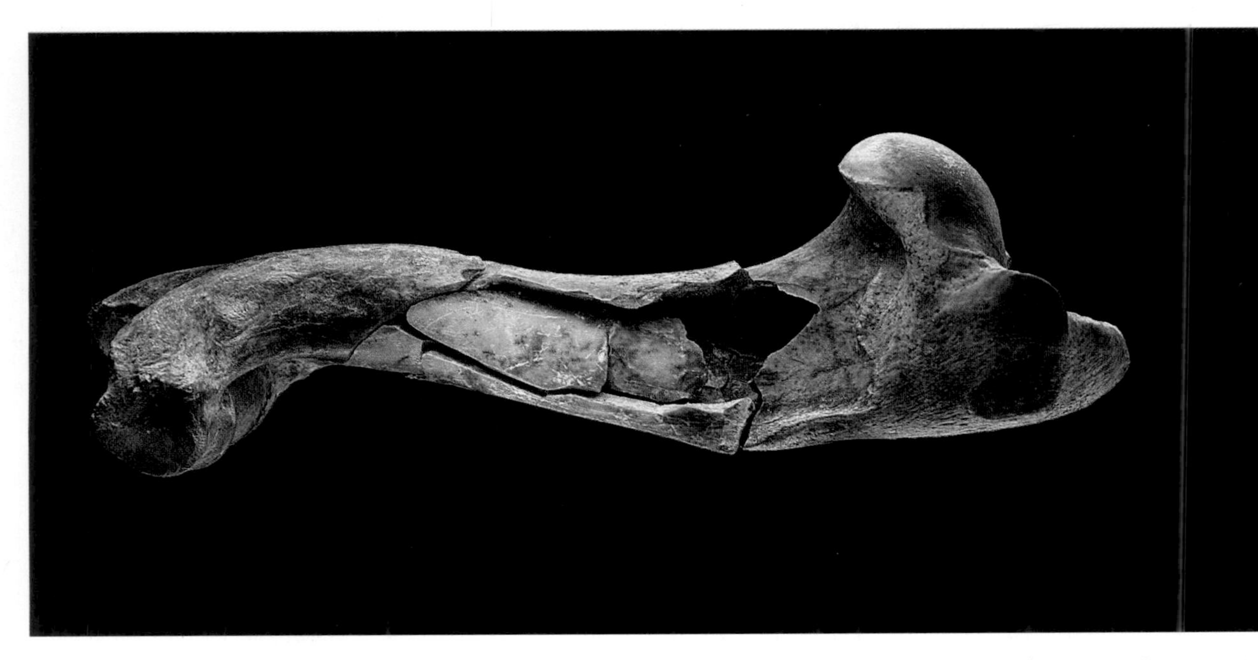

chewing surfaces of teeth, sometimes with the aid of a scanning electron microscope, has refined the picture by permitting quantitative analysis of dental microwear. A very high incidence of enamel pitting is documented in the teeth of *A. robustus* and *A. boisei*. Moreover, the pits and scratches on these teeth are significantly larger than those seen on *A. africanus* teeth. The frequency and size of enamel pits in *A. robustus* are reminiscent of the condition seen in mangabeys, organ-grinder monkeys, and in the orangutan, which consume very hard foods such as nuts, seeds, and fruits with tough rinds. The occlusal wear on *A. africanus* teeth, characterized by fewer pits and narrower scratches, suggests a different dietary preference. Similarities in enamel wear to patterns seen in primates like the spider monkey, which eats more mature, fleshy, softer fruits as well as leaves, indicate that *A. africanus* probably consumed less nuts and seeds than *A. robustus* or *A. boisei*. ◖ Dental wear in the South African australopithecines contrasts strongly with that seen in East African *A. afarensis*. In the South African *A. africanus* and the robust australopithecines, teeth were quickly worn flat after eruption, exposing large islands of dentine. In fact, the canine teeth are so heavily worn that they must have participated in some of the crushing and grinding functions of the postcanine teeth. In *A. afarensis*, not only do the canines exhibit limited occlusal wear, the posterior teeth show minimal wear even when the incisors are heavily worn. This suggests an emphasis on the anterior teeth for food preparation, perhaps of soft fruits, as is the case in chimpanzees. Microscopic examination reveals antemortem dental chippage in *A. afarensis*, probably caused by biting down on hard, small food objects like nuts. Close examination of the edges of the incisors show striations from front to back. It may be that some form of vegetation was stripped between the incisors in *A. afarensis*. ◖ Meat consumption in early humans must have been very limited. Dentally they did not have slicing and cutting teeth necessary for eating meat, and they lacked the necessary stone tools for processing it. Chimpanzees have been observed eating the meat of monkeys, small bush pigs, small antelopes, and even the young of their own kind. Chimpanzees are successful hunters in large part because of their strength and speed in the trees. Australopithecines were bipedal, relatively slow on the ground, and limited in their ability to pursue potential game into the trees because they lacked a grasping foot. ◖ It is highly likely that early hominids incorporated a wide variety of foodstuffs into their diets. Yet many items that may have been eaten, such as insects, which at times are eaten in great quantity by chimpanzees, would not have left any diagnostic signature on the very hard enamel. This would also be true for honey, eggs, worms, and small vertebrates such as rodents and reptiles. ◖ At the moment, details of dental wear, and by inference their diets, in more ancient hominids such as *A. anamensis* and *Ardipithecus ramidus* are not available. The molars of the former taxon are thick-enameled and have wear similar to that seen in *A. afarensis*, except that canines show heavy apical wear. The condition in *A. ramidus* is somewhat distinct, since it is the only putative hominid that has thin dental enamel, a feature more closely shared with the African apes. ◖ Conjectures about early hominid diet rely on inferences from dental evidence, studies of modern primate diets, remains of animal bones and associated tools at archeological sites, and information on what

Antelope humerus from Olduvai Gorge, Tanzania. Its shaft shattered to expose the marrow within, this bone from the FLK locality displays both stone tool cut marks and carnivore tooth marks. The array of tools and bones from this site has been used to construct differing scenarios of hunting or scavenging by early humans nearly 2 million years ago. Actual size. *Photograph by David Brill; courtesy of National Museum of Tanzania.*

eaters, such as horses, have tall teeth with chewing surfaces composed of alternating strips of enamel and dentine. Primates, by contrast, are in large part generalized in their feeding adaptations and therefore lack the specialized dental configurations seen in grazers and carnivores. ◖ Within the order Primates, hominids have teeth that are remarkably generalized, suggesting a wide-ranging omnivorous diet. However, unlike the African apes, which have thin dental enamel, hominid teeth have thick enamel. It is thought that thick enamel is the primitive condition—that is, the condition that has not been altered through evolutionary change. This conjecture is in keeping with the different evolutionary histories of apes and hominids. Apes may have had opportunity to evolve a thin enamel, whereas hominids may have retained the thick enamel from the last common ancestors of apes and humans. ◖ Body size also bears a relationship to dietary preference. For example, insectivores, with a high metabolic rate, expend a lot of energy capturing their prey and tend to be small-bodied. Leaf eaters, with lower metabolic rates (the gorilla is an extreme example here), have larger bodies. Interestingly, frugivores, or fruit eaters, tend to have relatively larger brains than folivores, or leaf eaters. Presumably, because fruits are seasonal and more regionally distributed than leaves, fruit eaters would need larger brains to process the more complex seasonal and geographic information about their environment. ◖ Another line of evidence comes from strontium-calcium ratios in hominid remains. Within the food web there are distinct differences between strontium-calcium ratios in the bodies of different species, which ingest these mineral isotopes with their food and incorporate them into their bones. Plants, a primary source on the food chain, have a high ratio, herbivores a lower one, and carnivores, which eat the herbivores, the lowest ratio. Attempts have been made to determine the value of these ratios in early hominid fossils as an aid to determining their food preferences. Although the effects of fossilization and burial may limit measurement of the strontium-calcium ratio, some interesting results have been obtained for *A. robustus*. Ratios determined for hominids from Swartkrans, South Africa, fall between those of leopards and baboons and suggest a more omnivorous diet rather than the strictly vegetarian one that was first supposed. ◖ These considerations paint in broad strokes the dietary preferences of early hominids, namely, they were opportunistic omnivores. Detailed examinations of the modern hunter-gatherers eat. Although the exact details of our ancestors' diets may never be known, they clearly developed effective strategies for feeding, and equally effective strategies for not being eaten themselves.

39 · Cannibalism

CHARGES of cannibalism among our ancestors have been made at different times throughout the history of paleoanthropology, with an accusing finger pointed at several species. From our modern, culturally civilized perspective, we tend to view cannibalism as an inhuman—perhaps the most inhuman—of acts, repellent and repugnant. Yet, if there is evidence for cannibalism deep in our past, we need to ponder it objectively. It sheds a light, however harsh, on one aspect of human nature. ◖ Among nonhuman primates, fifteen species have been documented engaging in cannibalism, and the behavior is fairly widespread among mammals. Males and females of our close ape relative, the chimpanzee, cannibalize infants. But without the benefits of direct observation, we have only enigmatic evidence from which to infer such behavior on the part of our ancestors. ◖ For instance, a bashed and broken adolescent *Australopithecus africanus* lower jaw, missing its front teeth, that was found at Makapansgat, South Africa, in 1948 prompted anatomist Raymond Dart to investigate this species's apparently violent nature. In his memoir, Dart declared: "*Australopithecus* lived a grim life. He ruthlessly killed other australopithecines and fed upon them as he would upon any other beast, young or old. " But the pattern of broken bones examined by Dart proved on later analysis to have been made by hyenas and other carnivores seeking fat-rich marrow, not by these predominantly herbivorous hominids. ◖ When Franz Weidenreich studied the *Homo erectus* fossils from Zhoukoudian, China, the cave home of Peking Man, in the 1930s, he noticed that there seemed to be too many skulls for the number of limb bones. The faces on some of the skulls had been broken off and the foramen magnum, the hole at the base of the skull through which the spinal cord passes, had been enlarged, as though someone or something had torn open the skull to consume the brain. The cave also preserved evidence of controlled fire, and many bones had been burned, so Weidenreich suggested that Peking Man had been a cannibal. Louis Leakey provided his own interpretation of Zhoukoudian, with Peking Man as the meal of modern humans who, he believed, lived at the site simultaneously. But, as at Makapansgat, it seems that hyenas were the culprits here, too. ◖ These examples illustrate the critical need to distinguish between patterns of bone breakage made by carnivores or other animals and that made by humans. Each leaves a distinctive signature on bone for the careful investigator to find. If it can be determined that early humans were breaking open human bones, it doesn't necessarily mean that cannibalism occurred. Cut marks may indicate ritual defleshing, such as scalping, and broken or burned bones may be part of a mortuary practice. What fossil or archeological evidence could reveal whether early humans ate other humans? ◖ A cranium from Bodo, Ethiopia (see page 94), belonging to *Homo heidelbergensis* displays diagnostic stone tool cut marks around the eye sockets, on the cheekbone, on the forehead, and on the top and back of the cranium. It shows no sign of chewing by carnivores. Because the bone had not begun to heal around the grooves sliced into it and because the marks pass under the rock matrix sticking to the skull, the cut marks were made either while this hominid lived or just after he died. Around 600,000 years ago, this individual was intentionally defleshed, in the earliest such incident known. But whether the butcher ate any of this flesh cannot be answered. ◖ The most recently proposed case for early cannibalism comes from Gran Dolina, Spain, where even more ancient remains of *H. heidelbergensis*, about 780,000 years old, have been recovered (see page 46). The excavators noticed striations on a skull fragment of hominid temporal bone and later found similar markings on a pair of toe bones. An examination of casts of the striations under a scanning electron microscope revealed the telltale V-shaped cross-section of stone tool cut marks like those observed on the Bodo specimen. The dozen cut marks on the temporal fragment occur on the mastoid crest, an attachment point for the sternocleidomastoid muscle, indicating that flesh had likely been removed from the bone. Other animal bones at Gran Dolina have identical defleshing and dismembering marks as well as impact fractures from hammerstones. In contrast, carnivore tooth marks occur on only a small percentage of bones from the cave, so it appears that hominids were mainly responsible for butchering these bones. ◖ Tim White, who spotted the cut marks on the Bodo specimen, and Nick Toth recently surveyed other examples of purported trauma in the more recent fossil record. Some specimens of European Neandertals provided contradictory conclusions about cannibalism in this species. Two specimens that have been cited as victims of cannibalism or ritualized defleshing are the Circeo I cranium from Grotta Guattari, Italy, and the child's cranium from Engis, Belgium. (Although not recognized on its discovery in 1829, the Engis specimen was in fact the first Neandertal, and thus the first hominid fossil, ever found.) Circeo I was missing the base of the skull when it was found in 1939, lying upside down in an alleged circle of stones. The story spread that this Neandertal's brain had been consumed in a cannibal feast. But the skull bears no cut marks, percussion fractures, or other indications of human-induced damage. It does, however, have several marks made by gnawing teeth. And the cave in which it lay was an ancient hyena den. ◖ As for Engis, the suspected cut marks on this cranium were made by humans, but not by any intending to eat the child. The marks, also seen on other Belgian Neandertal skulls, correspond to cranial tracing and measurement tools, the striations left by the sandpaper that was used to smooth the plaster during the reconstruction of missing bone, and scalpel damage inflicted as the molds were being removed to make casts of the fossil. They were all made by overeager nineteenth-century anthropologists. ◖ White and Toth's analysis of bones from the Croatian cave site of Krapina made a more convincing case for cannibalism and corroborated the opinion of the cave's original excavator. (see pages 95 and 211) The skeletons of several Neandertals were shattered and scattered throughout the site. Collected between 1895 and 1905, unfortunately without archeological techniques, the 850 human bones and 1,000 tools tell a chilling story. Some 800 of the bones reveal cut marks and fractures made by hammerstones, while none show any carnivore gnawing. The sides of the skulls were smashed in, and many meat-rich bones are missing, while fragile bones containing little nutritious marrow, such as the fibula of the lower leg, remain intact. It's a perplexing pattern, but Karl Gorjanovic-Kramberger, the excavator of Krapina, may have interpreted it correctly when he wrote in 1918: "These men ate their fellow tribesmen, and what's more, they cracked open the hollow bones and sucked out the marrow.... " A similar story may be made for the nearby Neandertal cave site of Vindija, where the skulls were also smashed in and upper arm bones bear cut marks. ◖ If Neandertals occasionally resorted to cannibalism, perhaps to avoid starvation, did this behavior distinguish them from modern humans? Apparently not. White also examined the fragmentary remains from the caves of Klasies River Mouth in South Africa, which preserved what may be some of the earliest members of our species. The small number of human fossils include a handful of lower jaw fragments, a dozen cranial fragments, and assorted bits of bone (see page 42). Many of the bones were burned, presumably while resting in one of the fire pits used by the early humans here. A piece of frontal bone from a skull shows the same distinctive cut marks above the eye socket as on the Bodo skull, and the bone was broken apart while still fresh. ◖ A much more recent case of prehistoric cannibalism comes from the Neolithic cave site of Fontbrégoua, France, which was

Cranium of *Homo heidelbergensis* from Bodo, Ethiopia (*above*). This specimen has several cut marks made while the bone was still fresh, so the skull was defleshed either before or shortly after death. Actual size. *Courtesy of Donald Johanson and National Museum of Ethiopia.*
Cut marks on the cheek bone of the Bodo cranium (*right*). These straight incisions could only have been made by stone artifact. Similar marks were found near the eye sockets and on the forehead and rear of this specimen. *Courtesy of Donald Johanson, Institute of Human Origins and National Museum of Ethiopia.*

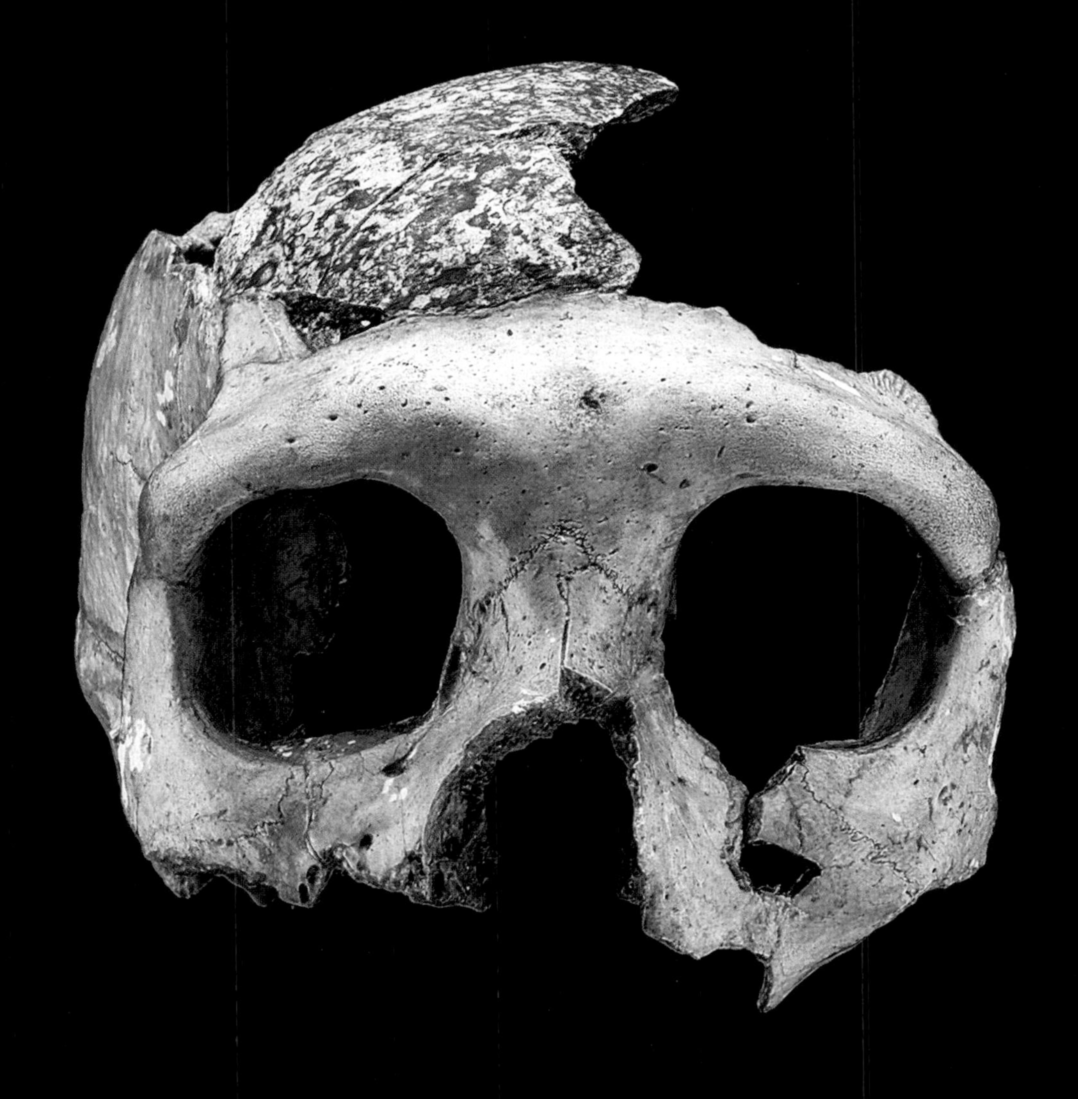

Partial cranium of *Homo neanderthalensis* from Krapina, Croatia. Judging from the skeletal representation and poor preservation of Neandertal bones from Krapina, this cave's occupants cannibalized the remains of their fellow residents. Actual size. *Photograph by David Brill; courtesy of Geolosko-Paleontologie Musej.*

excavated in the 1980s. About 6,000 years ago, broken bones from at least thirteen humans were disposed of in three piles. In ten separate piles were bones from domestic sheep and wild animals that had been broken and butchered in the same way, with cut marks in similar places and frequencies. The bones from animals consumed for food and those of humans were treated identically. Certain bones, such as meaty limb bone shafts and the braincase, are conspicuously absent from both human and animal piles or show up only as discarded scraps. The bones show no sign of having been cooked, but all other evidence indicates that filleted human meat and extracted marrow were consumed. ◖ Since cannibalism is such a controversial issue, anthropologists need to examine the evidence for it with care and caution. A set of criteria can be established, including cut marks, broken bones, the presence or absence of certain nutritiously valuable bones, and burning or other signs of cooking, as contextual clues that should be present in some combination for one to infer that human bones were being processed for nutrients. Even if careful analysis leads to the conclusion that humans ate their cohorts on occasion in the past, we will probably never know exactly why.

40 · Fire

HUMANS became adept manipulators of the environment in the course of our evolution, and one of the key steps in that process was the ability first to control, then create, fire. As a source of heat and light, fire provided protection from predators and shelter from inclement weather. Eventually, fire expanded the diet of early humans. Seeds and plant foods could be heated to break down toxins. Meat could be roasted to kill parasites and preserve the spoils of hunting or scavenging forays. Mastery of fire ultimately enabled our species to occupy the coldest reaches of the continents and may even have allowed humans to exploit a previously unused food supply by the thawing of frozen animal carcasses. Certainly, fire permitted meat to be smoked and dried to eat when other foods could not be had in harsh northern regions. For our ancestors, fire was the best thing since stone tools (sliced bread was still many millennia away). ◖ Despite its obvious importance as an implement of human culture, the origin of fire has been difficult to trace. As archeologists dig deeper into time, the evidence for fire becomes both scarcer and more ambiguous, and more time elapsed in which to erase what traces may have once existed. Typically, *Homo erectus* is credited with the first use of fire, in part because the earliest evidence falls within the time period when this species lived and because fire was considered essential for the widespread dispersal of *Homo erectus* outside of Africa. ◖ Claims for early human fire at around 1.4 million years ago at Chesowanja, Kenya, were based on the discovery of about forty flecks and lumps of burned clay at a site with animal bones and lava tools similar to the oldest stone tools from Olduvai Gorge and Koobi Fora. The excavators ruled out a natural brushfire as an explanation, although other observations suggest that tree stumps consumed by African bush fires could create a pattern like that found at Chesowanja. Lightning and volcanic heating could be alternative explanations for the baked clay. ◖ More compelling evidence for ancient fire comes from the South African cave site of Swartkrans. Excavation of the youngest layers in the cave turned up a relatively small percentage of burned bones from animals ranging from antelope to zebra (and even a few from the most common hominid at the site, *Australopithecus robustus*). The few hundred burned bones came from the same layer of sediment in a single corner of the cave deposit. Chemical analysis showed that these bones had been darkened by carbon residues. Microscopic comparisons with bones heated experimentally to a series of different temperatures determined that the fossils had been subjected to prolonged temperatures of between 315 and 480 degrees Celsius or even hotter, such as would have occurred in a campfire made from the local

Burned bone from Swartkrans, South Africa. A total of 270 burned bones excavated from Member 3 of this cave provides direct evidence that early humans tended fire nearly a million years ago. Actual sizes. *Courtesy of C.K. Brain, Transvaal Museum.*

firewood. Based on the relative abundance of hominid bones throughout the site, an australopithecine may have made the fires at Swartkrans, but since the burned bones occur only after the first half-million years or so of time captured at the site, when fossils of *Homo* also appear (see page 184), it is reasonable to conclude that the new hominid in the area, *Homo*, was responsible. ◖ Although the evidence from Swartkrans is intriguing, it is still an isolated occurrence. Perhaps fire had been controlled by hominids but not created, at least not as an everyday event. Further archeological evidence for fire does not appear until around 500,000 years ago. At the site of Zhoukoudian, China, where the famous Peking Man remains (see page 188) were found, *Homo erectus* apparently contained fire throughout a long period of occupancy during a cold, temperate climate similar to northern China's today. Four ash layers at the site range in thickness from about 1 to 6 meters and date to periods between 460,000 and 230,000 years ago. Charred Chinese hackberry seeds also occur in the cave deposits, along with possibly burned bones, artifacts, and charcoal, although some archeologists question the presence of actual hearths at this site. And it is structures like hearths that ultimately

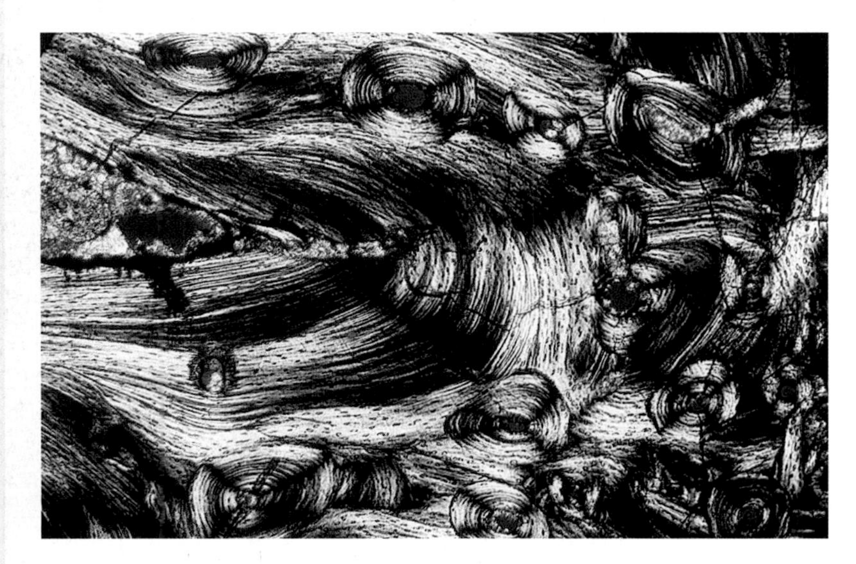

Photomicrograph of burned fossilized bone. In polarized light this thin-section through one of the Swartkrans burned bones reveals how the lamellar structure has been darkened by free carbon that formed while the fresh bone was heated. The same pattern occurred in experimental bones heated to between 300 and 400 degrees Celcius, a typical temperature in a campfire. *Courtesy of C.K. Brain, Transvaal Museum.*

provide unequivocal evidence for fire later in the archeological record. ◖ In Europe, for example, evidence for such a fire pit has just recently been excavated at Menez-Dregan on the southern coast of Brittany. Here, a thick concentration of charcoal and burned bones is enclosed by a ring of flat stone blocks. This has been interpreted as a hearth where the occupants may have roasted rhino meat over an open flame. Electron spin resonance dating of burned quartz places the age of the site between 380,000 and 465,000 years. If the date holds up, this could become the earliest evidence for controlled fire. To the south, on the French Riviera coast, the open-air site of Terra Amata contained hearthlike depressions that were lined on one side with rocks as if to make a windbreak for a fire that burned sometime between 400,000 and 200,000 years ago. Charcoal was found throughout the deposits at the site, and several burned mussel shells were recovered. ◖ Hearths did not become common until the Middle Paleolithic, or within the past 100,000 years. By that time, humans had mastered fire, and it must have achieved its important social role of bringing families and groups together and facilitating the exchange of ideas and information. Human use of fire in the Middle Paleolithic can be demonstrated in Africa, Europe, and the Near East. The Israeli cave of Kebara, for instance, was inhabited by Neandertals at least 60,000 years ago, and careful excavation revealed what the excavators called an impressive accumulation of flat and bowl-shaped hearths. The base of the hearths contained blackened, organic-rich silt with charcoal from local oak and carbonized seeds of wild peas. In addition to parching peas, the occupants of Kebara may have been roasting meat, judging from burned bone fragments found in the cave. After fires were put out, the ashes may have spread to warm the ground on which the Neandertals slept. ◖ By the Upper Paleolithic, around 40,000 years ago, fire was in common use for heating caves and dwellings. At sites such as Abri Pataud in Les Eyzies, France, hearths incorporated draft channels and warming stones for more efficient cooking. ◖ Whether or not fire first crept into our culture around a million years ago, it certainly became a force in human evolution within the past 500,000 years. Use of fire became more frequent within the past 200,000 years, and after 100,000 years ago fire began to serve several specialized functions in daily life. As a complement to our evolving paleolithic technology, fire was a critical cultural tool for our survival and spread as a species, and most importantly, for our social development. The fireside provided the place to share food and share thoughts, a role that it continues to fulfill on a winter's night.

41 · Shelter

THE IDEA of a home or a shelter where we retreat for peace, protection, or privacy is an essential part of our daily lives. Few of us can conceive of being homeless, of having no dwelling to return to after a journey of a single day or one of many months. Yet our ancestors lived without building themselves shelters for most of our evolutionary history. Although structures have been inferred from evidence found at a few sites with associated Acheulean tools—such as pavements of closely packed stones at Olorgesailie, Kenya, and Isimila, Tanzania, and a stone wall supporting a possible lean-to shelter against the cave wall at Lazaret, France—only in the later part of the Middle Paleolithic, around 60,000 years ago, does archeological evidence for the construction of shelters really become apparent. Even then, the evidence remains sparse and enigmatic. For instance, a single posthole was discovered from a Mousterian level at the long-occupied cave of Combe-Grenal, France, and excavators made a cast of the 21 centimeter-long wooden stake that once filled it. Nothing can be concluded, though, about what sort of structure this artifact supported or secured. Low stone walls have been reported from the sites of Cueva Morin, Spain, and Pech de l'Aze, France. In La Grotte du Renne at Arcy-sur-Cure, France, a stone wall and eleven postholes delineated the perimeter of an apparent hut covering more than 9 square meters. The postholes once held up mammoth tusks and limb bones, which may have been the supports for a roof. ◖ Despite these few examples, Middle Paleolithic people did not alter their environments to the extent that their Upper Paleolithic successors did, and that includes building unambiguous shelters at cave and open-air sites, often inferred from square and rectangular pavements of river cobbles that formed the base of structures. As modern humans moved out of environments in Europe rich in natural caves and began to occupy open-air sites at higher latitude during the past 40,000 years, shelters became critical for survival. ◖ At Dolni Vestonice in Moravia, Czech Republic, humans lived for five periods between 28,000 and 24,000 years ago. The site is famous both for an unusual triple burial discovered in 1986 and for the remains of five dwellings—the largest covering an area 9 meters by 15 meters—demarcated by postholes, mammoth bones, and blocks of limestone. The remains of two kilns reveal that these people were the first anywhere to experiment with ceramics, creating human and animal figurines that may have been purposefully exploded inside the ovens. ◖ Spectacular evidence of past shelters also comes from further east in Europe, specifically from sites in Ukraine on the central Russian plain between the Carpathian foothills and the Urals. Modern humans most likely moved into this environment to hunt the abundant herds of large herbivores—woolly mammoth, reindeer, horse, and bison—and they set up short and long-term camps in prominent river valleys. This was an extreme environment for humans, one marked by a frigid climate and harsh weather. Large mammals provided a vital source of food, certainly, but animal skins and furs must have been important for clothing, too. In view of the scarcity of trees at some sites, mammoth bones and reindeer antlers also provided handy construction materials. Ten Russian sites possess the ruins of mammoth bone structures, and eight other sites have the remains of structures made with additional materials. ◖ One of these sites, Molodova, on the Dnestr River, consists of several occupation levels containing numerous hearths, which are associated with mammoth bones arranged to create windbreaks. At the Middle Paleolithic site Molodova I, an oval arrangement of mammoth bones once stood as a shelter. The floor space inside had been cluttered with 29,000 flint flakes and fragments, hundreds of broken animal bone pieces, fifteen hearths, and a piece of red ochre. A slightly smaller and less clearly patterned arrangement of mammoth bones occurs at Molodova V, and this site has also preserved a dwelling roofed by reindeer antlers, which were presumably covered with animal skins. ◖ Reindeer antlers and mammoth bones were also

Cast of stake from Combe-Grenal, France. This cast was made from a posthole in a Mousterian layer of the cave site. The blunt tip indicates that the original wooden stake was pounded into hard ground to support a tent or windbreak. Actual size. *Photograph by David Brill; courtesy of Denise de Sonneville-Bordes, Université de Bordeaux I.*

incorporated into structures at Mezin, a site on the Desna River. Five bone concentrations found here have been interpreted as the remains of conical huts constructed with animal skin. Because bones from 116 mammoths of different geological ages were incorporated into the structures at Mezin, it is likely that the occupants mostly scavenged bones from mammoths that had died naturally, adding bones as needed from recently hunted animals. ◖ Another site, Yudinovo, had dwellings of a very different design: one was built around a base of two concentric rings of mammoth bones, with possible postholes drilled into some of the bones in the inner ring; elsewhere at the site, fifty-six mammoth skulls surrounded a large depression dug a half meter below ground level and divided by lines of bones into six partitions or "rooms" of a long house. ◖ The most impressive mammoth bone dwellings come from Mezhirich, a site southwest of Mezin on the Dnepr River where human occupation dates to between 18,000 and 14,000 years ago. This winter camp contained at least five bone houses. One of these had been built from 385 mammoth bones. A semicircle of skulls, topped by a second layer of skulls, pelves, and scapulae, formed the interior wall, and ninety-five mandibles, stacked chin down in rows, fortified the outer wall. Ivory tusks arched across the perimeter to support an animal skin roof. Beneath the bones of Dwelling Number One lay 4,600 flint tools, plus bone artifacts, charred bones, and scattered pieces of red ochre and amber for beads, all surrounding a central circular fire pit. Some bones placed upright around the pit may have been part of a barbecue. The entire shelter had been about 4.5 meters across. ◖ At each dwelling, the shapes of the bones were put to best advantage to create a sound structure. That each had a unique arrangement of bones implies an aesthetic sense among the builders, who attempted a variety of architectural styles. The builders of one dwelling adapted elements of construction from two other huts and added some individual touches. ◖ Building these houses was no easy task. A single mammoth skull with a small pair of tusks weighed more than 90 kilograms, and Mezhirich's Dwelling Number One contained about 20,700 kilograms (23 tons) of bones. Each house may have taken ten people at least four or five days to build. Such effort, plus the amount of accumulated debris from their daily lives, suggests that people stayed here, throughout long winters, for several years. The site's population at any time cannot be determined for certain, but a population of twenty-five has been estimated. Mezhirich was a full-fledged settlement, and in its buildings and material items we see a foreshadowing of the sedentary societies that became a more universal part of human life only 10,000 years ago, with the advent of agriculture.

42 · Clothing

AS WITH SHELTER, early humans had no need for clothing during most of their evolutionary history. They occupied tropical and subtropical regions and, at least until *Homo ergaster* and *Homo erectus* appeared, probably had a healthy coat of body hair. Judging from the proportions of the boy's skeleton from Nariokotome (see page 72), *Homo ergaster* had a tall, thin build similar to that of modern equatorial Africans; it may have been more energy efficient for this hominid to be relatively hairless in the tropical heat, and we have no evidence to conclude that *ergaster*, or even globe-trotting *Homo erectus*, wore clothes. ◖ The earliest hominid that is likely to have had attire is *Homo neanderthalensis*. Although there is no scrap of archeological evidence for Neandertal clothing, the distinctive sloping wear on Neandertal incisors may derive from their use as a vise to grip leather and sinews, perhaps during the curation of animal skins. Neandertal tools would have been useful for scraping mammal hides, and skins and furs would have helped them survive in often glacial environments. Limited evidence for Neandertal body adornments was uncovered in the Grotte du Renne at Arcy-sur-Cure, France. In addition to Châtelperronian stone artifacts were bone and antler tools and an intriguing set of eight plausible items of personal adornment, including carved and grooved teeth from deer and fox. ◖ Only at modern human archeological sites, however, do we find artifacts specifically suited for creating and wearing clothes. Bone needles almost indistinguishable from modern sewing needles have been found at 26,000 year-old sites in central Europe, and at western European sites dating to 23,000 years ago in the Solutrean period. Needles become more common during the succeeding Magdalenian period. The needle shown here comes from Enlene, France, a site best known for its thousands of portable art objects, including engraved, flat stones that were laid on the cave floor like tiles. Of course, the needles have proved more durable than the clothing they stitched, so we can only guess at how these outfits looked. ◖ Buttons made from bone or stone disks date to at least this time as well. At the Late Magdalenian site of Montastruc in the Dordogne region of France, an engraving shows the front of a human figure with a series of small circles running up the middle of the torso and chest. Round objects interpreted as buttons also have engraved animals on the surface, while other buttons were toggle-shaped. ◖ Body adornments, such as beads and pendants of bone, mammoth ivory, shell, amber, stone, and other natural objects, appear about 35,000 years ago, at the beginning of the Aurignacian period of the Upper Paleolithic. They occur scattered in large numbers at ancient campsites and in living areas. Beads probably served a variety of uses, including as buttons, necklaces, or bracelets, and were sewn directly onto clothing to add decorative texture. Body adornments were frequent features of early modern human graves, including those of Cro-Magnon (see page 100). ◖ Archeologist Randall White has reconstructed the stages by which humans manufactured ivory beads in southwest France during the Aurignacian period. The procedure began with four-inch stakes of mammoth ivory cut from the soft outer layer of a tusk and fashioned into a cylindrical rod as thick as a pencil or twig. Because discarded tusk fragments are rare at French archeological sites and intact mammoth tusks are absent, the ivory must have been transported from a distant source. The ivory sticks were incised and broken into shorter segments. The craftsperson whittled away layers of ivory to thin one end of a segment into a stem, then gouged a hole through the ivory at the stem's base using a pointed tool. Further grinding and

Bone needle in matrix from Enlene, France. Evidence of early human clothing has not survived in the archeological record, but tools specifically suited for tailoring have been preserved from as far back in time as 26,000 years ago. Actual size. *Photograph by David Brill; courtesy of Société Civile de Domaine de Pujol.*

polishing reduced and rounded the stem and the bulb at the opposite end of the segment until the hole was left near one edge of the finished bead. This technique created a cylindrical bead around a hole, rather than attempting to pierce an already finished bead. ◖ Perhaps the most famous example of early body adornment comes from Sunghir, an archeological site near Moscow that dates to about 24,000 years ago, where the burials of three individuals contained 10,000 ivory beads and pierced teeth. On the body of an elderly male, beads were arrayed in strands across the forehead and chest and along both legs. This pattern suggests that the beads had been sewn onto a hooded tunic, or perhaps a separate cap and jacket, and tailored pants. The remains of ivory bracelets and pendants and shell and tooth necklaces also decorated each grave. ◖ Undoubtedly, some sort of protective clothing would have been a necessity for humans to spread out across Ice Age Europe and as far north as the Russian steppe. A bone figurine found at Buret, Siberia, depicts a human figure wearing a hooded, parka-like outfit. These people may have dressed entirely in fur, because many furbearing mammals, including foxes and wolves, were hunted at these open-air sites. ◖ Because so little evidence of human clothing has survived at archeological sites, it is necessary to move beyond the time range of this book and jump to the end of the Late Stone Age for a glimpse of what earlier humans might have worn. The extraordinary discovery in 1991 of a Late Stone Age hunter-gatherer whose frozen body had been preserved by a glacier in the Tyrolean Alps provided a very rare and informative look at utilitarian clothing from more than 5,000 years ago. Archeologists carefully collected and reconstructed seven articles of attire preserved in bits and pieces along with the Iceman and his small tool kit. From head to toe, he wore a conical fur hat with a leather chin strap; a sleeveless deerskin tunic; a plaited grass cloak that stretched from shoulders to knees and was fringed to permit free leg movement; loose-fitting leather leggings that hung by straps from a belt and tucked into the shoes; a leather loincloth that protected a belt pouch containing tools and tinder; the pouch itself, which appears to be made of calf leather, possibly from the now extinct aurochs, an ancestor of domesticated cattle; and shoes made of oval pieces of leather bound with straps and stuffed with grass padding, held in place by a net of grass cords. ◖ The leather tunic or cape, probably tanned over a smoky fire, had been scraped on one side. It may have been reversible so that the fur side could be worn in or out, depending on the weather. Sinew and grass held together the several vertical strips of hide, and some seams show signs of a hasty repair with grass thread. In addition to deerskin, bear, ibex, and chamois hide may have been incorporated into the shirt. Although weaving was already an established technique by this time, the Iceman wore no woven clothing.

43 · Burial

SIGNS of purposeful burial do not appear until relatively late in the archeological record. We have widespread and excellent evidence for burials in excavated graves, often accompanied by grave goods and body adornments, beginning in the Upper Paleolithic, or around 40,000 years ago. The evidence for purposeful burial associated with Neandertal skeletons from the preceding Middle Paleolithic is more ambiguous, for these burials lack obvious signs of attendant ceremony or ritual. Even earlier, the rich trove of 300,000 year-old hominid fossils from the Sima de los Huesos in the Atapuerca Mountains of Spain (see page 204) may represent a case of deliberate disposal of corpses down a dark cave shaft, but there is no evidence here of individual burial. ◖ Beginning with the Middle Paleolithic, as people began to occupy caves and rockshelters more frequently, the odds increased that complete or nearly complete skeletons would be preserved intact. Thus, to determine if the bodies represent intentional burials, other evidence besides the flexed skeleton, such as excavated grave pits or accompanying grave goods, should be present. Unfortunately, there is ample opportunity for such information to be disturbed or lost between the time of burial and excavation, or during and after excavation. ◖ Among the Neandertal skeletons proposed as deliberate burials are specimens from Krapina, La Chapelle-aux-Saints, La Ferrassie, La Quina, Le Moustier, Regourdou, Roc de Marsal, and Spy, in Europe, and from Amud, Kebara, KiikKoba, Tabun, Teshik-Tash, and Shanidar in Asia. Some of these—the Krapina specimens and several from Shanidar—are more likely the hapless victims of cave ceiling collapses, while others may have been preserved through natural processes of burial. But there is more convincing evidence that such specimens as La Chapelle I, La Ferrassie 1 and 2 (found lying head to head) and four other individuals found within pits at that site, the young child from Roc de Marsal, the adult and infant from Amud, and the Kebara skeleton discovered in 1983, among others, were indeed deliberately buried by their contemporaries. ◖ Whether the act of burial reflects any religious or spiritual beliefs in Neandertals, an emotional attachment to specific individuals, or simply the fear of scavenging animals and the pragmatic need to remove a decaying body from a campsite cannot be determined. A commonly cited case of Neandertal ritual burial is Shanidar 4, known as the "Old Man," from the Shanidar Cave in Iraq. Soil samples collected from the grave revealed a high concentration of pollen from a broad range of colorful wildflowers, some with medicinal value. The scenario developed that this partially blind and crippled individual, who had obviously survived with the care and attention of others, had been attended by survivors, who cast flowers over his grave. With the 1960s still fresh in the cultural consciousness, the Shanidar Neandertals were called the first flower people. Yet it is not really possible to rule out wind as the source for depositing pollen atop the body or even two of the Iraqi excavation crew who wore flowers tucked into their sashes. ◖ Indeed, with the exception of Shanidar 4, Middle Paleolithic burials show a lack of special character, and what grave goods that do attend corpses—stone tools and animal bones, but never any art or adornments—could have already been present in the sediment used to cover a body. At La Chapelle-aux-Saints, for instance, the leg and foot bones of a bovid found near the body were interpreted as a haunch of meat that had been given as an offering of food for the deceased, and numerous nearby stone tools in the sediment were taken as suggestive evidence that the tomb had been the site of recurring funeral feasts by other Neandertals. Both conclusions are clearly speculative. ◖ In contrast to Neandertal graves, Upper Paleolithic burials of modern humans appear to be much more common (nearly 100 examples from Eurasia, versus about three dozen for the Middle Paleolithic Neandertals). Upper Paleolithic burials occur in both caves and open-air sites and often include a rich assortment of grave goods, such as stone and bone tools, shells, ivory beads or pendants, animal bones, and red ochre. The bodies in these burials are more often fully extended rather than in the flexed position of the Neandertals and are much more likely to occur as multiple burials, as in the double burial of an infant with the adult female Qafzeh IX (see page 239) or the enigmatic triple burial at Dolni Vestonice of a presumed female and two young males, one with a wooden pole penetrating his hip. ◖ The 20,000 year-old burial of a male known as the "Young Prince" at Arene Candide, Italy, exemplifies the elaborate nature of Upper Paleolithic burials. The body was dusted with red ochre and decorated with mammoth ivory pendants, four *bâtons de commandement*, shells that may have been linked in a bracelet and a 23-centimeter flint blade inserted in one

Cast of *Homo sapiens* burial at Arene Candide, Italy. In contrast to Neandertal burials, Upper Paleolithic graves commonly included artifacts, body adornments and sprinklings of red ochre. This reconstructed cast of the 20,000 year-old burial shows mammoth ivory pendants and a flint blade accompanying the body of a teenage boy. *Courtesy of Giacomo Giacobini, Universitá di Torino.*

hand. Red ochre is a recurring feature in Upper Paleolithic burials, although its symbolic meaning can only be guessed at. Its use was also widespread: the body of a male (see page 51) buried at Lake Mungo, Australia, around 30,000 years ago had been sprinkled with ochre.

44 · Art

IF ART is an attempt to imitate nature, our Upper Paleolithic ancestors were master artists. It is impossible to visit a cave like Lascaux in southwestern France or Altamira in northern Spain and not be moved by the images of horses, bison, deer, and other prehistoric animals painted on the ancient cave walls. Reaching across eons of time, these lifelike yet hauntingly impressionistic paintings immediately connect us with the artists who rendered their world on cave walls nearly 20,000 years ago. ¶ When the painted cave of Altamira first came to the attention of researchers, in 1880, the immediate reaction was that such sophisticated and well-executed paintings could not have been made by prehistoric people. With the discovery of other decorated caves in France, however, Upper Paleolithic art was confirmed to be genuine. Today more than 300 decorated caves are known in southwestern Europe that date from the Upper Paleolithic and provide a window on the aesthetic life of our forebears. Caves decorated with art are still being found, such as the cave at Chauvet, in the Ardeche, which dates to some 30,000 years ago and was discovered in December 1994. An even more remarkable discovery is the cave of Cosquer, near Marseilles, France. Cut off by rising sea levels when the glaciers melted, about 12,000 years ago, it was not seen again until found by a scuba diver in 1991 who discovered it at the end of a 150 meter submerged passageway. ¶ The Upper Paleolithic, roughly between 40,000 and 10,000 years ago, saw an explosion of human cultural activities. Our ancestors began to gain some mastery over nature and with it, perhaps, the confidence to celebrate nature. The earlier, survival-oriented existence was gradually replaced by one in which imagery, innovation, ceremony, and ritual were interwoven in highly complex patterns. Humans were beginning to cope with intangible fears, anxieties, and mysteries, perhaps in concert with an increased awareness of their own intellectual powers and consciousness. And as the Upper Paleolithic people spread throughout the world, they created art. Some art in Australia may be as much as 40,000 years old, and since it is still part of the Australian Aboriginal people's way of life, it is the oldest continuous art tradition in the world. Art from Africa dates back to nearly 30,000 years, but little has survived, for the painting was often done in areas exposed to the elements. ¶ The exact meaning of the art from this period may be lost forever, but the sophistication, elaboration, and widespread manifestations of art in Asia, Africa, Australia, and Europe attest to the importance of artistic activity in Upper Paleolithic times. Art was likely the product of professionals, and this suggests that their society enjoyed an economic surplus that freed certain individuals from purely sustenance labor. The images themselves, however, would have been deeply embedded in the broader cultural fabric of the group, representing the interests of all. ¶ One of the best-known and most extensively studied examples of cave art is the cave at Lascaux, in France. The immediate impression one gets on entering the Hall of the Bulls is that the art was carefully planned perhaps reflecting at least in part the intentions of a single artist. Oil lamps that provided illumination for the artists were found in the cave, and a piece of charcoal from the cave floor has been dated to 17,000 years ago. Holes in the cave walls may have been used to anchor some sort of scaffolding for the artists and their assistants. Some 17,000 years before Michelangelo painted the ceiling of the Sistine Chapel, an Upper Paleolithic artist was supported 6 meters above the cave floor to complete some of the paintings. ¶ The cavalcade of horses and bulls in Lascaux seems to be in motion, especially when viewed by the flickering illumination of an oil lamp. A mythical animal bearing two forward-jutting straight horns appears to command the performance. Some think it is a shaman draped in an animal skin. Caves have their own aura of mystery, and Lascaux may have been chosen because of its unique personality or because it had special significance to the group. ¶ The paintings at Lascaux reveal much naturalistic detail and the use of a variety of techniques and pigments. The brown and red ochre that appears in several hues on the walls could have been taken from the sediments in the floor of the cave. Manganese and charcoal were used for black. It took special skill to paint on the uneven, calcite-covered walls—mistakes could not be hidden. Outlines of even the largest animals were drawn by a sure hand in a space of appropriate size. Lines were drawn using an ochre crayon, and dots were made by stabbing at the wall with a pigment stick. ¶ In areas where the pigment appears diffuse and "soft," it may have been blown on, perhaps through a hollow bird bone; or the pigment may have been chewed in the mouth, then spit on the wall. The techniques of spitting or blowing a pigment onto the wall may have had special significance for the artist. Breath gives life, and French prehistorian Michel Lorblanchet conjectures that using the breath to decorate a wall bestowed "life" on the image. He speculates that, in a manner of speaking, the painter was transformed into the animal being painted. ¶ Although images of humans are rare in Paleolithic cave art, images of animals are plentiful and seem to interweave magical and realistic spheres. Some animals painted on Upper Paleolithic cave walls, such as horses and bison, appear to be speared. Were such depictions an attempt at sympathetic magic, to give the hunters dominion over prey and ensure hunting success? In other paintings, natural bulges on the cave walls were used to accentuate the belly of an animal and make it look pregnant. Perhaps these realistic animal representations were created in the hope that game would always be plentiful. Were they painted in the recesses of subterranean caves as a symbolic gesture to the belief that Earth was the womb of all life? ¶ At one French cave, Les Trois Frères, there is a fanciful creature known as the sorcerer. It wears a helmet of antlers and has owl eyes, a horse's tail, wolf ears, bear paws, and human feet and penis. The melding of natural life forms gives a general impression that this was a place of initiation where, under the spell of a shaman, individuals underwent certain rites of passage. Were some of the symbols and images the result of hallucinations as shamans entered a trancelike state? ¶ Cave wall art, although undoubtedly created for the entire society, nevertheless is of an invitational or ritualistic nature. Public to a degree, its very hiddenness kept it from being public to all. Public art in the form of monuments or generally acclaimed works is common in the world today, often reminding people of their belonging to a particular place or of having a shared history. Few such pieces of public art survive from the Upper Paleolithic, but one, in Cap Blanc, France, is quite impressive. A frieze of horses, carved in soft limestone under a rock overhang, is visible from the valley below. We can only speculate on its function—perhaps it was a visual reminder to the wandering bands of hunter-gatherers that this region belonged to a particular group of people. This kind of public art was for everyone, even those outside the social group of the artist, and it clearly served a different purpose from ritualistic art or private, individual art. ¶ Individual art, if it existed, would have belonged to the category of portable art. Portable art took on myriad forms: carvings made of stone, bone, antler, and ivory in the form of human heads; carvings of the entire female body with accentuated breasts and vulva, called "Venus" figurines, that served as fertility fetishes; carved animal heads and bodies; perforated animal bone, seashells, and teeth that were strung together as necklaces; an intricately decorated spear thrower or sculpted *bâton de commandement*, and so on. Such mobile art may have been very specific pieces that a person carried throughout life. Perhaps a certain object signified belonging to a

Bear head figurine from Isturitz, France. Human occupants of this site purposefully aligned the bones of cave bears and fashioned this realistic image of an animal that must have inspired awe and fear. Actual size. *Photograph by David Brill; courtesy of Musée des Antiquités Nationale.*

Bison figurine from La Madeleine, France. This head of a spear-thrower, which depicts a bison licking its flank, is one of the classic images of hand-held art and comes from The type site for the Magdalenian period. Actual size. *Photograph by David Brill; courtesy of Musée des Antiquités Nationale.*

Rock art from southeast Algeria (*left*). This image of a giraffe hunter was created by the Tuareg people perhaps as long as 3,000 years ago. *Photograph by David Coulson.*
Cave painting from Lascaux, France (*above*). Seventeen thousand years ago, an artist in the cave's rotunda created this face-off between two aurochs, an extinct cattle, each depicted with an associated symbol. A small horse appears between the aurochs' horns, and three stags can be seen below. *Courtesy of Norbert Aujoulat, Centre National de Préhistoire, Ministère de la Culture.*

particular clan, or served as the symbolic bond between two people, in the manner of a modern-day wedding ring. It is also probable that some owners regarded these pieces as talismans and attributed supernatural or protective powers to them. ◖ Some of the most intriguing examples of portable art are pieces that appear to be records of historical events. The changing seasons of the year are likely to be among those events recorded, and from La Vache we find a bone knife with, on one side, the face of a doe, water, and flowering plants. These images probably recorded springtime. On the opposite face a bison in autumn rut, dying flowers, and nuts suggest autumn. The meaning of an engraved bone plaque from Blanchard is less clear. It bears 29 sets of marks, arranged in a serpentine pattern, and has been interpreted as a record of phases of the moon 30,000 years ago. ◖ With the end of the Upper Paleolithic in Europe art became more improvisational. The first great efflorescence of prehistoric art occurred during the height of the last Ice Age. In Europe once the open steppe and grasslands began to disappear with the melting of the ice sheets and forests began to dominate the landscape, the Upper Paleolithic way of life gave way to agriculturalism.

45 · The Origins of Language

LANGUAGE is a distinctly human feature that all of us depend on daily. Language informs and enriches our world and our perceptions. It is the foundation on which all modern human behavior rests. Imagine human culture without language in all its manifestations: books, plays, operas, poetry, newspapers, television, movies, the Internet, casual conversations, and formal debates. Because language provides such a central part of our being, much effort has been spent in tracing its origins. ◖ Some paleoanthropologists have argued that language evolved almost overnight, emerging in modern humans about 50,000 years ago as part of a genetic mutation that suddenly hardwired the brain and permitted a cultural flowering seen throughout the archeological record of the Upper Paleolithic. Traditionally, though, language has been considered a more ancient innovation that must have evolved over millions of years, at least since the beginning of genus *Homo*. How can we decide between these disparate hypotheses? ◖ Fossil evidence, in the form of cranial endocasts that reveal the peaks and valleys on the surface of hominid brains, has been brought to bear on the question of when language evolved. Because surface morphology of the brain may not strictly correlate with internal function, however, drawing conclusions from endocasts proves difficult. Endocast experts look for asymmetry in the brain hemispheres and the presence of Broca's area, Wernicke's area, or other structures linked to language in modern humans. The presumed presence of certain sulci in these structures on endocasts has then been taken as evidence of language competence in various early hominids, including *Homo habilis* and even *Australopithecus africanus*. ◖ But interpretations of the presence and position of these critical structures differ, as do conclusions about the capacity for language. Wernicke's area proves to be especially tricky to identify in endocasts. As for Broca's area, traditionally viewed as the motor center for speech, recent data indicate that control centers for language reside in several regions of the brain and that Broca's area may more generally serve motor functions. ◖ Others have cited aspects of our primate heritage as evidence that language must have evolved early in our lineage. As social primates, hominids lived in large groups. Perhaps group size created a need to hold these groups together, with language providing the social glue. As a bonding mechanism, language, or at least an enhanced type of vocal communication, could have fulfilled the task more effectively than grooming does, while permitting the exchange of useful information. But other primates who live in large social troops and who communicate vocally still lack the equivalent of human language. Nevertheless, the extent of social communication in other animals indicates that human language must have likewise emerged in a social setting. ◖ Language evolution is probably intimately linked to brain evolution, and since our brain has been growing and reorganizing over the past 2 million years, it seems unlikely that language suddenly arose from some radical new mutation. Human brains could have been language-competent long before spoken languages appeared. The enlarging brain of early *Homo* no doubt was capable of complicated cognitive coordination and calculation and as such relied on and used skills important to language. Perhaps language evolved in tandem with our enlarging brain or was a cause, rather than a consequence, of brain enlargement during the Pleistocene. ◖ Yet the idea of early language runs into trouble when compared with archeological evidence. Although the first appearance of tools corresponds with the time to which some paleoanthropologists assign the origin of language, the technology of early *Homo*, the Oldowan and especially the Acheulean, shows no sign of innovation or diffusion of new ideas beyond a standard set of tool types and flaking techniques. More important, if language, which constitutes a symbolic use of signs to communicate and an imposition of symbolic meaning on reality, evolved early, why do we not find obvious archeological evidence of symbols until very recently, particularly within the past 40,000 to 50,000 years? ◖ The tools of this latter period show extreme variety and innovation in raw material, design, and function, plus regional styles and other features suggesting a role for language in developing and disseminating these new forms. What also appears around this time is art, both paintings and engravings as well as portable carvings. And art, of course, is inherently symbolic. Perhaps the appearance of full-blown phonetic language as we think of it today, with its syntax and symbols, made this possible. ◖ Does this mean that only modern humans among the hominids had the capacity for language? At least our close contemporaries, the Neandertals, probably also possessed language. Analysis of the Neandertal cranial base led to the hypothesis that the Neandertal larynx was too primitive to permit spoken language. In humans the larynx sits low in the throat, which facilitates uttering a wide range of sounds but makes us the only mammals incapable of simultaneously drinking and breathing, lest we run the risk of choking. Judging from their lack of cranial flexion, Neandertals had a high-sitting larynx and a more apelike vocal tract incapable of the full range of human sounds. ◖ Then a compelling piece of evidence for Neandertal language turned up in the burial of Kebara 2 in Israel. A nearly complete hyoid bone—the only one from the Middle Paleolithic until the skeletal discoveries from Atapuerca, Spain—was found beside the specimen's mandible. The only free-floating bone in the human body, the hyoid attaches to soft tissue of the larynx and anchors throat muscles important to speaking. Because the Kebara hyoid has an essentially modern morphology, as opposed to a chimpanzee hyoid, we might infer that this Neandertal had a modern-looking larynx and was capable of producing the modern range of spoken sounds or words that comprise language. ◖ From the question of when language appeared, we must consider the even more elusive but critical question of why it evolved at all. Some hypotheses have considered language to be a secondary occurrence rather than a target of natural selection. As linguist Steven Pinker points out, however, language itself contains clues that lead to the conclusion that language evolved as a specific adaptation. Language, whether spoken or written, exists in all human societies today and existed in all known past societies. All of these languages possess complex rules of grammar, and certain nonfunctional, universal rules also hold across these languages. This suggests that the unifying force is not culture but nature, in the form of the human brain. All societies seem to have the equal potential to learn language, as do all individuals within a given society. Most interestingly, between the ages of

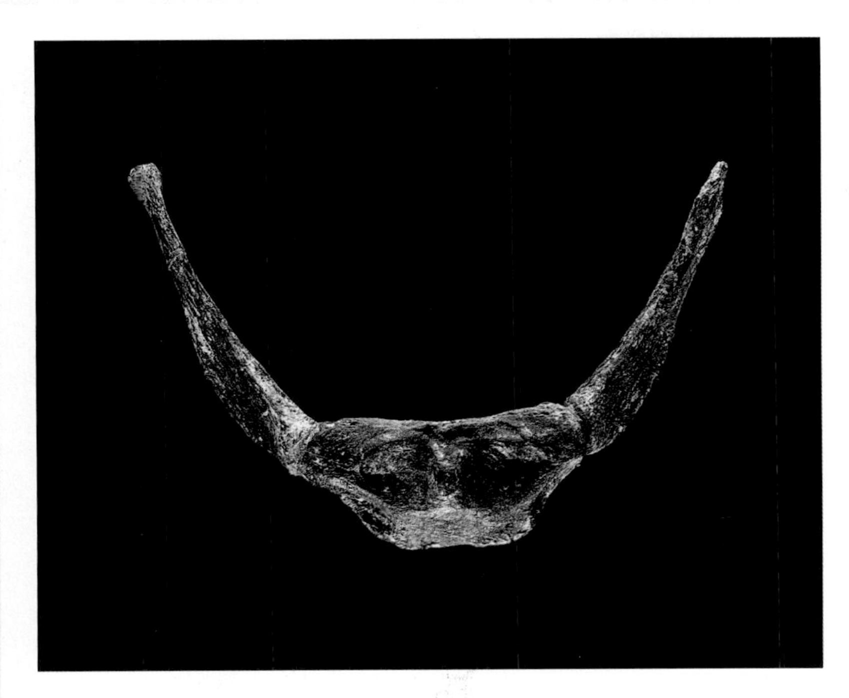

Hyoid of *Homo neanderthalensis* from Kebara, Israel. This rarely preserved throat bone closely resembles the hyoid of a modern human, which suggests that Neandertals shared the human capacity for spoken language. Actual size. *Photograph by David Brill; courtesy of Sackler School of Medicine, Tel Aviv University.*

two and three years, generally, children in all cultures begin to assimilate language naturally, without cues or classes, from the experiences and sensations around them. ◖ Like a good adaptation, language increases our reproductive fitness; it is essential to our strategies for obtaining mates. It allows us to exchange potentially life-saving information about our physical and social environments. Language has a complex anatomy and can be considered to be as complicated an organ as the vertebrate eye, which serves a specific function; language thus passes the test of complexity by design as to whether some structure or organ could be the product of natural selection. Language also appears to operate independently from the systems behind other cognitive processes; for instance, it can exist in the absence of intelligence, and vice versa. So language is unlikely to have evolved by chance, by random genetic drift, or by some process other than directed natural selection. It has been built into our biology as the most efficient and effective means to communicate our thoughts.

46 · The Problem of Consciousness

WE have looked at the evolutionary history of many parts of our bodies from the feet to the brain. But what about that apparently extrasomatic structure of the mind, or consciousness? Where does the brain end and the mind begin, or are they one and the same? Is it consciousness – more than bipedalism, language, or evolved culture – that really sets humans apart? ◖ First, what is consciousness? No single definition may suffice for such an elusive concept, but we can describe consciousness as self-awareness and self-reflection, the ability to feel pain or pleasure, the sensation of being alive and of being us, the sum of whatever passes through the mind. ◖ So, consciousness deals with the subjective experiences of our lives, and as such it differs from the logical cognition conducted by computers. Since the middle of the twentieth century, when mathematician and Enigma code-breaker Alan Turing posed the question of whether machines could think, researchers in artificial intelligence have devised generations of machines to find an answer. Significant doubt remains, though, as to whether a machine will ever experience subjective feelings or the sorts of emotions emoted by the supercomputer Hal in Stanley Kubrick's film *2001: A Space Odyssey*. As Robert Wright asked recently in *Time* magazine, about the chess-playing computer that challenged (unsuccessfully) world champion Garry Kasparov, "Could Deep Blue ever feel deeply blue?" ◖ Paleoanthropologists probably can make little contribution to solving the problem of consciousness. Feelings don't fossilize. Yet scholars from a surprisingly diverse range of disciplines – including philosophy, neurology, immunology, molecular biology, and physics, to name a few – have attempted to answer the vexing question posed here, usually be delving into their respective sciences for inspiration. As titles from some recent books on the subject show – *Consciousness Explained*, *The Problem of Consciousness*, *Consciousness Reconsidered* – opinion is divided on how conclusive these efforts have been. ◖ Two recent hypotheses of consciousness differ in the emphasis placed on feeling and thinking. One view, articulated by Nicholas Humphrey in *A History of the Mind*, holds that consciousness is nothing more or less than immediate sensory experience; sensation-arousing stimuli define who we are, how we feel, what we know. Philosopher Daniel Dennett, author of *Consciousness Explained*, argues that consciousness can be understood from the metaphor of a computer. He views the mind as the software to the brain's hardware, a program that writes a narrative of our experience, edited and compiled from multiple drafts of information streaming into the brain. In this view, the present moment of sensation is insignificant compared to the subsequent mental reflection and contemplation, from which meaning arises. Consciousness – the mind – is simply a product of the brain. ◖ Yet another hypothesis, named neural Darwinism, was posited by immunologist Gerald Edelman in response to the brain-as-computer model. Comparing the brain to the immune system, Edelman argues that shifting alliances of neurons compete in a process similar to natural selection that results in shaping the brain with selected stimuli from outside. A fourth hypothesis, proposed by physicist Roger Penrose, dismisses the computer metaphor for one drawn from quantum mechanics, proposing that the interaction of subatomic forces in the brain sparks our sense of self. ◖ Admittedly, neither of us has fully pondered the merits or shortcomings of these theories, but none of the answers seems particularly satisfactory. Consciousness, being inherently singular and subjective, is a tricky prospect for objective scientific analysis. Indeed, at least one philosopher contends that as products of evolution, our brains are simply too limited cognitively to grasp the concept of consciousness. Unlike bipedalism or language, physical and tangible phenomena, it is not clear how consciousness could act like an adaptation to increase our fitness for survival. Perhaps it doesn't, if consciousness is merely the sum of our sensations; what once may have been a critical component of our ability to survive may now instead add layers of richness to our lives. We need to close the gap between the physical and subjective realms of this topic before we can hope to reach an understanding of consciousness. Until then it remains, according to *Scientific American*, "biology's most profound riddle."

47 · Will Humans Become Extinct?

EXTINCTION. It's a weighty word that resounds with the deep tones of finality and inevitability. Extinction is as natural a process as speciation and evolution. Just as every individual life has its end, so every species, if we look back through the fossil record, ultimately comes to pass. We know relatively little about how extinction works, about its specific causes and broad consequences, but its influence on the course of evolution has been considerable. ◖ Virtually all species that have ever lived have gone extinct. The fossil record contains good data on some 250,000 past species extinctions. We can also recognize in the fossil record a series of mass extinctions that may have recurred every 26 million years for the

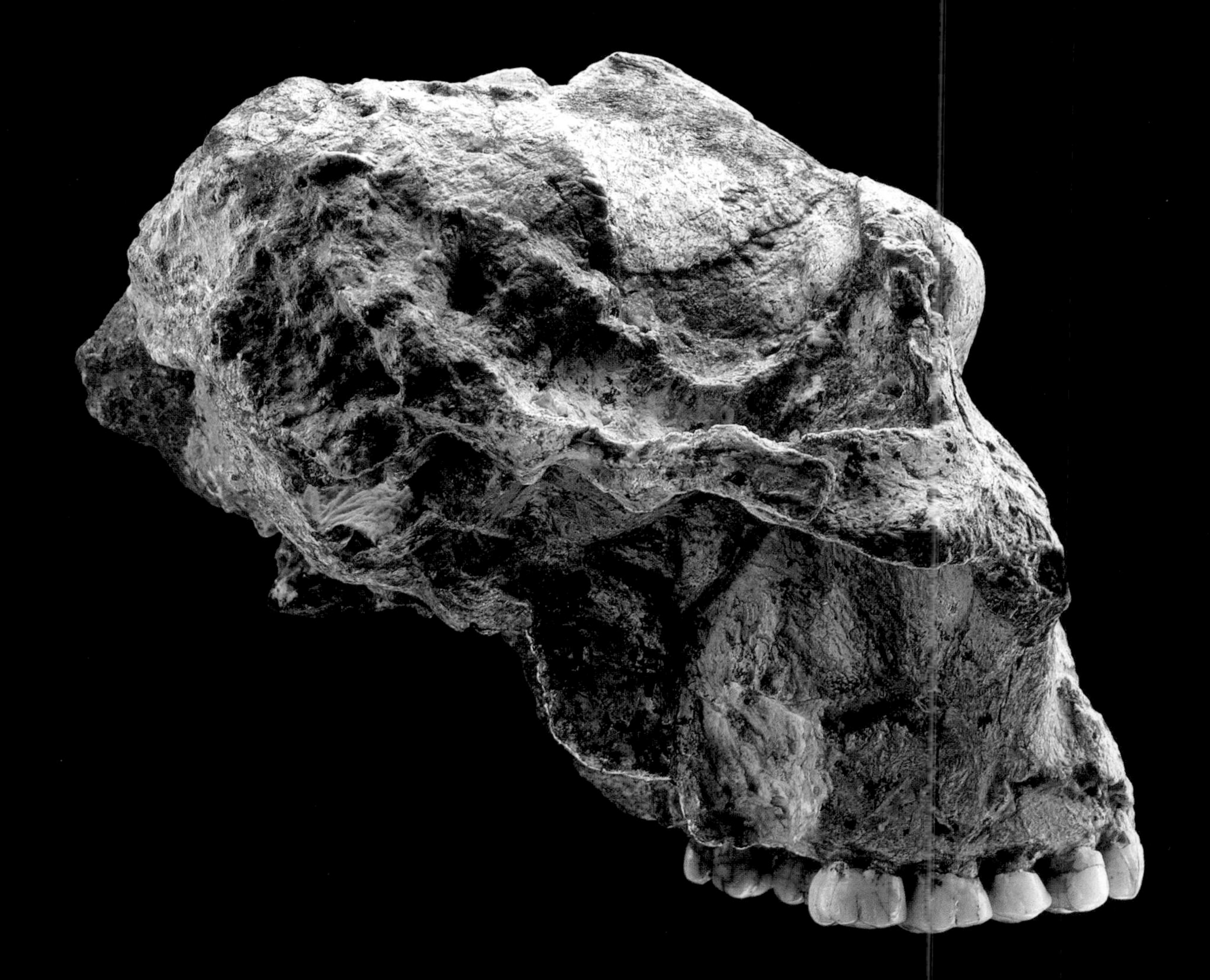

Cranium of *Australopithecus robustus* from Swartkrans, South Africa. This species, represented by the SK 48 specimen, appeared about 1.9 million years ago and went extinct between 1.6 and 1.0 million years ago. Actual size. *Photograph by David Brill; courtesy of Transvaal Museum.*

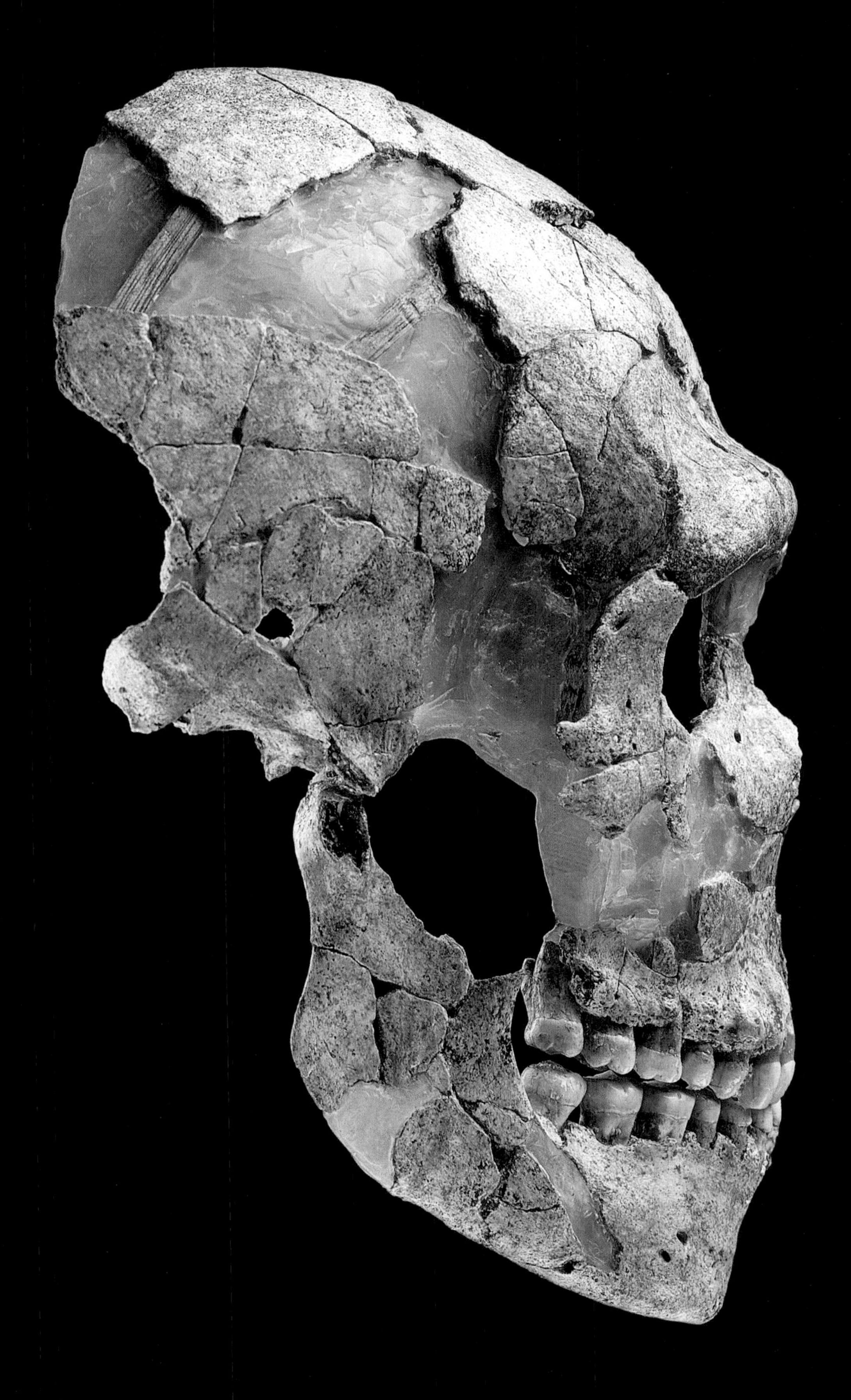

Skull of *Homo neanderthalensis* from Saint-Césaire, France. Recognizable Neandertals first appeared about 200,000 years ago but were extinct before 30,000 years ago. This 36,000 year-old specimen was one of the last known survivors. Actual size. *Photograph by David Brill; courtesy of Université de Bordeaux I.*

past 250 million years, leading paleontologists to seek evidence for cosmic catastrophes – such as impacts from periodically passing asteroids – as culprits of major extinctions. Massive volcanic eruptions and lava flows may also have been responsible, particularly for the Permian mass extinction about 250 million years ago, which wiped out between 75 and 95 percent of all life on Earth. ¶ The Permian was by far the largest of five past mass extinctions that left their mark in the fossil record, most recently the Cretaceous-Tertiary extinction 65 million years ago. This event eliminated the giant dinosaurs and opened new opportunities for the diversification and radiation of mammals, including primates. (Three other mass extinctions occurred during the Ordovician, Devonian, and Triassic periods, respectively 440, 365, and 210 million years ago.) Whatever may have triggered these events, they were devastating for species unable to cope, adapt, and survive. ¶ So, if we strictly consider the odds from the past, then yes, we are likely to go extinct. We are the sole survivors of a relatively small and unusual family of primates, which are a peculiar group of mammals. We have reached a position of unparalleled dominance in the natural world in terms of our use of diverse resources and ability to alter environments, often to detrimental effect. Biologists such as E. O. Wilson believe that by disturbing and removing natural habitats worldwide, we are perpetuating a sixth mass extinction that threatens much of the planet's biodiversity. While there is reason to think that we can have a long tenure on Earth (recall that *Australopithecus afarensis* lasted for around a million years), there are many indications from our behavior that perhaps our end will come, too. Evolution comes with no guarantees. ¶ Extinction has been an increasingly frequent factor in hominid evolution. The last known appearance of *A. afarensis* is in 3 million-year-old sediments at Hadar, Ethiopia, and no subsequent hominid species appears to have lived as long (with the possible exception of *Homo erectus*, if this species is defined to include fossils otherwise placed in the species *Homo ergaster*). After the extinction of *afarensis*, hominids diversified between 3 and 2 million years ago, with at least five species existing simultaneously by the end of this period. But after 2 million years ago, the hominid pattern switches from diversification to extinction. *Homo habilis* and *Homo rudolfensis* both appeared and disappeared before 1.5 million years ago. Between 1.5 and 1.0 million years ago, *Australopithecus boisei* and *A. robustus* went extinct. Within the last million years, *Homo erectus*, *H. heidelbergensis*, and *H. neanderthalensis* have all likewise gone extinct. ¶ As for us, the conditions for significant evolutionary change in our species have been greatly diminished, perhaps eliminated. Human populations are no longer isolated, and for the most part we have become one giant global gene pool. There may be little significant morphological change awaiting us under natural selection because we are also operating under the ameliorating influence of cultural evolution. Our culture allows us to be generally adaptable to environments and new conditions. Biologically we are, in many ways, still foraging the savannas, but culturally we are exploring outer space. Culture is our key survival strategy, as long as we can keep the planet intact and alive. If conditions became critical for our survival, would our brains, honed by 2 million years of biological and cultural evolution, be up for the challenge? (Our brains, by the way, are expensive organs to run and maintain, demanding about 20 percent of our body's energy intake. In the face of future environmental stresses and the continuing march toward global cultural homogenization, we may continue to see a decline in brain size, which has been shrinking, along with our overall stature, for at least the last 10,000 years.) ¶ Evolution, and the future, are inherently unpredictable. If environmental conditions suddenly change, or if new diseases and viruses or political anarchy and terrorism threaten significant numbers of people, who can say whether culture will see us through? But it has brought us to this point, where we are poised to both consider our past and contemplate our future. To quote Czech president Vaclav Havel, "For the first time in the history of man, the planet he inhabits is encompassed by a single global civilization.... [T]his makes the modern world an essentially dramatic place, with so many peoples in so many places resisting coexistence with each other. And yet its only chance for survival is precisely such coexistence. "

48 · The Place of Humans in Nature

For, after all, what is man in nature? A nothing compared with infinity, all when compared with nothing. A middle point between nothing and all. Infinitely far from understanding the extremes... equally incapable of seeing the nothing when he emerges and the infinity in which he is engulfed. – B. Pascal, *Pensées*

IN THE MAIN, this book has been concerned with the fossil evidence for human evolution. But study of the ancient past has yielded more than simply knowledge about our ancestors. Paleoanthropology has brought into the common marketplace of ideas Darwin's theories about evolution and extinction. From that broader perspective we are able to see *Homo sapiens* as one species among many, and to face our own possible extinction. In evolutionary terms, we are almost assured of extinction. As our perspective on our own species through time enlarges, a single question emerges into an ever brighter spotlight as the true core of our quest: What is our place in nature? ¶ There are some who take the extreme position that humans are intruders on the natural order and don't belong on Earth. But we are here, having survived the usual evolutionary processes of elimination, and we have equally as strong a warrant (not more) to be here as any other organism. But unlike any other creature that has ever lived, we have been endowed with a great intelligence, through which we have achieved unprecedented dominion over nature. And with this gift of intelligence comes the responsibility to use it well – as guardians of Earth and its life. ¶ If we hold up the fossil record of our ancestors to modern life, it is evident that we have become highly culturally dependent. Our link to nature has loosened. For example, as individuals, we no longer provision ourselves daily and directly from Earth's resources. Yet this dependence on culture for survival has occurred in only an instant of geological time. By contrast, millions of years went into shaping us physically, and biologically we have changed very little from our ancestors millions of years ago. ¶ Perhaps, in some manner of speaking, it is this imbalance in the clocks, an imbalance between our biological and cultural evolution, that is at the root of our modern dissatisfaction, our sense of unease and unrootedness, of being out of tune with nature. Cultural and technological evolution advances happen unbelievably quickly, but genetic change is glacially slow. Genetically, we are merely 1.6 percent different from chimpanzees, and we have been separated from them for 6 to 8 million years. How much closer must we be to the earliest *Homo*, which appeared more than 2 million years ago!
¶ Ancient hominid fossils like Lucy are a link to our common origin with the African apes; this is no longer contested. Yet the fossils have an even more important message for us: they are a testament to our link to the natural world. The more links we find, the closer to nature we see ourselves. We are, without doubt, part of the continuum of life. By living so thoroughly in a world of culture as we do, we tend to see ourselves as

Cave painting from Cosquer, France. Among the oldest European art, this image was painted about 27,000 years ago. Handprints may signify an artist's signature and indicate that Upper Paleolithic people were conscious of themselves and their environment. Actual size. *Photograph by J. Collina-Girard; courtesy of Jean Clottes, International Committee on Rock Art.*

distinct from nature. So, it is terribly important for us to be reminded that we are part of nature. We cannot ignore the natural world from which we evolved. ◖ The human time frame is generally limited to the life span of the reflective individual. We may, perhaps, appreciate the past of our parents and grandparents, and contemplate anxiously the future of our children and grandchildren. But this concern encompasses about a hundred-year span. To be good custodians of Earth, a responsibility our brains and adaptive capabilities impose on us, we must have the foresight to consider the extended future as well as the hindsight to take lessons from our ancient ancestors. ◖ Let us see what our past might indicate about our future. From what we know now, *A. afarensis*, Lucy's species, walked on the African continent for approximately 1 million years—about 50,000 generations. Anatomically modern humans have been around for roughly 100,000 years—only 5,000 generations, one-tenth the length of time that Lucy's species persisted. To equal the length of time that Lucy's species lived, we would need to survive for another 9,000 centuries, and by all estimates the next century alone will be a very tough one. We are a very recent addition to Earth's biomass. ◖ Knowing our place in nature enriches us beyond comprehension. Nature is familiar, it is in our genes. It is reawakened when we sit around a campfire and exchange stories, just as our ancestors did for hundreds of thousands of years when we were hunter-gatherers, living in tune with the natural world. If we are to continue for the next 9,000 centuries, we must abandon our arrogance and become the introspective species. The choices that we and our descendants will make must be ones that benefit not only us, but all of our fellow travelers in life. ◖ *Homo sapiens* is the most intelligent, the most dangerous, and the most cooperative of all animals that have ever existed, but we must understand that we are not the final product of 3 billion years of evolution on Earth. Our species, like all others, is an evolutionary work in progress. Unlike other species, however, we have some ability to control our fate. We have the know-how to influence how the game is played out.

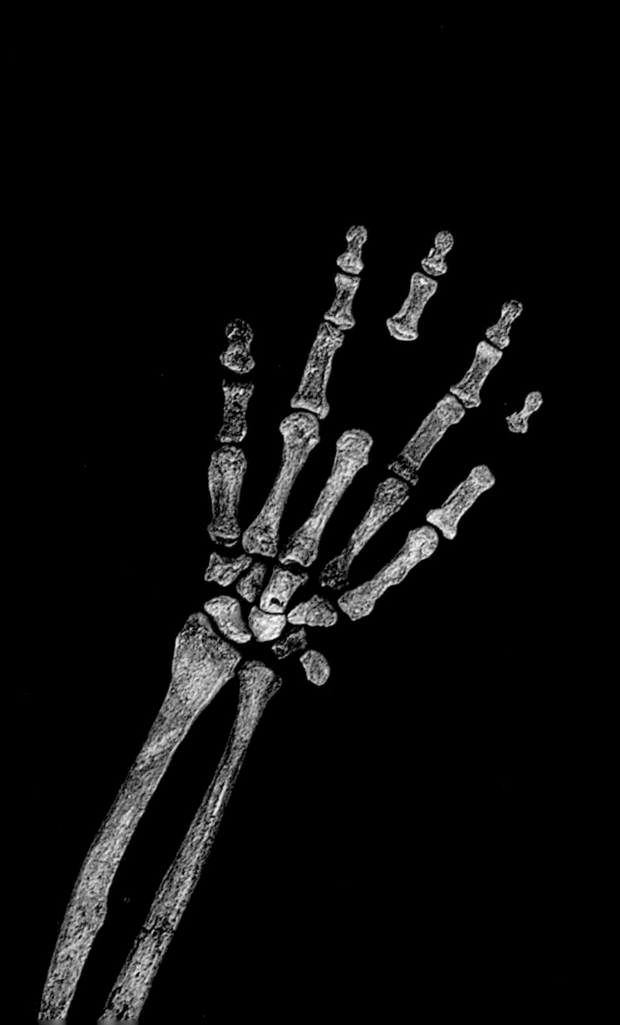

ENCOUNTERING THE EVIDENCE

Part 2

SPECIMEN	LOCALITY	AGE	DISCOVERER	DATE	PUBLICATION
Juvenile partial mandible	Aramis, Ethiopia	4.4 million years	Alamayehu Asfaw	December 20, 1992	White, T.D., G. Suwa, and B. Asfaw. 1994. *Australopithecus ramidus*, a new species of early hominid from Aramis, Ethiopia. *Nature* v. 371: 306-312

Ardipithecus ramidus

ARA-VP-1/129

Some 70,000 generations prior to Lucy's birth, an enigmatic but highly provocative and very apelike hominid walked the African landscape in what is now Ethiopia. Some 4.4 million years later its nearly complete skeleton may offer some intriguing new insights into a time when hominids were not that different from the common ancestor to our own zoological family, the Hominidae, and the African apes.

Little information has yet been made available about the "mystery skeleton" collected in 1994 and 1995 at Aramis in the Middle Awash region of Ethiopia, at locality ARA-VP-6/500, by an international team led by anthropologists Tim White and J. Desmond Clark from the University of California, Berkeley. Its bones are crushed and broken and still, in large part, encased in plaster jackets, awaiting reconstruction. Excavation of the skeleton was unusually demanding because the bones were tightly packed in a hardened clay. To prevent the bone from turning to powder, preservative had to be applied to each bone before the bone was removed from the ground. The slow, painstaking work of excavation often continued late into the night under illumination supplied by the headlights of a Toyota Land Cruiser.

The skeleton is remarkably complete; for example, it has seven out of the eight wrist bones and nearly all of the finger bones, which are long and curved. The pelvis, lower limb, and foot bones may reveal a locomotor mode unlike that of any living or extinct primate. Thus far the finders have been cautious in saying that *ramidus* was a biped, although the foramen magnum is situated fairly far forward, as is seen in a portion of the basicranium (ARA-VP-1/500), a condition usually considered indicative of bipedalism.

The fossil-rich beds of the Middle Awash were first recognized in the late 1960s by French geologist Maurice Taieb, and in the early 1980s a team led by Jon Kalb, an American geologist at the University of Texas, estimated the sediments in the Aramis region to be roughly 4.5 million years old. It was not until December 17, 1992, however, that the first hominid fossil, an upper right third molar, was found at Aramis by Gen Suwa, an anthropologist at the University of Tokyo, Japan. During the same field season this diagnostic mandible fragment with a deciduous lower first molar, known by the catalogue number ARA-VP-1/129, was discovered by Alemayehu Asfaw of the Ethiopian Ministry of Information and Culture.

Following another highly fruitful field season at Aramis, in September 1994 the Middle Awash research team officially announced a new species of *Australopithecus—A. ramidus.* An associated set of adult teeth, ARA-VP-6/1, was chosen as the holotype. The species is distinguished from other hominids by a number of anatomical features, including relatively large upper and lower canines, a chimp-like lower first deciduous molar, an apelike temporomandibular joint, thin dental enamel, and a markedly asymmetrical lower first premolar. The overall impression gained from the Aramis fossil collection is one of a significantly more primitive (more apelike) stage than that seen in later hominids.

Initially assigned to the genus *Australopithecus,* in a correction published in May 1995 in *Nature* the Aramis material was transferred to a new genus, *Ardipithecus.* In the Afar language, *ardi* means "ground" or "floor" while *-ramid* means "root"; *pithecus* is from the Greek and means "ape." The name reflects in its generic and specific parts the idea of a basal species for the Hominidae.

Announcement of a new species of hominid is bound to encounter a bumpy road, and this is already the case for *ramidus.* The accuracy of its geological age, its distinctiveness from other, already named species, and its place on the human family tree have been questioned (see page 38). Resolution of these ambiguities must await further detailed publication of the Aramis finds, but preparing, reconstructing, and analyzing the fossils may take several years.

The finds at Aramis have broken new ground and are among the first to open a window onto deposits more than 4.0 million years old. There is little question that *ramidus* will enrich our knowledge of a very distant time in human evolution. The Middle Awash is fertile territory for hominid hunters, who are already contemplating looking in geological strata dated to roughly 5 million years. Should hominoid fossils be found in such ancient horizons, it may be difficult to decide which ones are our ancestors and which were ancestral to the African apes.

***Ardipithecus ramidus*, ARA-VP-1/129.** The pointed crown of the deciduous molar in this right mandible fragment proved to be a critical feature in distinguishing this new species. Actual size. *Photograph copyright © 1994 by Tim D. White/Brill Atlanta.*

Australopithecines

Charles Darwin made a brave prediction in 1871 in *The Descent of Man*, when he wrote,

In each great region of the world the living mammals are closely related to the extinct species of the same region. It is, therefore, probable that Africa was formerly inhabited by extinct apes closely allied to the gorilla and chimpanzee; and as these two species are now man's nearest allies, it is somewhat more probable that our early progenitors lived on the African continent than elsewhere.

Vindication of this prediction did not come until nearly half a century after Darwin's death, when Raymond Dart, anatomist at the University of the Witwatersrand in Johannesburg, announced the discovery of a fossilized child's skull from the site of Taung in South Africa. In 1925, he placed the skull in a new taxon, calling it *Australopithecus africanus*. In the specimen he saw a mixture of apelike features such as a projecting face and very small brain (405 cc), but he also surmised from the ventral position of the foramen magnum (the hole at the base of the skull from which the spinal cord emerges) that the creature had walked upright and was therefore a human ancestor.

Dart's choice of the name *Australopithecus* is a mixture of Latin and Greek: *australo*, Latin for "southern," and *pithecus*, latinized Greek for "ape." These "southern apes" of Africa have turned out not to be confined to southern Africa, nor are they apes. However, because of the stringent rules of the International Code of Zoological Nomenclature, which govern the naming of taxa, Dart's name cannot be altered. *Australopithecus* is the valid generic designation for a diverse group of early hominids (members of the zoological family the Hominidae, which includes ourselves and our bipedal ancestors), who apparently did not make and use stone implements and were common to both southern and eastern Africa between roughly 4 and 1 million years ago.

Since Dart's coining of the genus, subsequent discoveries have been made which show that *Australopithecus* comprises a diverse group of early hominids, the seven species *anamensis, afarensis, africanus, robustus, aethiopicus*, and *boisei* and most recently *bahrelghazali*. These early hominids, collectively called the australopithecines and sometimes referred to as man-apes, reflect the initial radiation of our zoological family and have been found only in Africa. Although they are confined to sites in South and East Africa, with the exception of one specimen from Chad, it is most probable that they lived over a much broader area of Africa, but their remains did not, unfortunately, become fossilized. Although they possessed the cardinal feature for being placed in the Hominidae, bipedality, they are distinguished from our own genus *Homo* by having relatively small brains. *Australopithecus* brains generally were 500 cc or less, but a few specimens have been recorded with slightly larger brain volumes. *Homo* brains, on the other hand, are usually larger than 600 cc (one has been recorded as low as 510 cc) and range up to more than 2,000 cc. Modern *Homo sapiens* brains average 1,200 cc.

Beginning in 1936, the famed paleontologist Robert Broom, from the Transvaal Museum in Pretoria, South Africa, began to find additional australopithecine fossils at the site of Sterkfontein. Now numbering close to 400 specimens, these finds from Sterkfontein were first given a new name, *A. transvaalensis* (after the Transvaal region of South Africa), but they are now considered to be of the same species as the Taung Child and are placed in *A. africanus*.

Two other sites in southern Africa, Kromdraai and Swartkrans, yielded remains of a different type of australopithecine. In 1938, Broom recognized a fossil hominid from Kromdraai that differed from *A. africanus* in having a bony crest on the top of the skull, massive postcanine teeth, and a robustly built mandible. With his proclivity for coining new genus and species names for each of his discoveries, and wanting to emphasize the robust nature of the Kromdraai specimen, Broom designated the find *Paranthropus robustus*. *Para* is Greek for "near" or "alongside," and *anthropus* is latinized Greek for "man." Only twelve hominid specimens have been recovered from Kromdraai fossils, and although most paleoanthropologists recognize them as a discrete species, they are placed in the same genus as the Taung Child and referred to as *Australopithecus robustus*.

In 1948, Broom and his student John T. Robinson recovered more fossils of robust australopithecines from the site of Swartkrans, situated across an old river valley about 1.2 kilometers from Sterkfontein. True to form, Broom distinguished these finds by a new name: *Paranthropus crassidens* (*crassus* meaning "thick" or "solid" and *dens* meaning "tooth"). Long-term excavation at the site has recovered close to 300 australopithecine specimens from Swartkrans, making it one of the largest samples from a single site anywhere in Africa. Although some paleoanthropologists still believe that the Swartkrans hominids are a different species from those at Kromdraai, most researchers place the Swartkrans finds in *A. robustus*.

In the late 1940s, Dart undertook fieldwork at the site of Makapansgat in the northern Transvaal, where several dozen australopithecine fossils have now been found. In spite of the many anatomical similarities shared with the Sterkfontein hominids, Dart ascribed the Makapansgat fossils to a new species, *A. prometheus*. The species name is from the Greek Titan who stole fire from the heavens, and it was chosen because the bones had a dark coloration, presumably caused by being burned in fires made by the australopithecines. However, chemical analysis revealed that the dark coloration was due to staining by manganese dioxide. Currently, the Makapansgat hominids are placed in *A. africanus*.

In the nonhominid animal fossils from Makapansgat Dart saw a high incidence of horns, antelope mandibles, and certain long bones. He interpreted these as having been selectively collected and used by the australopithecines as tools and weapons. The long bones were used as clubs, he speculated, the horns as daggers, and the serrated edges of the teeth in antelope mandibles were employed as saws. He named this assemblage the Osteodontokeratic Culture (*osteo* means "bone," *donto* means "teeth," and *kerato* means "horn"). It is now believed that the bone accumulation at Makapansgat is better explained by the scavenging and hunting activities of hyenas, porcupines, and leopards.

Although the South African australopithecine cave sites cannot be precisely dated using radiometric techniques because there are no volcanic ashes or other datable deposits, a comparative chronology has been established using the presence and absence of time-specific mammalian species. The premise is simple: older geological layers have a

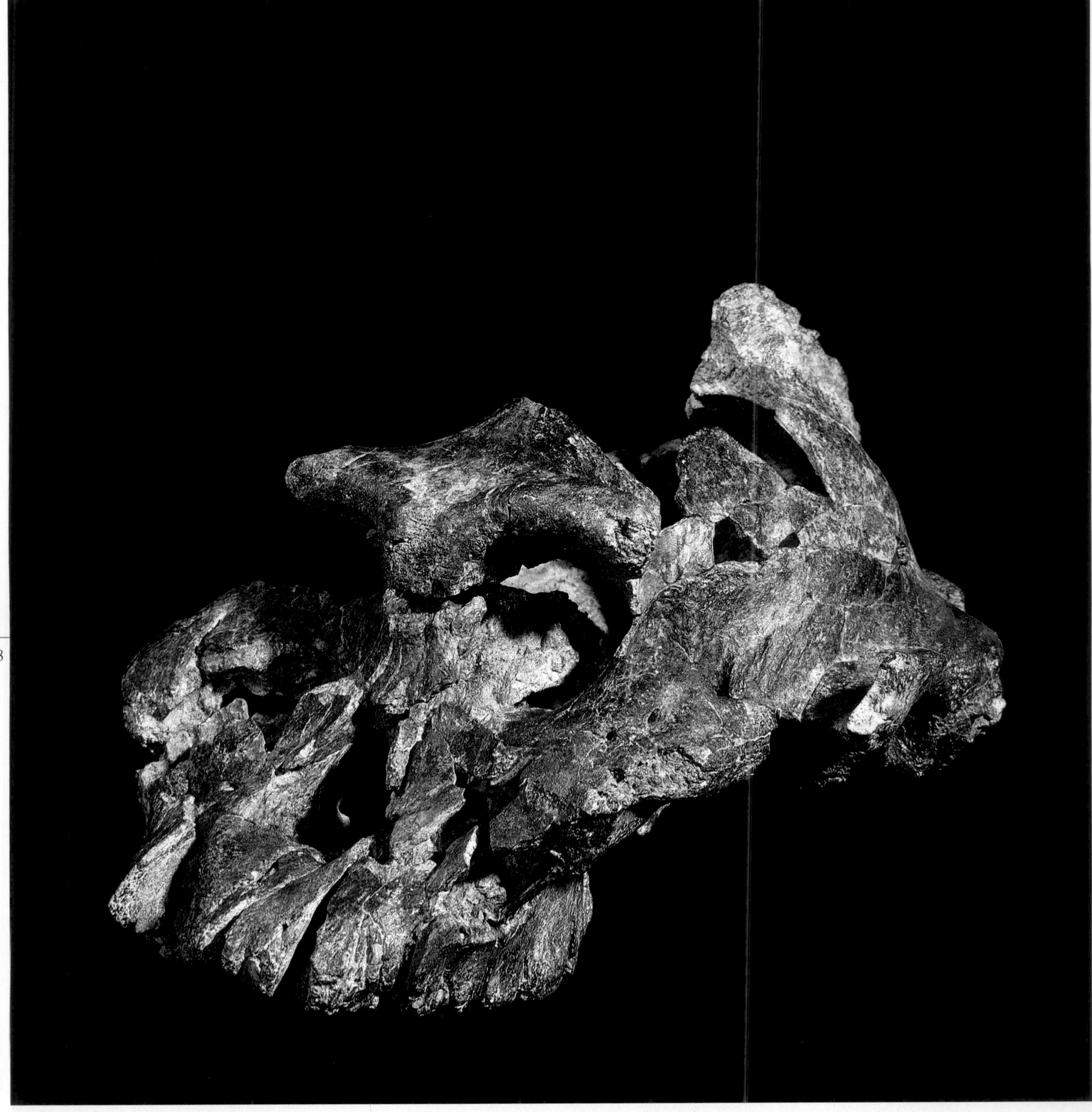

***Australopithecus aethiopicus*, KNM-WT 17000.**
This 2.5 million year-old cranium comes from the earliest known kind of robust australopithecine, a parallel branch of hominids that went extinct about a million years ago. Actual size.
Photograph by Robert I.M. Campbell; courtesy of National Museums of Kenya.

higher percentage of extinct forms and younger layers have more species of extant forms. Comparison of extant and extinct species found in the cave sites in South Africa, using this premise, gives the following chronological sequence for the sites, from the oldest to the youngest: Makapansgat, Sterkfontein, Taung, Kromdraai, and Swartkrans.

Because some animal species found in the South African sites are also known from radiometrically dated sites in East Africa, an approximate idea of the ages of the South African sites can be established using biostratigraphy. Some species of antelopes and monkeys, for example, are time diagnostic; that is, they are known only from specific time ranges. With this knowledge, approximate biostratigraphic ages have been suggested for the South African australopithecine sites: Makapansgat, 2.8 million years; Sterkfontein, 2.5 million years; Taung, 2.3 million years; Kromdraai, 2.0 million years; and Swartkrans, 1.8 to 1.0 million years.

In 1959, at Olduvai Gorge in northern Tanzania, Mary Leakey, a world-famous archeologist, found the first significant specimen in East Africa to be recognized as an australopithecine. The specimen was nicknamed "Nutcracker Man" because of the enormous cheek teeth. Louis Leakey, a pioneer of paleoanthropology in East Africa, initially dubbed the find *Zinjanthropus boisei*, but it is now called *A. boisei*. Sometimes referred to as a "hyper-robust" australopithecine, *boisei* is distinguished from its South African counterpart, *robustus*, by its massiveness, enormous cheek teeth, tall face, visor-like cheekbones, and other anatomical features. Numerous specimens of *boisei* have been recovered from sites in Ethiopia, Kenya, and Tanzania from a time interval between 2.3 and 1.4 million years ago.

One of the best-known species of australopithecine, *A. afarensis*, was named in 1978 by Donald Johanson, Tim White, and Yves Coppens, based on fossil finds from Laetoli, Tanzania, and Hadar, Ethiopia. This australopithecine, represented by more than 300 specimens that include most cranial and postcranial bones in the body, is distinguished by a unique suite of primitive cranial, dental, and mandibular anatomical features. Overall the skull is very apelike in appearance, dominated by a strongly projecting face. The neurocranium is quite small, containing a brain averaging roughly 430 cc in size. The species is best known from the famous 3.2 million-year-old Lucy skeleton, which is clearly bipedal but retains certain apelike features such as relatively long arms and curved finger and toe bones. There is almost universal agreement among paleoanthropologists that *afarensis*, now also known from Kenya, is the sole hominid species thus far recognized in the 3 to 4 million-year time slice.

Based on a toothless mandible from the Shungura Formation near the Omo River in southern Ethiopia, *A. aethiopicus* was named in 1968 by two French paleontologists. This taxon is now known from an undistorted and fairly complete cranium from west of Lake Turkana, in northern Kenya, called the Black Skull. This 2.5 million-year-old cranium, which possesses a large, flange-like, posteriorly placed sagittal crest atop the braincase and enormous cheek teeth (inferred from large tooth roots), has obvious affinities with the robust australopithecines. However, it is distinguished from all other species by having features reminiscent of *A. afarensis*, such as a projecting face, little flexion of the cranial base, and compound temporonuchal crests situated on the occipital (back) of the cranium. Even though less than half a dozen specimens have been identified, *aethiopicus*, dated to between 2.7 and 2.5 million years, is one of the most distinctive of all australopithecine species.

From two fossil sites in northern Kenya, Kanapoi and Allia Bay, twenty-one australopithecine specimens were assigned to *A. anamensis* by Meave Leakey, a zoologist at the National Museums of Kenya, and her colleagues. Slightly more ancient than *A. afarensis*, dating to between 3.9 and 4.2 million years ago, *anamensis* (*anam* is the Turkana word for "lake"), they believe, makes an ideal ancestor to *afarensis*. Although *anamensis* shares many anatomical details in the jaws and teeth with *afarensis*, the primitive, very receding mandibular symphysis (front of the mandible), narrow, parallel tooth rows, and the detailed anatomy of the teeth justify placing these finds in a novel species.

When initially published, fossil hominid remains from 4.4 million-year-old deposits from the site of Aramis in the Middle Awash region of Ethiopia were assigned to *Australopithecus ramidus* (*ramid* is from the Afar word for "root"). The remarkably primitive aspects of the teeth and jaws, such as the thin dental enamel, relatively large canines, and several other features, prompted the discoverers to transfer these finds to a new genus, *Ardipithecus ramidus*. In doing so, paleoanthropologists Tim White from Berkeley, Gen Suwa from Japan, and

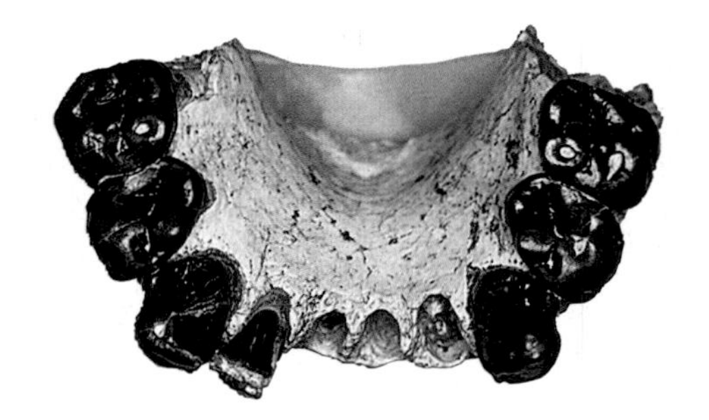

***Australopithecus bahrelghazali*, KT12/H1.**
Described as a new species in 1996, this mandible from Bahr el Ghazal, Chad, extends the range of australopithecines to 2,500 kilometers west of the Great Rift Valley. Actual size.
Courtesy of Michel Brunet, Université de Poitiers.

***Australopithecus africanus*, Sts 71 cranium and Sts 36 mandible.**
A child's skull from Taung served as the type specimen for this species in 1925, but several hundred specimens, including these two, have since been recovered from the site of Sterkfontein, South Africa. Actual size.
Photograph by David Brill; courtesy of Transvaal Museum.

Berhane Asfaw from Ethiopia removed the Aramis hominids from designation as an australopithecine.

The geographic distribution of australopithecines has always been hampered by lack of favorable geological deposits outside of the Great Rift Valley in East Africa and the cave sites in South Africa. But recently Michel Brunet, a French paleontologist at the University of Poitiers, reported the discovery of the front portion of a mandible with seven teeth from the Central African country of Chad, 2,500 kilometers west of the Rift Valley. The associated vertebrate fauna shares similarities with fauna from sites in East Africa dated to between 3.0 and 3.5 million years. Assigned to a new species, *Australopithecus bahrelghazali* (Bahr el Ghazal is a riverbed), the specimen's dental anatomy of the mandible is similar to that of *A. afarensis*, but the contour of the mandibular symphysis (chin area) is more modern.

Although it is clear that there is a diversity in australopithecines, not everyone is agreed on the phylogenetic relationships between them or even on their taxonomy. For some, the robusts are best placed in the genus *Paranthropus*, which includes *robustus*, *crassidens*, *boisei*, and *aethiopicus*. The nonrobust australopithecines are sometimes referred to as gracile australopithecines, probably a misnomer, since their bodies do not appear to be significantly more lightly built than those of the robusts. Using Dart's original appellation, the genus *Australopithecus* currently includes *anamensis*, *afarensis*, *bahrelghazali*, and *africanus*.

The rationale for maintaining a generic distinction for these early hominids was clearly articulated by John Robinson in 1972 when he considered the specialized cranial anatomy of *Paranthropus* (the robusts) as representing a specific dietary specialization for processing hard, tough, fibrous foods. The more generalized cranial morphology of *Australopithecus*, for Robinson, reflected a more omnivorous diet that incorporated vegetation as well as meat. This view, dubbed the dietary hypothesis, has been revived by paleoanthropologist Ron Clarke at the University of the Witwatersrand in Johannesburg. For these researchers a genus reflects a specific way of life or "adaptive zone." The species within each genus, *Paranthropus* and *Australopithecus*, simply reflect variations on the larger theme of the generic adaptation. While recognizing this point of view in this book, we have chosen to use only a single genus, *Australopithecus*.

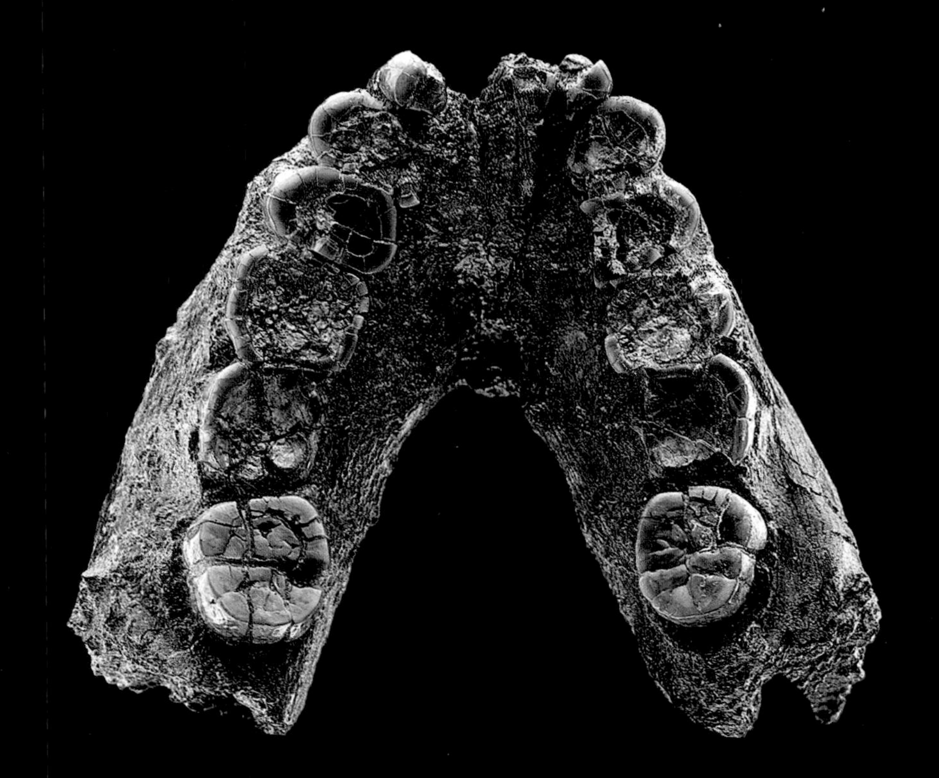

Australopithecus boisei, Omo L. 7a-125. An occlusal view of the mandible best illustrates the enormous premolars and molars found in this species. Actual size. *Photograph by David Brill; courtesy of National Museum of Ethiopia.*

SPECIMEN	LOCALITY	AGE	DISCOVERER	DATE	PUBLICATION
Adult mandible	Kanapoi, Kenya	4.1 million years	Peter Nzube	September 10, 1994	Leakey, M.G., C.S. Feibel, I. McDougall and A.C. Walker. New four-million-year-old species from Kanapoi and Allia Bay, Kenya. *Nature* (1995) v. 376: 565-571

Australopithecus anamensis

KNM-KP 29281 TYPE SPECIMEN

The wind-swept desert southwest of Lake Turkana (formerly Lake Rudolf) was first explored in 1965 when an expedition from the Museum of Comparative Zoology at Harvard University collected 4 million-year-old fossils from this area at a site called Kanapoi. Bryan Patterson, expedition leader, was the son of Lieutenant-Colonel Patterson, an Indian army officer who played a critical role in the construction of the railway from Mombasa to Uganda at the end of the nineteenth century and beginning of the twentieth. Patterson's group found only a single hominid, a left distal humerus, KNM-KP 271.

In 1965, recovery of a 4 million-year-old hominid, even an isolated specimen, drew considerable attention, but its taxonomic assignment was ambiguous. Because of its great age, some scientists referred the specimen to *Australopithecus*, but others pointed out anatomical affinities with *Homo*. As more has become known about the anatomy of early hominid humeri, it has become apparent that due to extensive overlap in anatomy between *Homo* and *Australopithecus*, it is impossible to assign the Kanapoi humerus to a particular genus with certainty. More diagnostic specimens were necessary to resolve the evolutionary affinities of the Kanapoi hominid.

Because of the remoteness of Kanapoi, fieldwork did not begin again until zoologist Meave Leakey of the National Museums of Kenya organized a research team in 1994. Her extensive field experience, gained in part by working with her husband, Richard Leakey, in the Lake Turkana Basin, provided a vital background for the work at Kanapoi. As other members of the search team, Meave Leakey selected Peter Nzube and Kamoya Kimeu, veteran fossil hominid finders from the National Museums of Kenya.

Nearly thirty years after the initial hominid find at Kanapoi, nine dental, cranial, and postcranial specimens were collected. The teeth and jaws exhibited anatomical features reminiscent of *A. afarensis*, but there were obvious differences. Although they were clearly best placed in *Australopithecus*, a host of primitive features demanded that a new species be erected for the hominids: *A. anamensis*. The species name derives from the Turkana word *anam*, which means "lake," and was chosen because of the proximity of Kanapoi to Lake Turkana, and as a reference to the paleolake, Lake Lonyumun, which existed in the area millions of years ago.

A partial tibia (KNM-KP 29285), consisting of proximal and distal ends, has anatomical features indicating bipedalism. The proximal condyles of the tibia, which articulate with the distal femur, are concave, as in humans, and the distal tibia, where it articulates with the ankle, has a thickening of the bone that acts as a built-in shock absorber during bipedal locomotion.

The type specimen (KNM-KP 29281), a mandible lacking the ascending rami but possessing a full complement of teeth, is rather small and narrow, reminiscent of the condition seen in Miocene apes. The tooth rows are even straighter and more parallel than in *A. afarensis*. In lateral view, the front of the mandible in *anamensis* is markedly receding, with the internal buttress, or torus, as it is called, heavily developed and elongated posteriorly. These and many other dental features substantiate claims of a more primitive status for the Kanapoi hominids than that seen in *afarensis* (see page 124).

An additional twelve fossil hominid specimens from Allia Bay, on the eastern shores of Lake Turkana, have been placed in the same species as those from Kanapoi. The sedimentary sequences at Kanapoi and Allia Bay have been very adequately dated using the argon-argon method. The majority of the vertebrate fossils at Kanapoi come from two levels. The lower one, dated to approximately 4.2 million years, is where the type mandible for *anamensis* was found. The upper one, containing Patterson's humerus and the tibia, is older than 3.5 and younger than 4.1 million years. The Allia Bay hominids are roughly 3.9 million years old.

It is not unusual that new discoveries such as those assigned to *A. anamensis* generate new questions. For example, the taxon as currently known exhibits an unusual combination of apelike and *Homo*-like characters not seen in other hominids. In *afarensis* both cranial and postcranial anatomy are apelike, but in *anamensis* the postcranial skeleton (tibia) has advanced *Homo*-like features while the cranial region recalls the Miocene apes. The significance of such a unique amalgam of traits will have to await recovery of additional fossils. However, the most significant aspect of *A. anamensis* is that this species, with a similar but more primitive anatomy than that of *A. afarensis*, makes it a good precursor to Lucy's species.

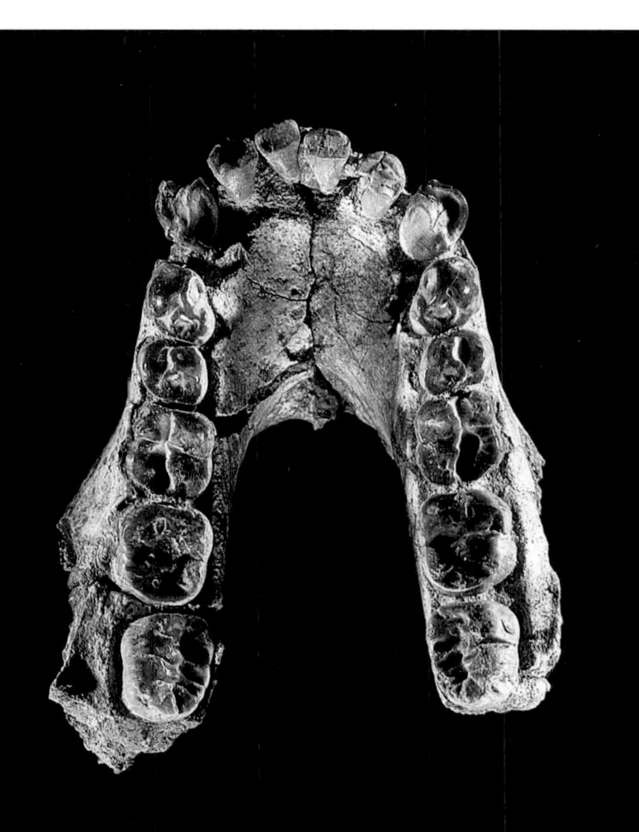

***Australopithecus anamensis*, KNM-KP 29281.**
Straight, parallel tooth rows, seen in occlusal view (*above*), and the receding symphysis beneath the front teeth in lateral view (*below*) distinguish this mandible from that of other hominid species. Actual size.
Photographs by Robert I.M. Campbell; courtesy of National Museums of Kenya.

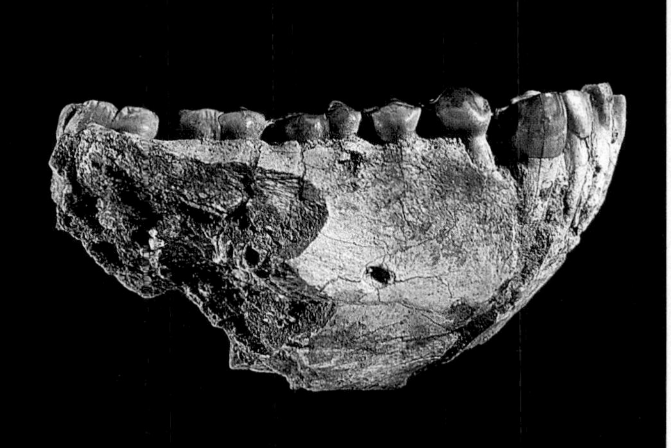

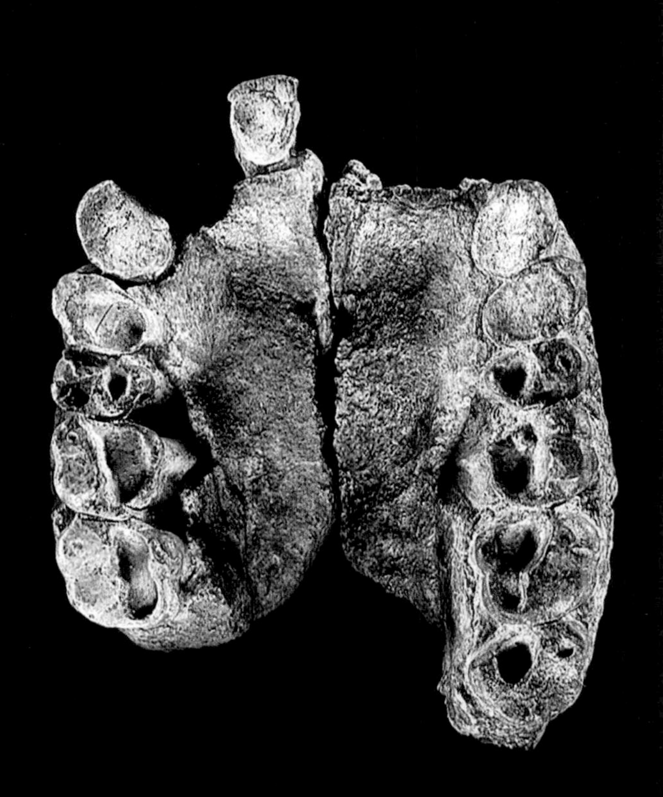

***Australopithecus anamensis*, KNM-KP 29283.**
In this species, the maxilla has a very shallow palate, seen in occlusal view (*above*), and the canine tooth with its robust root and crown, seen in lateral view (*below*), exceeds in size that of *A. afarensis*. Actual size.
Photographs by Robert I.M. Campbell; courtesy of National Museums of Kenya.

SPECIMEN	LOCALITY	AGE	DISCOVERER	DATE	PUBLICATION
Partial adult skeleton	Hadar, Ethiopia	3.2 million years	Donald Johanson	November 30, 1974	Taieb, M., D.C. Johanson, and Y. Coppens. 1975. Expédition internationale de l'Afar, Ethiopie (3 ème campagne 1974), découverte d'Hominidés plio-pléistocenes a Hadar. *C.R. Acad. Sci. Paris,* 281: 1297-1300.

Australopithecus afarensis

A.L. 288-1 *LUCY*

Most fossil finds are known simply by a catalogue number or the place name where the remains were found. However, in the case of Lucy, a partial skeleton, few outside the profession of paleoanthropology would recognize her from the catalogue entry Afar Locality (A.L.) 288-1.

A celebrity among fossils, Lucy is better known than her discoverer. She shows up in crossword puzzles, on "Jeopardy!," in cartoons, poems, rock music lyrics, feminist plays, and even as a tattoo. In Ethiopia, where she was found, the government issued a commemorative stamp with her Amharic name, Dinquinesh, which means "wonderful thing." In remote Ethiopian towns it is not unusual to find a "Lussy Bar" or "Lucy Cafe." The scientific name, *Australopithecus afarensis,* derives from the Afar region and the nomadic Muslim Afar people. The Afar take great pride in Lucy and some Afars, although Muslim, believe that the first human was Lucy, so that all humanity is descended from the Afars.

Worldwide, Lucy has become an ancestral ambassador of sorts, acting like a magnet, drawing people to the study of human origins. Even among those who know practically nothing about human evolution, Lucy is vaguely familiar. In fact, bringing up her name is like referring to a distant relative, which of course she is. The affectionate name given to the partial skeleton comes from the Beatles' song "Lucy in the Sky with Diamonds."

Although more complete skeletons and much older fossils than Lucy have now been found, she is still the touchstone, the reference point, to which other discoveries are compared. Fossil hominids are "older than" or "more complete than" Lucy, for example. And, most important, like the derivation of her name from the Latin *lux,* she has thrown much light on one of the earliest stages of human evolution.

Referred to a new species of *Australopithecus* in 1978, she made her debut at a Nobel Symposium on early hominids as *A. afarensis.* Her species appears to be the last common ancestor to the several branches of hominids that emerged between 2 and 3 million years ago. A long-lived species, extant between 3 and 4 million years ago, *afarensis* remains are presently recognized in Tanzania, Kenya, and Ethiopia. Lucy's kind left the magnificent footprints in a 3.5 million-year-old volcanic ash at Laetoli, Tanzania.

Lucy's skeleton consists of some 47 out of 207 bones, including parts of upper and lower limbs, the backbone, ribs, and the pelvis. With the exception of the mandible, the skull is represented only by five vault fragments, and most of the hand and foot bones are missing. Because there is no duplication of any skeletal element (for instance, there are not two right humeri), the remains are from a single individual.

The erupted third molar, or wisdom tooth, as well as the closed epiphyseal lines (growth lines) attest that she was a mature adult, despite her diminutive stature of just over 1 meter. Comparative observations of other fossils assigned to her species suggest that these ancestors were sexually dimorphic, and her small size is characteristic of her female status (see page 73).

The center of vigorous debate, Lucy has spawned a quarter century of research in paleoanthropology. For example, some primitive features such as her relatively long arms and curved hand bones suggests that she was still an agile arboreal climber. Others see her as a terrestrial biped and interpret these features as evolutionary baggage, left over from the time when her ancestors lived in trees. It was difficult at first to find a place for Lucy on the hominid family tree, but few today would deny her an important role in hominid evolution. To some she is the "mother of all humankind" and to others she is the "woman who shook up man's family tree."

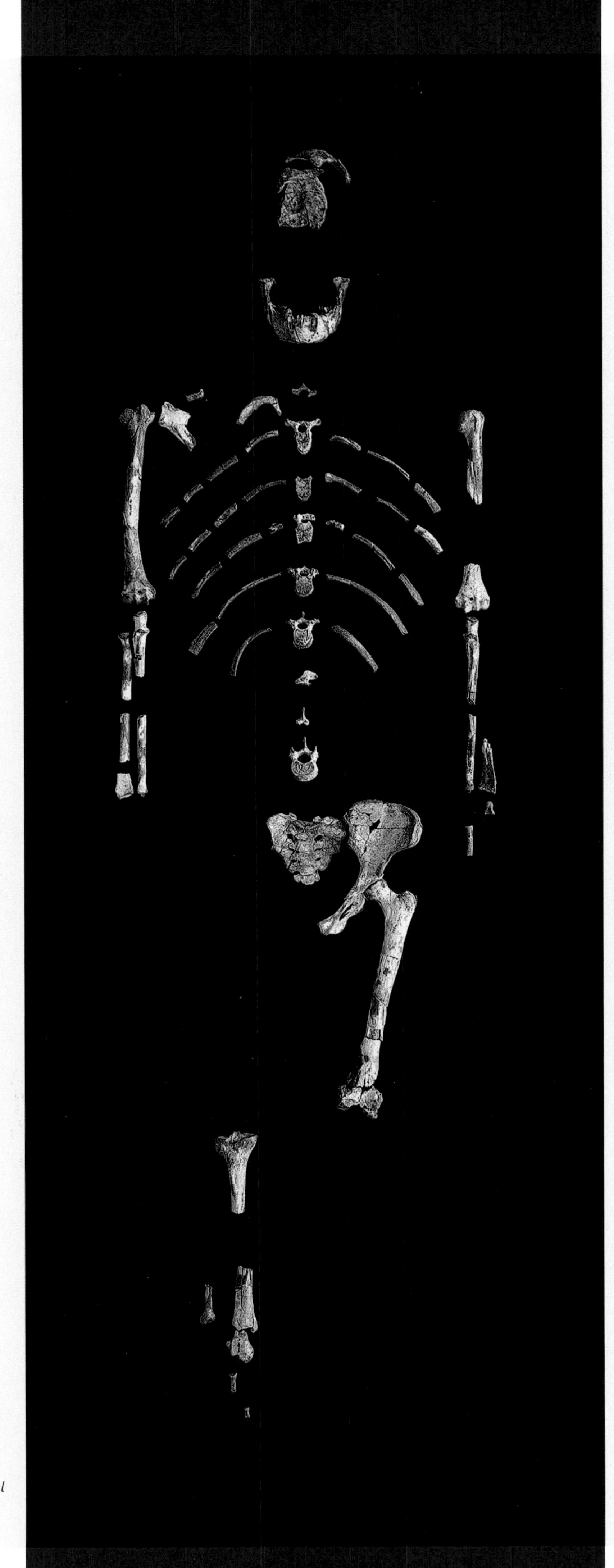

Skeleton of *Australopithecus afarensis* from Hadar, Ethiopia.
More than two decades after its discovery, the skeleton of Lucy, or A.L. 288-1, remains an important reference point to which older and younger fossils are compared.
Photograph by David Brill; courtesy of National Museum of Ethiopia.

SPECIMEN	LOCALITY	AGE	DISCOVERER	DATE	PUBLICATION
Fragments of 13 individuals	Hadar, Ethiopia	3.2 million years	Michael E. Bush	November 2, 1975	Taieb, M., D.C. Johanson, Y. Coppens, and J.-J. Tiercelin. 1978. Expédition internationale de l'Afar, Ethiopie (4 ème et 5 ème Campagne 1975-1977): Chronostratigraphie des gisements a hominidés pliocene de l'Hadar et correlations avec les sites prehistoriques da Kana Gona. *C.R. Acad. Sci. Paris*, 287: 459-461.

Australopithecus afarensis

A.L. 333 *THE FIRST FAMILY*

In the fall of 1975, about a year after Lucy was found, a unique discovery was made at Hadar. At Afar Locality (A.L.) 333, on a steep hillside, a number of hominid fossils were found eroding from a single geological horizon. At the outset it was thought that perhaps this was another partial skeleton, but when two identical left distal fibulae were collected, it was clear that more than one individual was represented. Following two field seasons of work at locality 333, more than 200 hominid fragments were recovered. Most were found during screening operations on the hillside, but seventeen specimens were excavated in situ.

Based on a count of mandible fragments and lower teeth, the minimum number of individuals represented at locality 333 is thirteen. Nine of them were adults and four were juveniles, the youngest (less than one year old) represented by an unerupted lower deciduous incisor (A.L. 333x-25).

Where geological strata are rich in fossil specimens, the assemblage usually consists of a mixture of different animal groups. In the case of locality 333, however, with the exception of a few fish and rodent remains, all the bones were hominid. In paleontology the study of death assemblages is called taphonomy, and when it is biased in such a way as at 333, it is referred to as a catastrophic assemblage. In other words, some disaster overcame a group of *afarensis,* which ultimately became buried in a single geological horizon.

The precise cause of the death assemblage has not been ascertained, but various scenarios such as a flash flood have been suggested. Close inspection of the bone surface reveals a total lack of carnivore damage, such as tooth marks or crushing, which rules out predation. Moreover, the articular ends of the bones are intact, not chewed off by scavengers. The bones have, however, been broken, perhaps by water transport before final deposition and fossilization. Lack of advanced weathering of the bone surfaces implies rapid burial.

Since the 333 collection is a catastrophic one, in all probability it samples a group of related individuals. This unique and important collection, therefore, allows some insights into the biology and structure of a single fossil hominid species not available from any other locality in Africa.

Aside from size, the 333 specimens are nearly identical in their anatomy. In fact, the entire size range of hominids found at Hadar and assigned to *A. afarensis* is represented in the 333 collection, adding strength to the notion that only a single species existed in the pre-3.0 million-year-old deposits at Hadar, and that this species, *afarensis,* was markedly sexually dimorphic.

A highly significant benefit gained from the 333 sample is the appreciation of growth and development in a fossil species. A number of fairly complete upper and lower jaws as well as a partial cranium (A.L. 333-105) of a child allow the tracing of development from youth to maturity. Some anatomical features, such as the shape of the nasal region and mandible, which distinguish adult *afarensis* specimens from other species of *Australopithecus* are already indicated in the immature specimens.

Ongoing excavations at locality 333 promise to permit a fuller understanding of the cause for such a remarkable accumulation of hominids. Geologically, the locality is capped by a resistant sandstone, which indicates an ancient meandering river. The geological layer from which the hominids derive is fairly fine-grained and may be a low-lying delta plain.

One final distinction for the hominids at 333 is their geological age. Recent argon-dating of the Hadar deposits brackets these hominids between two volcanic ashes. Precise laboratory analysis shows that the disaster that killed and interred the earliest evidence of our ancestors living in groups transpired between 3,180,000 and 3,210,000 years ago!

***Australopithecus afarensis*, A.L. 333-105.** Despite being crushed and distorted, this specimen, one of at least 13 individuals found at the 333 site of Hadar, Ethiopia, provides clues to the juvenile cranial anatomy of this species. Actual size. *Photograph by David Brill; courtesy of National Museum of Ethiopia.*

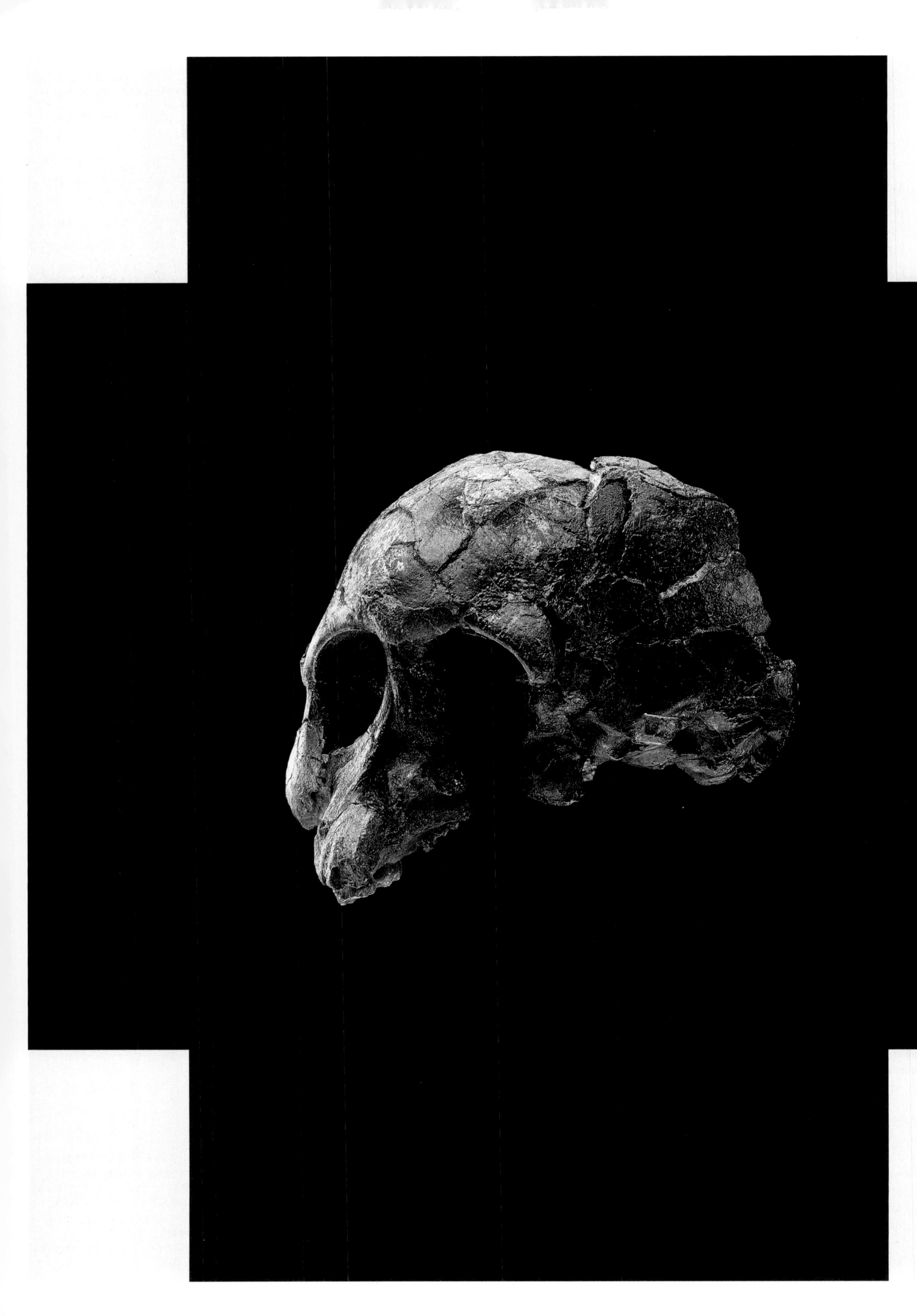

SPECIMEN	LOCALITY	AGE	DISCOVERER	DATE	PUBLICATION
Adult cranium	Hadar, Ethiopia	3.0 million years	Yoel Z. Rak	February 26, 1992	Kimbel, W.H., D.C. Johanson, and Y. Rak. 1994. The first skull and other new discoveries of *Australopithecus afarensis* at Hadar, Ethiopia. *Nature* v. 368: 449-451

Australopithecus afarensis

A.L. 444-2

Humans recognize each other by the distinctive constellation of features seen in our skulls, especially our faces. Although other parts of our anatomy are also unique to each of us, it is our face that immediately identifies us. This is also the case for fossil hominids, in which species are most easily identified by a unique combination of anatomical features in the skull. Paleoanthropologists, therefore, generally place much confidence in species for which skulls are known.

Although the vast majority of anatomical traits marshaled to support the announcement, in 1978, of *Australopithecus afarensis* as a new species are seen in the skull, acceptance of this species was not universal, owing in part to the lack of a fairly complete skull specimen. Nearly every anatomical region of the skull was known, but from fragments of different individuals. In 1983 these fragments formed the basis of a composite reconstruction of a male *A. afarensis*. But the lack of association of the different anatomical parts in a complete skull led some paleoanthropologists to suggest that more than one species of hominid was combined into the reconstruction. The implication was that the face of one species and the braincase of another had been assembled into one skull.

An opportunity to test the veracity of the composite skull reconstruction came with the discovery in 1992 of a fairly complete *A. afarensis* skull by Yoel Rak of Tel Aviv University, Israel. Thirteen major pieces of skull and hundreds of small fragments were found in a gully at Hadar. After these fragments were reassembled, the Afar Locality (A.L.) 444-2 skull closely resembled the composite reconstruction, supporting the hypothesis that only a single species was incorporated into the reconstruction.

The skull is slightly older that 3.0 million years and measurements of its overall size distinguish it as the largest *Australopithecus* skull ever found, yet its brain size is estimated to be only slightly more than 500 cc. Because of its size, big canine teeth, massive mandible (not pictured here), and strong muscle markings, the skull is presumed to be a male. Other specimens from Hadar, such as A.L. 417-1, with small canines and a less projecting (prognathic) face, are presumed females. The degree of difference between male and female *A. afarensis* specimens is similar to that seen between the sexes of great ape species.

Based on the heavy dental wear, A.L. 444-2 was an old individual, for much of the enamel is worn away, exposing large areas of dentine. The anterior teeth exhibit heavy wear, suggesting the stripping of vegetation and perhaps manipulation of food with the lips and anterior teeth. Such a view gains support from the posteriorly positioned but low sagittal crest. Fibers of the temporalis muscle toward the back of the skull are oriented fairly horizontally and were enlarged to resist the pulling forces generated by food preparation at the front of the prognathic face. The condition in *A. afarensis* is more like that seen in chimps and especially gorillas. This contrasts with the typical condition in robust australopithecines, where the anterior fibers of the temporalis muscle, acting vertically to generate powerful grinding forces between the cheek teeth, are sometimes so enlarged that an anteriorly placed sagittal crest is formed. In A.L. 444-2 a small, very low posteriorly placed sagittal crest is present.

Fortunately, the frontal region of the skull, a previously poorly known cranial region in *A. afarensis,* is well preserved in A.L. 444-2. Details of this anatomy, such as the low, sloping forehead and the bony torus above the eye orbits, add further to the distinctiveness of this species. Viewed anteriorly, the face with its squared off orbits more closely resembles a gorillas's face rather than a chimpanzee's. In addition to affirming the presence of only a single species at Hadar, the skull extends the temporal range of *A. afarensis* from 3.4 to 3.0 million years at this site.

Recovery of the A.L. 444-2 skull permits positive identification of a frontal bone found in 1981 at Belohdelie, a site situated roughly 72 kilometers directly south of Hadar. The Belohdelie specimen shares a series of diagnostic features with the A.L. 444-2 specimen such as a thick torus just above the orbits and absence of a sulcus behind the torus, so typical of chimpanzees. Because the Belchdelie frontal is dated to roughly 3.9 million years, the temporal range of *A. afarensis* is extended to 900,000 years, suggesting a long period of anatomical stasis for this region of the skull.

Using a fairly complete skull like A.L. 444-2, John Gurche, an artist trained in anthropology, was able to reconstruct, in three dimensions, a male *A. afarensis* skull. (see page 82) Beginning with a cast of the skull, and drawing on knowledge gained from numerous dissections of humans and apes, he sculpted layers of clay into the shape of muscles. After adding fatty tissue and salivary glands, he then positioned glass eyes and the nasal cartilage. Finally, he covered the entire reconstruction with pliable urethane for skin. Although such details as wrinkles, skin tone, and the placement of hair will always be open to debate, the resulting image is undoubtedly a close facsimile of a male of Lucy's species. At long last, *A. afarensis* received a face, something all of us can look at and appreciate how different that species was from our own. Yet, in spite of the overall apeness of the skull, there is a sense of concern in the eyes that reaches out to us across millions of years.

***Australopithecus afarensis*, A.L. 444-2.** Discovered in 1992, this is the first relatively complete adult cranium of *A. afarensis* and confirmed an earlier reconstruction made from the bones of several different individuals. Actual size.
Photograph by William H. Kimbel, Institute of Human Origins; courtesy of National Museum of Ethiopia.

SPECIMEN	LOCALITY	AGE	DISCOVERER	DATE	PUBLICATION
Adult female knee joint	Hadar, Ethiopia	3.4 million years	Donald C. Johanson	October 30, 1972	Johanson, D.C., and T. Taieb. 1976. A preliminary anatomical diagnosis of the first plio/pleistocene hominid discoveries in the central Afar, Ethiopia. *Am. J. Phys. Anthropol.* 45:217-234

Australopithecus afarensis
A.L. 129-1A+1B

During a brief visit of only a few days to the site of Hadar, Ethiopia, in 1972, an international team of scientists was stunned by the incredible number of well-preserved fossils eroding from the geological strata. Evaluation of some of the fossil fauna, particularly the pigs and elephants, suggested an age well in excess of 3 million years for the site. Only a handful of hominids dated to earlier than 3 million years had been found in Africa, and the team was hopeful that fossil hominids would eventually be found at Hadar. With great optimism, plans were made to launch the inaugural expedition to Hadar the following year.

Members of the International Afar Research Expedition, as it was then called, began a systematic survey of the Hadar badlands, with the paramount objective being the discovery of fossil hominids, for any significant finds could add immeasurably to a poorly known segment of time in hominid evolution. As fortune would have it, the first discovery of a hominid at the site was made in some of the oldest geological levels at Hadar.

A small fossil fragment was spotted poking out from soft sediments, and on closer inspection it turned out to be broken, exposing a cross section of bone. The diagnostic portion, the articular end, was hidden in the loose sediment, but after careful removal it was identified as the proximal (top) end of a tibia (A.L. 129-1b). Quite small in size, it could easily be mistaken for a monkey tibia. The tibia was left in the exact place where it had been found a slow survey on hands and knees led to the finding of a distal (bottom) end of a femur (A.L. 129-1a). It matched the color of fossilization in the tibia exactly, and when the two bones were fitted together, it was obvious that they were from the same individual. The articulating surfaces were perfectly congruent, having been molded to each other during the life of the individual roughly 3.4 million years ago.

The anatomy of the knee joint is a reliable indicator of locomotion, and from a number of diagnostic features it was apparent that this fossil knee was from a biped. Three obvious characters verified that it was a hominid knee: first, the femoral shaft rose at an angle that allowed the head of the femur to fit into the pelvis; second, the lateral condyle (one of two knobs on the femur, which sits on the tibia) was flattened and elongated from front to back, which enhances the transfer of body weight to the tibia during walking; and third, the lateral border of the patellar notch on the femur was raised, which prevented the patella (kneecap) from dislocating.

The immediate importance of the knee joint was that it confirmed the presence of hominids in the Hadar geological sequence and, at the time of discovery, provided the oldest evidence for a cardinal feature in human evolution—bipedality. The distal femur fits comfortably into one's palm, suggesting that the individual represented by the knee joint was fairly small, similar in size to Lucy. When first discovered, it was not possible to assign the specimen to a genus or species, but we know now that it belongs to *Australopithecus afarensis*.

The proximal (top) ends of the right and left femora were also found and are assumed to be from the same individual because they are identical in color and fossilization to the knee joint. Both proximal fragments are broken through the neck—a typical fracture pattern in modern humans who break their hip. Furthermore, the anterior and posterior surfaces of the bones show areas of crushing. The splintered nature of the damage suggests that it was inflicted when the bone was still fresh, most likely by a carnivore. Even more interesting is the fact that the left proximal femur fragment was found about 18 meters away, suggesting that perhaps these bones were scattered by carnivore activity on the prehistoric landscape.

Although the Hadar knee joint is no longer the oldest evidence for hominid bipedality, its discovery at Hadar in 1973 provided the impetus for continuing research not only at this important fossil site, but in other regions of the Afar Triangle as well.

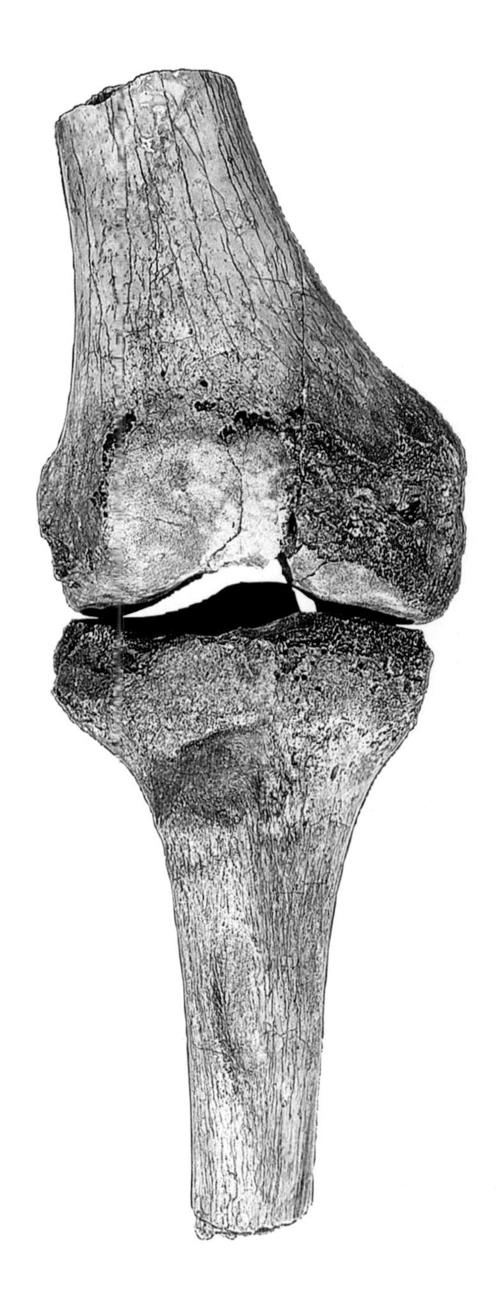

***Australopithecus afarensis*, A.L. 129-1a+1b.** The first hominid fossil found at Hadar, Ethiopia, this femur and tibia preserve a complete knee joint lacking the knee cap, which indicates that this species walked on two legs. Actual size.
Courtesy of Donald Johanson, Institute of Human Origins; and National Museum of Ethiopia.

SPECIMEN	LOCALITY	AGE	DISCOVERER	DATE	PUBLICATION
Adult mandible	Laetoli, Tanzania	3.6 million years	Maundu Muluila	1974	Leakey, M.D., R.L. Hay, G.H. Curtis, R.E. Drake, M.K. Jackes, and T.D. White. 1976. Fossil hominids from the Laetolil Beds, Tanzania. *Nature* 262: 460-465. Leakey, M.D., and R.L. Hay. 1979. Pliocene footprints in the Lactolil Beds at Laetoli, northern Tanzania. *Nature* 278: 317-328.

Australopithecus afarensis

L.H.-4 TYPE SPECIMEN

FOSSIL HOMINID FOOTPRINTS

The preconceptions we carry with us, no matter how scientifically objective we try to be, can strongly influence the way we conduct research. This was probably the case when Louis Leakey visited the fossil site of Laetoli, Tanzania, in 1935, in search of possible hominid ancestors. Although the site is rich in fossil mammalian remains, Leakey spent little time there, for the absence of stone artifacts signaled to him that there could not possibly be hominid remains at the site. Humans are distinct because we make tools, and Olduvai Gorge, some 30 kilometers to the north, where stone tools were oozing out of the geological layers, held much more promise for finding human ancestor remains.

After studying with Sir Arthur Keith, then England's most accomplished and respected anatomist, Leakey was convinced that "true man" did indeed have a very ancient ancestry. Keith was fanatically dedicated to the veracity of the Piltdown skull, which had been found in 1912 in a gravel pit in Sussex, England. There, a hominid skull with a brain of modern size had been recovered in association with the teeth of extinct animals, with an age of 5 million years. The jaw, however, was like that of a primitive ape. The combination of a modern-appearing cranium and a primitive apelike jaw, now known to be a hoax, justified Keith's view that it was the brain that led the way in human evolution.

As for the teacher, so for the student: Leakey took the view of a very ancient occurrence for "true man" back with him to his native Kenya, and when he learned of the discovery at Olduvai Gorge, in neighboring Tanzania, of a human skeleton, which was found by the noted German paleontologist Hans Reck, from Berlin, Leakey was certain that the find would support Keith's views. In 1931, Leakey and Reck mounted an expedition to Olduvai, where Leakey immediately found stone tools in abundance. He also found something else he was looking for—a very ancient but modern-looking hominid, Olduvai Hominid (OH) 1, in association with stone tools. Back in England, Keith was elated and congratulated Louis Leakey on his discovery. The die was now cast that would continue to color Leakey's belief in very ancient "true *Homo*," right up to the time of his death.

Even though it was soon discovered that the Olduvai skeleton was the burial of a modern Maasai into older geological horizons, Leakey was not deterred. At the sites of Kanam and Kanjera, in Kenya, he recovered remains of anatomically modern humans in deposits of presumed great antiquity. However, geological investigation showed that the finds were also intrusive burials of modern humans into older sediments. The Piltdown hoax was unveiled in 1953, by anatomists Joseph Weiner and Wilfred Le Gros Clark of Oxford University and Kenneth Oakley, an archeologist at the British Museum of Natural History. The Piltdown specimen was a practical joke: the cranium of a modern human and the mandible of a modern orangutan had been buried together, along with the bones of extinct animals.

Perhaps it was Louis Leakey's a priori assumption about the nature of early "true man" that explains why he did not recognize a left lower hominid canine collected at Laetoli in 1935 along with numerous other Pliocene vertebrate fossils. The tooth was too primitive, not modern in form, and there were no associated stone tools. The tooth, misidentified as that of a monkey, rested in obscurity until it was recognized at the Natural History Museum in London as a hominid, and published in *Science* in 1981.

Except for a brief period in 1939, when the German explorer Ludwig Kohl-Larsen recovered two hominid specimens at Laetoli (the Maasai word for a red lily), little attention was paid to the potential of the site for elucidating our past. However, in 1974, Mary Leakey's friend George Dove, who owned the Lake Ndutu Lodge, some 40 kilometers from Olduvai, brought to Mary Leakey's attention his discovery of fossil teeth in a load of sand he had collected for building. He and Mary Leakey traced the source of the sand back to Laetoli. In 1974 she returned to the site, which led to the discovery of some thirty hominid specimens.

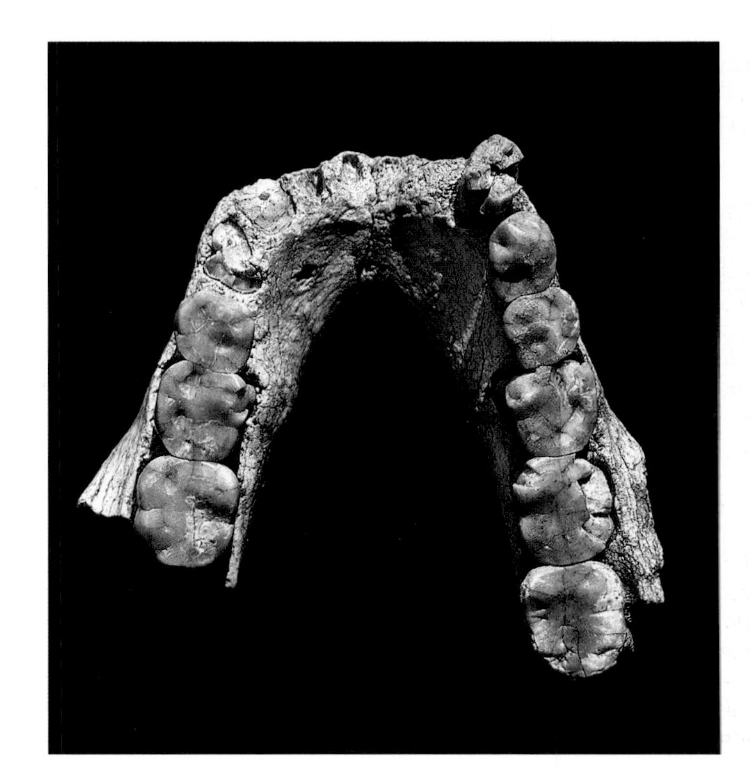

Australopithecus afarensis, LH 4.
This mandible was chosen as the type specimen for this species to affirm the connection between it and other fossils from Laetoli, Tanzania with hominid fossils from Hadar, Ethiopia, 1,500 kilometers away. Actual size. *Courtesy of Donald Johanson, Institute of Human Origins; and National Museums of Kenya*

Geological studies at Laetoli confirmed a date of 3.6 million years for the hominids, roughly equivalent to the date for the hominids at Hadar. This dictated a much closer examination and comparison of the Laetoli hominids with those from Hadar by Donald Johanson and Tim White, now of Berkeley, California. It was soon apparent that the hominids from the two sites, separated by roughly 1,500 kilometers, were nearly identical in their anatomy and should properly be placed in the same species. A whole suite of anatomical features in the teeth, jaws, and cranial material highlighted the australopithecine affinities of the Hadar and Laetoli hominids. However, the more primitive character states (see page 119) in the specimens resulted in the recognition, in 1978, of a novel species, *A. afarensis*. Although the Hadar specimens were more complete, the L.H.-4 mandible, lacking the ascending rami but containing nine teeth, was selected to be the flagship fossil for the species in 1978 because of its distinctive and diagnostic anatomy, as well as the fact that detailed descriptions and photographs of it had already been published. Furthermore, choosing a Laetoli specimen for the holotype of the larger Hadar collection helped solidify the connection between Laetoli and Hadar hominids.

While the fossil hominids collected at Hadar and Laetoli were attracting headlines, a totally unanticipated discovery in 1976 at Laetoli later would distinguish the site as one of the true wonders of the prehistoric world. In a volcanic ash, dated to roughly 3.6 million years, thousands of exquisitely preserved animal footprints were found. While the layer of volcanic ash, Tuff 7, was still wet, monkeys, antelopes, elephants, two species of rhinos, three-toed horses, a small cat, giraffes, guinea fowl, francolins, and even perhaps a passing dung beetle left their imprints in the ash.

It was, however, the 1978 discovery by Paul Abell, a geochemist, of undeniable hominid footprints at Laetoli that ignited the imagination of scientists and lay people alike. At first the discovery was met with disbelief, but after the hominid nature of the prints was verified, excavations in 1978 and 1979 uncovered a 27-meter-long trackway with more than sixty-nine hominid footprints.

After detailed inspection, there was no doubt that the imprints were made by a hominid. The impression in the ash revealed a strong heel strike, and the deep indentation made by the great toe was identical to one modern humans would leave in beach sand during toe-off. But most important about the great toe was that it was in line with the lateral four toes, and not divergent as in a quadrupedal primate like a monkey. In some of the clearer, better-defined prints, even the longitudinal arch of the foot and the ball of the foot were visible.

Which hominid made these footprints? The answer seems obvious, because the only hominid present in the Laetoli deposits was *A. afarensis*, and by inference the footprints must have been made by members of this species. One scientist, Russell Tuttle, anatomist at the University of Chicago, looked at the foot fossils from Hadar and said they were too large to fit into the Laetoli impressions. The Laetoli prints, according to Tuttle, were so modern that they could not have been made by a large-footed *A. afarensis* with somewhat curved toes. The implication was that another hominid, more *Homo*-like, made the prints, but strangely, not a single bone of such a hominid has been found at Laetoli. One would also have to explain why *A. afarensis* left bones at Laetoli but no footprints.

To address Tuttle's assertions, anthropologists Gen Suwa at the University of Tokyo, Japan, and Tim White at the University of California, Berkeley, took a closer look at the Hadar foot bones in 1983. They scaled the anatomy of the bones down to Lucy's size, and the reconstructed foot fit perfectly into the Laetoli prints. Until the phantom hominid at Laetoli, who left footprints and no fossil remains behind, is found, the best bet is to infer that *A. afarensis* was responsible for the Laetoli footprint trail. To find *afarensis* footprints was nothing short of a miracle!

In-depth geological study of the Laetoli strata by Richard Hay, geologist at the University of Illinois, revealed that the volcanic eruption that produced the ash in which the footprints were preserved occurred at the end of the dry season, when the grass had been grazed down to a stubble. The pocked surface, a result of the impact of falling raindrops, indicated that the rainy season had started. Higher up in the geological sequence, apparently deeper into the rainy season, heavier rainfall washed away many of the smaller prints, but game trails left by large migrating herds of antelopes are evident.

It took a unique series of events to create this marvelous portrait of the past. The volcano Sadiman spat out a cloud of ash with the consistency of fine beach sand. The ash blanketed the ground like new-fallen snow. Then, it rained. The ash became mushy, and animals left their impressions in the mud. The sun came out and quickly dried the mud. Because the ash was rich in carbonates, it hardened into an almost cement-like layer. Another puff of ash, and the footprints were sealed for posterity. Sadiman was not quiet until some 16 to 20 centimeters of layered ash had accumulated. The final event occurred 3.6 million years later, when scientists recognized the Footprint Tuff that erosion had exposed.

We will never know what Lucy's relatives thought when Sadiman began to erupt. The footprint trail, however, shows a steady progression from south to north of two hominids, perhaps walking side by side. One set of prints is large, the other small. Were they male and female? Were the smaller prints made by a child? Partway along the trail, the hominids appear to have paused, turned, and looked westward. What caught their attention? The answer is lost in time, but after the pause they resumed walking in the original direction—as if they knew exactly where they were going.

***Australopithecus afarensis*, Laetoli footprint.** The site of Laetoli, Tanzania attracted worldwide attention after the discovery in 1978 of a hominid footprint trail that demonstrated a humanlike gait for this early hominid. Actual size.
Photograph by John Reader, Science Source/Photo Researchers.

SPECIMEN	LOCALITY	AGE	DISCOVERERS	DATE	PUBLICATION
Adult cranium	Sterkfontein, South Africa	2.5 million years	Robert Broom and John T. Robinson	April 18, 1947	Broom, R. 1947. Discovery of a new skull of the South African ape-man, *Plesianthropus. Nature* v. 159: 672

Australopithecus africanus

STS 5 *MRS. PLES*

Raymond Dart's 1925 publication of the Taung Child (see page 142) as a new kind of human ancestor was not well received. Instead of eliciting praise, the announcement drew strong criticism from nearly everyone except paleontologist Robert Broom. Broom, one of the more eccentric characters ever to have worked in the field of paleoanthropology, burst into Dart's lab just after publication of *A. africanus* and fell to his knees "in adoration of our ancestor," as he put it.

Robert Broom, a Scotsman, arrived in South Africa in 1897 via Australia, drawn by his fascination with the mammal-like reptiles of the Karoo Desert. Supporting himself with a medical position, he collected, cleaned, drew, and published extensively. In 1925, the year Dart announced the Taung Child, Broom was fifty-eight and had 250 publications to his name. The level of his output was almost incomprehensible: he named some seventy new genera and close to 200 new species of reptiles.

Broom caught the hominid fever, but his medical work and the Great Depression prevented him from doing much about it. Then, in 1934, he was given a post at the Transvaal Museum in Pretoria in paleontology and physical anthropology. He continued to focus on reptiles, publishing 16 papers in 18 months, but in 1936 he vowed to find an adult version of the Taung Child.

Broom was led by two of Dart's students to a cave being mined for limestone, some 64 kilometers southwest of Johannesburg. G. W. Barlow, who was in charge of the quarrying operation, on the side sold to tourists fossils that were found at the cave, known as Sterkfontein. Broom told Barlow to keep a keen eye open for anything even vaguely resembling a hominid.

On August 17, 1936, only eight days after Broom's appeal, he was presented with two thirds of an endocast, not unlike that of the Taung Child. Broom searched through the broken breccia and found the base of a skull, parts of the vault, some teeth, and a badly crushed maxilla. Here was the hominid he wanted. With a proclivity for naming new taxa, he dubbed the find, TM 1511, *Australopithecus transvaalensis* (interestingly, the name is mentioned only in a figure caption), but in 1938 he placed it in *Plesianthropus transvaalensis*, "near man from the Transvaal."

During World War II, fossil hunting essentially ceased, but in 1947 Broom, now over eighty years old, and his assistant John T. Robinson reinitiated work at Sterkfontein. The bone breccia at the site is so consolidated that they used dynamite to blast open the deposits. On April 18, after the dust had cleared, they found an adult skull of *Australopithecus* in the breccia. The blast had split the skull into two major fragments across the braincase, exposing a crystal-lined brain cavity.

After weeks of laboratory preparation and cleaning, the specimen, Sts 5, was found to be a nearly complete cranium, lacking teeth. Robinson and Broom concluded that it was the skull of a middle-aged female, and since then it has been known as "Mrs. Ples." From examination of anatomical details on the inside base of the skull and the bones in the orbit, they concluded in June that "these small-brained man-like beings were very nearly human."

In some ways the recovery of "Mrs. Ples" was a vital turning point in the broader acceptance of the South African australopithecines as hominids. With an adult cranium like Sts 5, the case could no longer be made that the Taung Child was simply a juvenile ape. Sts 5 demonstrated without doubt that had the Taung Child grown up, it would not have developed into an ape.

Some of Broom's more cavalier approaches to excavation, such as his lack of attention to stratigraphic details, drew criticism from the Historical Monuments Commission. In fact, he had been forbidden to work at Sterkfontein, but he defied the ruling. Again the Commission banned him, but scientific and public outcry quickly forced a reversal of the ban, allowing him to further his excavations at Sterkfontein.

***Australopithecus africanus*, Sts 5** (see also page 3).
Although it has long carried the nickname "Mrs. Ples," this cranium actually belongs to a male according to recent anatomical studies. Note its very projecting lower face in lateral view. Actual size.
Photograph by David Brill; courtesy of Transvaal Museum.

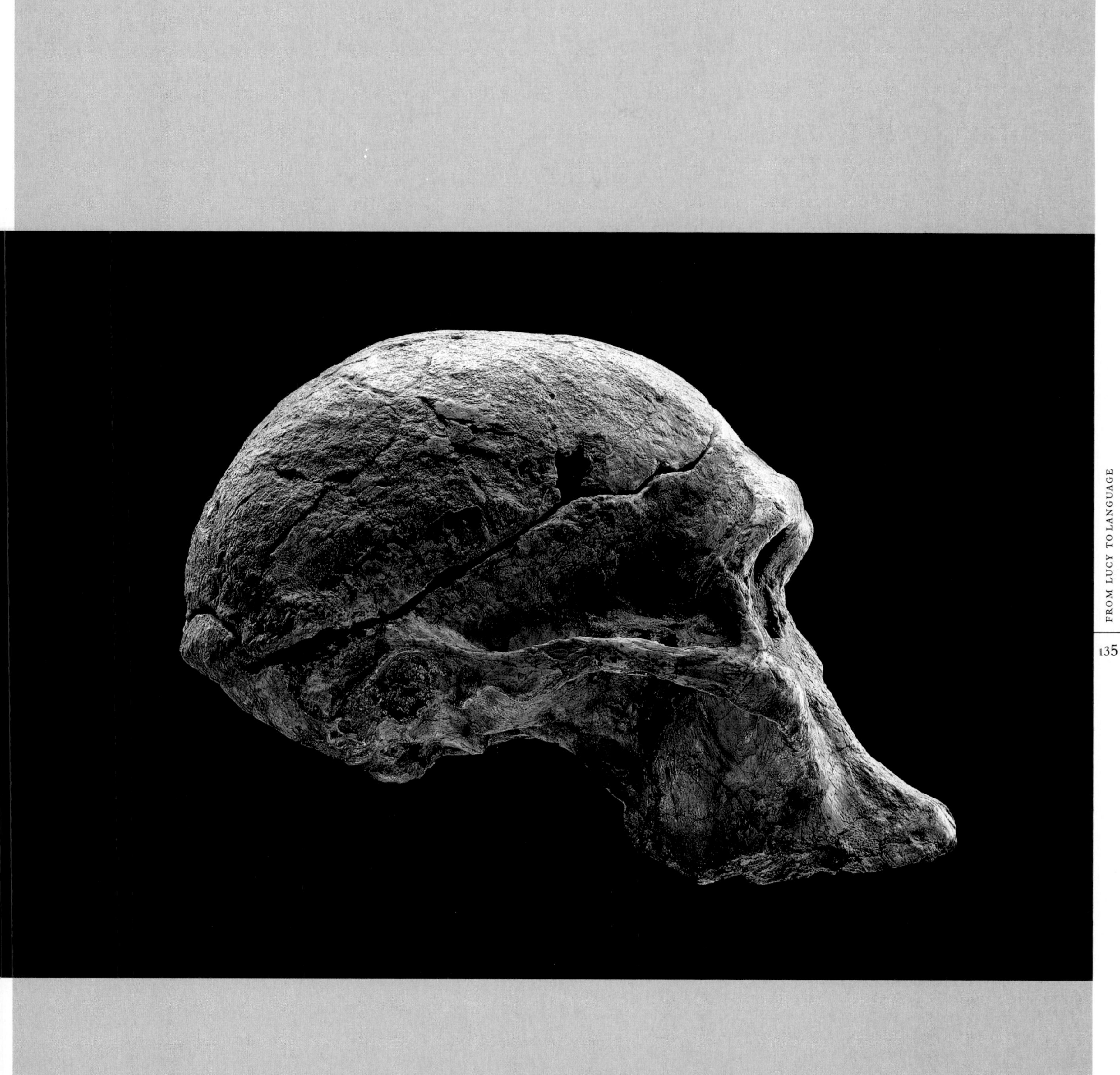

SPECIMEN	LOCALITY	AGE	DISCOVERERS	DATE	PUBLICATION
Partial adult skeleton	Sterkfontein, South Africa	2.5 million years	Robert Broom and John T. Robinson	August 1, 1947	Broom, R., J.T. Robinson, and G.W.H. Schepers. 1950. Sterkfontein Ape-man *Plesianthropus*. *Mem. Transvaal Mus.* no. 4.

Australopithecus africanus
STS 14

In 1947, following his short period of banishment from the important fossil cave site of Sterkfontein by the Historical Monuments Commission (see page 134), paleontologist Robert Broom was more determined than ever to find significant hominid fossils at the site. On August 1, he and his assistant at the TransvaalMuseum, John Robinson, later distinguished by his all-encompassing study of the dentition of the australopithecines, blasted out a slab of cave breccia containing a portion of a thigh bone, several vertebrae, and, most important, both innominates (hip bones) of an australopithecine. This was a remarkable find when judged by any criterion. It was also the vital evidence Broom needed to convince those who doubted that the australopithecines were indeed hominids. This partial skeleton attested to the bipedal nature of these early creatures, which assured them a place in the family Hominidae.

Teeth and jaws are always abundant at early hominid sites, teeth because they contain the hardest substance in the body, enamel, and jaws because the bone surrounding the teeth is so compact and dense. This is fortunate, because teeth and jaws are extremely useful for understanding dietary adaptations and taxonomic affinities of hominid remains (see page 28). The more delicate parts of the skeleton, however, such as the vertebrae, ribs, and pelvis, tend to be a rarity. The paper-thin bone, especially of the pelvic blades, is easily broken and destroyed before being buried and ultimately fossilized. Vertebrae have the unique hydrodynamic property of easily floating away from a decaying carcass and seldom become fossilized. Ribs, containing nourishing marrow, are readily crunched up as hors d'oeuvres by hungry scavengers.

The August 1947 find received the catalogue number Sts 14. After extensive laboratory work, a partial sacrum, fifteen consecutive vertebrae, and four ribs were extracted by meticulously chipping away the hard matrix. Comparisons of the Sts 14 pelvis with a modern human pelvis revealed slight differences, as was to be expected, but the overall anatomy was distinctly different from that of any ape.

The iliac blade is short and wide, with a well-developed sciatic notch and a strong anterior inferior iliac spine. Broom was quick to point out that this was undeniable proof of the hominid affinities of the australopithecines and confirmed the bipedal nature of these early creatures.

Because the pelvis was noticeably small, Broom and Robinson considered the specimen to be female. The pelvis differs from a modern human pelvis in having a forward projecting anterior superior spine, a very small articular surface for the sacrum, and a marked outward flare of the iliac blades. Robinson concluded that this individual probably had wide hips and a bulging abdomen.

Unlike modern humans, who normally have five lumbar vertebrae, Sts 14 had six. The lumbar region in the modern African apes tends to be reduced, with the number of lumbar vertebrae varying from three to five but averaging between three and four. In Sts 14 the first lumbar vertebra is transitional with a rib facet, like a thoracic vertebra, but with superior articular facets typical of a lumbar vertebra. The six lumbar vertebrae show increased dorsal wedging from the higher to the lower vertebrae, consistent with a well-developed lumbar curve (lordosis).

In 1950 Broom and Robinson provided only preliminary descriptions of Sts 14, and more detailed study was not published by Robinson until 1972. There is always pressure to publish new finds. It is a delicate balance between satisfying those awaiting publication and not publishing too hastily, leaving oneself open to criticism that the information is incomplete. Broom was acutely aware of this problem, and in 1950 he wrote, in an obviously defensive mode, "We think it much preferable to issue even inadequate descriptions and let other workers know something of our finds than to keep them secret for 10 years or more." Broom was reacting to scientists who held off publishing their finds for many years but who were swift to criticize those, like himself, who did publish quickly.

Reading Broom's publications, one gets a sense of urgency, no doubt in response to his advancing years. In the end he was fanatically driven to finish his monograph on the Swartkrans hominids. On April 6, 1951, after completing the final corrections, he allegedly said, "Now that's finished...and so am I." He died that evening.

***Australopithecus africanus*, Sts 14.**
Remains of the vertebrae and pelvis are quite rare in the early human fossil record, so this specimen was important in establishing that australopithecines were more humanlike than apelike below the neck.
Photograph by John Reader, Science Source/Photo Researchers.

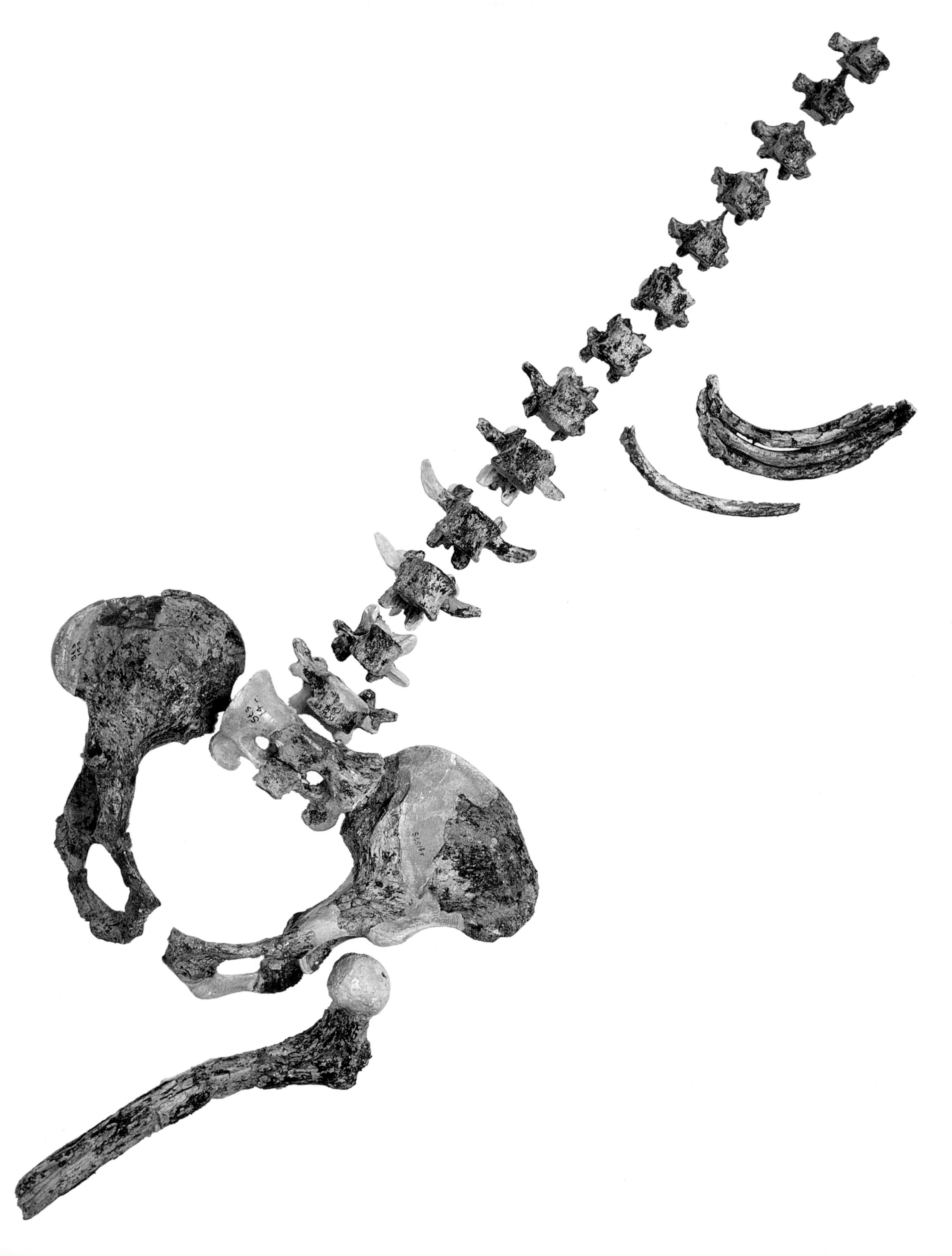

SPECIMEN	LOCALITY	AGE	DISCOVERERS	DATE	PUBLICATION
Adult cranium and mandible	Sterkfontein, South Africa	2.5 million years	Robert Broom and John T. Robinson	November 13, 1947; August 10, 1948	Broom, R., Robinson J.T., and G.W.H. Schepers. 1950. Sterkfontein Ape-man *Plesianthropus*. *Trans. Mus. Mem.* no. 4; Broom, R., and J.T. Robinson. 1949. A new mandible of the ape-man *Plesianthropus transvaalensis*. *Am. J. Phys. Anthropol.* 7:123-127

Australopithecus africanus

STS 71 AND STS 36

The 1947-49 excavations at Sterkfontein, under the direction of Robert Broom, distinguished paleontologist at the Transvaal Museum, and his student John Robinson, resulted in the discovery of seventy early hominid specimens. Work at the cave proceeded at a rapid pace, and in 1950 Broom and Robinson, along with G.W.H. Schepers, an anatomist from the University of the Witwatersrand in Johannesburg, published detailed descriptions of these finds in a Transvaal monograph. Originally catalogued as Skull No. 7, one of the better preserved crania at Sterkfontein, and now known as Sts 71, this specimen was an important addition to the hominid species at the site. Sts 71 consists of more than half of the face and the entire right side of the braincase, permitting a cranial capacity estimate of 428 cc. In lateral view, and probably as a result of slow, plastic deformation during fossilization, the cranium appears more globular, less elongated, than "Mrs. Ples" (Sts 5), which has a cranial capacity of 485 cc.

In a figure caption Broom referred to Sts 71 as a female. It was a strange assignment because the facial robusticity, especially the forwardly placed root of the zygomatic process (where the cheekbone leaves the side of the face) and the large size of the postcanine dentition, is more indicative of a male status. An interesting resolution of the correct identification of the sex of Sts 71 came in 1972 when John Wallace, the late student of Phillip Tobias, professor emeritus of anatomy at the University of the Witwatersrand, completed his doctoral thesis on the form and function of the South African australopithecines.

Wallace knew that some of the upper and lower dentitions from the South African caves, such as Sts 52a (maxilla) + 52b (mandible), were from the same individuals, since details of their occlusion and of their occlusal wear patterns matched. He identified ten individuals for which he was able to match upper and lower dentitions. Nine were from the cave of Swartkrans, with the sole specimen from Sterkfontein being the association of the cranium, Sts 71, with the mandible, Sts 36 (see page 138). As in Sts 71, the teeth in Sts 36 were heavily worn, exposing large islands of dentine. In an evaluation of the Sts 36 mandible, Broom and Robinson concluded that the jaw was male because of its massive size and very large teeth. It is this important association of the Sts 71 cranium and the Sts 36 mandible that offers a striking picture of a male skull from Sterkfontein.

Recognition of Sts 71 as male solved one problem but created another. Compared with female faces at Sterkfontein, Sts 5 and Sts 52, the facial profile of Sts 71 is less prognathic. This is unusual, because among the modern apes the males are regularly more prognathic than the females. If sexual dimorphism cannot explain the variation in facial morphology seen at Sterkfontein, then, according to paleoanthropologists William Kimbel of the Institute of Human Origins and Tim White of the University of California, it is possible that more than one hominid species may be present in the collection.

Substantial cranial variation in the Sterkfontein sample is further indicated by the undescribed cranium Stw 505 (Stw designates Sterkfontein, University of the Witwatersrand excavations), found in 1989. (see page 141) This specimen is most unusual because its estimated cranial capacity is greater than 600 cc, considerably larger than the mean of 452 cc for six adult *A. africanus* crania. Morphologically the Stw 505 cranium is very similar in shape to other crania from Sterkfontein (especially Sts 71) and the tooth roots suggest massive cheek teeth and very reduced anterior teeth. The root of the zygomatic (cheekbone) is very thick, and there is even a hint of a low sagittal crest toward the back of the cranium.

The continued reevaluation of specimens such as Sts 71, which have been known for quite sometime, is an excellent example of how interpretations may change as a result of more detailed study. If Sts 71 and the associated mandible Sts 36 represent a species distinct from *A. africanus*, it may be extremely challenging to sort the Sterkfontein fossil hominid specimens into the two different species, because they are so similar in so many respects.

Australopithecus africanus, Sts 71.
A lateral view (see following page) shows the braincase of this male cranium, with a cranial capacity of 428 cc, and a less projecting face than that of Sts 5. Actual size.
Photograph by David Brill; courtesy of Transvaal Museum.

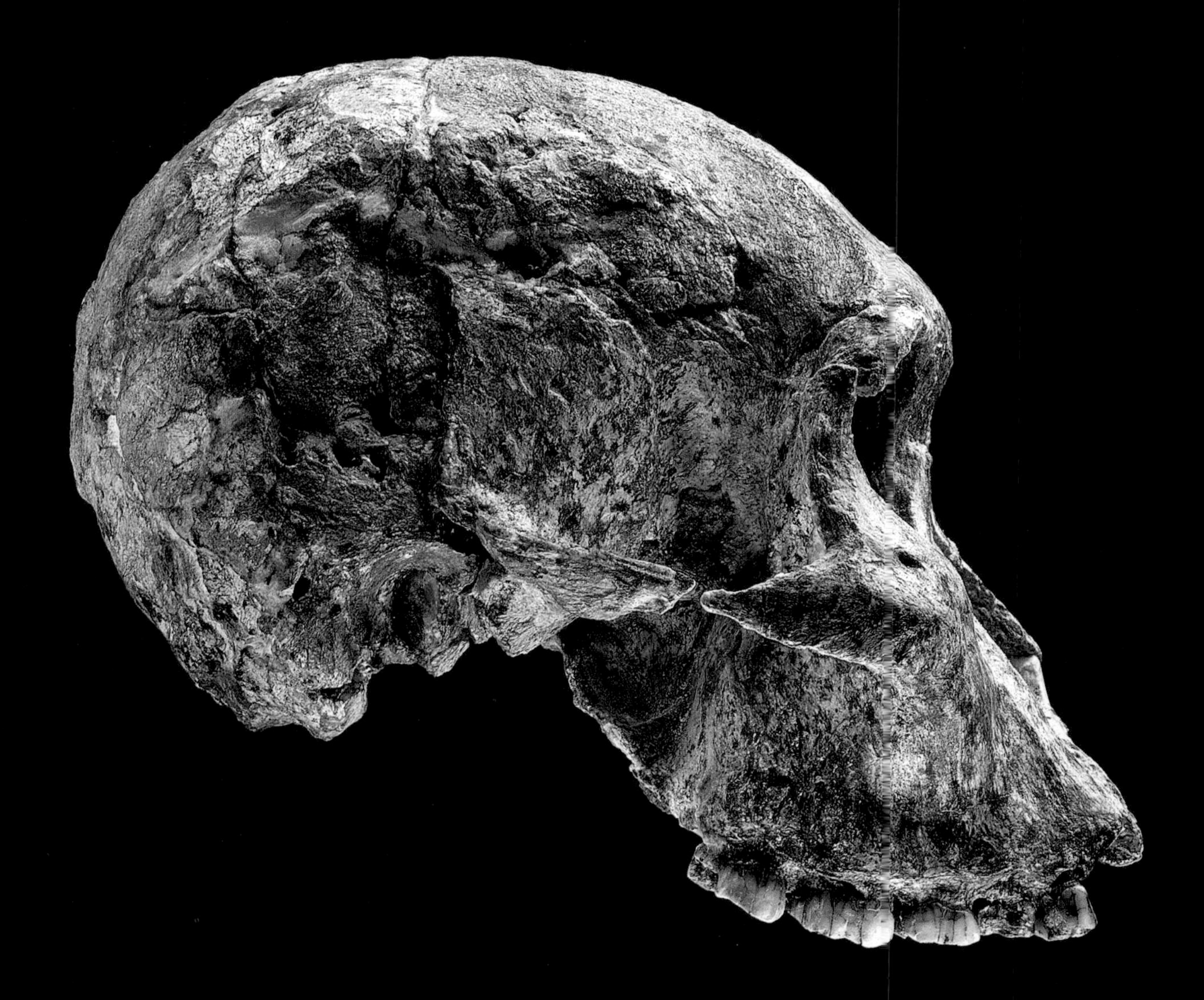

***Australopithecus africanus*, Sts 71**
(see previous page). Actual size.
Photograph by David Brill; courtesy of Transvaal Museum.

***Australopithecus africanus*, Stw 505.**
Presently undescribed, this specimen found in 1989 has an unusually large cranial capacity—greater than 600 cc—for *Australopithecus*, underscoring the amount of variation present in the Sterkfontein hominids. Actual size.
Photograph by Ron Clarke, University of the Witwatersrand.

SPECIMEN	LOCALITY	AGE	DISCOVERERS	DATE	PUBLICATION
Juvenile skull	Taung, South Africa	ca. 2.3 million years	M. de Bruyn	October 1924	Dart, R. 1925. *Australopithecus africanus.* The man-ape of South Africa. *Nature* v. 115: 195-199

Australopithecus africanus

TAUNG CHILD TYPE SPECIMEN

At a town called Taung, then located in the South African protectorate of Bechuanaland, the Northern Lime Company was actively mining limestone. M. de Bruyn, a quarryman who was overseeing the mining activities, knew of anatomy professor Raymond Dart's keen interest in the fossil animals that occasionally turned up in the dolomitic limestone. He saved these fossils and from time to time sent a box or two to Dart at the University of the Witwatersrand in Johannesburg. Little did de Bruyn know that his shipment of specimens collected in the fall of 1924 contained something even more valuable than the diamonds being found at Kimberley, some 130 kilometers to the north. In that shipment Dart recognized an endocranial cast that differed from those of the usual baboons found at the site. Most of the face and an attached lower jaw were preserved, and an endocast fit perfectly into the front part of the skull. There was no mistake: the anatomy confirmed his initial impulse that the Taung specimen was clearly not a monkey. After more than two months of carefully cleaning away the limestone, Dart wrested from the block of breccia the skull of an immature primate that could only be an early hominid. On February 7, 1925, in the pages of *Nature*, he announced evidence that harkened back to Darwin's prediction that Africa would eventually yield remains of the earliest stages of human evolution.

In a bold stroke, Dart named the first new genus in paleoanthropology *Australopithecus.* He chose the Taung specimen as the holotype for the species *Australopithecus africanus.* Despite mixing Latin, *australo*, with latinized Greek, *pithecus*, his name for this "southern ape of Africa" has stood the test of time.

This "man-ape of South Africa", as Dart referred to it, contained quite a number of human-like features. These included a rounded, high forehead lacking browridges, delicate cheekbones, a relatively flat profile in lateral view, and a lightly built mandible. The child's estimated cranial capacity is 405 cc, with a projected adult size of 440 cc. The teeth were also rather modern looking, lacking the space between the canine and the first lower premolar that is seen in the apes, and the canine was small and did not project much above the adjacent teeth. The foramen magnum (the hole in the base of the skull from which the spinal cord emerges) was forwardly placed on the base of the skull and not positioned toward the back, as in quadrupeds. This anatomical arrangement convinced Dart that the Taung Child was bipedal.

Once published, grave doubts and outright dismissal of Dart's claims issued forth from the established British anthropological community. For one thing, the find was all wrong: it had the jaw of a human and the brain of an ape, just the reverse of the situation predicted by those who saw the brain as leading the way in human evolution. After all, the English already had Piltdown Man, with an enlarged brain and apelike jaw, and how could an English fossil be cast aside in favor of one from darkest Africa?

One of the most widespread criticisms of Dart's Taung Child was merely that it was a child. The first permanent molar was just beginning to erupt, attesting to the juvenile nature of the fossil. Because most of the distinguishing features such as large canines, a sloping forehead, a large jaw, and a projecting face appear later in the growth of apes, it was thought unacceptable to use an immature specimen to diagnose a new species of ancient hominid. Given a chance, the Taung Child might have grown up to be an ape.

Additional circumstances were stacked against acceptance of the Taung Child as a human ancestor. Dart was considered young and inexperienced. Few scientists actually traveled the long distance to Johannesburg to see the original, and casts were not easily available. Even when Dart traveled with the Taung specimen to England, he was overshadowed by the more eloquent expositions on the Peking finds, which were beginning to take center stage.

Unfortunately, no other hominid specimens have ever been found at Taung, despite recently renewed excavations. Why was only one specimen recovered from the site? Puncture marks and depression fractures on the Taung specimen are similar to those seen in animal bones found in the nests of eagles. It is possible that the Taung Child represents the leftovers from the meal of a large bird of prey.

For whatever reason, Dart's monograph on the Taung Child, except for the passage on the teeth, was rejected by the Royal Society. Adding insult to injury, the influential English anatomist Sir Arthur Keith and the Austrian paleontologist Othenio Abel each published approximately 100 pages on the Taung specimen, with Keith concluding it was a chimpanzee and Abel that it was a gorilla.

Perhaps for these as well as other reasons, Dart chose not to pursue discovery of other fossil evidence to bolster his ideas about Taung, but instead dedicated himself to developing the anatomy department at the University of the Witwatersrand. It was not until adult specimens of *A. africanus* were found at sites like Sterkfontein (see page 134) twenty years later that Dart's views about the Taung Child were confirmed. Oddly, the type specimen for *Australopithecus africanus* still languishes undescribed in a university vault, more than seventy years after its discovery.

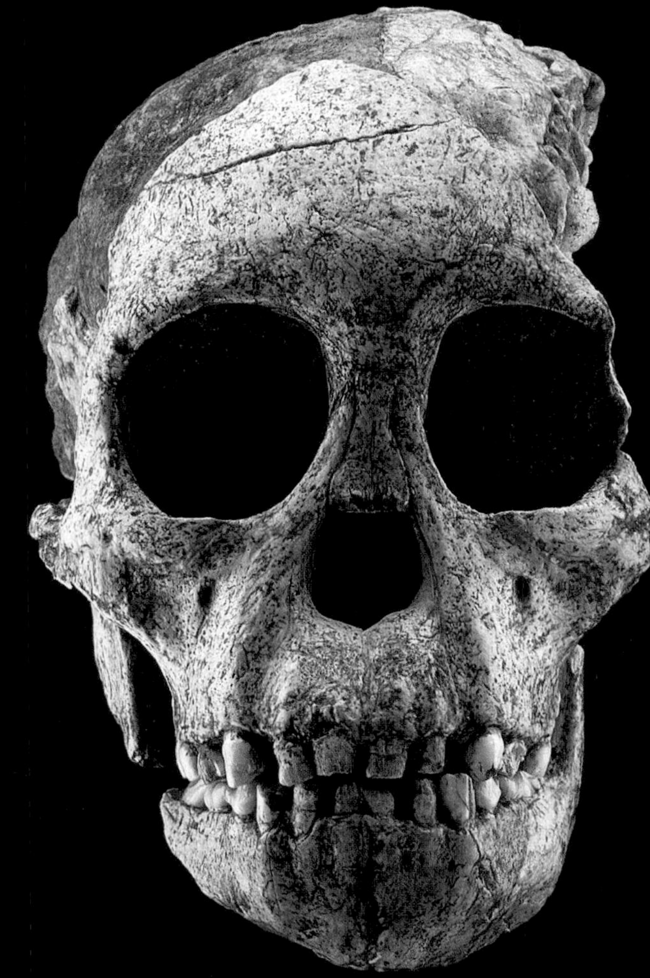

***Australopithecus africanus*, Taung child** (see also page 79).
The first early hominid found in Africa, this skull provided the basis for a new genus and species. Note that the first molar has only partially erupted, indicating that this individual died as a juvenile. Actual size.
Photographs by David Brill; courtesy of University of the Witwatersrand.

SPECIMEN	LOCALITY	AGE	DISCOVERER	DATE	PUBLICATION
Adult partial cranium and mandible	Kromdraai, South Africa	ca. 2.0 million years	Gert Terblanche	June 8, 1938	Broom, R. 1938. The Pleistocene anthropoid apes of South Africa. *Nature.* 142: 377-379; 897-899

Australopithecus robustus

TM 1517 TYPE SPECIMEN

After the initial discovery of an australopithecine at Sterkfontein, in 1936, Robert Broom made repeated visits to the lime quarry to see if Barlow had located any more hominid specimens. Broom purchased some eighteen additional fossil hominids from Barlow, but most were much more fragmentary than the original endocast and partial cranium. However, one specimen, TM 1513, a distal femur, was quite complete, and from its anatomy, especially the carrying angle of the femoral shaft and the elongated lateral condyle, Broom became convinced that *Plesianthropus transvaalensis* was bipedal.

On a visit to Sterkfontein on June 8, 1938, Broom bought, for two pounds, a maxillary fragment containing the first molar. This specimen was of particular interest to him for it was quite large with round, puffy cusps that he surmised might represent a species different from the *transvaalensis* fossils recovered earlier from the site. Broom further noticed that the matrix adhering to the maxilla was different from that at Sterkfontein, and he asked Barlow where the specimen had been collected. A week later Barlow finally admitted that the specimen had been given to him by a schoolboy who worked as a guide at the cave on Sundays.

Broom immediately went off to visit the boy's home and found that Gert Terblanche was at school. He was eager to find the boy, since fresh breaks on the maxilla suggested that additional fragments might be found at the place of discovery. Tracking the boy down at school, Broom purchased four additional teeth from him and, after lecturing the school on the cave sites, he was led by Gert to a place called Kromdraai, located only 1.5 kilometers east-northeast of Sterkfontein.

Just as Broom had suspected, more fragments were found on the hillside where the initial find had been made. These fragments included most of a palate with teeth, the left side of a cranium with the zygomatic arch, and the right half of a mandible with the premolars and molars. Broom's original hunch was correct: the hominid from Kromdraai was quite different from the one at Sterkfontein.

The Kromdraai specimen, known as Transvaal Museum (TM) 1517, had a larger face and more powerful jaws housing much larger premolars and molars. Broom was quick to publish, and in August 1938, just slightly more than two months after the initial find at Kromdraai, TM 1517 became the holotype for *Paranthropus robustus*. For the genus name Broom combined Greek terms meaning "beside man," and to emphasize the more massive nature of the fossils he chose the Latin *robustus*, meaning "strongly and stoutly built," for the species designation. (In this book we use *Australopithecus* in place of *Paranthropus*, but more and more paleoanthropologists are returning to Broom's genus name for the robust australopithecines.)

When World War II brought an end to the mining operation at Sterkfontein, Broom turned his attention to laboratory work. He chipped away at blocks of breccia from Kromdraai and found hand and foot bones, a right elbow joint, and an ankle bone, the talus. Broom became preoccupied with completing a monograph on the australopithecines, and he even made the bold assertion that they belonged in their own zoological subfamily, the Australopithecinae. His insightful descriptions of the fossil hominids continue to be invaluable reference for anyone working in paleoanthropology. Descriptions, thought by some to be fairly fanciful, of the australopithecine endocasts were presented in Part II of the monograph by G.W.H. Schepers, an anatomist, and one of Dart's students, the same boy who had originally led Broom to Sterkfontein in 1936.

Broom's monograph, published on January 31, 1946, received the U.S. National Academy of Sciences award as the most important book of the year in biology and went a long way toward altering the view that the South African ape-men were not human ancestors. The year 1946 was also a pivotal year for paleoanthropology, because Sir Wilfred E. Le Gros Clark, renowned professor of anatomy at Oxford University, made a careful study of the original australopithecine fossils and became convinced that they were indeed human ancestors. Le Gros Clark's stamp of approval carried substantial weight, and at the First Pan-African Congress, convened by Louis Leakey in January 1947 in Nairobi, he championed referral of the australopithecines to the Hominidae.

***Australopithecus robustus*, TM 1517.**
The large face, jaws and teeth of this specimen relative to *A. africanus* convinced Robert Broom that it belonged to a different species, the first of the robust australopithecines to be discovered. Actual size.
Photograph by John Reader, Science Source/Photo Researchers.

SPECIMEN	LOCALITY	AGE	DISCOVERERS	DATE	PUBLICATION
Adult cranium	Sterkfontein, South Africa	ca. 2.5 million years	Alun Hughes	June 6, 1984	Clarke, R.J. 1988. A new *Australopithecus* cranium from Sterkfontein and its bearing on the ancestry of *Paranthropus*. In *Evolutionary History of the "Robust" Australopithecines*, F.E. Grine, ed., pp. 285-292

Australopithecus sp.
STW 252

Most paleoanthropologists consider the large sample of fossil hominids from the Transvaal cave known as Sterkfontein as belonging to a single species, *Australopithecus africanus*. But the recovery of a fragmented partial cranium in 1984, catalogued as Stw 252, from the site raises the possibility of multiple species at Sterkfontein as some investigators had already suggested (see page 138).

Although the geological age of Stw 252 cannot be determined with any degree of accuracy since it was extracted from an undated cave deposit, University of the Witwatersrand paleoanthropologist Ron Clarke reported that it is from deposits deep in the cave, raising the possibility that it is older than many other Sterkfontein specimens. Clarke has studied and reconstructed Stw 252, which consists of nearly a complete upper dentition, most of the palate, small fragments of the face, and portions of the frontal, parietal, and occipital bones. He noted aspects of the anatomy of the specimen which differ significantly from typical *A. africanus* specimens such as Sts 5 (see page 134) and more closely resemble the condition in *Paranthropus*. (Clarke strongly advocates retention of paleontologist Robert Broom's generic designation for the robust australopithecines, which in this book are designated *Australopithecus*.) These features are a thin supraorbital margin, temporal lines which converge toward the midline atop the cranium, a hint of a frontal trigone (a flat hollowed area on the frontal bone, on the midline, just above the nasal bones), and a relatively flat face.

Clarke also noted the unusual combination of very large anterior teeth and very large posterior teeth in Stw 252 which distinguishes this specimen from other australopithecines. The maxillary anterior teeth are much larger than any other Sterkfontein hominid, and in fact larger than all other australopithecines from South Africa. The canine of Stw 252 is remarkably large, as well as very pointed and projecting. The cheek teeth, premolars and molars, are very large with "puffy cusps" and by and large their dimensions fall into the size range of robust australopithecines, exceeding

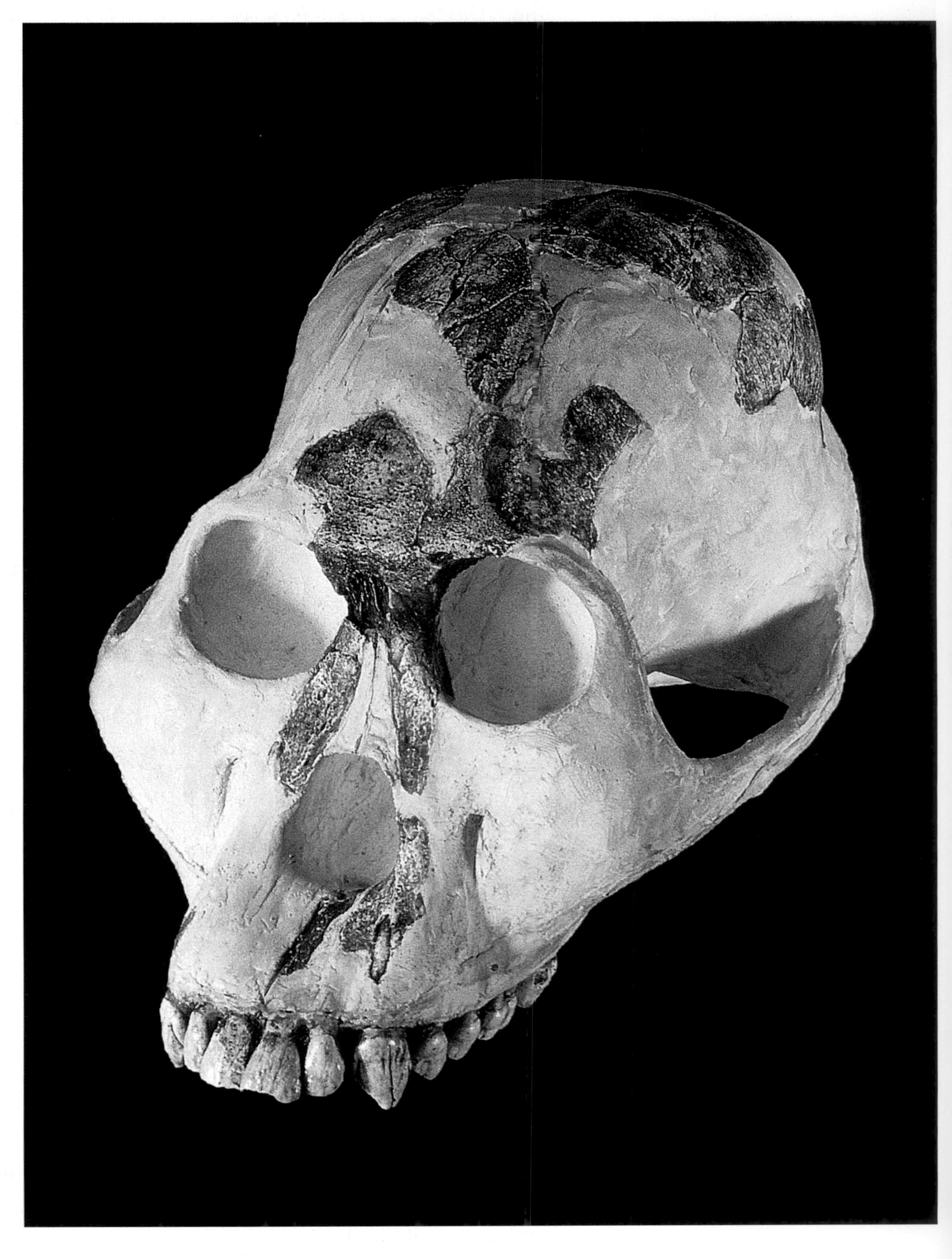

those of the more gracile *A. africanus*. Clarke contends that Stw 252 is a precursor to the robust australopithecines, and although he does not put it into a new species, he leans strongly in favor of this designation.

Typical robust australopithecines are characterized by having greatly expanded back teeth, associated with heavy mastication, and reduced front teeth. Clarke postulates that Stw 252 samples an early part of the robust lineage when natural selection had increased cheek tooth size, but had not yet reduced the anterior dentition. This condition is similar to that seen in the Black Skull (see page 152) which, judging from the tooth roots, had large anterior and posterior teeth like Stw 252. Unlike the Black Skull, Stw 252 lacks the bladelike sagittal crest, reflecting the marked enlargement of the muscles of mastication called the temporalis muscles.

The large anterior teeth are in many ways reminiscent of those seen in the east African species *A. afarensis*, notably the large canine similar to a specimen from the site of Laetoli, in Tanzania, dated to 3.5 million years. And like *afarensis*, Stw 252 has a diastema, a gap in the tooth row, between the canine and the first upper premolar. The cheek teeth of *afarensis* are, however, dwarfed in comparison with the large molars and premolars of Stw 252.

Stw 252, along with the Black Skull, contributes to the notion that in the evolution of robust australopithecines the sequence of morphological change was first enlargement of the crushing and grinding cheek teeth, and only later the reduction of the anterior teeth. Both the Black Skull and Stw 252 have prognathic (projecting) mid-faces with enlarged teeth, not unlike the more ancestral condition seen in *A. afarensis*. One interpretation, therefore, is that an *afarensis*-like hominid may have been ancestral to both Stw 252 at Sterkfontein and the Black Skull (see page 152) in eastern Africa.

***Australopithecus* sp., StW 252 cast (*left*) and fossil fragments (*right*).**
The case for a second species at Sterkfontein is strengthened by this recent discovery, reconstructed from the original teeth and cranial fragments shown here. It has a flat face and other features similar to robust australopithecines, but the combination of large front and back teeth is unlike any other members of this genus. Actual sizes.
Photographs by Ron Clarke, University of the Witwatersrand.

	SPECIMEN	LOCALITY	AGE	DISCOVERERS	DATE	PUBLICATION
SK 6	Adolescent mandible	Swartkrans, South Africa	1.5-2.0 million years	Robert Broom and John T. Robinson	November 16-26, 1948	Broom, R. 1949. Another new type of fossil ape-man. *Nature.* 163: 57
SK 48	Adult cranium	Swartkrans, South Africa	1.5-2.0 million years	Fourie	June 30, 1950	Broom, R., and J.T. Robinson. 1952. Swartkrans Ape-man, *Parathropus Crassidens. Trans. Mus. Mem.* no. 6.
SK 79	Adult cranium	Swartkrans, South Africa	1.5-2.0 million years	Robert Broom and John T. Robinson	1949	Robinson, J.T. 1956. The Dentition of the Austrolopitho-pithecinae. *Trans. Mus. Mem.* no. 9.

Australopithecus robustus

SK 6 TYPE SPECIMEN / SK 48 / SK 79

Funding for paleoanthropological research has never been abundant, and whereas institutional and governmental research grants do cover a portion of the cost, most scientists sooner or later must turn to private sources for financial support. This was especially true in the early days of the science, and it was definitely the case for the Scottish paleontologist Robert Broom, when he worked at the Transvaal Museum in South Africa. In 1948, sadly in need of funding, he began working with a wealthy young American by the name of Wendell Phillips, who, according to Broom, had "more money and egotism than scientific ability." Phillips was leading and financing the University of California African Expedition and was eager to find ape-man fossils for the university.

Broom, having worked for many years at Sterkfontein, and highly knowledgeable about the entire valley, knew of another cave site, situated only 1,170 meters directly west of Sterkfontein, called Swartkrans. Hoping to find hominids there he initiated work in November 1948. Almost immediately most of the left half of an adolescent hominid mandible was found, containing five cheek teeth, as well as the isolated right second premolar and three molars.

It was immediately obvious to Broom that the massive jaw and large, thick-enameled teeth were quite different from those found across the valley at Sterkfontein. Broom succumbed to his usual temptation to give an entirely new genus name to the jaw, and less than two months later he published the mandible, SK 6, as the holotype of *Paranthropus crassidens*. The species name combines the Latin *crassus*, meaning "thick" or "solid," and *dens*, meaning "tooth." Broom was struck by the puffy cusps and the thick-enameled caps on the dental crowns.

Although most paleoanthropologists now place the Swartkrans remains in *A. robustus*, there is strong sentiment for restoration of *Paranthropus* as a distinct genus, and based on detailed study by Fred Grine, a paleoanthropologist at the State University of New York at Stony Brook, who considered especially the deciduous teeth, the Swartkrans remains may be a different species from the *P. robustus* that Broom had named eleven years earlier from a hominid fossil found at the cave of Kromdraai (see page 144).

Broom's excavations at Swartkrans were handsomely rewarded, for the hominid collection was dominated by teeth and jaws. His work at Swartkrans is an excellent example of the interruption of serious scientific research by economic interests. Although priority was given to commercial mining of the cave for calcite, Broom, intrepid as always, scoured the breccia piles, which were growing rapidly, owing to the use of heavy charges of explosives at the site. On June 30, 1950, a "fine skull" was blasted out of the deposits. Only slightly crushed, but somewhat damaged in the explosion, the SK 48 specimen contained the right canine, first premolar, and left three molars.

The importance of this cranium, SK 48, was that it added significant knowledge about the distinctive morphology of the robust australopithecines. Considered a female by Broom, SK 48 sports a slight sagittal crest, and in lateral view the zygomatic arches are massive and project far forwards, hiding the sunken nasal area. The canine is quite small, as is the entire region for the incisors, while the posterior teeth are relatively large—a typical robust australopithecine condition.

The Transvaal cave sites were not places of occupation but simply traps that collected bones that fell into them and ultimately fossilized them in very hard cave breccia. The slow process of burial and fossilization often put tremendous pressure on the bones, cracking and distorting them. An excellent example of this can be seen in SK 79, where only portions of the face are preserved (see page 4).

Even in death Broom would not be silenced, for in March 1952, nearly a year after his death, a 123-page monograph entitled *Swartkrans Ape-Man, Paranthropus crassidens*, with numerous drawings and plates, was published as Transvaal Museum Memoir No. 6, authored by Broom and Robinson. Robinson continued to work at Swartkrans for only a year after Broom's death. Fortunately, however, under the able leadership of C. K. Brain, former director of the Transvaal Museum, work began again in 1966. Brain replaced the destructive dynamiting of the cave site. He developed an excavation technique employing metal wedges that were placed in holes drilled into the breccia and driven in with a 16-pound hammer. The resulting breccia blocks were carefully broken using hammers and chisels. When a promising bit of fossil was detected, smaller and more controllable drills were used to remove the breccia.

After 26 years, Brain ceased his excavations at Swartkrans, and in September 1992 the site was declared a National Monument, ensuring its protection.

***Australopithecus robustus*, SK 6.**
Robert Broom named designated this mandible as the type specimen of *Paranthropus crassidens*, and many paleoanthropologists choose to classify all robust australopithecines in the genus *Paranthropus*. Actual size.
Photograph by John Reader, Science Source/Photo Researchers.

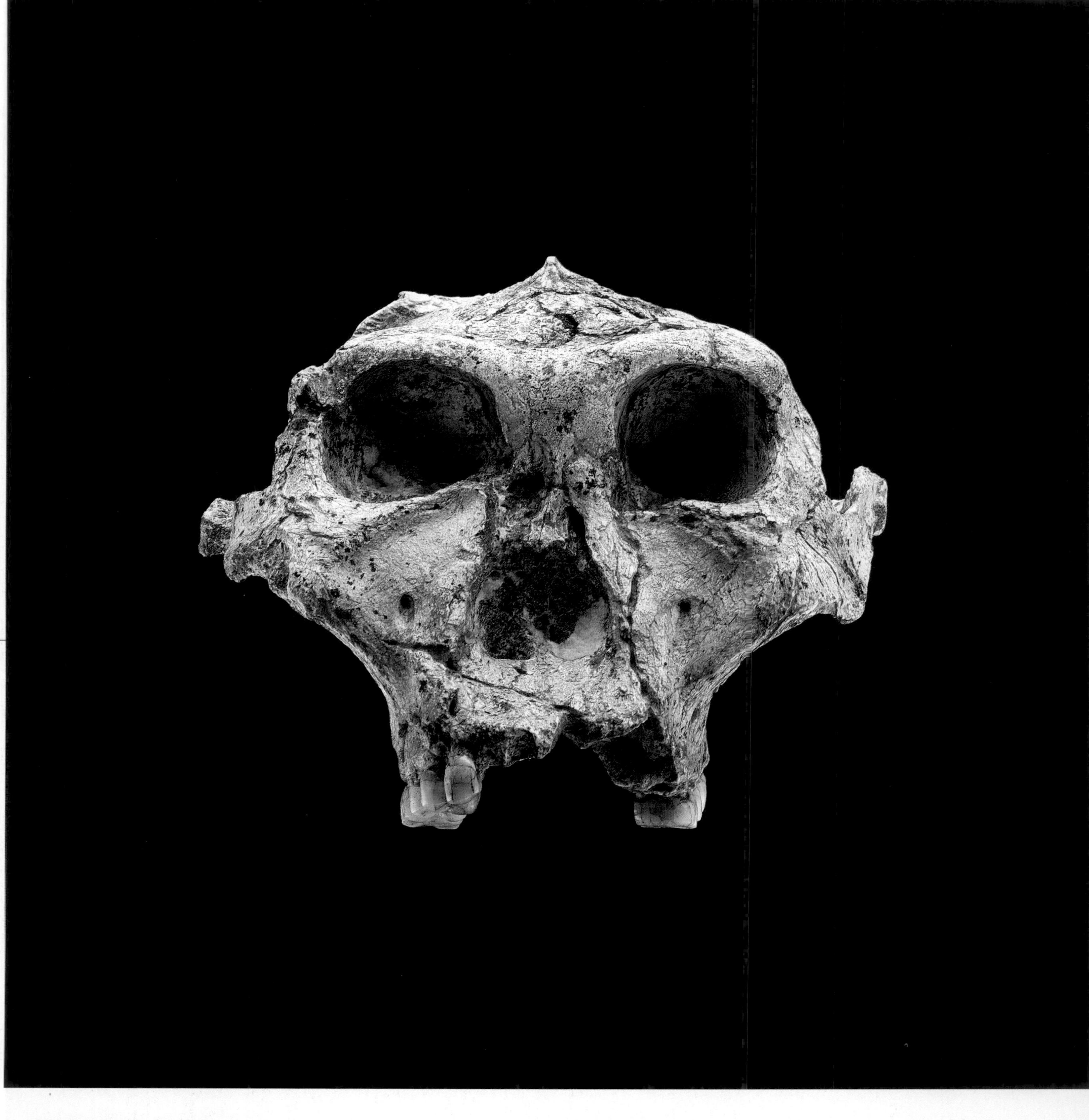

***Australopithecus robustus*, SK 48** (see previous page, and see also page 108). The frontal view (*above*) shows the slight sagittal crest and broad, flat face of this specimen, and the basal view (*opposite*) displays the characteristically small canine and enlarged rear teeth. Actual size. *Photograph by David Brill; courtesy of Transvaal Museum.*

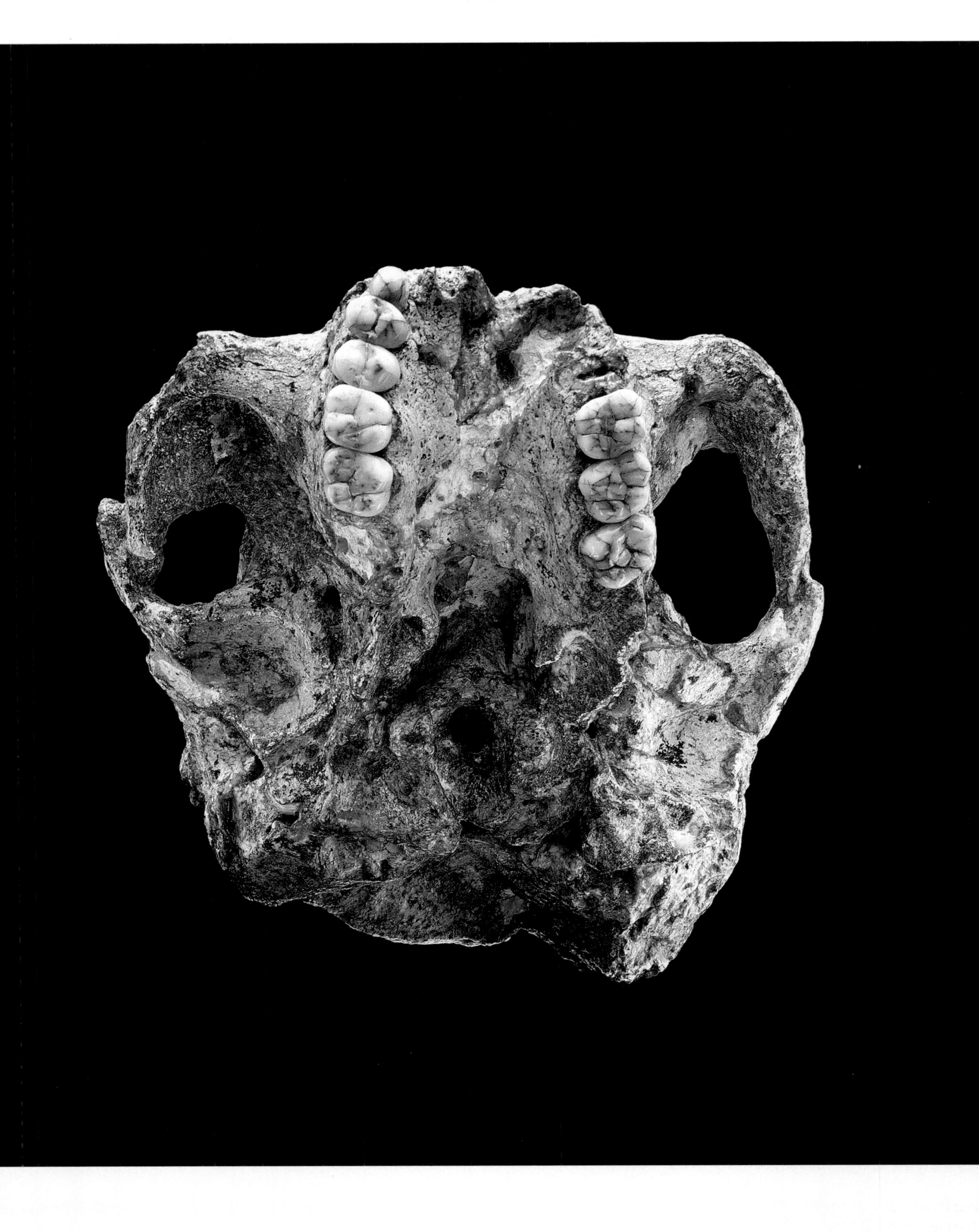

SPECIMEN	LOCALITY	AGE	DISCOVERER	DATE	PUBLICATION
Adult cranium	Lake Turkana, Kenya	2.5 million years	Alan C. Walker	August 29, 1985	Walker, A.C., R.E. Leakey, J.M. Harris, and F.H. Brown. 1986. 2.5-Myr *Australopithecus boisei* from west of Lake Turkana, Kenya. *Nature* v. 322: 517-522.

Australopithecus aethiopicus

KNM-WT 17000 *BLACK SKULL*

The Black Skull, so called because manganese-rich minerals had stained the fossil blue-black, is a dramatic example of species diversity in hominid evolution. Here is a specimen, KNM-WT 17000, recovered from west of Lake Turkana and dated to 2.5 million years, which belongs to a distinct species, *Australopithecus aethiopicus*, and appears to have absolutely nothing to do with our genus, *Homo*. Even though it is not on a direct evolutionary line to modern humans, the Black Skull has much to tell us about the speed of morphological change, the character of that change, and the possibility of multiple lineages in hominid evolution.

The Black Skull is most likely an early example of a very successful group of australopithecines that were geographically widespread and temporally successful but ultimately went extinct. Known as robust australopithecines, these fascinating bipeds developed a host of masticatory specializations, such as massive jaws, huge crushing and grinding cheek teeth, and sometimes sagittal crests, useful in processing vast amounts of low-quality food. The best-known examples are Robert Broom's *Paranthropus robustus*, from South Africa (see page 144), and Louis Leakey's *Zinjanthropus boisei*, from East Africa (see page 156), now both placed in the genus *Australopithecus*.

When the Black Skull was announced, the geometry of the human family tree resembled a Y, with *A. afarensis* as the stem species and ancestral to two divergent lineages: one leading to robust australopithecines and extinction and the other to our own genus, *Homo*. Because of the general lack of fossil hominids in the interval between 2 and 3 million years ago, the discovery of a fairly complete cranium from this time range promised to throw light on this dark period in hominid evolution.

A. aethiopicus possesses a host of primitive features reminiscent of its presumed ancestor, *A. afarensis*. For example, the face is quite prognathic (projecting), the cranial capacity is very small (410 cc), and cresting features, especially on the back of the skull, are typical of *A. afarensis*. On the other hand, there are a number of derived features, such as a prominent sagittal crest, a flat and concave face, and markedly expanded cheek teeth (indicated by the preserved molar and premolar roots), that are characteristic of geologically younger robust australopithecine species.

Interpretations of the amalgam of primitive and advanced features in the Black Skull are divided. The discoverers placed KNM-WT 17000 in *Australopithecus boisei*, choosing to emphasize the few derived anatomical features shared between them. They argued that the lineage of robusts in East Africa was continuous and that to avoid the difficult choice of where to slice the lineage into different species, the Black Skull should simply be considered a more ancient representative of *A. boisei*.

On the other hand, paleoanthropologists William Kimbel, Tim White, and Donald Johanson, from Berkeley, California, compared some thirty-two cranial features observed in KNM-WT 17000 with other species of *Australopithecus* and came to a different conclusion. They noted that whereas only two features were shared with *A. boisei*, twelve were shared with *A. afarensis* (of the remaining, six were shared with *A. africanus, robustus*, and *boisei* and twelve with *A. robustus* and *boisei*).

Based on the strength of the derived robust australopithecine features in KNM-WT 17000, the option of calling it *A. afarensis* was simply not defensible. Furthermore, the argon-argon date of 2.5 million years for the skull placed it midway between *afarensis* and *boisei*. It was therefore concluded that 17000 was deserving of the species name *aethiopicus* . So, how was the name *aethiopicus* chosen for a fossil find from Kenya?

Almost forgotten, an edentulous mandible from the Shungura Formation in southern Ethiopia, west of the Omo River, that had been found in 1967 by a French expedition, suddenly took on new meaning. Initially this 2.5 million-year-old mandible was assigned to *Paraustralopithecus aethiopicus* by French paleontologists Camille Arambourg (now deceased) and Yves Coppens at the Collège de France. They thought the V-shaped jaw, among other features, distinguished it from other robust forms, but the majority of paleoanthropologists ignored the new name. Now resurrected, the Omo 18-1967-18 specimen, although a mandible and therefore not directly comparable with a cranium (17000), provided a species name (the genus designation was dropped) for the spectacular Lake Turkana specimen: *A. aethiopicus*. (see page 155)

Aside from the nomenclatural debates surrounding the find, the evolutionary implications of 17000 are most intriguing. Because of its antiquity it might be an ancestor to *boisei, robustus*, or both species. Even more interesting is the observation that since *A. africanus* does not have the primitive traits seen in *afarensis* and *aethiopicus*, it can no longer be a precursor to all later robusts. This dictates addition of a third branch to the family tree.

It is now probable that *A. africanus* gave rise to *A. robustus* in southern Africa and that *A. aethiopicus* evolved into *A. boisei* in eastern Africa. If this is borne out by further finds, it implies a case of parallel evolution. In other words, robust australopithecines whose ancestors diverged from a common ancestor, *A. afarensis*, subsequently evolved similar adaptations independently, presumably in response to environmental change and subsequent dietary specialization.

There is a thought-provoking ramification of parallel evolution. The evolutionary specialization of the robusts was uncommonly successful in that they survived, over a very large geographic area, for as much as 1.5 million years, yet they met a dead end. Even though their adaptation was highly successful and apparently even arose twice in different lineages, this did not assure survival for the robust australopithecines.

***Australopithecus aethiopicus*, KNM-WT 17000** (see also page 118).
Compared to other robust australopithecines, the striking so-called Black Skull has a very projecting face, seen in lateral view, a tall sagittal crest along the midline of the cranium, and compound bony crests at the rear. Actual size.
Photograph by Robert I.M. Campbell; courtesy of National Museums of Kenya.

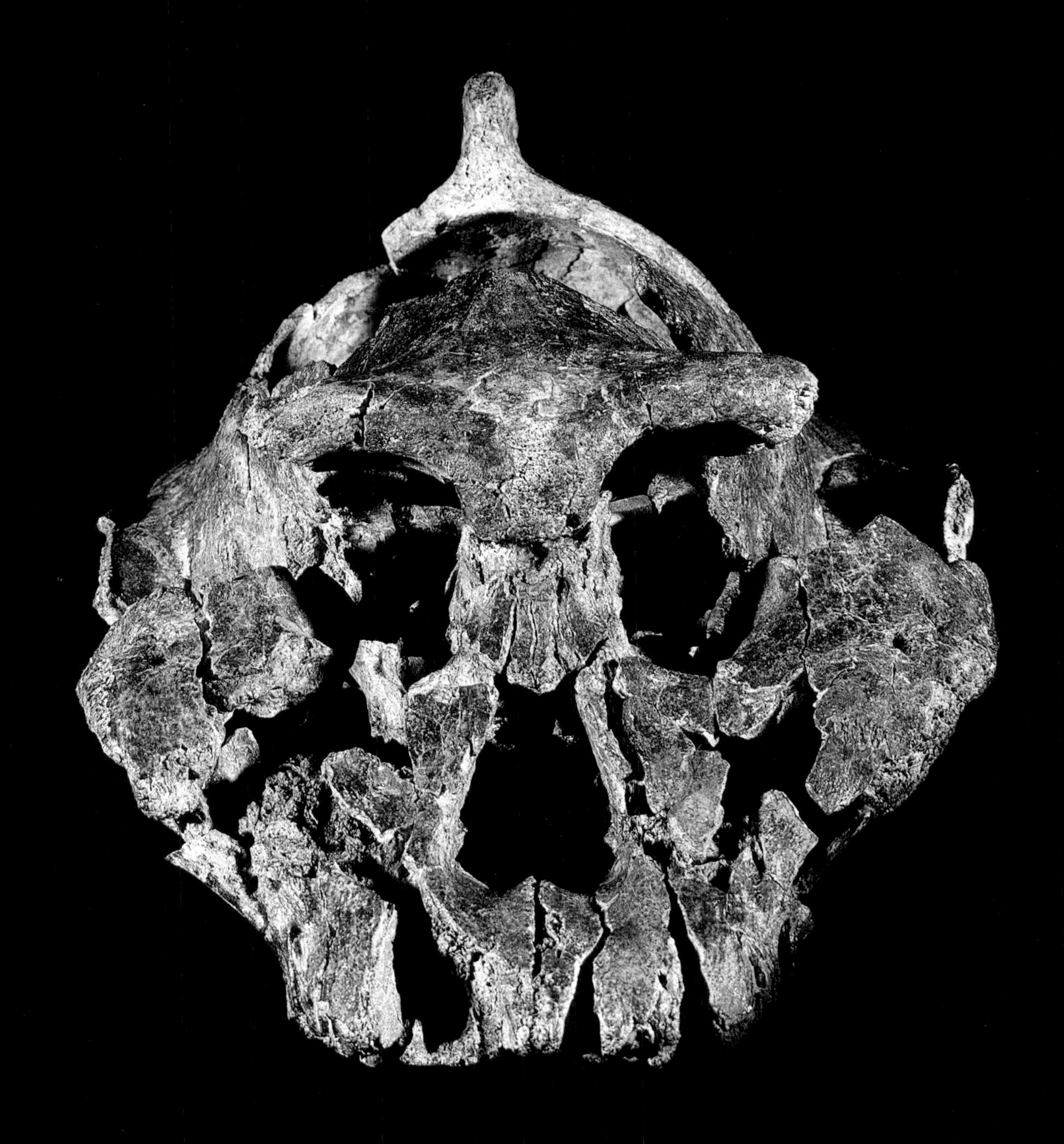

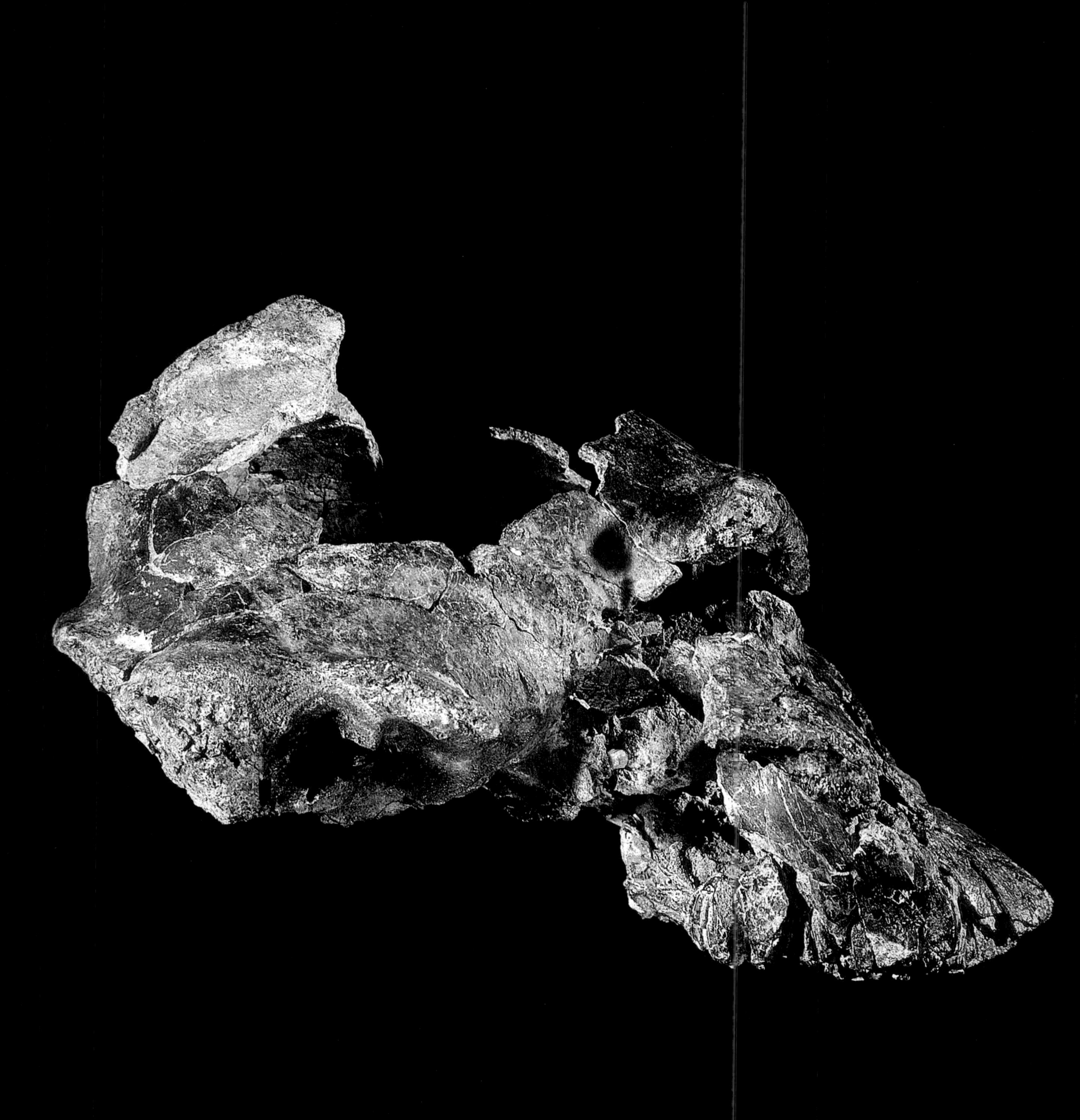

***Australopithecus aethiopicus*, KNM-WT 17000**
(see previous page). Actual size.
Photograph by Robert I.M. Campbell; courtesy of National Museums of Kenya.

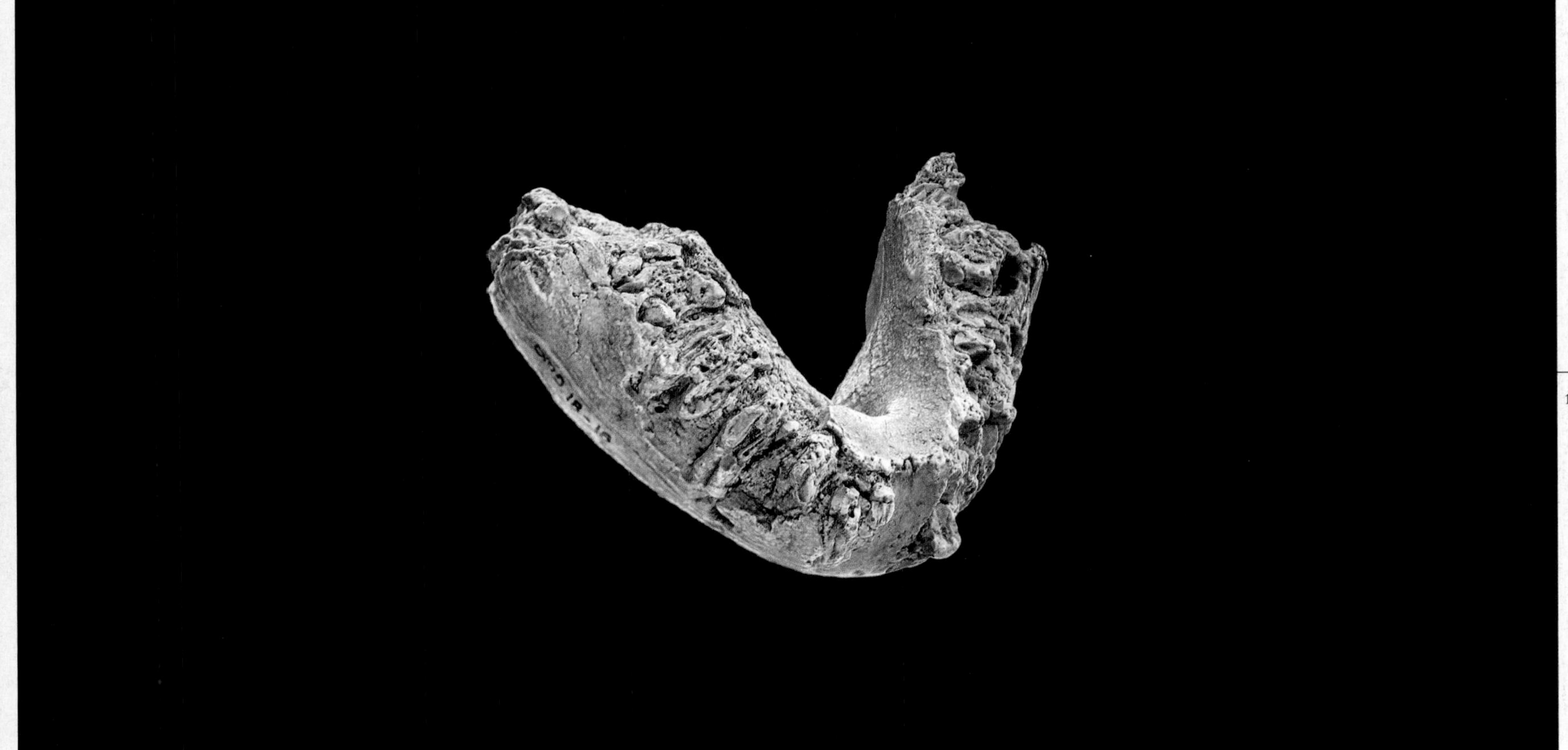

***Australopithecus aethiopicus*, Omo 18 (cast).**
This toothless V-shaped mandible found in Ethiopia in 1967 may belong to the same species as the KNM-WT 17000 cranium, as both specimens are 2.5 million years old. Actual size.
Photograph by David Brill; courtesy of Donald Johanson, Institute of Human Origins.

SPECIMEN	LOCALITY	AGE	DISCOVERER	DATE	PUBLICATION
Adult cranium	Olduvai Gorge, Tanzania	1.8 million years	Mary D. Leakey	July 17, 1959	Leakey, L.S.B. 1959. A new fossil skull from Olduvai. *Nature* v. 184:491-493.

Australopithecus boisei

OH 5 TYPE SPECIMEN *ZINJ · NUTCRACKER MAN*

Too often, important hominid fossil finds lie securely locked away with nothing more than a brief initial announcement in an obscure scientific journal. This was certainly not the case for the type specimen of the species *Australopithecus boisei*, discovered by Mary Leakey in 1959, almost exactly a century after Darwin published *On the Origin of Species*. Soon after its discovery, on the edge of the Serengeti Plain at Olduvai Gorge in northern Tanzania, Mary and her husband Louis Leakey placed the wonderfully complete cranium in the hands of a remarkable anatomist, Professor Phillip V. Tobias. After years of dedicated descriptive, comparative, and interpretive work, in 1967 Tobias published a 264-page monograph on the find, a landmark in paleoanthropology.

Discovery of the celebrated specimen from Olduvai Gorge was a critical event in paleoanthropology. Not only did it launch modern paleoanthropology as a multi-interdisciplinary endeavor (see page 21), but it was the pivotal find that focused attention on East Africa, resulting in a seemingly endless series of hominid discoveries in the Great Rift Valley.

Louis Leakey, virtually the embodiment of human paleontology, believed that humans, large brained and toolmaking, originated millions of years ago. In fact, it was his initial discovery of tools at Olduvai Gorge in 1931 that convinced him that hominid fossils would eventually be found at the site. For Louis, tools were the defining feature of being human. How ironic, then, that the landmark find at Olduvai would be an *Australopithecus*—too small brained and primitive to be the toolmaker.

Most revealing about Louis Leakey's convictions are his first impressions of the skull, which he recorded on July 17, 1959, in a field notebook. Despite the obvious australopithecine features, such as small brain size and a well-developed masticatory system, he called the find *Titanohomo mirabilis* ("miraculous giant man"). Leakey considered the skull "near man," the fabricator of stone tools and therefore our direct ancestor. Some scientists might have accepted the find as the toolmaker, but to Leakey the Olduvai toolmaker could not be an *Australopithecus*.

Less than one month after the discovery, Leakey, as sole author, published in the pages of *Nature* a new genus and species for the Olduvai skull: *Zinjanthropus boisei*. The species name derives from one of Leakey's benefactors, Charles Boise, who helped finance the Olduvai work. Zinj is an old Arabic name for East Africa, and *anthropus* comes from the Greek for "man." Leakey's claim that Zinj was a new genus and a direct ancestor of modern humans generated little support among paleoanthropologists. However, the great geological antiquity of the cranium—at first only thought to be in excess of 600,000 years old, it is now dated to 1.8 million years—its completeness, and the simple fact that stone artifacts derived from the same geological horizons were all reasons to rejoice when Leakey and Zinj made their appearance at the University of Chicago's Darwin Centennial, celebrating the anniversary of *The Origin of Species*.

More than 100 specimens of teeth, mandibles, and some fairly complete crania of *Australopithecus boisei*, as it is now known, have been found in Ethiopia, Tanzania, and Kenya. The oldest of these was unearthed at Omo, Ethiopia, and is dated to about 2.3 million years ago (L. 74a-21, a fragmentary mandible) with the youngest, from Olduvai Gorge, dated to about 1.2 million years (OH 3 and OH 38, isolated teeth).

A. boisei was a truly impressive creature, dominated by a massive skull with a broad, concave face—a face like no other in human evolution. Zinj resembled its cousin in South Africa, *A. robustus*, but *boisei* was "hyper-robust" in cranial adaptations. Although males and females showed marked sexual dimorphism (for example, OH 5 was a male and KNM-ER 732 was a female), the identical masticatory anatomy is diagnostic of both sexes. Males had prominent crests on the skull, especially a longitudinal crest along the skull midline, for anchoring huge temporalis muscles. These are the ones you feel on the side of your skull when you move your jaw up and down. Strong facial buttressing, seen in prominent, flaring cheekbones, projected anteriorly to hide the nasal area in lateral view. The gum-chewing muscles, the masseters, on the side of the face were bulging and massive.

Enormous molars, four times the size of our own, with low cusp relief and fairly flat surfaces were deeply set into the jaws by massive roots. The greatly reduced incisors and canines suggest that slicing and piercing were not significant in eating. To afford enhanced power to the chewing muscles, the mandible, in some instances ten times as thick as our own, was retracted and placed under the braincase, allowing for the production of more powerful vertical forces by the chewing muscles. The repositioning of the mandible and the palate produce a flat, slightly dished face.

The deep, thick mandible is a response to large masticatory forces that were necessary for processing low-quality food. In short, here was a creature in which a craniofacial architecture had been honed over generations to produce the most efficient chewing machine ever—the Cuisinart of human evolution. From the powerful vertical forces evident in the skull and jaw comes this individual's affectionate nickname, "Nutcracker Man."

Louis Leakey's suggestion that Zinj was a distinctive sort of early human ancestor is now universally accepted, even though the genus name, *Zinjanthropus*, has been dropped in favor of *Australopithecus*. Detailed examination of other finds, especially from Koobi Fora, substantiate the unique facial skeleton of *A. boisei*. In a notable study of comparative and functional anatomy, *The Australopithecine Face*, Yoel Rak defined a host of morphological features found in the face that make *boisei* a unique species. The palate is strongly retracted; the zygomatic (cheek) bones have migrated forward, extending into a visor-like support for the masseter muscles; and the supraorbital tori slope away from the midline, giving the face a "sad" expression.

A. boisei was the end point of an evolutionary trajectory that can now be traced back to 2.5 million years ago (see *Australopithecus aethiopicus*, page 152).

Extinction of the robust australopithecines may have been due to changes in the environment that made it more difficult for them to compete with other animals for diminishing food resources. Perhaps the diversification and population increases of baboons were important factors. Or perhaps the robusts were easy prey for the different members of the carnivore guild, which was developing its modern character. C. K. Brain showed that the robusts at Swartkrans in South Africa appear to have often been taken by leopards, as is evidenced in the puncture marks in one cranium from the site. Most likely the robusts made the evolutionary mistake of becoming too specialized, superbly adapted at what they did but not adaptable enough to keep up with the changes around them.

***Australopithecus boisei*, OH 5** (see also pages 5 and 74).
The most famous fossil from Olduvai Gorge, Tanzania, this cranium, nicknamed "Zinj," belongs to a specialized East African hyper-robust australopithecine. Actual size.
Photographs by David Brill; courtesy of National Museum of Tanzania.

SPECIMEN	LOCALITY	AGE	DISCOVERERS	DATE	PUBLICATION
Adult male cranium and adult female cranium	Koobi Fora, Kenya	1.7 million years	Richard Leakey and H. Mutua	1969/1970	Leakey, R. 1970. New hominid remains and early artifacts from North Kenya. *Nature* v. 226: 223-4; Leakey, R. 1971. Further evidence of lower Pleistocene hominids from East Rudolf, north Kenya. *Nature* v. 231: 241-245

Australopithecus boisei

KNM-ER 406
KNM-ER 732

It took the discovery of two important crania, KNM-ER 406 and KNM-ER 732, from Koobi Fora, Kenya, to resolve a controversial hypothesis proposed in the 1960s by University of Michigan anthropologist Milford H. Wolpoff. Wolpoff championed the proposition that all South African australopithecines belonged to a single species. His reasoning was that the differences in tooth size, robusticity, cresting patterns, and facial shape were merely a reflection of sexual dimorphism (size and shape differences seen in the two sexes of one species). For Wolpoff, the males had been assigned to *A. robustus* and the females to *A. africanus.*

There were a number of obvious criticisms of what became known as the single species hypothesis. First, why did all the females (*A. africanus*) live and die at Sterkfontein and all the males (*A. robustus*) at Swartkrans? Second, why did the males wait half a million years to assemble at Swartkrans for a communal death? Despite these obvious problems in interpretation, Wolpoff stressed the high degree of overlap in morphology between *A. africanus* and *A. robustus* and continued to promulgate the single species hypothesis.

A solution to the single species versus multiple species argument required the recovery of an enlarged fossil hominid record from a well-dated geological sequence. The highly fossiliferous deposits east of Lake Turkana in northern Kenya, known as Koobi Fora, fit the bill perfectly, and in 1968 Richard Leakey, director of the National Museums of Kenya, initiated a series of highly successful expeditions to the region. In late August of the next year, Leakey found a virtually complete but edentulous cranium. The specimen, KNM-ER 406, although partially encased in sandstone, exposed sufficient anatomy to warrant placement in *A. boisei*, initially named after Olduvai Hominid 5 (see page 156).

KNM-ER 406 shares with OH 5 the following anatomical features: (1) sagittal and nuchal crests; (2) a deep palate with massive tooth roots and presumably very large cheek teeth; (3) a dish-shaped face that was astonishingly wide (due to the flaring cheekbones) but short in height; (4) just behind the thin supraorbital tori, a frontal bone that is severely pinched (postorbital constriction), and immediately above the nasal bones, a projecting area known as the glabella, behind which is a flattened area called the frontal trigone; (5) a heart-shaped foramen magnum (as is also seen in OH 5); and (6) the root of the zygomatic (cheekbone) placed far forward over the second upper premolar.

Evidence for bone disease is relatively rare in early hominids, but KNM-ER 406 has a small, round hole on the frontal bone, just behind the left orbit. Apparently this was a pathology of some sort and may have been a metastatic abscess.

In 1970 a partial cranium catalogued as KNM-ER 732, sometimes referred to as a demicranium since a large portion of the left half is missing, was found at Koobi Fora in geological deposits identical in age to the 1.7 million-year-old KNM-ER 406 specimen. Although clearly smaller in size and lacking the sagittal and nuchal crests of KNM-ER 406, the 732 cranium otherwise displayed the suite of anatomical traits typical of *A. boisei.* These features include: (1) a prominent glabella, (2) a frontal trigone, (3) a dish-shaped face, (4) a forwardly placed zygomatic root, (5) a very wide face, owing to the flaring zygomatics, and (6) strong postorbital constriction. Both crania have thin vault bones, typical of the australopithecines, with reconstructed cranial capacities of 510 cc for KNM-ER 406 and 500 cc for KNM-ER 732.

Employing the great ape model of sexual dimorphism, in which male chimps and, especially, male gorillas have larger, more heavily built crania than females, it is possible to assess the differences between KNM-ER 406 and 732. These two crania share an overwhelming number of anatomical characteristics. Those absent in KNM-ER 732, such as sagittal and nuchal crests, are precisely those missing in female great ape skulls. Therefore, the most parsimonious explanation of the difference in size between these two specimens is that KNM-ER 406 is a male and KNM-ER 732 is a female *A. boisei.*

In large part it was the recovery of these two crania from Koobi Fora that demonstrated without doubt the presence of sexual dimorphism in the australopithecines. Employing this model of sexual dimorphism seen in *A. boisei*, it was possible to reexamine the South African australopithecine sample. This resulted in two important conclusions: first, the anatomical differences between the Sterkfontein and Swartkrans samples were more marked than those seen in a single species such as *A. boisei*, and second, at each of these sites in South Africa, male and female specimens could be identified using as a guide the differences in size and rugosity seen in KNM-ER 406 and 732. The single species hypothesis was now effectively dead.

***Australopithecus boisei*, KNM-ER 406.** Note the flat face, enormous arching cheek bones, and prominent crest atop this male robust australopithecine cranium. Actual size. *Photograph by David Brill; courtesy of National Museums of Kenya.*

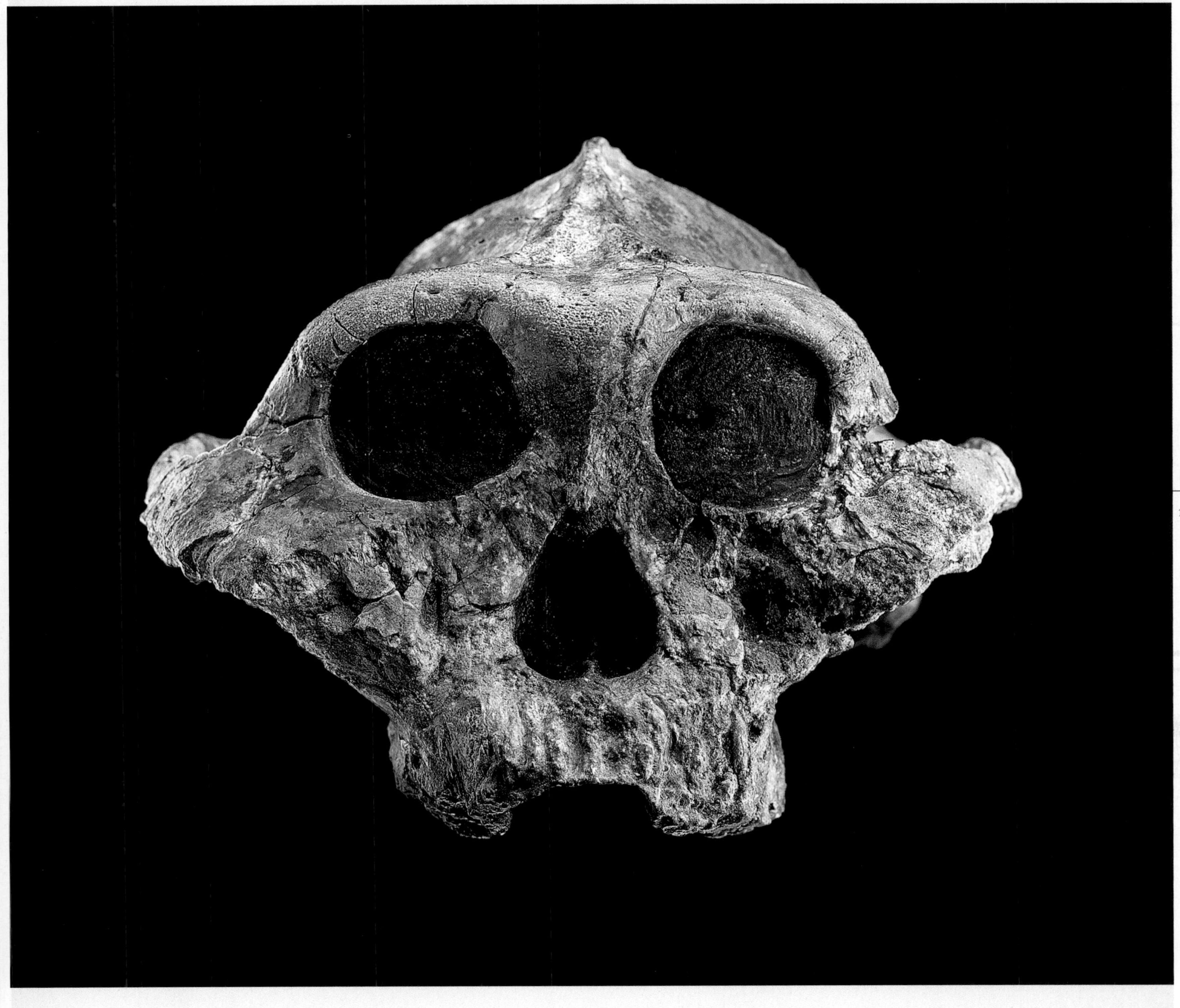

***Australopithecus boisei*, KNM-ER 406**
(see previous page). Actual size.
Photograph by David Brill; courtesy of National Museums of Kenya.

***Australopithecus boisei*, KNM-ER 732.**
In a case of strong sexual dimorphism, an apparent female cranium of the same species has a similar brain size but much smaller facial features and no crests. Actual size.
Photograph by David Brill; courtesy of National Museums of Kenya.

HOMO

For decades since its initial discovery in 1924, our understanding of *Australopithecus* greatly overshadowed knowledge of our own genus, *Homo*. Until the early 1960s, the oldest known species of *Homo* was *Homo erectus*, named by Dutch anatomist Eugène Dubois following his 1891 find of a skullcap in Java. What is emerging now as a result of discoveries of *Homo* fossils, particularly in East Africa, is a more comprehensive look at the diversity of early *Homo* during Pliocene and Pleistocene times (roughly 1.5 to 2.5 million years ago). At long last the significant temporal and morphological gap separating *H. erectus* and the australopithecines is beginning to be bridged. Yet at this stage of our understanding, because of the paucity of specimens, paleoanthropologists are far from agreeing on the roots and diversity of early *Homo*.

The australopithecines are characterized as having relatively small brains, large cheek teeth, a postcranial skeleton with some apelike features, and an absence of culture. In contrast, species of the genus *Homo* have relatively and absolutely large brains, a more modern postcranial skeleton, a significant reduction in tooth and jaw size, and, most important, culture.

The first mention of an early *Homo* in Africa that was distinct from *Homo erectus* came in 1964 with the announcement of *Homo habilis* from Olduvai Gorge, Tanzania. For the type specimen, Louis Leakey, Phillip Tobias, and John Napier chose Olduvai Hominid (OH) 7, a mandible associated with parts of the cranial vault and some postcranial bones. Although their landmark paper drew attention to features different from *Australopithecus* such as the narrow cheek teeth and a human-like foot, their main reason for putting the Olduvai hominids into *Homo* was brain expansion. Until their article appeared in *Nature*, a cerebral Rubicon of anywhere between 700 and 800 cc had existed as the lower limit for the genus *Homo*. But in order to include the Olduvai specimen in *Homo*, which had an estimated cranial capacity of 680 cc, Leakey, Tobias, and Napier lowered the cerebral Rubicon to 600 cc. They also stressed a nonanatomical rationale for placing OH 7 in *Homo*—the presumed ability of these hominids to manufacture the stone tools found at the site. With this in mind it was Raymond Dart, author of *Australopithecus*, who suggested the name *habilis*, which implies "able, handy, mentally skilful [sic], vigorous," resulting in the popular moniker for the species, "handy man."

The overwhelming emphasis placed on the supposed cultural abilities of handy man in defining a species did not sit well with many paleoanthropologists. A major objection was that another hominid, *A. boisei*, a robust australopithecine, was already known from the same 1.8 million-year time stratum that had yielded the *habilis* material, and many critics thought it impossible to determine which hominid was responsible for the tools. According to most paleoanthropologists, the naming of a species should rest on its anatomical distinctiveness and not on presumed cultural abilities.

Louis Leakey led the charge on this issue, for not only did he believe that "man makes tools" but, even more important, that "tools maketh man." *Habilis* was his man, and by the time of his death, in 1972, Louis Leakey had embraced the idea that *H. habilis* led directly to *H. sapiens*, putting *H. erectus* onto a side branch.

Acceptance of *H. habilis* was far from universal, with some researchers more willing to expand the definition of *Australopithecus* to include the Olduvai specimens and others thinking they were simply earlier representatives of *Homo erectus*. Additional discoveries from Olduvai, the Lake Turkana basin, and South Africa bolstered the notion of early *Homo*. Especially strong vindication came in 1972, when a fairly complete cranium, KNM-ER 1470, was recovered east of Lake Turkana (formerly Lake Rudolf) at Koobi Fora in northern Kenya. Unfortunately, the teeth were not preserved, but with a cranial capacity of just over 750 cc, nearly everyone accepted 1470 as evidence of *Homo* at approximately 1.9 million years, roughly equivalent to the age of *H. habilis* at Olduvai Gorge.

Other important Pliocene-Pleistocene *Homo* specimens include a lightly built mandible (KNM-ER 992) and a small toothed cranium (KNM-ER 1813), also from Koobi Fora, which were assigned to *H. habilis*. Some specimens, like the wonderfully complete adolescent male skeleton (KNM-WT 15000) and two crania (KNM-ER 3733 and 3883), were judged to have affinities with *Homo erectus*.

Not everyone thought that these specimens fell comfortably into *habilis* or *erectus*. Australian anthropologist Colin Groves and his Hungarian colleague Vratislav Mazák concluded in 1975 that the KNM-ER 992 mandible, because of its very small cheek teeth, belonged to a new species, *Homo ergaster*. An obvious reference to the stone tools found in the same geological horizon as the mandible, *ergaster* is from the Greek for "workman". Recognizing this species designation, University of Liverpool anatomist Bernard Wood, an expert on early *Homo*, now includes KNM-WT 15000 and KNM-ER 3383 and 3733 in *H. ergaster*.

By announcing 1470 as *Homo*, but not placing it in a species, Richard Leakey, then director of the Kenya National Museums, left the door open for someone to assign it to a new species. This happened in 1986, when a Russian anthropologist, Valerii Alexeev, selected 1470 as the type specimen for a new species, *Homo rudolfensis* (he called it *Pithecanthropus rudolfensis*, but the genus name, no longer in use, was replaced by *Homo*). In spite of the incompleteness of Alexeev's description and his unfamiliarity with the original specimen, the name has stuck and is now in common usage.

An interesting new wrinkle in the understanding of *H. habilis* came in 1986 with the recovery of a partial skeleton at Olduvai Gorge, OH 62. Although very fragmentary, OH 62 presents the first definitive association of upper and lower limbs of *H. habilis*, which, surprisingly enough, indicate that the body build was rather apelike. The arms are relatively long compared to the legs, reminiscent of the condition in *A. afarensis* and very unlike the modern body build paleoanthropologists had envisioned.

The KNM-WT 15000 *H. ergaster* skeleton has, in contrast a postcranial skeleton that is modern-like in size and proportions. Unfortunately, the postcranial skeleton of *H. rudolfensis* is largely unknown, with the possible exception of two large femurs (KNM-ER 1482 and 1471). The size variation in early *Homo* has also been interpreted as representing sexual dimorphism, with the smaller specimens (*habilis*) being female and the larger ones (*rudolfensis*) male. Other detailed studies of facial and cranial anatomy suggest that KNM-ER 1813 and KNM-ER 1470 are too distinct to belong in a single species.

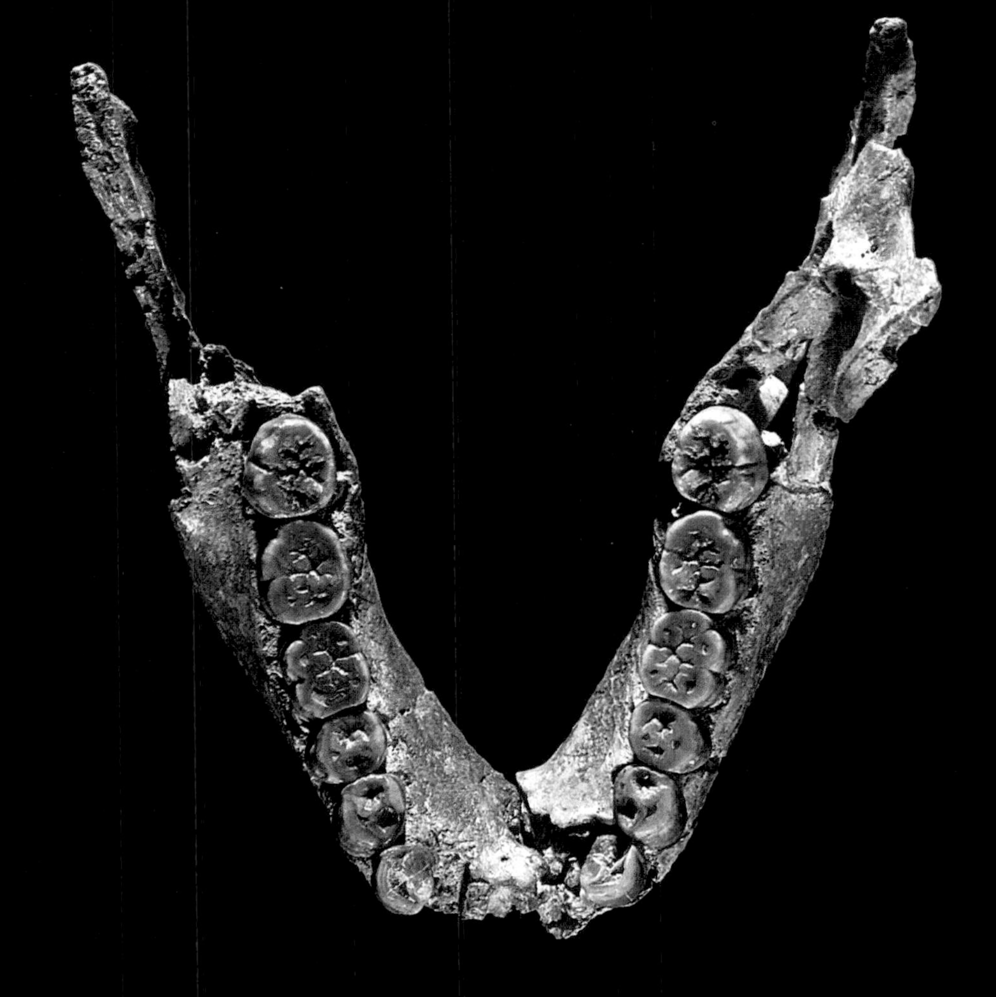

***Homo ergaster*, KNM-ER 992.**
Based on the small size of its teeth, this partial mandible became the type specimen for the species *Homo ergaster*, which is also represented by the cranium KNM-ER 3733 and the skeleton KNM-WT 15000. Actual size.
Photograph by Robert I.M. Campbell; courtesy of National Museums of Kenya.

The current appreciation of early *Homo* in Africa suggests three plausible species. *Homo habilis* shows brain expansion relative to its small body size, but its postcranial skeleton is quite *Australopithecus*-like. A second species, *Homo rudolfensis*, with substantial brain expansion, has cranial features like pneumatization (large air cells in certain areas like the mastoid), a broad midface, large cheek teeth (as judged from the tooth roots), and relatively thick dental enamel—characteristics that are also *Australopithecus*-like. The third species, *Homo ergaster*, now acknowledged to be distinct from *H. erectus*, possesses a combination of a modern body build, large absolute and relative brain size, reduced teeth and jaws, and an apparent posture and locomotor abilities more like those of later *Homo*. Bernard Wood has concluded that *H. ergaster* is the most likely choice of an ancestor to later species of *Homo*.

For the moment, the evolutionary roots of *Homo* are still poorly understood, but they will ultimately be found in pre-2 million-year-old deposits. Despite the widely held view that *A. africanus* makes a good candidate for ancestor to *Homo*, equally convincing arguments can be mounted to support a unique link between *africanus* and *A. robustus* (see page 38). Should this be the case, then the three species of Pliocene-Pleistocene *Homo* are without an identifiable predecessor.

From the Pliocene (before 2 million years ago), there are precious few specimens attributable to *Homo*. Claims for early *Homo*, dated to roughly 2.5 million years, have been made for specimens from Lake Baringo, Kenya (a temporal bone), Uraha, Malawi (a mandible), and Sterkfontein, South Africa (a partial cranium). But there is a general lack of agreement as to the dating of these specimens. The oldest well-dated specimen of *Homo* is A.L. 666-1 (see page 168), from Hadar, Ethiopia at 2.3 million years. This maxilla is not identical to any named species of *Homo*, but it does have affinities with *H. habilis*. Perhaps the A.L. 666-1 maxilla, 400,000 years older than other previously well-dated *Homo* specimens will lead the way toward clarifying the origins of our own genus.

Should further discoveries substantiate the presence of more than one species of early *Homo*, it may then be the case that *Homo* underwent an adaptive radiation. From the temporal distribution of the three proposed species, it would appear that *H. rudolfensis* is the most ancient, followed by *H. habilis* and finally *H. ergaster*. The evolutionary relationships between these three species and the Hadar *Homo* are extremely difficult to ascertain because of the relatively few specimens known for early *Homo*.

If *H. ergaster* gave rise to the later *Homo* species *heidelbergensis, neanderthalensis*, and *sapiens*, there is a considerable temporal gap between the most recent *ergaster*, at about 1.5 million years, and the oldest *heidelbergensis*, at about 0.8 million years. This gap is occupied by what is customarily referred to as *H. erectus*, but some paleoanthropologists, such as Ian Tattersall, of the American Museum of Natural History, suggest that *erectus* is too specialized to be an ancestor to modern peoples.

Homo heidelbergensis was long relegated to the dustbin, after having been named by Otto Schoetensack in 1908, based on the mandible from Mauer, near Heidelberg, Germany. The specimen lacks an exact geological age but it is a strong candidate for being among the oldest hominids in Europe, at about half million years. Other specimens that might reasonably be assigned to *H. heidelbergensis* include Arago, in France, Atapuerca, in Spain, Petralona, in Greece, Kabwe and Bodo, in Africa, and perhaps Steinheim, in Germany, and Ndutu, in Tanzania. Neandertals, with their distinctive anatomy, are considered here to be a separate species, *Homo neanderthalensis*, which died out around 30,000 years ago.

Modern humans, *Homo sapiens*, probably arose in Africa between 200,000 and 100,000 years ago. This species is the only surviving hominid species of the genus, in fact the last surviving member of the zoological family the Hominidae. (Ironically, *Homo sapiens* is the only hominid species for which there is no type specimen.) Acceptance of a relatively recent origin for *sapiens*, the so-called "out of Africa" model (see page 46), implies that the Asian *H. erectus* is not an ancestor to modern-day *Homo*.

This short review of the genus *Homo* serves to stress the complexity in the evolution of this genus. This is particularly true for the very earliest stages of the genus, when its evolution has customarily been thought to be uncomplicated and straightforward. Species diversity within *Homo* again draws attention to the view that the evolution of modern humans is not a directional or unilineal process but, as for other mammalian groups, one that exhibits branching and diversification. It is now necessary to dedicate as much attention to understanding the diversity in the genus *Homo* as has been afforded *Australopithecus*.

***Homo erectus*, Peking Man reconstruction.** A third of the known fossils from this species come from the site of Zhoukoudian, China, but most of the original specimens, including those used in this reconstruction, have been lost. Actual size.
Photograph by David Brill; courtesy of American Museum of Natural History.

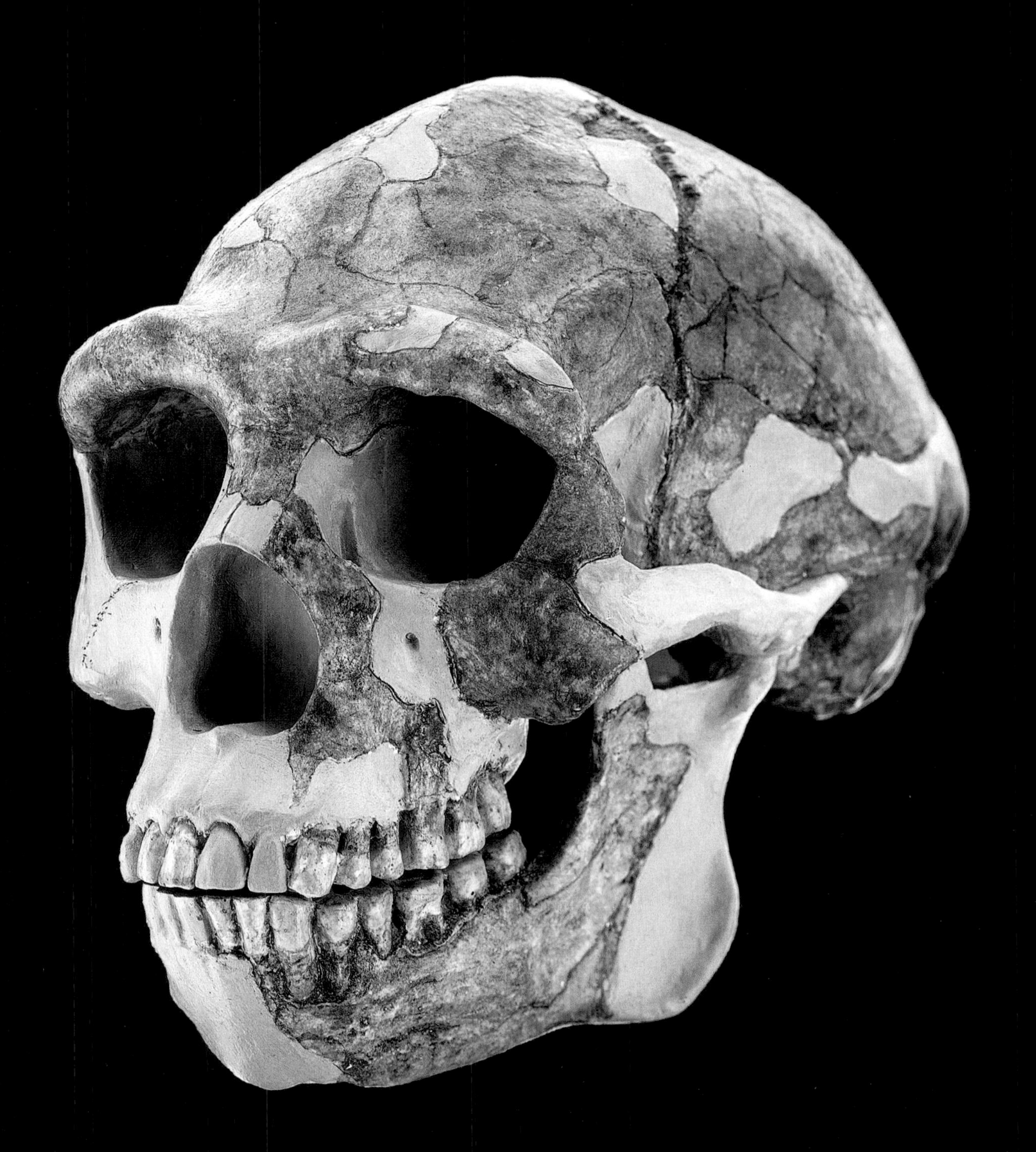

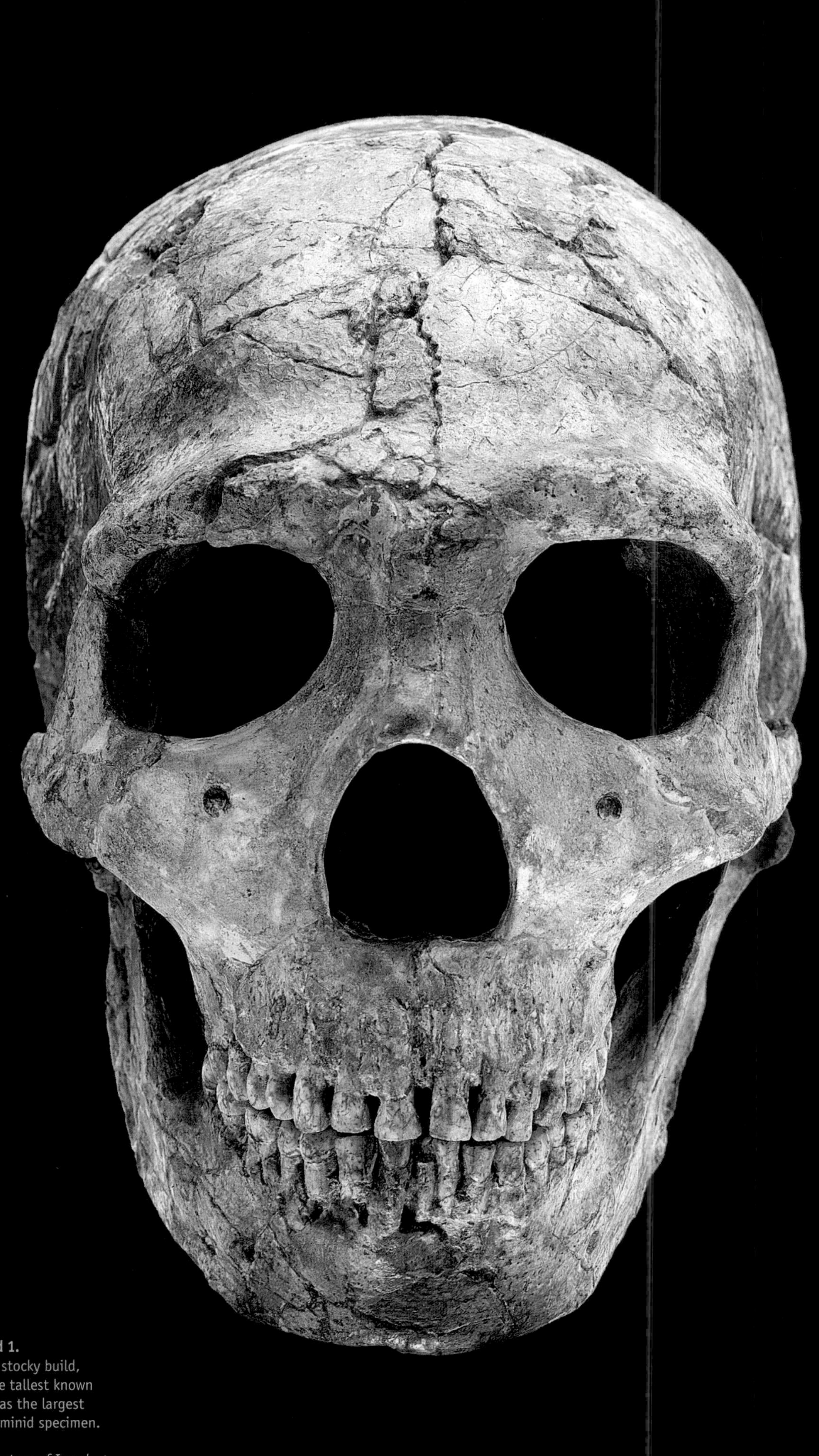

***Homo neanderthalensis*, Amud 1.**
Neandertals tended to have a stocky build, but the Amud 1 skeleton is the tallest known individual—1.8 meters—and has the largest brain capacity of any fossil hominid specimen. Actual size.
Photograph by David Brill; courtesy of Israel Antiquities Authority, Rockefeller Museum.

***Homo sapiens*, Cro-Magnon I.**
Skeletons excavated from the French rock-shelter of Cro-Magnon have come to characterize, at least in popular literature, the earliest modern humans in Europe. Actual size.
Photograph by David Brill; courtesy of Musé de l'Homme.

SPECIMEN	LOCALITY	AGE	DISCOVERERS	DATE	PUBLICATION
Adult maxilla	Hadar, Ethiopia	2.3 million years	Ali Yesuf and Maumin Allahendu	November 2, 1994	Kimbel, W.H., R.C. Walter, D.C. Johanson, J.L. Aronson, Z. Assefa, G.G. Eck, E. Hovers, C.W. Marean, Y. Rak, K.E. Reed, C. Vondra, T. Yemane, D. York, Y. Chen, N.M. Evensen, and P.E. Smith. 1996. Late Pliocene *Homo* and Oldowan tools from the Hadar Formation (Kada Hadar Member), Ethiopia. *J. Hum. Evol* 30 in press

Homo sp.

A.L. 666-1

A surprising discovery was made at Hadar, Ethiopia, on November 2, 1994, when an unprepossessing hominid maxilla (upper jaw) was collected in an area called the Makaamitalu. Unlike the 323 other hominid specimens from Hadar, all of which have been attributed to *Australopithecus afarensis*, this specimen, catalogued as A.L. 666-1, had a distinctive parabola-shaped dental arch that immediately identified it as belonging to *Homo*.

The maxilla, found in two halves, was cleanly broken along the midline (intermaxillary suture), allowing the two parts to be easily fitted back together. The initial find was made on the slope of a steep knoll by Ali Yesuf and Maumin Allahendu, two Afar members of the Hadar Research Project from the Institute of Human Origins in Berkeley, California. Some thirty pieces of tooth crowns and roots as well as bits of the maxilla itself were recovered during careful surface collection and sieving operations at the locality. These pieces were all fitted back into the maxilla and included the right canine to first molar and left lateral incisor to second molar.

The anatomy of the 666 specimen is clearly distinct from other maxillas from Hadar assigned to *A. afarensis*. In *afarensis* the maxilla is shallow and narrow with a rectangular dental arch, and there is marked prognathism (projection) below the nasal opening. In contrast, the 666 maxilla is relatively deep and wide with a bowl-shaped dental arch and exhibits only slight prognathism. Notably these features in the 666 specimen are common in species recognized as *Homo* rather than *Australopithecus*.

Also scattered on the side of the knoll where the maxilla was found were some twenty manufactured stone flakes and cores (see page 90). These artifacts were very fresh with sharp edges, and, like the maxilla, presumably had not been on the surface long. Made predominantly of basalt and chert, the tools are most similar to those classified in the Oldowan industry, named after initial finds made at Olduvai Gorge, Tanzania.

A 2-square-meter excavation was made into the knoll in an attempt to locate the precise horizon from which the maxilla and artifacts came. In a layer of silt identical to the silt matrix adhering to the maxilla, a total of fourteen additional artifacts, similar to those on the surface, and three bone fragments were recovered. In patina and color these bones match the maxilla. In addition, a fossilized root cast in the sinus of the maxilla resembles the numerous root casts found in the excavation. It is therefore highly likely that the surface material came from the same horizon that yielded the in situ artifacts and bone fragments.

Geological studies of the locality in which 666 was found confirm that the artifact-bearing level is situated roughly 80 centimeters below a well-dated volcanic ash known as BKT-3. A very precise date of 2.33 ± .07 million years for BKT-3 was determined utilizing the single-crystal laser fusion technique (see page 26).

A date of 2.3 million years for the 666 maxilla is significant because no other occurrence of *Homo* in Africa is definitely dated to older than 1.9 million years. (An older date of 2.5 million years for a mandible from Malawi is imprecise because it is based on associated vertebrate species that range over a considerable time period.) The anatomy of A.L. 666-1 is not identical to other species of *Homo*: *habilis*, *rudolfensis*, or *ergaster*. When more complete remains are found at the site, it will be possible to determine if the maxilla belongs to one of these species or perhaps a new one.

The importance of the A.L. 666 discoveries at Hadar is that this is the oldest known definitive association of hominid remains with stone tools and the oldest well-dated evidence for the genus *Homo*. Further finds of *Homo* will add substantially to our understanding of the roots of our own genus.

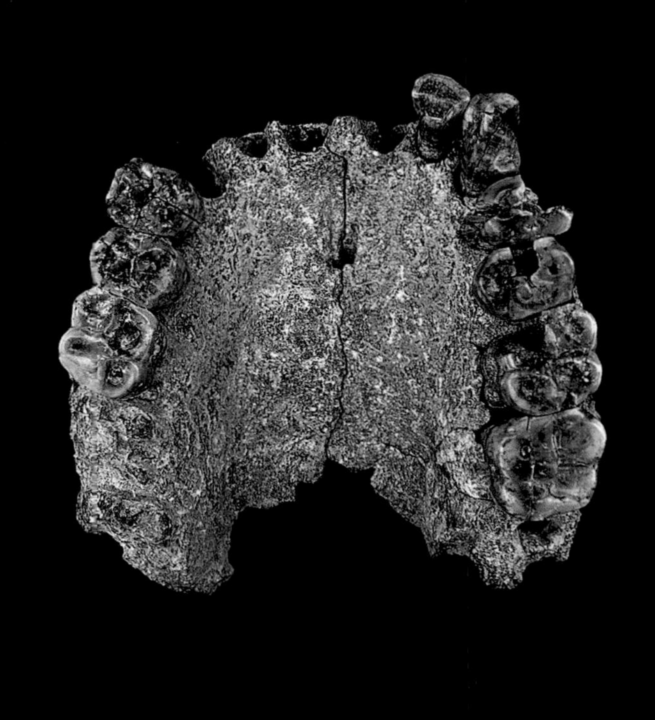

Homo **sp., A.L. 666-1 (*top*) and *Australopithecus afarensis*, A.L. 200-1 (*bottom*).**
Two maxillae from Hadar, Ethiopia show very different features. The more narrow, rectangular specimen with a shallow palate belongs to *A. afarensis*, while the more recently discovered fossil is a new species of *Homo*. Actual size.
Courtesy of Donald Johanson, Institute of Human Origins; and National Museum of Ethiopia

Homo **sp., A.L. 666-1 (*top*) and *Australopithecus afarensis*, A.L. 200-1 (*bottom*).**
A lateral view reveals further differences between these specimens, particularly the less projecting alveolar region of the *Homo* maxilla, which is the oldest well-dated fossil of our genus. Actual size.
Photograph by William Kimbel, Institute of Human Origins; courtesy of National Museum of Ethiopia.

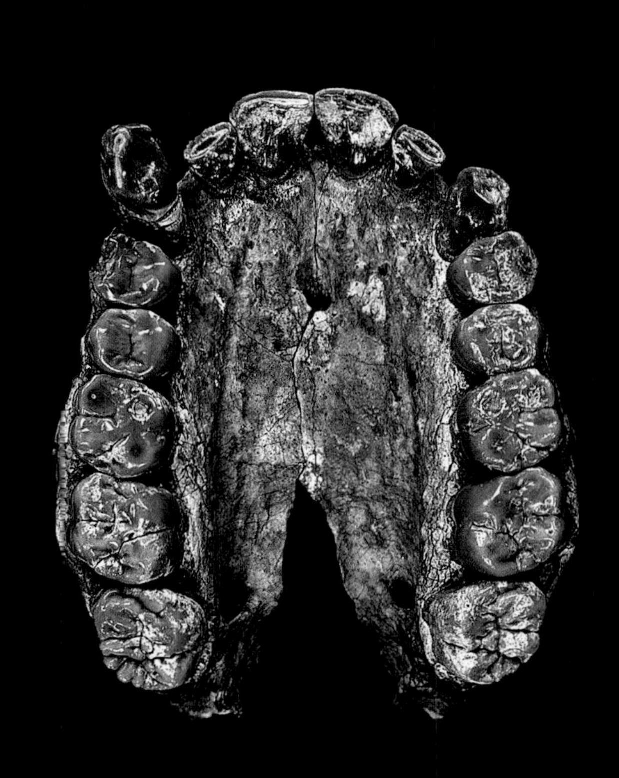

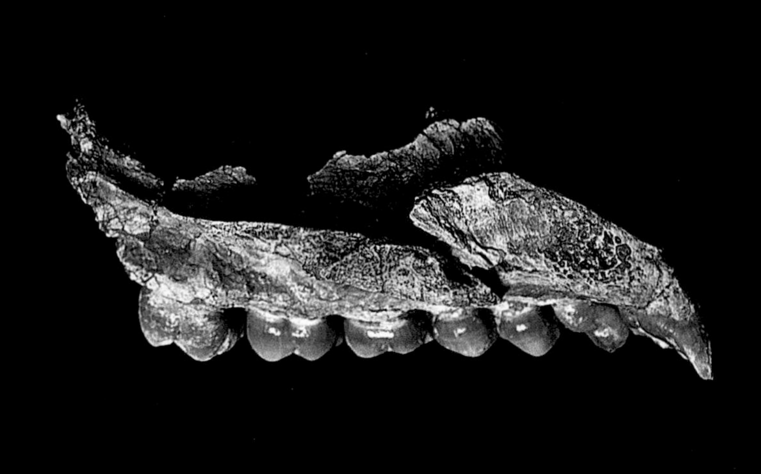

SPECIMEN	LOCALITY	AGE	DISCOVERER	DATE	PUBLICATION
Juvenile male partial skeleton	Olduvai Gorge, Tanzania	1.75 million years	Jonathan Leakey	November 4, 1960	Leakey, L.S.B., P.V. Tobias, and J.R. Napier. 1964. Recent discoveries of fossil hominids in Tanganyika; at Olduvai and near Lake Natron. *Nature* 202(4927): 7-9

Homo habilis

OH 7 TYPE SPECIMEN

OH 7 serves as the holotype for *Homo habilis*: the definitive single specimen used to describe the distinguishing attributes of this species, which has traditionally been placed at the root of our genus, *Homo*. The story of its discovery and analysis illustrates the process of naming a new hominid species and the obstacles that often block scientific acceptance of the new name.

The specimen consists of two dozen bones and fourteen teeth that, judging from their proximity, similar size, and lack of duplication, come from the same individual: a nearly complete left parietal bone, a fragmented right parietal, most of the mandibular body, and all of the lower teeth, from the incisors back to the right first molar and left second molar. Twenty-one finger, hand, and wrist bones and an upper molar, all found nearby, probably come from the same skeleton, a juvenile that died at the age of ten to twelve years. OH 7 was nicknamed "Jonny's Child" in honor of the discoverer, Louis and Mary Leakey's oldest son.

Although OH 7 was selected to represent its species, it was not the first *Homo habilis* fossil found at Olduvai Gorge. In 1959 Heslon Mukiri, one of the Leakeys' fossil hunters, came across a molar and premolar at another site in Bed I, the oldest of Olduvai's major geological deposits. Weeks after Mukiri's discovery, however, Mary Leakey uncovered the spectacular OH 5 cranium (see page 156), a find that temporarily overshadowed the significance of the two teeth. With the discovery of OH 7 in 1960, attention again turned to the apparent presence of a more gracile hominid that lived contemporaneously with the robust australopithecine represented by OH 5 and that may have made the site's many Oldowan stone tools instead of OH 5. (The more complete OH 7 became the holotype for *H. habilis*, and the two teeth and a mandibular fragment were designated OH 4.)

Louis Leakey informally referred to the OH 7 bones as "pre-*Zinjanthropus*," but he quickly became convinced that the fossils belonged to an early form of *Homo*. To help describe the bones, he enlisted paleoanthropologist Phillip Tobias and anatomist John Napier, who remained more cautious in their conclusions until detailed study could be made. Tobias noted the parietals' large size and determined that OH 7 had possessed a significantly larger brain than had *Australopithecus africanus* or *A. boisei*, yet much smaller than the brain of *Homo erectus* from Java and China. From a partial endocast, Tobias obtained a cranial capacity of 363 cc and estimated that the total cranial capacity would have been around 674 cc, or 50 percent larger than the average for six *A. africanus* crania.

Establishing such an obvious difference in brain size was a first step toward designating a new species. Further clues came from the teeth, the shape of which fell outside the known range for *A. africanus* and came much closer to later members of *Homo*. The incisors of OH 7 were relatively large compared to both *Australopithecus* and *H. erectus*. The premolars and molars appeared too narrow and elongated to belong to any australopithecine. The hand bones also more closely resembled other species of *Homo*, as did a nearly complete set of foot bones recovered nearby but from a different skeleton.

The combined evidence from three distinct parts of the skeleton, then, pointed toward this specimen being something new and different. Additional fossils found at Olduvai late in 1963—the specimens OH 13, 14, 15, and 16—clinched the argument that a second hominid species had lived beside *A. boisei*. In January 1964, more than three years after the discovery of OH 7, Leakey, Tobias, and Napier announced their new species of *Homo* with a name suggested by Raymond Dart, who had named the genus *Australopithecus* almost forty years earlier. *Homo habilis* means "handy man," a reference to this species's presumed aptitude for toolmaking.

After the name was published, several prominent anthropologists challenged its validity. The new fossils, they argued, were not distinct enough from *Australopithecus africanus* (or, alternatively, from *Homo erectus*) to be a separate species, but rather were some sort of subspecific variety. Other names and interpretations were introduced and debated, but *habilis* eventually became accepted in the late 1970s by a majority of paleoanthropologists. In large measure, acceptance came after discovery of the 1470 cranium (see page 177), which, ironically, has since been convincingly proposed as belonging to a second species of early *Homo*.

***Homo habilis*, OH 7.**
This mandible is one of two dozen bones from a juvenile skeleton found at Olduvai Gorge, Tanzania, that comprise the type specimen of this species. The relatively large incisors and narrow premolars and molars provided dental clues that this was a new kind of hominid. Actual size.
Photograph by John Reader, Science Source/Photo Researchers.

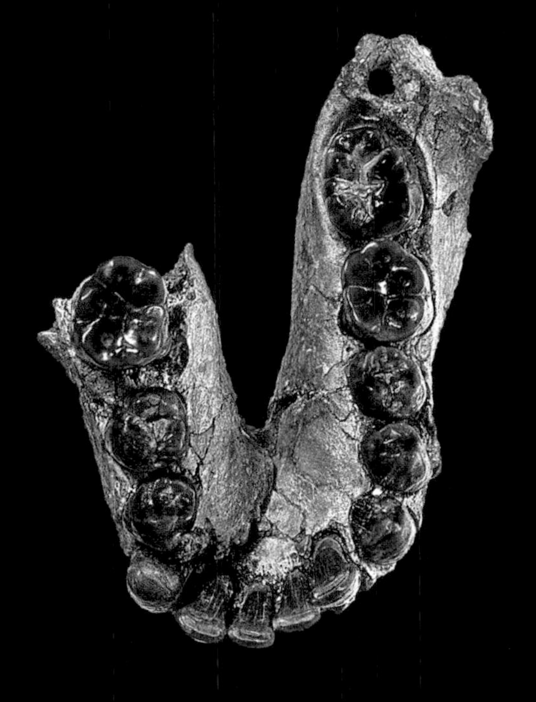

SPECIMEN	LOCALITY	AGE	DISCOVERER	DATE	PUBLICATION
Adult female cranium	Olduvai Gorge, Tanzania	ca. 1.8 million years	Peter Nzube	October 1968	Leakey, M.D., R.J. Clarke, and L.S.B. Leakey. 1971. New hominid skull from Bed I, Olduvai Gorge, Tanzania. *Nature* 232:308-312

Homo habilis

OH 24

Having enough distinctive fossil evidence is an important first step toward designating a new hominid species. For those scientists who considered it hasty to name the species *Homo habilis* from more fragmentary cranial fossils such as OH 7 (see page 170), this specimen provided important corroborating evidence for the species's validity. We include it here for that reason, and because it constitutes the oldest hominid from Olduvai Gorge and, with the exception of OH 5 (see page 156), the most complete cranium ever found there.

When it was found the fractured and collapsed braincase, cemented together with a coating of limestone, gave little hint of the specimen's value. Paleoanthropologist Phillip Tobias, co-author of the paper announcing *habilis*, remarked, on seeing the fossil, "Only Twiggy has been that flat!" The British model's name stuck as a nickname for OH 24.

Paleoanthropologist Ron Clarke's prolonged and painstaking reconstruction with dental pick, drill, and hammer restored as much of the original anatomical form as possible to OH 24. More than 100 tiny fragments could not be put back into place, and the cranium remains somewhat distorted. The top is still flattened, and the base is depressed around the foramen magnum. Behind the browridges, the vault should rise more vertically than it does. Despite these shortcomings, the specimen can still tell us a lot about this hominid.

All the cranial bones are thin and lack the robusticity that tends to characterize australopithecine crania. Relative to australopithecines, the braincase has expanded from side to side, so that OH 24 approaches the striking parietal breadth of OH 7 (see page 170), but these bones of the braincase are shorter vertically than those of the *habilis* type specimen. The cranial capacity of OH 24 falls just under 600 cc, the minimum value for *Homo*, but the low estimate is probably due to the cranium's distortion.

The increased size of the braincase was countered by a reduction of the face, a pattern that continued with our species. From a short and relatively straight upper face, the maxilla of OH 24 slopes forward, imparting a hollowed profile like the face of *Australopithecus africanus* (see Sts 5, page 134), although it is less projecting than in that species. The face approaches that of *A. boisei* in breadth but is not nearly so flat as a robust's face.

Tooth crowns and roots in this specimen are small. The missing incisor and canine teeth probably eroded down the slope where the fossil was found long before its recovery. Two premolars and five molars have been preserved. Judging from the state of tooth eruption—the third molars had recently erupted and show no trace of wear—this individual was an adolescent or young adult at death.

In features of both the cranium and the teeth, OH 24 resembles more closely the specimen OH 13 than the presumed male specimen OH 7, even though OH 24 is closer in geological age to the latter. The sides of the cranium in OH 24 are clearly smaller than the parietal bones in OH 7. This suggests that the anatomy of early *Homo* incorporated significant individual and sexual variation.

Homo habilis, OH 24.
Although it is heavily reconstructed, this cranium constituted important additional evidence in support of *Homo habilis* being a valid species. Actual size.
Photograph by David Brill; courtesy of Institute of Human Origins.

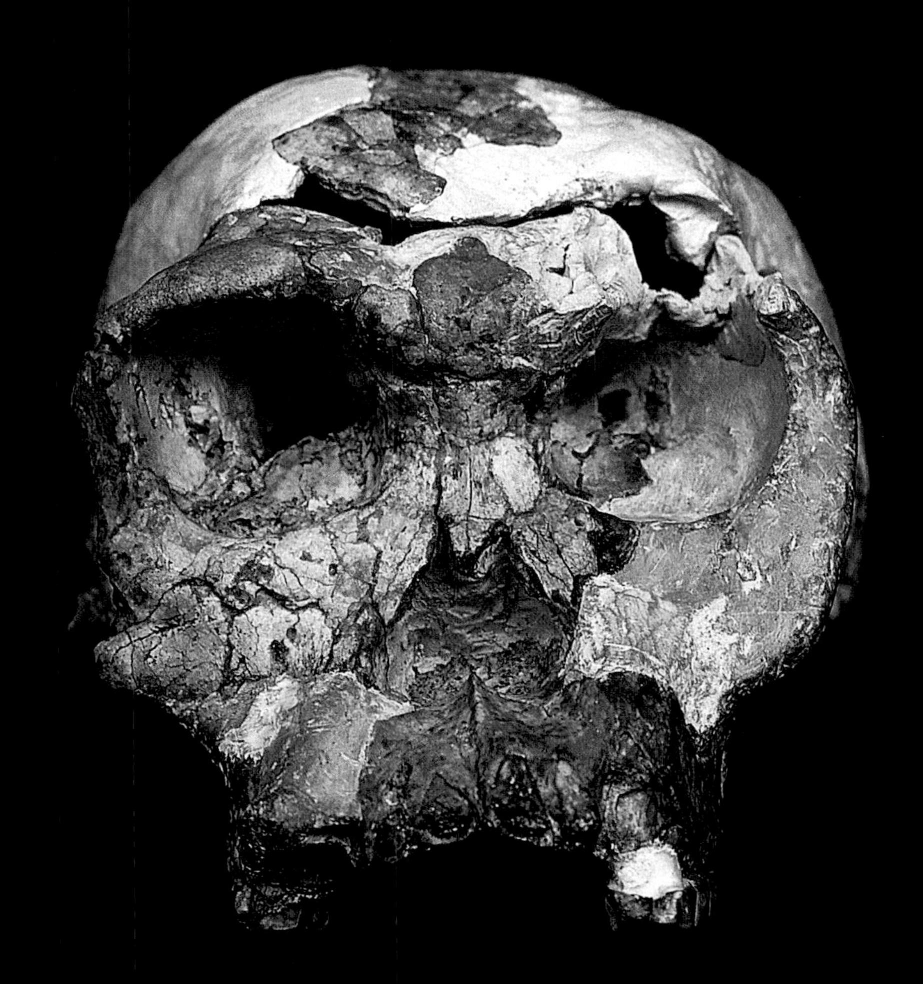

SPECIMEN	LOCALITY	AGE	DISCOVERER	DATE	PUBLICATION
Adult cranium	Koobi Fora, Kenya	1.9 million years	Kamoya Kimeu	1973	Leakey, R.E.F. 1974. Further evidence of Lower Pleistocene hominids from East Rudolf, North Kenya, 1973. *Nature* 248:653-656

Homo habilis
KNM-ER 1813

The discovery of a diminutive cranium at Koobi Fora posed a dilemma disproportionate to the specimen's size. A year earlier, KNM-ER 1470 (see page 177) had been found, revealing that a large-brained, large-faced, big-toothed species of *Homo* had inhabited Koobi Fora close to 2 million years ago. Then came this specimen of essentially equal antiquity and with a similar bell-shaped braincase but with a small face, small teeth, and a much smaller brain. Its small size was not due to immaturity, for the third molar had fully erupted and shows wear.

Could 1813 be a female of the same species as the male 1470, as some have suggested, or is the story more complicated? Although their obvious size differences make it likely that 1470 and 1813 represent respectively a male and female, it is increasingly unlikely that they belong to the same species. The differences in braincase size, facial size and shape, and overall robusticity are too great to ignore or to be explained by sexual variation. Instead, there were at least two species of early *Homo*, only one of which survived and led to *Homo erectus* and later to modern humans.

The smallest of the several hominid crania found at Lake Turkana, 1813 also has a slightly smaller brain capacity than any of the Olduvai *Homo* fossils. Its brain volume was about 510 cc (just above the australopithecine average and below the generally accepted cutoff point of 600 cc for *Homo*), compared to 1470's cranial capacity of 775 cc.

Although the nasal bones of this specimen have been crushed and the entire face is skewed somewhat to the left from its true anatomical position, the right side of the face is mostly complete. The upper jaw is particularly well preserved, with an intact set of left teeth from the canine to the third molar. Both the short, lightly built face and the small, arched, and rounded supraorbital torus are quite distinct from 1470's anatomy. A peculiar rounded protuberance on the back of the 1813 cranium may be the beginning of a transverse torus, as occurs in *Homo erectus*, so this feature could link 1813 with later species of *Homo*.

Although it can be readily contrasted with 1470, 1813 can be more easily compared to the less complete Olduvai crania generally included within *Homo habilis*. In size and shape, the teeth of 1813, as well as the palate and parts of the skull, strongly resemble those of OH 13. The 1813 cranium also shows affinities with the crushed cranium of OH 24 (see page 172): both are of similar overall size and have a short face, small eye sockets, nasal bones and cheekbones placed low on the face, and a projection of the face beneath the nasal opening. The dimensions of the parietal and occipital bones are similar in all three specimens.

Because of these similarities, we have opted to include KNM-ER 1813 in *Homo habilis*, following the classification of paleoanthropologist Bernard Wood. Richard Leakey initially concluded that 1813 was closest to the South African species *Australopithecus africanus*. He has more recently avoided putting a taxonomic label on 1813 other than to say that it and OH 13 should not be called *Homo habilis*, a name he applies to the 1470 cranium. But anatomy and stratigraphy support the idea that 1813 belongs in *habilis* and that this species—on the basis of facial proportions and the shape of the cheekbones and browridge, among other features—makes a better ancestor than *rudolfensis* does to all later species of *Homo*, including modern humans.

***Homo habilis*, KNM-ER 1813** (see also page 6). Similar in size and appearance to OH 24, this cranium from Koobi Fora, Kenya has been placed in the same species. The small face, teeth, and braincase of this specimen distinguish it from other Koobi Fora crania, which belong to two different species of early *Homo*. Actual size.
Photograph by David Brill; courtesy of National Museums of Kenya.

SPECIMEN	LOCALITY	AGE	DISCOVERER	DATE	PUBLICATION
Partial adult skeleton	Olduvai Gorge, Tanzania	1.8 million years	Tim D. White	July 21, 1986	Johanson, D.C., F.T. Masao, G.G. Eck, T.D. White, R.C. Walter, W.H. Kimbel, B. Asfaw, P. Manega, P. Ndessokia, and G. Suwa. 1987. New partial skeleton of *Homo habilis* from Olduvai Gorge, Tanzania. *Nature*. 327: 205-209

Homo habilis

OH 62

After decades of painstaking research at Olduvai Gorge, Mary Leakey retired from fieldwork to complete scientific publication of her excavations. The untiring efforts of Louis and Mary Leakey assured that no stone would be left unturned in the search for fossil and archeological clues in this canyon, cut into the flat and generally featureless Serengeti Plain of Tanzania. After each rainy season, the slopes and gullies of the gorge were systematically searched for any new evidence that might have come to the surface as a result of erosion. Owing to the compacted and lightly cemented Olduvai deposits, erosion was slow, and after so many years of surface survey the chances of making an important discovery like *Zinjanthropus* were vanishingly small.

This was the setting when the Institute of Human Origins was invited to assist the Tanzanian Department of Antiquities in reopening work at Olduvai in 1985. The team was well aware of the odds against making a significant find. However, late in the afternoon of July 21, 1986, only three days into the expedition, a hominid fossil was found in an area of the gorge immediately adjacent to a dirt road that had led literally tens of thousands of tourists and scientists into the gorge.

Northern Tanzania, especially Ngorongoro Crater and the Serengeti, draws an endless stream of tourists who come on safari to observe and photograph African animals. On this tourist circuit lies the gem of Olduvai Gorge. After a visit to a small museum detailing the work at Olduvai, guides lead tourists into the gorge to visit localities where the Leakeys made important discoveries, such as the "Zinj" site where a stone plinth marks the exact spot of discovery.

How ironic that sitting on the surface of the ground, a mere 25 meters off the road, was a highly fragmented, 1.8 million-year-old partial skeleton. After recognition of the first fragment of the skeleton, a proximal right ulna, a major effort was put into an arduous search for additional skeletal elements. Because it was the sixty-second hominid to be found at Olduvai, the specimen was given the designation Olduvai Hominid 62, or OH 62. Screening of all the loose sediments in the immediate area resulted in the recovery of more than 18,000 bone and tooth fragments over an area of about 40 square meters. Most of these were non-hominid remains, but 302 were identified as belonging to OH 62.

Compared with a skeleton like Lucy or the Black Skull, OH 62 was scrappy. The teeth were hopelessly splintered into such tiny fragments that, with few exceptions, it was not possible to reassemble a complete tooth crown. It was equally impossible to reassemble the cranial vault fragments into anything even remotely resembling a skull. However, portions of a right arm, including most of a humerus and parts of the ulna and radius, were recovered. Part of the left femur was also recovered, including the femoral neck and some of the shaft. Most important, thirty-two fragments were successfully glued together to form most of the maxilla, or upper jaw.

It was the maxilla that permitted identification of OH 62. This portion of the facial skeleton most closely resembled specimens from Olduvai and elsewhere that had been assigned to *Homo habilis*. Because of this, as well as the complete lack of robust australopithecine specializations, such as megadont molars, OH 62 was attributed to *H. habilis*.

OH 62 represents the first time that upper and lower limb elements of *H. habilis* were securely associated. The third molar had erupted, and from the heavily worn occlusal surfaces of the teeth it was clear that OH 62 was a relatively old adult. From the diminutive size of the limb bones, especially the femur, which is even smaller than Lucy's, it was postulated that OH 62 was a female. In fact, OH 62 may be the smallest adult fossil hominid ever found, with an estimated stature of about 1 meter.

The most startling aspect of OH 62 became evident when body proportions were calculated for the upper and lower limbs. Fairly accurate estimates of total limb length for the humerus and the femur, both incomplete, could be calculated. The humerofemoral index of 95 percent indicated that the humerus was 95 percent the length of the femur: a very long arm. In modern humans this index is roughly 70 percent, while in a quadruped like a chimpanzee it is 100 percent (that is, the humerus and femur are of equal length). Such apelike proportions for *Homo habilis* were unanticipated.

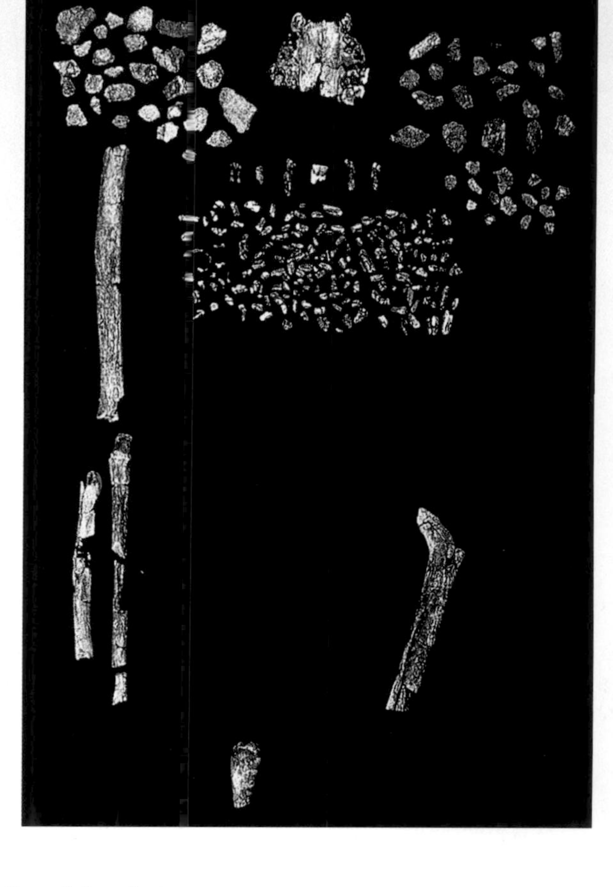

***Homo habilis*, OH 62.**
Partially pieced together from more than 300 fragments, this tiny skeleton permitted an estimate of body proportions which revealed that this hominid had very long arms compared to its legs, like Lucy and African apes. *Courtesy of Donald Johanson, Institute of Human Origins.*

It was previously thought that in *H. habilis*, body proportions would be more modern. The implication was clear: this specimen, OH 62, had limb proportions reminiscent of the primitive condition seen in *A. afarensis* (Lucy). If *H. habilis* was to be considered an ancestor to *H. ergaster/erectus* at 1.6 million years old, then not only would body size have to increase rather considerably, but the relationship between upper and lower limbs would also have to change dramatically. All this would have had to occur over a mere 200,000 years of time. Not an impossibility, but evolution would have had to have been fairly rapid.

OH 62 raises a number of additional important issues. If this is a female *Homo habilis*, as postulated, which other hominids in East Africa represent the males? If the larger femora (KNM-ER 1471 and 1482) from Lake Turkana are from male individuals, then sexual dimorphism is on par with that seen in *A. afarensis*—something that had not been anticipated. The discovery of OH 62 has added to the confusion surrounding the diversity in early *Homo* (see page 162). According to Bernard Wood, an anatomist at Liverpool University, England, *H. habilis*, as classically represented by finds at Olduvai Gorge, appears to represent a species distinct from *H. ergaster* and *H. rudolfensis*. Although it appears that early *Homo* may be more speciose than formerly appreciated, the sorting out of the different species will have to await recovery of more complete *Homo* specimens, ideally with cranial and postcranial elements preserved in the same individuals.

SPECIMEN	LOCALITY	AGE	DISCOVERER	DATE	PUBLICATION
Adult cranium	Koobi Fora, Kenya	1.8 to 1.9 million years	Bernard Ngeneo	August 1972	Leakey, R.E.F. 1973. Evidence for an advanced Plio-Pleistocene hominid from East Rudolf, Kenya. *Nature* 242: 447-450

Homo rudolfensis

KNM-ER 1470 TYPE SPECIMEN

The famous cranium of KNM-ER 1470, which graced the cover of Richard Leakey and Roger Lewin's best-selling book *Origins*, brought Richard Leakey instant fame and vindicated Louis Leakey's belief that a large-brained species of *Homo* inhabited East Africa millions of years ago. Louis, who saw the specimen only four days before he died, carried to his grave the deep-seated conviction of his teacher, Arthur Keith, that our genus had a great antiquity dating back millions of years, and he refused to accept an ancestral role in our lineage for any australopithecine. Although often seen as the epitome of *Homo habilis*, the species Louis helped name and that was dearest to his heart, 1470 may deserve a new identity and reveal a more complicated pattern of evolution in the early days of *Homo*.

In his initial description of the fossil, Richard Leakey chose to label 1470 an indeterminate species of *Homo* rather than include it within *Homo habilis*, primarily because it was thought to be 2.9 million years old, or a million years older than the *habilis* fossils from Olduvai Gorge. This age was based on an estimate of 2.6 million years for the KBS Tuff, a volcanic ash layer at Koobi Fora that lay above the specimen. But it turned out that the age initially calculated for the tuff was made inaccurate by samples contaminated by older volcanic rocks; the real age was only 1.8 million years, and suddenly KNM-ER 1470 became the same age as *Homo habilis*.

The cranium was reconstructed from more than 150 fragments by zoologist Meave Leakey into two major pieces that constitute the specimen's most striking features: a large braincase and a broad, flat face. Some have pointed out minor features of the face and cranial shape that could link this specimen to *Australopithecus*, but the bulk of its traits and a brain volume of 775 cc support its placement within *Homo*. Whether 1470 really belongs within *habilis* has become a matter of heated debate.

Compared with the smaller Koobi Fora cranium KNM-ER 1813 (see page 174), for instance, there is only a slight supraorbital torus across the forehead with no sulcus or depression behind it; 1470's face is much longer, with the upper part narrower than the middle, and the upper jaw is squared off rather than rounded, with a very short, shallow palate. The cranium lacks the crests and heavy muscle markings that characterize australopithecine skulls. Although its tooth crowns were not preserved, the remaining roots and sockets reveal that this individual had very large incisors and canines and moderate premolars and molars.

Other features of 1470's anatomy are a marked constriction of the braincase behind the eye sockets (but less than occurs in robust australopithecines), a bulging frontal bone that rises steeply to meet the square parietal bones forming the thin-walled sides of the braincase, and an occipital bone that is smoothly rounded rather than flexed as in *Homo erectus*.

What features 1470 shares with *habilis* occur in other species of *Homo*, and we have already noted several important differences between 1470 and *habilis* that apparently are not due to sex, time, or geography. If the smaller specimens from Olduvai and Koobi Fora constitute *Homo habilis*, then perhaps 1470 belongs to a separate species.

In 1986, the scientific name *Homo rudolfensis* was proposed by Valerii Alexeev for KNM-ER 1470. This new species has been identified with a few fossils recovered from Koobi Fora in sediments from the slim slice of time between 1.9 and 1.8 million years ago. Other specimens attributed to *Homo rudolfensis* include the cranial remains KNM-ER 1590 and KNM-ER 3732, and the lower jaw KNM-ER 1802. By acknowledging 1470 as a separate species, we concur with the view that at least two species of early *Homo* lived contemporaneously in East Africa. The evolution of *Homo* was not a simple linear story from *habilis* to *erectus* to *sapiens*, and we must now decide whether *habilis* or *rudolfensis* makes a more likely ancestor for the rest of our lineage.

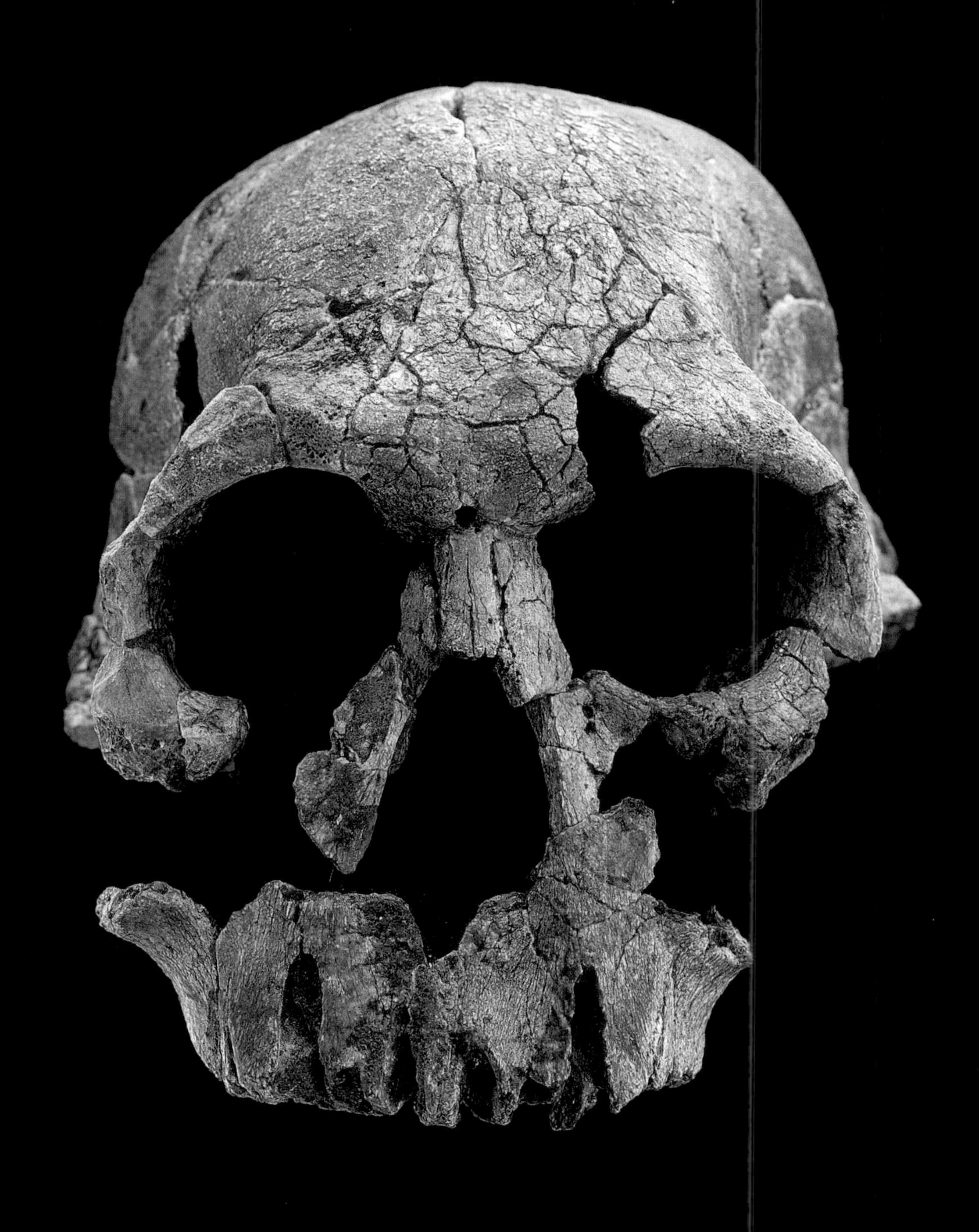

***Homo habilis*, KNM-ER 1470** (see previous page).
Compared to the cranium KNM-ER 1813, of similar age and found at the same site, this specimen, seen here in frontal and lateral views, has a long, flat face, a short, squared palate in the upper jaw, and a much larger cranial capacity. Actual size.
Photographs by David Brill; courtesy of National Museums of Kenya.

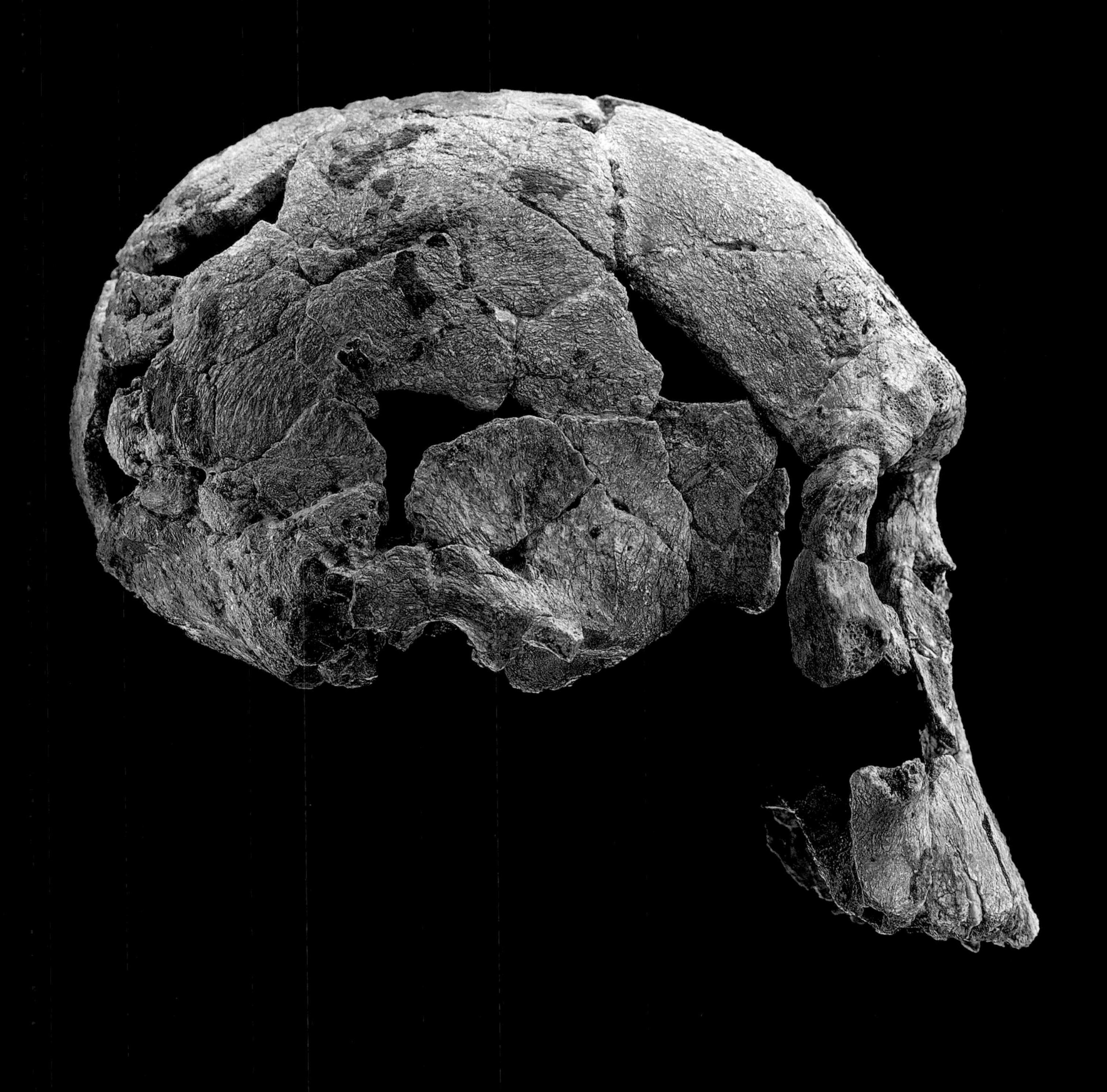

SPECIMEN	LOCALITY	AGE	DISCOVERER	DATE	PUBLICATION
Adult cranium	Koobi Fora, Kenya	1.75 million years	Bernard Ngeneo	1975	Leakey, R.E.F. 1976. New hominid fossils from the Koobi Fora formation in Northern Kenya. *Nature* 261:574-576

Homo ergaster
KNM-ER 3733

The exquisitely well-preserved cranium of *Homo ergaster*, KNM-ER 3733, confirmed the coexistence of *Homo* with robust australopithecines in East Africa and thus mooted the single species hypothesis for human evolution (see page 53). Until the 1984 excavation of the KNM-WT 15000 skeleton (see page 182), KNM-ER 3733 was the best example of this species. The double-arched browridge atop the eye sockets barely protruded from the ground, but that was enough for Bernard Ngeneo, a member of the "Hominid Gang" of Kenyan fossil finders. The fragmented remains of the face and upper jaw were unearthed nearby, but the lower jaw was never found.

Because the anatomical features of the face are markedly less robust than those of the juvenile male KNM-WT 15000, found on the opposite side of Lake Turkana, the 3733 cranium can be identified as a female with confidence. It had also reached maturity, a conclusion based on the closed sutures between the cranial bones, the degree of dental wear, and the eruption of the third molars.

From the side, KNM-ER 3733 displays the low cranial vault profile characteristic of Asian *Homo erectus*, as well as a swelling or keeling along the midline atop the cranium, a round torus across the occipital bone at the rear, and a cranial base wider than the top of the cranium. In overall size, 3733, with a brain capacity of 850 cc, compares with the Zhoukoudian specimens (see page 188), and the sides of the braincase are flattened instead of arching as in modern humans. However, 3733 does lack some features that characterize *Homo erectus* in Java and China, including thick skull bones, an angular torus, and an obvious sulcus, or depression, behind the browridge. Such differences may warrant placing this and other African fossils in a separate species, *Homo ergaster*, which was originally named for another fossil from Koobi Fora, the mandible KNM-ER 992.

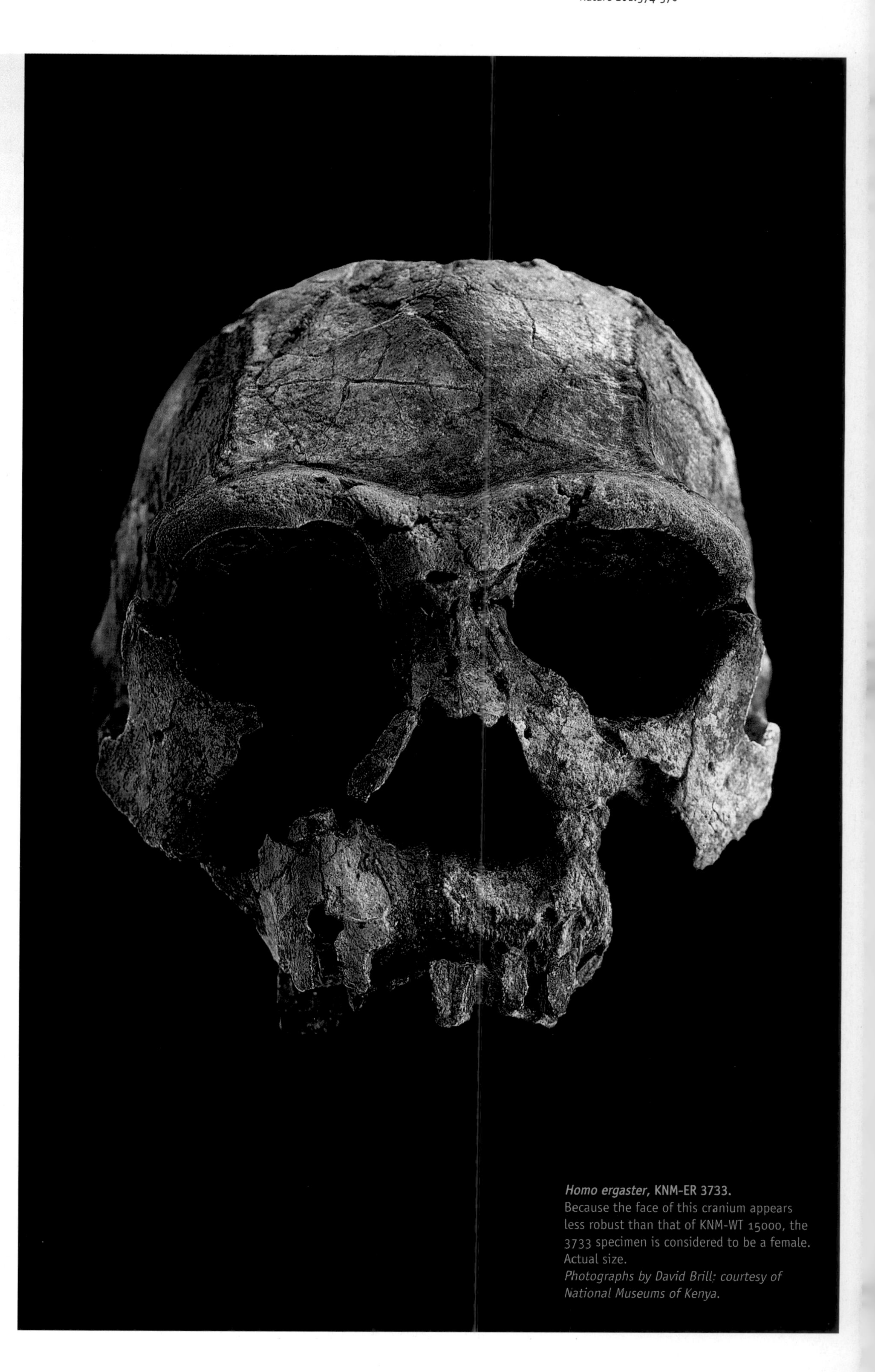

Homo ergaster, KNM-ER 3733.
Because the face of this cranium appears less robust than that of KNM-WT 15000, the 3733 specimen is considered to be a female. Actual size.
Photographs by David Brill: courtesy of National Museums of Kenya.

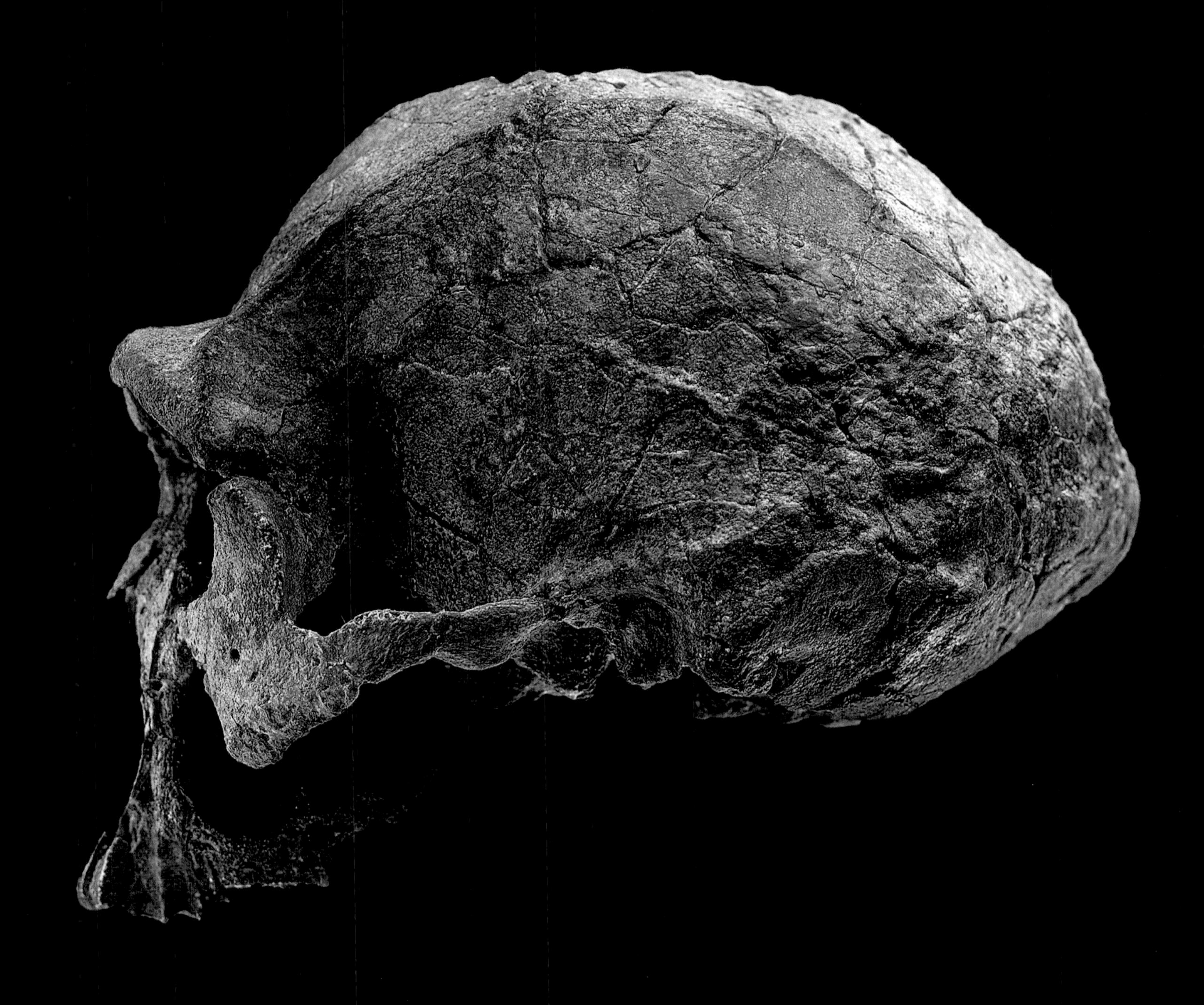

SPECIMEN	LOCALITY	AGE	DISCOVERER	DATE	PUBLICATION
Juvenile male skeleton	Nariokotome, Kenya	1.6 million years	Kamoya Kimeu	August 22, 1984	Brown, F., J. Harris, R. Leakey, and A. Walker. 1985. Early *Homo erectus* skeleton from west Lake Turkana, Kenya. *Nature* 316:788-792

Homo ergaster

KNM-WT 15000

The initial discovery of a tiny cranial fragment on a slope covered with lava pebbles in Nariokotome, Kenya, was a modest start to the eventual recovery of this unparalleled specimen, the most complete skeleton of any early hominid discovered to date and a rich source for research. This is the first early human fossil from before 100,000 years ago with a skull complete enough to precisely measure brain size and with enough of the postcranial skeleton preserved to enable an accurate estimate of body size, and thus the testing of ideas about relative brain size and growth and development. Moreover, the eighty pieces of postcranial bones could help answer questions about limb proportions, locomotion, maturation, gestation, and perhaps whether this hominid had language. Many of the postcranial bones for this species, such as the ribs, were found for the first time with this skeleton from Nariokotome. Experts on all parts of the skeleton analyzed this specimen in the decade after its unearthing by paleoanthropologists Richard Leakey, Alan Walker, and their team.

The individual was a boy who apparently died in early adolescence (see page 78 for details on estimating his age at death) on the edge of a shallow delta, where his body was covered rapidly by sediments and preserved. Although some large animal, perhaps a hippopotamus, had trampled and scattered some of the bones, the skeleton was remarkably well preserved. Had he lived to adulthood, the Nariokotome boy would have stood over 1.8 meters tall and weighed nearly 68 kilograms. He had already reached a height of more than 1.5 meters and a weight of around 47 kilograms. He was tall and thin, in body shape and limb proportions resembling present-day equatorial Africans. Despite his youth, the boy's limbs nearly matched the mean measurements for white North American adult males. This species was apparently much larger than any earlier hominid (see page 72 for a photograph of the complete skeleton).

The skull was reconstructed from about seventy pieces, not including the teeth, nearly all of which were recovered. The tooth morphology mirrors that of Chinese *Homo erectus* specimens (see page 188). Features of the skull (a maximum cranial breadth far back, a moderate supratoral sulcus behind the supraorbital torus) recall other *erectus* specimens. Compared to the African specimen OH 7 (see page 170), KNM-WT 15000 has a much smaller supraorbital torus, possibly due to the latter's immaturity. The endocranial volume is 880 cc, slightly larger than that of KNM-ER 3733 (see page 180) and less than that of OH 7. As a mature adult, the boy's brain size would probably have reached about 909 cc, which would place him between the smaller Kenyan specimens and the larger Chinese *Homo erectus* specimens from Zhoukoudian.

KNM-WT 15000 displays some obvious differences from a modern human skeleton. These differences include longer spines on the vertebrae and a more constricted canal for the spinal cord that limited the number of nerves to the thoracic cavity and may have reduced the ability to regulate air passing from the lungs to the mouth (which in turn could have rendered the boy incapable of speech); a narrow pelvis that may have been more efficiently designed for walking and running than our own (see page 76 for the implications of KNM-WT 15000's narrow pelvis for birth and infant development in the species); and an elongated neck on the femur, a primitive feature also found in australopithecines. Overall, though, KNM-WT 15000 demonstrates that hominids by this time had departed from the apelike australopithecine body plan of our early evolution and were rapidly approaching the body and brain size that characterize modern humans.

***Homo ergaster*, KNM-WT 15000** (see also page 72).
The boy from Nariokotome, WT 15000, has a skull complete enough to accurately measure brain size. The 80 additional bones recovered from his skeleton allow an estimate of body size and convey much information about this species' biology. Actual size.
Photograph by David Brill; courtesy of National Museums of Kenya.

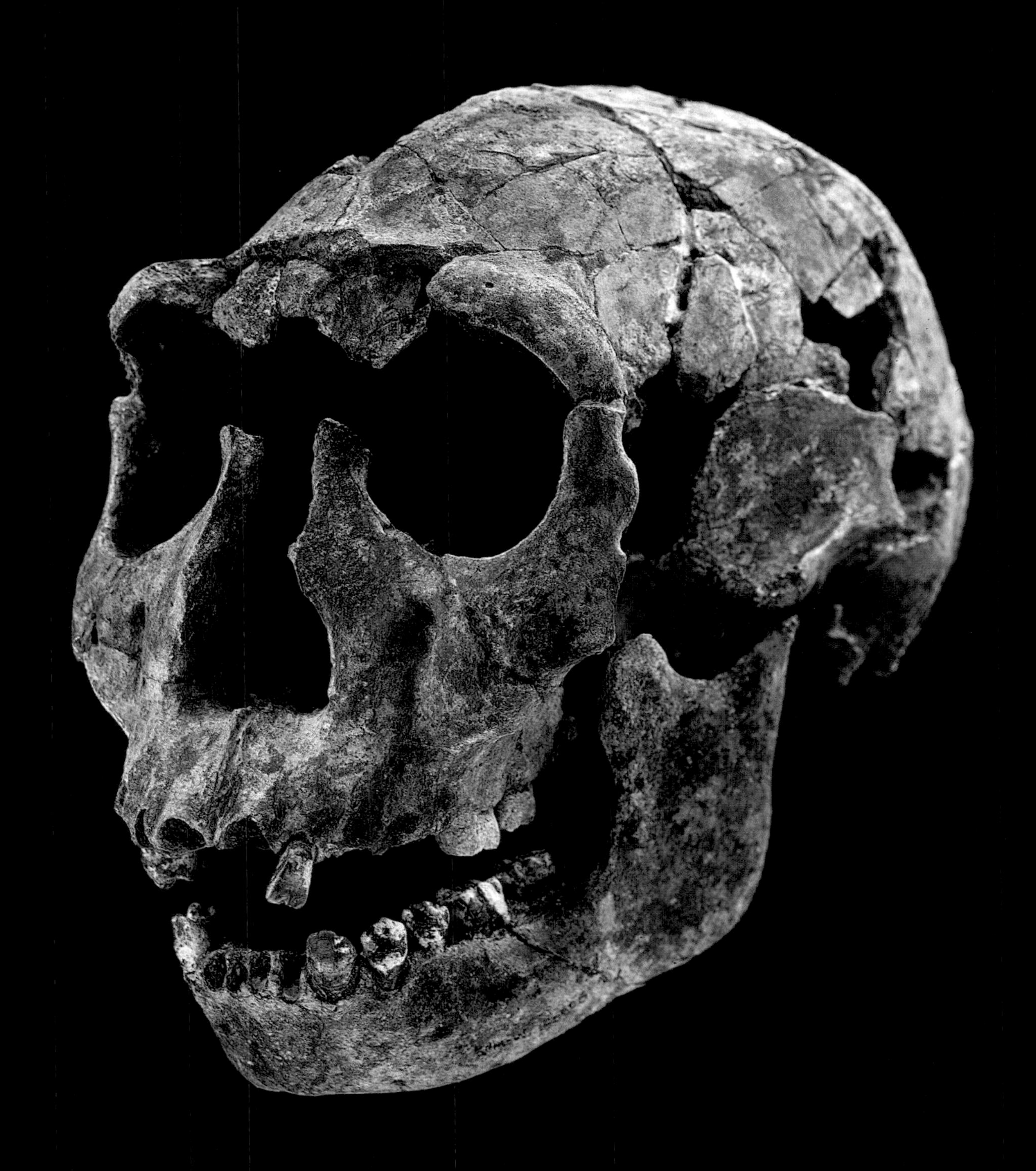

SPECIMEN	LOCALITY	AGE	DISCOVERER	DATE	PUBLICATION
Adult partial cranium	Swartkrans, South Africa	ca. 1.5 million years	Ronald Clarke	July 23, 1969	Clarke, R.J., F.C. Howell, and C.K. Brain. 1970. More evidence of an advanced hominid at Swartkrans. *Nature* 225: 1219-1222

Homo ergaster

SK 847

Not all human fossil discoveries are made in the field. Some are made while reexamining museum specimens in light of discoveries made subsequent to the specimens' collection. The cranium identified as Swartkrans (SK) 847, the best example of early *Homo* from South Africa and perhaps from one of the first users of fire, is a case in point. While inspecting the collections of the Transvaal Museum in Pretoria in 1969, paleoanthropologist Ron Clarke noticed that among the hominid fossil remains from Swartkrans were two pieces of a cranium, a facial fragment and the temporal bone, that looked very different from the robust australopithecine fossils that surrounded them. Clarke found that the two pieces fit together and thus came from the same individual.

Next, Clarke realized that the facial fragment also fit perfectly with part of a maxilla, SK 80, that had been described by Robert Broom and John Robinson in the early 1950s as representing a separate hominid species at Swartkrans from the robust australopithecines, one that they named *Telanthropus capensis* (which Robinson later included within *Homo erectus*). Now Clarke had most of the left side of a face, the cheekbone, and part of the side and base of a cranium from a single individual, and he knew that Broom and Robinson had been right. The cave at Swartkrans has yielded the bulk of the known robust australopithecine remains—bones from at least eighty-five individuals of *Australopithecus robustus*—but Clarke's serendipity confirmed that a second type of early human had lived at the site. Clarke wrote his doctoral dissertation on this cranium.

SK 847's salient facial features include a relatively short and narrow face, a pronounced browridge or supraorbital torus that is thick both in the middle and to the sides, moderate constriction of the cranium behind the eye socket, an obvious supratoral sulcus, and a sharply sloping frontal bone. In addition, the specimen has delicate, curved cheekbones and rounded, forward-projecting nasal bones. In all of these features, SK 847 contrasts strongly with the anatomy of both *Australopithecus robustus*, such as SK 48 and SK 79 (see page 148), and *Australopithecus africanus*, such as Sts 5 (see page 134).

Furthermore, SK 847 possesses a short palate and small temporomandibular joint (the area where the lower jaw connects to the cranium) that could only fit a small, short lower jaw and not the typically massive mandible of a robust australopithecine. In fact, although it comes from a different individual, the mandible SK 15 makes a good match for SK 847 and also happens to be the type specimen used to name *Telanthropus*.

Despite all the anatomical evidence suggesting that SK 847 belonged to *Homo*, some paleoanthropologists maintained, largely by invoking the single species hypothesis (see page 158), that all the hominids from Swartkrans were of the same species and that this specimen was simply a small robust australopithecine. But the facial anatomy of SK 847 can be clearly distinguished from that of a presumed female robust australopithecine, KNM-ER 732 (see pages 73 and 161). A much more favorable comparison, however, can be made between SK 847 and another Koobi Fora specimen, KNM-ER 3733 (see page 180), which has also been classified as *Homo ergaster* or African *Homo erectus*.

The presence of *Homo* at Swartkrans raises an interesting issue. Should we assume that this hominid—rather than the robust one whose bones constitute at least 95 percent of the hominid fossils from the site—was responsible for the stone tools and the evidence of controlled fire (see pages 96-97) found in the cave? Despite the statistical odds, it seems a reasonable conclusion. Just as there is no clear association at any site of stone tools and robust australopithecine bones, even though the hands of *Australopithecus robustus* had the necessary musculature and precision grip to flake stone, so there is no evidence elsewhere linking this species to the creation or curation of fire.

***Homo ergaster*, SK 847.**
South African cave sites are known for preserving large numbers of australopithecine fossils, but this is one of the much rarer examples of early *Homo*. Actual size.
Photograph by David Brill; courtesy of Transvaal Museum.

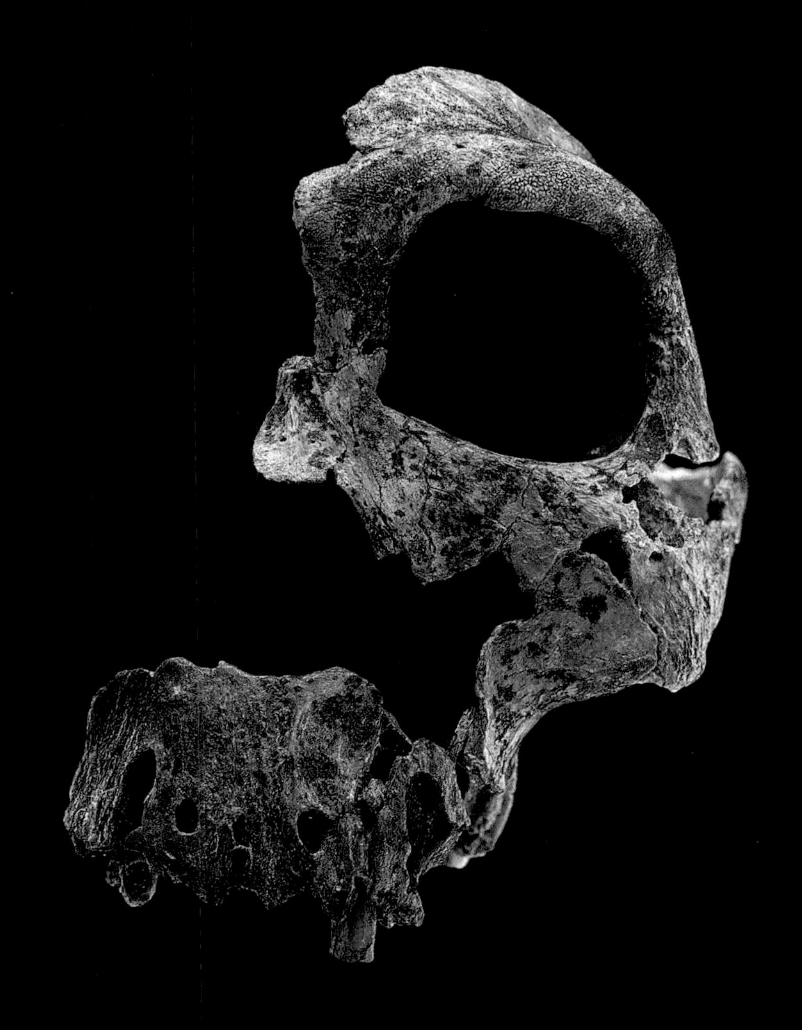

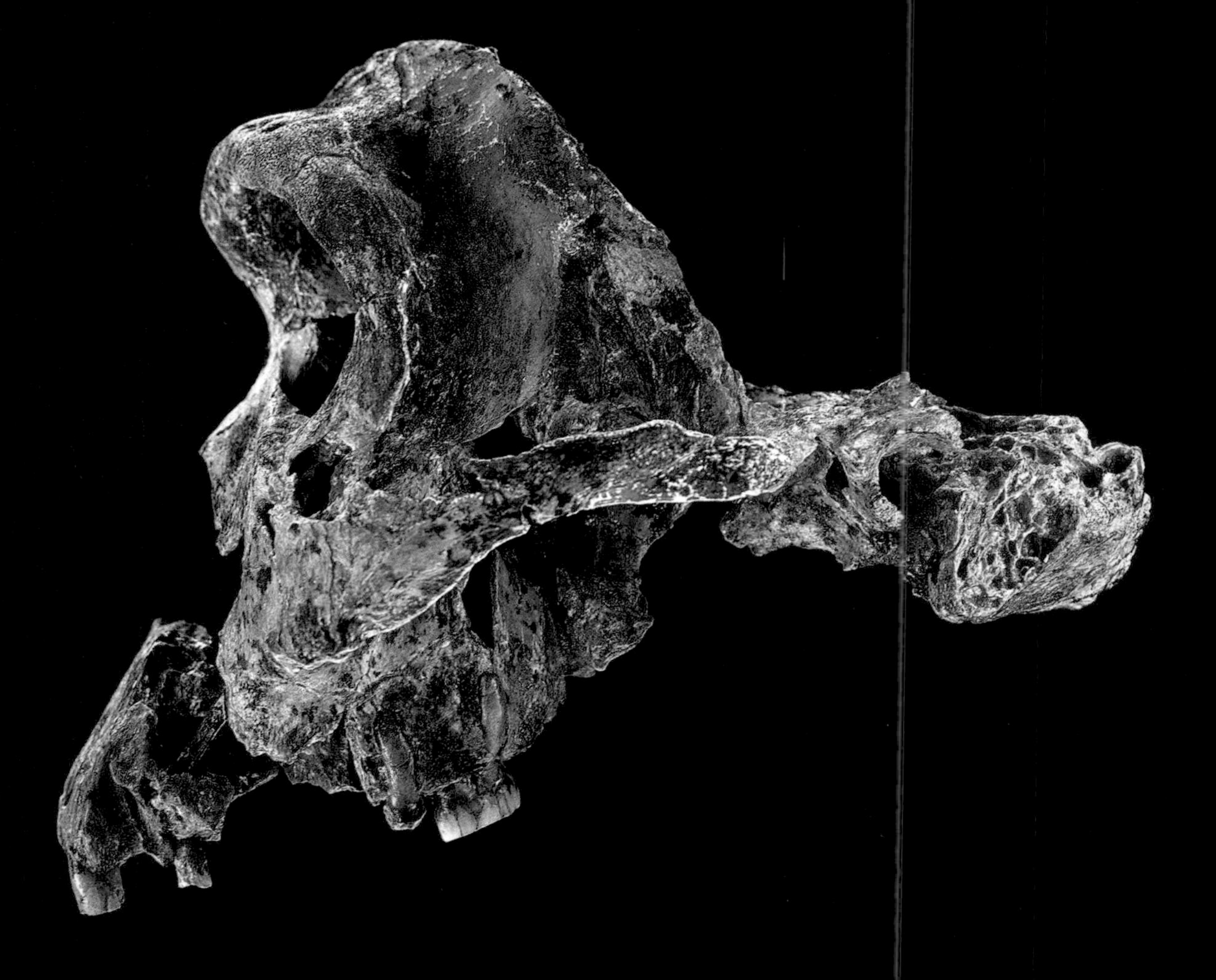

***Homo ergaster*, SK 847** (see previous page).
Actual size. *Photograph by David Brill; courtesy of Transvaal Museum.*

SPECIMEN	LOCALITY	AGE	DISCOVERER	DATE	PUBLICATION
Adult partial cranium	Trinil, Java, Indonesia	ca. 500,000 years	Eugène Dubois	October 1891	Dubois, E. 1894. Pithecanthropus erectus, *eine menschenaehnliche Übergangsform aus Java* (Landesdruckerei, Batavia).

Homo erectus

TRINIL 2 TYPE SPECIMEN *JAVA MAN*

If the discovery of a skullcap and assorted bones in the Neander Valley initiated paleoanthropology as an endeavor, the specimen known as Trinil 2 was the first fossil to suggest our ancestors' antiquity and geographic spread. Its discoverer, Eugène Dubois, set out from Holland to find the missing link between apes and humans and succeeded in making the first hominid discovery outside of Europe. Trinil 2, or Java Man, became the holotype specimen of *Homo erectus*.

Inspired by British biologist Alfred Russel Wallace's conviction that clues to our origins lay in Southeast Asia, Dubois enlisted as an army surgeon in the Royal Dutch East Indies Army and became an avocational fossil hunter in Sumatra. He had little luck there, but in 1890 he continued his search on Java, along the bank of the Solo River.

Success came with the unearthing of this thick, mineralized cranium consisting of a flat frontal bone, much of both parietals, and the upper portion of the occipital bone. The pronounced supraorbital torus and the constriction behind it are striking features of this specimen. Much of the surface anatomy has worn smooth, but the extremely flat forehead has an obvious keel along the bone's midline. A pathological femur subsequently found upstream from the cranium may or may not belong to the same individual and has a remarkably modern-looking form.

In 1894, Dubois named his Java Man *Pithecanthropus erectus*, taking the genus name coined by biologist Ernst Haeckel for a hypothetical human ancestor. Since the 1950s, when evolutionary theorist Ernst Mayr proposed that the Javan hominids and the roughly contemporaneous fossils of Peking Man could be placed in a single species, the fossils have been identified as *Homo erectus*. Further discoveries in Java have turned up remains from a total of about forty individuals of this species, and an equal number have come from China, mainly from the site of Zhoukoudian (see page 188).

No tools have ever been found associated with the fossils of *H. erectus* in Java. This is curious, because elsewhere the species is associated with the conspicuous and ubiquitous heavy-duty butchering artifacts of the Acheulean industry. Some have proposed that this hominid in Indonesia and East Asia relied on cutting tools made from abundant bamboo. Alternatively, in light of the very ancient dates recently announced for two *H. erectus* specimens from Modjokerto and Sangiran (see page 191), it may well be that this species left Africa before the Acheulean had even evolved there. Acheulean tools spread outside of Africa with subsequent emigrants but never penetrated far into Asia. Despite Dubois's early success and that of subsequent fossil hunters there, Asia has not turned out to be the cradle of humankind. Darwin, not Wallace, had it right that we should seek our ultimate origins in Africa.

***Homo erectus*, Trinil 2.**
The first hominid fossil found outside of Europe, Trinil 2 focused the search for our origins in Asia until older fossils began to be discovered in Africa. Actual size.
Photograph by John Reader, Science Source/Photo Researchers.

SPECIMEN	LOCALITY	AGE	DISCOVERERS	DATE	PUBLICATION
Adult skull reconstruction	Zhoukoudian Cave, China	400,000-500,000 years	W.C. Pei and the Cenozoic Research Laboratory	1928-1937 (specimens used in reconstruction)	Weidenreich, F. 1943. The skull of *Sinantropus pekinensis:* a comparative study of a primitive skull. *Palaeontologia Sinila* New Series D, Ne. 10 Geological Survey of China, Pehpei, ChungKing

Homo erectus
PEKING MAN

The cave of Zhoukoudian, or Dragon Bone Hill, about 40 kilometers south of Beijing, China, has yielded the largest collection of *Homo erectus* fossils from any one place. Accounting for a third of the known fossils from this species, the bones from forty individuals provided a rich trove for research: five skullcaps, several cranial and facial fragments, eleven mandibles, and 147 teeth. The fossils met a tragic and mysterious end: all of the original fossils, save for two teeth sent to Sweden in the 1920s, vanished in December 1941 after being packed for shipment to the United States in the wake of the Japanese invasion of China during World War II. Postwar excavations turned up a few more teeth, cranial, jaw, and limb bone fragments, but the rest were gone. Fortunately, in anticipation of the invasion, exacting casts of each specimen had been made.

Paleoanthropologists have just put a new face on this famous old fossil. The skull shown here is a recent reconstruction by Gary Sawyer and Ian Tattersall of the American Museum of Natural History, that departs significantly from the original reconstruction made by German anatomist Franz Weidenreich and his assistant Lucille Swan in the 1930s. The original reconstruction used a cranium and lower jaw from two females and a probably female maxilla. The new reconstruction takes advantage of previously ignored bones from males, and thus finally affords a look at Peking Man himself.

Bones from four individuals were used in the new reconstruction. The skullcap from Skull XII, which included nasal bones and the rim of the left eye socket, a partial maxilla from Skull XIV, and two facial fragments from Skull X created a nearly complete left side of the face. The mandible was reconstructed using the left and right fragments GI and GII and following the bone's bilateral symmetry to make a mirror image for missing parts from the opposite side. The complete lower jaw could then guide reconstruction of the midface so that teeth and other points of contact were aligned correctly. Isolated teeth were added to complete the dentition in both jaws.

The result is a larger cranium with a more massive and projecting face overall and a broader, taller nasal region. Peking Man now more closely resembles the anatomy of *erectus* specimens from elsewhere.

The Zhoukoudian fossils were excavated beginning in the 1920s and given the name *Sinanthropus pekinensis* by Canadian physician Davidson Black based on a few isolated teeth (all the fossils were later lumped within the species *Homo erectus*). The first skullcap was found in 1929, and as more fossils accumulated in the following decade, Weidenreich made extensive studies of them that contributed to his multiregional view of human evolution by his recognition of twelve anatomical features that he believed Peking Man shared with modern Chinese. His series of monographs on Zhoukoudian, published between 1936 and 1943, remain definitive, and we can thank his foresight in bringing all of the master molds and casts—made before the original fossils became lost—with him to the American Museum of Natural History, where they are still kept today.

The five skullcaps have a mean cranial capacity of 1,043 cc. The supraorbital torus of Peking Man is smaller than that of OH 7 or Sangiran 17 from Java. Occipital bones from Zhoukoudian are strongly flexed (note the back of the skull in lateral view) with a broad torus across the bone's width. These specimens are also characterized by flat, thick, rectangular parietal bones, massive facial bones, and bulky mandibles.

Zhoukoudian contains a rich record of fauna and archeology that attests to the cave's occupation for more than 200,000 years. Hominids seem to have alternated with carnivores at the site, perhaps occasionally competing for food and shelter at the same time. Bones belonging to ninety-seven species of mammals and sixty-two kinds of birds have been excavated. At least 17,000 stone tools were made by the inhabitants, predominantly from quartz, with smaller percentages of rock crystal, sandstone, and flint artifacts. Zhoukoudian also preserved what until recently was the earliest evidence of the human use of fire (see page 96).

***Homo erectus*, original cast of Peking Man** (see also pages 7 and 165).
Franz Weidenreich's original cast of cranium XII from Zhoukoudian, China provided the braincase and upper face for a new reconstruction of Peking Man's skull. Actual size.
Photograph by David Brill; courtesy of American Museum of Natural History.

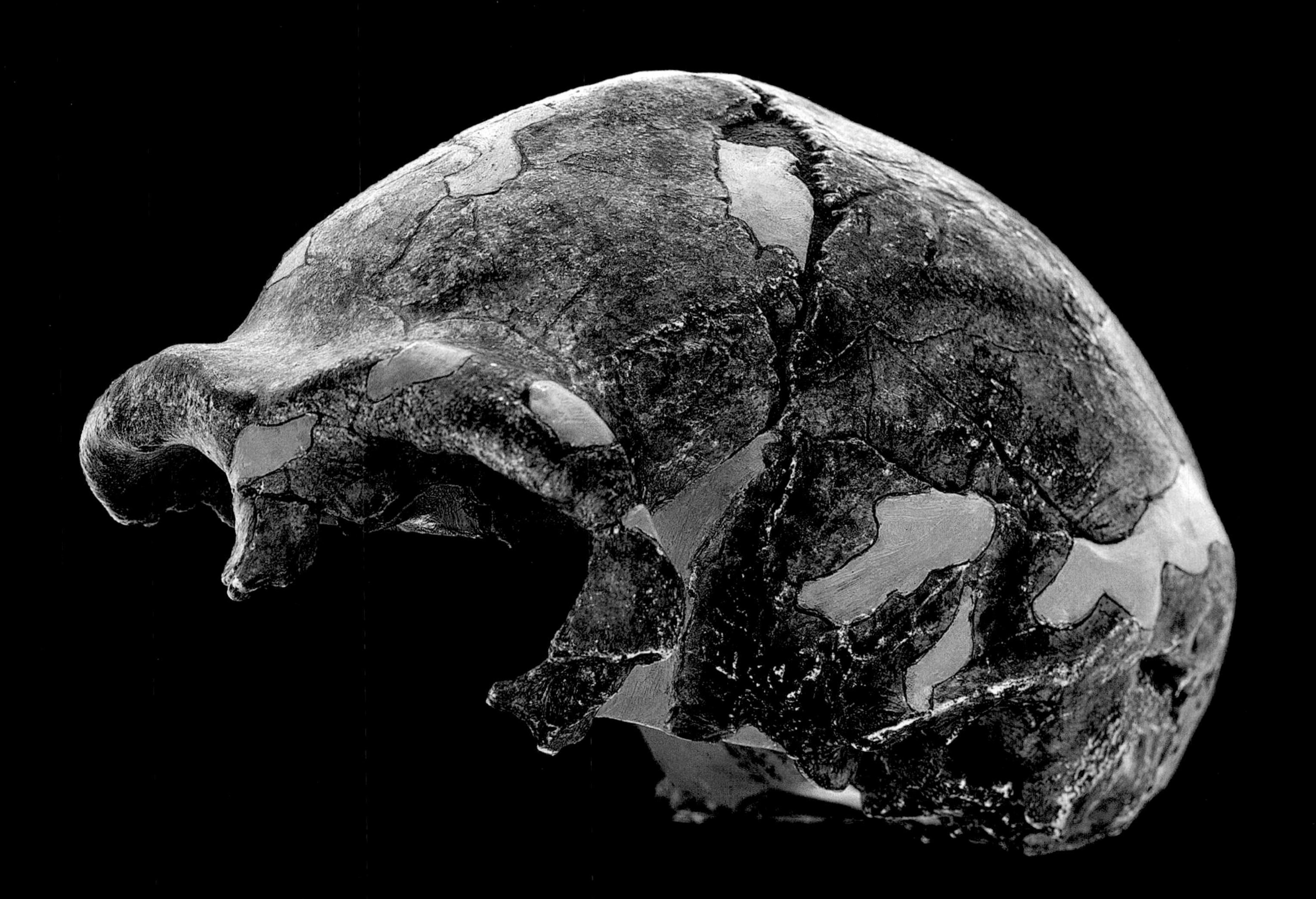

Homo erectus, reconstructed skull of Peking Man (see previous page).
This revised reconstruction gives Peking Man a more massive, projecting face and broader nose than earlier versions and appears more similar to *Homo erectus* fossils from elsewhere in Asia. Actual size.
Photograph by David Brill; courtesy of American Museum of Natural History.

SPECIMEN	LOCALITY	AGE	DISCOVERER	DATE	PUBLICATION
Adult male cranium	Sangiran, Java, Indonesia	ca. 800,000 years	Mr. Towikromo	September 13, 1969	Sartono, S. 1971. Observations on a new skull of *Pithecanthropus erectus* (Pithecanthropus VIII) from Sangiran, Central Java. *Proc. Acad. Sci. Amst. B*, 74, 185-194

Homo erectus

SANGIRAN 17

Eighty years elapsed after Eugène Dubois discovered his famous fossil skullcap at Trinil (see page 187) before paleoanthropologists could finally gaze into the face of Java Man. Although other fossil hunters subsequently found complete crania, skullcaps, and cranial fragments from a dozen individuals, all lacked the facial skeleton. Then, in 1969, a farmer cultivating his land struck the side of a skull embedded in the sandstone soil. His blow opened a large hole in the fossil, but the fragments were collected, along with the more intact bone, which was heavily mineralized and had a rusty brown color from iron oxide. Once it was reconstructed, Sangiran 17 constituted the best-preserved hominid cranium from Java and the only known adult male *Homo erectus* from anywhere. But by providing the first face of Indonesian *Homo erectus*, the specimen took on a central role in the multiregional model for the origin of *Homo sapiens*.

This model hypothesizes that *Homo erectus* evolved in place in Java and accumulated anatomical traits that were then passed on to its descendant species, *Homo sapiens*. These traits can be traced through time in various fossils in Java and even to a population of modern humans that migrated from Java to Australia perhaps 50,000 years ago. A separate regional lineage is said to link *erectus* and *sapiens* fossils in China, including specimens from Zhoukoudian (see page 188) and Dali (see page 234), and it is speculated that another migration took members of our species from China into Australia at around the same time.

In Java, this direct line of evolution allegedly begins with the Sangiran specimens and continues with specimens from Sambungmacnan and the much younger crania from Ngandong, all the way to present-day Javanese. Some of the cited stable anatomical traits include a long, relatively flat frontal bone; a projecting face with massive, flat cheekbones; a distinct ridge, called a zygomaxillary tuberosity, at the base of the cheekbone; a rounded edge to the bottom of the eye sockets; and the lack of a clear demarcation between the nasal region and the lower face. Similar features supposedly carry over to much younger Australian fossils such as the partial cranium WLH 50 from Willandra Lakes and the skeletons from Kow Swamp (see page 247), the latter being only 10,000 to 14,000 years old. Many of these facial features are adaptations for heavy chewing power.

Other characteristics visible in Sangiran 17 that distinguish Indonesian *Homo erectus* from other populations of the species and that figure in the multiregional model include the very thick bones of the braincase, which is flattened along the sides; a maximum breadth at the base of the cranium; reduced development of the frontal and parietal lobes of the brain (with a cranial capacity of 1,029 cc, Sangiran 17 is toward the high end of the range in brain size); and prominent muscle markings along the sides and back of the cranium.

Originally the multiregional model suggested that *erectus* had been evolving in China and Java for a million years. But new dates from Javan fossils—including some hominid skull fragments found at Sangiran in the 1970s, now estimated by the argon-argon technique to be 1.66 million years old, although Sangiran 17 is a much younger specimen—would push back the beginning of this species's isolation in Java to nearly 2 million years ago. Since the exact geological layer where the Java specimens is unknown, there is serious doubt about their association with the 1.66 million year old volcanic rocks. However, multiregional evolution proponents are adapting their ideas to the new dates, but 2 million years of local evolution is too long a period to consider this *erectus* population as a plausible modern human ancestor. No other example from hominid evolution exists to support the idea that this population evolved in place, with little or no gene flow from elsewhere, for nearly 2 million years.

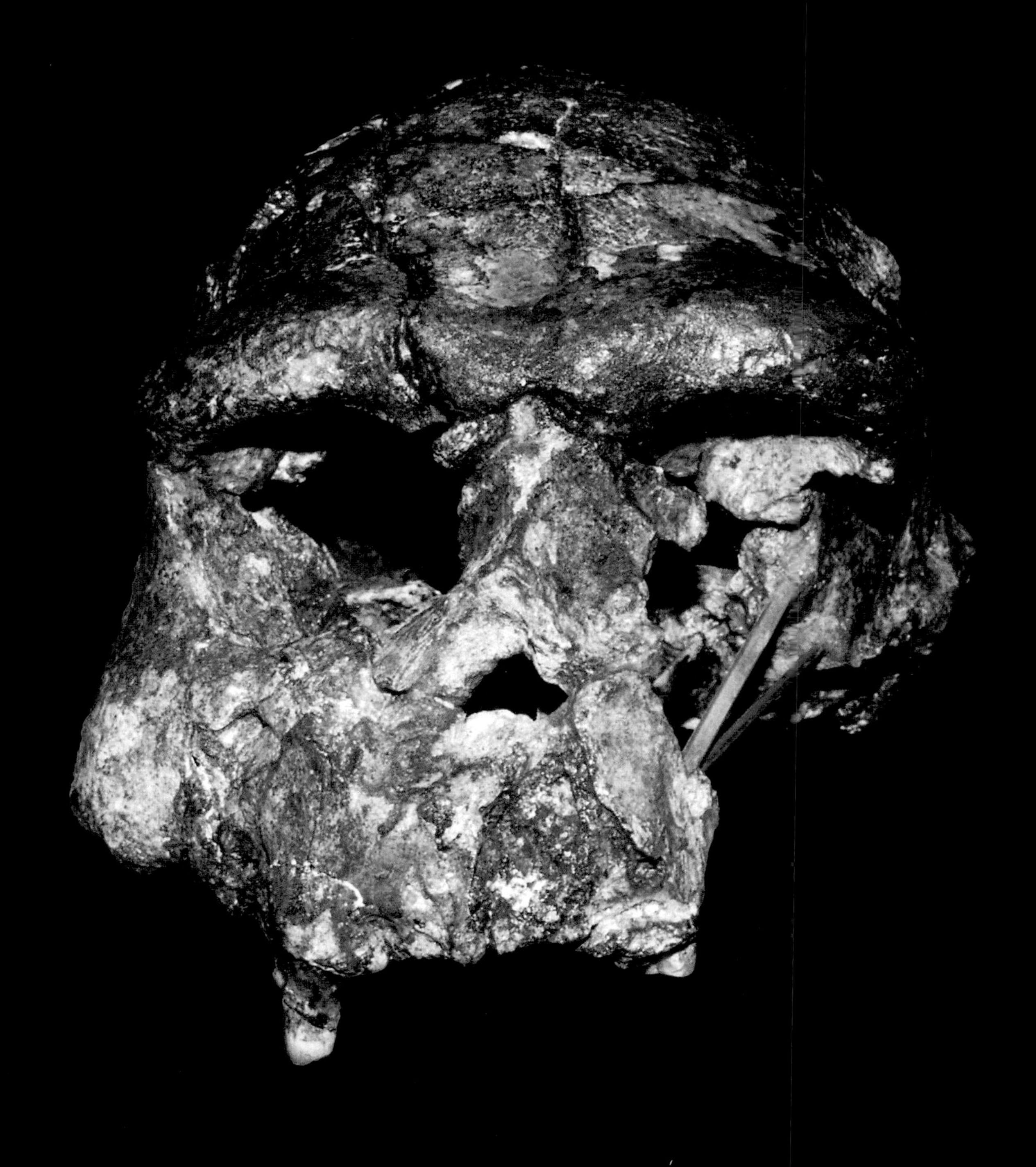

***Homo erectus*, Sangiran 17** (see previous page). This most complete specimen of Java Man (frontal, left, and lateral, right) displays a flat forehead and cheekbones, projecting face, and a braincase that is flattened along the sides and broadest at the base—all features that distinguish Indonesian *Homo erectus*. Actual size. *Courtesy of Frachroel Aziz, Geological Research and Development Centre, Indonesia.*

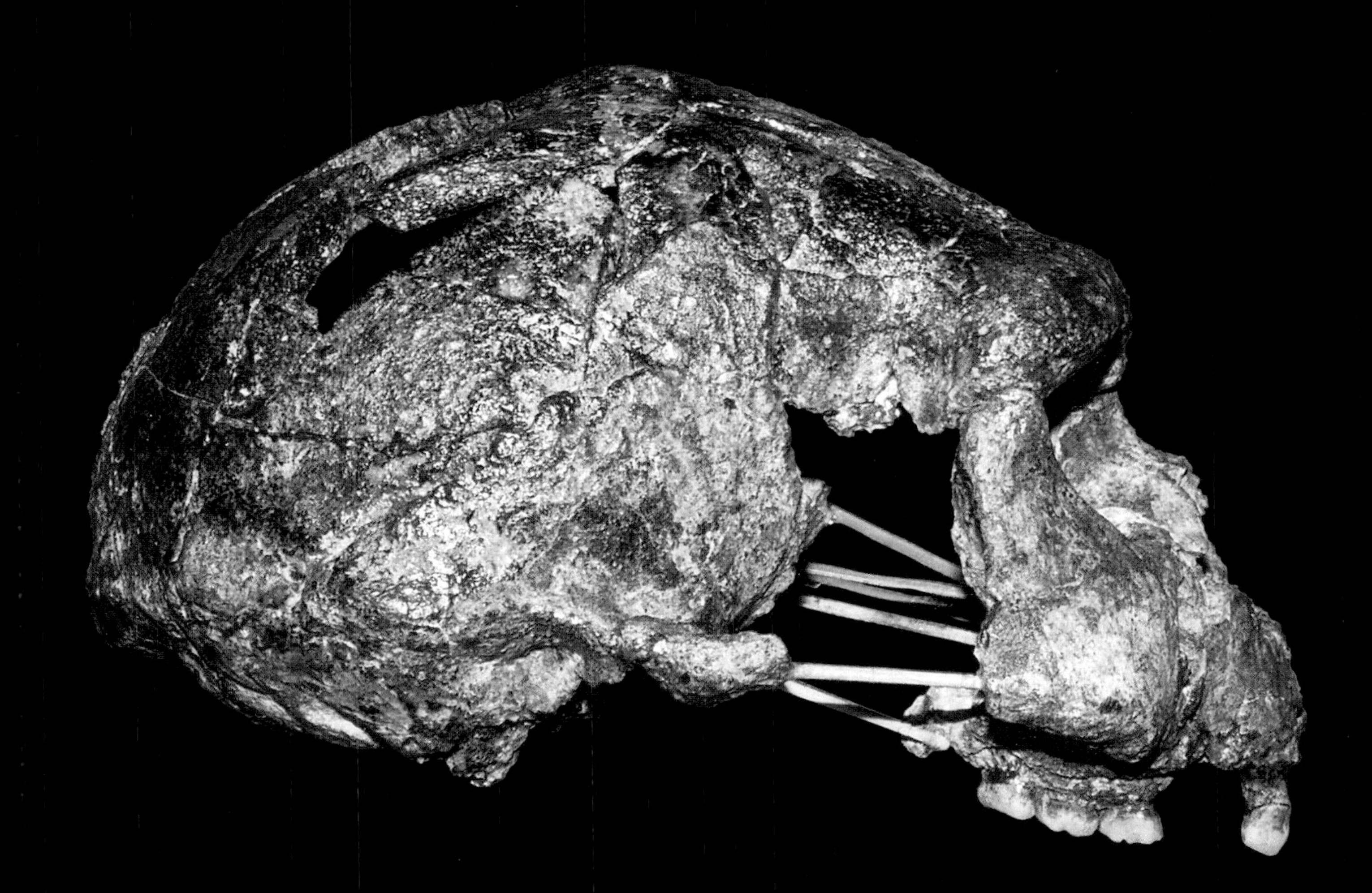

SPECIMEN	LOCALITY	AGE	DISCOVERERS	DATE	PUBLICATION
Adult cranium	Bodo d'Ar, Ethiopia	600,000 years	Alemayhew Asfaw, Paul Whitehead, and Craig Wood	October 15 and 23. 1976	Conroy, G.C., C.J. Jolly, D. Cramer, and J.E. Kalb. 1978. Newly discovered fossil hominid skull from the Afar depression, Ethiopia. *Nature* 276: 67-70

Homo heidelbergensis
BODO CRANIUM

Creationists love to argue that paleoanthropologists lack transitional fossils to show that one hominid species evolved into another. The specimen known as Bodo, after its place of discovery in Bodo d'Ar, Ethiopia, refutes that argument. It possesses a range of anatomical features typical of different species of *Homo* and as such does not fit easily into any one species. Even as this specimen captures a biological transition in progress, the stone tools collected at Bodo reflect an unfolding cultural transition.

Bodo sports the biggest face known in the human fossil record. In 1981, five years after this massive cranium was found, the left lower rear corner of a parietal bone from the skull of a second individual was recovered from Bodo d'Ar, and even this small fragment reveals the robust skull structure of early humans at this site. Part of an upper arm, or humerus, found at Bodo d'Ar in 1990, however, is smaller than that of many modern humans, perhaps reflecting size differences between ancient males and females in this population.

Despite its broader, more massive face, Bodo bears a striking resemblance to the younger specimen from Kabwe, or Broken Hill, commonly called Rhodesian Man (see page 208). Both have a broad face and a thick, prominent ridge, or supraorbital torus, over the eye sockets. Like many *Homo erectus* specimens, Bodo has a bony midline keel atop the cranium. Its *sapiens*-like features include the nasal bones, the mandibular fossa (a shallow depression in front of the ear hole where the lower jaw attaches), and the forehead or frontal bone. More important for proponents of the view that modern humans evolved first and only in Africa before spreading around the world, Bodo has anatomical affinities with the Petralona specimen from Greece (see page 200).

When the specimen was discovered, its age was thought to be only 350,000 years, contemporaneous with other European specimens of *Homo heidelbergensis*. New dates reported in 1994 for the Bodo d'Ar site have increased the estimated age of this skull to around 600,000 years, within the time frame of *H. erectus.* But Bodo's anatomy has advanced beyond that of its *erectus* contemporaries in Asia, including those at the Peking Man site of Zhoukoudian.

The site at Bodo d'Ar provides an extremely rare snapshot of simultaneous biological and cultural evolution. Near where the cranium was found, stone tools—Acheulean hand axes and cleavers—litter the ground, along with the bones of hippos, baboons, and antelopes. The numerous lava tools recovered from the same river sands as the human fossils document a technological shift from the more simple single-faced cores and flakes of the Developed Oldowan industry to the bifacial, heavy-duty artifacts of the succeeding Acheulean industry. Curiously, this transition at Bodo d'Ar occurred very late, since elsewhere in Ethiopia at Konso-Gardula, Africa's earliest Acheulean tools have been found, dating to about 1.7 million years ago.

Humans may have been butchering hippos at some of the archeological sites near Bodo, but stone tools were apparently used on Bodo Man himself. Distinctive cut marks discovered on several parts of the cranium after the bone was cleaned indicate that Bodo Man was the victim of defleshing and butchery, either before his death or shortly thereafter (see page 93).

***Homo heidelbergensis*, Bodo** (see also page 94). This immense specimen, with the largest face in the human fossil record, possesses a mix of primitive anatomical features, such as the thick browridge and cranial wall, and more modern ones, including the shape of the forehead and nasal bones. Actual size.
Courtesy of Donald Johanson, Institute of Human Origins; and National Museum of Ethiopia.

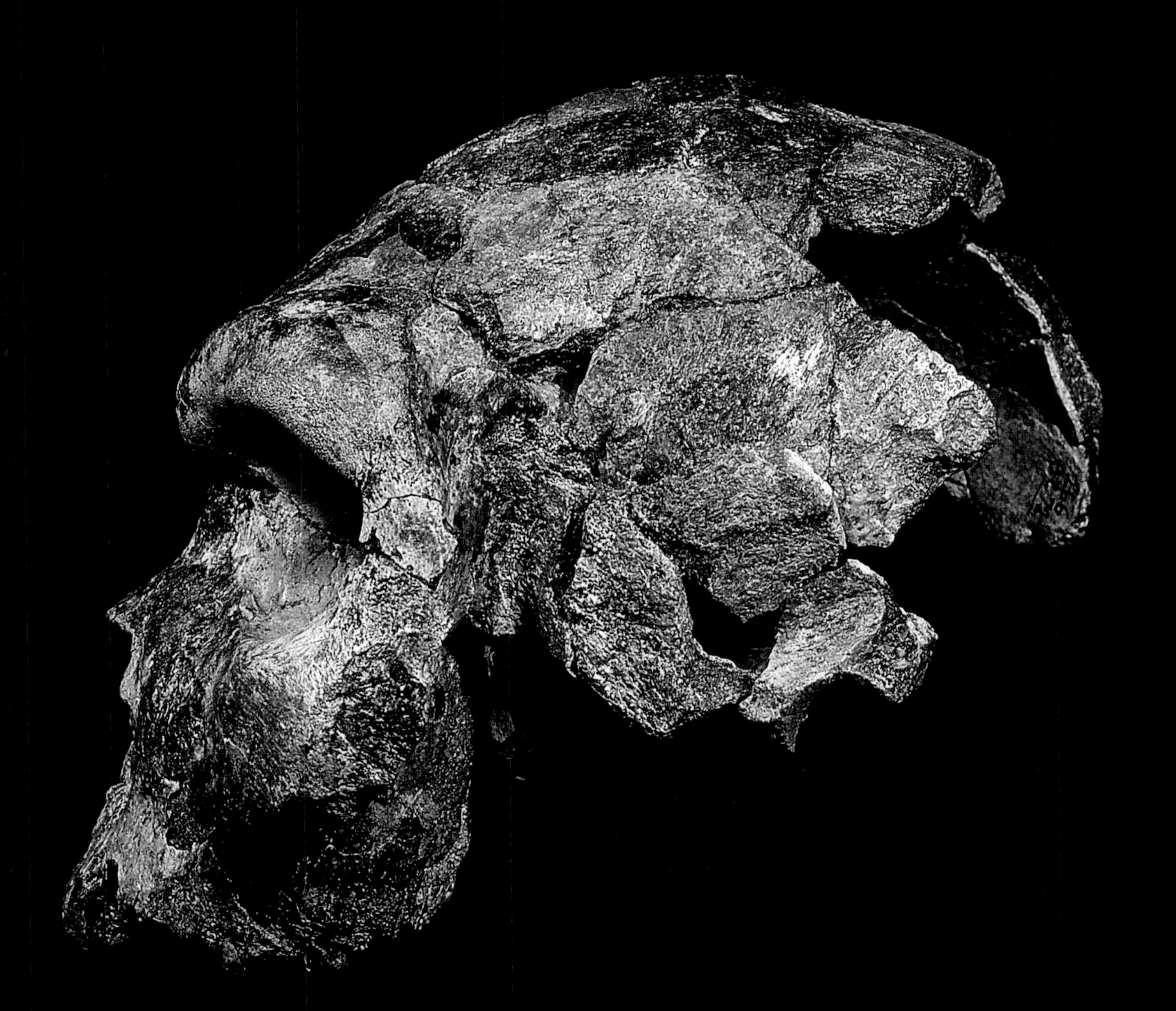

SPECIMEN	LOCALITY	AGE	DISCOVERER	DATE	PUBLICATION
Adult mandible	Mauer sand pits, Germany	ca. 400,000 to 500,000 years	Workman for Joseph Rosch	October 21, 1907	Schoetensack, O. 1908. *Der Unterkeifer des* Homo heidelbergensis *aus den Sanden von Mauer bei Heidelberg,* 1-67 (Wilhelm Engleman, Leipzig)

Homo heidelbergensis

MAUER 1 TYPE SPECIMEN

Until the 1990s, this robust jawbone had been the oldest known hominid fossil in Europe. Although the recently discovered mandible from Dmanisi, Georgia, and fossils from Gran Dolina, Spain (see page 46), eclipse the Mauer specimen in age, this fossil remains one of the earliest Europeans. Also known as Heidelberg Man, the mandible is the type specimen of *Homo heidelbergensis,* a scientific name that has recently gained currency and refers to the species at the base of the lineage that led to, and terminated with, the Neandertals.

When this fossil was found near the village of Mauer, a few kilometers southeast of Heidelberg, it validated the long-held conviction of paleontologist Otto Schoetensack. The river sands deposited at the Mauer quarry were known to contain the remains of extinct mammals—rhino, elephant, bear, bison, deer, and horse among them—and were thought to date deep into the Pleistocene. Schoetensack believed that the gravel pits at Mauer might yield the remains of some Pleistocene human, so he made frequent train trips to the site from Heidelberg. He had to wait twenty years, but finally a worker discovered this mandible in a layer that had been buried by nearly 24 meters of deposits. Schoetensack completed and published his extensive monograph on the mandible just a year later. Five years after the discovery he died.

Although Schoetensack created the name without justifying it by describing the unique anatomical features of this species, there are features that seem to set *H. heidelbergensis* apart from *Homo erectus,* Neandertals, and modern humans. In the case of Mauer 1 the anatomy is clearly more primitive than that of either Neandertals or modern humans. There is no projecting chin, and the symphysis at the front of the massive mandible slopes down and back from the teeth. The specimen possesses a surprisingly broad ramus, the vertical portion that connects the jaw to the cranium, which anchored strong chewing muscles. Other than taurodontism, a combination of enlarged pulp cavities and fused roots, the completely preserved teeth show no typical Neandertal traits, and the large molars are small for *H. erectus* teeth but overlap those of some early modern humans.

Although no unambiguous tools were found with Heidelberg Man (some bone fragments and pebbles have been argued to bear signs of hominid use), he was thought to be a contemporary of the people who made the Acheulean tools that have been found elsewhere in western Europe, and to have lived during the warm period between the first two glaciations of Pleistocene Europe. The exact age of the specimen, however, remains somewhat uncertain.

In a bit of hyperbole, Schoetensack wrote that apart from the teeth of this fossil, "Even an expert could not be blamed if he hesitated to accept it as human." Echoing Schoetensack's sentiments, English anatomist Arthur Keith later wrote, "From the very first, anatomists have been struck by the apparent discrepancy between the `humanity' of the teeth and the massive power—almost bestiality—of the jaw itself." These two authorities considered Mauer to be an early and primitive type of Neandertal, a view that has been strengthened by the recovery of subsequent fossils in Europe.

Homo heidelbergensis, **Mauer 1.**
The type specimen for this species, the mandible of Heidelberg Man dates to nearly half a million years ago and remains one of the oldest human fossils from Europe. Note the absence of a chin in front and the very broad ascending ramus at the rear of the bone. Actual size.
Photograph by John Reader, Science Source/Photo Researchers.

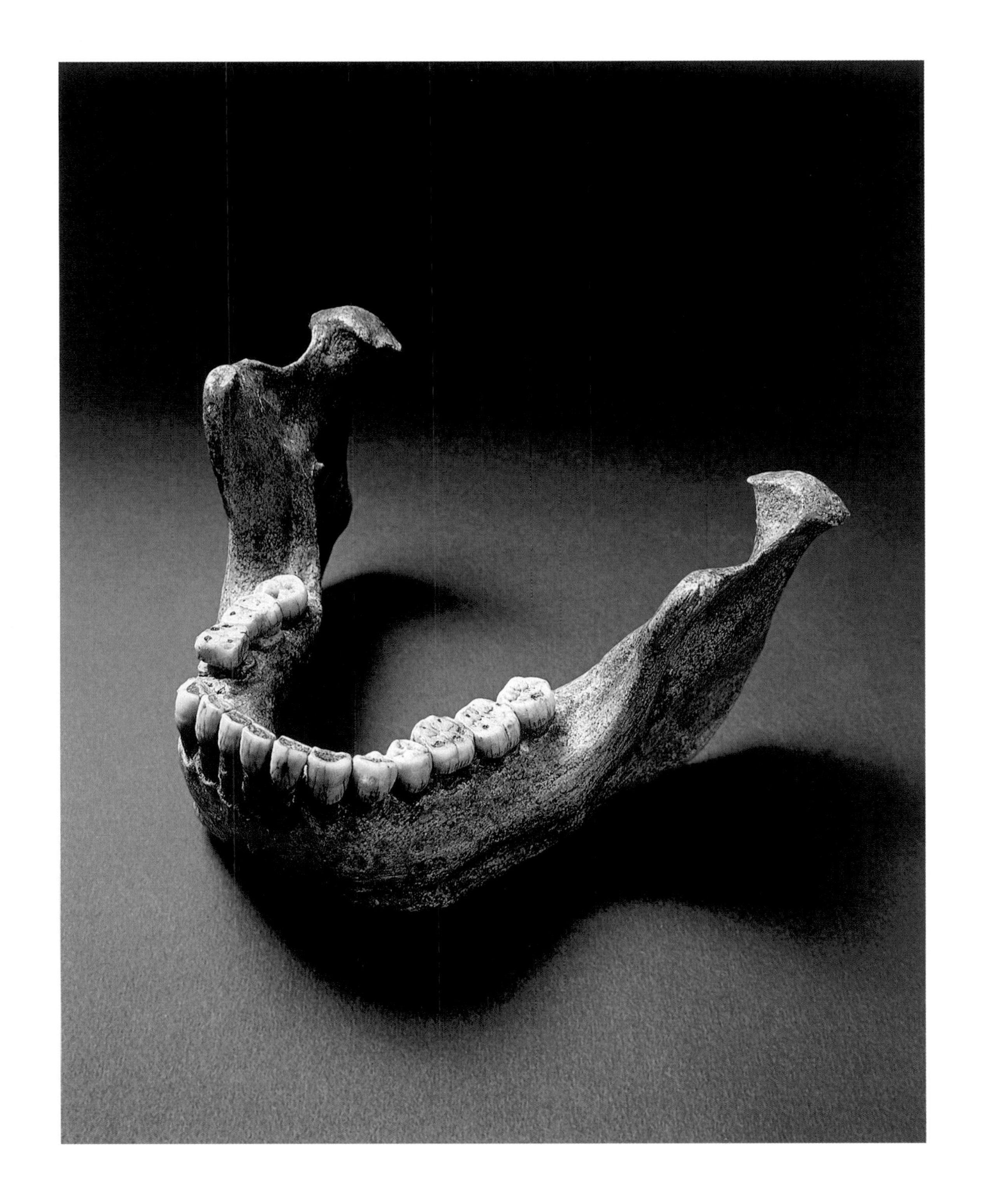

SPECIMEN	LOCALITY	AGE	DISCOVERER	DATE	PUBLICATION
Adult cranium	Caune de l'Arago, Tautavel, France	ca. 400,000 years	Henry de Lumley	1971	de Lumley, H., and M.-A. de Lumley. 1971. Découverte de restes humairs anténéandertaliens datés du début de Riss á la Caune de l'Arago (Tautavel, Pyrénées-Orientales). *C.R. Acad. Sci. Paris* 272:1729-1742

Homo heidelbergensis

ARAGO XXI

An impressive limestone cave in the eastern Pyrenees, perched above the Verdouble River, Arago has yielded about sixty human fossils since excavation began in 1964. These have included fourteen teeth and some finger bones, but the most spectacular fossils are a large hip bone and the cranium known as Arago XXI. Often referred to as Tautavel Man, the cranium has traditionally been considered that of a young male because of its size and robust facial features.

Despite its obvious distortion, Arago XXI is important for representing the robust end of anatomical variation in the early humans of Europe during the Middle Pleistocene (from about 700,000 to 200,000 years ago). Arago XXI possesses a fairly complete face, with five molar teeth, and part of the braincase. A prominent browridge frames the slightly projecting face. Behind the browridge, a deep sulcus, or depression, separates the face from the long, flattened forehead, and the cranium narrows behind the eye sockets (a feature called postorbital constriction). The sides of the cranium, the parietal bones, display an angular torus, a trait usually associated with *Homo erectus.*

This specimen has in fact been classified by its discoverers to that species. The hip bone from Arago also shows similarities to bones belonging to *H. erectus* times from Zhoukoudian, in China, Koobi Fora, in Kenya, and the Olduvai Gorge, in Tanzania. Two chinless lower jaws from Arago, with distinct sizes that could reflect differences between males and females, have also been compared with *H. erectus* specimens.

But there is some doubt whether *Homo erectus* ever entered Europe (see page 46), and other aspects of Arago XXI's anatomy argue against its placement in this species. For instance, the frontal, or forehead, bone of Arago is broader than that of a typical *erectus*, has less postorbital constriction, and shows no sagittal keel along the midline of the bone. Arago has a more straight-sided braincase, and its estimated brain size of 1,166 cc exceeds the known range for *erectus.*

Like Petralona 1 (see page 200) or the Steinheim cranium, the Arago specimen can instead be considered part of the "archaic" European population preceding the Neandertals, a population that would be expected to retain some primitive traits from its *erectus* ancestors. In many respects, the Steinheim cranium resembles a smaller version of the Arago cranium, with a similar frontal bone and facial anatomy, although the Steinheim cranium has a more projecting upper jaw and hollowed cheekbones. We therefore include Arago XXI in *Homo heidelbergensis*, a species showing early signs of adapting to the Pleistocene glacial environments of western Europe by evolving the incipient signs of a Neandertal physique, especially in the face.

***Homo heidelbergensis*, Arago XXI.**
Arago XXI represents the high end of variation in size and robusticity evident in European crania after 500,000 years ago and before the appearance of Neandertals. Note the degree of cranial constriction behind the eye sockets. Actual size.
Photograph by David Brill; courtesy Musée de l'Homme.

SPECIMEN	LOCALITY	AGE	DISCOVERERS	DATE	PUBLICATION
Adult cranium	Katsika Hill, Petralona, Greece	300,000-400,000 years	J. Malkotsis, J. Stathis, B. Avaramis, C. Sarijanides, and C. St. Hantzarides	September 16, 1960	Kokkoros, P., and A. Kanellis. 1960. Découverte d'un crane d'homme paléolithique dans peninsule Chalcidique. *Anthropologie* 64:132-47

Homo heidelbergensis

PETRALONA 1

In a cave of vaulted galleries full of hanging stalactites and climbing stalagmites, the cranium of Petralona 1 was found hanging suspended in a stalagmite 23 centimeters above the ground. Early reports that the rest of the skeleton lay nearby could be apocryphal, for no skeleton was ever recovered. This is a shame, for the remarkably well-preserved cranium has proved to be one of Europe's most enigmatic human fossils, its identity and geological age as uncertain as the stories surrounding its discovery. This specimen underscores the difficulty of trying to pin a species designation—an inherently dynamic, biological concept—to a static and singular fossil.

Petralona 1 is very transitional in form, with some Neandertal-like features and others that are much more primitive. The cranium looks as though a Neandertal face had been grafted to the braincase and rear of a cranium from some other species. In fact, it was originally classified as a Neandertal but later was claimed to be *Homo erectus*. The best match for Petralona's odd anatomy, though, comes from other European specimens of *Homo heidelbergensis* such as Arago XXI (see page 198) and the recently discovered Atapuerca crania (see page 204).

The Neandertal-like features of Petralona's face include the double-arched browridge rimming the upper eye sockets like a pair of spectacles and the broad nasal opening, which became exaggerated in later "classic" Neandertals. The cheekbones are inflated like those of Neandertals, whereas *Homo sapiens* has distinctive, hollowed-out cheekbones (see Cro-Magnon I, page 244). An important difference from Neandertals is that the middle of Petralona's face does not project forward. Overall the face, especially the upper half, is massive and broad compared to any Neandertal, and the upper jaw has a wide palate that would be too broad to fit even the lower jaw from Mauer (see page 196). As for the rest of the cranium, the thick occipital bone at the rear, with its prominent transverse torus, or bar, for anchoring muscles resembles what is seen in a typical *Homo erectus*. But the expanded braincase is quite unlike *erectus*, and the estimated cranial capacity of 1,220 cc compares with the largest *erectus* brains and smallest Neandertal brains.

Petralona 1 was originally thought to be only 70,000 years old, as young as many Neandertal remains. Later estimates increased its antiquity tenfold, but the actual age most likely falls in the middle of these extremes. A pair of analytical techniques, electron spin resonance and uranium series dating (see page 26), have been tried to determine the specimen's age by dating the calcite that covered the cranium and other stratigraphic layers in the cave. The results give a minimum age for Petralona 1 of 200,000 years, but the specimen's primitive morphology indicates that its true age is closer to twice that figure.

***Homo heidelbergensis*, Petralona 1** (see also page 8).
Another transitional form like Bodo, Petralona 1 possesses a Neandertal-like face, including a double-arched browridge and full cheekbones, but lacks Neandertal traits on the braincase or rear of the cranium. Actual size.
Photograph by David Brill; courtesy Paleontological Museum, University of Thessaloniki.

SPECIMEN	LOCALITY	AGE	DISCOVERER	DATE	PUBLICATION
Adult female cranium	Sigrist gravel pit, Steinheim, Germany	ca. 250,000 years	Karl Sigrist, Jr.	July 24, 1933	Berckhemer, F. 1933. Ein Menschen-Schädel aus den diluvialen Schottern von Steinheim a.d. Murr. *Anthropol. Anz.* 10:318-321

Homo heidelbergensis

STEINHEIM

A curious mosaic of primitive and advanced traits, the Steinheim cranium is the odd man (or, more likely from its size and anatomy, woman) out among Middle Pleistocene crania. It lacks the robust cranial characters of other *heidelbergensis* specimens like Arago XXI (see page 198) and Petralona 1 (see page 200), yet it is not strictly a Neandertal either. Unlike the Petralona 1 cranium, with its Neandertal-like face and primitive rear, Steinheim shows just the opposite pattern by possessing Neandertal traits only at the back of the cranium, such as the depression in the occipital bone called a suprainiac fossa.

Steinheim figured in the pre-sapiens hypothesis, first proposed by anatomists Sir Arthur Keith and Marcellin Boule and defended by their students, according to which modern humans must have had a very ancient ancestry, perhaps dating back millions of years, and the Neandertals and other archaic fossils had nothing to do with it. The remains of Piltdown Man fitted nicely into this scheme until they were exposed as a hoax. The Steinheim individual in turn was seen as the base of a relatively late-branching Neandertal stem that became an evolutionary dead end. The pre-sapiens view has since been discredited: there are no ancient modern humans in Europe.

Although Steinheim can be considered a plausible Neandertal ancestor—and we have opted to include it in *Homo heidelbergensis*—in some features it rather anticipates our own species. It retains some primitive features, including the marked supraorbital torus beneath the forehead and a cranial capacity of around 1,100 cc. (Steinheim was smaller brained than its approximate contemporary, the partial cranium from Swanscombe, England, and a cranial capacity of 1,100 cc is quite small for a Neandertal.) In certain traits of the face and the shape of flexion of the cranial base, the Steinheim cranium more closely resembles *Homo sapiens* than *Homo neanderthalensis*. Although warped and distorted from postmortem damage, the face clearly appears flatter than a Neandertal's and has a canine fossa, the slight depression beside the nasal opening, a trait not found in Nean-

dertals. Other modern traits include the large frontal sinus, the straight, expanded parietal bones, and small third molars. The mastoid process, the round protuberance at the base of the skull behind the ear canal, lacks the pronounced crests typically found on the mastoids of Neandertals as a result of the heavy forces that Neandertals placed on their front teeth. No other parts of the skeleton or any stone tools that could provide further clues to its identity accompanied the cranium.

***Homo heidelbergensis*, Steinheim.**
In contrast to the Petralona specimen, Steinheim has some Neandertal traits on the rear of the cranium combined with the flatter face, hollowed cheekbone, and small third molars of a modern human. Actual size.
Courtesy of Staatliches Museum für Naturkunde.

SPECIMEN	LOCALITY	AGE	DISCOVERER	DATE	PUBLICATION
Adult skull	Sima de los Huesos, Sierra de Atapuerca, Spain	ca. 300,000 years	Juan-Luis Arsuaga	July 8, 1992 and July 24, 1993	Arsuaga, J.-L., I. Martinez, A. Gracia, J.-M. Carretero, and E. Carbonell. 1993. Three new human skulls from the Sima de Los Huesos Middle Pleistocene site in Sierra de Atapuerca, *Nature* 362: 534-537

Homo heidelbergensis
ATAPUERCA 5

Atapuerca 5 is the most complete premodern skull in the fossil record. It is even more complete than the Cro-Magnon remains, which are nearly ten times younger. More important, this skull and more than 700 other human fossils from this site give the first comprehensive glimpse of Neandertals in the making.

Located at the bottom of a 15-meter shaft, the Sima de los Huesos, or "pit of the bones," is a remarkable site. This tiny, low-ceilinged chamber has yielded the remains of at least thirty individuals, including children, adolescents, and adults. Every bone in the skeleton is represented, even the fragile hyoid, previously found only with the Kebara Neandertal skeleton (see page 218). More than 70 percent of all human postcranial bones from the entire Middle Pleistocene (the period spanning 700,000 to 200,000 years ago) come from here, so Atapuerca offers an unprecedented opportunity to study variation due to age and sex in a single early human population from this time.

Speleologists stumbled upon the chamber in 1976 while mapping the cave system. They were followed by a Spanish excavation team, which spent six years removing tons of sediment from the chamber and searching for human bone fragments among thousands of pieces of cave bear bones before they hit paleontological paydirt. Such small finds as bones from the tips of fingers convinced the crew that the pit contained complete human skeletons.

Working under wet, cold, cramped conditions in the chamber for only a few hours at a time, five people suspended above the ground on wooden planks carefully carve away wet clay to expose the delicate, easily shattered bones. The fossils are put in boxes, which are then placed inside padded bags and packed in backpacks to be carried out of the cave, where they are allowed to dry and harden.

In 1992 the complete calvarium of Cranium 4 was found, cause for a champagne celebration in the cave. On the last day of fieldwork that year, the team uncovered the calvarium of Cranium 5 nearby. Returning to the site one last time to close up for the season, the team decided to dig a little more and soon found the face that fit Cranium 5. In 1993 they found a lower jaw for Cranium 5 and completed the skull.

Atapuerca 5 has a broad, bulky face with the widest nasal opening of the human fossil record. The cranium is relatively small and round. Its brain capacity, 1,125 cc, is smaller than that of any adult from Atapuerca (and smaller than almost every hominid brain from the Middle Pleistocene of Africa or Eurasia), but the upper canine from this skull is the biggest in the collection, indicating a wide range of size variation among individuals. Cranium 4, in contrast, may have the largest known brain capacity, 1,390 cc, of any Middle Pleistocene human fossil. These brains far surpassed those of *Homo erectus* in size and were close to the size of Neandertal brains. The degree of size difference between Cranium 4 and Cranium 5 is comparable to that between the crania from Steinheim (see page 202) and Petralona (see page 200).

Certain traits in the Atapuerca crania foreshadow the features of "classic" European Neandertals, including the prominent double-arched browridge above the eyes, the projecting middle face (particularly noticeable on Skull 5), a well-developed nuchal torus, or bar, on the rear of the braincase, worn front teeth, and, in Skull 5, a retromolar space, the gap behind the third molar that comes from the middle of the face being pulled forward. Skull 5 lacks a canine fossa (the hollowing of the cheekbone above the canine that occurs in modern humans but not in Neandertals, giving the latter an inflated look to the cheekbones). Another specimen in the collection does, however, possess a canine fossa.

In other traits, the Atapuerca population shows little tendency in the Neandertal direction. The crania recovered from the site are high and round in side view, rather than long and low like a typical Neandertal cranium, and they are broadest at the base. The mastoid process on the base of the cranium behind the ear opening is prominent and projecting except among juveniles, in which it resembles the Neandertal condition. The Atapuerca occipital bones also lack a protruding bun of bone and a suprainiac fossa, an elliptical depression on the bone.

The Atapuerca fossils capture an early stage of isolated evolution on the European continent that would culminate in the emergence and extinction of Neandertals. Although the bones were not found in association with tools or other evidence of habitation and were not deliberately buried, they may have entered the pit by human hands, perhaps foreshadowing another Neandertal behavioral trait, the burying of their dead.

Homo heidelbergensis, Atapuerca 4.
Unlike the relatively small cranial capacity of cranium 5, Atapuerca 4 has the largest brain capacity, 1,390 cc, of any Middle Pleistocene human fossil. When it was found, the excavators celebrated with champagne in the cramped cave. Actual size.
Photograph by Javier Trueba, Madrid Scientific Films; courtesy of Juan-Luis Arsuaga.

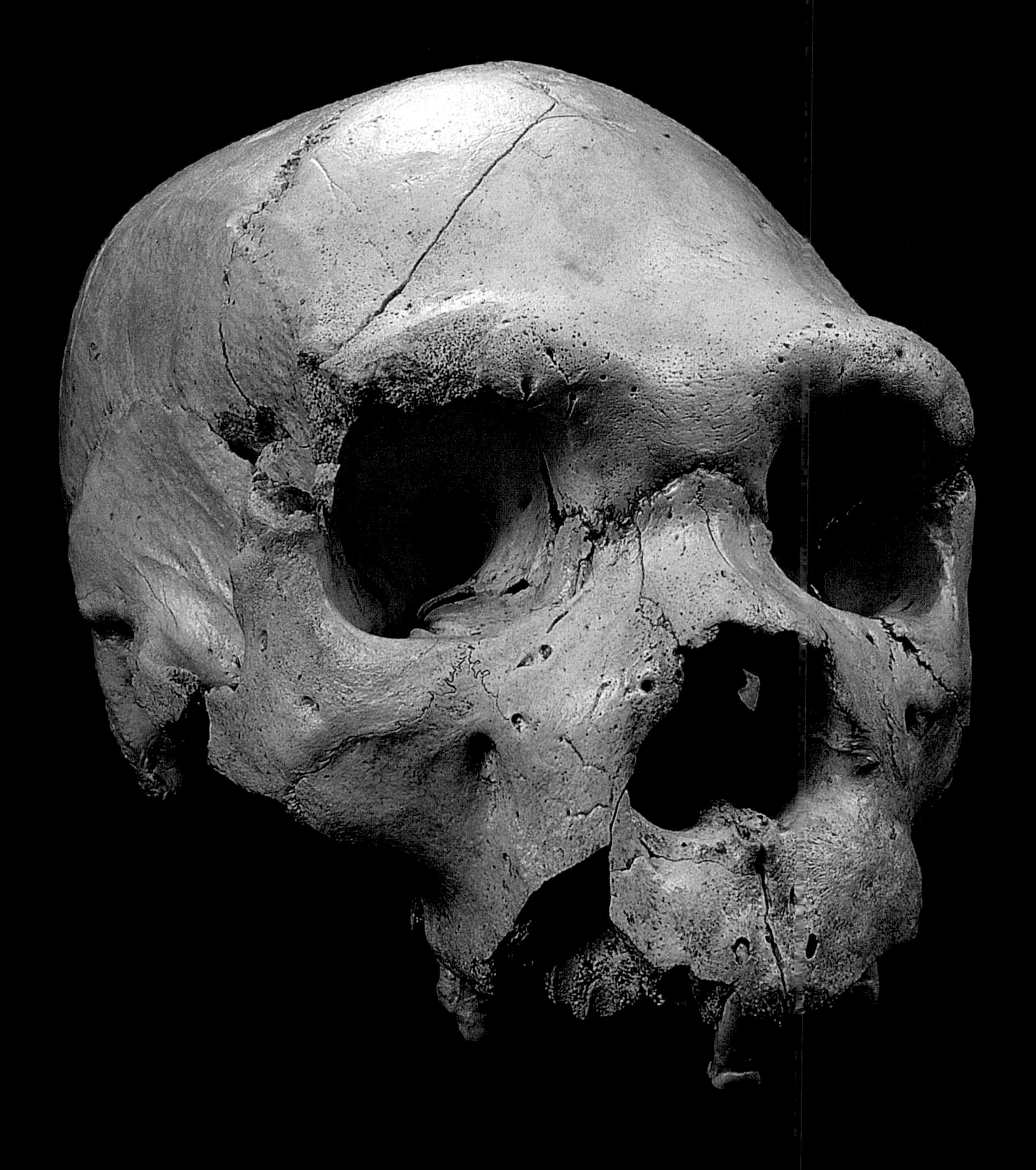

***Homo heidelbergensis,* Atapuerca 5** (see previous page).
The most complete skull (frontal, *left,* and lateral, *right*) from a rich Spanish cave site, Atapuerca 5 displays such incipient Neandertal traits as a projecting mid-face, double-arched browridge, inflated cheekbones, and a gap behind the third molar. Actual size.
Photographs by Javier Trueba, Madrid Scientific Films; courtesy of Juan-Luis Arsuaga.

SPECIMEN	LOCALITY	AGE	DISCOVERER	DATE	PUBLICATION
Adult cranium	Kabwe, Zambia	ca. 300,000 years	Tom Zwigelaar	June 17, 1921	Woodward, A.S. 1921. A new cave man from Rhodesia, South Africa. *Nature* 108(2716): 371-372

Homo heidelbergensis
BROKEN HILL 1

The quest for lead and zinc in a vast cave beneath a limestone kopje led to the discovery of this famous specimen, the first fossil of any human ancestor to be found in Africa. As such, it marked the start of paleoanthropologists' continuing quest for human origins on that continent. Tucked away in the wall at the base of the cave, 27 meters beneath the surface, the specimen known as Broken Hill 1 was brought to light in 1921 by miner Tom Zwigelaar, who reportedly hoisted the hefty cranium onto a pole as a way of prodding his men to work harder. A later search for the lower jaw turned up some modern-looking limb bones that came from different, possibly less ancient individuals. Soon the well-preserved fossil was delivered to anatomist Arthur Smith Woodward, in London, who described it in the journal *Nature* as a new species, *Homo rhodesiensis*, or Rhodesian Man.

Ever since the discovery of the Broken Hill cranium, several "archaic" human specimens have turned up in Africa, and we choose to include these with several European specimens in the species *Homo heidelbergensis*. Like Bodo (see page 144) and other fossils, Broken Hill 1 may be an individual from the ancient African population from which our species first evolved.

The Broken Hill, or Kabwe, specimen was once thought to be only 40,000 years old, based on an assessment of the associated stone tools (that assessment was later revised). Thus, American anthropologist Carleton Coon, who constructed an ambitious but flawed categorization of the world's races, used the cranium in his 1962 book *The Origin of Races* as evidence that Africans remained at a *Homo erectus* level of evolution at a time when *Homo sapiens* had already appeared in Europe. But evidence from other vertebrate fauna at the site suggests that Broken Hill 1 is at least 125,000 years old, and probably much older, so its primitive features make sense, in light of its obvious antiquity. Rather than being the contemporary of the very modern-looking Cro-Magnon specimens (see page 244), Broken Hill 1 is closer in age to the Petralona 1 cranium (see page 200).

Woodward noted some similarities between the large, heavy face of Broken Hill 1 and that of the Neandertal found at La Chapelle-aux-Saints, but he considered the shape of the Broken Hill specimen's braincase to be "much more ordinarily human." It has a low, sloping forehead and a long cranium that held a brain approaching 1,300 cc in size (significantly larger than the average for *Homo erectus*). In 1925, Woodward's colleague, Sir Arthur Keith, was impressed enough by this specimen to devote to it two chapters in the second volume of his revised *The Antiquity of Man*. He wrote that Broken Hill 1 revealed that "the wild dreams of the Darwinists have a solid basis in fact" and provided "for the first time a glimpse of our ancestral state."

Keith thought that the strikingly massive browridge over the eyes could not be explained as merely an adaptation to heavy chewing and speculated that, like the large canines of male gorillas, this was a secondary sex characteristic for males to attract mates. But there is no evidence that this was the case.

The specimen displays some disease and wounding. Ten of the sixteen upper teeth contain cavities, and abscesses formed in the jaw. A partially healed, quarter-inch-diameter wound above and in front of the left ear opening may have been inflicted by a sharp instrument or by carnivore teeth.

***Homo heidelbergensis*, Broken Hill 1.**
The first hominid fossil to be found in Africa, Broken Hill 1 resembles the Bodo cranium with its robust, primitive facial features. Ten of its teeth contain cavities, and a partially healed wound penetrated the bone by the left ear. Actual size.
Photograph by John Reader, Science Source/Photo Researchers.

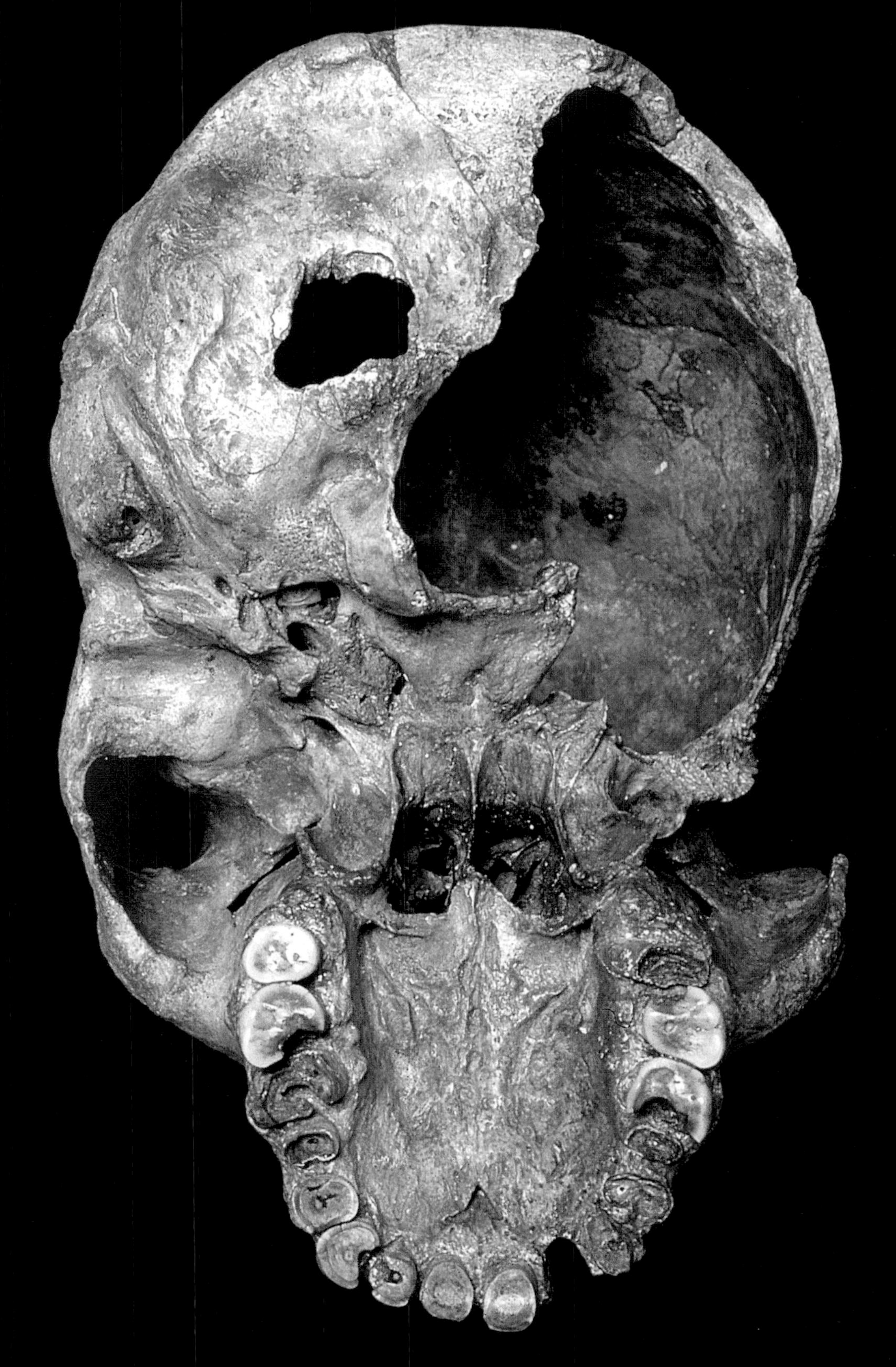

***Homo heidelbergensis*, Broken Hill 1** (see previous page). Actual size.
Photograph by John Reader, Science Source/Photo Researchers.

SPECIMEN	LOCALITY	AGE	DISCOVERER	DATE	PUBLICATION
Adult female partial cranium	Krapina cave, Croatia	130,000 years	Karl Gorjanovic-Kramberger	August 23, 1899	Gorjanovic-Kramberger, K. 1906. *Der diluviale Mensch von Krapina in Kroatien* (C.W. Kreicels Verlag, Wiesbaden)

Homo neanderthalensis
KRAPINA C

Paleoanthropologists typically work with scattered pieces of skulls and skeletons. Sometimes a nearly or fully complete skeleton is found. On very rare occasions, one site yields an entire ancient population for study. That is the case at Krapina, a limestone cave in the mountains of Hrvatsko Zagorje, Croatia, where the largest known sample of Neandertal remains has been found. Males and females, children to adults, and almost every part of the skeleton are represented among the more than 850 human fossils from up to eighty individuals, most of whom died between the ages of sixteen and twenty-four years. Three thousand animal bones and a thousand stone tools were also recovered. Because many of the hominid bones are broken into small pieces, determining exactly which bones go with which individuals has been a mostly insurmountable challenge since the turn-of-the-century excavations, but five crania have been partially reconstructed—Krapina C being the most complete.

As should be expected from such a large sample, the Krapina fossils exhibit considerable variation in size and anatomy, particularly in the teeth, lower jaws, and certain cranial features. The sample of 279 teeth includes front teeth with large crowns and molars that show the Neandertal trait of taurodontism, or an enlarged pulp chamber and fused roots. Such cranial traits as the projecting midface, a retromolar space in the lower jaw, and an occipital bun align the Krapina sample with other, more recent European Neandertals, as do postcranial bones revealing the Krapina people to have been barrel-chested with muscular forearms and powerful hands.

In general, however, the Krapina fossils lack the classic anatomy of later Neandertals from further west, such as La Ferrassie (see page 226). Neither are they quite like the Near East Neandertals. Compared to "classic" Neandertals, the Krapina individuals tended to be more lightly built but to have large faces, widely separated eye sockets, and broad crania. Some had higher foreheads and limb bones that closely resemble those of modern humans. The intermediate nature of the anatomy has been cited as evidence that the Krapina Neandertals evolved directly into the modern human populations of Central Europe, but evidence is lacking from elsewhere in Europe for such a transitional scenario.

The fragmentary state of human fossils from Krapina and another Croatian cave site, Vindija, as well as the presence of stone tool cut marks on certain bones strongly suggests that some of these Neandertals were butchered and possibly cannibalized (see page 93). Debate on this issue has continued ever since the initial excavator, Karl Gorjanovic-Kramberger, concluded that the pattern of bone breakage and the burning of some bones provided evidence of cannibalism. Some of the breakage may have come from falling rock debris, but falling rocks cannot explain why only the elbow ends of the humeri are present and not the shoulder ends of this marrow-rich upper arm bone. Meaty and marrow-filled femora are missing from the sample, except for one shaft fragment from a child. And there is no sign of carnivore chewing on the bones that remain. In addition to obvious cut marks, some bones show concoidal scars, the rippling fracture pattern that is a distinctive signature of blows from a human stone artifact, further evidence that human bones were actively processed for the nutrients they contained.

***Homo neanderthalensis*, Krapina C** (see also page 95).
Krapina C is the most complete of five crania from this Croatian cave, which preserved highly fragmentary remains from a population of about 80 individuals, from children to adults. This specimen shows the typically broad, lightly built face of these particular Neandertals. Actual size.
Photograph by David Brill; courtesy of Geolosko-Paleontologi Musej.

SPECIMEN	LOCALITY	AGE	DISCOVERER	DATE	PUBLICATION
Adult female cranium	Saccopastore quarry, Rome, Italy	ca. 120,000 years	Mario Grazioli	May 13, 1929	Sergi, S. 1929. La scoperta di un cranio del tipo di Neanderthal presso Roma, *Rivista di Antropologia* 28:457-462

Homo neanderthalensis

SACCOPASTORE 1

With its lightly built cranium, the specimen known as Saccopastore 1, found in the Saccopastore quarry in Rome, resembles early modern humans almost as much as it does the "classic" Neandertals that appeared in Europe 60,000 years later. That fact gave Saccopastore 1 a pivotal place in the pre-Neandertal hypothesis developed by Italian anthropologist Sergio Sergi, who first studied and described this specimen. Sergi proposed that the evolutionary line leading from an anatomically generalized "pre-Neandertal" type of early human split into two branches, one leading to later Neandertals and the other to modern *Homo sapiens*. He based this idea on the resemblance of Saccopastore to specimens from Steinheim (see page 202), Swanscombe, Fontéchevade, and Ehringsdorf. The Swanscombe and Steinheim individuals formed the pre-Neandertal base, with the specimens from Saccopastore, Krapina, and Ehringsdorf occupying the Neandertal branch and the cranial fragments from Fontéchevade on the branch to modern humans. This idea, which came to dominate the previously popular pre-sapiens hypothesis (see page 43), made it acceptable for archaic-looking early humans to be viewed as modern human ancestors, although the western European Neandertals were still seen as an evolutionary dead end. This scenario is partially right: Neandertals were the end product of isolated evolution in Europe from *Homo heidelbergensis*, but it is not clear that modern *Homo sapiens* descended from any pre-Neandertal stock.

Missing only its browridges, Saccopastore 1 preserves the most complete evidence for an early Neandertal from the Riss-Würm interglacial period (between 127,000 to 115,000 years ago), making it comparable in geological age to the large but highly fragmented Neandertal population from Krapina (see page 211). Six years after this female cranium was found with Mousterian tools at a gravel quarry along a tributary of the Tiber River, a companion specimen was found by anthropologists Alberto Blanc and Abbé Henri Breuil during a visit to the site. Saccopastore 2 is a more robust male represented by the cranial base and pieces of a face that more closely resembles the Petralona 1 cranium (see page 200) than a typical Neandertal. Both specimens reveal that early Neandertal crania contained many generalized features.

Yet they are unmistakably Neandertals. Saccopastore 1 has a low cranial vault and a projecting midface with a broad nasal opening. It exhibits all the typical Neandertal features from the rear and base of the skull—including a suprainiac fossa and occipitomastoid crest—except the occipital bun. Unlike most Neandertals, however, Saccopastore 1's occipital bone appears rounded, and the cranial base appears more flexed than in such "classic" Neandertal specimens as those from La Chapelle-aux-Saints and La Ferrassie. This latter feature may have implications (see page 106) for Neandertals' capacity to use spoken language.

***Homo neanderthalensis,* Saccopastore 1.** A female member of an early Neandertal population, this specimen has a typically broad nasal opening and low forehead, as seen in frontal view. From the side, the low cranial vault and projecting mid-face are clearly visible, along with the flexed cranial base. *Courtesy of Giorgio Manzi, Museo di Antropologia of the University of Rome "La Sapienza".*

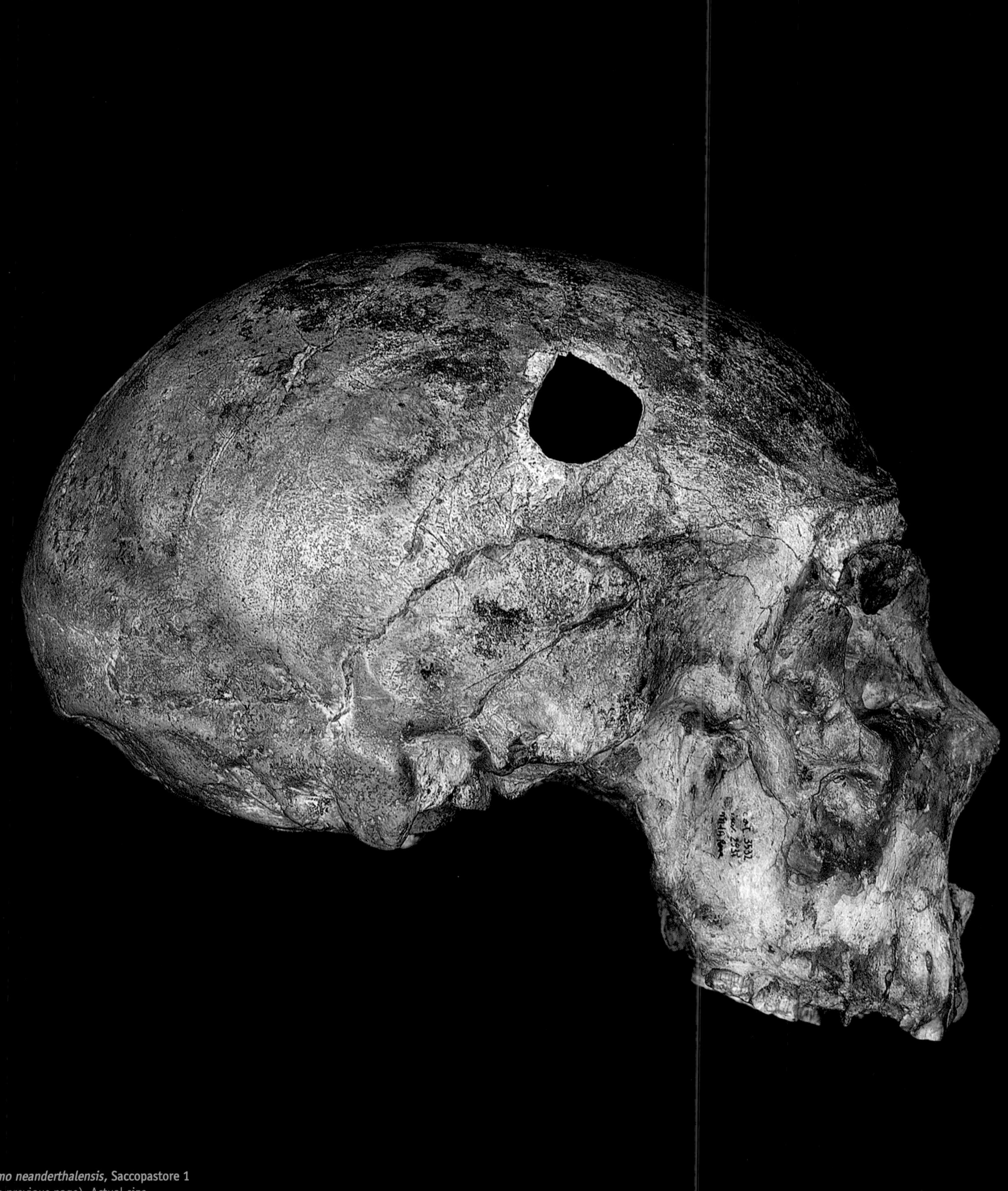

***Homo neanderthalensis*, Saccopastore 1**
(see previous page). Actual size.
Courtesy of Giorgio Manzi, Museo di Antropologia of the University of Rome "La Sapienza".

SPECIMEN	LOCALITY	AGE	DISCOVERER	DATE	PUBLICATION
Juvenile partial skeleton	Teshik-Tash, Uzbekistan	ca. 70,000 years	Alexei Okladnikov	July 4, 1938	Gremyatsky, M.A., and M.F. Nestourkh, editors. 1949. *Teshik-Tash: Paleolithic Man* (Moscow University Publishers, Moscow) [in Russian]

Homo neanderthalensis

TESHIK-TASH

The skeleton known as Teshik-Tash, after its place of discovery in Uzbekistan, defines the easternmost extent of the Neandertals' known geographic range. Some 3,200 kilometers from the nearest Neandertal in Europe and 1,600 kilometers from his conspecifics in the Shanidar cave of Iraq, this young boy lay in a cave due south of Samarkand at an altitude of nearly 1.6 kilometers in the rugged and remote Gissar mountain range. The Teshik-Tash specimen demonstrates that Neandertals inhabited isolated and extreme environments.

Teshik-Tash was the first Paleolithic site in Central Asia to be excavated, but other nearby cave sites indicate a long human history in the region. Discovery of the skeleton, its bones yellowed by the surrounding sediment, came at the beginning of a two-year excavation. The cave contained five separate occupation layers and a dozen hearths, some of which had clusters of broken bones and wild goat horns and stone flakes and core tools nearby.

The skeleton had apparently been buried at the base of the thickest and archeologically richest occupation layer, along the cave's western wall, with the feet pointed toward the entrance. The shallow pit in which it lay protected the skeleton from falling rocks that shattered bones in the layer immediately above the corpse, but the pressure of overlying sediments flattened the skull. Fortunately, the cranium was well preserved and could be reconstructed from about 150 pieces.

The Teshik-Tash boy died at around age nine, but he had reached sufficient maturity to have developed some of the distinctive features of Neandertal anatomy. These included a large face and nasal region, a developing browridge, a receding forehead, a long cranium, and a lower jaw lacking a bony chin. His cranial capacity was around 1,500 cc, high for the boy's age by modern human standards.

Various parts of the postcranial skeleton, including one neck vertebra, several ribs, a humerus, the clavicles or collarbones, a femur, a tibia, and the fibulae (the smaller of the lower leg bones), lay scattered near the cranium. The ends of both the humerus and femur had been gnawed off, and a coprolite (fossilized scat) lay near the skeleton, suggesting that a hyena or other carnivore had dug up the burial and removed some of the bones. No artifacts had been included with the body.

The most striking feature of the grave was the presence of six pairs of large bony horn cores from Siberian ibex, or mountain goat, that had been placed point down in a circle surrounding the skull, and a few other bones. A small fire had been lit briefly beside the body. These clues have made Teshik-Tash a frequently cited example of Neandertal ritual burial (see page 100).

It is difficult to know whether these horns were intentionally placed around the corpse in some symbolic gesture. Perhaps the horns were tools that were used to bury the boy and were then discarded, serving no ritualistic purpose. Or the proximity of the horn cores to the skeleton may be fortuitous. Ibex horns and bones are very common throughout the site; of 769 bones found in the cave from mammals other than rodents, 761 of these belonged to ibex. Judging from such prevalence, ibex was the animal of choice hunted by the Neandertal inhabitants, and villagers in this remote region still relied on goat hunting for subsistence as recently as the late 1930s, when this skeleton was found. Whether or not the Neandertals of Teshik-Tash practiced a cult of the dead and a cult of wild goats, they depended on these agile, majestic mammals to survive here.

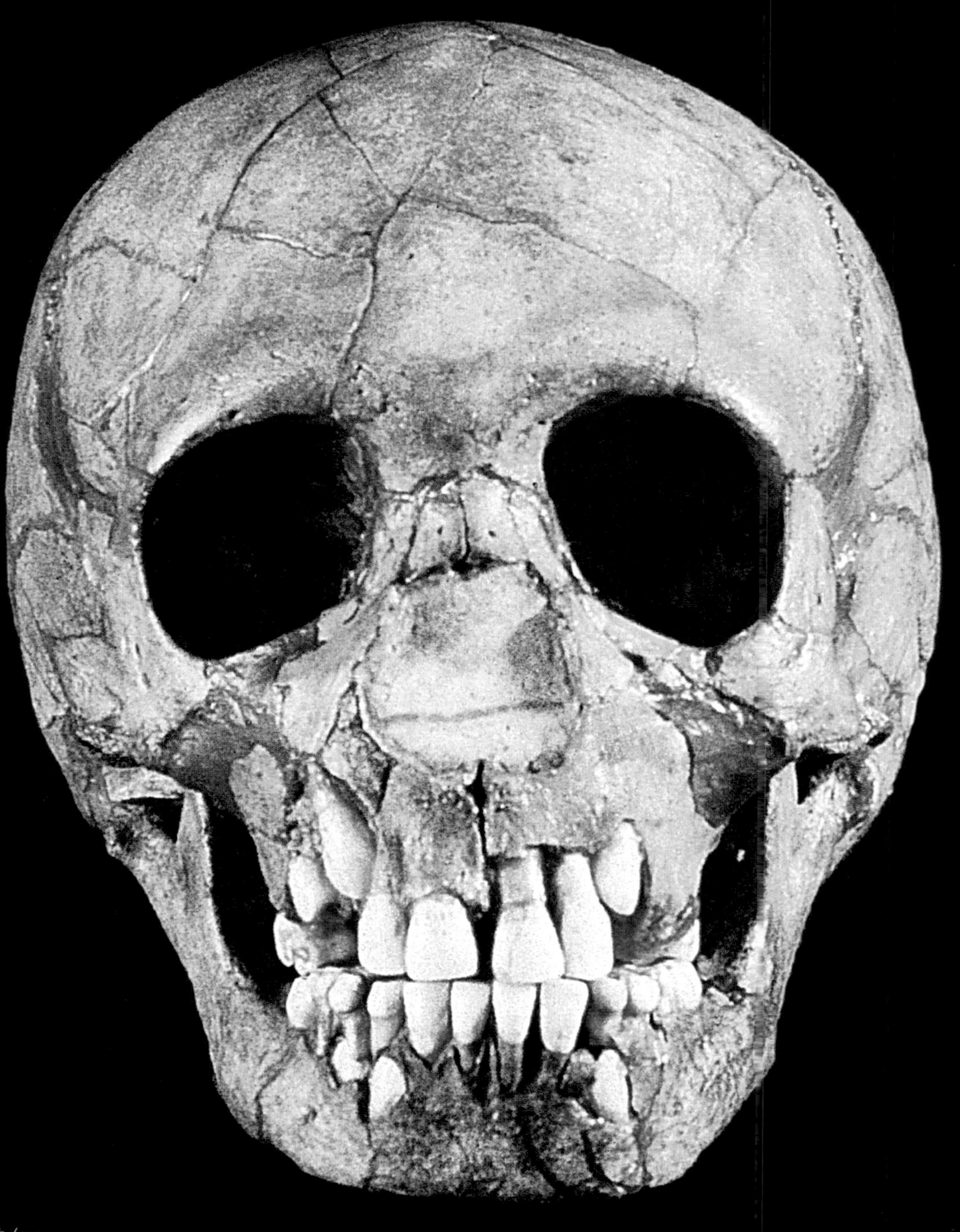

***Homo neanderthalensis,* Teshik-Tash** (see previous page).
This child's skull (frontal, *left,* and lateral, *right*) and accompanying skeleton represents the easternmost Neandertal yet found. Even at a young age, the specimen exhibits such distinctive Neandertal features as the long, low cranium, large nasal opening, a developing browridge, and a lower jaw lacking a chin. Actual size.
Photographs by Andrei Mauer; courtesy of Institute and Museum of Anthropology, Moscow State University.

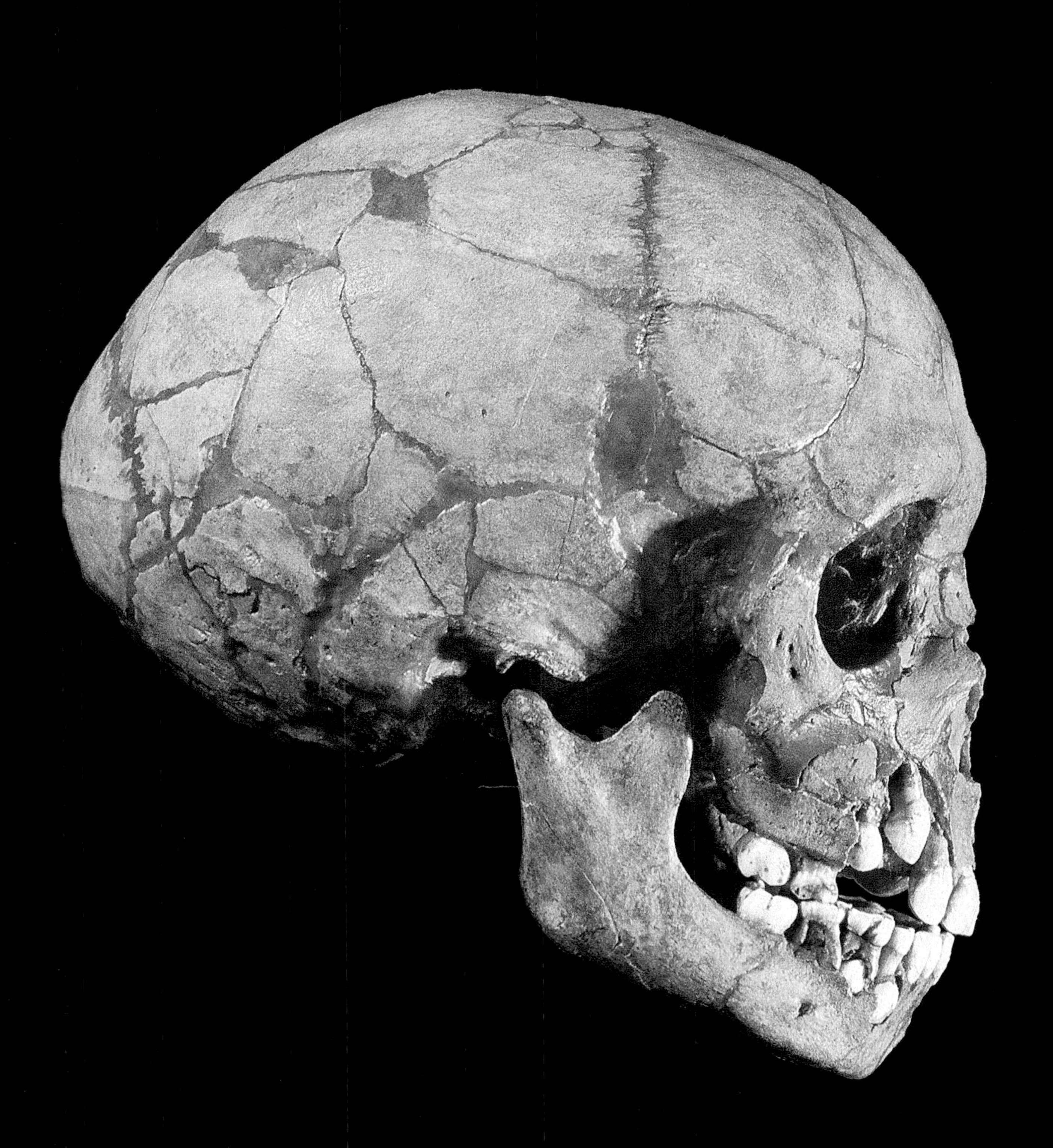

SPECIMEN	LOCALITY	AGE	DISCOVERER	DATE	PUBLICATION
Adult male skeleton	Kebara Cave, Israel	ca. 60,000 years	Lynne Schepartz	October 1983	Arensburg, B., O. Bar Yosef, M. Chech, P. Goldberg, H. Laville, L. Meignen, Y. Rak, E. Tchernov, A.M. Tillier, and B. Vandermeersch. 1985. Une sépulture néanderthalien dans la grotte de Kebara (Israel). *Compte Rendus des Séances de l'Academie des Sciences* (Paris), Série II, 300:227-230

Homo neanderthalensis

KEBARA 2

Nicknamed "Moshe" in honor of Moshe Stekelis, a previous excavator of this cave site, the Kebara 2 specimen is a virtually complete skeleton from the mandible on down. In fact, it is the most complete Neandertal specimen known, and it includes the first complete set of ribs, vertebrae, and pelvis ever found.

Another preservation first for Kebara 2 is the hyoid bone, the only bone in the human body that connects to no other bones. Rooted in the cartilage surrounding the larynx, the hyoid anchors throat muscles necessary for speech. The discovery in this specimen of a hyoid bone identical to that of modern humans has important implications for the Neandertals' capacity for language (see page 107).

Moshe's skeleton was discovered on the edge of a test pit dug during initial excavation during the 1960s (which revealed the fragmentary infant skeleton labeled Kebara 1). In an apparent burial, he had been placed on his back inside a shallow pit, with the right arm laid across his chest and the left arm resting on his abdomen. He was probably between the ages of 25 and 35 when he died, and there are no clues in the bones to death by violence or disease. Mysteriously, Moshe's cranium has vanished, possibly carried off by a carnivore or buried elsewhere in the cave. Only one upper third molar was found. The right leg and the lower half of the left leg are also missing.

Although we cannot regard his face, Kebara 2 has clear similarities to skeletons from Amud, Tabun, and Shanidar, but it is more robust than all of them. At 1.7 meters, the individual was taller than a typical European Neandertal. The massive mandible, with a complete set of teeth, possesses the retromolar space common to Neandertals and lacks a chin. Other parts of the skeleton, such as the hyoid and vertebrae, are indistinguishable in size and shape from those of modern humans. The fifth lumbar vertebra, at the base of the spinal column, for instance, has the same modern modifications for bipedalism found in our own spines.

The complete pelvis also speaks to this hominid's posture and locomotion. With a longer distance between the hip joints on the sides and the joint of the pubic bones in front of the pelvis, Neandertals had their center of gravity shifted forward and may have lacked the degree of cushioning and shock absorption found in a modern human pelvis.

Besides this spectacular fossil specimen, the Kebara cave preserved a rich archeological record that offers a detailed look at the lives of Near East Neandertals, who occupied the site from before 60,000 years ago until at least 48,000 years ago. (Less frequent human occupation occurred during the Upper Paleolithic, and consequently carnivore remains are more common from this time period.) More than 25,000 stone tools at least 2.5 centimeters in size were collected from the site. These represent the Levallois industry typical of this time period and generally associated with Neandertal remains. The Neandertals preferred fine-grained flints, mostly collected within a few miles of the cave, for their tools, and they used efficient flaking techniques to make the most of their raw material. Half of the triangular points and flakes that have been analyzed for signs of wear bear impact fractures, suggesting that these tools had been hafted to wooden shafts and then heaved as projectiles. Other tools have wear traces associated with woodworking and cutting. Curiously, the Kebara artifacts closely resemble stone tools excavated from the Israeli cave of Qafzeh, but the more ancient skeletons buried at Qafzeh (see page 239) are clearly modern humans rather than Neandertals. Why two distinct populations, different species, would share the same culture remains a mystery.

Numerous round and oval hearths were excavated in the cave, along with layers where grassy and woody vegetation was burned. Pieces of burned flint retrieved from the hearths proved crucial in dating the site and the skeleton by the thermoluminescence technique. Locally obtained oak wood fueled the hearth fires, which were apparently used to parch wild peas and perhaps to roast gazelle and deer meat. Garbage dumps full of broken animal bones and waste from stone tool manufacture accumulated along the cave's north wall, away from the central living area. The picture that emerges from this broad range of archeological evidence suggests that the dwellers of Kebara were far more technologically capable and sophisticated than Neandertals have often been portrayed.

***Homo neanderthalensis*, Kebara 2.** No cranium was found with this skeleton buried in an Israeli cave, but Kebara 2 is nonetheless the most complete Neandertal specimen known and includes the first set of ribs, vertebrae, and pelvis ever found. *Photograph by David Brill; courtesy of Sackler School of Medicine, Tel Aviv University.*

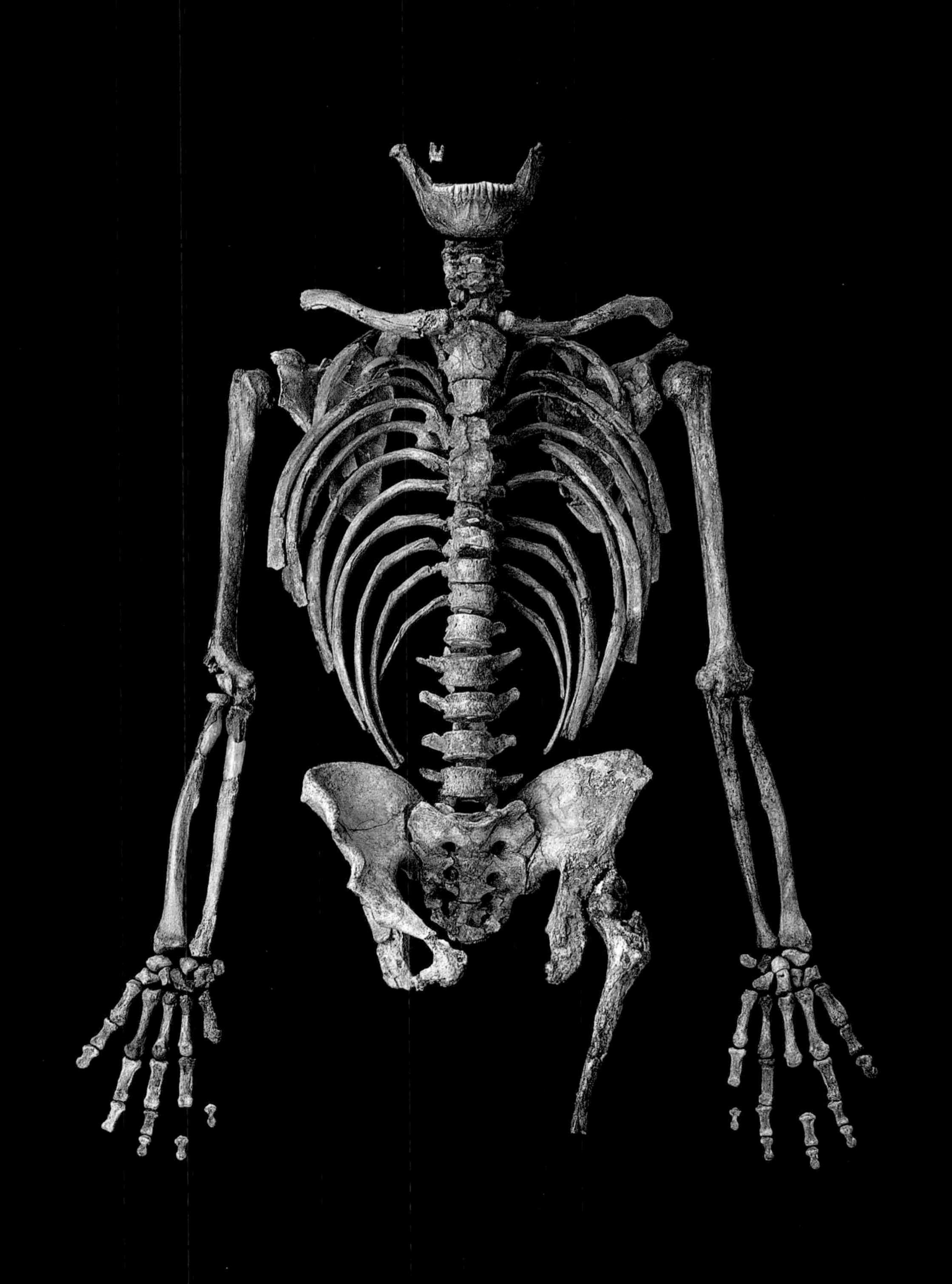

SPECIMEN	LOCALITY	AGE	DISCOVERERS	DATE	PUBLICATION
Adult male skeleton	Amud Cave, Israel	40,000-50,000 years	Hisashi Suzuki	June 28, 1961	Suzuki, H., and F. Takai, editors. 1970. *The Amud Man and His Cave Site* (University of Tokyo Press, Tokyo)

Homo neanderthalensis

AMUD 1

The adult male hominid skeleton found in Amud Cave, Israel, can be described by two superlatives. At more than 1.8 meters, the individual is the tallest Neandertal known, and the skull enclosed the largest brain—a whopping 1,740 cc—of any known fossil hominid. Judging from the degree of closure in the sutures between the cranial bones, he probably died at around age 25.

The shattered skeleton lay on its left side with its limbs flexed, at the top of the Middle Paleolithic level, surrounded by younger Upper Paleolithic tools and even younger pottery. The pale gray bones had not completely fossilized and proved fragile in the cave's soft soil. The skull, which had been crushed from the side, was found first and was so encrusted with limestone rubble that it was nearly mistaken for a chunk of fallen cave ceiling. Unfortunately, the palate and much of the diagnostic facial region is missing, but the enormous lower jaw is intact. The jaws contain a complete set of thirty-two teeth, which are small for such a large individual. Many parts are less complete: the vertebrae, pelvis and right lower limbs, for instance, were badly damaged or missing.

Amud 1's anatomy presents an eclectic mix of features. Although clearly a Neandertal, it is not a "classic" Neandertal such as the most famous European specimens. Amud 1 shows closest affinity to the Neandertals of Shanidar Cave in Iraq (the skull was reconstructed using Shanidar I as a guide) and Tabun, Israel, but it also has some similarities to the Skhul and Qafzeh populations of early modern *Homo sapiens.*

Although the large, long, narrow face falls within the range of European Neandertal dimensions, there are differences in the details. The browridge above the eyes is more slender and angles backward on each side of the face. The eye sockets have sharply defined margins, as in modern humans, rather than the typically rounded edges of Neandertals. The maxilla appears less inflated in the cheeks than can be seen in the Neandertal from La Chapelle-aux-Saints or even in specimens from Shanidar, and there is a more marked chin at the front of the mandible than is typical of Neandertals.

The mix of Neandertal and modern features continues on the cranium. The cranium is wide and long; it is longer than in any modern human and longer than in the biggest European Neandertal, from La Ferrassie. The mastoid process of the temporal bone, which protrudes like a knob beneath the ear opening, approaches modern human size and is larger than the mastoid process in the Neandertals at La Chapelle-aux-Saints and Gibraltar. In rear view, the cranium is perfectly round, like a bowling ball—a typical Neandertal trait—but the occipital bone combines a Neandertal-like torus, or bar, of bone across its width with a sharply curved overall shape that resembles a modern human cranium.

Amud is Hebrew for "pillar" and refers to a stone pinnacle near the cave entrance. The cave was perched about 30 meters above the streambed of the Wadi Amud, through which water flows to the Sea of Galilee. A nearby perennial spring may have also attracted Neandertals to the site. Initial attempts to date the Neandertal occupation of the cave by the radiocarbon method fell far short of the real age; more recent estimates using the electron spin resonance technique on a mammal tooth suggest an age of between 40,000 and 50,000 years, relatively late in the Neandertals' time on Earth. Perhaps the combination of a relatively young age and peculiar anatomy indicate that Amud 1 is a more evolved form of Neandertal than its immediate European predecessors; or it may simply be a variant due to geographic separation.

***Homo neanderthalensis*, Amud 1** (see also page 116).
Though it lacks the important mid-face region, this specimen can be identified as a Neandertal, resembling those from other Near East sites. Note the retromolar gap behind the tooth row in the lower jaw. Actual size.
Photograph by David Brill; courtesy Israel Antiquities Authority, Rockefeller Museum.

SPECIMEN	LOCALITY	AGE	DISCOVERERS	DATE	PUBLICATION
Partial infant skeleton	Amud Cave, Israel	50,000 to 60,000 years	Tina Hietala and Yoel Rak	June 9, 1992	Rak, Y., W.H. Kimbel, and E. Hovers. 1994. A Neandertal infant from Amud Cave, Israel, *Journal of Human Evolution* 26: 313-324

Homo neanderthalensis

AMUD 7

Renewed excavation at Amud Cave in the early 1990s unearthed the remains of four humans. The bones indicate that these individuals had all died in the first year of life except for a child of about eight years, represented by a single tooth. The most complete specimen, a tiny newborn's skeleton catalogued as Amud 6, had been buried just on the edge of a Middle Paleolithic layer, but radiocarbon dating of Amud 6 determined that this infant was a modern human who had died between 680 and 880 A.D. and whose grave had been dug into older layers of the site.

Amud 7, found the following year in 1992, had been buried even lower in the stratigraphic sequence of the cave than the male Neandertal skeleton of Amud 1 (see page 220) that had been discovered in 1961. Amud 7, therefore, dates without question to Neandertal times, specifically between 50,000 and 60,000 years ago. Based on the degree of tooth eruption, the infant died when it was just ten months old.

Although the collapsed cranium of Amud 7 includes only the occipital, parietal, and temporal bones, the lower jaw, or mandible, is relatively complete, and the ribs and vertebrae are well preserved. Found lying on its right side in a niche on the cave's north wall, the skeleton's articulation, especially that of the intact hand and foot bones, suggests that this was also an intentional burial. Intriguingly, a red deer's upper jaw leaned against what remained of the infant's pelvis. Two early modern human burials at the nearby cave sites of Qafzeh and Skhul also had associated animal bones (see Skhul V, page 242), but if the deer jaw had been placed beside the Amud infant, it would mark the first known occurrence in the Levant of grave goods associated with a Neandertal.

Analysis of the Amud 7 skeleton has revealed some previously unrecognized features that appear to be unique to Neandertals and should prove useful in identifying other fossil remains to this species. For instance, the foramen magnum, the hole in the base of the cranium through which the spinal cord passes, is extremely elongated and oval shaped in Amud 7, whereas modern humans retain the more primitive round shape (shared with most primates and many other mammals). A similarly elongated and oval foramen magnum can be seen in juvenile Neandertal crania from Engis, La Quina, and Teshik-Tash (see page 215).

Three more distinctive Neandertal traits occur in the mandible of Amud 7. First, there is no bony chin as in modern humans, so, when viewed from below, the front of the Amud baby's jaw appears squared off rather than pointed. Second, the U-shaped notch on top of the mandible's vertical ramus ends in the middle of the condyle, the knob that articulates the jaw with the cranium, and not on the side of the condyle as in all other hominids. Third, a prominent lipped tubercle or bump on the inner surface of the ramus marks the attachment of the medial pterygoid muscle. This muscle aids in chewing, and the uppermost muscle fibers appear to have been particularly well developed in Neandertals, as indicated by the rugose muscle marks on this side of the ramus that end at the medial pterygoid tubercle, which is absent in other early humans.

That such features appear even on the skull of a young infant indicates that they are genetically determined traits and reaffirms the many anatomical differences between Neandertals and modern humans. If babies can be so easily distinguished by the traits, it is additional evidence that Neandertals indeed constitute a separate species from modern humans.

***Homo neanderthalensis*, Amud 7.** Remains of a ten-month-old infant excavated from Amud cave contain some features unique to Neandertals, including an oval foramen magnum at the base of the cranium. *Photograph by David Brill.*

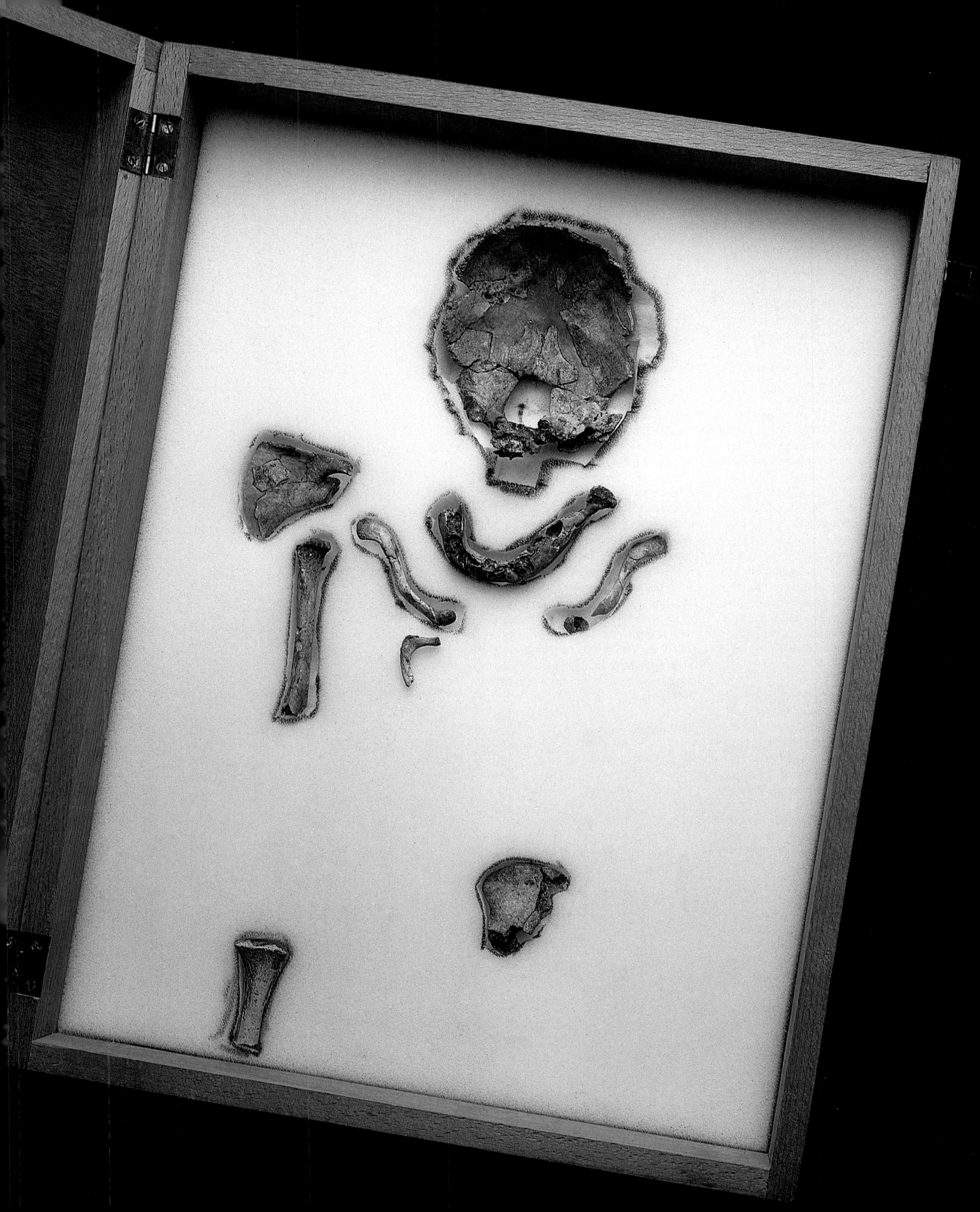

SPECIMEN	LOCALITY	AGE	DISCOVERERS	DATE	PUBLICATION
Adult male skeleton	Bouffia Bonneval, La Chapelle-aux-Saints, France	ca. 50,000 years	Amadee and Jean Bouyssonie and Josef Bonneval	August 3, 1908	Boule, M. 1908. L'Homme fossile de La Chapelle-aux-Saints (Covrèze). *C. R. Acad. Sci. Paris* 147:1349-1352

Homo neanderthalensis
LA CHAPELLE-AUX-SAINTS

The most complete Neandertal specimen known when it was found, the skeleton of a nearly toothless old man of La Chapelle-aux-Saints came to symbolize Neandertalness, but in the errant view of Neandertals as shuffling, brutish cavemen—a complete misrepresentation of their anatomy, gait, and intelligence. Marcellin Boule's in-depth study of this skeleton, published between 1909 and 1912, singlehandedly created this lingering and damaging image. Boule correctly noted that a large suite of skeletal features distinguished the Neandertals, but his unfortunate description resulted in Neandertals being considered more closely related to apes than to modern humans. By effectively making the La Chapelle-aux-Saints individual a reference specimen for its species, he left no place for Neandertals in our evolutionary lineage. This influential and persuasive study maligned Neandertals for decades and helped put the pre-sapiens hypothesis (see page 43) at center stage in the emerging debate over intellect and brain size in the hominid family tree.

Boule misinterpreted several pathological aspects of the skeleton and other features that reflect adaptation to a cold environment as being primitive and apelike. Among the pathological parts are a deformed left hip, a crushed toe, severe arthritis in the neck vertebrae, a broken rib, and a damaged kneecap. So unwavering was Boule in his bias that he noted the immense brain capacity of the La Chapelle individual—1,625 cc, well in excess of the modern human mean—but nonetheless discounted Neandertals' mental aptitude in the face of so many other "primitive" traits.

Reevaluation of this skeleton by anatomists William Straus and A.J.E. Cave in the 1950s showed how the deforming arthritis had skewed Boule's view of Neandertal gait. Neandertals were suddenly embraced and became all too readily included as a subspecies of human. But this Neandertal renaissance has since given way to a growing consensus that this was a separate species, a successful and highly derived—not primitive—one that ultimately went extinct. There was not enough time for Neandertals to have evolved into modern humans in Europe; they could not have been our immediate ancestors.

More recently, the La Chapelle-aux-Saints specimen has figured prominently in a debate over whether Neandertals possessed the equivalent of modern spoken language. It was argued that because the cranium had an unusually flat base, the larynx would have sat too high in the throat of Neandertals for them to pronounce the vowels a, i, and u. The base of a modern human cranium, once past infancy, becomes flexed, which lowers the larynx in the throat and permits a broader range of sounds to pass from the pharynx. A more recent reconstruction of the cranium of the La Chapelle-aux-Saints individual resulted in greater base flexion than Boule allowed in his reconstruction, but it still appears to have a flatter cranial base than in modern humans. Exactly what conclusion can be drawn from this feature remains unclear, but perhaps it is time to refrain from reading further Neandertal generalities into the diseased and damaged specimen from La Chapelle-aux-Saints.

***Homo neanderthalensis*, La Chapelle-aux-Saints.** The aged, pathological skeleton from La Chapelle formed the basis of a pervasive, but errant, view of Neandertals as shuffling, stupid brutes. The resorption of tooth sockets in both jaws, arthritis, and broken bones are just a few of the ailments that afflicted this individual. Actual size.
Photograph by John Reader, Science Source/Photo Researchers.

SPECIMEN	LOCALITY	AGE	DISCOVERERS	DATE	PUBLICATION
Adult male skeleton	La Ferrassie, France	ca. 50,000 years	Denis Peyrony and Louis Capitan	September 17, 1909	Capitan, L., and D. Peyrony. 1909. Deux squelettes humains au milieu de foyers de l'époque moustérienne. *Revue anthrop.* 19:402-409

Homo neanderthalensis

LA FERRASSIE 1

The adult male skeleton catalogued as La Ferrassie 1 best exhibits the "classic" Neandertal anatomy that evolved in glacier-covered western Europe midway between this species's appearance and extinction. All the defining Neandertal features appear in the cranium of La Ferrassie 1: the receding forehead, the long, low vault of the braincase, the globular shape when viewed from behind, the prominent, double-arched browridge, the projecting midface and backward-swept cheekbones, the weakly developed chin, the heavily worn front teeth, the retromolar gap behind the tooth row (resulting from the teeth having been pulled forward with the face), and the huge brain capacity (in this case more than 1,600 cc). The limbs show the Neandertal tendency for stout, thick bones with large joints.

Classic Neandertals constitute the clearest example in human evolution of a distinctive and unique set of anatomical features characterizing a population. Although seemingly trivial when considered individually, these shared features compose a consistent pattern that helps to define the Neandertals as an evolutionary unit—a distinct species from modern humans and other hominids. Some of the features visible in La Ferrassie 1 include, in lateral view, the mastoid tuberosity behind the ear opening and above the knoblike mastoid process at the base of the skull, and the occipitomastoid crest immediately behind the mastoid process; and, in rear view, an occipital torus, a horizontal bar of bone, on the cranium, and just above this torus an elliptical depression called the suprainiac fossa.

Of all the Neandertal traits present in this specimen, the teeth tell a particularly interesting story. In addition to abscesses and bone recession in the jaws, the teeth of La Ferrassie 1 are dramatically worn down, to the point that many of the enamel crowns have disappeared and dentine or pulp cavities are exposed, especially on the lower left teeth. In the upper jaw, the teeth on the right side are most severely worn. Grooves along the back of the teeth indicate that the lower jaw moved in a predominantly horizontal chewing motion rather than a vertical one, and the teeth were grinding coarse, gritty foods.

Much of the damage to the front teeth may stem from their use as extra hands. A comparison of the incisors of La Ferrassie 1 with teeth from gorillas (strict herbivores with a tough, fibrous diet) and Eskimos (who eat the least vegetation of any human population or nonhuman primate) for microscopic surface damage showed that tooth wear in the Neandertal closely resembled that of Eskimos. La Ferrassie's incisors have rounded edges with superficial flakes and gouges and deeper pits down to the dentine, as well as several fine, linear scratches. Eskimos use their teeth as tools, to hold everything from harness lines to sealskin boots in a viselike grip. Apparently Neandertals also used their teeth to clamp down on bulky objects, and to an even greater extent than modern Eskimos.

In addition to the nearly complete skeleton of a middle-aged male, the La Ferrassie rockshelter has yielded a largely intact adult female skeleton and the remains of five children ranging in age from prenatal to ten years: in composite, the largest set of juvenile human fossils from any site in France. The skeletons occupied six graves. The adult male and female were found lying head to head, and the skull from one child's skeleton had been removed and buried separately beneath a stone slab marked with curious depressions. Doubts had persisted about the reported Neandertal burial from La Chapelle-aux-Saints (see page 224), found a few years earlier, but the collective evidence from La Ferrassie confirmed that Neandertals buried their dead.

Soon after their discovery, Marcellin Boule used the La Ferrassie 1 and 2 skeletons to study missing bones for his infamous analysis of the La Chapelle-aux-Saints specimen. No one thoroughly studied the collection of La Ferrassie fossils until Jean-Louis Heim completed the first detailed descriptions, which were published as a monograph in 1976. Thanks to Heim's work and subsequent studies on this group of specimens, we can assemble a few facts about Neandertal life.

***Homo neanderthalensis*, La Ferrassie 1** (see also page 9).
Extreme, sloping wear on this male specimen's front teeth, some with dentine exposed, reflect a horizontal chewing motion and the use of teeth as an extra pair of hands to grip animal skins or other objects like a vise. Actual size. *Photograph by David Brill; courtesy Musée de l'Homme.*

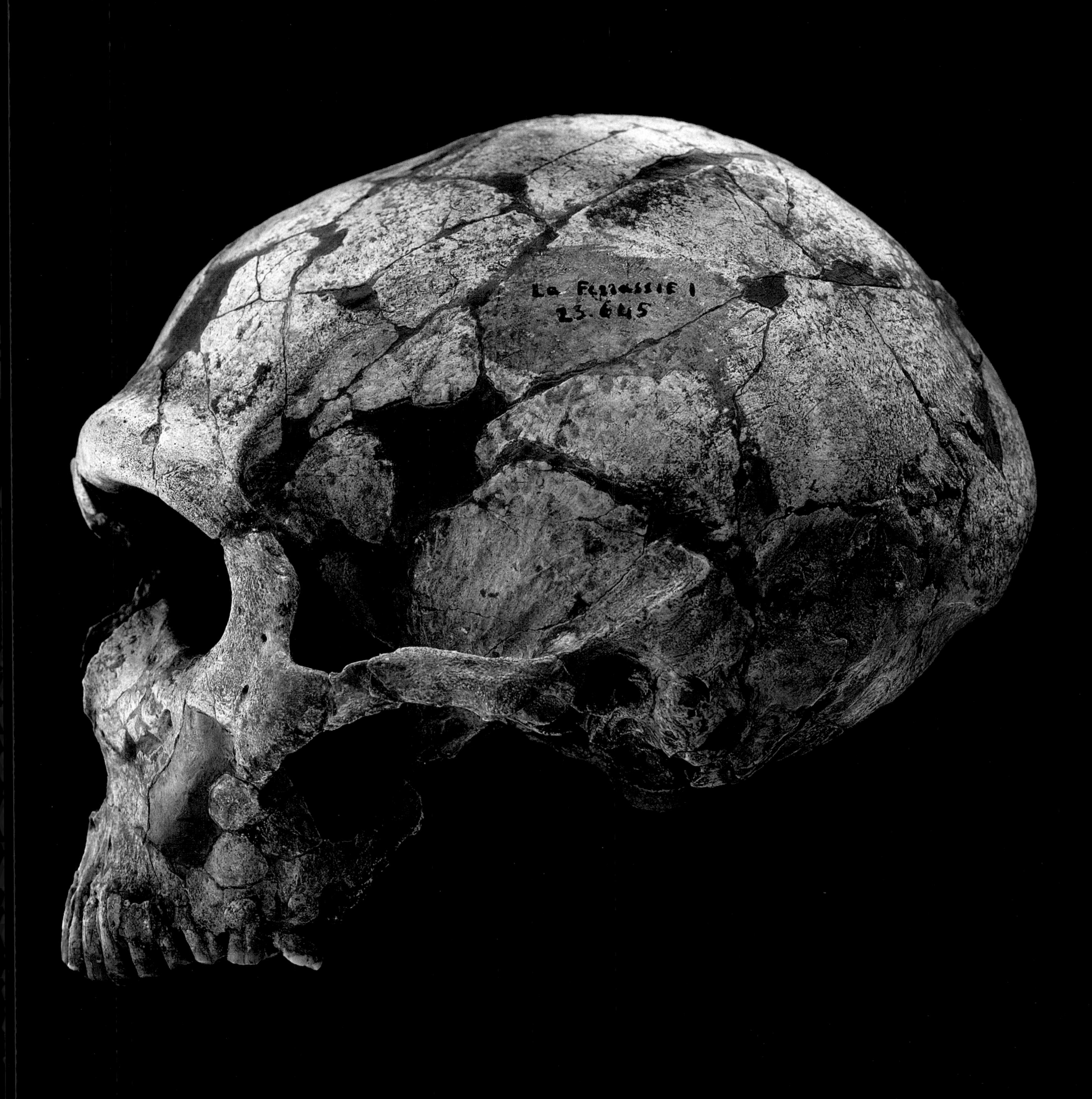
La Ferrassie 1
23.645

SPECIMEN	LOCALITY	AGE	DISCOVERERS	DATE	PUBLICATION
Adult calotte	Feldhofer grotto, Neander Valley, Germany	ca. 40,000-50,000 years	Unknown	August 1856	Fuhlrott, C. von. 1859. Menschliche Üebereste aus einer Felsengrotte des Düsselthals. *Verh. naturk. Ver. der preuss. Rheinl.* 16:131-153

Homo neanderthalensis

NEANDERTAL 1 TYPE SPECIMEN

The discovery and study of a partial adult hominid skeleton from the Neander Valley in Germany marked the start of paleoanthropology as a science and the beginning of efforts to understand our evolutionary past. Although a few other Neandertal specimens, such as those from Engis and Gibraltar (see page 230), had been found before limestone quarry workers uncovered this skeleton, the Neandertal 1 individual was the first to be recognized as something truly different. It was so different, in fact, that it became the first fossil hominid species to be named, when, in 1863, geologist William King proposed *Homo neanderthalensis* at a meeting of the British Association. King even stated in print that Neandertals might deserve their own genus. No one thinks so today, but the appellation has stood the tests of time and subsequent evidence. Today paleoanthropologists differ over whether *neanderthalensis* should be treated as a separate species or merely as a subspecies of *Homo sapiens*.

The name Neandertal comes from the valley near Düsseldorf where these bones were found. The valley had been named in memory of a seventeenth-century composer and vicar, Joachim Neumann, who took the adopted name Neander, meaning "new man." Thal (with a silent h) means "valley" in German, but the spelling changed early in the twentieth century to tal. Neandertal is still spelled both with and without the h.

When the workmen's shovels struck bone at Feldhofer in 1856, they uncovered first the top of a cranium. Then they found the two femora, the three right arm bones, two of the left arm bones, part of the left ilium, and fragments of a shoulder blade and ribs. Perhaps more of the skeleton lay in the cave mud, but only the largest bones were collected and saved for a local teacher and amateur naturalist, Johann Karl Fuhlrott. It is sobering to think that the opportunity to recover a complete Neandertal skeleton may have been missed, but the workers thought the bones came from a cave bear. Fuhlrott, however, suspected that the Feldhofer fossils represented unique pieces of the human past. He left their description to anatomist Hermann Schaaffhausen, and their joint announcement appeared in 1857, two years before Charles Darwin published his revolutionary work, *On the Origin of Species*.

Schaaffhausen noted the thick, well-developed muscle markings and ridges on the Neandertal bones. Even more striking was the oval shape of the skullcap, with its low, receding forehead and prominent, curved browridge. Because this appearance was unlike that of any human skull, the Neandertal cranium was labeled "apelike."

If Neandertal 1 signaled the birth of paleoanthropology, it also sparked the sort of intense controversy that has come to characterize this science. Prominent German scientists attributed the Neandertal's bowed thigh bones to habitual horse-riding and a case of rickets. The browridges, it was thought, resulted from prolonged frowning in pain from a poorly healed fracture of the left ulna. Such spurious arguments framed Neandertal 1 as a diseased modern human, perhaps a Cossack cavalryman, rather than some hitherto unknown primitive species. But reason prevailed, and although the validity of Neandertal Man was challenged in the country of his discovery, acceptance was more forthcoming in England. Thomas Henry Huxley commented on the Neandertal bones in his 1863 essays on man's place in nature, but it was King in the same year who dared go out on a limb and give these fossils the identity that we still recognize today.

***Homo neanderthalensis*, Neandertal 1.** Although it was not the first Neandertal fossil found, discovery of this skullcap in 1856 eventually led to the recognition of Neandertals as an ancient, extinct relative and began the ongoing debate about their place in our ancestry. Actual size.
Courtesy of Rheinisches Landesmuseum Bonn.

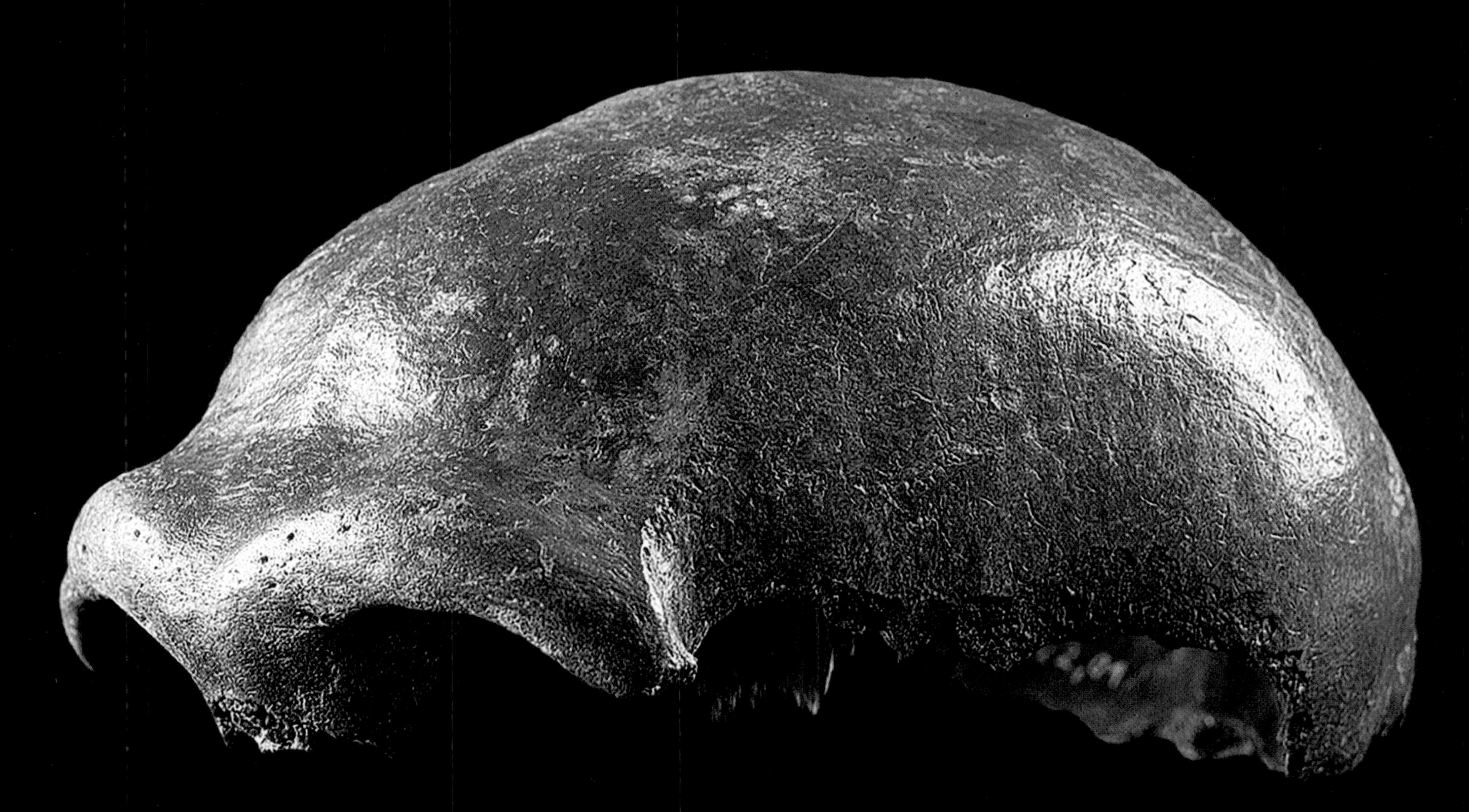

SPECIMEN	LOCALITY	AGE	DISCOVERER	DATE	PUBLICATION
Adult female cranium	Forbes' Quarry, Gibraltar	Uncertain	Unknown	Lieutenant Flint	Busk, G. Pithecoid Priscan Man from Gibraltar, *The Reader*. July 23, 1864

Homo neanderthalensis

GIBRALTAR 1

The individual represented by a female cranium found on Gibraltar in 1848 could be called the forgotten Neandertal. The impressive and remarkably complete cranium was found eight years before the discovery of the skullcap and limb bones from Feldhofer, Germany (see page 228), that gave us the name Neandertal. Because no one knew what to make of it at the time, the Gibraltar specimen languished for sixteen years before its significance was recognized. Even then, it received little attention until 1907, when it was finally described in detail, but by a geologist rather than an anatomist.

The exact location and circumstances of its discovery are unclear. A Captain Brome, who ran the military prison on Gibraltar, was an amateur fossil collector and employed prisoners to explore the local caves (a transgression that cost Brome his position). Apparently this cranium turned up in the course of construction on the Mediterranean island sometime before March 3, 1848, when brief mention of the specimen appeared in the minutes of the Gibraltar Scientific Society. There were no accompanying stratigraphic, archeological, or faunal data that might help determine its geological age.

Fortunately, in 1863, the cranium was sent to George Busk, the London zoologist who in 1861 had translated Hermann Schaaffhausen and Johann Fuhlrott's initial description of the Feldhofer Neandertal finds into English. Despite the stony matrix that covered the cranium, Busk recognized the Gibraltar specimen as a Neandertal. He collaborated with paleontologist Hugh Falconer in presenting the find to the British Association in 1869. That same year, French anatomist Paul Broca examined the Gibraltar specimen and pronounced it a Neandertal. Falconer described Gibraltar as "a very low type of humanity—very low and savage, and of extreme antiquity—but still man" and enthusiastically suggested several names for the specimen, including *Homo calpicus*, from Calfe, an ancient name for Gibraltar.

Gibraltar 1 was not the first Neandertal specimen ever found. That distinction goes to the child's skull from Engis Cave, Belgium, found in 1829 or 1830, the significance of which also went unrecognized, in part because influential French paleontologist Georges Cuvier dismissed the antiquity of Engis. However, Gibraltar 1 was the first complete adult cranium. At the rear and base of the cranium, Gibraltar 1 displays such Neandertal traits as a projecting occipital bone with a suprainiac fossa and a distinctive crest behind the round mastoid process of the temporal bone. This specimen also had the face that the Feldhofer specimen lacked, and many distinctive Neandertal features occur in the face. It is remarkable that, without a face to study, William King recognized the Feldhofer fossils as different enough to warrant the species name *neanderthalensis*. Had King waited to publish his description, he might have been made aware of Busk's possession and thus saved this female Neandertal from enduring obscurity.

***Homo neanderthalensis*, Gibraltar 1.** The first complete adult Neandertal cranium found, this female specimen has the large projecting face and receding cheekbones that distinguishes this species. Actual size. *Photograph by John Reader, Science Source/Photo Researchers.*

SPECIMEN	LOCALITY	AGE	DISCOVERER	DATE	PUBLICATION
Partial adult skeleton	Pierrot's Rock, Charente-Maritime, France	36,000 years	François Lévêque	July 27, 1979	Lévêque, F., and B. Vandermeersch. 1980. Les découvertes de restes humains dans un horizon castelperronien de Saint-Césaire (Charente-Maritime). *Bull. Soc. prehist. francaise* 77:35

Homo neanderthalensis
SAINT-CÉSAIRE

Once the sole contender for "last Neandertal," this specimen now must relinquish that distinction to the Neandertal lower jaw recovered from Zafarraya, Spain, in the early 1980s but recently dated to 33,400 years ago and to a 34,000 year-old Neandertal temporal bone from Arcy-sur-Cure, France. The Saint-Césaire skeleton nonetheless holds special significance in the debate surrounding the ultimate fate of Neandertals.

Excavation of the rockshelter began in 1976 after stone tools turned up in the course of widening the road for a mushroom-growing operation in the limestone caves of Pierrot's Rock. Many mammal bones and some stone tools from both Middle and Upper Paleolithic technologies were uncovered, along with the Neandertal.

The skeleton was found flexed into a small oval burial posture. The remains consist of the right half of a skull, some ribs, a shoulder blade, two robust arm bones, and fragments of the kneecap and shin bones. The skull reveals typical Neandertal traits, including the absence of a fossa, or shallow hollowing, above the upper canine, a gap in the tooth row behind the third molar (called a retromolar space), and the lack of a chin on the lower jaw.

Although the age of the site and the specimen had initially been estimated by comparisons of the fauna and archeology with other sites of known age, Saint-Césaire generated excitement in 1991 after burned flints associated with the skeleton had been dated by the thermoluminescence technique to 36,300 years, plus or minus 2,700 years. The implication of this date and the even younger ones from Zafarraya and Arcy-sur-Cure is that Neandertals and *Homo sapiens*, the Cro-Magnon, overlapped in Western Europe for up to 10,000 years. The nature of their coexistence—whether it was peaceful or violent, intimate or distant—has been the subject of much dispute and speculation. Perhaps any interactions played out differently in different regions.

Although there may have been ample time for cultural convergence, this overlap appears too brief for Neandertals to have evolved the modern morphology of Cro-Magnons. It has been suggested that the reduced amount of midface projection in the Saint-Césaire individual as compared to earlier western European Neandertals could indicate hybridization with *Homo sapiens*. Despite the difficulty of recognizing species—not to mention hybrids—from fossils alone, judging from their clearly disparate anatomies these groups were too biologically distinct to have shared anything more than culture.

The Saint-Césaire rock-shelter provides intriguing evidence about the late culture of Neandertals. This is only one of two sites where identifiable human remains have been found in association with distinctive Châtelperronian tools, including points and backed blades. The Châtelperronian industry found in France and Spain displays features of both the preceding Mousterian technology of the Middle Paleolithic, generally associated with Neandertals, and the later Aurignacian industry, usually viewed as the first stage of Upper Paleolithic technology and associated with modern *Homo sapiens*. Before the discovery of the Saint-Césaire individual, Châtelperronian tools had often been attributed to the hands and minds of modern *Homo sapiens*, but apparently such tools were the product of Neandertal industriousness.

One interpretation of this distinctive industry sees it as the Neandertals' attempt to mimic and master the newfangled technology that arrived in Europe with modern human immigrants. It remains unclear if the development of the Châtelperronian industry occurred in an atmosphere of cooperation or competition, but Saint-Césaire captures part of the dynamic physical and cultural transition among human populations in Europe between 30,000 and 40,000 years ago.

***Homo neanderthalensis*, Saint-Césaire.** Note the absence of a depression in the cheekbone above the canine, indicating that this skull had the Neandertal trait of inflated cheekbones. Other Neandertal traits are clearly visible in a lateral view (see page 109) of the mandible, including a retromolar gap by the ascending ramus and the absence of a chin. Actual size.
Photograph by David Brill; courtesy of Université de Bordeaux I.

SPECIMEN	LOCALITY	AGE	DISCOVERER	DATE	PUBLICATION
Adult male cranium	Dali, Shaanxi Province, China	ca. 200,000 years	Liu Shuntang	March 1978	Wu, X. 1981. A well-preserved cranium of an archaic type of early *Homo sapiens* from Dali, China. *Scientia Sinica* 241:530-539

Homo sapiens

DALI

Outside of Africa, the adult male cranium found at Dali, in China, is the best candidate for the earliest modern human. This specimen plays a crucial part in the multiregional model for the origin of *Homo sapiens*. According to this model (see page 46), the Dali cranium and an older Middle Pleistocene cranium and skeleton from Jinniushan in China's Liaoning Province constitute a link between the earlier *Homo erectus* fossils of Zhoukoudian (see page 108) and modern Chinese and illustrate longterm regional continuity in evolution.

In most cranial measurements, Dali falls between *H. erectus* and modern *H. sapiens*. Like *H. erectus*, Dali has a low, long, thick-walled cranium with a large and very thick browridge over the eyes. The rugged nuchal region at the rear of the cranium has a prominent torus, and on the top of the cranium is a slight sagittal keel.

Dali differs from *H. erectus* in being broadest at a higher point on the cranium and having less constriction behind the eye sockets. The estimated cranial capacity of the Dali specimen, 1,120 cc, is somewhat greater than that for the Zhoukoudian crania. The face presages the small, flat faces and prominent cheekbones of modern Chinese. Unfortunately, the absence of front teeth precludes checking for shovel-shaped incisors, a common trait in Asian populations today. Its forward-facing cheekbones gave Dali a flatter face than many archaic humans from Europe (such as *Homo heidelbergensis*) or Africa, and certainly much flatter than a Neandertal face. Although the face is relatively squat, deformation of the lower face during burial makes it difficult to measure the facial height accurately. In life, this face was longer and more projecting.

Despite these progressive features, a straightforward ancestral scenario with the Dali specimen being a link between earlier and later Chinese hominids cannot be proved. In some respects, it is just a typical Middle Pleistocene face, with resemblances to the modern humans of Qafzeh (see page 239). Analyses of skull shape reveal distinct differences between

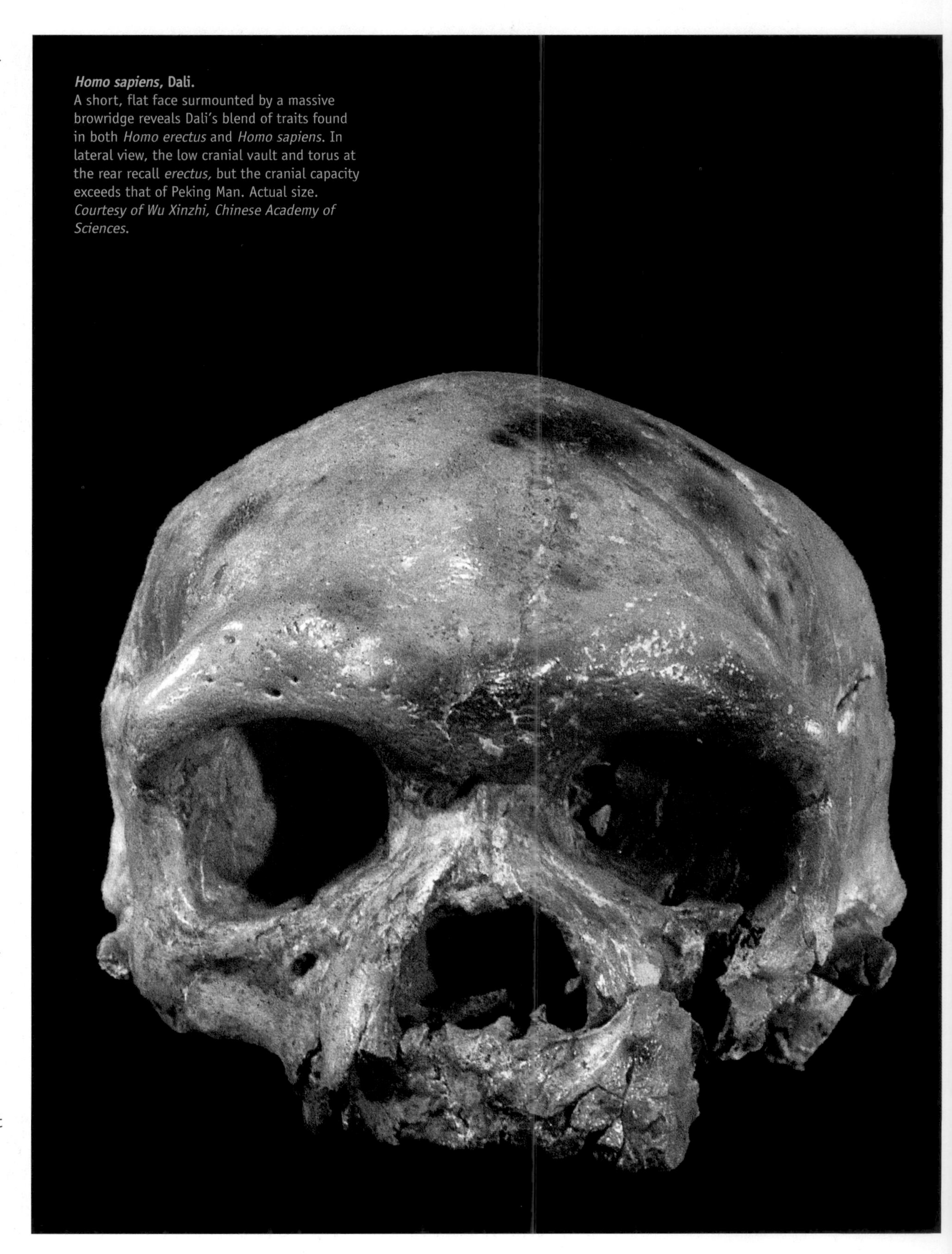

***Homo sapiens*, Dali.**
A short, flat face surmounted by a massive browridge reveals Dali's blend of traits found in both *Homo erectus* and *Homo sapiens*. In lateral view, the low cranial vault and torus at the rear recall *erectus*, but the cranial capacity exceeds that of Peking Man. Actual size.
Courtesy of Wu Xinzhi, Chinese Academy of Sciences.

Dali and both more recent modern humans in China (including the Upper Cave crania from Zhoukoudian) and contemporary Chinese populations. In fact, in skull shape the Dali specimen more closely resembles modern Europeans than Asians and shares similarities with late Middle Pleistocene fossils from Africa (including those from Omo, page 236). Rather than prolonged regional evolution in China, the shape of the Dali skull could reflect the spread of *Homo heidelbergensis* into Asia from Europe or Africa. If its age, estimated by the uranium series technique applied to ox teeth as 209,000 years plus or minus 23,000 years, is accurate, then Dali probably preceded the emergence from Africa of modern *Homo sapiens*.

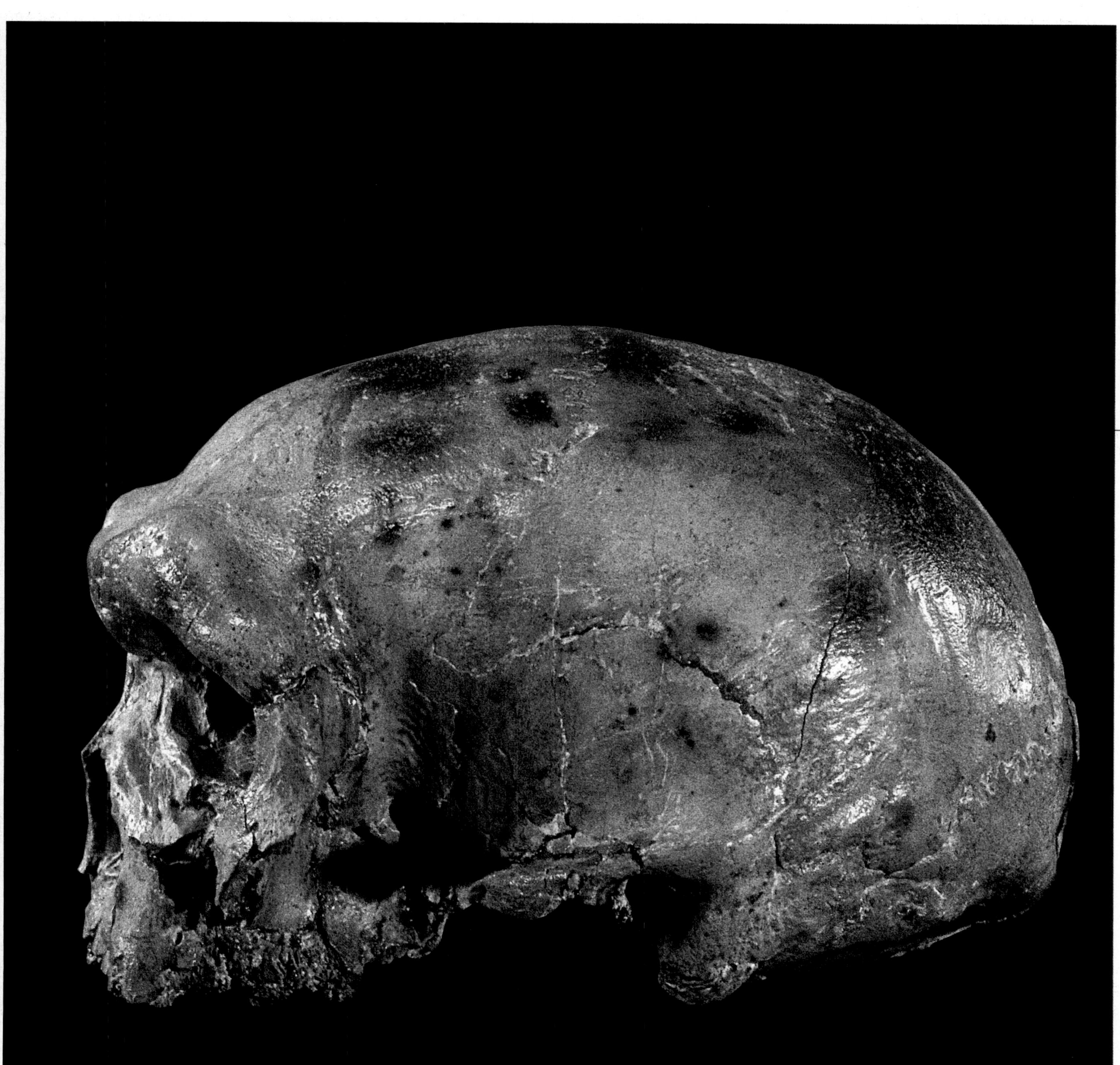

SPECIMEN	LOCALITY	AGE	DISCOVERER	DATE	PUBLICATION
Partial adult skeleton and cranium	Kibish, Omo Basin, Ethiopia	ca. 130,000 years	Kamoya Kimeu	1967	Leakey, R.E.F., K.W. Butzer, and M.H. Day. 1969. Early *Homo sapiens* remains from the Omo River region of Southwest Ethiopia, *Nature* 222:1132-1138

Homo sapiens

OMO I AND OMO II

Undeniably modern in its anatomy, the specimen from the Omo Basin in Ethiopia catalogued as Omo I has become a critical piece of evidence for those who argue that *Homo sapiens* evolved first, and relatively recently, in Africa before spreading into the rest of the world. At the time of its discovery, Omo I doubled the known duration of time that our species existed. Determining the age of this specimen, however, has proved difficult. It falls outside the range of time adequately addressed by the radiocarbon method, and the uranium series date from mollusk shells of 130,000 years is tentative until it can be confirmed by another technique.

In addition to the skull, the associated postcranial bones, from a shoulder, arm, hand, ribs, spine, legs, and foot, display fully modern human anatomy. A small number of stone tools and broken animal bones, as well as a complete buffalo skeleton, were also found nearby.

The obvious modern traits of the Omo I skull include the long and curved parietal bones of the expanded braincase, where the cranium reaches its maximum breadth, coupled with a short, broad face and high forehead. Its prominent browridge tapers at the sides instead of forming a consistently thick bar as in more archaic humans. The facial bones are fragmentary, but when the upper jaw is pieced together it reveals a modern-looking, U-shaped palate. The lower jaw possesses a chin, and the pair of worn teeth that survived appear modern in size and shape. Little of the cranial base was preserved, but a fortuitous break in the petrous region of the temporal bone—the hardest bone in the human skull, located internally from the ear canal—allowed a cast to form of the cochlea and semicircular canals of the inner ear.

Another specimen of presumably comparable age, Omo II, is a faceless cranium that displays some markedly different, more archaic anatomy. More heavily built than Omo I, this cranium has rugged muscle markings, a recessed forehead, and a conspicuous occipital torus, or bar, across the back. However, it shares with Omo I the modern traits of long, arched parietal bones along the sides of the braincase and of being broader at the top than the base. The estimated brain size for Omo II is 1,435 cc. Omo I, although more difficult to measure because of its incomplete preservation, had a brain at least as large, and well within the modern human range. But the striking morphological differences between Omo I and Omo II raise the question of whether either specimen was artificially intruded into the layer from which they were unearthed. They may not sample a single, contemporaneous population.

Homo sapiens, Omo I (see also page 45). At 130,000 years, the skull and partial skeleton of Omo I is one of the oldest known modern human fossils. Actual size. *Photograph courtesy of Michael Day.*

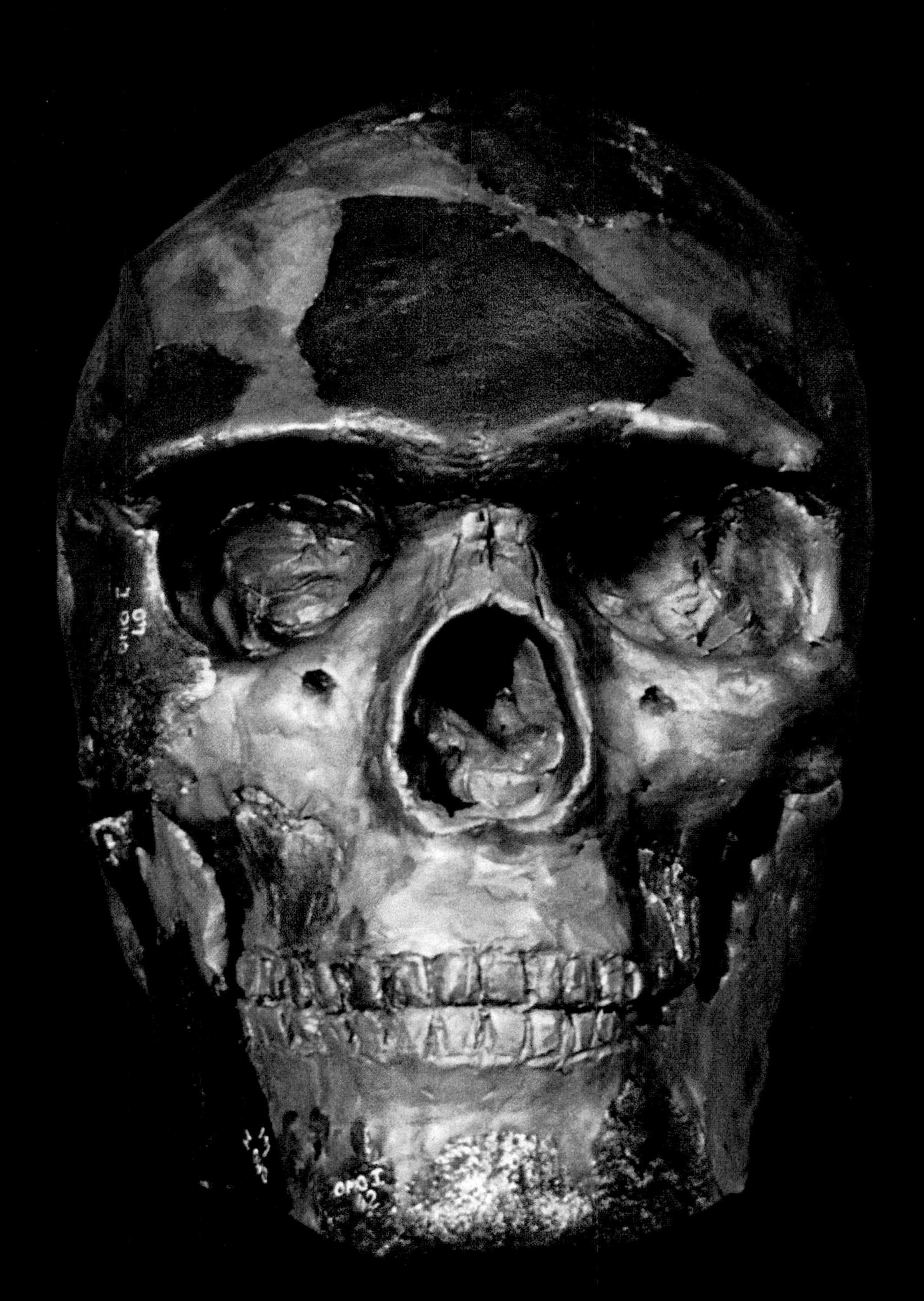

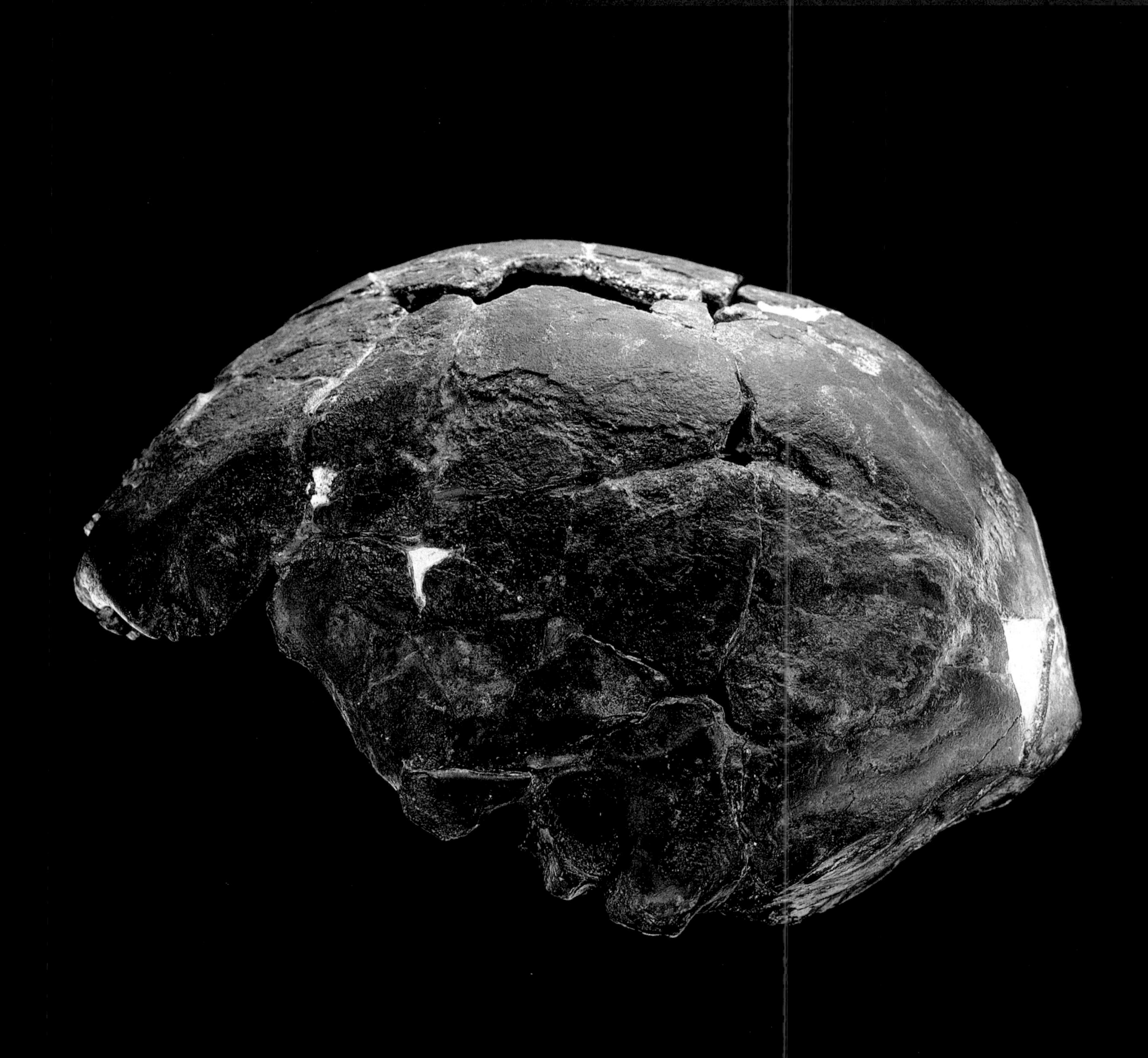

***Homo sapiens*, Omo II** (see previous page). The companion cranium from Omo-Kibish lacks a face and is more heavily built with rugged muscle markings and a receding forehead. Actual size.
Photograph by David Brill; courtesy of National Museum of Ethiopia.

SPECIMEN	LOCALITY	AGE	DISCOVERER	DATE	PUBLICATION
Adult female skeleton	Qafzeh cave, Israel	ca. 90,000-100,000 years	Bernard Vandermeersch	1969	Vandermeersch, B. 1969. Les nouveaux squellettes mostériens découverts à Qafzeh (Israël) et leur signification, *C.R. Acad. Sci. Paris* 268:2562-2565

Homo sapiens

QAFZEH IX

The woman whose remains were found in Qafzeh cave, Israel, in 1969 is one of the oldest known modern humans. Like Skhul V (see page 242), she may be a member of the population that gave rise to all anatomically modern *Homo sapiens* outside of Africa. This specimen is the most complete of the twenty-one skeletons of infants, children, adolescents, and adults that were buried in Qafzeh cave. Seven individuals were excavated in the 1930s, and further excavation outside the cave mouth between 1965 and 1980 uncovered the remains of at least fourteen additional individuals represented by fragments and by eight partial skeletons, including Qafzeh IX.

The individual died at around age 20 and was part of a double burial. Her skeleton lay on its left side, and the skeleton of a very young child lay beside her flexed lower legs. After the burial's discovery, an Israeli Air Force helicopter gently lifted both skeletons, still inside a one-ton block of rock-hard breccia that had been wrapped in plaster for protection, and delivered them to a laboratory where the bones could be removed more carefully.

In the 1950s, paleoanthropologist Clark Howell recognized the significance of the initial Qafzeh specimens when he compared them to those from Skhul and described both populations as "proto Cro-Magnons," to emphasize their modern-looking anatomy. The Qafzeh fossils took on increased significance in the 1980s after two new dating techniques revealed the site's antiquity to be more than twice most previous estimates. The thermoluminescence technique dated Qafzeh to 92,000 years ago, and estimates obtained by the electron spin resonance technique place it between 100,000 and 120,000 years ago. The combination of these early dates and the skeletons' mostly modern morphology means that these specimens approach the ancestral form for our species, if genetic evidence is right that we emerged within the past 200,000 years (see page 43). Moreover, the Qafzeh cave is close to Africa, which lends support to the genetic and fossil evidence suggesting that modern humans first arose on that continent.

The reconstructed skull of Qafzeh IX shows some deformation due to pressure from surrounding sediment during burial, but much of the anatomy can be clearly observed and described. The cranial wall is thinner than a Neandertal's and comparable to the mean for modern Europeans. In comparison with contemporary and younger Neandertals from the Levant, such as those from Tabun, Kebara, and Amud, the cranium of Qafzeh IX has a high forehead, a high, parallel-sided braincase, and a reduced browridge. The facial skeleton and lower jaw are marked by the presence of a canine fossa, a flat midface, the partial development of a bony chin, and the absence of a gap behind the third molar—all features that characterize modern humans. As for Skhul V, the lower face of Qafzeh IX projects far forward to accommodate its large teeth. Both this specimen and the male individual Qafzeh VI have a cranial capacity of about 1,554 cc—higher than even the modern-day average for our species. The postcranial skeletons are essentially indistinguishable from our own.

***Homo sapiens*, Qafzeh IX** (see previous page). The skeleton of a young child lay beside the flexed legs of this adult female, one of the earliest members of our species. The high forehead, parallel-sided braincase, and reduced browridge of Qafzeh (frontal, *left*, and lateral, *right*) can be contrasted with the Neandertal from nearby Amud (see pages 116 and 230). Actual size.
Photographs by David Brill; courtesy of Israel Antiquities Authority, Rockefeller Museum.

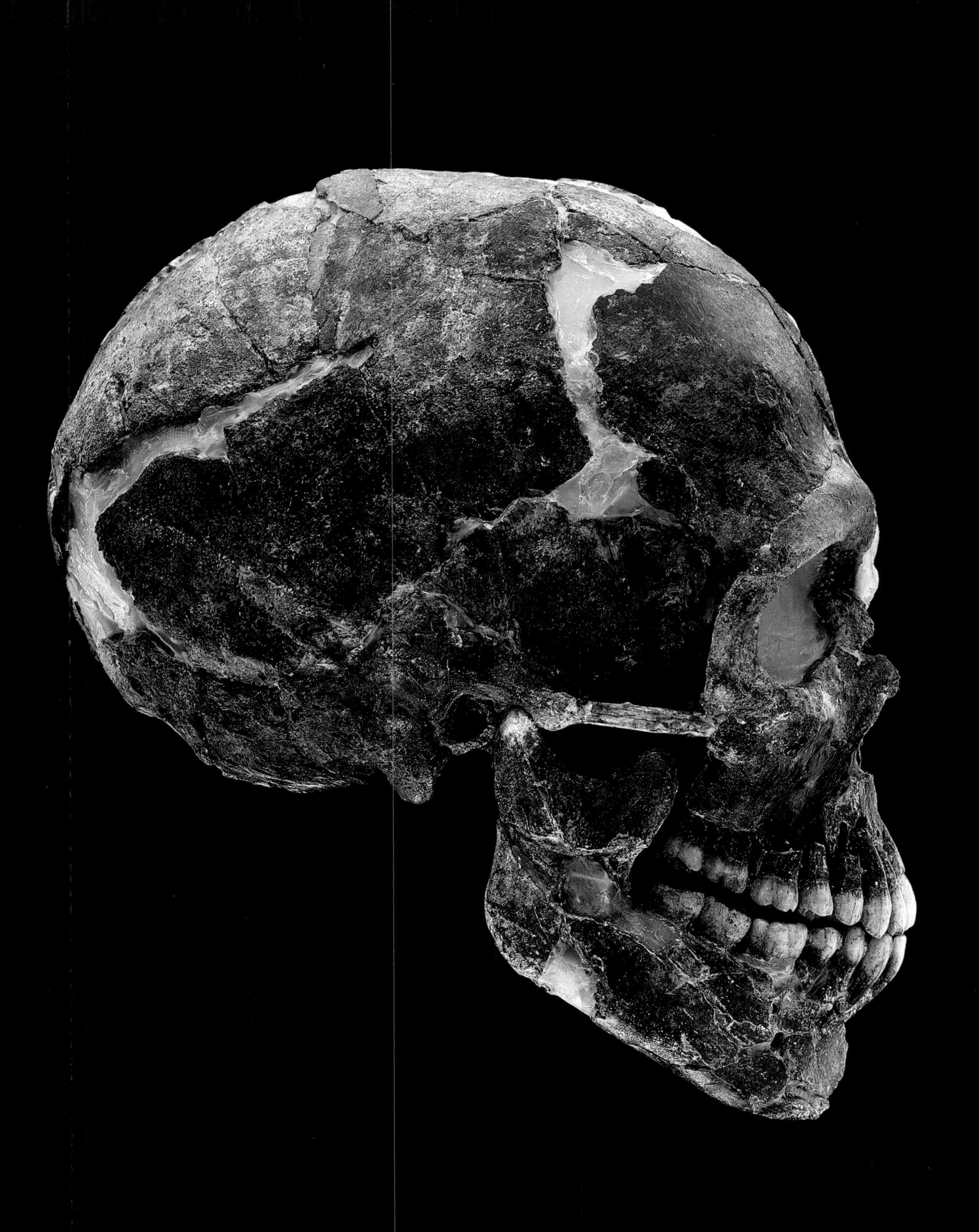

SPECIMEN	LOCALITY	AGE	DISCOVERERS	DATE	PUBLICATION
Adult male skeleton	Skhul cave, Mount Carmel, Israel	ca. 90,000 years	Theodore McCown and Hallum Movius Jr.	May 2, 1932	McCown, T.D., and A. Keith. 1939. The fossil remains from the Levalloiso-Mousterian. *The Stone Age of Mount Carmel,* vol. II (The Clarendon Press, Oxford)

Homo sapiens
SKHUL V

The adult male specimen known as Skhul V and nine other adults and children excavated from the cave of Skhul, in Israel, may represent, along with the people from the nearby cave of Qafzeh (see page 239), the ancestral population of modern humans that later spread out to occupy the globe. The evidence from Skhul and Qafzeh shows that humans appeared in the Near East long before they set foot in Europe, and it will be crucial in solving the mystery of modern human origins.

Originally, Skhul was thought to date to only about 40,000 years ago, based on comparisons of the faunal remains and tools found at the site with those found at the adjacent site of Tabun. This relatively late date meant that the more ancient Neandertals who occupied Tabun might have had time to evolve into the more modern-looking people at Skhul and Qafzeh. In the late 1980s, the application of new dating techniques made it clear that the Skhul group was in fact at least twice as old as previously thought. These individuals were the Tabun people's contemporaries, and they preceded other Neandertals in the Near East and in much of Europe. It suddenly seemed far less plausible that the Neandertals had evolved into the modern populations.

The remains of eight males and two females were intentionally buried in the cave at a level that also harbored nearly 10,000 Mousterian stone tools. The Skhul V individual lay on his back, turned to the right, with the chin pressed against the chest and legs tightly flexed. The left arm stretched across the body, and the hand apparently once clasped the mandible of a wild boar, the only evidence from these burials of a grave offering.

Skhul V is the tallest male and has the most complete skull, but it is missing the middle part of the face. From the wear on the teeth (half of the first molar crowns are worn down to the dentine layer) and the sutures on the skull, the approximate age at death of this individual was 30 to 40 years.

The Skhul people combine modern and primitive features in the skull and skeleton, but the anatomy is overwhelmingly similar to that of modern humans and contrasts particularly with the anatomy of the "classic" European Neandertals. For example, Skhul V possesses a high vault in the front of the cranium, a rounded occipital (unlike the flattened nuchal area in Neandertals) at the rear, and a modern-like flex to the cranial base. The chin is less apparent than in other individuals from Skhul. Notable differences between this individual and an average modern human skull are the prominent browridge and the prognathic lower face, which projects like a muzzle from beneath the slender cheekbones. The teeth show signs of abscesses and gum disease, and there is evidence of rheumatoid arthritis at the temporomandibular joint where the lower jaw connects to the cranium.

Through a small opening on the top of the skull, a working space was created through which a chisel and drill could be inserted. The limestone breccia was laboriously removed from inside the skull in order to make an endocast of the cranial cavity. The cast reveals a brain that was basically modern in general shape and in the proportions of the brain lobes. Removing the matrix also permitted measurement of the cranial capacity, which was around 1,518 cc, slightly below the mean value for modern Europeans.

Besides the skull, the preserved remains of Skhul V include some vertebrae and ribs, most of the left scapula, the right clavicle and part of the left clavicle, both humeri, the right radius and a shaft fragment from the left, the right ulna and the left ulnar shaft, some bones from both hands, the right ilium and half of the ischium, most of the right femur and part of the left femur, parts of the right and left tibiae, most of the left fibula, and a few bones of the left foot. These limb bones tend to be long and slender rather than stout and curved as in Neandertals.

Theodore McCown and Arthur Keith, who described the fossils, noted the differences from Neandertals in the Skhul sample. They viewed the Skhul anatomy as a forerunner to that seen in specimens such as Cro-Magnon I (see page 244), but McCown and Keith concluded that Skhul and Tabun sampled a single, variable population. Others have subsequently interpreted Skhul V's anatomy as showing signs of hybridization between modern and Neandertal populations. Hybridization is difficult to demonstrate in fossils, and even if it did happen rarely, it would not mean that Neandertals and modern humans were a single species. The Tabun individuals clearly differed from those at Skhul, who were undoubtedly on the cusp of becoming modern humans.

***Homo sapiens,* Skhul V** (see also page 10). Contemporaries of the people from Qafzeh, the inhabitants of Skhul cave likewise possessed a very modern human anatomy. Unlike humans today, this male skull lacks a chin and has a more projecting lower face. Actual size. *Photograph by David Brill; courtesy of Peabody Museum of Archaeology and Ethnology, Harvard University.*

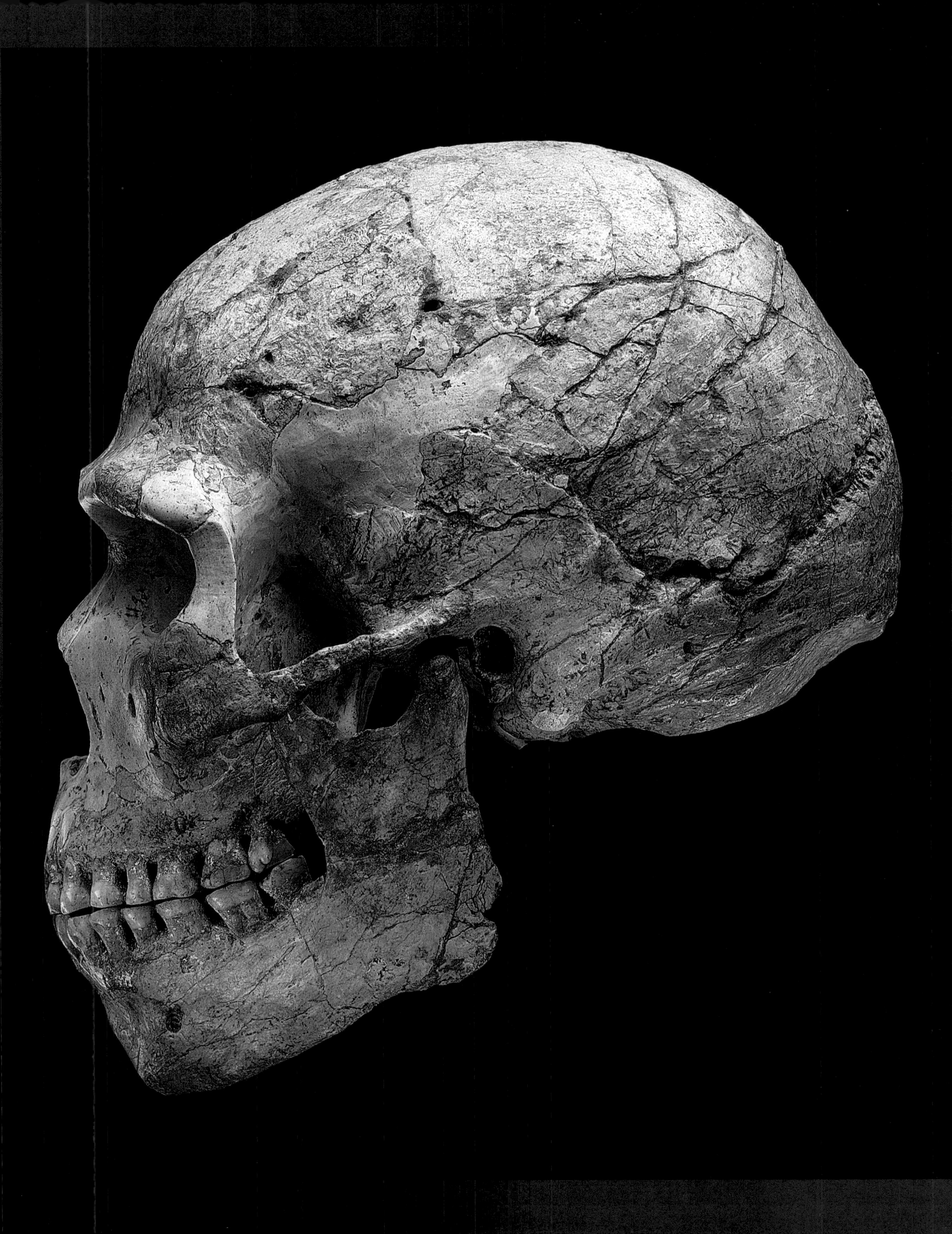

SPECIMEN	LOCALITY	AGE	DISCOVERERS	DATE	PUBLICATION
Adult male skeleton	Abri Cro-Magnon, Les Eyzies, France	30,000-32,000 years	Louis Lartet and Henry Christy	March 1868	Jones, T.R., editor. 1868. On the human skulls and bones found in the cave of Cro-Magnon, near Les Eyzies. *Reliquiae aquitanicae*

Homo sapiens
CRO-MAGNON I

To the public and to many anthropologists this rockshelter in Les Eyzies has become synonymous with modern humans. The anatomy of the individuals found at Cro-Magnon, France, was essentially our own. They were, however, not the first modern humans to evolve, nor were they entirely representative of human populations across Europe at the time when they lived. Nonetheless, when we gaze at the fossils from Cro-Magnon, we clearly see a reflection of ourselves. These were the type of people who painted the walls of caves and carved delicate figures in ivory.

Workmen constructing a railway line and station for the town of Les Eyzies (Cro-Magnon means "big cliff," referring to the limestone massif that rises above the town), now often labeled the capital of prehistory, discovered five skeletons representing three adult males, an adult female, and one infant. The bodies apparently had been deliberately buried in a single grave, along with body adornments: pierced shells and animal teeth that had probably been worn as necklaces or pendants. Bones from reindeer, bison, woolly mammoth, and other mammals and stone blades and knives belonging to the Aurignacian industry (the earliest style of Upper Paleolithic tools) completed the trove, which geologist Louis Lartet and banker Henry Christy excavated at the rockshelter. These men sorted and studied the human bones that had been removed and inadvertently scrambled by the railway workers.

The earliest definitive modern human from western Europe, Cro-Magnon I, also dubbed the "Old Man," has a face pitted from a fungal infection and probably died in middle age. Except for the teeth and the condyles of the lower jaw, his skull is complete. It shows such classic modern human features as a high, rounded cranium, a steep forehead, a very large brain capacity (over 1,600 cc), a short face with rectangular eye sockets, a tall and narrow nasal opening, a parabolic palate, and a prominent chin. However, the Cro-Magnon specimens do display variation in their skeletons, especially in the size and robustness of the browridge and the occipital bone of the skull.

Nonetheless, Cro-Magnon I was used to generalize about the physical features of all Cro-Magnons, or early Europeans other than the Neandertals and their ancestors. French paleoanthropologist Marcellin Boule, as an example, compared Cro-Magnon with the Neandertal from La Chapelle-aux-Saints (see page 224), who came across as a stumbling, brutish, primitive dead end. By comparison, Cro-Magnon, who walked upright, thought sentient thoughts, and created art, was unnecessarily valorized.

The Cro-Magnon skeletons reveal several ailments. A few have fused neck vertebrae, and the adult female survived with a fractured skull. Such injuries indicate not only that the individuals lived hard lives, but that their companions cared for them.

Present-day Europeans have departed in anatomy from the skull shapes found at Cro-Magnon. The initial modern human immigrants, including the people of Cro-Magnon, appear more similar to modern Africans and other subtropical populations than to those of temperate northern latitudes, based on analyses that used two dozen cranial measurements to characterize overall skull size and shape. This resemblance to subtropical populations suggests that Cro-Magnon I and his fellows migrated from some warmer clime, probably Africa or the Near East.

***Homo sapiens*, Cro-Magnon I.**
The 30,000 year-old cranium of Cro-Magnon I exhibits a number of definitive modern human traits, including the squat face with hollowed cheekbones and projecting nasal bones, sharply defined eye sockets, a high forehead, and curved parietal bones along the braincase, where the greatest cranial breadth occurs. Actual size.
Photograph by David Brill; courtesy of Musée de l'Homme.

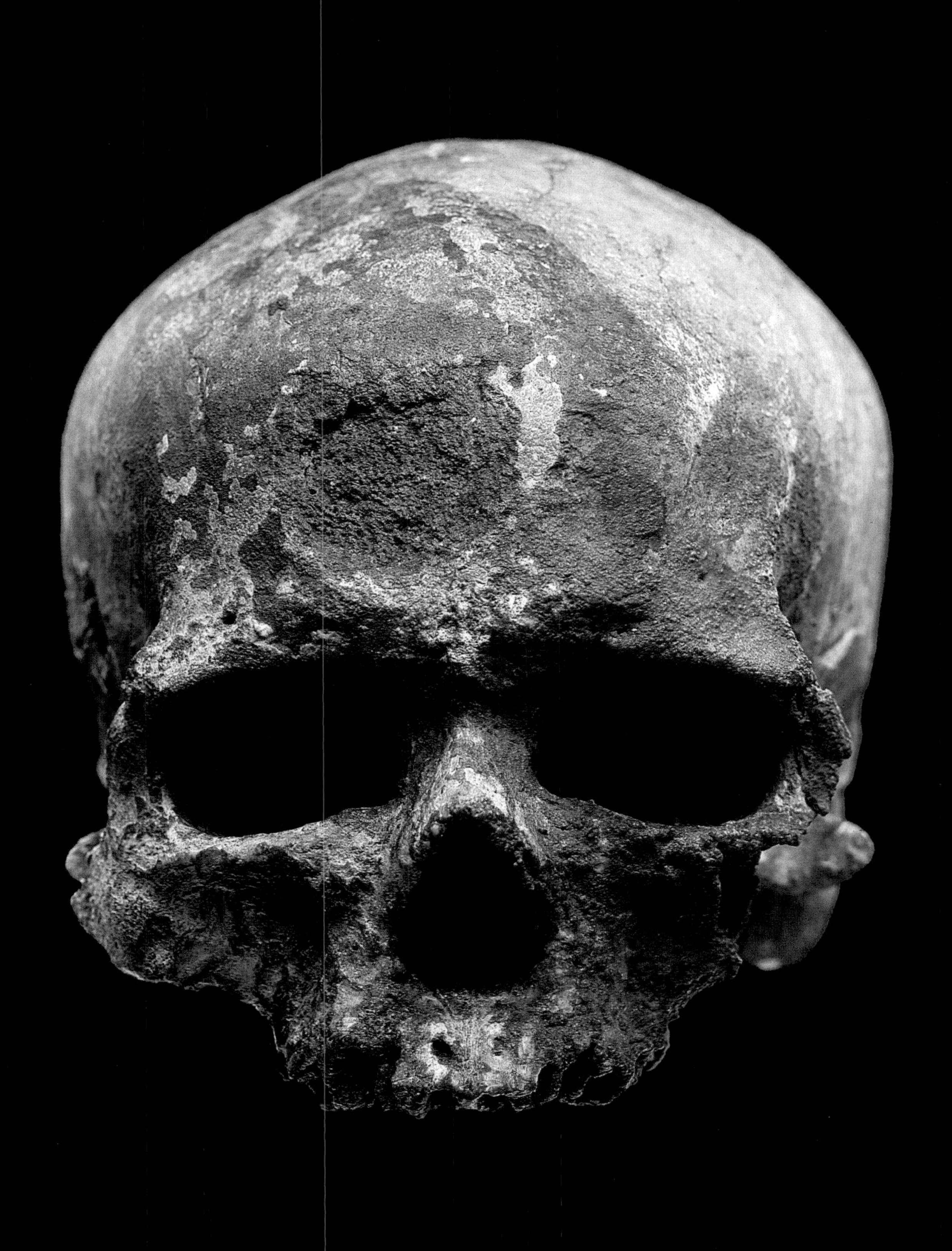

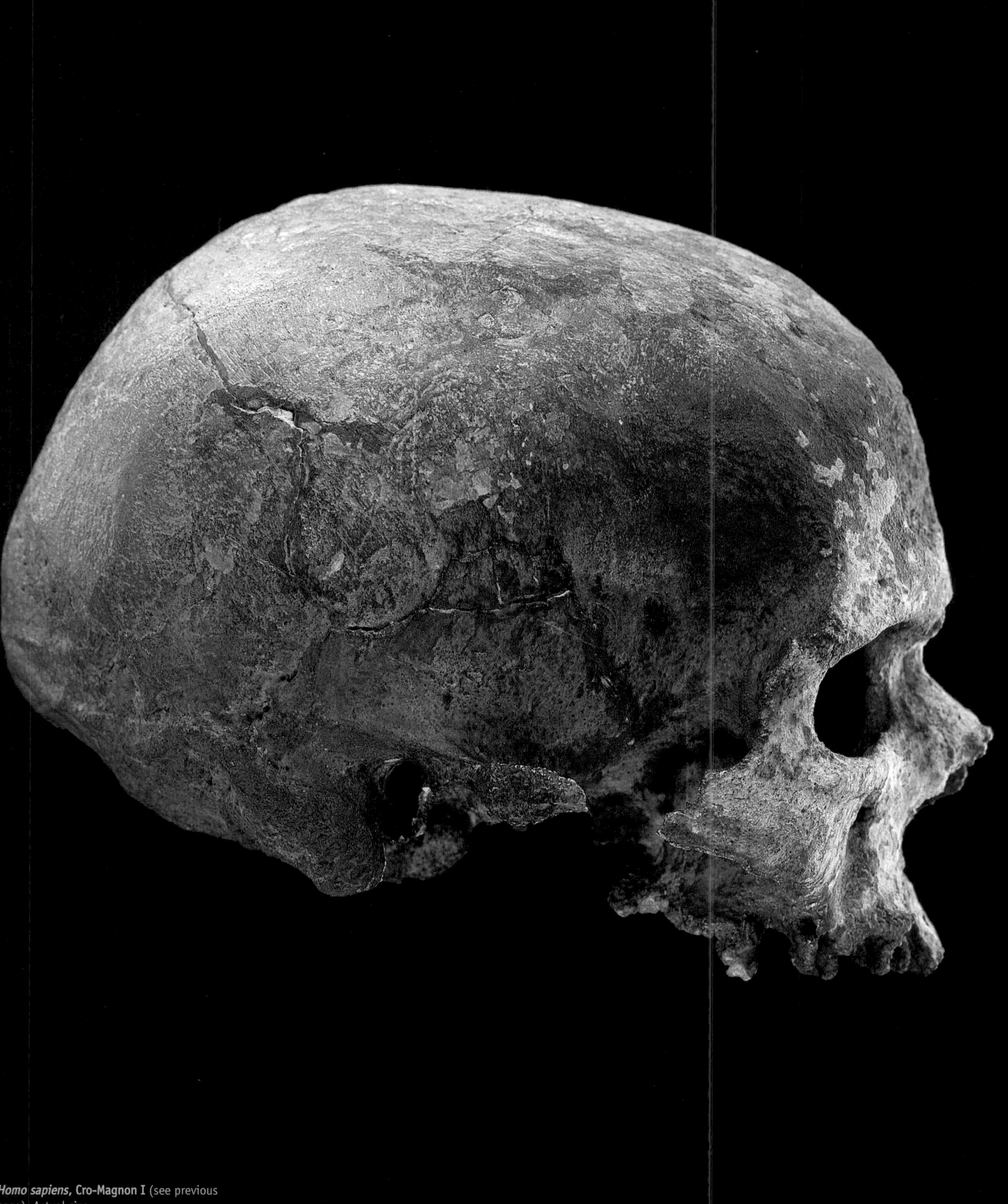

***Homo sapiens*, Cro-Magnon I** (see previous page). Actual size.
Photograph by David Brill; courtesy of Musée de l'Homme.

SPECIMEN	LOCALITY	AGE	DISCOVERERS	DATE	PUBLICATION
Adult male skeleton	Kow Swamp, Victoria, Australia	10,000 years	Alan Thorne and Phillip Macumber	October 10, 1967	Thorne, A.G. and P.G. Macumber. 1972. Discoveries of Late Pleistocene Man at Kow Swamp, Australia. *Nature* 238: 316-319

Homo sapiens

KOW SWAMP 1

The primitive anatomy of the face and front half of the cranium of Kow Swamp 1 poses a puzzle for so recent a member of our species. The flat, sloping forehead, massive eyebrow ridges, broad cheekbones, and projecting lower face distinguish this specimen from modern Aborigines. Kow Swamp 1 was part of an isolated remnant population in Australia that may have retained some archaic *Homo sapiens* traits, or, as its discoverers contend, these distinctive features may link the Kow Swamp people in a direct line of descent from *Homo erectus* in Java, where similar-looking fossils date to nearly a million years ago.

The archaic features stood out when a carbonate-encrusted partial skeleton caught anthropologist Alan Thorne's eye at the National Museum of Victoria in 1967. He mounted an expedition the following year to Kow Swamp, a freshwater lake near the Murray River, where he found and unearthed the rest of the bones belonging to this robust male, Kow Swamp 1. Kow Swamp's windblown silts have since yielded the remains of at least forty individuals who lived between 9,500 and 14,000 years ago. Adults, juveniles, and infants are represented in the burials, and some skeletons were adorned with animal bone, shell, ivory beads, and marsupial teeth. One body had been cremated, but the other skeletons lay in varying positions: fully extended or flexed partially or tightly. Kow Swamp 1 and another male individual, Kow Swamp 5, constitute the most complete skeletons from the site.

Thorne and colleague Milford Wolpoff, as part of their multiregional model of modern human origins, hypothesize that the Kow Swamp skeletons represent the recent end of an "out of Java" sequence of fossils that begins with the *Homo erectus* specimen Sangiran 17 (see page 191). Kow Swamp 1, Kow Swamp 5, and Sangiran 17 share a large but short projecting face and flat forehead, a thick cranial vault, and such details as a rounding of the lower side border of the eye socket and the absence of a marked division between the nasal floor and the lower face. These and other similarities suggest the presence of regional morphological continuity among Australasian hominids during the last million years.

Other parts of the skeleton seem to support a different story. In rear view, for instance, the Kow Swamp skulls have the high, straight sides of a typical modern human skull rather than the characteristic squat *erectus* shape seen in Sangiran 17. An analysis of thigh bones in the Kow Swamp collection found that the femur is completely modern in shape and has a thin-walled shaft. These femora lack both the thick cortical bone and the high "waist," or point of minimum breadth on the shaft, that distinguish an *erectus* femur. Some studies of the Kow Swamp crania, particularly that of Kow Swamp 5, have concluded that the distinctive anatomy may stem from these individuals having undergone cranial deformation as part of a cultural ritual that involved prolonged pressing or binding of the head. Frontal bone compression has been practiced by modern populations in parts of Australia and the Pacific, and such cultural factors or perhaps unknown environmental factors could account for the Kow Swamp group's resemblance to Javanese *Homo erectus*.

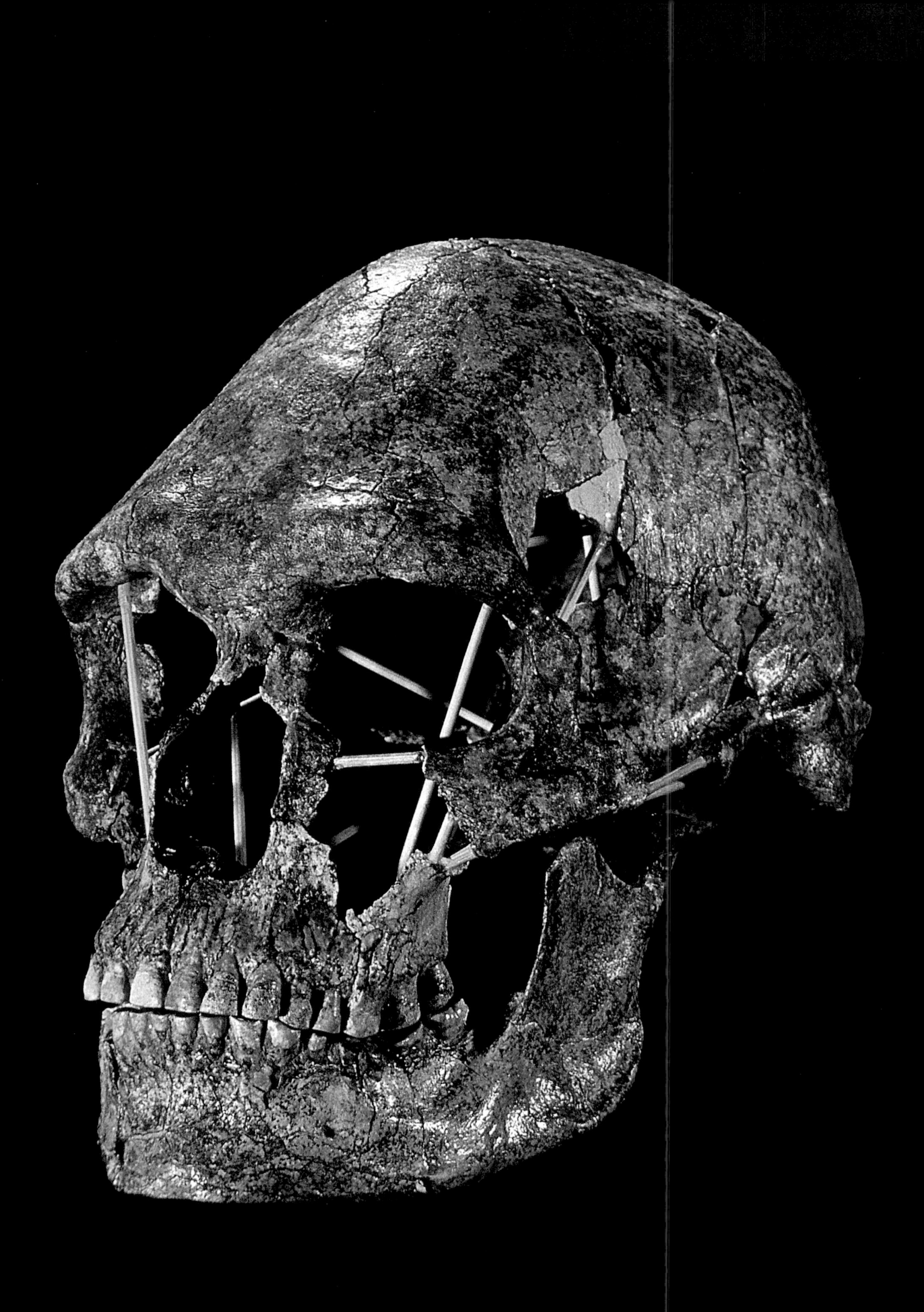

***Homo sapiens*, Kow Swamp 1** (see previous page). Actual size.
Courtesy of Alan Thorne, Australian National University.

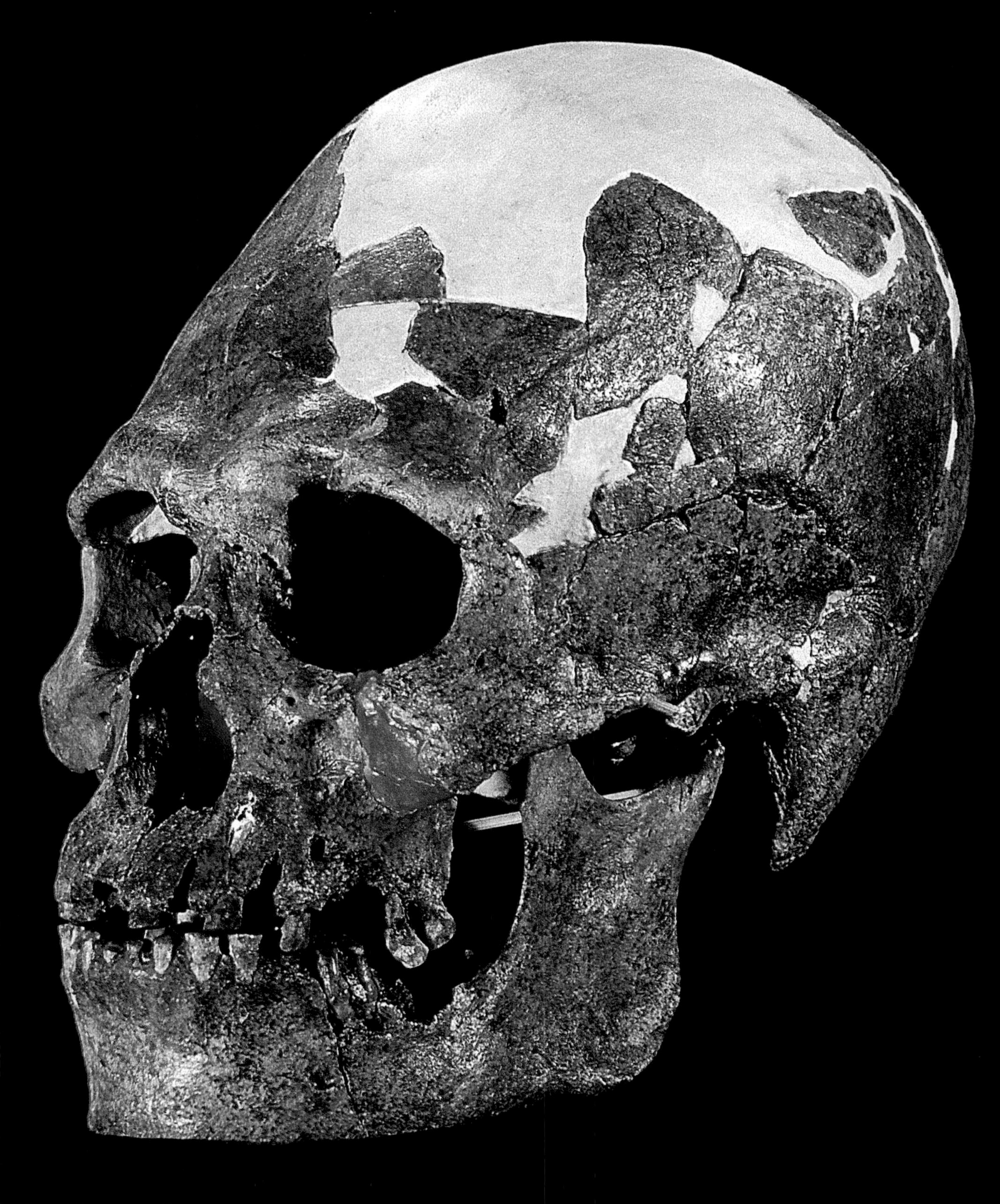

***Homo sapiens*, Kow Swamp 5** (see page 248). Another male specimen from Kow Swamp displays a similar range of primitive features as Kow Swamp 1. Are these due to certain cultural or environmental factors or did this population descend directly from *Homo erectus* in Indonesia? Actual size. *Courtesy of Alan Thorne, Australian National University.*

PALEOLITHIC TECHNOLOGY

Technology represents an important hallmark of humanness, and tracing the origin and evolution of technology is a critical part of paleoanthropology. Fewer than twenty animal species have been observed using tools in the wild, and among the primates, only humans and chimpanzees habitually use tools. Early humans employed sophisticated cognition in their selection and shaping of raw materials into stone tools, and in a broad sense stone technology proceeded from relatively rudimentary implements to more elaborate types that demanded increasingly complex manufacturing techniques.

The production and use of stone tools has not been associated with any of the earliest hominids, the australopithecines, although australopithecines may well have used other sorts of tools. For instance, bony horn cores of antelopes excavated from Swartkrans, South Africa, have strange striations running vertically and horizontally near each bone's rounded tip. These markings may have resulted from the use of these bones by some hominid as digging sticks to extract bulbs and tubers from rocky soil beneath scree slopes near the cave site, and the vast majority of hominid fossils from Swartkrans belong to *Australopithecus robustus*. But stone tools may be an innovation and adaptation that was confined to our genus, *Homo*. Early humans began to use stone tools as extensions of their bodies to modify or manipulate other objects or elements of their environment, and this became a significant part of our ecological adaptation, to the extent that paleolithic technology seems to have evolved in parallel with the expanding brain and enhanced social behavior of *Homo*. We summarize here the characteristics of the four major categories of paleolithic industry, their artifact types, and the processes by which these stone and bone tools were made.

Oldowan

The earliest record of human stone technology dates to about 2.4 million years ago and comes from Gona and the Omo Basin, both in Ethiopia. At 2.3 million years old, basalt and chert flakes and a *Homo* maxilla from the Makaamitalu region of Hadar, Ethiopia (see page 89), represent the oldest known association of a hominid fossil with stone tools. Tools from each of these sites belong to the Oldowan industry, named and defined by Mary Leakey in the 1960s based on her extensive excavations at Olduvai Gorge, Tanzania. (Oldowan is the adjectival form of the word Olduvai.) Oldowan tools continue to appear in the archeological record of East Africa until about 1.5 million years ago. They are most commonly attributed to *Homo habilis*, but Oldowan tools could have been made by other species, such as *Homo rudolfensis*, from Koobi Fora, Kenya.

These crude chopping and scraping implements and flakes represent the dawn of human culture and may constitute the first personal possessions. The most conspicuous artifacts among the Oldowan industry are simply flaked cores made from pebbles or chunks of rock, typically quartz or basalt. Mary Leakey described several types of these cores, from which a few flakes had been struck, and named them for their shape or presumed function. These types include hammerstones (often unmodified cobbles used to strike flakes from other rocks or to break open bones), unifacial and bifacial (flaked on one or both sides, respectively) choppers, heavy- and light-duty scrapers, and spheroids. A related industry known as the Developed Oldowan appeared about 1.5 million years ago and is noted for having relatively fewer choppers and bifaces and more scrapers, spheroids, and subspheroids. Oldowan and Developed Oldowan artifacts persist in the archeological record of Africa and overlap extensively in time with the succeeding Acheulean industry.

Archeologist Nicholas Toth has argued convincingly that Oldowan core forms were not the end products but rather the means to the end. Cores provided the raw material for producing sharp-edged flakes, and it was these flakes that became the primary tools for cutting open carcasses or slicing sinews in the quest for meat and bone marrow. The peculiar and sometimes ubiquitous spheroids may also not have been an intentional end product. Experiments with angular quartz chunks demonstrated that their repeated use as a hammerstone to flake other rocks converts the chunks into objects closely resembling spheroids after just a few hours, which suggests that hammerstones were reused and most likely kept and transported by early hominids.

If spheroids were an inadvertent result of rock bashing, other Oldowan tools bear specific marks of deliberate manufacture, such as the striking platform where a hammerstone hits a core, or the bulb of percussion on the inner surface of a flake taken from the core. But Oldowan technology involved minimum-effort techniques for flaking rock, without the apparent conventions and rules for manufacturing artifacts that characterize subsequent archeological industries. The basic Oldowan flaking technique was a hard-hammer percussion technique in which a smooth, rounded stone was wielded as a hammer to remove a flake from a core. The flake scar left on the core then provided a relatively flat surface with an acute angle—the optimal striking platform for removing a second flake. Alternative means of making Oldowan artifacts were the anvil technique, which involved striking a core on a stationary stone anvil, and the bipolar technique, which used a hammerstone to flake a core held against an anvil.

Oldowan chopper, Gadeb, Ethiopia (*top*). Oldowan artifacts were manufactured between about 2.4 and 1.5 million years ago. One of the primary tools were cores like this one from which a few sharp flakes had been struck. Actual size.
Photograph by David Brill; courtesy of National Museum of Ethiopia.

Horn core tool, Swartkrans, South Africa (*left*). Although bone tools do not become common until much later in the archeological record, this antelope horn core appears to have been used as a digging stick in rocky soil, since it has criss-crossing striations near its blunt tip that have been replicated in modern experiments. Actual size.
Photograph by David Brill; courtesy of Transvaal Museum.

Bone point, Swartkrans, South Africa (*bottom*). Another bone tool from the same cave site may be as old as 2 million years. Actual size.
Photograph by David Brill; courtesy of Transvaal Museum.

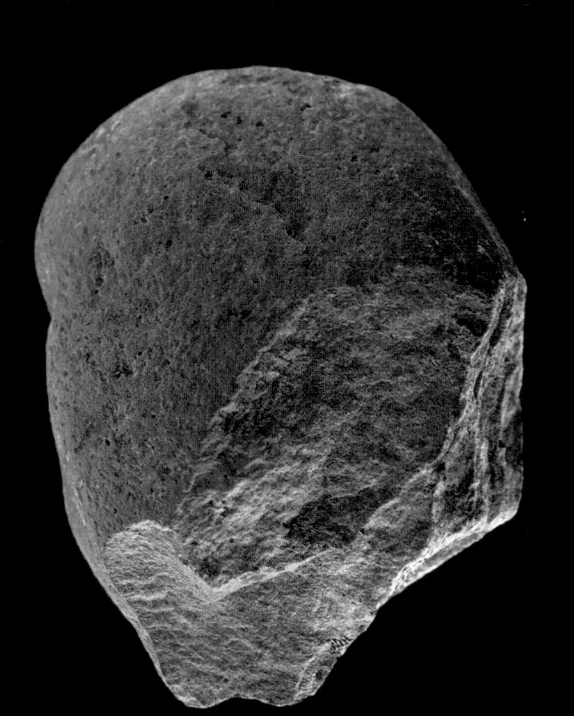

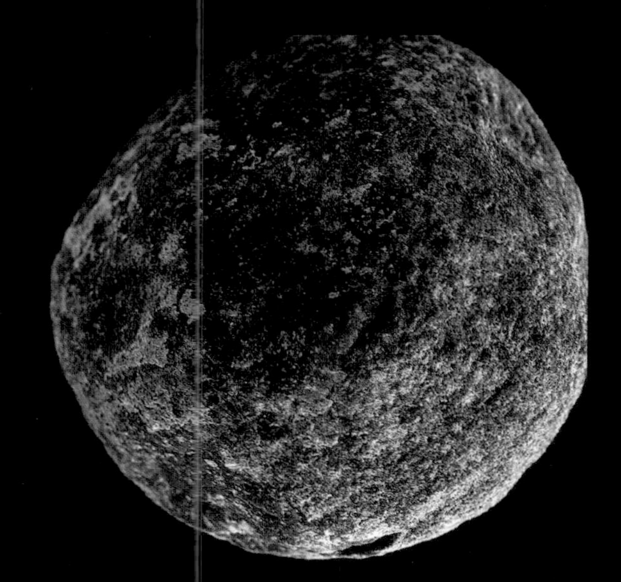

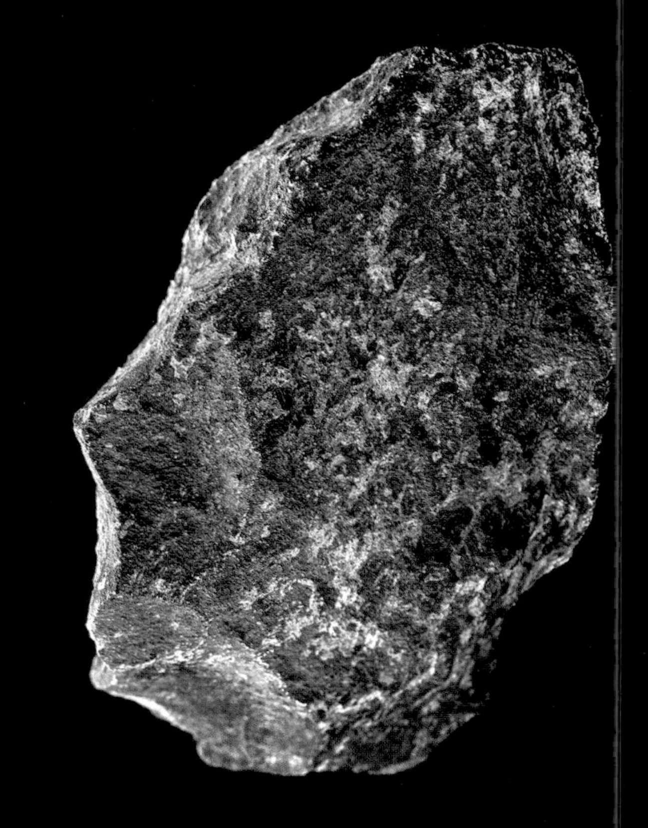

Oldowan end chopper, Olduvai Gorge, Tanzania (*top left*).
The name Oldowan comes from Olduvai Gorge, where Mary Leakey defined and described the industry and classified tools, such as this end chopper from Olduvai Bed I, by their form or apparent function. Actual size.
Photograph by David Brill; courtesy of National Museum of Tanzania.

Heavy-duty scraper, Olduvai Gorge, Tanzania (*top right*).
The steep, flaked edge of this kind of stone artifact led to its classification as a scraper, but other research suggests that the flakes themselves, rather than these chunky rock cores, were the primary tools. Actual size.
Photograph by David Brill; courtesy of National Museum of Tanzania.

Spheroid, Olduvai Gorge, Tanzania (*bottom*).
Ubiquitous at some East African sites, spheroids are probably just the unintended by-product of repeatedly bashing an angular hunk of quartz as a hammerstone to remove flakes from other rocks. Actual size.
Photograph by David Brill; courtesy of National Museum of Tanzania.

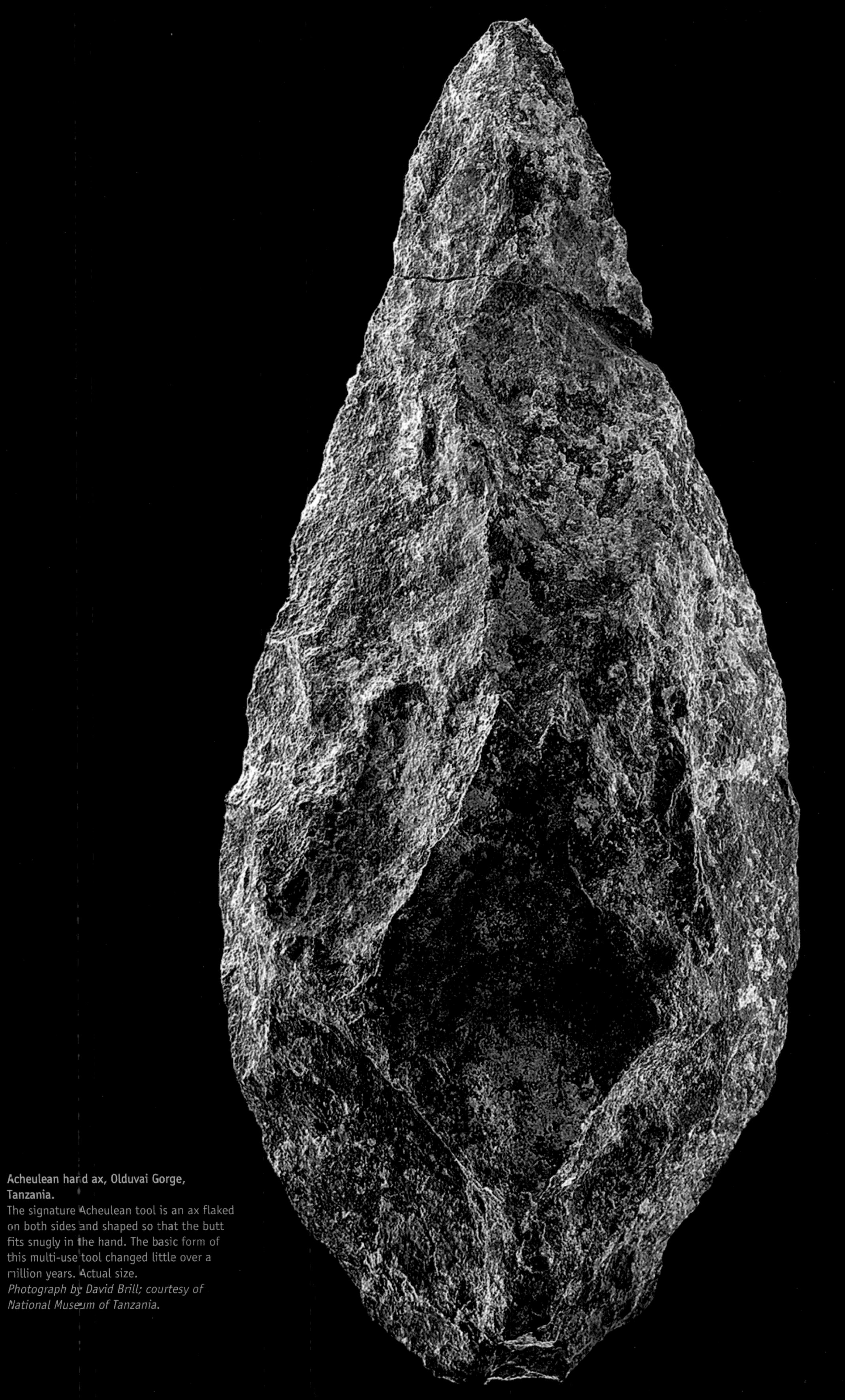

Acheulean hand ax, Olduvai Gorge, Tanzania.
The signature Acheulean tool is an ax flaked on both sides and shaped so that the butt fits snugly in the hand. The basic form of this multi-use tool changed little over a million years. Actual size.
Photograph by David Brill; courtesy of National Museum of Tanzania.

Acheulean

Named for the type archeological site of Saint-Acheul, France, this industry specialized in large, heavy-duty, sharp-edged tools. Analysis of microscopic wear traces on the working edges of these tools suggests that they primarily served in butchery and woodworking tasks. Acheulean tools are usually flaked all over both sides of a rock (quartzite, lava, chert, and flint were commonly used), hence the generic term biface. At some sites these tools look crude and chunky, at others they appear elegant and elongate, but the Acheulean reveals a degree of standardization in production technique and artifact form lacking in the Oldowan industry. This technological uniformity lasted for more than a million years in a region stretching from Africa through much of Europe, the Near East, and India. This major difference from the Oldowan industry signals a shift from simple, sharp flakes to specialized, functional tools. The major specific tool types include pointed hand axes, picks, and flat-edged cleavers. Crafting these tools required a complex set of procedures at each step, from finding a suitable core to the difficult process of flaking, trimming, and thinning the core to produce a pointed end for a hand ax or a truncated tip for a cleaver. Despite the elaborate manufacturing process, hand axes and cleavers make up a considerable percentage of the total archeological assemblage at most Acheulean sites.

Acheulean tools first appeared around 1.4 million years ago. The oldest known occurrence is from Konso-Gardula, Ethiopia, where abundant Acheulean tools over 1.3 million years old were found in 1991 along with a mandible of *Homo ergaster*. Other sites with early Acheulean tools of similar age are Olduvai Gorge, Tanzania, and Gadeb, Ethiopia. Tools from the earliest archeological sites in Europe more closely resemble the Oldowan than the Acheulean, suggesting that the first African migrants lacked a hand ax-based industry, but by 500,000 years ago the Acheulean industry proper had penetrated into Europe, where it continued until after 200,000 years ago. In France, Acheulean-like tools from a variant industry called the Tayacian are associated with remains of *Homo heidelbergensis* at the cave site of Arago (see page 98). Other Acheulean sites with fossils from this hominid species include Steinheim, Germany (see page 202), and Swanscombe, England. Acheulean tools apparently never reached East Asia, perhaps because more suitable raw materials for tools, such as bamboo, were plentiful, or because geographic barriers precluded biological and cultural diffusion between West and East Asia.

It took great skill and strength to master the making of Acheulean tools. The risky first step of striking a huge flake from a boulder with considerable force provided the raw form for a biface. This flake would then be worked with a hammerstone to remove smaller flakes alternately from each side, gradually whittling down the thickest areas and creating a more symmetrical shape. The toolmaker switched to a soft hammer of bone or antler or wood in order to remove thinner flakes and form a consistent edge to the biface.

Around a million years ago, more Acheulean assemblages became dominated by slim, symmetrical bifaces, especially the classic teardrop and lanceolate hand axes. Some incredibly oversized examples of Acheulean hand axes and picks come from the site of Isimila in Tanzania, tools so unwieldy that it taxes the imagination to picture them in practical use. At sites such as Olorgesailie, Kenya, where visitors on a raised wooden walkway can observe an archeological floor littered with hand axes, cleavers, and other tools, the incredible abundance of artifacts conjures images of an Acheulean assembly line.

Acheulean cleaver, Bihorel oest, France (*left*).
Another standard bifacial tool is the cleaver, made from a single large stone flake that is thinned and truncated to form a straight, broad tip. Actual size.
Photograph by David Brill; courtesy of Denise de Sonneville-Bordes, Université de Bordeaux I.

Acheulean lanceolate hand ax, Briqueterie, France (*right*).
Acheulean artifacts appear in Europe after 500,000 years ago and often adopt elongate, symmetrical shapes, such as this example crafted from flint. Actual size.
Photograph by David Brill; courtesy of Université de Bordeaux I.

Mousterian

The sort of core preparation that typified Acheulean toolmaking continued in the succeeding Mousterian industry, although the resulting tools were much smaller and had a wider range of shapes and uses. Named for the site of Le Moustier, France, where the remains of an adult and infant Neandertal were found, this industry appeared around 200,000 years ago (and thus overlapped with the Acheulean for thousands of years) and persisted until about 40,000 years ago. It occurred in various regional forms throughout Europe and in the Near East and Africa in essentially the same area where Acheulean tools have been found. In Europe, these artifacts are most closely associated with *Homo neanderthalensis*, but elsewhere, such as at the Near Eastern sites of Kebara (see page 218), Tabun, Qafzeh (see page 239), and Skhul (see page 242), Mousterian tools were made by both Neandertals and early *Homo sapiens*.

Many Mousterian toolmakers utilized either of two main techniques to prepare a stone core for the removal of a single, large flake of predetermined shape and thickness, which could then be shaped into a versatile range of tools by the process of retouching, or by the removal of many tiny flakes to form a new functional edge or to resharpen a dulled edge. These flaking techniques are jointly known as Levallois, for a Paris suburb where the technique was first identified in excavated artifacts. Although sometimes regarded as wasteful because only one flake could be produced, Levallois techniques in fact aimed to get as much cutting edge as possible from a core. The first technique began with a discoidal rock that was flaked around its circumference to create a faceted platform for the removal of an oval flake, forming a Levallois tortoise core (so named because the rounded top and flat bottom of the finished core resemble a tortoise's carapace). The resulting flake would often be retouched along one or both sides to form a scraper, which was used to work hides and wood. The second Levallois core technique also focused on preparing the core for a single flake, but the flake was triangular and pointed and probably served as the business end of projectiles or spears.

Other tools found in the Mousterian industry include notched flakes, denticulates (flakes with a rough, serrated edge), and flake blades similar to what would come to characterize Upper Paleolithic industries. When they were available near a hominid site, fine-grained flints were often chosen as raw material for making these Mousterian artifacts. One of the more unusual Mousterian tools comes from a North African industry called the Aterian, which may date to between 75,000 and 100,000 years ago. Although made with traditional Levallois techniques, Aterian points are notable for the squared-off tang protruding from the base that must have been used to haft this tool to the end of a wooden shaft as a spear point or arrowhead, an innovation that would be carried to new heights in the Upper Paleolithic.

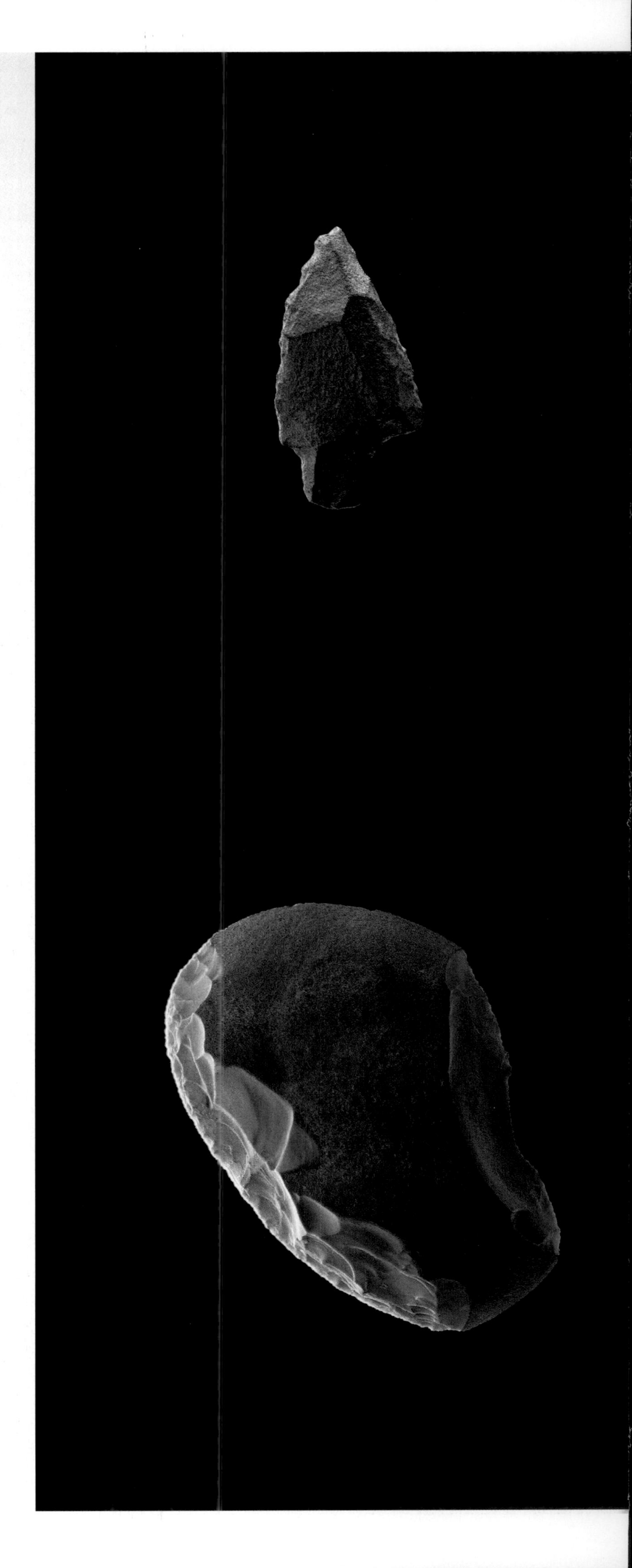

Aterian point, Colomb-Bechar, France (*top left*).
The tang at the base of this stone point identifies it as part of the variant Aterian industry. The point may have been hafted to the end of a stick to create a spear. Actual size.
Photograph by David Brill; courtesy of André Debenath, Université de Bordeaux I.

Double-sided scraper with Quina retouch, Combe-Grenal, France (*bottom left*).
Up to eighty percent of tools in the Quina variant of the Mousterian industry consists of scrapers, often with convex edges that have been retouched, or reshaped, by removing a series of very small flakes. Actual size.
Photograph by David Brill; courtesy of Universitee de Bordeaux I.

Mousterian point, Houppeville, France (*top right*).
A large pointed flake struck from a carefully prepared stone core is a typical tool from the Mousterian industry, which lasted from 200,000 to 40,000 years ago. The points may have been fashioned into projectiles. Actual size.
Photograph by David Brill; courtesy of Denise de Sonneville-Bordes, Université de Bordeaux I.

Levallois core and point, Le Tillet, France (*bottom right*).
This flint core reveals deliberate flaking around its edge to prepare a striking platform at the top so that this pointed flake would be removed without damage by the blow from another stone. Actual size.
Photograph by David Brill; courtesy of Denise de Sonneville-Bordes, Université de Bordeaux I.

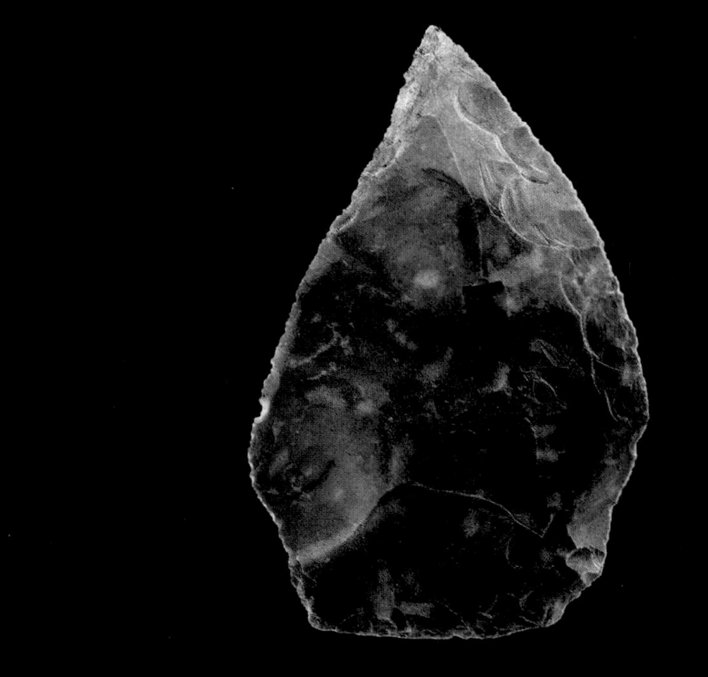

Upper Paleolithic

Diversity and specialization mark the archeological record of the Upper Paleolithic, in stark contrast to the technology of the Mousterian and every other preceding industry. Upper Paleolithic tools are more easily categorized and recognizable as having specific functions than those of any other paleolithic industry. This technological departure from the past, corresponded with the first signs of accelerated cultural evolution (and physically these toolmakers looked much like we do today). The most characteristic Upper Paleolithic tools were made from thin blades struck from cores. Blades are defined as flakes that are at least twice as long as their width. This technique greatly increased the number of cutting edges that could be obtained from a single core. Often, blades were broken and reshaped into microliths—small, geometrically shaped flakes that were hafted. One common tool from this industry, the burin, possessed a chisel-like engraving edge that facilitated the working of bone. Specialized bone and antler tools appear frequently in Upper Paleolithic archeological sites. Innovations in Upper Paleolithic technology and culture led to other aspects of human existence becoming more common or highly developed, such as the use of fire, burial of the dead, construction of clothing and shelter, and the creation of art.

The Upper Paleolithic spanned the period from 40,000 to 10,000 years ago in Europe. This industry probably started in western Asia and Africa at about the same time, although some African evidence suggests a much earlier origin there for the sorts of innovations that characterize the Upper Paleolithic. Barbed bone harpoons and points have been excavated from the Katanda site along Zaire's Semliki River, and these artifacts, which strongly resemble classic Upper Paleolithic bone tools from western Europe, are estimated to be as old as 90,000 years, which would place them firmly within the preceding Middle Stone Age. And the site of Kapthurin, Kenya, has yielded blades and blade cores reminiscent of Upper Paleolithic technique that may be 240,000 years old.

Unlike previous industries, the Upper Paleolithic quickly diversified, displaying distinctive regional styles. The earliest Upper Paleolithic industry was the Aurignacian (from 40,000 to 28,000 years ago), which was named after the Aurignac rockshelter in the Pyrenees foothills where such tools were first found in 1860. Aurignacian implements accompanied the modern human burials at Cro-Magnon and have been found at many sites across Europe. In the Near East, the Aurignacian spans the period from at least 32,000 to 17,000 years ago. Aurignacian assemblages can be characterized by the prevalence of end scrapers, burins, distinctive bone points, ivory beads and tooth necklaces, and some abstract human and animal figurines, including the recently discovered Dancing Venus of Gelgenberg, Austria, a flat figurine of a woman in green serpentine. France's earliest known cave paintings, from Chauvet and Cosquer, date to the late Aurignacian, 32,000 and 27,000 years ago, respectively.

Another Upper Paleolithic industry contemporary with the Aurignacian was the Châtelperronian, named for the French cave site of Châtelperron. This industry, which combined an evolved Mousterian technology with the use of blade and bone tools, can be confidently attributed to *Homo neanderthalensis* based on the association of both the Saint-Césaire skeleton (see page 232) and a juvenile Neandertal temporal bone from Arcy-sur-Cure, France, with Châtelperronian tools. This industry may have evolved in parallel with the Aurignacian or been adopted by Neandertals after the introduction of the Aurignacian to western Europe. The Châtelperronian industry apparently disappeared with the Neandertals around 34,000 years ago, while the Aurignacian and all later phases of Upper Paleolithic technology were created by *Homo sapiens.*

The Gravettian industry (from 28,000 to 22,000 years ago) added backed blades (backing refers to the broadening of one side of the blade by pressure-flaking that edge) and beveled-based bone points, which served as a new and more streamlined kind of spear tip, to the Upper Paleolithic tool kit. During this period, ivory beads became body adornments for burials, and the first of the Venus figurines, voluptuously depicted women carved in ivory, probably appeared in eastern, central, and western Europe. The brief Solutrean period (from about 21,000 to 19,000 years ago) featured incredible flint craftsmanship, best exemplified by bifacially flaked, leaf-shaped knives that were heated over a flame to permit the necessary precision flaking without snapping the object in two. This period of spectacular stoneworking both appears and disappears abruptly in the archeological record of France.

Perhaps the heyday of the Upper Paleolithic came with the Magdalenian industry (from 18,000 to 12,000 years ago), which is most notable for its wall art, the spectacular painted caves of Lascaux, Altamira, and other sites. Named for the French rockshelter La Madeleine, this period saw an increase in the use of microliths, which could be interchangeably hafted to make a range of composite tools, including arrows, as well as a prevalence of multibarbed bone harpoon heads, and spear throwers of wood, bone, or antler, which enhanced the speed and distance which a propelled spear could travel. All of these advances suggest much greater skill and sophistication for hunting many types of game.

Magdalenian biconical bone point, Abri Faustin, France (*left*).
Bone points appear in the earliest Upper Paleolithic period, after 40,000 years ago, but this example comes from the Magdalenian period, which began 18,000 years ago. Actual size.
Photograph by David Brill; courtesy of Michael Lenoir, Université de Bordeaux I.
Perigordian flint blade, Corbiac, France (*right*).
The most characteristic stone tool of the Upper Paleolithic, long blades provided a starting point for crafting microlithic flakes that were often combined into composite tools or used for a variety of specialized functions. Actual size.
Photograph by David Brill; courtesy of Denise de Sonneville-Bordes; Université de Bordeaux I.

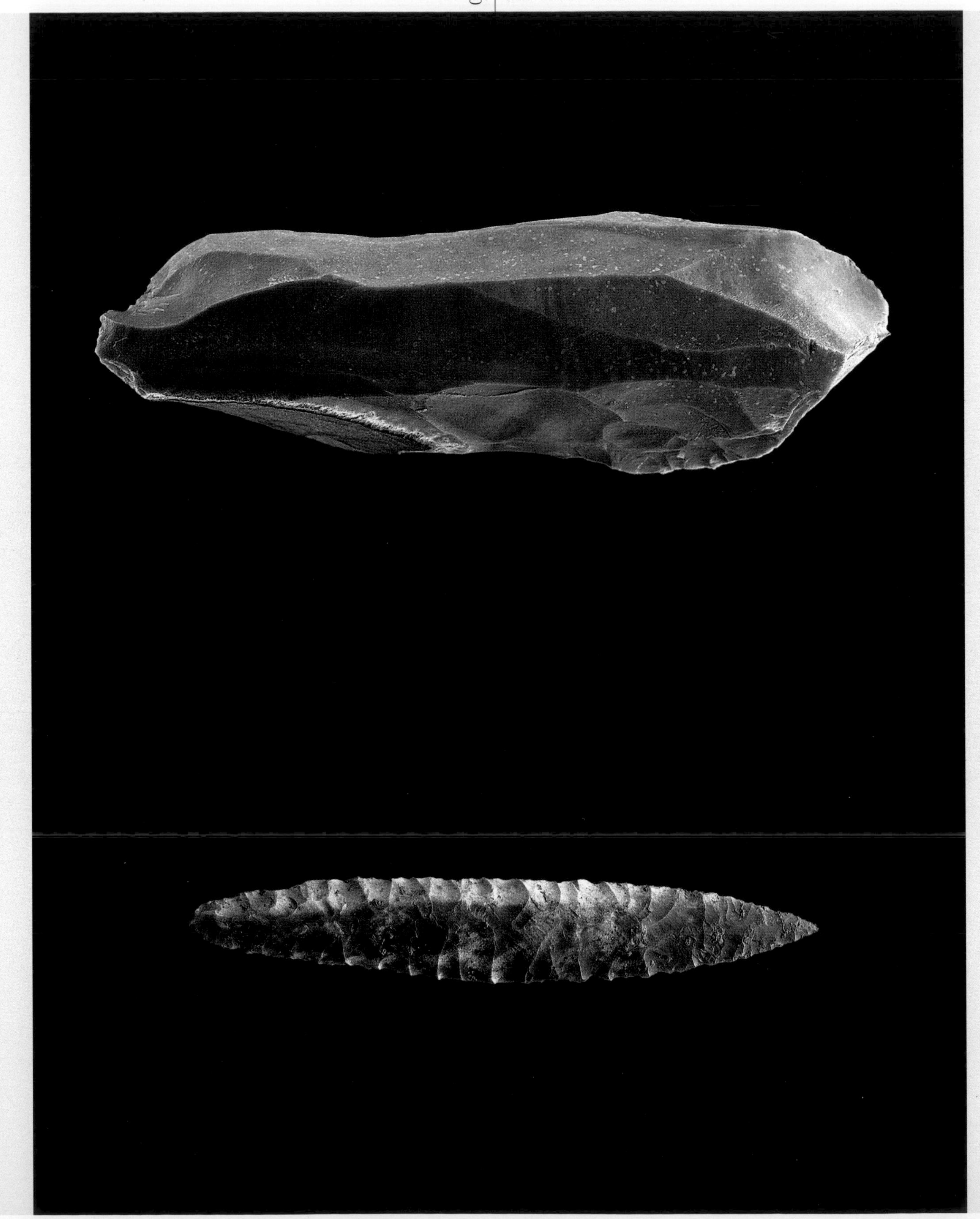

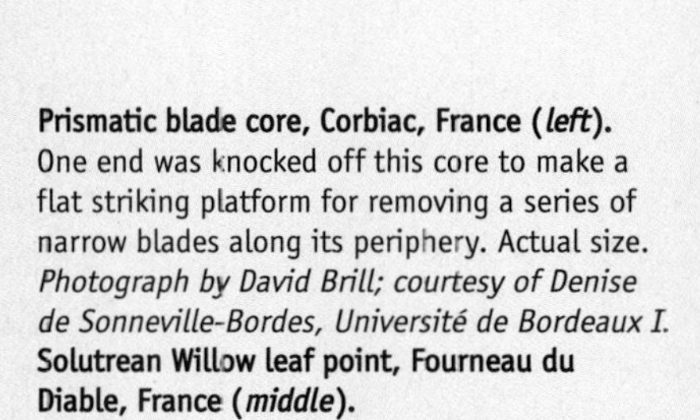

Prismatic blade core, Corbiac, France (*left*).
One end was knocked off this core to make a flat striking platform for removing a series of narrow blades along its periphery. Actual size.
Photograph by David Brill; courtesy of Denise de Sonneville-Bordes, Université de Bordeaux I.

Solutrean Willow leaf point, Fourneau du Diable, France (*middle*).
This beautiful, bifacial knife dates to around 20,000 years ago during a brief flowering of flint craftsmanship. It may have had greater ceremonial than functional use. Actual size.
Photograph by David Brill; courtesy of Université de Bordeaux I.

Magdalenian Double-row barbed harpoon, Le Morin, France (*right*).
Bone harpoons became common toward the end of the Upper Paleolithic and indicate that humans were exploiting a range of new food resources. In addition to such fishing gear, arrows and specialized spear-throwers were prevalent. Actual size.
Photograph by David Brill; courtesy of R. Deffarge, Université de Bordeaux I.

Appendix 1

TYPE SPECIMENS FOR HOMINID SPECIES

SPECIES	SPECIMEN NO.	SPECIMEN	PAGE NO.
Ardipithecus ramidus	ARA-VP-6/1	Assoc. set of teeth	see *116*
Australopithecus praegens	KNM-T1 13150	Adult mandible	*39*
A. anamensis	KNM-KP 29281	Adult mandible	*123*
A. bahrelghazali	KT 12/H1	Adult mandible	*119*
A. afarensis	L.H.-4	Adult mandible	*131*
A. africanus	Taung	Juvenile skull	*79 and 143*
A. crassidens	SK 6	Adolescent mandible	*149*
A. robustus	TM 1517	Adult partial cranium and mandible	*145*
A. aethiopicus	Omo 18	Adult mandible	*155*
A. boisei	OH 5	Adult cranium	*5, 30, 74 and 157*
Homo rudolfensis	KNM-ER 1470	Adult cranium	*178 and 179*
H. habilis	OH 7	Juvenile male partial skeleton	*171*
H. ergaster	KNM-ER 992	Adult mandible	*163*
H. erectus	Trinil 2	Adult partial cranium	*187*
H. heidelbergensis	Mauer 1	Adult mandible	*197*
H. neanderthalensis	Neanderthal 1	Adult partial cranium	*229*
H. sapiens	none		

The type specimen of a species is a particular specimen to which the species name was first properly applied. The rules governing the proper procedure for naming a species are found in the International Code of Zoological Nomenclature. In the case of a single specimen from a site, such as the Chad hominid, KT 12/H1, there is no ambiguity about which specific individual was used to designate the new binomial (meaning two names, the genus and the species); this specimen is properly called the holotype.

Appendix 2

Hominid Fossil and Archeological Sites

1 Altamira
2 Amud
3 Arago
4 Aramis
5 Arcy-sur-Cure
6 Arene Candide
7 Atapuerca
8 Bahr el Ghazal
9 Bodo
10 Border Cave
11 Broken Hill
12 Chauvet
13 Clovis
14 Combe-Grenal
15 Cro-Magnon
16 Dali
17 Dmanisi
18 Dolní Vestonice
19 Gadeb
20 Gibraltar
21 Hadar
22 Kanapoi
23 Debara
24 Klasies River Mouth
25 Koobi Fora
26 Kow Swamp
27 Krapina
28 Kromdraai
29 La Chapelle-aux-Saints
30 La Ferrassie
31 La Madeleine
32 Laetoli
33 Lake Mungo
34 Lascaux
35 Le Moustier
36 Lothagam
37 Makapansgat
38 Mauer
39 Meadowcroft Rockshelter
40 Middle Awash
41 Modjokerto
42 Monte Alegre
43 Monte Verde
44 Neandertal
45 Olduvai
46 Omo
47 Petralona
48 Qafzeh
49 Saccopastore
50 St. Acheul
51 Saint-Césaire
52 Sangiran
53 Shanidar
54 Skhul
55 Steinheim
56 Sterkfontein
57 Swanscombe
58 Swartkrans
59 Tabarin
60 Tabun
61 Taunq
62 Terra Amata
63 Teshik-Tash
64 Trinil
65 West Turkana
66 Zhoukoudian

ACKNOWLEDGMENTS

This book would not have been possible without the extraordinary dedication of the many researchers in the field and in the laboratory who have dedicated their lives towards a more complete understanding of humanity's past. Field workers, worldwide, have often operated under less than ideal circumstances, exposing themselves to all sorts of hardships and dangers, focusing solely on the goal of finding and recovering the fossil and archeological evidence left behind by our ancestors. There is no way to measure the endless hours scientists have spent in the laboratory to tease every ounce of information from this evidence. There is still much to know about our ancestry, and most assuredly by the time this book graces the shelves of bookstores, teams, already hard at work, will add important discoveries to those presented here.

José Conde, of Studio Pepin, Tokyo, must be congratulated for his elegant design and thoughtfulness in presenting our words and pictures in a captivating and appealing manner.

Majorie Pannell, copyeditor, has done a marvelous job of blending our two writing styles into a readable and illuminating text, and Diana Salles, illustrator, has provided important drawings which are of great help in guiding the reader.

Special assistance was given by Ian Tattersall, Gary Sawyer, Joanna Grand, Anibal Rodriguez, and Paul Goldstein of the American Museum of Natural History. The American Museum is a national treasure, and the generous help provided by our friends there is a reflection of how truly wonderful this museum really is.

We are grateful to Meave Leakey and William Anyonge of the National Museums of Kenya, where some of the most important fossil hominids (and numerous other vertebrate fossils, many on display) are housed, for permitting us to include photographs, some for the very first time, of recent discoveries of early *Australopithecus*. Thanks to Robert I.M. Campbell of Nairobi, Kenya, for his excellent photography of the Kenyan fossils, often under extreme time constraints.

A very special thanks to Enrico Ferorelli of New York City for his companionship at Hadar, his gracious cooperation, and insightful photographic eye.

Thanks to Maryellen Ruvolo, Harvard University, for providing advance copies of unpublished research papers.

Special thanks to Paul G. Bahn, world expert on rock art, for his critical comments on paleolithic art.

We wish to extend our sincere gratitude to the following individuals for their assistance in providing photographs or access to original specimens for photography: David Coulson, Nairobi; Steven Gerard, Photo Researchers, New York; Rose Taylor, Science Photo Library, London; Michael Day, Natural History Museum, London; David Hunt, Richard Thorington, and Chip Clark at the National Museum of Natural History, Washington D.C.; Lindsay Hooper, South African Museum, Cape Town; Juan-Luis Arsuaga, Universidad Complutense de Madrid; Javier Trueba, Madrid Scientific Films, Madrid; Wu Xinchi, Institute of Vertebrate Paleontology and Paleoanthropology, Beijing; Alan Thorne, Australian National University, Canberra; Fachroel Aziz, Geological Research and Development Centre, Bandung, Indonesia; Anna C. Roosevelt, Field Museum of Natural History, Chicago; Gerald Newslands, High River, Alberta; Jean Clottes, International Committee on Rock Art, France; Lena Godina, Moscow State University; Chris Dean, University College, London: Bob Brain, Transvaal Museum, Pretoria; Tom Dillehay, Univesity of Kentucky, Louisville; James Adovasio and David Pedler, Mercyhurst Archaeological Institute; Andrew Hill, Yale University, New Haven; Carola Lang and Daniela Schere, Staatliches Museum für Naturkunde, Stuttgart; Norbert Aujoulat, Centre National de Prehistoire, France; Michel Brunet, Université de Poitiers, France; Giorgio Manzi, Museo di Anthropologia of the University of Rome "La Sapienza"; Hoyer von Prittwitz, Rheinishches Landesmuseum, Bonn; Giacomo Giacobini, Universita di Torino; Eligio Vacca, Bari State University; John Gurche, Denver Museum of Natural History; Jean-Jacques Hublin, Musee de l'Homme, Paris; Owen Lovejoy, Kent State University; Lyman Jellema and Bruce Latimer, Cleveland Museum of Natural History; John Reader, Richmond, England; Jay Matternes, Fairfax, Virginia; Yves Coppens, College de France, Paris; Romulo Fialdini, Museo Goeldi, Brazil; Teuku Jacob, Gadjah Mada University, Indonesia; and Tim White, University of California, Berkeley.

Thanks to the following individuals for their expert assistance in the printing and publishing of this book: Fabio Bortolazzi, Fulvio Forcellini, and Bert Paolucci, Editoriale Bortolazzi-Stei, Verona; William S. Rosen, Janice Easton, and Marie Florio, Simon and Schuster Editions, New York; Cheryl Brant, Witwatersrand University Press, Johannesburg; and Michael Dover, Clare Currie, and Caroline Earle, Weidenfeld & Nicolson, London.

I (DCJ) would like to extend my personal gratitude to my closest colleagues at the Institute of Human Origins for their continuing assistance and shared fascination with paleoanthropology. William H. Kimbel, Robert C. Walter, Eric E. Meikle, Ann M. Blair, Michelle T. Nolan, Kaye E. Reed, Yoel Z. Rak, and Gerald G. Eck have contributed more than they will ever know to this venture.

I am deeply indebted to the Institute of Human Origins' Board of Directors who have provided the moral and financial means for us to continue to pursue one of the most fascinating of all quests—Human Origins.

Appreciation is expressed to the Ethiopian Ministry of Information and Culture and the Center for Research and Conservation of Cultural Heritage for their assistance.

Our spouses deserve a great deal of admiration for all they have weathered during the genesis of this book. Melissa Merz read portions of the manuscript and assisted with the index. Lenora Carey Johanson provided espressos, kept the fax machine operational, and led the cheer leading squad.

We owe a deep debt of gratitude to Peter N. Nevraumont and Ann J. Perrini of Nevraumont Publishing Company for approaching us with this project and enthusiastically encouraging us to pursue and—ultimately—complete it. Their insight, guidance, and attention to detail inspired us, and they have contributed substantially to the quality of this book.

SELECTED REFERENCES

The references cited here were consulted during the writing of this book and are intended to guide readers who wish to know more detail about the subjects covered in this book.
References with asterisks contain extensive bibliographies, a compendium of edited articles, or general overviews of hominid evolution.

PART I: *Central Issues of Paleoanthropology*

1. The Human Creature

Diamond, Jared. 1992. *The Third Chimpanzee.* New York: Harper Collins.

2. The Quest for Origins

*Bowler, Peter J. 1986. *Theories of Human Evolution: A Century of Debate, 1844-1944.* Baltimore, Johns Hopkins University Press.

Landau, Misia. 1991. *Narratives of Human Evolution.* New Haven: Yale University Press.

3. Is Human Evolution Different?

Bonner, John T. 1980. *The Evolution of Culture in Animals.* Princeton: Princeton University Press.

Lumsden, Charles, J., and Edward O. Wilson. 1983. *Promethean Fire.* Cambridge: Harvard University Press.

Wilson, Edward O. 1975. *Sociobiology: The New Synthesis.* Cambridge: Harvard University Press.

4. The Science of Paleoanthropology

Howell, F. Clark. 1967. "Recent advances in human evolutionary studies." *The Quarterly Review of Biology* 42:471-513.

Johanson, Donald C. 1996 (in press). "The Strategy of Paleoanthropology: Early African Hominids." *Yearbook of Physical Anthropology.*

5. The Early Human Fossil Record

*Klein, Richard G. 1989. *The Human Career.* Chicago: University of Chicago Press.

6. Discovering Early Human Fossil Sites

Asfaw, Berhane, Cynthia Ebinger, David Harding, Tim D. White, and Giday WoldeGabriel. 1990. "Space based imagery in paleoanthropological research: an Ethiopian example." *National Geographic Research* 6:418-434.

*Johanson, Donald C., and Maitland A. Edey. 1981. *Lucy: The Beginnings of Humankind.* New York: Simon and Schuster.

7. Recovering the Remains of Early Humans

Fagan, Brian M. 1978. *In the Beginning: An Introduction to Archaeology.* Boston: Little, Brown.

*Walker, Alan C., and Pat Shipman. 1996. *The Wisdom of the Bones.* New York: Alfred A. Knopf.

8. Dating Fossils and Artifacts

Lewin, Roger. 1991. "Rock of ages – cleft by laser." *New Scientist* 131(1788):36-40.

Marshall, Eliot. 1990. "Paleoanthropology Gets Physical." *Science* 247:798-801.

Shreeve, James. 1992. "The Dating Game." *Discover* 13(9):76-83.

9. Climate and Human Evolution

deMenocal, Peter B. 1995. "Plio-Pleistocene African Climate." *Science* 270:53-58.

Hill, Andrew. 1987. "Causes of perceived faunal change in the later Neogene of East Africa." *Journal of Human Evolution* 16:583-596.

Kingston, John D., Bruno D. Marino and Andrew Hill. 1994. "Isotopic Evidence for Neogene Hominid Paleoenvironments in the Kenya Rift Valley." *Science* 264:955-959.

*Vrba, Elisabeth S., George H. Denton, Timothy C. Partridge and Lloyd H. Burckle, editors. 1995. *Paleoclimate and Evolution with Emphasis on Human Origins.* New Haven: Yale University Press.

10. Teeth

*Aiello, Leslie, and Christopher Dean. 1990. *Human Evolutionary Anatomy.* London: Academic Press.

Beynon, Alan D., and M. Christopher Dean. 1988. "Distinct dental development patterns in early fossil hominids." *Nature* 335:509-514.

Hillson, S. 1986. *Teeth.* Cambridge: Cambridge University Press.

Macho, Gabriele A., and Bernard A. Wood. 1995. "The role of time and timing in hominid dental evolution." *Evolutionary Anthropology* 4:17-31.

*Martin, R.D. 1990. *Primate Origins and Evolution.* Princeton: Princeton University Press.

Swindler, Daris R. 1976. *Dentition of Living Primates.* London: Academic Press.

White, Tim D. 1991. *Human Osteology.* San Diego: Academic Press.

11. Proteins, DNA, and Human Evolution

Sarich, Vincent M. and Allan C. Wilson. 1967. "Immunological Time Scale for Hominid Evolution." *Science* 158:1200-1203.

Sibley, Charles G. and Jon E. Ahlquist. 1984. "The Phylogeny of the Hominoid Primates, as Indicated by DNA-DNA Hybridization." *Journal of Molecular Evolution* 20:2-15.

12. Why is Paleoanthropology So Contentious?

*Lewin, Roger. 1987. *Bones of Contention: Controversies in the Search for Human Origins.* New York: Simon and Schuster.

*Tuttle, Russell H. 1988. "What's new in African paleoanthropology?" *Ann. Rev. Anthropol.* 17:391-426.

13. Our Closest Living Relatives

King, Mary-Claire and Allan C. Wilson. 1975. "Evolution at Two Levels in Humans and Chimpanzees." *Science* 188:107-116.

Ruvolo, Maryellen. 1995. "Seeing the forest and the trees." *Am. J. Phys. Anthropol.* 98:211-232.

14. The Last Common Ancestor of Apes and Humans

Andrews, Peter. 1987. "Aspects of hominoid phylogeny." In Colin Patterson, editor. *Molecules and Morphology in Evolution: Conflict or Compromise.* 21-53. Cambridge: Cambridge University Press.

Andrews, Peter, and J. E. Cronin 1982. "The relationships of *Sivapithecus* and *Ramapithecus* and the evolution of the orang-utan." *Nature* 297:541-546.

Benefit, Brenda R., and Monte L. McCrossin. 1995. "Miocene hominoids and hominid origins." *Annu. Rev. Anthropol.* 24:237-56.

*Ciochon, Russell L., and Robert S. Corruccini, editors. 1983. *New Interpretations of Ape and Human Ancestry.* New York: Plenum Press.

Darwin, Charles. 1871. *The Descent of Man and Selection in Relation to Sex.* New York: Appleton.

Greenfield, Leonard O. 1979. "On the adaptive pattern of '*Ramapithecus*'." *Am. J. Phys. Anthropol.* 50:527-548.

Greenfield, Leonard O. 1980. "A late divergence hypothesis." *Am. J. Phys. Anthropol.* 52:351-166.

McHenry, Henry M. 1984. "The common ancestor." In Randall L. Susman, editor. *The Pygmy Chimpanzee.* 201-230. New York: Plenum.

Pilbeam, David. 1982. "New hominoid skull material from the Miocene of Pakistan." *Nature* 295:323-234.

Simons, Elwyn L. 1977. "Ramapithecus." *Scientific American* 236(5):28-35.

15. Drawing the Human Family Tree

*Johanson, Donald C., and Tim D. White. 1979. "A systematic assessment of early African hominids " *Science* 203:321-30.

Skelton, Randall R., and Henry M. McHenry. 1992. "Evolutionary relationships among early hominids." *Journal of Human Evolution* 23:309-349

*Tattersall, Ian. 1995. *The Fossil Trail.* New York: Oxford University Press.

Wood, Bernard A. 1992. "Origin and evolution of the genus *Homo*." *Nature* 355:783-790.

——. 1994. "The oldest hominid yet." *Nature* 371:280-281.

16. African Genesis

Ferguson, Walter W. 1989. "Taxonomic status of the hominid mandible KNM-ER TI 13150 from the middle Pliocene of Tabarin, in Kenya." *Primates* 30:383-387.

Hill, Andrew, and Steven Ward. 1988. "Origin of the Hominidae: The record of African large hominoid evolution between 14 My and 4 My." *Yearbook of Physical Anthropology* 31:49-83.

Leakey, Meave G., Craig S. Feibel, Ian McDougall, and Alan C. Walker. 1995. "New four-million-year-old hominid species from Kanapoi and Allia Bay, Kenya." *Nature* 376:565-571.

White, Tim D., Gen Suwa, and Berhane Asfaw. 1994. "*Australopithecus ramidus*, a new species of early hominid from Aramis, Ethiopia. *Nature* 371:306-312

17. Early versus Modern Humans

*Johanson, Donald, Lenora Johanson, and Blake Edgar. 1994. *Ancestors: In Search of Human Origins.* New York: Villard Books.

*Jurmain, Robert, and Harry Nelson. 1994. *Introduction to Physical Anthropology.* Sixth Edition. Minneapolis/St. Paul: West Publishing Co.

*Tattersall, Ian. 1995. *The Fossil Trail.* New York: Oxford University Press.

18. Eve, and Adam

Ayala, Francisco J. 1995. "The Myth of Eve: Molecular Biology and Human Origins." *Science* 270:1930-1936.

Hammer, Michael F. 1995. "A recent common ancestry for human Y chromosomes." *Nature* 378:376-378.

Ruvolo, Maryellen. 1996. "A New Approach to Studying Modern Human Origins: Hypothesis Testing with Coalescence Time Distributions." *Molecular Phylogenetics and Evolution* 5(1):202-219.

Tishkoff, S.A., E. Dietzsch, W. Speed, A.J. Pakstis, J.R. Kidd, K. Cheung, B. Bonné-Tamir, A.S. Santachiara-Benerecetti, P. Moral, M. Krings, S. Pääbo, E. Watson, N. Risch, T. Jenkins, and K.K. Kidd. 1996. "Global Patterns of Linkage Disequilibrium at the CD4 Locus and Modern Human Origins." *Science* 271:1380-1387.

Whitfield, L. Simon, J.E. Sulston, and P.N. Goodfellow. 1995. "Sequence variation of the human Y chromosome." *Nature* 378:379-380.

Wilson, Allan C., and Rebecca L. Cann. 1992. "The Recent African Genesis of Humans." *Scientific American* 266(4):68-73.

19. The Earliest Fossil Evidence of Anatomically Modern Humans

Bar-Yosef, Ofer, and Bernard Vandermeersch. 1993. "Modern Humans in the Levant." *Scientific American* 267(4):94-100

Klein, Richard G. 1994. "The problem of modern human origins." In Matthew H. Nitecki and Doris V. Nitecki, editors. *Origins of Anatomically Modern Humans.* 3-17. New York: Plenum Press.

——. 1995. "Anatomy, Behavior, and modern human origins." *Journal of World History* 9:167-198

*Mellars, Paul, and Chris Stringer, editors. 1989. *The Human Revolution: Behavioural and Biological Perspectives on the Origins of Modern Humans.* Princeton: Princeton Univ. Press.

20. Out of Africa

Carbonell, E., J.M. Bermúdez de Castro, J.L. Arsuaga, J.C. Díez, A. Rosas, G. Cuenca-Bescós, R. Sala, M. Mosquera, and X.P. Rodriguez. 1995. "Lower Pleistocene Hominids and Artifacts from Atapuerca-TD6 (Spain)." *Science* 269:826-830.

Gabunia, L., and A. Vekua. 1995. "A Plio-Pleistocene hominid from Dmanisi, East Georgia, Caucasus." *Nature* 373:509-512.

Gutin, JoAnn C. 1995. "Remains in Spain Now Reign As Oldest Europeans." *Science* 269: 754-755.

Parés, Josep M., and A. Pérez-González. 1995. "Paleomagnetic Age for Hominid Fossils in Atapuerca Archaeological Site, Spain." *Science* 269: 830-832.

Shreeve, James. 1994. "*Erectus* Rising." *Discover* 15(9):80-89.

Swisher, C.C. III, G.H. Curtis, T. Jacob, A.G. Getty, A. Suprijo, Widiasmoro. 1994. "Age of the Earliest Known Hominids in Java, Indonesia." *Science* 263:1118-1121.

21. The First Americans

Adovasio, J.M. and Ronald C. Carlisle. 1986. "Pennsylvania Pioneers." *Natural History* 95(12):20-27.

Dillehay, Tom D. 1987. "By the Banks of the Chinchihuapi." *Natural History* 96(4):8-11.

Marshall, Eliot. 1990. "Clovis Counter-revolution." *Science* 249:738-741.

——. 1992. "The Perils of a Deeply Held Point of View." *Science* 257:621-622.

Meltzer, David. 1995. "Stones of contention." *New Scientist* 146(1983):31-35.

Morell, Virginia. 1990. "Confusion in Earliest America." *Science* 248:439-441.

Roosevelt, A.C., M. Lima da Costa, C. Lopes Machado, M. Michab, N. Mercier, H. Valladas, J. Feathers, W. Barnett, M. Imazio da Silveira, A. Henderson, J. Silva, B. Chernoff, D.S. Reese, J.A. Holman, N. Toth, K. Schick. 1996. "Paleoindian Cave Dwellers in the Amazon: The Peopling of the Americas." *Science* 272:373-384.

22. Peopling the Globe

Cavalli-Sforza, Luigi Luca and Francisco Cavalli-Sforza. 1995. *The Great Human Diasporas.* New York: Addison-Wesley (Helix Books).

Gamble, Clive. 1994. *Timewalkers: The Prehistory of Global Colonization.* Cambridge: Harvard University Press.

Roberts, Richard G., R. Jones, N.A. Spooner, M.J. Head, A.S. Murray and M.A. Smith. 1994. "The Human Colonisation of Australia: Optical Dates of 53,000 and 60,000 Years Bracket Human Arrival at Deaf Adder Gorge, Northern Territory." *Quaternary Geochronology* 13:575-583.

23. Defining Human Species

Dawkins, Richard. 1995. *River Out of Eden.* New York: Basic Books.

*Eldredge, Niles. 1985. *Unfinished Synthesis.* New York: Oxford University Press.

*Kimbel, William H., and Lawrence B. Martin, editors. 1993. *Species, Species Concepts and Primate Evolution.* New York: Plenum Press.

*Meikle, W. Eric, and Sue Taylor Parker. 1994. *Naming our Ancestors.* Prospect Heights: Waveland Press.

Tattersall, Ian. 1986. "Species recognition in human paleontology." *Journal of Human Evolution* 15:165-75.

24. Co-Existing Human Species

Bower, Bruce. 1995. "Pruning the Family Tree." *Science News* 148:154-155.

Walker, Alan C. 1976. "*Australopithecus*, *Homo erectus* and the single species hypothesis." *Nature* 261:572-574.

25. Human Diversity Today and 26. What is Race?

Brace, C. Loring. 1995. "A Four-Letter Word Called "Race." Paper presented at the annual meeting of the American Association for the Advancement of Science.

*Marks, Jonathan. 1995. *Human Biodiversity: Genes, Race, and History.* New York: Aldine de Gruyter.

Vines, Gail. 1995. "Genes in Black and White." *New Scientist* 147(1985):34-37.
Wills, Christopher. 1994. "The skin we're in." *Discover* 15(11):76-81.

27. The Size of Early Humans

*Jungers, William L., editor. 1985. *Size and Scaling in Primate Biology.* New York: Plenum Press.
McHenry, Henry M. 1992a. "How big were early hominids?" *Evolutionary Anthropology*, 1:15-20.
——. 1992b. "Body size and proportions in early hominids." *Am. J. Phys. Anthropol.* 87:407-431.
Robinson, John T. 1972. *Early Hominid Posture and Locomotion.* Chicago: University of Chicago Press.

28. Sexual Dimorphism

Frayer, David W., and Milford H. Wolpoff. 1985. "Sexual Dimorphism." *Ann. Rev. Anthropol.* 14:429-73.
McHenry, Henry M. 1991. "Sexual dimorphism in *Australopithecus afarensis*." *Journal of Human Evolution* 20:21-32.
Plavcan, J. Michael, and Carel P. van Schaik. 1993/94. "Canine dimorphism." *Evolutionary Anthropology* 2:208-214.
Plavcan, J. Michael, Carel P. van Schaik, and P.M. Kappeler. 1995. "Competition, coalitions and canine size in primates." *Journal of Human Evolution* 28:245-276.

29. Gestation

Fischman, Joshua. 1994. "Putting a New Spin on the Birth of Human Birth." *Science* 264: 1082-1083.
Rak, Yoel, and Baruch Arensburg. 1987. "Kebara 2 Neanderthal pelvis: First look at a complete inlet." *Am. Journal Phys.. Anthropol.* 73: 227-231.
Trinkaus, Erik. 1984. "Neandertal Pubic Morphology and Gestation Length." *Current Anthropology* 25(4):509-514.

30. Maturation

Beynon, Alan D., and Bernard A. Wood. 1987. "Patterns and rates of enamel growth in the molar teeth of early hominids." *Nature* 326:493-496.
Bromage, Timothy G. and M. Christopher Dean. 1985. "Re-evaluation of the age at death of immature fossil hominids." *Nature* 317:525-527.
Mann, Alan E. 1975. *Some Paleodemographic Aspects of the South African Australopithecines.* Philadelphia: University of Pennsylvania Publications in Anthropology 1.
Shipman, Pat. 1987. "An Age-Old Question: Why did the Human Lineage Survive." *Discover* 8(4):60-64.
Smith, B. Holly. 1986. "Dental Development in *Australopithecus* and early *Homo*." *Nature* 323:327-330.

31. Evolution of the Human Brain

Bilsborough, Alan 1973. "A multivariate study of evolutionary change in the the hominid cranial vault and some evolution rates." *Journal of Human Evolution* 2:387-404.
Deacon, Terrence W. 1990. In J.A. Hawkins and M. Gell-Mann, editors. *The Evolution of Human Languages.* New York: Addison-Wesley.
Passingham, Richard. 1982. *The Human Primate.* Oxford and San Francisco: W.H. Freeman.
Wills, Christopher. 1993. *The Runaway Brain: The Evolution of Human Uniqueness.* New York: Basic Books.

32. Reconstructing the Appearance of Early Humans

Johanson, Donald C. 1996. "Face-to-Face with Lucy's Family." *National Geographic Magazine* 189(3):96-117.
Rensberger, Boyce. 1981. "Facing the Past." *Science 81*. 2(8):40-51.
Waters, Tom. 1990. "Almost Human." *Discover.* 11(5):42-45.

33. Primate Societies and Early Human Social Behavior

Ghiglieri, Michael P. 1989. "Hominoid Sociobiology and Hominid Social Evolution." In Paul G. Heltne and Linda A. Marquardt, editors. *Understanding Chimpanzees.* 370-379. Cambridge: Harvard University Press.
Wrangham, Richard W. 1987. "The Significance of African apes for reconstructing human social evolution." In Warren G. Kinzey, editor. *The Evolution of Human Behavior: Primate Models.* 51-71. Albany: State University of New York Press.

34. Evidence for Bipedalism

Coppens, Yves, and Brigitte Senut, editors. 1991. *Origine(s) de la Bipédie chez les Hominidés.* Paris: Cahiers de Paléoanthropologie.
Leakey, Mary D., and John M. Harris, editors. 1987. *Laetoli: A Pliocene Site in Northern Tanzania.* Oxford: Clarendon Press.
Lovejoy, C. Owen. 1988. "Evolution of Human Walking." *Scientific American* 256(5): 118-125.
Stern, Jack T. Jr., and Randall L. Susman. 1983. "The locomotor anatomy of *Australopithecus afarensis*." *Am J. Phys. Anthropol.* 60:279-317.
Susman, Randall L., Jack T. Stern, and William L. Jungers. 1984. "Arboreality and bipedality in the Hadar hominids." *Folia primatolgica* 43:113-156.
White, Tim D., and Gen Suwa. 1987. "Hominid footprints at Laetoli: facts and interpretations." *Am. J. Phys. Anthropol.* 73:485-515.

35. The Origins of Bipedalism

Chaplin, George, Nina G. Jablonski, and N. Timothy Cable. 1994. "Physiology, thermoregulation and bipedalism." *Journal of Human Evolution* 27:497-510.
Hrdy, Sarah B. and William Bennett. 1981. "Lucy's husband: What did he stand for?" *Harvard Magazine* July-August:7-9, 46.
Jablonski, Nina G., and George Chaplin. 1993. "Origin of habitual terrestrial bipedalism in the ancestor of the Hominidae." *Journal of Human Evolution* 24:259-280.
Lovejoy, C. Owen. 1981. "The origin of man." *Science* 211:341-350.
——. 1993. "Modeling human origins: are we sexy because we're smart, or smart because we're sexy?" In D. Tab Rasmussen, editor. *The Origin and Evolution of Humans and Humanness.* Boston: Jones and Bartlett Publisher.
Rodman, Peter S., and Henry M. McHenry. 1980. "Bioenergetics and the origin of hominid bipedalism." *Am. J. Phys. Anthropol.* 52:103-106
Shreeve, James. 1996. "Sunset on the Savanna." *Discover* 17(7):116-125.
Wheeler, Peter E. 1988. "Stand tall and stay cool." *New Scientist* 1612:62-65.

36. The Oldest Stone Tools

Kimbel, W.H., R.C. Walter, D.C. Johanson, J.L. Aronson, Z. Assefa, G.G. Eck, E. Hovers, C.W. Marean, R. Bobe-Quinteros, Y. Rak, K.E. Reed, C. Vondra, T. Yemane, D. York, Y. Chen, N.M. Evensen, and P.E. Smith. 1996 (in press). "Late Pliocene *Homo* and Oldowan tools from the Hadar Formation (Kada Hadar Member), Ethiopia." *Journal of Human Evolution.*
*Leakey, Mary D. 1971. *Olduvai Gorge: Excavations in Beds I and II, 1960-1963.* Cambridge: Cambridge University Press.
Roche, Hèlène, and Jean-Jacques Tiercelin. 1977. "Découverte d'une industrie lithique ancienne in situ dans la formation d'Hadar, Afar central, Éthiopie." *Comptes Rendus des séances de l'Academie des Sciences.* (Paris) 284:1871-1874.
*Schick, Kathy D., and Nicholas Toth. 1993. *Making Silent Stones Speak.* New York: Simon and Schuster.

37. Hunters, Gatherers, or Scavengers?

Binford, Lewis R. 1981. *Bones: Ancient Men and Modern Myths.* New York: Academic Press.
——. "Fact and fiction about the *Zinjanthropus* floor: data, arguments, and interpretations." *Current Anthropology* 29:123-149.
Blumenschine, Robert J. 1987. "Characteristics of an early hominid scavenging niche." *Current Anthropology* 28:383-407.
——. 1991. "Breakfast at Olorgesailie: The natural history approach to early stone age archaeology." *Journal of Evolution* 21:307-327.
Blumenschine, Robert J., and John A. Cavallo. 1992. "Scavenging and human evolution." *Scientific American* 265(10):90-96.
Brain, Charles K. 1981. *The Hunters or the Hunted?* Chicago: University of Chicago Press.
Bunn, Henry T., and Ellen M. Kroll. 1986. "Systematic butchery by Plio/Pleistocene hominids at Olduvai Gorge, Tanzania." *Current Anthropology* 27:431-452.
Issac, Glynn Ll. 1978. "Food sharing and human evolution: archaeological evidence from the Plio-Pleistocene of East Africa " Journal of Anthropological Research 34:311-325.
*Lee, Richard B., and Irven DeVore. 1968. *Man the Hunter.* Chicago: Aldine.
Shipman, Pat, and Alan C. Walker. 1989. "The costs of becoming a predator." *Journal of Human Evolution* 18:373-392.
Tooby, John, and Irven DeVore. 1987. "The reconstruction of hominid behavioral evolution through strategic modelling." In Warren G. Kinzey, editor. *The Evolution of Human Behavior: Primate models.* 183-237. Albany: State University of New York Press.

38. Diet

Benyon, Alan D. and Bernard A. Wood. 1986. "Variations in enamel thickness and structure in East African hominids." *Am. J. Phys. Anthropol.* 70:177-194.
Grine, Fred E. 1987. "Quantitative analysis of occlusal microwear in *Australopithecus* and *Paranthropus*." *Scanning Microscopy* 1:647-656.
Grine, Fred E., and Richard F. Kay. 1988. "Early hominid diets from quantitative image analysis of dental microwear." *Nature* 333:765-768.
Kay, Richard F. 1975. "The functional adaptations of primate molar teeth." *Am. J. of Phys. Anthropol.* 43:195-215.
Ryan, Alan S., and Donald C. Johanson. 1989. "Anterior dental microwear in *Australopithecus afarensis*: comparisons with human and non human primates." *Journal of Human Evolution* 18:235-268.
Teaford, Mark F. 1994. "Dental microwear and dental function." *Evolutionary Anthropology* 3:17-30.
Walker, Alan C. 1981. "Diet and teeth." *Phil. Trans. Roy. Soc. Lond.* B 292:57-64.

39. Cannibalism

Fernández-Jalvo, Yolanda, J.C. Díez, J.M. Bermúdez de Castro, E. Carbonell and J.L. Arsuaga. 1996. "Evidence of Early Cannibalism" *Science* 217:277-278?
Villa, Paola, C. Bouville, J. Courtin, D. Helmer, E. Mahieu, P. Shipman, G. Belluomini, M. Branca. 1986. "Cannibalism in the Neolithic." *Science* 233:431-437.
Villa, Paola and E. Mahieu. 1991. "Breakage patterns of human long bones." *Journal of Human Evolution* 21:27-48.
White, Tim D. 1986. "Cut Marks on the Bodo Cranium: A Case of Prehistoric Defleshing." *Am. J. Phys. Anthropol.* 69:503-509.
White, Tim D. and Nicholas Toth. 1989 "Engis: Preparation Damage, Not Ancient Cutmarks." *Am. J. Phys. Anthropol.* 78:361-367.

40. Fire

Brain, Charles K. and Andrew Sillen. 1988. "Evidence from the Swartkrans Cave for the Earliest Use of Fire." *Nature* 336:464-466.
Fischman, Joshua. 1996. "A Fireplace in France." *Discover* 17(1):69.
Gowlett, J.A.J., J.W.K. Harris, D. Walton and B.A. Wood. 1981. "Early archaeological sites, hominid remains and traces of fire from Chesowanja, Kenya." *Nature* 294:125-129.
James, Steven R. 1989. "Hominid Use of Fire in the Lower and Middle Pleistocene." *Current Anthropology* 30(1):1-26.
Straus, Lawrence Guy. 1989. "On Early Hominid Use of Fire." *Current Anthropology* 30(4):488-491.

41. Shelter

Bordes, François. 1972. *A Tale of Two Caves.* New York: Harper and Row.
Gladkih, Mikhail I., Ninelj L. Kornietz and Olga Soffer. 1984. "Mammoth Bone Dwellings on the Russian Plain." *Scientific American* 251(5):164-170.
Klein, Richard G. 1973. *Ice Age Hunters of the Ukraine.* Chicago: The University of Chicago Press.

42. Clothing

Spindler, Konrad. 1994. *The Man in the Ice.* New York: Harmony Books.
White, Randall. 1986. *Dark Caves, Bright Visions: Life in Ice Age Europe.* New York: W.W. Norton.

43. Burial

Chase, Philip G. and Harold C. Dibble. 1987. "Middle Paleolithic Symbolism: A Review of Current Evidence and Interpretations." *Journal of Anthropological Archaeology* 6:263-296.
Gargett, Robert H. 1989. "Grave Shortcomings: The Evidence for Neandertal Burial." *Current Anthropology* 30(2):157-190.
Harrold, Francis B. 1980. "A comparitive analysis of Eurasian Paleolithic burials." *World Archaeology* 12(2):195-211.

44. Art

*Bahn, Paul G., and Jean Vertut. 1988. *Images of the Ice Age.* New Yorks: Facts on File.
Chauvet, Jean Marie, Eliette Brunel Deschamps, and Christian Hillaire. 1996. *Dawn of Art: The Chauvet Cave.* New York: Harry N. Abrams.
Clottes, Jean, and Jean Courtin. 1996. *The Cave Beneath the Sea.* New York: Harry N. Abrams.
Lewis-Williams, J. David. 1981. *Believing and Seeing: Symbolic Meanings in southern San Rock Paintings.* New York: Academic Press.
Lorblanchet, Michel. 1988. "From the cave art of the reindeer hunters to the rock art of the kangaroo hunters." *L'Anthropologie*, 92:271-316.
*Marshack, Alexander. 1991. *The Roots of Civilization.* Mount Kisco, Moyer Bell Ltd.

45. The Origins of Language

Arensburg, Baruch, Anne-Marie Tillier, Bernard Vandermeersch, Henri Duday, Lynne A. Schepartz and Yoel Rak. 1989. "A Middle Paleolithic human hyoid bone." *Nature* 338:758-760.
Noble, William and Iain Davidson. 1991. "The Evolutionary Emergence of Modern Human Behaviour: Language and its Archaeology." *Man* 26(2):223-254.
Pinker, Steven. 1994. *The Language Instinct: How the Mind Creates Language.* New York: William Morrow.

46. The Problem of Consciousness

Bower, Bruce. 1992. "Consciousness Raising." *Science News* 142:232-235.
Dennett, Daniel C. 1991. *Consciousness Explained.* Boston: Little, Brown.
Horgan, John. 1994. "Can Science Explain Consciousness?" *Scientific American* 268(7):88-94.
Humphrey, Nicholas. 1992. *A History of the Mind.* New York: Simon & Schuster.
Wright, Robert. 1996. "Can Machines Think?" *Time* 147(13):50-57.

47. Will Humans Become Extinct?

McKibben, Bill. 1989. *The End of Nature.* New York: Random House.
Nitecki, Matthew H., editor. 1984. *Extinctions.* Chicago: The University of Chicago Press.
Ward, Peter. 1994. *The End of Evolution: On Mass Extinctions and the Preservation of Biodiveristy.* New York: Bantam Books.
Wilson, Edward O. 1992. *The Diversity of Life.* Cambridge: Harvard University Press.

48. Place of Humans in Nature

Huxley, Thomas H. 1863. *Evidence as to Man's Place in Nature.* London: Williams and Norgate.

Ardipithecus ramidus, ARA-VP-1/129

Day, Michael H. 1995. "Remarkable delay." *Nature* 376:111.

Kalb, Jon E., Clifford J. Jolly, Elizabeth B. Oswald, and Paul F. Whitehead. 1984. "Early hominid habitation in Ethiopia." *American Scientist* March-April 72:168-178.

Kappelman, John, and John G. Fleagle. 1995. "Age of early hominids." *Nature* 376:558-559.

WoldeGabriel, Giday, Tim D. White, Gen Suwa, Paul Renne, Jean de Heinzelin, William K. Hart, and Grant Heiken. 1994. "Ecological and temporal placement of early Pliocene hominids at Aramis, Ethiopia." *Nature* 371:330-333.

White, Tim D., Gen Suwa, and Berhane Asfaw. 1995. "*Australopithecus ramidus*, a new species of early hominid from Aramis, Ethiopia." *Nature* 375:88.

Australopithecines

Broom, Robert, and John T. Robinson 1950. *Further Evidence of the Structure of the Sterkfontein Ape-Man* Plesianthropus. Transvaal Mus. Memoir 4:11-84.

——. 1952. *Swartkrans Ape-Man:* Paranthropus crassidens. Transvaal Mus. Memoir 6:1-123.

Broom, Robert, and G.W.H. Schepers. 1946. *The South African Fossil Ape-Men. The Australopithecinae.* Transvaal Mus. Memoir 2:1-271.

Brunet, Michel, Alain Beauvilain, Yves Coppens, Emile Heintz, Aladji H.E. Moutaye, and David Pilbeam. 1995. "The first australopithecine 2,500 kilometres west of the Rift Valley (Chad). *Nature* 378:273-275.

Brunet, Michel, Alain Beauvilain, Yves Coppens, Emile Heintz, Aladji H.E. Moutaye, and David Pilbeam. 1996. "*Australopithecus bahrelghazali*, une nouvelle espèce d'Hominidé ancien de la région de Koro Toro (Tchad)." *Comptes Rendus des séances de l'Academie des Sciences.*Paris 322:907-913.

Clark, W.E. Le Gros. 1967. *Man-Apes or Ape-Men? The Story of Discoveries in* Africa. New York: Holt, Rinehart and Winston.

Grine, Fred E. 1993. "Australopithecine taxonomy and phylogeny: historical background and recent interpretation." In Russell L. Ciochon and John G. Fleagle, editors *The Human Evolution Source Book.* 145-175 Englewood Cliffs, Prentice Hall.

Grine, Fred E., editor. 1988. *Evolutionary History of the "Robust" Australopithecines.* New York: Aldine de Gruyter.

Howell, F. Clark. 1978. "Hominidae." In Vincent J. Maglio and H.B.S. Cooke, editors. *Evolution of African Mammals.* 154-428. Cambridge: Harvard University Press.

Johanson, Donald C., and Tim D. White. 1979. "A systematic assessment of early African hominids." *Science* 202:3321-330.

Rak, Yoel. 1983. *The Australopithecine Face.* New York: Academic Press.

Reed, Charles A. 1983. "A short history of the discovery and early study of the Australopithecines: the first find to the death of Robert Broom (1924-1951)." In Kathleen J. Reichs, editor. *Hominid Origins: Inquiries Past and Present.* 1-77 Washington, D.C.: University Press of America.

Robinson, John T. 1956. *The Dentition of the Australopithecinae.* Transvaal Mus. Memoir No.9:1-179.

Tobias, Phillip V. 1968. *The Cranium and Maxillary Dentition of Australopithecus (Zinjanthropus) boisei. Olduvai Gorge.* Vol. 2. Cambridge: Cambridge University Press.

Tobias, Phillip V. 1988. "*Australopithecus afarensis*" and *A. africanus*: critique and an alternative hypothesis." *Palaeontologia Africana* 23:1-17.

Wallace, John A. 1972. *The Dentition of the south African Early Hominids: A study of form and Function.* Ph.D. Dissertation, The University of the Witwatersrand.

——. 1974. "Dietary adaptations of *Australopithecus* and early *Homo*. In Russell H. Tuttle, editor. *Paleoanthropology, Morphology and Paleoecology.* 204-223. The Hague: Mouton Publishers.

White, Tim D., Donald C. Johanson, and William H. Kimbel. 1981. "*Australopithecus africanus*: its phyletic position reconsidered." *South African Journal of Science* 77:445-470.

Australopithecus anamensis, KNM-KP 29281

Coffing, Katherine, Craig Feibel, Meave Leakey, and Alan Walker. 1994. "Four-million-year-old hominids from east Lake Turkana, Kenya." *Am. J. Phys. Anthropol.* 93:55-65.

Leakey, Meave. 1995. "The farthest horizon." *National Geographic Magazine* 188:38-51.

Australopithecus afarensis, A.L. 288-1, Lucy

Johanson, Donald C., and Maitland A. Edey. 1981. *Lucy: The Beginnings of Humankind.* New York: Simon and Schuster.

Johanson, Donald C., C. Owen Lovejoy, William H. Kimbel, Tim D. White, Steven C. Ward, Michael E. Bush, Bruce M. Latimer, and Yves Coppens. 1982. "Morphology of the Pliocene partial hominid skeleton (A.L. 288-1) from the Hadar Formation, Ethiopia." *Am J. Phys. Anthropol.* 57: 403-451.

Australopithecus afarensis, A.L. 333, The First Family

Johanson, Donald C. 1976. "Ethiopia yields first "family" of early man." *National Geographic Magazine* 150:791-811.

Kimbel, William H., Donald C. Johanson, and Yves Coppens. 1982. "Pliocene hominid cranial remains from the Hadar Formation, Ethiopia." *Am. J. Phys. Anthropol.* 57:453-499.

White, Tim D., and Donald C. Johanson. 1989. "The hominid composition of Afar locality 333: some preliminary observations. In Giacomo Giacobini, editor. *Hominidae.* 97-101. Milan: Jaca Book.

Australopithecus afarensis, AL 444-2

Johanson, Donald C. 1996. "Face-to-face with Lucy's family." *National Geographic Magazine*, 189:96-117.

Kimbel, William H., Tim D. White, and Donald C. Johanson. 1984. "Cranial morphology of *Australopithecus afarensis*: a comparative study based on composite reconstruction of the adult skull." *Am. J. Phys. Anthropol.* 64:337-388.

Australopithecus afarensis, A.L. 129-1a+1b

Johanson, Donald C., C. Owen Lovejoy, and Kingsbury G. Heiple. 1976. "Functional implications of the Afar knee joint. *Am. J. Phys. Anthropol.* 45:188.

Tardieu, Christine. 1991. "Étude comparative des déplacements du centre de gravité du corps pendant la marche par une nouvelle méthode d'analyse tridemensionnelle. Mise à l'épreuve d'une hypothèse évolutive. In Yves Coppens, and Brigitte Senut, editors. 49-58 *Origine(s) de la Bipédie chez les Hominidés.* Paris: Cahiers de paléoanthropologie.

Australopithecus afarensis, LH 4, Fossil Hominid Footprints

Feibel, Craig S., Neville Agnew, Bruce Latimer, Martha Demas, Fiona Marshall, Simon A.C. Waane, and Peter Schmid. 1995. "The Laetoli hominid footprints—a preliminary report on the conservation and scientific restudy." *Evolutionary Anthropology* 4:149-154.

Hay, Richard L., and Mary D. Leakey. 1982. "The fossil footprints of Laetoli." *Scientific American* 246(2):50-57.

Johanson, Donald C., Tim D. White, and Yves Coppens. 1978. "A new species of the genus *Australopithecus* (Primates: Hominidae) from the Pliocene of Eastern Africa " *Kirtlandia* No. 28:1-14.

*Leakey, Mary D., and John M. Harris, editors. 1987. *Laetoli: A Pliocene Site in Northern Tanzania.* Oxford: Clarendon Press.

White, Tim D. 1977. "New fossil hominids from Laetoli, Tanzania." *Am. J. Phys. Anthropol.* 46:197-230.

Australopithecus africanus, Sts 5, Mrs. Ples

Rak, Yoel. 1983. *The Australopithecine Face.* New York: Academic Press.

Australopithecus africanus, STS 14

Abitbol, M. Maurice. 1995. "Reconstruction of the STS 14 (*Australopithecus africanus*) pelvis." *Am. J. Phys. Anthropol.* 96:143-158.

Robinson, John T. 1972. *Early Hominid Posture and Locomotion.* Chicago: University of Chicago Press.

Australopithecus africanus, Sts 71 and Sts 36

Rak, Yoel. 1983. *The Australopithecine Face.* New York: Academic Press.

Australopithecus africanus, Taung Child

Berger, Lee R., and Ronald J. Clarke. 1995. "Eagle involvement in accumulation of the Taung child fauna." *Journal of Human Evolution* 29:275-299

Broom, Robert 1925. "Some notes on the Taungs skull." *Nature* 115:569-571.

Dart, Raymond A. 1967. *Adventures with the Missing Link.* Philadelphia: The Institutes Press.

Tobias, Phillip V. 1992. "New researches at Sterkfontein and Taung with a note on Piltdown and its relevance to the history of paleo-anthropology." *Trans. Roy. soc. S. Afr.* 48:1-14.

Australopithecus africanus, TM 1517

Rak, Yoel. 1983. *The Australopithecine Face.* New York: Academic Press.

Robinson, John T. 1956. *The Dentition of the Australopithecinae.* Transvaal Mus. Memoir No.9:1-179.

Australopithecus africanus, Stw 252

Clarke, Ron J. 1996 (in press). "The genus *Paranthropus*: What's in a name?" In Meikle, W. Eric, F. Clark Howell, and Nina G. Jablonski editors. *Contemporary Issues in Human Evolution.* San Francisco: California Academy of Sciences.

Australopithecus robustus, SK6, SK 48, and SK 79

Rak, Yoel. 1983. *The Australopithecine Face.* New York: Academic Press.

Robinson, John T. 1956. *The Dentition of the Australopithecinae.* Transvaal Mus. Memoir No.9:1-179.

Australopithecus aethiopicus, KNM-WT 17000, Black Skull

Arambourg, Camille, and Yves Coppens. 1968. "Sur la découverte dans le Pléistocène inférieur de la vallé de l'Omo (Éthiopie) d'une mandibule d'Australopithécien. *Comptes Rendus des séances de l'Academie des Sciences.* (Paris) 265:589-590.

Arambourg, Camille, and Yves Coppens. 1968. "Découverte d'un Australopithécien nouveau dans les gisements de l'Omo (Ethiopia)." *South African Journal of Science* 64:58-59.

Kimbel, William H., Tim D. White, and Donald C. Johanson. 1988. "Implications of KNM-WT 17000 for the evolution of "Robust" *Australopithecus*." In Fred E. Grine, editor. *Evolutionary History of the "Robust" Australopithecines.* 259-268. New York: Aldine de Gruyter.

Leakey, Richard E. F., and Roger Lewin. 1992. *Origins Reconsidered.* New York: Doubleday.

Australopithecus boisei OH 5, Nutcracker Man

*Tobias, Phillip V. 1968. *The Cranium and Maxillary Dentition of Australopithecus (Zinjanthropus) boisei. Olduvai Gorge.* Vol. 2. Cambridge, Cambridge Univ. Press.

Australopithecus boisei, KNM-ER 406, and KNM-ER 732

Walker, Alan C., and Richard E.F. Leakey. 1978. "The hominids of East Turkana." *Scientific American* 239(2):54-66.

Homo

Kramer, Andrew, Steven M. Donnelly, James H. Kidder, Stephen D. Ousley, and Stephen M. Olah. 1995. "Craniometric variation in large-bodied hominoids: testing the single-species hypothesis for *Homo habilis*." *Journal of Human Evolution* 29:443-462.

Miller, Joseph A. 1991. "Does brain size variability provide evidence for multiple species in *Homo habilis*?" *Am. J. Phys. Anthropol.* 84:385-398.

Stringer, Chris B. 1986. "The credibility of *Homo habilis*." In Bernard A. Wood, Lawrence Martin and Peter Andrews editors. *Major Topic in Primate and Human Evolution.* 266-294, Cambridge: Cambridge University Press.

*Tobias, Phillip V. 1991. *Olduvai Gorge: Vol 4. The skulls, endocasts and teeth of* Homo habilis. Cambridge: Cambridge University Press.

*Wood, Bernard A. 1991. *Koobi Fora Research Project. Vol. 4: Hominid Cranial Remains.* Oxford: Clarendon Press.

——. 1992. "Origin and evolution of the genus *Homo*." *Nature* 355:783-790.

——. 1993. "Early *Homo*. How many species?" In William H. Kimbel and Lawrence B. Martin, editors. *Species, Species Concepts, and Primate Evolution.* 485-522. New York: Plenum Press.

Homo habilis, OH 7 and OH 24

Leakey, Louis S.B., P.V. Tobias and J.R. Napier. 1964. "A New Species of Genus *Homo* from Olduvai Gorge." *Nature* 202(4927):7-9.

Leakey, Mary D., Ronald J. Clarke and Louis S.B. Leakey. 1971. "New Hominid Skull from Bed I, Olduvai Gorge, Tanzania." *Nature* 232:308-312.

Rightmire, G. Philip. 1993. "Variation Among Early Homo Crania From Olduvai Gorge and the Koobi Fora Region." *American Journal of Physical Anthropology* 90(1):1-33.

Tobias, Phillip V. 1991. *Olduvai Gorge: The Skulls, Endocasts and Teeth of* Homo habilis (volume 4). Cambridge: Cambridge University Press.

Homo habilis, KNM-ER 1813

Leakey, R.E.F. 1974. "Further evidence of Lower Pleistocene hominids from East Rudolf, North Kenya, 1973." *Nature* 248: 653-656.

Leakey, Richard and Roger Lewin. 1992. *Origins Reconsidered: In Search of What Makes Us Human.* New York: Doubleday.

Wood, Bernard A. 1991. *Koobi Fora Research Project Volume 4: Hominid Cranial Remains.* Oxford: Oxford University Press.

Homo habilis, OH 62

Hartwig-Scherer, S. 1993. "Body weight prediction in early fossil hominids: Towards a taxon-"independent" approach." *Am. J. of Physical Anthropol.* 92:17-36.

Johanson, Donald C., and James Shreeve. 1989. *Lucy's Child: The Discovery of a Human Ancestor.* New York: William Morrow.

Homo rudolfensis, KNM-ER 1470

Leakey, Richard E.F. 1973. "Evidence for an Advanced Plio-Pleistocene Hominid from East Rudolf, Kenya." *Nature* 242: 447-450.

Wood, Bernard A. 1991. *Koobi Fora Research Project* (Volume 4). Hominid Cranial Remains. Oxford: Oxford University Press.

Homo ergaster, KNM-ER 3733

Leakey, Richard E.F. 1976. "New hominid fossils from the Koobi Fora formation in Northern Kenya." *Nature* 261:574-576.

Homo ergaster, KNM-WT 15000

Brown, Frank, John Harris, Richard Leakey and Alan Walker. 1985. "Early *Homo erectus* skeleton from west Lake Turkana, Kenya." *Nature* 316: 788-792.

Walker, Alan, and Richard Leakey, editors. 1993. *The Nariokotome* Homo erectus *Skeleton.* Cambridge: Harvard University Press.

Homo ergaster, SK 847

Clarke, Ronald J., and F. Clark Howell. 1972. "Affinities of the Swartkrans 847 Hominid Cranium." *Am J. Phys. Anthropol.* 37(3): 319-335.

Clarke, R.J., F. Clark Howell, and C.K. Brain. 1970. "More Evidence of an Advanced Hominid at Swartkrans." *Nature* 225: 1219-1222.

Homo erectus, Trinil 2, Java Man

Dubois, Eugène 1926. "On the principal characters of the cranium and the brain, the mandible and the teeth of *Pithecanthropus erectus*." *Proc. Acad. Sci. Amst.* 27:265-278.

Homo erectus, Peking Man

Rukang, Wu,and Lin Shenglong. 1983. "Peking Man." *Scientific American* 248(6):86-94.

Tattersall, Ian and Gary J. Sawyer. 1996. "The Skull of Sinanthropus from Zhoukoudian, China: A New Reconstruction." *Journal of Human Evolution* (in press).

Weidenreich, Franz. 1943. "The Skull of *Sinanthropus pekinensis*: a comparative study on a primitive hominid skull." *Palaeontologia Sinica*, New Series D, 10:1-485.

Homo erectus, Sangiran 17

Jacob, Teuku. 1975. "Morphology and paleoecology of early man in Java." In Russell H. Tuttle, editor. *Paleoanthropology, Morphology and Paleoecology*. 311-326. The Hague: Mouton Publishers.

Sartono, S. 1975. "Implications arising from *Pithecanthropus* VIII." In Russell H. Tuttle, editor. *Paleoanthropology, Morphology and Paleoecology*. 327-360. The Hague: Mouton Publishers.

Sartono, S. 1972. "Discovery of Another Hominid Skull at Sangiran, Central Java." *Current Anthropology* 13(1):124-125.

Homo heidelbergensis, Bodo

Clark, J.D., J. de Heinzelin, K.D. Schick, W.K. Hart, T.D. White, G. Woldegabriel, R.C. Walter, G. Suwa, B. Asfaw, E. Vrba ,and Y. H-Selassie. 1994. "African *Homo erectus* : Old Radiometric Ages and Young Oldowan Assemblages in the Middle Awash Valley, Ethiopia." *Science* 264:1907-1909.

Conroy, Glenn C., C.J. Jolly, D. Cramer, and J.E. Kalb. 1978. "Newly discovered fossil hominid skull from the Afar depression, Ethiopia." *Nature* 276:67-70.

Homo heidelbergensis, Mauer 1

Kraatz, Reinhart. 1985 In Eric Delson, editor. *Ancestors: The Hard Evidence*. New York: Alan R. Liss.

Schoetensack, Otto. 1908. *Der Unterkiefer des* Homo heidelbergensis *aus den Sanden von Mauer bei Heidelberg*. Leipzig: Wilhelm Engelmann.

Homo heidelbergensis, Arago XXI

Lumley, Henry de, editor. 1979. *L'Homme de Tautavel*. Dossiers de l'Archéologie 36.

Homo heidelbergensis, Petralona 1

Kokkoros, P., and A. Kanellis. 1960. "Découverte d'un crane d'homme paléolithique dans la peninsule Chalcidique." *Anthropologie* 64: 132-147.

Poulianos, A.N. 1971. "Petralona: A Middle Pleistocene cave in Greece." *Archaeology* 24:6-11.

Stringer, Christopher B. 1974. "A Multivariate Study of the Petralona Skull." *Journal of Human Evolution* 3:397-404.

Homo heidelbergensis, Steinheim

Adam, Karl Dietrich. 1985. "The chronological and systematic poition of the Steinheim skull." In Eric Delson, editor. *Ancestors: The Hard Evidence*. 272-276. New York: Alan R. Liss.

Homo heidelbergensis, Atapuerca 5

Arsuaga, Juan-Luis, I. Martínez, A. Gracia, J.-M. Carretero and E. Carbonell. 1993. "Three new human skulls from the Sima de los Huesos Middle Pleistocene site in Sierra de Atapuerca, Spain." *Nature* 362: 534-537.

Stringer, Christopher B 1993. "Secrets of the Pit of the Bones." *Nature* 362:501-502.

Homo heidelbergensis, Broken Hill 1

Keith, Arthur. 1926. *The Antiquity of Man*. London: Williams and Norgate (second edition).

Klein, Richard G. 1973. "Geological Antiquity of Rhodesian Man." *Nature* 244:311-312.

Woodward, Arthur S. 1921. "A New Cave Man from Rhodesia, South Africa." *Nature* 108(2716):371-372.

Homo neanderthalensis, Krapina C

Smith, Fred H. 1976. *The Neandertal remains from Krapina: A descriptive and comparative study*. Univ. Tenn. Dep. Anthrop. Rep. Invest. 15:1-359.

Homo neanderthalensis, Saccopastore 1

Manzi, Giorgio, and Pietro Passarello. 1991. "Anténéandertaliens et Néandertaliens du Latium (Italie Centrale)" *L'Anthropologie* 95(2/3):501-522.

Homo neanderthalensis, Teshik-Tash

Movius, Hallam L. Jr. 1953. "The Mousterian Cave of Teshik-Tash, Southeastern Uzbekistan, Central Asia." *American School of Preshistoric Research Bulletin* 17: 11-71.

Homo neanderthalensis, Kebara 2

Bar-Yosef, Ofer, B. Vandermeersch, B. Arensburg, A. Belfer-Cohen, P. Goldberg, H. Laville, L. Meignen, Y. Rak, J.D. Speth, E. Tchernov, A-M. Tillier, and S. Weiner. 1992. "The Excavations in Kebara Cave, Mt. Carmel." *Current Anthropology* 33(5): 497-550.

Homo neanderthalensis, Amud 1

Suzuki, Hisashi, and F. Takai, editors. 1970. *The Amud Man and His Cave Site*. Tokyo: The University of Tokyo.

Homo neanderthalensis, Amud 7

Rak, Yoel, William H. Kimbel, and Erella Hovers. 1994. "A Neandertal infant from Amud Cave, Israel." *Journal of Human Evolution* 26: 313-324.

Homo neanderthalensis, La Chapelle-aux-Saints

Boule, Marcellin. 1911-1913. "L'homme fossile de La Chapelle-aux-Saints." *Annales de Paléontologie* 6-8.

Straus, William L., Jr. and A.J.E. Cave. 1957. "Pathology and the Posture of Neanderthal Man." *Quarterly Review of Biology* 32(4):348-363.

Homo neanderthalensis, Ferrassie 1

Heim, Jean-Louis. 1976. "Les hommes fossiles de la Ferrassie I." *Archives de l'Institut de Paléontologie Humaine* 35:1-331.

Puech, Pierre-François. 1981. "Tooth Wear in La Ferassie Man." *Current Anthropology*: 22(4):424-430.

Homo neanderthalensis, Neandertal 1

King, William. 1864. "The Reputed Fossil Man of the Neanderthal." *Quarterly Journal of Science* 1:88-97.

Schaafhausen, Hermann. 1858. "Zur Kenntnis der ältesten Rassenschädel." *Archiv. Anat. Phys. wiss. Medicin* 453-478.

Homo neanderthalensis, Gibraltar 1

Keith, Arthur 1911. "The early history of the Gibraltar cranium." *Nature* 87: 313-314.

Homo neanderthalensis, St.-Césaire

ApSimon, A.M. 1980. "The last neanderthal in France?" *Nature* 287:271-272.

Mardis, Scott E. 1995. "The Last Neanderthals." *Archaeology* 48(6):12-13.

Mercier, N., H. Valladas, J-L. Joron, J-L. Reyss, F. Leveque, and B. Vandermeersch. 1991. "Thermoluminescence dating of the late Neanderthal remains from Saint-Césaire." *Nature* 351:737-739.

Stringer, Christopher B. and Rainer Grün. 1991. "Time for the last Neanderthals." *Nature* 351:701-702.

Homo sapiens, Dali

Stringer, Christopher B. 1992. "Reconstructing recent human evolution." *Phil. Trans. R. Soc. Lond.* B 337:217-224.

Wu, Xinchi and Frank E. Poirier. 1995. *Human Evolution in China: A Metric Description of the Fossils and a Review of the Sites*. New York: Oxford University Press.

Homo sapiens, Omo I and Omo II

Leakey, Richard E.F., Karl W. Butzer, and Michael H. Day. 1969. "Early *Homo sapiens* Remains from the Omo River Region of South-west Ethiopia." *Nature* 222:1132-1138.

Homo sapiens, Qafzeh IX

Vandermeersch, Bernard. 1981. *Les Hommes Fossiles de Qafzeh*. Paris: Editions du Centre National de la Recherche Scientifique.

Homo sapiens, Skhul V

McCown, Theodore D., and Sir Arthur Keith. 1939. *The Stone Age of Mount Carmel (volume II)*. Oxford: The Clarendon Press.

Homo sapiens, Cro-Magnon 1

Lartet, Eduard, and Henri Christy. 1868. In T.R. Jones, editor. *Reliquiae aquitanicae*. London: Williams and Norgate.

Stringer, C.B., J.-J. Hublin and B. Vandermeersch. 1984. In F.H. Smith and F. Spencer, editors. *The Origin of Modern Humans: A World Survey of the Fossil Evidence*. New York: Alan R. Liss, 1984.

Homo sapiens, Kow Swamp 1

Kennedy, Gail E. 1984. "Are the Kow Swamp Hominids 'Archaic'?" *Am. J. Phys. Anthropol.* 65:163-168.

Thorne, Alan G. and P.G. Macumber. 1972. "Discoveries of Late Pleistocene Man at Kow Swamp, Australia." *Nature* 238 316-319.

Paleolithic Technology

Asfaw, Berhane, Y. Beyene, G. Suwa, R.C. Walter, T.D. White, G. WoldeGabriel and T. Yemane. 1992. "The earliest Acheulean from Konso-Gardula." *Nature* 360:732-734.

Gutin, JoAnn. 1995. "Do Kenya Tools Root Birth of Modern Thought in Africa?" *Science* 270:1118-1119.

Hublin, Jean-Jacques, F. Spoor, M. Braun, F. Zonneveld, and S. Condemi. 1996. "A late Neanderthal associated with Upper Palaeolithic artefacts." *Nature* 381:224-226.

*Schick, Kathy D., and Nicholas Toth. 1993. *Making Silent Stones Speak: Human Evolution and the Dawn of Technology*. New York: Simon and Schuster.

Wymer, John. 1982. *The Paleolithic Age*. London: Croom Helm.

* *General References*

Aiello, Leslie, and M. Christopher Dean. 1990. *An Introduction to Human Evolutionary Anatomy*. London: Academic Press.

Ciochon, Russell, and John G. Fleagle, editors. 1987. *Primate Evolution and Human Origins*. New York: Aldine de Gruyter.

Ciochon, Russell, and John G. Fleagle, editors. 1993. *The Human Evolution Source Book*. Englewood Cliffs: Prentice Hall.

Day, Michael H. 1986. *Guide to Fossil Man*. New York: Cassell (fourth edition).

Delson, Eric, editor. 1985. *Ancestors: The Hard Evidence*. New York: Alan R. Liss.

Johanson, Donald and Maitland Edey. 1981. *Lucy: The Beginnings of Humankind*. New York: Simon and Schuster.

Johanson, Donald, Lenora Johanson and Blake Edgar. 1994. *Ancestors: In Search of Human Origins*. New York: Villard Books.

Jones, Steve, Robert Martin and David Pilbeam, editors. 1992. *The Cambridge Encyclopedia of Human Evolution*. New York: Cambridge University Press.

Klein, Richard G. 1989. *The Human Career: Human Biological and Cultural Origins*. Chicago: The University of Chicago Press.

Martin, Robert D. 1990. *Primate Origins and Evolution*. Princeton: Princeton University Press.

Mayr, Ernst. 1982. *The Growth of Biological Thought: Diversity, Evolution, and Inheritance*. Cambridge: Harvard University Press.

Meikle, W. Eric, F. Clark Howell, and Nina G. Jablonski, editors. 1996. *Contemporary Issues in Human Evolution*. San Francisco: California Academy of Sciences.

Milner, Richard. 1993. *The Encyclopedia of Evolution: Humanity's Search for Its Origins*. New York: Henry Holt (revised edition).

Reader, John. 1981. *Missing Links: The Hunt for Earliest Man*. London: Collins.

Rightmire, G. Philip. 1990. *The Evolution of Homo erectus: Comparative anatomical studies of an extinct human species*. Cambridge: Cambridge University Press.

Sherratt, Andrew, ed. 1980. *The Cambridge Encyclopedia of Archaeology*. New York: Crown Publishers.

Shreeve, James. 1995. *The Neandertal Enigma: Solving the Mystery of Modern Human Origins*. New York: William Morrow.

Stringer, Christopher and Clive Gamble. 1993. *In Search of the Neanderthals*. London: Thames and Hudson.

Stringer, Christopher, and Robin McKie. 1996. *African Exodus: The Origins of Modern Humanity*. London: Cape.

Tattersall, Ian. 1995. *The Last Neandertal: The Rise, Success, and Mysterious Extinction of Our Closest Human Relatives*. New York: Macmillan.

——. 1995. *The Fossil Trail: How We Know What We Think We Know about Human Evolution*. New York: Oxford University Press.

Tattersall, Ian, Eric Delson, and John Van Couvering, editors. 1988. *Encyclopedia of Human Evolution and Prehistory*. New York: Garland Publishing.

Tobias, Phillip V. ed. 1985. *Hominid Evolution: Past, Present and Future*. New York: Alan R. Liss.

Trinkaus, Erik and Pat Shipman. 1992. *The Neandertals: Changing the Image of Mankind*. New York: Alfred A. Knopf.

Wood, Bernard, Lawrence Martin, and Peter Andrews, editors. 1986. *Major Topics in Primate and Human Evolution*. Cambridge: Cambridge University Press.

INDEX

Abel, Othenio 142
Abell, Paul 132
Abri Faustin 258
Abri Pataud 97
Acheulean
  absence in East Africa 187, 254
  cleaver 254, *255*
  hand ax *253*, 254, *255*
Acheulean artifacts, oldest known 28
Acheulean industry 25, 46, 90, 97, 106, 187, 191, 196, 250, 254, 256
Afar depression 25
Ahlquist, Jon 31
A.L. 129-1a+1b 130, *130*
A.L. 200-1 *169*
A.L. 288-1 23, 124, *125*. *See also* Lucy
  pelvis 87, *87*
A.L. 333 23, 126
A.L. 333-105 126, *127*
A.L. 417-1 128
A.L. 444-2 28, *129*
  reconstruction of *82*, 83
A.L. 666 90
  artifact *90*
A.L. 666-1 164, 168, *169*
Alexeev, Valerii 162, 177
Allahendu, Maumin 168
Allia Bay 23, 119, 122
Altamira 102, 258
Altamura skeleton *24*, 25
Amud cave 100, 218, 220, 222, 239
Amud 1 *10*, *166*, 220, *221*, 222
Amud 6 222
Amud 7 222, *223*
Andrews, Peter 33
Ape behavior, implications for last common ancestor 83, 86
Ape DNA 18
Arago 46, 164, 198, 254
Arago XXI 198, *199*, 200, 202
Arambourg, Camille 152
Aramis 23, 40
ARA-VP-1/129 116, *116*
ARA-VP-1/500 116
ARA-VP-6/1 116
Ardipithecus 39
Ardipithecus ramidus 23, 32, 38, 40, 40, 53, 92, 116, *116*, 119
Arene Candide 100
Arrows 258
Art 102, 106. *See also* Rock painting
  emergence of 52
  in Africa 102, *104*
  in Australia 102
  in Europe 102
  in the Americas *48*, 49
Asfaw, Alemayehu 116
Asfaw, Berhane 121
Atapuerca 46, 106, 164, 200, 204
  discovery of 25
Atapuerca 4 204, *205*
Atapuerca 5 204, *206*, *207*
Aterian 256
Aterian point *256*
Aurignac 258
Aurignacian 99, 244, 258
Australia 49-52, 102, 247
Australopithecine
  body weight 40
  culture 21
Australopithecus 38, 168
  derivation of 117
  first 25
  species of 40, 117, 121
Australopithecus aethiopicus 23, 38, *118*, 119, 152, *153*, *154*, *155*, 156
Australopithecus afarensis 2, 23, 25, 32, 37, 38, 40, 52, 53, 57, 73, 76, 92, 119, 121, 122, *125*, 126, *127*, 128, *129*, *130*, *131*, 132, 147, 152, 162, 168, *169*
  duration of 111, 112
  evidence of bipedalism 86, 87, *87*
  reconstruction *82*, 83, 128
  teeth and jaws *29*
Australopithecus africanus *3*, 23, 38, 57, 73, 76, 78, *79*, 86, 91, 92, 93, 106, 117, *120*, 134, *135*, 136, *137*, 138, *139*, *140*, *141*, 142, *143*, 152, 158, 164, 170, 172, 174, 184
  endocasts *81*
  pelvis 136, *137*
Australopithecus anamensis 23, 32, 38, *40*, 52, 53, 92, 119, 122
Australopithecus bahrelghazali *119*, 121
Australopithecus boisei *5*, 23, *30*, 38, 52, 53, *54*, 57, *74*, *75*, 92, 119, *121*, 152, 156, *157*, 158, *159*, *160*, *161*, 162, 170, 172
  extinction of 111
Australopithecus praegens 40
Australopithecus robustus *4*, 23, 38, 52, 57, 91, 92, 96, *109*, 117, 119, 144, *145*, 148, *149*, *150*, *151*, 152, 158, 164, 184, 250
  extinction of 111
Australopithecus sp. 146, *146*, 147, *147*

Baboon 73
Barlow, G. W. 134, 144
Bâton de commandement 100, 102
Beads 99
Belohdelie 23, 128
Bihorel oest 254
Binford, Lewis 91
Biocultural feedback 21
Biological species concept 52
Biostratigraphy 22
Bipedalism 18, 32, 40
  compared to quadrupedalism 88
  evidence for 130, 132, *133*
  features associated with 86-88
  origins of 88
Bison figurine *103*
BKT-1 tuff *27*
Black skull. *See* KNM-WT 17000
Black, Davidson 188
Blanc, Alberto 212
Blanchard 106
Blumenschine, Rob 91
Bodo 164, 208
Bodo cranium 93, *94*, 194, *195*,
  cut marks on 93 *94*
Body adornments 99, 100
Body proportions
  of African apes 32
  of *Homo habilis* 176
  of *Homo ergaster* 182
Boise, Charles 156
Bone point *251*, 258, *259*
Bonobo 89
  social behavior 86
Border Cave 43
Border Cave 1 *44*
Boule, Marcellin 43, 202, 224, 226, 244
Boxgrove 46
Brace, C. Loring 158
Brain endocasts 81
Brain expansion, distinguishing *Homo* 37
Brain size
  ape and human 76
  cerebral Rubicon 162
  decline in modern humans 111
  in *Australopithecus* 117
  in *Homo* 117
  increase during Pleistocene 81, 83
  of hominids 80
  of modern humans 80
  of primates 80
Brain, C. K. 148, 156
Breuil, Abbé Henri 212
Briqueterie 254
Broca's area 80, 106
Broken Hill. *See* Kabwe
Broken Hill 1 208, *209*, *210*
Broom, Robert 117, 134, 136, 138, 144, 146, 148, 152, 184
Brunet, Michel 121
Buret 100
Burial 100-102
  artifacts associated with 99
  at Arene Candide 100, *101*
  at Dolni Vestonice 97, 100
  at Kow Swamp 247
  at La Ferrassie 226
  at Lake Mungo *51*, 102
  at Sunghir 100
  at Teshik-Tash 215
Buttons 99

Canine dimorphism 73
Cann, Rebecca 41
Cannibalism 93, 96
Cap Blanc 102
Cavalli-Sforza, Luigi Luca 41
Cave bear figurine *103*
Cave, A. J. E. 224
Caverna da Pedra Pintada 49
Cavities-in Broken Hill 1 208, *209*
Ceramics 97
Chad 39, 119, 121
Châtelperron 258
Châtelperronian 99, 258
Chauvet 25, 102, 258
Chesowanja 96
Chimpanzee 73
  cannibalism 93
  diversity in behavior 83
  genetic similarity to humans 111
  hunting and meat eating 92
  social behavior 86
  tool use 89, 90
Chimpanzee skull *34*, *35*
Christy, Henry 244
Circeo I 93
Cladistics 37
Cladogram *38*
Clark, J. Desmond 116
Clarke, Ron 121, 146, 172, 184
Climate, influence on human evolution 27-28
Clothing 99-100
Clovis point 47
Cognitive neuroscience 80
Colomb-Bechar 257
Combe-Grenal 97, 257
Competitive exclusion principle 53
Consciousness 107
Coon, Carleton 56, 208
Coppens, Yves 119, 152
Corbiac 258, 261
Cosquer 25, 102, *108*, 258
Creationism 31-32
Cretaceous-Tertiary extinction 111
Cro-Magnon 43, 49, 99, 244, 258
  discovery of 25

Cro-Magnon fossils 204, 208
Cro-Magnon I *167*, 200, 242, 244, *245*, *246*
Cueva Morin 97
Culture 43

Dali 234, *234*, *235*
Dart, Raymond 86, 93, 117, 134, 142, 162, 170
Darwin, Charles 33, 73, 117, 156, 187
 evolutionary theory 31
Dating 22, 26-27
 absolute dating 26
 accelerator mass spectrometry radiocarbon dating 26
 amino acid racemization 27
 biostratigraphy 26
 electron spin resonance 27, 97, 200, 220, 239
 First Family fossils 27
 fission-track 27
 KBS Tuff 26
 optically stimulated luminescence 27, 49
 paleomagnetism 27, 46, 47
 potassium-argon 27
 radiocarbon 26, 49, 220
 relative dating 26
 sample from Hadar *27*
 single-crystal laser-fusion argon-argon 27, 46, 126, 152, 168
 Sterkfontein 26
 superposition 26
 Swartkrans 26
 techniques 43
 thermoluminescence 27, 49, 218, 239
 uranium series 27, 200, 234, 236
De Bruyn, M. 142
Dean, Christopher 78
Dennett, Daniel 107
Descent with modification 52
Devonian 111
Diamond, Jared 18
Digging sticks 250, *251*
Dmanisi 46, 196
DNA 21, 30-31, 56
 Ape 18
 DNA-DNA hybridization 31
 Gorilla 32
 mitochondrial 32, 41
DNA, nuclear 41, 49
 Chimpanzee and Bonobo 32
Dolni Vestonice 97
Dove, George 131
Dubois, Eugène 37, 162, 187, 191

Edelman, Gerald 107
Ehringsdorf 212
Electrophoresis 33
Endogamy 86
Engis 93, 222
Eve hypothesis 41
Evolution 37
 biological 21
 common ancestor 32
 cultural 21, 111
 divergence of humans and African apes 31
 divergence of Old World monkeys and hominoids 31
 human 30-31
 influence of climate on 27-28
 molecular 30
 relationship between human and ape 32
Excavation of early human remains 25-26
Exogamy 86
Extinction 53, 107, 111
 evidence in fossil record 28

Fejej 23, 40
Fire 96-97
FLK I 91
Folsom point 47
Fontbrégoua 93, 96
Fontéchevade 212
Foramen magnum 86, 142, 222
Fort Ternan 33
Fossil Record, Hominid 22-25
Fossil sites, early human 25
Fourneau du Diable 261
Frankfurt Horizontal 83

Gadeb 254
Galley Hill 43
Gene-culture coevolution 21
Genetic drift 53
Geochronologist 22, 27
Gesher Benot Ya'aqov 46
Gestation 76
Ghiglieri, Michael, 86
Gibraltar 220
Gigantopithecus 30
Gona 90, 250
Gona artifacts *90*
Gongwangling 46
Goodman, Morris 31
Gorilla 32
 social behavior 86
Gorilla gorilla beringei *84*, *85*
Gorilla, mountain *84*, *85*
Gorjanovic-Kramberger, Karl 93, 211
Gran Dolina 23, 46, 196
Gran Dolina fossil *46*
 cut marks on 93
Gravettian 258
Great Rift Valley 21, *23*, 25, 38
Grimaldi 43
Grine, Fred 148
Grotta Guattari 93
Grotte du Renne. *See* Arcy-sur-Cure
Groves, Colin 162
Gurche, John 83, 128

Hadar *22*, 23, 25, 28, 86, 119, 126, 128, 130, 164, 168, 250
Haeckel, Ernst 37, 187
Hammerstone *90*, 250
Havel, Vaclav 111
Hay, Richard 132
Hearths 96-97
Heidelberg 25
Heidelberg Man 196
Heim, Jean-Louis 226
Henneberg, Maciej 56
Home base hypothesis 91
Hominid
 body weight 57, 73
 diet 91-92
 evidence of cannibalism 93
 social behavior 89
 stature 57
 subsistence behavior 90-91
 tooth enamel 92
Hominid species, coexistence 53, 56
Hominidae 18, 33, 40, 116, 117, 144, 164
Homo 57, 106, 111, 162, 164, 168
 cranial capacity 40
 earliest fossil 28
 oldest dated fossil 164, 168, *169*
 sexual variation in 172
 species of 40
 tool use by 250
 use of fire 96-97
Homo, early 55-56
 number of species 37
Homo erectus 7, 23, 28, 38, 41 46, 49, 91, 93, 96, 111, 162, 164, 170, 174, 180, 184, 187, *187*, 188, *189*, *190*, 191, *192*, *193*, 198, 200, 204, 208, 234, 247
Homo ergaster 23, 38, 46, 53, 55, *72*, 73, 78, 90, 99, 162, *163*, 164, 168, 180, *180*, *181*, 182, *183*, 184, *185*, *186*, 254
Homo habilis 6, 23, 38, 52, 73, 90, 91, 106, 162, 164, 168, 170, *171*, 172, 174, *175*, 176, *176*, 177, 250, 111
Homo heidelbergensis *8*, 23, 38, 41, 46, *46*, 47, 93, 164, 194, *195*, 195, *197*, 198, *199*, 200, *201*, 202, *202* 203, 204, *205*, *206*, *207*, 208, *209*, *210*, 212, 234, 235, 254
Homo neanderthalensis *9*, *10*, 23, *24*, 38, 56, *76-77*, 95, 107, *110*, 111, 164, *166*, 211, *211*, 212, *213*, *214*, 215, *216*, *217*, 218, *219*, 220, 221, 222, *223*, 256, 258
Homo rudolfensis 23, 38, 90, 111, 162, 164, 174, 168, 177, *178* 179, 250
Homo sapiens 18, *44*, *45*, *51*, 38, *42*, 56, *58-71*, 162, 164, *167*, 200, 202, 208, 212, 234, *234*, *235*, 236, *237*, *238*, 239, *240*, *241*, 242, *243*, 244, *245*, *246*, 247, *248*, *249*, 256, 258
 distinguishing features 41
 duration of 112
Homo sp. 168, *169*
Houppeville 257
Howell, F. Clark 239
Huia 73
Human
 ape comparisons 18
 DNA 18
 closest living relatives 32-33
 coexistence with neandertal 27
 skeleton *19*
 skull *20*
Human and ape-last common ancestor 18, 28, 30, 33, 37, 39, 41, 86
Human and African ape-genetic similarity 18, 31, 32-33, 40, 111
Humphrey, Nicholas 107
Hunting hypothesis 90
Huxley, Thomas Henry 32
Hybridization, between modern humans and Neandertals 56
Hyoid bone 218
 evidence for language 106, *107*

Ice Age 106
Iceman 100
Interspecific variation 52
Isaac, Glynn 90
Isimila 97, 254
Isturitz *11*, *103*

Java Man 37, 41, 187, 191
Jinniushan 234
Johanson, Donald *18*, 119, 132, 152

Kabwe 164, 191, 208
Kalb, Jon 116
Kanam 131
Kanapoi 23, 40, 52, 119, 122
Kanjera 131
Kanzi 89
Kapthurin 258
Kasparov, Garry 107
Katanda 258
Kattwinkel, Wilhelm 25
Kebara 97, 100, 239, 256
Kebara 1 218
Kebara 2 78, 204, 218, *219*
 hyoid 106, *107*
 pelvis *76-77*
Keith, Sir Arthur 43, 131, 142, 177, 196, 202, 208, 242
Kiik-Koba 100
Kimbel, William 138, 152
Kimeu, Kamoya 122

Klasies River Mouth 43, 93
Klasies River Mouth fossils *42*
KNM-ER 406 23, 53, *54*, 56, 158, *159*, *160*
KNM-ER 732 *75*, 156, 158, *161*, 184
KNM-ER 820 80
KNM-ER 992 23, 162, *163*, 180
KNM-ER 1470 23, 26, 162, 164, 170, 174, 177, *178*, *179*
KNM-ER 1471 162, 176
KNM-ER 1482 23, 162, 176
KNM-ER 1590 80, 177
KNM-ER 1802 23, 177
KNM-ER 1813 *6*, 23, 162, 174, *175*, 177
KNM-ER 3732 177
KNM-ER 3733 53, *55*, 56, 162, 180,*180*, *181*, 182, 184
KNM-ER 377 23
KNM-ER 3883 23, 162
KNM-KP 271 122
KNM-KP 29281 122, *123*
KNM-KP 29283 *123*
KNM-KP 29285 *40*, 122
KNM-WT 15000 23, *72*, 73, 78, 162, 180, 182, *183*
  age estimate 80
KNM-WT 17000 28, *118*, 147, 152, *153*, *154*
Kohl-Larsen, Ludwig 131
Konso-Gardula 28, 191, 254
Koobi Fora 23, 26, 53, 90, 96, 156, 158, 162, 174, 177, 180, 198, 80
Kow Swamp 191, 247
Kow Swamp 1 247, *248*
Kow Swamp 5 247, *249*
Krapina 93, 100, 211, 212
Krapina C *95*, 211, *211*
Krapina Neandertal fossil *23*
Kromdraai 117, 119, 144
Ksar Akil 43
KT12/H1 *119*
Kubrick, Stanley 107

La Chapelle-aux-Saints 43, 100, 208, 212, 220, 224, *225*, 226, 244
La Ferrassie 100, 211, 212, 220
La Ferrassie 1 *9*, 226, *227*
La Madeleine *103*, 258
La Quina 100, 222
La Vache 106
Laetoli 23, 119, 124, 131-132
Laetoli footprints 87, 132, *133*
Lake Mungo 102
Lake Turkana 23, 40
Language 106-7
Lartet, Louis 244
Lascaux 102,*105*, 258
Late Stone Age 100
Lazaret 97
Le Gros Clark, Sir Wilfred 131, 144
Le Morin 261
Le Moustier 100, 256
Le Tillet 257
Leakey, Louis 33, 43, 89, 93, 131, 144, 162, 170, 176, 177
Leakey, Mary 119, 131, 156, 170, 176, 250
Leakey, Meave 40, 119, 122, 177
Leakey, Richard 122, 158, 162, 174, 177, 182
Les Trois Frères 102
Levallois core and point *257*
Levallois technique 218, 256
Lewin, Roger 177
Lewis, G. Edward 33
LH 4 131, *131*
Linnaeus, Carolus 18, 40, 52
Locomotion, of last common ancestor 37
Lorblanchet, Michel 102
Lothagam 23, 38
Lothagam mandible *39*
Lovejoy, C. Owen 89
Lucy 21, 23, 25, 37, 76, 111, 119, 124, *125*, 130
  body weight 57
  pelvis 87, *87*
  teeth 30
Lumsden, Charles 21

Magdalenian 99, 258
Maka femur *2*
Makapansgat 23, 93, 117, 119
Malakunanja II 51
Mammoth bone structures 97, 99
Mann, Alan 78
Mass extinction 107, 111
Matternes, Jay 83
Maturation
  ape 78
  australopithecine pattern 30
  hominid 78
  human 78
  Neandertal 80
Mauer 1 25, 46, 164, 196, *197*, 200
Mauer mandible. *See* Mauer 1
Mayr, Ernst 187
Mazák, Vratislav 162
McCown, Theodore 242
Meadowcroft Rockshelter 47
Meadowcroft Rockshelter artifact *49*
Menez-Dregan 97
Mezhirich 99
Mezin 99
Microliths 258
Middle Awash 23, 40, 116
Middle Paleolithic 97, 100, 220, 222
Middle Pleistocene 23, 198, 202, 204, 234
Middle Stone Age 43
Migration 41, 49
Miocene 33, 37, 122
Missing link 33
Modern Evolutionary Synthesis 52
Modern human
  aesthetic sense 99
  closest living relative 31
  earliest Americans 47, 49
  earliest fossil evidence 43
  evidence of cannibalism 93
  genetic diversity 43
  genetic variation 56
  homogenization of 38
  image in art 102
  population size 52
Modern human origin, timing of 41
Modjokerto 23, 46, 187
Molecular clock 33, 41
Molodova 97
Montagu, Ashley 31
Montastruc 99
Monte Alegre artifact *49*
Monte Verde 47
Monte Verde artifacts *47*
Mousterian industry 43, 212, 242, 256, 258
Mousterian point *257*
Mousterian scraper *256*
Mrs. Ples. *See* Sts 5
Mukiri, Heslon 170
Multiregional model of human origins 188, 191, 234, 247
Mungo III *51*
Mutation 41, 53

Napier, John 162, 170
Nariokotome 80, 99, 182
Natural selection 53, 83, 86, 89, 106, 107
Nauwalabila I 52
Ndutu 164
Neander Valley 187
Neandertal 32, 196, 200, 202, 239
  as separate species 224, 226
  birth canal 78
  brain size 83
  burials 100
  capacity for language 106, 212, 218, 224
  "classic anatomy" 211, 212, 220, 226, 242
  coexistence with modern humans 37
  evidence of cannibalism 93
  first 25
  hybridization with modern humans 242
  largest fossil sample 211
  most complete specimen 218, *219*
  pelvis 76
  tooth wear 226
  use of fire 97
  wear on teeth 99
Needles, bone 99, *99*
Neolithic 93
Neural Darwinism 107
Ngandong 23, 191
Ngeneo, Bernard 180
Nzube, Peter 122

Oakley, Kenneth 131
OH 1 131
OH 3 156
OH 4 170
OH 5 5, 23, *30*, *74*, 156, *157*, 170, 172
OH 7 162, 170, *171*, 172
OH 9 182, 188
OH 13 172, 174
OH 13-16 170
OH 24 172, *173*, 174
OH 38 156
OH 62 73, 162, 176, *176*
Oldowan
  chopper 250, *251*, *252*
  Developed Oldowan 191, 250
  scraper *252*
  spheroid *252*
Oldowan industry 89, 90, 106, 168, 250, 254
Olduvai Gorge *23*, 23, 25, 27, 46, 52, 53, 89, 91, 96, 119, 131, 156, 162, 168, 170, 172, 176, 177, 198, 250, 251, 252, 253, 254
Olorgesailie 97, 254
Omo 23, 90, 156, 234, 250
Omo I 43, *45*, 236, *237*
Omo II 43, 236, *238*
Omo 18 23, 152, *155*
Omo L. 7a-125 *121*
Omo-Kibish 43
Ordovician 111
Osteodontokeratic culture 117
Out of Africa model of human origins 236, 239

Paleoanthropologist 22
Paleoanthropology 18-22, 31-32
Paleobotanist 22
Paleontologist 22
Palynologist 22
Pan 52
Pan paniscus 32
Pan troglodytes 32, *34*, *35*
Paranthropus 117, 121, 144, 146, 152
Paranthropus crassidens 117, 148
Paraustralopithecus 152
Pascal, Blaise 111
Patterson, Bryan 122
Pauling, Linus 31
Pech de l'Aze 97
Pedra Furada Rockshelter 49
Peking Man 7, 41, 93, 96, *165*, 182, 188, *189*, *190*
Pendejo Cave 49
Penrose, Roger 107
Perikymata 78

Permian 111
Petralona 46, 164, 191
Petralona 1 *8*, 198, 200, *201*, 202, 204, 208, 212
Phillips, Wendell 148
Phyletic gradualism 53
Phylogenetic tree *38*
Phylogeny 37-38
Pigments, in rock painting 102
Pilbeam, David 33
Piltdown Man 43, 131, 142, 202
Pinker, Steven 106
Pithecanthropus 37, 162, 187
Pleistocene 106, 162, 196
  Lower 80
  Middle 80
Pleistocene overkill hypothesis 52
Plesianthropus 134
Pliocene 131, 162, 164
Pongidae 18, 40
Pongo 33
Posthole, as evidence of shelter 97, *98*
Pre-Neandertal hypothesis 212
Pre-sapiens hypothesis 202, 212, 224
Pre-sapiens theory 43
Primate 18
  communication 106
  reproductive behavior 73
Proteins, immunological reaction technique 30-31
Punctuated equilibrium 53

Qafzeh 43, 218, 220, 222, 234, 239, 239, 242, 256
Qafzeh IX 100, 239, *240*, *241*
Qafzeh VI 239
Quadrupedalism 86

Race 56-57
Rak, Yoel 128, 156
Ramapithecus 30, 33, 37
  bipedalism 33
Reck, Hans 131
Recognition species concept 52
Reconstruction
  A. afarensis skeleton *88*
  H. erectus *165*
Red ochre 100, 102
Regourdou 100
Rhodesian Man 208
Robinson, John T. 117, 121, 134, 136, 138, 184
Robust australopithecine 23, 28, 37
  teeth 30
Roc de Marsal 100
Rock art-Algeria *104*
Rock painting
  Australia *50*, *113*
  Brazil *48*
  Lascaux *105*
Ruvelo, Maryellen 41

Saccopastore 1 212, *213*, *214*
Saccopastore 2 212
Sadiman 132
Saint-Acheul 254
Saint-Césaire 258
Saint-Césaire skull *110*
Sambungmachan 191
Sangiran 23, 46, 187, 191
Sangiran 17 188, 191, *192*, *193*, 247
Sarich, Vincent 31, 33
Satellite imagery 22, 25
Sawyer, Gary 188
Schepers, G. W. H. 138, 144
Schoetensack, Otto 164, 196
Secondary altriciality 76
Serengeti 91, 176
Sergi, Sergio 212
Sexual dimorphism 40, 52, 73, 158, 162, 176
Sexual selection 73
Shanidar 100, 215, 218, 220
Shanidar 1 220
Shanidar 4 100
Shelter 97, 99
Sibley, Charles 31
Sima de los Huesos. *See* Atapuerca
Simons, Elwyn 33
Sinanthropus 188
Single species hypothesis 53, 158, 180, 184
Sivapithecus 33, *36*
Siwalik Hills 33
SK 6 148, *149*
SK 15 184
SK 48 *109*, 148, *150*, *151*, 184
SK 79 *4*, 148, 184
SK 80 184
SK 847 23, 184, *185*, *186*
Skhul 43, 220, 222, 256
Skhul V 222, 239, 242, *243*
Smith, Holly 78
Solutrean 99, 258
Spear-thrower *103*, 258
Speciation 38, 53
  evidence in fossil record 28
Spy 100
Steinheim 254
Steinheim cranium 164,198, 202 *202*, *203*, 204, 212
Stekelis, Moshe 218
Sterkfontein 23, 38, 117, 119, 134, 136, 138, 142, 144, 146, 148, 158, 164
Stone tools 250, *251*, *252*, *253*, 254, *255*, 256, *257*, 258, *259*, *260*, *261*
  cut marks *91*, 211, 191
  earliest 89-90
Stoneking, Mark 41
Straus, William 224
Striae of Retzius 78
Strontium-calcium ratio in bone 92
Sts 5 *3*, 134, *135*, 138, 146, 184
Sts 14 136, *137*
Sts 36 *120*, 138
Sts 52 a+b 138
Sts 71 *120*, 138, *139*, *140*
Stw 252 146, *146*, 147, *147*
Stw 505 138, *141*
Sunghir 100
Suwa, Gen 116, 121, 132
Swan, Lucille 188
Swanscombe 202, 212, 254
Swartkrans 23, 78, 92, 117, 119, 136, 148, 156, 158, 184, 250, 251
  evidence for fire 96, *96*, *97*

Tabarin 23, 39
Tabarin mandible *39*
Tabun 100, 218, 220, 239, 242, 256
Taieb, Maurice 25, 116
Taphonomy 126
Tattersall, Ian 164, 188
Taung 23, 25, 78, 117, 119, 142
Taung skull *79*, 134, 142, *143*
  evidence of bipedalism 87
Technology, evolution of in Paleolithic 250
Teeth
  Dryopithecus pattern 30
  abundance in fossil record 136
  as evidence of diet 91-92
  Australopithecus 30
  development 78
  hominid 28
  microwear 92
  Old World monkeys and apes 28
Telanthropus 184
Templeton, Alan 41
Terblanche, Gert 144
Terra Amata 97
Teshik-Tash 100, 215, *216*, *217*, 222
Thackeray, Francis 56
Thorne, Alan 247
Titanohomo 156
TM 1511 134
TM 1513 144
TM 1517 144, *145*
Tobias, Phillip 138, 156, 162, 170, 172
Toth, Nicholas 93, 250
Triassic 111
Trinil 23, 187, 191
Trinil 2 187, *187*
Trinkaus, Erik 78
Tugen Hills 28
Turing, Alan 107
Turnover pulse hypothesis 28
Tuttle, Russell 132
Twiggy 172

'Ubeidiya 46
Upper Paleolithic 18, 43, 47, 83, 91, 97, 99, 100, 102, 106, 218, 220, 244
  blade 258, *259*, *260*
  culture 21
  harpoon 258, *261*
Upper Paleolithic industry 256, 258
UR 501 23
Uraha 164

Vallois, Henri 43
Venus figurines 102, 258
Venus of Gelgenberg 258
Vindija 93, 211
von Koenigswald, Ralph 30
von Linné, Carl 18
Vrba, Elisabeth 28

Walker, Alan 33, 182
Wallace, Alfred Russel 187
Wallace, John 138
Washburn, Sherwood 21
Weidenreich, Franz 93, 188
Weiner, Joseph 131
Wernicke's area 80, 106
West Turkana 23
Wheeler, Peter 88
White, Randall 99
White, Tim 40, 93, 116, 119, 121, 132, 138, 152
Willow-leaf point 258, *260*
Wills, Christopher 80
Wilson, Allan 31, 41
Wilson, Edward O. 21, 111
WLH 50 191
Wolpoff, Milford H. 158, 247
Wood, Bernard 162, 174, 176
Woodward, Arthur Smith 208
Wrangham, Richard 83, 86
Wright, Robert 107

X chromosome 41

Y chromosome 41
Yesuf, Ali 168
Yuanmou 46
Yudinovo 99

Zhoukoudian 23, 93, 96, 180, 182, 187, 188, 191, 198, 234, 235
Zinjanthropus 119, 156
Zuckerkandl, Emile 31
Zwigelaar, Tom 208